Double Award

AS Level for AQA

Health &
Social Care

Series editor:
Neil Moonie

www.heinemann.co.uk
✓ Free online support
✓ Useful weblinks
✓ 24 hour online ordering

01865 888058

Heinemann

Inspiring generations

Heinemann Educational Publishers
Halley Court, Jordan Hill, Oxford OX2 8EJ
Part of Harcourt Education

Heinemann is a registered trademark of
Harcourt Education Limited

First published 2005

10 09 08 07 06 05
10 9 8 7 6 5 4 3 2 1

British Library Cataloguing in Publication Data is available
from the British Library on request.

10-digit ISBN: 0 435471 55 4
13-digit ISBN: 978 0 435471 55

Edited by Neil Moonie
Designed Lorraine Inglis
Typeset and illustrated by TechType

Original illustrations © Harcourt Education Limited, 2005

Cover design by Wooden Ark Studios

Printed by Scotprint

Cover photo: © Getty Images

Picture research by Ginny Stroud-Lewis

Acknowledgements
Every effort has been made to contact copyright holders of material reproduced in this book. Any omissions will be
rectified in subsequent printings if notice is given to the publishers.

Websites
There are links to relevant websites in this book. In order to ensure that the links are up to date, that the links work,
and that the sites are not inadvertently linked to sites that could be considered offensive, we have made the links
available on the Heinemann website at www.heinemann.co.uk/hotlinks. When you access the site the express code
is 1554P.

Please note that the examples of websites suggested in this book were up to date at the time of writing. It is essential
for tutors to preview each site before using it to ensure that the URL is still accurate and the content is appropriate.
We suggest that tutors bookmark useful sites and consider enabling students to access them through the school or
college intranet.

Contents

Introduction

This book has been written to support students who are studying for the double award AS level GCE using the course structure designed by AQA. The book is designed to support the following AS level Units:

Unit 1   Effective Caring (externally assessed)

Unit 2   Effective Communication (internally assessed)

Unit 3   Health, Illness and Disease (internally assessed)

Unit 4   Child Development (externally assessed)

Unit 5   Nutrition and Dietetics (externally assessed)

Unit 6   Common Diseases and Disorders (externally assessed)

Unit 7   Needs and Provision for Elderly Clients (internally assessed)

Unit 8   Needs and Provision for Early Years Clients (internally assessed)

Unit 9   Complimentary Therapies (internally assessed)

Unit 10   Psychological Perspectives (internally assessed)

Candidates undertaking the Advanced Subsidiary (AS) level double award must take units 1, 2 and 3. They must then take at least one unit from units 4, 5, and 6. Up to two units may be selected from units 7, 8, 9 and 10. This book has been organised to cover each of the available units. Headings are designed to make it easy to follow the content of each unit and to find the information needed to achieve a high grade. As well as providing information, each unit is designed to stimulate the development of the thinking skills needed to achieve an advanced level award.

Assessment

Each unit will be assessed by coursework or by an external test set and marked by AQA. Detailed guidance for coursework assessment and external test requirements can be found in the unit specifications and at the AQA web site at www.aqa.org.uk. This book has been designed to support students to achieve high grades as set out in AQA standards and guidance available during 2004/ 2005.

Special features of this book

Throughout the text there are a number of features that are designed to encourage reflection and to help students make links between theory and practice. In particular this book has been designed to encourage a depth of learning and understanding and to encourage students to go beyond a surface level of descriptive writing. The special features of this book include:

Think it over

The feature is designed to provide thought provoking questions that will encourage reflective thinking, or possibly reflection involving discussion with others.

Did you know?

Interesting facts or snippets of information included to encourage reflective thinking.

Key skills

Some activities which could contribute towards evidence for key skills are identified using this heading.

Scenario

We have used this term in place of the more traditional term 'case study' because the idea of people being perceived as 'cases' does not fit easily with the notion of empowerment – a key feature of current government policy. Scenarios are presented throughout the units to help explain the significance of theoretical ideas to Health, Social Care and Early Years settings.

Consider this

This feature appears at the end of each section and presents a brief scenario followed by a series of questions. These questions are designed to encourage reflection and analysis of the issues covered within the section.

Key concept

Because the authors believe that the development of analytic and evaluative skills requires the ability to use concepts, the authors have identified key concepts and offered a brief explanation of how these terms might be used.

Assessment guidance

At the end of each unit there is a 'how you will be assessed' section that provides either sample test material for externally assessed units or outline guidance and ideas designed to help students achieve the highest grades when preparing internally assessed coursework.

Glossary

This book contains a useful glossary to provide fast reference for key terms and concepts used within the units.

References

There is a full list of references used within each unit together with useful websites at the end of each unit.

Author details

Neil Moonie, former Deputy Director of the Department of Social Services, Health and Education in a College of Further and Higher Education. Chartered Psychologist, part-time lecturer and contributor to a wide range of textbooks and learning resources in the field of health and social care. Editor of Heinemann's GNVQ Intermediate and Advanced textbooks on health and social care since 1993 and editor of the 2000 Standards AVCE textbook.

Siân Lavers is a lecturer at a College of Further Education, teaching on the Levels Two and Three Health and Social Care Programmes, the BTEC National Diploma in Early Years and the CIEH Foundation Food Hygiene Certificate. She has contributed to several text books on Health and Social Care, S/NVQ 3 Care and Key Skills.

Dee Spencer-Perkins began her social services career in research, moving on to become a trainer and then a training manager. She is a Chartered Member of the Chartered Institute of Personnel and Development, and now works as an independent trainer, consultant and writer specialising in language and communication. Dee also has a keen interest in disability issues.

Beryl Stretch, former Head of Health and Social Care in a large College of Further Education. Currently part of the senior examining board for Edexcel, GCE and GCSE Health and Social Care. Former external and internal verifier for VCE, GNVQ, NVQ programmes and examiner for GCSE Human Biology. Contributor to several bestselling textbooks on health and social Care at all levels.

Laura Asbridge has trained as a general nurse, neonatal intensive care nurse and Midwife. She has worked in many hospitals from London to Botswana. She now works as a course manager in Health and Social Care and a lecturer in A level Psychology, at a college of Further Education. She has been working with Edexcel developing the New BTEC First in Health and care course and as a script marker.

Penny Tassoni is an education consultant, writer and trainer specialising in early years' education. She also works as a reviser for the lead awarding body for childcare and education awards. Penny trained and worked as an early years and primary teacher before lecturing in a FE college on a range of childhood studies courses. Penny has written and contributed to a wide range of best selling books on early years.

Acknowledgements

Dee Spencer-Perkins would like to thank the following for their help and advice:
Rob Dyson (Scope), Beth Tarlton (Norah Fry Research Centre), Clara Scammell, Karen Sharpe, Bernard Yu (Havering PCT), Adrian Coggins (Royston, Buntingford and Bishop's Stortford PCT), and also Richard Abbott, Barbara Brown, Emma Burnham, Roger Carruthers, Rosemary Cunningham, Violetta Etheridge, Gail Lincoln, Lynne Lytton, Josephine O'Gorman, Shashi Sharma, Joannah Weightman, and Janet Wilkinson.

Laura Asbridge's acknowledgements go:
To Beth Howard at Heinemann whose gentle coercion encouraged me to take up writing and to my supportive husband who didn't allow me to succumb to doubts.

The authors and publisher would like to thank all those who have granted permission to reproduce copyright material.

Crown copyright material is reproduced with the permission of the Controller of HMSO; National Day Nurseries Association; British Toy and HobbyAssociation; Coeliac Society; Institute of Child Health; Age Concern; British Psychological Society; Gingerbread; Save the Children; NSPCC; The Prince of Wales's Foundation for Integrated Health

The authors and publisher would like to thank the following for permission to reproduce photographs:

Alamy Images/archivberlin Fotoagentur GmbH/page 7; Alamy Images/Peter Titmuss/page 8; Richard Smith/ page 12; Harcourt Education (UK schools)/page 29; Alamy Images/Photofusion Picture Library/page 38; Alamy Images/page 41; Science Photo LIbrary/DR KARI LOUNATMAA/page 43; Richard Smith/page 44; Alamy Images/Janine Wiedel Photolibrary/page 45 (1); Richard Smith/page 45 (2); Richard Smith/page 50; Alamy Images/page 57; Harcourt Education/Jules Selmes/page 68; Richard Smith/page 79; Getty Images/Stone/page 81; Harcourt Education/page 88; Corbis nrf/page 102; Harcourt Education/Jules Selmes/page 107 (1); Photodisc/page 107 (2); Corbis/page 108; Photodisc/page 111; Harcourt Education/(UK Schools)/page 112; Harcourt Education/Tudor Photography (UK schools)/page 113; Alamy Images/Janine Wiedel Photolibrary/page 124; Science Photo Library/DR. E. WALKER/page 127; Science Photo Library/PARVIZ M. POUR/page 128; Alamy Images/Swerve/page 145; Harcourt Education/Tudor Photography/page 178; Harcourt Education/Tudor Photography/page 181; Harcourt Education/Jules Selmes/page 185; Alamy Images/page 185; Harcourt Education/Tudor Photography/page 185; Ginny Stroud-Lewis/page 187; Science Photo Library/BIOPHOTO ASSOCIATES/page 188; Ginny Stroud-Lewis/page 191; Science Photo Library/DR P. MARAZZI/page 217; Science Photo Libray/ZEPHYR/page 221; Corbis/page 229; Science Photo Library/Mark Thomas/page 232; Science Photo Library/WESTERN OPHTHALMIC HOSPITAL/page 235; Corbis/page 263; Alamy Images/Stock Connection/page 264; Richard Smith/page 273; Sally and Richard Greenhill/page 275; Sally and Richard Greenhill/page 302; Science Photo Library/MAURO FERMARIELLO/page 324; Alamy Images/Eddie Gerald/page 328; Corbis/Owen Franken/page 329; Science Photo Library/HATTIE YOUNG/page 329; Alamy Images/Mike Kipling Photography/page 368; unknown/page 372; Science Photo Library/page 376; Sally and Richard Greenhill/page 378; Science Photo Library/WILL MCINTYRE/page 381; Sally and Richard Greenhill/page 384

Every effort has been made to contact copyright holders of material produced in this book. Any omissions will be rectified in subsequent printings if notice is given to the publishers.

Effective caring

You will learn about:

Introduction

This unit introduces you to a selection of services which are provided for individuals in health and social care. It also covers factors that are necessary for a good quality of life and some of the skills and techniques which carers may use to ensure they treat service users well.

How you will be assessed

This unit is externally assessed through a written examination comprising four compulsory structured questions.

1.1 Life quality factors

There are many factors to take into account that enable people to enjoy a good quality of life. A common set of principles and values called the care value base was devised in 1992. The care value base is intended to provide guidelines for health and social care workers to ensure that the care they provide to service users is appropriate and takes into account individual needs and preferences.

There are three main areas of health and social care that are affected by the care value base. These are:

* fostering equality and diversity
* fostering people's rights and responsibilities
* maintaining confidentiality of information.

These can be further divided into five main elements:

* anti-discriminatory practice
* confidentiality
* individual rights
* personal beliefs and identity
* effective communication.

Psychological life quality factors

There are many factors that can affect a person's quality of life. Basic needs such as food and water, warmth and safety and security are physical factors, but psychological factors (including those shown in Figure 1.1) also play a large part in how people feel about their lives.

Occupation

Being occupied, or having something to do, whether it is paid work, volunteer work or taking part in a hobby or sporting activity, helps people to

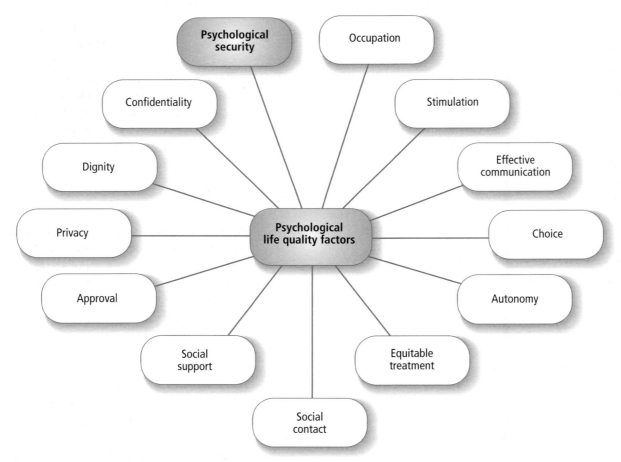

FIGURE 1.1 *Psychological factors that affect the quality of life*

feel that their existence is worthwhile. Certain activities provide people with status and this can be an important factor, as it helps to build self-confidence and self-esteem. Success at work or being the star player on a sports team will contribute to a general feeling of well-being, especially if what a person does is valued by others. This may also bring other benefits such as improving fitness levels or developing a wider social circle.

Stimulation

When people are stimulated by work or a particular interest, their minds are active and they feel challenged and motivated by what they are doing. Boredom can quickly set in when individuals feel that they have nothing to do, and this can develop into apathy – the less a person does, the less he or she wants to do, which can lead to depression. This can be a problem in some care settings, especially if a resident has previously lived a full and independent life. It is important to find out about an individual's interests and to try to provide appropriate stimulation for each service user.

Effective communication

Being able to communicate effectively provides many benefits. It allows for social contact and can help people to meet new friends by exchanging information. A carer who has good communication skills is able to provide information to service users, which can be used to improve their quality of life. This allows them to:

∗ find out, or be given information about their treatment, future opportunities or prospects

∗ be given coherent explanations for their condition and future treatment

∗ ask questions and receive answers

∗ be listened to.

All of these factors will help the service user to feel that their views and wishes are valued.

Choice

Having choice is linked to effective communication. Individuals only have choice when they know that there is more than one option to consider and make a decision about.

Choice provides a certain amount of power and a sense of freedom. Some choices may be quite minor such as being able to choose when, where and what you eat, but some are major decisions such as choosing a career or deciding whether or not to move house. For older people, a major decision may be about going into residential care. In order to make an informed choice the individual will need to know what options are available and practicalities such as cost, location and facilities. However, in some care settings service users may not have a great deal of choice in some matters.

Autonomy

Autonomy is the ability to have control over one's life and the opportunity to make one's own decisions. When people have the freedom to make choices about their life without being coerced, they are said to be autonomous.

Equitable treatment

This is the absence of unfair discrimination. In practice what it means is that a service user can receive treatment that is fair and not significantly better or worse than the treatment given to another person. Therefore, an individual, who because of his or her circumstances has a greater need than the individual in the next room, will receive that care regardless of the cost or resources needed.

Social contact

Social contact is the opportunity to be with other people. People who do not have any form of social contact can easily become isolated, which can lead to depression. Some people have a lot of social contact and are members of many different social groups, depending on their interests or work. This helps to develop a sense of self because such individuals have a sense of belonging.

Social support

This allows individuals to be provided with support from people whom they trust, such as friends and family. This can help to provide individuals with emotional security. Some people do not have family or many friends and may rely on social support from advocates or care workers.

Approval

When individuals know that their actions gain approval, affection or praise from others, they develop a sense of self-esteem.

Privacy

All service users have the right to privacy. This is particularly important if service users are receiving treatment that might be embarrassing, if they wish to be undisturbed, or if they wish to speak confidentially to a care worker. Maintaining privacy for service users shows respect for their wishes and can lead to a sense of trust developing between carers and service users.

Dignity

Being shown respect allows service users dignity. Providing care that does not demean individuals increases their self-esteem.

Confidentiality

The maintenance of confidentiality is a vital aspect of caring for others. Ensuring that sensitive information about a service user is not given to anyone who does not have the right to know it, helps to maintain an atmosphere of trust between carer and service user.

Psychological security

Psychological security means that individuals will not be afraid or anxious about any aspect of their life. Anyone who is facing a major life change may be worried about the consequences of the decisions they are making. Reassurance and effective communication can help to relieve any fears.

Physical life quality factors

A good quality of life can be influenced by factors that can be grouped together using the term 'physical life quality factors'. These include aspects of exercise, nutrition, safety, hygiene, comfort and being free from pain, as shown in Figure 1.2. For example, service users will feel that the caring they receive is not very effective if they are poorly fed and in pain.

Exercise

When we think of exercise, mental images of

Consider this

The Poplars is a large residential nursing and care home on the outskirts of a large town. Public transport links into the town centre are good and many staff and visitors use the bus on a daily basis. Although the rooms are clean and comfortable, few of the staff have any qualifications and only mandatory training such as moving and handling and fire training is provided. A new manager was appointed three days ago and she is shocked by the staff's lack of knowledge. Several incidents have been brought to her attention, which she feels must receive her immediate attention. Some of the incidents are listed below. Describe which psychological life quality factors are missing in these situations.

1. A visitor hears two of the care assistants talking on the bus. One says, 'I don't know how Mrs Smith has coped until now with looking after her husband, especially since she was diagnosed with breast cancer six months ago.'

2. Mrs Johnston's daughter arrives to visit and finds her sitting on a commode in her room with the door wide open.

3. Mr Brown was admitted to The Poplars a week ago and was told that the policy is that all service users are in bed by 8.30 pm. His favourite programme is on at 9.00 pm. He does not have a television in his room.

4. Mrs Davison is reluctant to receive care from Julia, the care assistant on duty. She calls her a nosy cow and tries to hit her.

---

gymnastic activity or school physical education tends to prevail in most people's minds. This is not necessarily what we mean when we consider exercise in terms of effective caring. However, this also does not mean that hydrotherapy, exercising in water and remedial gymnastics, for example, should be excluded in the overall consideration of exercise in this regard.

It has been known for a long time that adequate physical activity is crucially important both in society as a whole (see Unit 3.2 on page 107) and as part of daily living within the caring professional role.

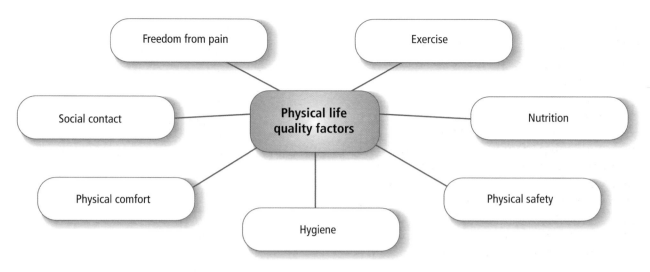

FIGURE 1.2 *Physical factors that affect the quality of life*

Infants need to exercise their limbs to promote sitting, crawling and walking. They love to be laid on a rug or blanket, without the encumbrance of a nappy, and kick their legs and wave their arms in sheer pleasure. Adding stimulation such as suspended toys and sound-making devices fills them with joy and promotes relaxation and sleep.

Infants may be given some time lying on their back and the front, and carers will often be surprised by how much an infant will change position even though there is as yet no strength in the limbs. This type of activity can start from only a few weeks old, as long as the infant is not left for too long and is content.

Later on, they should be given opportunities to support their weight on the legs and arms as in the crouch position, with their legs tucked up and arms bent at the elbow. An infant will soon let the carer know if it is unhappy. From 8–9 months of age onwards, under careful supervision, infants should be allowed to pull themselves up using a steady support such as heavy furniture; and this will promote walking at around age 13–15 months. Now and again, it is found that carers (usually paid) who are looking after more than one or two children will not encourage movement in these ways because a crawling and walking child needs more attention and vigilance. This is obviously something that needs to be given attention to and guarded against most carefully. Children also need fresh air, stimulation and short walks (carers may find it useful to take the buggy on walks as well for when fatigue sets in). The carer should ensure that there is some form of restraint like a wrist strap or harness and reins because very young children have no sense of danger or road sense.

Children are more active than adults, but whether older children now get enough exercise to receive the full range of health benefits is unknown. We have learned (in a government paper) that 33 per cent of boys and around 40 per cent of girls undertake such low physical activity levels that in the future this may affect their health experience. (*At least five a week: evidence on the impact of physical activity and its relationship to health,* Chief Medical Officer of Health 2004).

Children at school should have at least one hour of moderately intense physical activity each day; and at least twice a week activities such as chasing games, skipping, running, jumping and gymnastics should be included to increase the density of bones and develop muscle strength.

> ✴ DID YOU KNOW?
>
> Currently, the only time that many children are intensely physically active occurs at school, and as play areas become less available and journeys to school are by bus or car, it is feared that this is far from adequate. Socio-economic factors also become important as leisure centre activity and team participation becomes expensive in time and money.

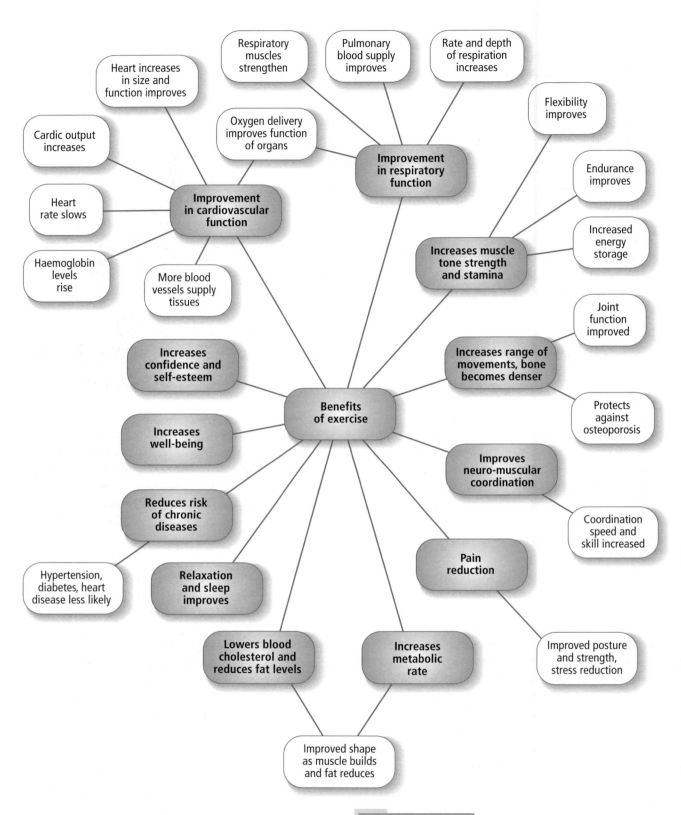

FIGURE 1.3 *The benefits of exercise*

Think it over...

Looking at Figure 1.3, choose a service user group and prioritise the benefits for that group.

Stuart is nearly seven years old; his parents saved enough money to send him and his brother to a football scheme in the summer holidays. He displayed a talent for football and was offered the opportunity to go to a football academy run by a premier league team in the area. Stuart is performing well and loves the sport, but training takes place a fair distance away on three nights of the week and often matches take place on Sundays. With three children in the family and two working parents without their own transport, life is becoming difficult. Stuart's 12-year-old sister gets bored watching Stuart play football and his brother also feels that he is not getting any attention. Stuart's parents feel that it is costing too much time and money to promote his sport and fear that they will soon be forced to give up the training. They are also worried about the effect on their other two children.

Competitive sports and other substantial ways of exercising are important sources of psychological well-being for most young adults and children, bringing improvements in mood, reduced tension and anxiety as well as social and emotional benefits. Young people with difficult, challenging and anti-social behaviour might change with a purposeful outlet for energy and emotion. Walking to school and cycling needs to be supported and encouraged with walking 'buses' and safer cycle paths.

Disabled people are now catered for in a way that has never happened before. There are workout videos and DVDs for people with developmental disabilities, multiple sclerosis, mental health problems, people recovering from heart attacks and strokes. Tai Chi, bowls, weight lifting, Bocce (Italian lawn bowling) and basketball are all prominent activities for those service users who have disabilities.

It seems that the only barrier to the creation of specialised exercise products is a lack of awareness. The Internet has proved to be a real asset for disabled service users in that it enables them to access products that are specific to their requirements. Some service users who require specialised physical activity sessions may attend physiotherapy departments in their local hospitals and occupational therapists will also help in their rehabilitation. However, there are still plenty of opportunities to raise the quality of life for disabled people who have long been ignored.

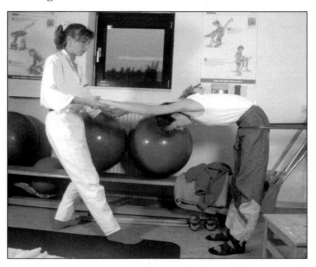

Exercising in a physiotherapy unit

People who sit or lie too long in one position may develop bed or pressure sores where the skin lies over a bone prominence; this happens because the body weight prevents the blood supply delivering oxygen and nutrients to the tissues. When the tissues break down because of inadequate blood supplies, the resulting sore can be difficult and slow to heal. Infection is a risk and major surgery may be required, as this can be life threatening.

Although aids such as sheepskins and foam cushions are useful to those suffering with bed or pressure sores, the priority for service users is to move and change position. Service users often need reminding to do this and encouraging their motivation is important. Wheelchair users are encouraged to lift themselves on their forearms from time to time to relieve the pressure.

Physical activity slows the loss of bone mineral density in older adults; it may delay the progression of osteoarthritis and delay the onset of low back pain. It is also helpful to those people who have had joint replacements.

Housework is an excellent physical activity and wheelchair users and other service users can assist in this form of activity in residential accommodation. People in later adulthood clearly should be offered tasks commensurate with their abilities and capacities but at the same time should not sit in the same chair, day after day, watching television. An old adage used frequently in care is 'Use it or lose it'.

This is unfortunately very true, particularly with respect to mobility. Every time you perform a task for someone who could do it for him or herself, perhaps with difficulty or very slowly, you have moved that individual one step closer to dependency.

Some people, largely through ignorance, express dissatisfaction at seeing an older or disabled service user in care having to perform tasks for themselves. We must never be tempted to stop maintaining or increasing independence and mobility. Walking is the most important form of exercise and increasingly small goals must be incorporated into daily living. Mobility aids, patience, encouragement and support

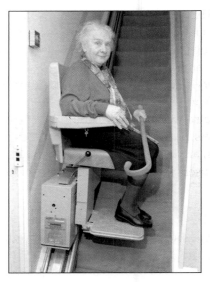

An older person being supported with mobility

must be part of physical activity for older service users.

One research study by Jirovek (1991) concluded that a daily exercise routine for older, mentally frail service users promoted greater mobility and continence. Many elderly service users deemed to have incontinence merely cannot get to the lavatory in time and using a commode chair to get there and walking back improves continence substantially.

The importance of assisting older service users to walk within their capabilities cannot be emphasised enough.

Nutrition

This is the process by which an individual takes in and uses food. As well as eating to survive and being aware of the current interest in the relationship between food and physical health, it is important to remember that food forms a major part of social and cultural living. A carer must help in promoting a pleasant social environment for service users when they are eating. The dining area should be cheerful with tablecloths, napkins, place mats and condiments, as eating food in well-organised surroundings helps to stimulate the appetite and foster good table manners.

Service users should choose their own food from a menu with assistance, where necessary, to promote preferences and any special dietary needs. This will include cultural, ethnic and religious requirements when appropriate.

Fasting is also important in certain religious festivals and carers need to be aware that urging some service users to participate in mealtimes may offend them.

It is also worth remembering that important life events, such as christenings, weddings and funerals, are usually celebrated by sharing food. Service users in care may miss these events and be disinclined to participate in normal meals.

You will find more information on nutrition and malnutrition in Unit 3 on page 104.

Babies and toddlers who do not grow at an expected rate are said to fail to thrive.

Under-nourishment may arise from home problems such as a poor relationship between mother and child or even neglect. Delayed social, emotional and intellectual skills as well as poor growth, tend to occur in deprived children. There is a possibility that a child in a stable family who is receiving adequate nutrition yet fails to thrive may be suffering from serious physical disorders.

Several studies comparing dietary intake and growth have concluded that the quality and quantity of food intake declines with poverty. In poor families, where genetic factors can be discounted, the oldest child tends to be taller than younger siblings and a possible explanation is that the larger the family the smaller the quantity of shared food. Many mothers will go without food so that their children will eat. In Britain, there are still families in poverty suffering from malnourishment but so, too, are some affluent families, not from lack of food but the wrong type of food. Malnutrition arises when any component of food is taken in incorrect quantities. Too much fat, salt and sugar in the diet, very often from convenience foods, can lead to obesity, see Unit 3, page 104.

With all life stages, input should equal output – that is to say that the amount of food taken in must equal the amount of energy expended. With an increasingly sedentary population, input is tending to vastly exceed output, resulting in an overweight or obese population with long-term effects.

Adults need to vary their food habits in accordance with their lifestyles. With the decline of heavy agricultural labour and the mining and manufacturing industries, together with the increase of electronic and service industries, the myth that a working man needs a hearty meal when he comes home from work is no longer valid for most families. The meal portions in care establishments are a frequent source of complaint and service users often supplement the food provided with food gifts from visitors and family. Although public service meals are provided to a restricted budget, service users are clearly used to a larger quantity of food. Food habits are hard to give up and at home, meal providers tend to serve the same portions regardless of changes in circumstances.

Ill people and those with poor appetites, in particular, need to have food presented in an attractive way and not be over-faced with large quantities. Food should have a pleasant smell and taste, as well as appearance. Some people may be on special diets, such as patients who suffer from coeliac disease, renal failure and phenylketonuria; it is easy to become disaffected with a diet in these circumstances and service users may consume outlawed food or become disinterested in food as a result.

Carers need to be well informed about nutritional needs, as some service users may enter a caring establishment with lifelong eating habits that are less than healthy. However, common sense needs to prevail; if service users have reached later adulthood, despite 'unhealthy' diets, perhaps high in fat, salt and sugar, they may be deprived of important calories and fat-soluble vitamins (Vitamins A, D, E and K) with enforced change, and they certainly would not feel very happy. Elderly service users may have lost some sense of smell and/or taste; they may have problems with swallowing and either poorly fitting or a complete lack of teeth, leading ultimately to problems with nutrition.

Service users entering residential care frequently do so because they have been unable to care for themselves in the recent past. Consequently, such service users may have forgotten to eat for long periods or eat bizarre combinations of food. Such difficulties will usually clear up in a few weeks but special requirements such as extra protein and vitamins may be required temporarily.

Individuals who have suffered a stroke may need food cut up in small pieces and special cutlery aids to assist with nutrition. Visually impaired service users may require food to be placed in particular plate locations and others may require fluids to drink to help with swallowing drier foods. All elderly service users should be encouraged to drink plenty of fluids;

they tend to restrict their fluid intake if they are anxious about incontinence.

Physical safety and hygiene

The key word here is probably vigilance; a carer must always be alert for risks and hazards. When you are caring for an individual or group of service users you cannot let any harm befall them. Service users would not be in care unless they were in need of someone to look after them. They may be too young, in later adulthood, disabled, ill or infirm service users.

There must be safe limits for infants' and toddlers' activities and safe toys for them to play with. Suitable precautions should be taken to guard against infection and any child who has an infection cared for with minimal risk to others. Sometimes this is difficult, as many infections have long incubation periods and children can pass on the disease before adults are aware of its existence. In this case, parents and guardians must be made aware of the possibility of an infection being spread.

Crockery and utensils must be washed well in hot water and detergent and babies' feeding bottles must be sterilised. Waste materials such as dirty nappies must be bagged and disposed of safely and all spills cleared up immediately. Some minor accidents and tumbles will inevitably occur because youngsters are by nature inquisitive and adventurous; parents need to be informed so that they, in turn, can keep a watchful eye on their children at home.

It is not sufficient to notice hazards, you must deal with them properly and promptly or make the area as safe as possible by using warning signs, closing down or closing off the hazard, and reporting it immediately to a supervisor. You should use common sense regarding the hazards you can manage and those you cannot do anything about due to your own lack of knowledge and expertise.

For example, you can mop up spilt water, remove furniture from corridors or pick up fallen objects, but do not try to repair broken equipment or deal with hazardous materials unless you have had special training. You should pay particular attention to trailing electrical flexes, worn furnishings and floor coverings, broken or faulty equipment, slippery floors and any obstructions to exits and fire escapes.

Just as you would do in your own home, challenge and check out everyone you meet who you are not familiar with. Do not assume that because visitors are wearing some type of uniform on, they are bona fides – this is the most common way for people who are 'up to no good' to gain access into care establishments that are usually not locked. Ask for proof of identity. Nowadays, most organisations provide identity badges or cards, and it may be necessary to call the organisation that the individual claims to be representing to check on authenticity. Many old people have been 'conned' by criminals, who state that they are from the council, utility services or similar, and have suffered greatly as a result.

Elderly people are vulnerable because they are too trusting. Often they come from communities where doors were left unlocked so that neighbours could come and go.

Some service users may have valuable property that should be safeguarded; such items should be placed in safety and a record kept that includes a description of each one. Supervisors should be aware of any service users who keep large sums of money or valuables so that they may be made aware of the risks and responsibilities associated with refusing to use the facilities for safekeeping.

You also need to guard against aggressive or violent people; these may be visitors or service users (and sometimes carers themselves). Ensure that you are not alone, be close to an exit door and/or emergency alarm and never give out information that you are not permitted to give.

It is not advisable to lift service users manually or use lifting equipment unless a qualified person has trained you. You may permanently damage yourself, colleagues or service users.

It is essential that carers of all service users, not just infants and children, ensure that they always wash their hands carefully, particularly before and after:

* preparing and handling food
* assisting with the toilet
* assisting with personal hygiene
* disposing of any waste material such as nappies, bedpans and urine bottles
* any medical procedure
* touching animals, pets
* cleaning
* touching any contaminated material.

* DID YOU KNOW?

There are three types of hand washing:

* social – using soap and water
* antiseptic – using an antiseptic detergent solution or alcohol rub
* surgical – washing with an antiseptic detergent for at least 3 minutes.

Carers frequently report washing their hands more often than they are observed to do. In many cases, the hands are not washed very carefully; the areas between the fingers are usually poorly cleaned, and the thumb, palm creases and tips of the middle and ring fingers are often not carefully washed. If carers themselves do not wash their hands carefully or provide advice to service users, particularly children, infection will continue to be spread in this way.

Hand washing

There has been a lot of bad publicity about the lack of clean hospitals and the rising number of cases of MRSA infection, resulting in serious damage to people's health and a significant number of deaths. The media attention has caused the government some considerable embarrassment and resulted in a number of changes in the way hospitals are cleaned. This is a wake-up call for all care establishments that physical safety and cleanliness are of paramount importance in ensuring that the health of service users is not put at risk through shoddy work and bad practice. Kitchen and food hygiene must be included in this too; there have been numerous reports of food poisoning cases from hospitals, residential establishments, nurseries and schools in the past. In some cases, deaths of infants and older people have occurred, as these are the most vulnerable groups for food poisoning illness.

Physical comfort

Infants and young children who cannot express themselves verbally may cry when uncomfortable with pain, dirty nappies, stickiness or dirt; but it is subject to individual emotion and experience. Some children never seem to mind and others get distressed easily. Lack of emotion is no excuse for not dealing with a situation that can lead to skin complaints and infections.

Children who are articulate will say when they are uncomfortable and so will adults.

A service user who cannot get adequate rest, relaxation or sleep may become irritable, depressed and bad-tempered. Mental activities become less accurate and medication omitted or mistaken. Different people require different periods of sleep and some people like to stay up into the small hours of the morning and sleep until noon, while others are up early and ready to go to bed around 10.00 or 11.00 pm.

FIGURE 1.4 *Hospital is often not a restful place*

Many people complain of being unable to rest during a stay in hospital; there are others around you, lights on, people talking quietly, the telephone rings constantly, the bed and bedding feels different and cleaners arrive early in the morning (see Figure 1.4). Service users often say that they need to go home to get a rest!

Some things you can do to make a service user comfortable at night:

∗ provide physical and mental exercise during the day

∗ make sure that the room is not too cold or too hot

∗ use the lavatory before getting into bed

∗ relieve anxieties as much as possible

∗ warm, preferably milky drink before bed-time

∗ keep noise and light down to a minimum

∗ make bed comfortable with support pillows as necessary

∗ avoid stimulants such as caffeine, spicy food and alcohol late in the evening.

A quiet, resting period should also be scheduled into daylight hours and many establishments will have their own strategy for this. Open visiting can be a problem. Visitors who arrive just as service users are settling down, for example, may not be aware of the disturbance they cause; this may present the opportunity for a carer to suggest a slightly earlier or later time for visiting.

Service users should be able to choose their own clothing for comfort although a carer can make helpful suggestions.

It is important when lifting and moving service users to discuss what you are going to do, obtain consent and talk about how they can assist and cooperate. A service user must not be treated like a carcass of meat that is moved from one place to another and must be comfortable with the procedure.

Freedom from pain

Management of pain is an important part of caring for someone, but you may not always know about the pain. Some people can bear strong pain and others cannot bear slight pain; it is a very personal experience comprising both physical and emotional factors. You should be aware of the need to ask if a service user is in pain if they are unusually quiet, distressed, tense, fidgeting or sweating. Some service users will put up with the pain for quite some time, as they do not want to bother people, other service users are frightened of pain and will tell you straight away. It is also important to be aware of the difficulties that might be faced in expressing symptoms of pain by people with learning disabilities, speech and hearing problems and those who do not have English as their first language.

Always listen sympathetically to service users who complain of pain and ask whether you can assist them in some way. When someone is used to a particular type of pain, they may have a remedy that works for them such as curling up with a hot-water bottle or taking two Paracetamol tablets. Always refer the service user to a supervisor and check that it is all right to manage the pain as the service user wishes. Sometimes, if an investigation is being carried out, pain relief might be withheld so that the medical team can assess the situation accurately. On other occasions, particularly with an accident or injury, there might be the possibility of a surgical operation and it would be dangerous to provide medication, however simple.

Sometimes a service user in pain can be helped by moving into a better position, massaging the area affected or by the application of warmth or cold (ice pack). Chronic muscular pain can be helped by a TENS machine (transcutaneous electrical nerve stimulation) and the service user can walk about while this is happening.

Walking about and talking to others helps some people, while others like a warm bath or carrying out a task to take the mind off the pain.

There are several 'alternative therapies' that many service users rely upon, such as acupuncture, reflexology, meditation, yoga and aromatherapy. These should be part of the total care package and should be openly discussed with the medical team.

There are also various medications that provide pain relief such as Aspirin, Codeine, Paracetamol, combinations of these, Ibruprofen and morphine derivatives. Qualified, experienced carers only should administer these drugs.

Think it over...

Research one alternative therapy and evaluate its effectiveness in the management of pain.

1.2 Treating people well

You have just learned what life quality factors are. The term 'treating people well' means providing life quality factors that match the needs and personality of the individual. An example of this would be to ensure that any individual who is capable of expressing a preference should be offered choice, such as what to eat at mealtimes. Every individual is different and should be treated with equality. This does not, however, mean treating everyone the same.

There are ethical and practical reasons why people should be treated well. Care workers who provide care for others have an ethical duty to ensure that the care they provide safeguards the interests of the individuals and maintains as good a quality of life as possible.

In practical terms, treating people well leads to a good working relationship which is based on trust. If service users are treated well they trust those providing the care and behave cooperatively. If carers are treated with respect by those for whom they are providing care, they will make sure that they do the same in return.

There are many ways in which people can be treated badly, which has a negative effect on their self-esteem and self-confidence.

Ways in which people can be treated badly

Neglect

Neglect means to leave someone uncared for. In a care setting this could mean not meeting physical needs such as, for example, failing to provide care in helping individuals to use the lavatory, washing or feeding them. Neglect could also involve not meeting psychological needs such as communication or safety and security. Any of these could lead to an individual feeling unvalued and will create feelings of low self-esteem. It may also lead to a feeling of fear and insecurity. In a home care setting where the main carer may be a relative with little or no experience, an individual may be neglected because of a lack of knowledge, rather than a deliberate act of cruelty.

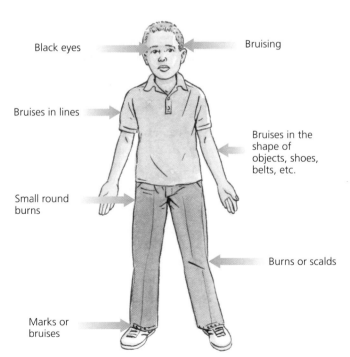

Black eyes
Bruising
Bruises in lines
Bruises in the shape of objects, shoes, belts, etc.
Small round burns
Burns or scalds
Marks or bruises

FIGURE 1.5A *Ways in which children can be abused*

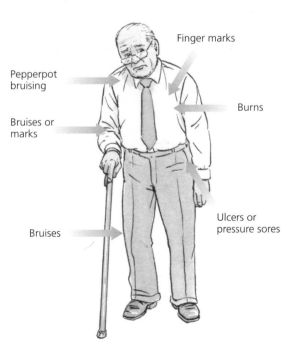

Finger marks
Pepperpot bruising
Burns
Bruises or marks
Bruises
Ulcers or pressure sores

B *Ways in which older people can be abused*

> The Department of Health (1999: 5) defines child neglect as:
>
> *'the persistent failure to meet a child's basic physical and/or psychological needs, likely to result in the serious impairment of the child's health or development. It may involve a parent or carer failing to provide adequate food, shelter and clothing, failing to protect a child from physical harm or danger, or the failure to ensure access to appropriate medical care or treatment. It may also include neglect of, or unresponsiveness to, a child's basic emotional needs'.*
>
> Source: www.nspcc.org.uk/inform

✱ DID YOU KNOW?

Since its launch in 1986, the charity Childline has counselled over one million children and young people.

Over 1,000 volunteers provide a 24-hour helpline for children in distress or danger. There are eleven counselling centres in the United Kingdom and about 4,000 children call Childline every day but only about 2,300 will get through due to lack of funds.

Rejection

Rejection of someone means not accepting them. Reasons for rejecting people may be based on unacceptable behaviour or their not conforming to recognised norms and values. New mothers who suffer from post-natal depression can reject their babies and this can cause long-term relationship problems between them and their child if they are not offered support.

Hostility

A carer who is hostile to a service user will be unable to create a good working relationship with that individual. Hostility may be due to a lack of understanding about the individual or a fundamental disagreement regarding his or her beliefs and values. Of course, it is also possible for a service user to be hostile towards a care worker, especially if the individual feels that his or her way of life is being threatened.

Punishment

Punishment is the application of sanctions against someone if it is believed that they have committed an act which is not acceptable. It is never acceptable for a carer to punish a service user for a real or imagined misdemeanour, especially if the individual is already in a vulnerable position which might result in fear. A carer must always remember that they may find themselves in a position of power and this must never be abused.

Bullying

Bullying is defined as deliberately hurtful behaviour, repeated over a period of time.

The Andrea Adams Trust defines bullying as:

* unwarranted, humiliating, offensive behaviour towards an individual or groups of employees
* persistently negative malicious attacks on personal or professional performance which are typically unpredictable, unfair, irrational and often unseen
* an abuse of power or position that can cause such anxiety that people gradually lose all belief in themselves, suffering physical ill health and mental distress as a direct result
* the use of position or power to coerce others by fear or persecution, or to oppress them by force or threat.

Source www.channel4.com/health

The above definitions relate to bullying in the workplace, but can just as easily apply to care settings. It is not only service users who might be bullied. They might bully staff, or staff might bully other staff. In any of these cases, a difficult working environment may result and can severely affect an individual's self-esteem and self-confidence.

Violence

Violence is never acceptable in care settings. Notwithstanding the very real danger of physical harm being done to someone, the fear of harm can lead to withdrawal and depression. It might cause individuals to behave in a way that is quite different to their normal pattern of behaviour and this might be the first sign to a care worker that there is a problem.

Unfair discrimination

Unfair discrimination can occur on the basis of gender, sexuality, ethnicity, religion, social class, age and impairment. None of these are acceptable in a care environment and there are Acts of Parliament such as the Sex Discrimination Act 1975, the Disability Discrimination Act 1995 and the Race Relations Act 1976 which are in place to ensure equality for everyone. People who are discriminated against may not receive the care and support that they need and will feel unvalued. This is another aspect of bad treatment that will affect people's self-esteem and self-confidence.

Summary

This section has provided an overview of factors that can result in people being treated badly. All are unacceptable but this is especially the case in care work. The negative consequences are very far-reaching and an older vulnerable person may never fully recover from the effects.

Consider this

The Patterson family all live in the same street in a rather rundown area. Joe and Mandy are 28 and 26 years old and have four children, Josh aged nine, Jenny aged seven and twins Julie and James aged five. Two doors away are James senior and Peggy, Joe's parents who look after Betty, Peggy's mother who is 82 years old. Betty has been widowed for 15 years and has become increasingly frail. Her hearing and sight are both poor and she is waiting for a cataract operation. She is also in the early stages of Alzheimer's disease. Peggy is Betty's main carer, but she also looks after the children after school from 3.00 pm until 5.30 pm when Mandy finishes work at the local shoe shop. Joe works shifts and alternates weekly between 8.00 am to 5.00 pm and 3.00 pm to 11.00 pm. Money is tight for both households and Peggy often feels under great pressure. She is worried about how she will cope as Betty's condition deteriorates.

One day Sheila, the district nurse, makes a routine home visit to Betty to see how she is. She takes Betty's blood pressure and notices that she has bruises on her upper arms. She appears distressed and tearful. When she is unable to say how they happened, Sheila asks Peggy. Betty immediately becomes defensive and denies all knowledge of the bruises. When pressed, Peggy becomes verbally abusive and orders Sheila out of the house.

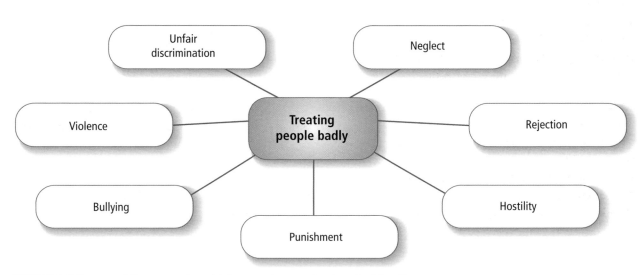

FIGURE 1.6 *Some of the ways in which people may be treated badly*

Mandy has recently noticed that Jenny is very quiet and withdrawn. When she tries to ask her what is wrong, she says that she is fine. Mandy has noticed that two of the Christmas presents she saved hard to buy her are nowhere in the house. Jenny is unable to provide an explanation for their disappearance. Josh has mentioned that he does not think that Jenny is very happy at school and does not appear to have any friends, but is unwilling or unable to say more.

1. Which individuals do you think might be being treated badly, in what way and who by?

2. What suggestions do you think Sheila could make to overcome some of the problems that have resulted in some members of the family being treated badly?

3. Which other professionals could be involved in helping the family to resolve their problems?

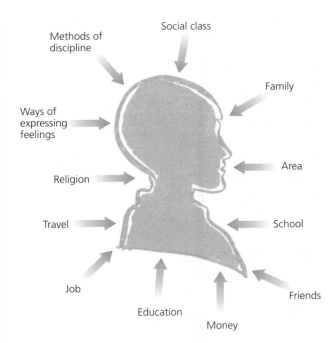

FIGURE 1.7 *People differ in their attitudes to others*

Barriers to treating people well – attitudes and prejudices

There can be different barriers that can cause difficulties when trying to treat people well. These can include:

* barriers internal to carers

* service user barriers.

Barriers internal to carers

Attitudes and prejudices

Barriers can arise when carers have attitudes and prejudices that do not coincide with those of service users. Prejudice involves the use of stereotypes to try to explain or categorise particular groups in society. A carer's background and upbringing will help to develop beliefs, values and norms that might not be the same as some of the individuals that they are employed to look after. Attitudes and prejudices that people hold can often have been an influence since an early age. For example, if someone is brought up from an early age to believe that black or Asian people are inferior to white people, then when

older, that individual might value them less and provide an inferior level of care. It is important that carers are aware of their background and beliefs and use this in a positive way to provide the best possible care to service users.

Think it over...

An important part of being an effective carer is being able to reflect on your practice and think about how you behave towards others and why. Think about the situations you have observed at your work experience placement. Do the care workers treat some service users differently than others? In what way is the treatment different? What do you think might be the reasons for this? Use Figure 1.6 to help you to identify some of the factors you might have come across.

Stereotyping

Stereotyping is using a range of characteristics or labels to describe a person or a group of people. This type of labelling is often negative and unfair; for example, a person who is overweight might be perceived as lazy and slow, or a young black man may be seen as being a drug-using criminal. However, every person is an individual and will have different characteristics, both positive and negative. Stereotyping may lead to discrimination, as a person's perception about a group of people, whether it is gender, sexuality, social class or race, will influence how that individual interacts with them. Although stereotyping can be an easy way of categorising people and making sense of the world, it is important to remember that all people are individual and unique, with individual and unique needs which must be met.

Lack of motivation

One of the keys to good team work is to ensure that all the members of the team are motivated. Having a set purpose and clear goals that everyone works towards will provide the 'glue' that holds the team together. In addition, individual motivation of team members will depend on each person having the opportunity to have his or her needs met, whether this is through training or taking on particular responsibilities that the individual is interested in.

Lack of motivation can arise when there is no common purpose and care workers become disenchanted or demoralised with the work they are doing. This may lead to a reduction in the quality of care that is provided to service users, and service users who become aware of this may feel that they are not sufficiently valued.

One of the ways in which motivation can be maintained is to ensure that there are sufficient

Think it over...

Think about the activities you do now or have done in the past. This could be school work or further study, hobbies or sport. Were your activities carried out alone or as part of a team? Think about how you feel or felt about each of the activities you undertake now or undertook in the past. Do you think that your level of motivation influenced how successful you were, and did working alone or as part of a team influence your motivation? Can you think of reasons for your answers?

challenges for the team that will allow everyone to remain motivated and keep morale high. Setting challenges that will improve the quality of the care being offered will give service users a sense of well-being and value.

Conformity with inappropriate workplace norms

When a child starts school or an individual begins a new job, they become socialised into the norms of the establishment that they have joined. This means that they will learn the rules and routines that are considered to be normal and acceptable modes of behaviour. Some care workers can have negative experiences if they have worked in a care setting that does not pay sufficient attention to the types of behaviour that are acceptable. An example of this would be communicating in a way with service users and colleagues that might be seen as rude or lacking in respect. This may involve verbal or non-verbal communication, and inappropriate physical contact can make a service user feel very uncomfortable.

Pre-occupation with own needs

Sometimes staff can become pre-occupied with their own needs and fail to put the needs of their service users first. An example of this would be a situation in which a care assistant who is due to go off duty in five minutes is asked by a service user to be helped to the toilet. The care assistant says that she is going off duty in five minutes and will ask another member of staff to help her. However, she forgets to do so and half an hour later another care assistant goes to see the resident and finds her very distressed as she has wet herself. Putting her own needs first resulted in a very distressing situation for her service user, and although the care assistant has the right to get off duty on time, she also has a responsibility to ensure that all her service users receive appropriate care promptly, and she should have remembered to communicate her service user's need to another member of staff before leaving. Although it can be difficult to put aside one's own needs and wishes, care workers must always be aware that the needs of service users must take priority over their own needs.

Lack of skill

Lack of skill can occur for a variety of reasons. It can occur as a result of inexperience, lack of training or an inability to reach the level of skill that is required of an effective care worker. Carers have a responsibility to identify their training needs and ask their manager to meet these needs. Senior carers and managers also have a responsibility to ensure that all mandatory training is provided, such as fire and manual handling training, and they should also identify any other training needs that are considered necessary for staff to carry out their duties in a proper manner.

Although it can be difficult for a carer to accept that they do not have the skills necessary to provide the level of care that is needed by some individuals, it can sometimes be kinder for a manager to point this out. If there is little appreciable sign of improvement after a set amount of time and considerable attempts to provide training, it might be appropriate to encourage a carer who is lacking some or all of the above skills to consider an alternative career. Managers do have a responsibility to ensure that the carers they employ have the skills and knowledge to provide high-quality care to service users, and they must be confident of this.

Service user barriers

Lack of status and power

There are different groups in society who are perceived or perceive themselves as being less valuable than others. These can be people with disabilities, older people or people with mental health problems. Status helps people to define how people are treated by others and how they see themselves. It is linked to the roles people have, and if an individual feels that he or she does not have a defined role, then they may also feel that they have little or no status in society.

There are cultural differences in the way that different groups of people are accorded status. In China, high status is awarded to the elder members of a family because they are seen by the other members as having wisdom and experience. In the United Kingdom, there is less respect

shown to older people and they are seen as being needy and dependent. This can lead to feelings of insecurity and low self-esteem. It can be a confusing time for an older person who is no longer able to care for him or herself at home and has to enter residential care. Such individuals may feel that any status or power that they had in their working life has disappeared, and may put up barriers that make them resistant to receiving care from others.

It is very important for care professionals to make sure that they use good communication skills with their service users, so gaining a lot of information about them including their likes and dislikes; this will enable the carers to ensure that service users' needs can be met and they can be provided with choice and the opportunity to maintain some of the interests they had before entering residential care. This will in turn help to maintain their self-esteem and self-confidence, and gradually any barriers can be broken down.

Concealing real needs

Many service users will conceal what their real needs or worries are because they do not want to be a nuisance to those who look after them. Other reasons for concealing their real needs might be embarrassment if they find it difficult to talk about intimate problems. This may especially be the case for older ladies who might feel very uncomfortable discussing such subjects, especially if they may have to do so with a young male doctor or carer. Often, an individual will present with an entirely different problem and it will depend upon the skills of the carer to identify whether there is a greater problem that they are reluctant to talk about.

Tendency to exaggerate

Some service users will exaggerate their illness, needs or concerns in order to guarantee appropriate care. Sometimes this will be an attention-seeking device if an individual is lonely and feels in need of care or social contact. Although an individual may exaggerate, it is important that care workers do not trivialise their concerns, which may be very real to the individual concerned.

Hostile or obstructive behaviour

Sometimes individuals will display hostile or obstructive behaviour to carers or to other service users. This may be due to a medical condition such as dementia, or to fear about what is happening to them. Service uses may lash out as a form of defence or because they are frustrated at not being able to voice their concerns in a way that can be understood. Behaviour can be obstructive if a person is denying that they have a problem and need support. Under no circumstances should carers put themselves at risk if service users become violent when attempting to resist the provision of care. It is never worth putting oneself at risk. In such a situation the carer should immediately consult with a senior member of staff to discuss whether alternatives could or should be offered.

Summary

This section has looked at how to treat people well and the barriers that might arise that might prevent such treatment. It is important to remember that all elements of the care value base must be taken into account to ensure the good treatment of service users.

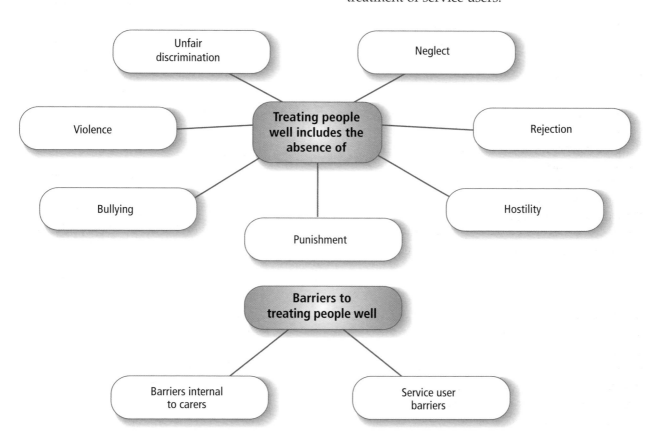

FIGURE 1.8 *How to treat people well*

Mary has just started work in a residential home for adults with learning difficulties. Sarah, one of the senior carers, has been asked to spend the shift with her showing her round the home and introducing her to the service users. During the tour, Mary starts to become a little worried about what she is seeing. Several of the residents look dirty and unkempt and one or two are sitting alone in their rooms with apparently nothing to do. Mary notices that one of them is blind. Another resident is displaying aggressive behaviour to others in the television room and two members of staff are attempting to restrain him. They are shouting at him and telling him that he is being very naughty.

In the dining room two of the carers are having their coffee and smoking in front of residents. Even though one of the residents is asking them to play a board game, the staff just say, 'Go away, Joe, we're having coffee – we need a break from you sometimes, you know.'

As they complete their tour of the home, Mary says to Sarah that she is surprised at the disrespectful way that the carers speak to the residents, and that she has noticed that some of the residents seem withdrawn and a little afraid of the staff. Sarah replies that it's just teasing and a bit of a laugh and that none of the residents have complained about the way they are spoken to, and in any case they're all 'retarded and don't notice'.

1. What factors can you identify that might indicate that the residents are not being treated well?

2. Why is this behaviour from the staff unacceptable?

3. Why might the residents be afraid of the staff?

4. What do you think Mary should do?

5. What do you think the management should do?

1.3 Caring skills and techniques

Promoting the optimal environment for supporting service users

Carers develop special skills and techniques in order to promote the optimal environment for supporting service users and making a difference to their health and daily activities. These abilities come with training and practice and need to form part of every carer's self-assessment and reflection cycle. It is useful to keep notes on the outcomes of practice and to consider how techniques can be improved.

> **Key concept**
>
> *Social perception* is the ability to recognise accurately how service users are feeling, their needs and intentions.

Perception

Perceptions can be accurate and inaccurate and we must be aware of making assumptions that are wrong. Prejudices arise from assumptions and we must guard against falling into the trap of discrimination and stereotyping. It is commonly recognised that the verbal component of a one-to-one conversation is less than 35 per cent and mostly information-giving while over 65 per cent is non-verbal and provides all manner of clues about a variety of subjects. A good carer is intuitive and can pick up and receive non-verbal signals that may actually be in conflict with the spoken words.

To communicate effectively, there must be eye-to-eye contact; we are all familiar with an individual who finds it uncomfortable to meet one's gaze. In Western culture this is taken to mean that the person is keeping information back or being less than truthful. We must be aware of different cultures, however, because in Japan, for instance, most people gaze at the neck rather than the face because it is considered to be offensive. Conversely, people who hold your gaze for a considerable length of time are interested in you or hostile towards you. The size of the pupils of the eye provides the clue; dilated pupils signify interest whereas negative, aggressive feelings constrict the pupils. You need to practice interpreting signs such as these.

Service users, for example, may put up barriers towards you by crossing their arms and/or legs (known as a closed position); in doing so they demonstrate that they may be defensive and are withdrawing from the conversation. An open position with legs slightly apart and arms relaxed, often with the palms uppermost, may be associated with an honest and truthful display (see Figure 1.9).

Service users who pick imaginary fluff from their clothes while looking towards the floor are showing a very common sign of disapproval with the content of the communication, and those who pick at their cuffs, buttons and watches may be displaying nervousness. Service users who are anxious will rarely have their hands open; it is far more likely that they will have a closed fist that shows white knuckles. Even though the words used indicate that the service users are not worried, the behaviour described here and biting the lips would indicate otherwise. Anxious people may look paler than usual, be more distracted and seem quieter than usual.

Service users who feel 'down' or depressed frequently have their head bent down and eyes on the floor; their gait is more shuffling and they take smaller steps, their clothing tends to be coloured grey, brown or black and they make little effort to look nice.

FIGURE 1.9 *Body posture can indicate attitude to others*

Observation

Observation is rather like the Advanced Motoring Test, where the examiner expects you to be aware of your surroundings for quite some distance ahead and behind you, regardless of whether it forms an immediate threat or not. You are expected to be pro-active in any given situation rather than retro-active. Being pro-active means that you are anticipating or thinking ahead about what might happen and the potential response is already forming; to be retro-active, on the other hand, means responding to a situation that has already happened.

Once again, skills like these need practice and reflection and then consideration about whether action should be taken. You might ask yourself questions similar to the following while you are carrying out your normal daily work tasks:

* Were any service users acting differently?
* Were any service users particularly drowsy or alert?
* Did the appetites of service users change?
* Did physical measurements of body temperature or blood pressure vary more than usual?
* Can I account for noticeable changes?
* How long have these changes been apparent?
* Do I need to record the changes, refer to colleagues or respond to the variation?
* At what time intervals do I need to repeat my observations?
* Am I missing something important?
* Did I miss anything that a colleague noticed?
* Why did I fail to notice?

Questions such as these with their responses (logged into a notebook) will assist the personal and professional development of any carer and promote valuable reflective skills.

Communication

This is not just talking or chatting to service users; indeed, it is one of the hardest skills to acquire and needs constant practice and reflection, too. Many professional carers never acquire the skills of communication to the levels desired because it is difficult, requiring constructive criticism and honest feedback from others that only a few are prepared to ask for and act upon.

The special type of listening promoted by carers is called active listening and there are many people who justifiably believe that you cannot be an effective communicator without first being an active listener. The term means that you are being active not passive in the way in which you listen; this is demonstrated by giving wholehearted attention, nodding encouragingly, prompting where necessary, clarifying any difficulties and by generally being supportive. You will find more detail about listening skills in Unit 2.

When we communicate we impart information and this may be managed more effectively if we invite questions from the audience. Sometimes speakers feel threatened by questions because they find it difficult to give answers or do not know the answer. Admit openly and honestly if you do not know the answer – do not guess or try to drive the question in a different direction without giving the answer – everyone knows what you are trying to do and will appreciate an honest reply. We have all met politicians and salespersons that have their own agendas and rarely provide direct answers to questions, particularly when they sense criticism, and they do not convince us of their credibility. Offer to search for the answer if at all possible and to return, but do not say this if you have no intention of doing so.

It is of paramount importance that you match the way you give information to the style of the service user or service user group. For example, when talking to a child or a service user with learning difficulties, it is necessary to use simple short sentences that convey the message in a positive way. For older people, especially if they have hearing difficulties, it is essential to let them see both your eyes and lips; it is usually not necessary to shout but to speak clearly and slowly. Be prepared to repeat your words, as understanding can be slower. Never use the sort of language you would use to a child; it would be quite wrong and older people may become very irritated by it.

Listen and observe how experienced carers communicate with different service users and do not be afraid to ask questions or ask for feedback.

It is also polite, especially if you are a young person, to ask the service user how he or she would like to be addressed. Just because another carer calls someone by his or her first name, you must not assume that it is all right for you to do so. Many older people may prefer to be called Mrs Smith, rather than Maggie, by someone much younger whom they have only just met. When in doubt, do not ask your friend – ask the service user.

FIGURE 1.10 *Make sure people understand your meaning*

Encouraging behaviour that promotes health and well-being

Encouraging service users to reinforce behaviour that increases their health and well-being (known as adaptive behaviour) is an important skill for carers. We all like praise and encouragement and will remember the occasion far longer, which increases the chances that the behaviour will be repeated and eventually become the norm. Carers should not remonstrate with service users when their behaviour is not likely to increase their well-being (known as maladaptive behaviour). The

Think it over...

Style of language must also match the service user group. Sally, who was on work experience in a residential home, was engaged in a conversation with Mrs Booth, aged 89 years; they were discussing a new cardigan, which Mrs Booth's daughter had brought on a visit the day before. Mrs Booth puzzled over Sally's comment that the cardigan was 'cool' and decided that she would never wear the garment on cold days.

Think about other fashionable language traits and how they might be misinterpreted by an older generation of service users.

Think it over...

Sally, who was in the last three months of pregnancy with her first child, was on the verge of being allowed to go home after being brought into antenatal care because her blood pressure was higher than it should be. Carer A met Sally re-entering the ward and stopped to speak with her. During the conversation, the carer could see the bulge of a cigarette packet in Sally's dressing gown and could smell tobacco smoke on her breath. How would you proceed with the conversation knowing that smoking increases blood pressure and seriously affects the unborn child? Practice the conversation with a colleague and ask how he or she felt.

carer can, however, gently provide information about the effects of the maladaptive behaviour, remembering that each individual is unique and free to choose.

Think it over...

Mabel Thomson, an elderly widow, had a very poor appetite following a stroke. Her medical team thought that the stroke had affected the area of her brain that controlled appetite. Consequently, already frail, she was losing weight; one day her carer noticed that she had managed to eat half of her supper and praised her by saying that she had done very well. On another occasion, an inexperienced carer gently chastised her because she had left half her meal, telling her that she would never get better if she did not eat her supper. Comment on the merits of the two carers.

Creating trust

Creating trust is vital if caring is to be a true partnership between carer and service user. A throwaway line such as 'See you later' or 'I'll be back to hear about yesterday's visit' is taken seriously by the service user, who often has little to do but wait expectantly for the carer to return. This is often seen to be of no significance by the carer beset by a hundred other issues, but the service user feels let down and of no consequence. It is far better not to not make such statements but wait and see if other duties permit, and then say 'I have a few spare minutes to hear about your visit yesterday'.

Carers and doctors, in particular, seem to have no understanding of the way in which service users or their families dissect words.

Think it over...

Mrs T telephoned the ward to see how her husband was after his heart bypass surgery. She had been told that there was no point in visiting that day, as he would be under the influence of the anaesthetic until the morning; but this did not stop her from feeling very anxious. The carer who answered the telephone paused to examine notes on a computer screen and replied that 'he was as well as could be expected'. Mrs T thanked him for the information, said she was sorry to have troubled them and put the telephone down. As she made herself a cup of tea, she thought about the reply: 'What did it mean?' 'Was Mr T not expected to recover, was he extremely ill or had some complication arisen?' Mrs T did not sleep that night because the carer's response worried her so much. How could the carer have answered Mrs T and not caused her so much anxiety?

Service users and their carers may develop special relationships when the service user reveals confidences.

Think it over...

A service user may tell a carer that she is sad that her daughter is a drug addict and had an abortion last year. She would have liked to be a grandmother. The carer tells her colleague that the daughter, who lives close to the friend, is a drug addict. Later, the colleague asks the service user if she is worried about her daughter and the service user immediately knows that her confidences have been breached. Although she does not bring up the issue with her carer, she never trusts her with information again. What are the implications for the care relationship?

In the scenario above the carer has breached confidentiality; the information had no bearing on the care of the service user and the carer had no right to pass it on to anyone without the consent of the service user. At the very least, the carer should have been disciplined and could have lost her job as a result. Every care organisation should have a policy on confidentiality, which employees must abide by.

As carers, we have the obligation to be consistent in our approach. Service users may feel angry and resentful if maladaptive behaviour is condoned one day, as it is ignored due to pressure of work, and when repeated the next day, the issue is taken up.

Tommy loves water play in the nursery, but he can behave badly towards other children. Yesterday, he threw a plastic cup full of water over Sarah and was forbidden to play with water again. Today, he joined the water play again and threw water over Mollie. The carer made him promise not to do it again and he continued with water play.

What effects would this inconsistency have on Sarah, Mollie and Tommy?

FIGURE 1.11 *Children in a nursery at water play*

Reducing negative feelings and behaviours of service users and others, avoiding and defusing conflict

Earlier, we looked at reflective caring and the need to notice changes in behaviour. You might notice that someone is becoming emotionally disturbed and be able to take him or her into a quiet room to enquire if they are worried about something, so managing the situation in a pro-active way. When conflict arises more suddenly, it is also wise to take the individual to a quiet place, to talk without an audience. Some people relish an audience and 'play to the gallery'. The physical act of moving also provides a few

moments in which the individual may become calmer. Always keep calm yourself and try to appear confident, but do not attempt to argue or glare at the other person; dropping eye contact from time to time may also be useful. Going to fetch a supervisor, if appropriate, will give yet more time to quieten down and time to consider the issues. Use any counselling skills that you have acquired, particularly active listening skills, paraphrasing and reviewing until you are quite clear about the complaint. Use empathy and try to convey understanding of the situation; there may be a release of emotion such as crying and this release is often succeeded by a quieter period.

When appropriate, touching a hand or arm may convey a caring attitude, but be aware of any cultural differences regarding touch and any sexual implications. Never promise action that you cannot fulfil to get out of a difficult situation, and if you promise to speak to someone else (with the service user's permission) then do so promptly, again without specifying that they will take action.

Sam was angry. He had taken his girlfriend into A&E because she was feeling unwell, her breathing was fast and shallow and her pulse was racing. The duty medical officer asked her to breathe into a bag and several hours later sent her home having diagnosed a 'panic attack'. Two weeks later, in a different location, there was a repeat attack and this time it led to hospitalisation and a minor operation to amend the rhythm of her heart. Sam returned to the first hospital, demanding that the A&E doctor was sacked.

How would you manage Sam's anger?

Gaining compliance

This is getting someone to agree with a recommended course of action. Trying to simply persuade someone to do something usually does not work because there is no basis for agreement, only one individual trying to influence another. When that person is not present, the persuasion loses impact and the request is discarded. An individual needs information, usually in the form of reasoning or a limited number of choices in order to proceed with the request. For example, trying to persuade a service user to stop smoking will not work, but providing information on the health risks of smoking might. If this is still deemed to be too difficult, then alternatives can be offered such as reducing the number of cigarettes smoked over time with targets, providing 'patches', changing daily habits and introducing a new specific physical activity are limited choices that may be tried.

Eye contact and facial expression

These are very important in gaining compliance, because you will learn to 'read' a service user's gaze as agreeing or not. For example, an elderly male resident refuses to bathe and his table companions have complained that his body odour puts them off eating. Nobody wants to sit near him at meal times. Tom's carer decides that she will try to resolve the situation and talks to Tom in a quiet room, sitting in an open position with full eye contact to gain his attention.

Carer: 'Tom, other residents have said that your body odour prevents them enjoying their food.'

Tom: 'Who says I smell?'

Carer: 'That is not important, what is important is your personal hygiene is offending some other residents.'

Tom: 'I don't like bathing.'

Carer: 'I appreciate that, but it is necessary to wash regularly to prevent body odour caused by bacteria on the skin.'

Tom: 'I ain't got no bacteria.'

Carer: 'Everybody has bacteria on their skin, Tom, and if left too long, they produce smells, and they can cause skin infections.'

Tom: 'I don't like getting in and out of the bath, and I don't like those hoists.'

Carer: 'All right, Tom, how about a shower, where you can stand up?'

Tom: ' Well . . .'

Carer 'What about once a week?'

Tom: 'Will that stop people complaining about me?'

Carer: 'I'm sure it will, Tom, and a shower is very refreshing, you can have a special stool to sit on if you would like to.'

Tom: 'There's always someone grumbling about something.'

Carer: 'Tom, can we agree that you will take a weekly shower on, say, Tuesdays and more often if you feel like it?'

Tom: 'Oh! I suppose so.'

Tom is still a little grudging in his reply, so it is very important that eye contact is held and the last carer's statement repeated if necessary.

FIGURE 1.12 *An elderly man enjoying a sit-down shower*

Think it over...

Using the scenario above, analyse the exchange between Tom and the carer in the light of caring skills and techniques. Would you have tackled the issue differently? Justify your comments.

How might the carer follow through after the first shower day?

Eye contact and a pleasant facial expression are also important to gain someone's attention. Earlier, in the section on avoiding conflict, we discussed the importance of not glaring and even dropping eye contact when dealing with an angry person.

Disengagement

Disengagement means breaking an exchange for a short period, perhaps by going to call someone else or moving to a different location. This often has the power to calm down a heated exchange. Disengagement has been mentioned before in the section on avoiding conflict – see page 27.

Physical contact

Touching a service user's hand or arm, or putting an arm around someone's back, can be very reassuring and provides emotional security. A direct look with a smile and a touch will also show that you approve of a situation. Touching someone with whom you are unfamiliar, an individual from a different culture or a person who might consider touch to have a sexual connotation, is not to be recommended. As a carer, you will learn to resist using touch until you are sure that it will not be misinterpreted.

'Did you see that? He stroked my arm – I think he fancies me!'

FIGURE 1.13 *Touching may be misinterpreted*

Distraction

This can be used to divert a service user from worrying about something too much or when they are in pain. A service user may be taught to use distraction when necessary. It may be more powerful when taught through the senses, such as concentrating on pictures or photographs and imagining sunshine or cold winds, sounds like birds singing or smells of fish and chips. This type of therapy can be combined with muscle relaxation and massage. Closing the eyes or having a blindfold can help the imagination.

The pain or the anxiety does not disappear but the mind is able to shut it out for a period, perhaps while painkillers take effect.

Modelling

This means showing only socially acceptable behaviour in a situation in the hope that a service user will learn to act in a similar way. A simple form of modelling might entail greeting service users with a warm smile and a cheery 'Good morning' on entering the room. After a few mornings, service users will greet you in the same way and often be the first to do so.

Working alongside service users

This can be a wonderful way to cement caring relationships and stimulate discussion. Playing with infants and children provides insights into the way that they relate to certain things and it has been particularly useful to use doll play in cases of suspected child abuse. People in late adulthood can be encouraged to do housework and cooking alongside caring staff to stimulate

Playing with children reveals the way they relate to others

mental activities and physical abilities. Young carers themselves can learn a lot about home-making from older people too!

Showing approval

Giving praise by making remarks such as 'Well done' or 'You look very nice today' is really valuable inside a caring relationship for it shows you noticed the effort the service user has made. Every one of us responds to praise and it is even more important with service users in care to show that they have been recognised as being human too. It is all too easy to fall into a de-humanising situation when you are doing your work. The difference here is that you are dealing with human beings with feelings.

Just because someone has a disability, illness or vulnerability does not mean that we can cease to value individuals as unique with wants, needs and hopes of their own. Just as you seek approval from parents, friends and family, service users seek approval from those nearest to them – their carers.

Setting challenges

Challenge in the form of small achievable targets is also part of the human condition. We continually set ourselves small challenges every day; for example, tomorrow I will try to get the lawn mowed, the ironing/washing done, that essay written that I have been meaning to get down to. Service users also need to be set small challenges to avoid becoming institutionalised; these may be quite simple, such as:

* walking a little bit further
* managing more personal hygiene
* playing a game
* listening to music
* doing more housework
* eating more fruit and vegetables
* spending less time in bed
* drinking more fluids.

Many other challenges may be set depending on the age, ability and experience of the service user.

Targets should always have a purpose and they are more likely to be successful when service users clearly understand the underlying reasons are for their benefit.

1.4 Services

Formal care

Many different types of services are available to potential and actual service users. Different individuals will have very differing needs and a variety of services should be available to meet those needs.

NHS services

NHS services can broadly be described as primary, secondary and tertiary. Primary services could be described as front-line services and are often the first point of contact for individuals in need. Often this is done by self-referral, that is the individual contacts the service him or herself, such as the general practitioner or the dentist. Sometimes individuals will be referred by others, such as relatives, if they are unable to do so for themselves. Secondary services are usually services to which individuals are referred by another health or social care professional. An example of this would be a lady who is suffering from arthritis in her hip. She goes to see her GP, who then refers her to an orthopaedic surgeon for further assessment and treatment. Secondary care generally focuses on hospital care, day surgeries and out-patient treatment. Tertiary care is usually specialised care such as intensive care services or long-term care such as rehabilitation or care for older people.

Community services include nursing and therapy services: district nurses, health visitors and community psychiatric nurses, for example; therapy services such as physiotherapy, occupational therapy and speech therapy and dental and optical services.

GP consultation, diagnosis and treatment

Individuals usually refer themselves to the general practitioner when they feel unwell. They will be asked to describe their symptoms and from this the GP will usually be able to make a diagnosis. It may be necessary to undertake various tests to make the diagnosis, some of which can be done at the surgery. These will include taking observations such as temperature, pulse, respiration rate and blood pressure, or taking a urine, faeces or blood sample. Generally these will need to be sent off to a laboratory for analysis, although some preliminary tests such as testing urine for glucose can be done at the surgery.

Once the GP has made a diagnosis, he or she will be able to start treatment to alleviate or cure the problem. Not all problems can be cured, but often relief can be given by different types of treatment, and the GP can refer service users to other health or social care professionals for further treatment or therapy.

Hospital services

Accident and emergency services are usually situated in large hospitals that have support services, which can be used to provide further treatment or services for individuals. People in need of emergency treatment can self-refer, or they may be referred to an accident and emergency department by a GP. Depending on the severity of the problem, individuals may be treated and discharged or may need to be admitted for further treatment. Diagnostic tools are generally more sophisticated, with more facilities available than at a GP surgery. Very ill or severely injured patients may require further diagnosis or treatment such as MRI scans or life support.

Day surgery

Day surgery is exactly what the name suggests. Individuals are admitted to a day surgery unit where they receive treatment and are discharged on the same day. This option will be considered for minor surgery; for example, some gynaecological treatments or dental extractions. Day surgery has a number of advantages, such as avoiding the need for nervous patients to spend the night in hospital, and relieving the burden on beds that might be needed for people requiring a longer stay in hospital. After-care advice must be clearly given and it must be stressed to day surgery patients that this must be followed. It is all too easy for people to believe that because their treatment has not required a stay in hospital they do not need to take time to recover. Even a small amount of general anaesthetic can make a person feel very tired for a couple of days, and many day surgery procedures will cause pain and discomfort.

Diagnosis and treatment by a hospital consultant

If a GP feels unable to provide the appropriate support and treatment for individuals, then he or she will refer them to a hospital consultant for further treatment. This is generally a senior doctor who has trained in a particular speciality for several years and is considered to be an expert in his or her field. A consultant will head a team of doctors, some of whom will still be undergoing training. Although the consultant will take overall charge of the diagnosis and treatment of patients, much of the day-to-day management of the care will be undertaken by other members of the team, and there may not be a guarantee that an operation or procedure will be carried out by the consultant in charge.

Community nursing

Community nurses provide care in the community and may provide general care or more specialised services depending on the needs of service users. District nurses are registered nurses who have an additional qualification. They may be in charge of a team of health care assistants, who provide day-to-day care in people's homes. They are usually based at GP surgeries or health centres. District nurses work closely with general practitioners and, in addition to providing care, may organise the provision of special equipment for their service users.

Community psychiatric nurses are nurses who are trained in mental-health nursing and may also have other qualifications such as a Diploma in Community Psychiatric Nursing and training in counselling and family therapy. Their role is to provide support to people who are experiencing problems in their lives or who have serious mental illnesses such as depression or schizophrenia.

Community midwives provide ante-natal and post-natal care in the community. Although most babies are born in hospital today, some mothers prefer to have their baby at home and will then require the services of the community midwife for a home delivery. Generally the midwife will take care of mother and baby for the first ten days of the baby's life, before referring them on to the health visitor.

Health Visitor

The Health Visitor is a registered nurse with special training in the assessment of the health needs of individuals, families and the community. The primary role is to promote health and tackle inequality across all age groups. Their main work is related to babies and children under five years of age. They take over the care of mother and baby when the baby is about ten days old. They run clinics, usually at GP surgeries or health centres, to monitor the children's health and undertake regular developmental checks to ensure that an individual child is developing within normal limits. The checks include hearing and sight tests. The role of the health visitor is set to change within the next few years.

Advice from NHS Direct

NHS Direct is a nurse-led 24-hour service that provides health care information and advice to the public in England on the diagnosis and treatment of common conditions through a telephone helpline and an online service. People can access the website through www.heinemann.co.uk/hotlinks (express code 1554P) to find out how to identify symptoms and by working out the course of action that is best for them. The self-help guide is also available in the back of all new Thomson Local directories.

NHS Direct Wales is a bilingual telephone help line which provides 24 hours health advice and information to people who live in Wales. The help line is manned by nurses and health information advisers who can give advice on what to do if someone is ill.

In Scotland NHS24 is a new service that became available to the whole of Scotland at the end of 2004. It is similar to NHS Direct but has the particular needs of the Scottish people in mind.

Informal care

Informal care is that given to a person in need by someone who is not paid to provide the care. Informal care is provided by a relative, neighbour or friend but can also be provided by voluntary groups such as charities or church groups.

Carers will provide all sorts of care to those they are looking after. These include:

* helping people to get up and go to bed
* helping with personal hygiene needs
* helping with toileting
* preparing food and drink
* giving medicines
* providing transport.

It is important for health care professionals to be aware that informal carers can experience high levels of stress because caring for someone, even if it is a close family member, is tiring emotionally and physically. Carers need support so that they can continue to provide the necessary care. This may include:

* having time off
* receiving satisfactory and reliable services to help them
* recognition of their role.

Early years

A variety of early years provision is available for pre-school children. This can be provided by the local authority, voluntary or private sectors. The government has pledged to provide pre-school care for all three- and four-year-olds who require it. This can take place in a variety of settings as long as it is registered by government regulatory bodies and is inspected regularly. The child registers with an early years setting, which receives funding for him or her. The minimum requirement of a part-time place is five two-and-a-half-hour sessions every week over 33 weeks (usually divided into 11-week terms). Parents have an element of choice about what type of childcare provision they have for their children. If, for example, they choose to place their child in a private fee-paying day nursery, then they will have to pay for any costs over and above the amount that is awarded for their child.

Day nurseries

These will provide full- or part-time day care for

---

* DID YOU KNOW?

In April 2001 there were 5.9 million informal carers in the United Kingdom. The majority of these carers were female (3.4 million compared with 2.5 million males). Around a quarter of both male and female carers were aged 45 to 54 with around a fifth of carers falling in each of the adjacent age groups (35 to 44 and 55 to 64).

Two-thirds of all carers were caring for less than 20 hours per week and a fifth were caring for 50 hours or more. Women were slightly more likely than men to be caring for 50 hours or more, while men were slightly more likely than women to be caring for less than 20 hours. However, of those aged 85 and over, male carers were more likely than female carers to be caring for 50 hours or more (54 per cent compared with 47 per cent).

In 2001 there were 179,000 male carers and 169,000 female carers aged 75 and over – representing 12 per cent of men within this age group and 7 per cent of women. Older men are more likely than older women to be married and therefore a larger proportion of men are able to provide care to their spouses, as well as receive care. Older women are more likely than older men to be living alone and are therefore more likely to receive care from personal social services. In Great Britain, although there was little difference between the proportions of men and women receiving home help in most age groups, a greater proportion of women than men aged 85 and over received private or local authority home help in 2001/02.

Source: Social Trends 34, 2004

children up to school age, often because parents work. They are usually private and parents pay fees. Children are given the opportunity to learn and to socialise with others.

> ### ✳ DID YOU KNOW?
>
> Over 750,000 children are cared for by day nurseries.
>
> In total 1.7 million children use day care.
>
> There are over 12,000 day nurseries in England and Wales.
>
> An estimated 25 per cent of nurseries also provide out of school care for 5–11-year-olds.
>
> Source: National Day Nurseries Association (www.ndna.org.uk)

Crèche

Crèches offer occasional care for children under the age of 8 years to give their parents the opportunity to have some time to themselves to pursue their own interests, such as going to the gym or going shopping. Parents are not usually required to stay with their child, but some may ask that the parents do not leave the building, for example in leisure centres. Crèches have to be registered if they run for more than two hours per day.

Playgroup

Playgroups are run on a not-for-profit basis and are most often managed by parent management committees. The committee employs a trained manager and trained childcare workers, but there will be parents who are involved in the day-to-day running of the service. Half the staff must be trained. Playgroups charge fees, but these are low and the average fee is approximately £3.50 for a three-hour-long session. Playgroups are registered and inspected every year.

Nursery school

A nursery school is a school for pre-school-age children, which is run independently from any other school. Nursery schools have their own head teacher and staff, which include teachers, nursery nurses and classroom assistants. A nursery school has to be registered with the

government regulatory bodies and is inspected every year. It will almost certainly offer a government-approved early years curriculum. There are state nursery schools, which are free, and private nursery schools where fees are paid, although a three- or four-year-old may be entitled to a free part-time place. If a child has a free part-time place and parents wish the child to attend full-time, they would have to pay the extra cost of doing so.

Care of elderly people

In November 2003, the House of Lords Select Committee on Economic Affairs produced a report *Aspects of an Ageing Population*, and it stated that:

> 'The population of the United Kingdom is ageing. In 2001, for the first time in the United Kingdom, there were more people aged over 60 than under 16. By 2051, an estimated one in four people will be aged over 65. Much debate on the ageing population has focused on the challenges it presents. We believe that, just as society has adjusted to accommodate the demographic changes that have been experienced so far, so too will it adjust to accommodate the challenges of the future.'

The fact that the population is ageing will in the future provide great challenges for health and social care services, as it is probable that the needs of older people will grow. Currently, various types of provision exist that has been designed to meet the needs of older people.

Nursing and residential home care

Nursing homes are for people who have an infirmity, illness or injury that means that they require regular nursing care, which cannot be provided for them at home, and can only be provided by a registered nurse. All nursing homes must be registered and regularly inspected by the appropriate health authority, although nursing home care is usually provided by the private or voluntary sector, and not by the NHS.

Residential homes are for people who do not require nursing care but are no longer able to cope with living independently, even if they have the support of formal or informal carers.

Residential homes are provided by the local authority or private or voluntary services and all have to be registered with the appropriate social services.

Some homes are dual-registered and offer both types of care. It is important that individuals needing care are aware of the difference in the type of care offered and choose, or are helped to choose, the most appropriate care for their needs.

Day care

Day care is a valuable service offered to older people who are still able to live at home, either alone or with other members of the family, but may spend long periods of time alone during the day. It may be provided by volunteers or by the local authority. A day centre will usually provide transport to and from the centre, a range of activities and a meal. This can be a lifeline for older people who may be lonely or may have experienced abuse or neglect. Participation in the activities at a day centre, whether it is using hairdressing facilities, going on outings or even just meeting new people who become friends, will give elderly people new interests, a sense of belonging and increased self-esteem and self-confidence.

Home (domiciliary) care

There may be reasons why an individual might choose to remain living at home and receive care and support from various services. They may feel that they are still able to live at home with extra support and do not like the thought that they may lose their independence by going into residential accommodation. Many services can be provided in the community, including nursing care, help with personal hygiene or dressing, meals on wheels or a home food delivery service such as Wiltshire Farm Foods that supply ready-made frozen meals, mobile shops, library services and hairdressers. Many companies provide personal alarm systems for those who live alone. This is usually a device that is worn round the neck with a call button that when pressed, will connect with a call centre which will forward the call to a GP, relative or the ambulance service.

Needs assessment

Whenever a request is made for care for an older person, an assessment of needs should be made. This is to ensure that individual needs are identified and can be met. If an individual is thinking of going into residential care, then a needs assessment will be made to ascertain whether residential care is the only option or whether the individual would be able to stay living in his or her own home with more help and support. The assessment of needs will be made by the local social services department in the case of residential care, and by social services and a qualified health professional in the case of nursing home care.

Social services will also assess the financial status of the potential service user and this will determine whether or not the individual is entitled to some help with the cost of the fees. However, if an individual has more than £16,000 worth of assets, he or she will be expected to pay the full cost of the fees.

The needs of services users can change and needs may have to be reassessed on a regular basis. This will include a reassessment of financial status, as residential care is very expensive and a service user may find that their assets soon disappear. Once their total assets drop below £16,000 they may become entitled to help with paying the fees.

Special needs

Children and young people who have special needs such as a learning difficulty or a physical disability may have particular needs that can best be met in a special school that has the facilities and specialist staff to meet their needs. In addition to providing education, some special schools that cater for pupils with profound and multiple learning difficulties will also provide other services such as physiotherapy, speech and language therapy, sensory rooms and possibly even a hydrotherapy pool. Some special schools are for primary aged children, but some will provide education from early years to 16 or 19 years of age.

Support within mainstream schools

The Education Act 1993 stated that children with special education needs should normally be educated at mainstream schools if this is what the parents want. As a result of this, many more children with special needs are being integrated into mainstream schools. However, there are mixed feelings about this strategy which is being promoted by the government. Some people support the strategy wholeheartedly because they feel that mainstream inclusion has a positive effect on children with learning difficulties, but others feel that a child with specific educational needs may not receive the specialist support that they need, although they will often have one-to-one support from a classroom assistant. There is a fear among some parents that a child with learning difficulties may feel intimidated by the fact that they are underachieving compared with other children in the class. Children with behavioural difficulties can also cause disruption in a mainstream classroom and some would argue that this will affect the learning of all children in that class.

Summary

This section has described different types of services that are available across generations. Although each service has been described individually it is important to remember that some individuals will require care from a multidisciplinary team who work together to provide a variety of services to those in need.

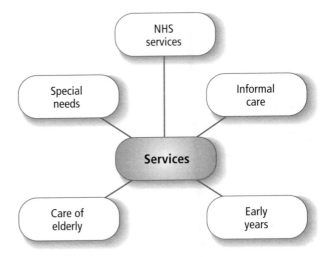

FIGURE 1.15 *Unit 1.4 summary*

Consider this

Undertake a survey of your local area to identify how much of the provision described above is available. Undertake research to find out what services are available and for which service user groups.

Find in local newspapers any articles that relate to proposed changes to existing provision. Make sure that you identify arguments for and against the proposed changes.

1. How many different services are available?

2. What proposed changes to services did your newspaper research identify?

3. What was the reaction to the proposed changes?

1.5 Access to services

Ways in which access to services can be achieved

Different ways in which services may be accessed include:

* self-referral
* referral by a third party
* recommendation of a professional
* recall.

Self-referral

People are only able to refer themselves to services if they know that they exist. There are a variety of ways that they can find out about what is available, such as general publicity through television and newspapers, from leaflets and posters in public places and by word of mouth. Normally services for which self-referral is made are GPs, dentists, opticians or private services. People may also refer themselves to social services if they feel that they have a need, although their needs will be assessed by qualified personnel to determine whether it is sufficient to require support.

Referral by a third party

People can be referred for primary or social services by a relative, neighbour or friend. Third-party referrals can be anonymous if the person referring prefers it. Another type of third-party referral can be from one service to another, such as a district nurse referring a service user to social services.

Recommendation of a professional

Some services can only be accessed by referral from a professional. One very commonly used example of this is referral by a GP to a hospital consultant or other specialist hospital service. There are other examples of professional referral, such as the referral of a child by a teacher to an educational psychologist.

Recall

Some services will provide a recall service. This is an automatic service that comes into operation after an individual has registered with a service such as a dentist or optician, or for screening services such as breast cancer screening or cervical smear testing.

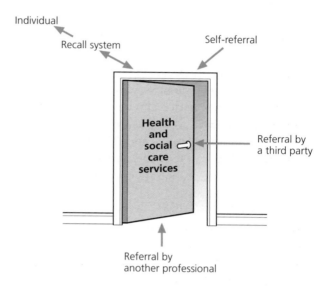

FIGURE 1.16 *Opening the door to health and social care services*

Barriers to access

There are different ways in which service users encounter barriers to receiving care from health and social care services. These are discussed below.

Inadequate resources

If there is inadequate funding and service capacity, this means that there are not enough resources to provide the care needed. This can result in delays in getting an appointment to see a general practitioner or in referral to secondary services. Staff shortages or shortage of beds can cause delays in receiving treatment and surgery, causing multiple cancellations for some individuals. Delays in receiving social service funding for residential care might result in a reduced level of care or delay in much needed care being provided. There is little that can be done about this by individual service users, but those who can afford to pay for private treatment may find that they are able to receive treatment more quickly.

Ignorance

Many people and their relatives might be completely unaware of services that may be available to them. Even if they are aware of the services, they may have no idea of how to access them. Developments in ICT, greater computer literacy and more widespread use of the Internet have helped to make information more available. In addition, public information announcements on the television are becoming more common and more people are aware of services such as NHS Direct where information can be gained by telephone or online. If people are receiving care or support from one service, careful questioning of the individual might lead the care professional to discover other needs that are not being met.

Physical difficulties

Individuals in need of services may be physically unable to access them. This may be because they live a long distance from the services they require and do not have their own transport or access to public transport. People who work full-time and have difficulty getting time off for appointments during the day may delay much needed consultations, especially if the service they require does not offer appointments before 9.00 am or after 5.00 pm.

Disabled or older people may not be able to access services due to mobility problems. If they are wheelchair users or have poor mobility, they might not be able to use public transport and may have no one they can ask to help them. Hospital car services provided by volunteers can be used to transport people to and from hospital for treatment or out-patient clinics, and social services can provide transport to take people to day centres. Various companies can provide motorised scooters for elderly people to help them to maintain their mobility, although requirements may be much simpler, such as the provision of walking sticks, frames or other mobility aids.

Communication

There are different ways in which communication can cause barriers to accessing services. If carers and service users do not have a common language it can be difficult (if not impossible) to exchange information. Service users with sensory impairments such as deafness or blindness might be prevented from accessing important information that might affect their care or physical or mental well-being. People who are illiterate will not be able to read written information and may be too embarrassed about

Reception areas should be designed to assist communication

their level of literacy to ask someone to help them. Any of these service users will suffer from inability to access services if the information they need is not available for them in suitable forms. Information could be provided in different languages and in Braille or on cassette tape. Interpreters, picture boards or signing could also be used.

Summary

In this section you have learned about the ways in which barriers can prevent full access to services that individuals require. With careful planning and knowledge of the different ways of providing information many of these barriers can be overcome. Provision of information in the right format can provide a better service to such individuals.

FIGURE 1.17 *Barriers to access*

Consider this

Mrs Singh is a 25-year-old Asian woman who came to live in the United Kingdom when her parents arranged her marriage four years ago. She received a basic level of education until the age of 14 but worked to help support her family until the marriage was arranged. She lives in a large city with a big Asian population and only mixes with other Asian women. As a result, she does not speak any English, only Punjabi. She has a son aged 18 months. She has just found a lump in her breast and is very worried about it. She finds it difficult to talk to her husband about such intimate matters and is reluctant to discuss it with him, partly because he works very long hours. She has confided in her next-door neighbour Mrs Kaur, who works at the local health centre. Mrs Kaur speaks Punjabi and some English and confides in the district nurse. She wants advice on how to help Mrs Singh.

1. What advice could the district nurse offer to Mrs Kaur?

2. How could the district nurse ensure that Mrs Singh receives treatment without delay?

3. What resources might the district nurse have access to that will help to provide an efficient and personalised service for Mrs Singh?

1.6 Rights and responsibilities of service users

The NHS Plan

The Prime Minister Tony Blair launched '*The NHS Plan*' in July 2000 to explain how extra funding will be used to improve the NHS. '*Your Guide to the NHS*' helped to explain how the changes will affect service users, what to expect now and in the future. The following information replaces *The Patient's Charter*, an influential document widely circulated in the 1990s. The guide (at the time of writing) may be difficult to obtain and consequently may be updated in the future.

One of the sections sets out the NHS core principles and the commitment to service users of the desire for the NHS to be a high quality health service with established aims.

The aims are listed below:

* The NHS will provide a universal service for all based on clinical need, not ability to pay

* The NHS will provide a comprehensive range of services

* The NHS will shape its services around the needs and preferences of individual patients, their families and their carers

* The NHS will respond to different needs of different populations

* The NHS will work continuously to improve quality services and to minimise errors

* The NHS will support and value its staff

* Public funds for healthcare will be devoted solely to NHS patients

* The NHS will work together with others to ensure a seamless service for patients

* The NHS will help keep people healthy and work to reduce health inequalities

* The NHS will respect the confidentiality of individual patients and provide open access to information about services, treatment and performance.

Think it over...

Consider the implications of this list of core principals for a service user and a carer in the employment of the NHS.

What does 'responding to the different needs of different populations' mean?

Discuss what you understand by 'a seamless service'.

In what ways can the NHS work to reduce health inequalities?

How can performance be judged?

Explain how confidentiality of individual patients can be respected.

Carry out a small investigation of people you know who use the services of the NHS and find out if they are aware of open access to information about services, treatment and performance.

Your commitment to the NHS

Key concept

The NHS is anxious to conserve resources and cut wastage so that all may benefit from the service. *Your Guide to the NHS* includes advice for service users using the service to participate in this regard. The guide also advises service users on ways to stay healthy and how to contact different sections of the NHS.

The NHS will work better if you use the service responsibly. Recommendations are made that you should:

* do what you can to look after your own health, and follow a healthy lifestyle.

* care for yourself when appropriate. (For example, you can treat yourself at home for common ailments such as coughs, colds and sore throats.)

* give blood if you are able, and carry an organ donor card or special needs card or bracelet.

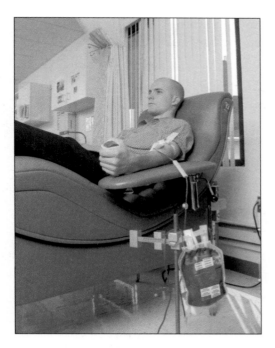

Give blood if you are able to

* listen carefully to advice on your treatment and medication. Tell the doctor about any treatments you are already taking.

* treat NHS staff, fellow patients, carers and visitors politely, and with respect. They will not accept violence, racial, sexual or verbal harassment from service users.

* keep your appointment or let the GP, dentist, clinic or hospital know as soon as possible if you cannot make it. Book routine appointments in plenty of time.

* return any equipment that is no longer needed such as crutches.

* pay NHS prescription charges and any other charges promptly when they are due and claim financial benefits or exemptions from these charges correctly.

* use this guide ('Your Guide to the NHS') to help you find the services you need.

Consider this

This is guidance for NHS service users in general. Carry out a small investigation of one or more of the bullet points, finding out whether service users know about the guidance and whether or not they abide by the principles listed. For example, you could find out whether your sample keeps appointments or treat themselves for minor ailments, donates blood or carries donor cards. Analyse your results and draw conclusions as far as you are able for a small sample. Discuss whether you think a larger sample would provide similar results.

1.7 Risks and safe working

Most occupations have some risks attached to them and workers should be trained correctly in procedures that should be taken to minimise those risks. Care workers, in particular, encounter risks because they are looking after elderly, ill or disadvantaged people and it is very important to take special protective care of their own health.

Blood-borne viruses, antibiotic-resistant bacteria, lifting injuries and violent service users are some of the major risks facing care workers.

Blood-borne viruses

HIV

The risk of contracting HIV (human immunodeficiency virus) is low providing that basic precautions are observed. Social contact has no risk attached. Sexual contact, inoculation, pregnancy/childbirth or contact with body fluids can spread the infection when there is a break in the skin or mucous membrane. Body fluids can be semen, breast milk, vaginal secretions, saliva and most importantly blood.

The most likely occurrence leading to infection of a care worker is needlestick injury. This is when a used syringe needle is accidentally plunged into a carer's own skin.

Syringe needles, scalpels and other sharp instruments used in care are collectively known as 'sharps' and special disposal methods are employed in all relevant care establishments. This is usually in a yellow 'sharps' container conforming to Department of Health standards. Other precautions are:

* strict observation of the establishment's policy on handling of equipment and material

* never replacing the needle sheath after use because this can often be the cause of needlestick injury

* leaving the needle on the syringe to minimise aerosol dispersal

* not removing scalpel blades with fingers (use forceps)

* regularly sealing sharps containers and sending for disposal (clearly labelled 'infection hazard') – daily is recommended

* wearing disposable gloves when handling sharps

* using electric shavers or depilatory cream for hair removal

* using disposable equipment whenever possible and autoclaving non-disposable items, again clearly labelled.

HIV infection continues to increase, so an increasing number of people will come into contact with carers. Many HIV positive people have no symptoms so it is wise to use gloves and plastic aprons for everyone when dealing with soiled bed linen, soiled dressings, collection of samples involving bodily fluids, intravenous drug administration, catheter care, urine bottles and bedpans. The wearing of gloves should not preclude effective hand-washing.

Normal toilet use will flush infected material away. There is no need to separate crockery from individuals with the infection unless there are open sores in the mouth or bleeding areas. Carers with cuts and abrasions should cover these with waterproof dressings and those with eczema excluded from the care of HIV+ individuals.

All body fluid splashes should be washed off immediately and if there is a perceived risk of splashing close to the face and mouth, face visors may be worn.

Soiled linen should be double-bagged (the inner bag is water-soluble and does not need to be opened) and washed at very high temperatures. The outer bag is coloured according to the organisation's guidelines.

Many HIV+ individuals suffer from feelings of discrimination and isolation so it is important to practice anti-discriminatory care and sensitivity and to remember confidentiality. HIV has a long incubation period so it is wise to use gloves and take precautions when dealing with any potential contaminated materials.

Hepatitis

There are three types of hepatitis, known as (infective) hepatitis A, (serum) hepatitis B and C; all are caused by viruses and can be serious conditions. Hepatitis A arises from poor hygiene (mouth to anus) or from infected food or drink. Hepatitis B and C are contracted through contact with infected blood or blood products and in this way have similarities with HIV infection. Immunisations are available for care workers deemed to be at risk and they should take the opportunity for added protection.

Protective measures for hepatitis are the same as those described for HIV infection.

Methicillin-resistant *Staphylococcus aureus* (MRSA)

> **Key concept**
>
> *Staphylococcus aureus* are common bacteria normally colonising the skin. Strains of these bacteria have always shown an ability to be resistant to antibiotics. Methicillin, an antibiotic, was first used in the 1960s and strains of Methicillin soon started to appear; these bacteria are now called MRSA.

Some strains spread more easily than others and some people are more vulnerable than others. Media publicity surrounding service users who contract MRSA has concentrated on those who have entered hospitals for minor surgical procedures and died, or lost limbs as a result of MRSA infections.

Politicians, both past and present, are blamed for dirty hospitals associated with MRSA and poor contract cleaning to reduce costs. The Secretary of State for Health has declared that

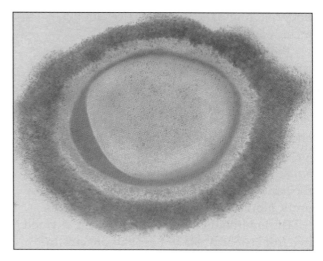

The Staphylococcus aureus bacteria

MRSA infection levels are beginning to decline as new measures take effect (March 2005).

MRSA is resistant to all penicillin drugs and can be resistant to other antibiotics as well; this means that only a small range of other antibiotics is available to treat service users who have these infections. These can be difficult to give, expensive and toxic to the service user. MRSA complications are unpredictable, so taking a standardised approach appropriate for all service users is not possible.

Some people carry MRSA on and in their bodies without harmful effects, but those who are more vulnerable can have life-threatening complications. Vulnerable people who are most at risk include:

* people in intensive care units
* surgical patients who have undergone invasive procedures
* service users who have had recent antibiotic treatment
* service users who have just been in hospital.

It is not known how many people in the community carry MRSA; certainly many people visiting those in hospital will be carriers of MRSA and some care workers themselves will be MRSA+. There is also potential infection in residential and nursing homes and their care staff. It makes sense that basic principles of care must underpin foundations for practice and this includes preventing cross-infection.

The most important principles behind the control of cross-infection are effective hand washing and good hygiene.

Good-quality soap, running clean water and careful drying are often all that is necessary for effective hand hygiene. However, most at-risk areas in hospitals now provide a suitable antiseptic/detergent soap and alcohol gel rub for the hands. This is available for care staff, service users and visitors to use at appropriate times.

The environment must be kept clean, dry and free from rubbish. Many hospitals are able to provide guidance leaflets for staff, service users and visitors.

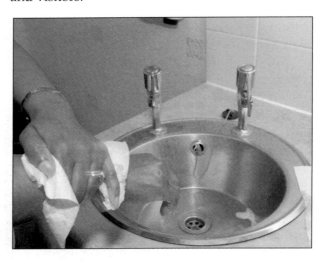

FIGURE 1.19 *Effective hand-washing prevents cross-infection*

Think it over...

Discuss the appropriate times for effective hand washing, bearing in mind the normal location of MRSA bacteria and the likely contaminated material from MRSA+ service users. You will find more useful information on page 10.

Matrons have been appointed to oversee cleanliness in care establishments, particularly where contract cleaners are still in place. Other establishments have taken back their own cleaning in order to have more control. In November 2004, Dr John Reid Secretary of State for Health gave an undertaking to halve the rates of MRSA infection by 2008 and charged Primary Health Care Trusts with the responsibility.

Think it over...

Talk to people you know, service users or those who visit relatives or friends in care establishments and ask them about cleanliness and tidiness in the wards. Collect media articles on MRSA and dirty hospitals and find out through government statistics whether MRSA is in decline.

Lifting injuries

Lifting injuries have been one of the main problems of care workers for decades. You should never try to move or lift a service user without correct training by an authorised tutor of moving and handling techniques. You must decline politely if you are not trained since you would place both your service user and yourself at risk of permanent damage. This is particularly so if you are an adolescent or young adult as your skeleton is still forming.

Think it over...

You should be aware of the following acts, regulations and polices:

* Health and Safety at Work Act (1974)
* Manual Handling Operations Regulations (1992)
* RCN guidelines for moving and handling
* European guidelines on moving and handling (various)
* Management of HASAW (1992)
* Lifting Operations and Lifting Equipment Regulations (1998)
* Local policies in the care establishment that you visit or do a work placement in.

Studying manual handling from a guide or textbook is not a substitute for the training course.

Imagine you are trying to learn how to ride a bicycle. No amount of reading can enable you to get on a cycle and ride perfectly straight away. The volume of legislation identifies the degree of concern that governments, trade unions, employers and employees have over lifting injuries. Although the problem exists in many professions, care workers have experienced a greater incidence of injury than any other.

People do not come in neat tidy packages, service users have fears and anxieties about being moved and many service users were not encouraged to help themselves, as is the case now. In the past, lifting aids were not numerous; most care workers were young women with unsuitable uniforms for lifting. Everything is relatively different today. Manual handling is kept to a minimum with whole-body or near whole-body lifts being eliminated for safety. Lifting aids are plentiful and carers are trained in their use. When manual lifts are unavoidable, trained carers work in teams and nurses, in particular, are encouraged to wear trousers so that more suitable stances can be taken for weight-bearing. Beds are now more moveable and the height is easy to adjust.

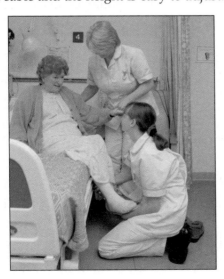

Nurses wearing trousers

Certain people in each hospital location or sub-location are designated to oversee the manual handling and most carers, after being trained, are required to undergo regular refresher courses to ensure that no bad habits have crept into their procedures.

Before an unavoidable lift, the risks are assessed and a plan is formulated; this includes the use of mechanical aids and the number of helpers. The team and the service user must be fully informed about each step of the lift. When the service user is able to give assistance, this is incorporated into the plan. A fully informed service user is more relaxed and cooperative and knows what to expect.

> ✳ DID YOU KNOW?
>
> Many lift types used in the past, such as the Drag lift and the Australian lift have now been condemned by the Royal College of Nursing, so keeping up to date with the latest thinking has never been more important.
>
> Most injuries caused by lifting affect the lower back and previously most nurses had been affected by low back pain at some time in their careers.

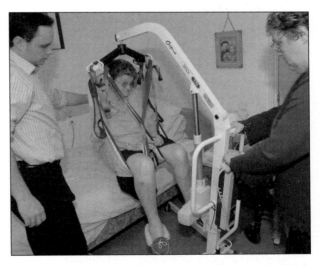

A service user being lifted using mechanical aids

Violence from service users

We all live in what appears to be a more violent and aggressive society and this is clearly shown in the increasing number of violent and aggressive incidents that care workers have to deal with on a daily basis. Nurses appear to be more than five times at risk of abusive behaviour than those who work in other occupations. The majority of unacceptable behaviour stems from service users in accident and emergency units and psychiatric wards. Community nurses are also vulnerable as they work in service users' homes but no care department seems to be exempt. Verbal abuse is the most common but minor and severe injuries occur as well.

Many care establishments, particularly hospitals open 24 hours, have invested in closed-circuit television and this has proved to be a deterrent. Service users who are intoxicated with alcohol also form one of the main problems in A&E units.

Some primary health care trusts refuse to treat service users who abuse staff (see also 'Your commitment to the NHS' on page 40) for a set period of time, often one year. Letters are sent to the service user's GP to confirm this.

As a learner, you should not be working on your own with a service user in a restricted space, but you should still know the basic precautions for your own safety.

Inappropriate behaviour is behaviour not usually seen in the care setting; often distressing, sometimes violent, occasionally oppressive or simply ignoring the needs of others around are examples of such behaviour. Inappropriate behaviour can come from service users, visitors or care workers. In some cases you will be able to understand why the individual is acting in this manner, in other cases you will not. Understanding the reasons or circumstances behind the behaviour does not change its unacceptability. In most cases you will be able to refer the matter to a supervisor, as you should not be working on your own. There are certain generic guidelines for dealing with inappropriate behaviour, but you must realise that each situation will be unique and sizing up the problem quickly will help.

Try to anticipate trouble and defuse it before it happens; knowing your service users will help you to do this.

Think it over...

Mr J, an ex-army man with a brusque manner, is a service user in the residential home in which you are working for two weeks' vocational placement. He likes to sit in a particular chair to watch the television in the communal living room. A new service user, Mrs M, came into the room straight after the evening meal, and occupied Mr J's chair. Mrs M is a timid service user, who has become prone to bouts of weeping since her husband died. You anticipate the problem that might arise when Mr J enters. How will you approach Mrs M and what might you say to her? Is it necessary to refer the matter to a supervisor?

Although Mr J is brusque and may distress Mrs M a great deal he is not likely to be violent. Most of the generic guidelines above will be appropriate for dealing with violent people as well, but in addition you will need to know:

* how to get out of the space as quickly as possible
* how to summon help – sound an alarm, shout for help, call security or police
* not to let an attacker get between you and the door
* remove any potential weapons if it is easy to do so.

Above all, keep yourself safe; you are a student and not trained to deal with attackers. Even if there are other people such as service users in the room, as an untrained person you will be more use bringing trained staff to their aid.

Think it over...

Find out about the appropriate steps to take in your placement when dealing with aggression and violence by reading the policy document and observing how other people manage sensitive situations.

Generic guidelines for dealing with inappropriate behaviour

1. Try to assess the size of the problem as quickly as possible and consider the approach you will use
2. Get help if there is not enough care staff around
3. Keep calm
4. Think clearly
5. Be clear in what you say
6. Try to get the service user into a private area
7. Repeat the request and give your reason but don't enter into an argument
8. Use frequent eye contact but don't stare
9. Be assertive but not aggressive
10. Give your service user personal space
11. Empathise with the service user
12. Let the service user back down in a way that will not belittle or humiliate them

Abuse

Sitting alongside inappropriate behaviour, there is the problem of abuse. This can be in many forms as shown in Figure 1.20.

FIGURE 1.20 *Some forms of abuse*

Consider this

Over a period of three months collect cuttings/photocopies from newspapers or magazines, or refer to TV documentaries related to different forms of abuse. Obtain a copy of one placement's policy on dealing with abuse.

In a small group discuss a selection of cases in the following ways:

* Which service user group was being abused?

* How many service users were involved?

* Who were the abusers?

* What type of care setting was involved?

* How long did the abuse continue?

* What were the likely short- and long-term effects on the service user?

* What signs might you have noticed if you had been working in that care setting?

* Why do you think the abuse started?

* What could you have done about it? (Your placement policy can be used here.)

You might find it helpful to repeat this exercise again using different cases before your study programme is finished to reinforce the importance of awareness of abuse.

UNIT 1 ASSESSMENT

You will be assessed on your knowledge, understanding and skills relating to effective caring through a written examination of one and a half hours.

Test questions

1. What factors must care workers take into account if they wish to ensure that their way of communicating is effective? (4)

2. Describe how distraction can be used to help a service user combat chronic pain. (3)

3. Explain the value of setting challenges for an older adult recovering from a hip replacement. (4)

4. A newly employed care worker takes a phone call from a man claiming to be Mr Sanderson, the son of a resident. He says that he has heard that his mother is very ill and wants to know what is wrong with her. What factors should the care worker take into account and what action should he or she take? (3)

5. Mrs B has had her operation cancelled twice; this time she had been prepared for theatre in the morning before being told that it had been cancelled again. Mr B has arrived to visit his wife and found that he is to take her home again without surgery. He is furious and threatens to punch the nearest person on duty, which is you. Explain how you would manage the situation. (5)

6. Ten year old George has just arrived home from school very excited because he has won a national prize in a story writing competition. His mother is watching day-time television and tells him not to disturb her. When he tries to get her to listen, she shouts that she has already told him not to disturb her and sends him to his bedroom. Explain how she is not treating George well. (5)

7. Identify and explain the precautions you would take helping a nurse colleague to change the soiled linen from a bed of a service user who has recently had surgery and is known to have hepatitis B. (5)

8. Define primary, secondary and tertiary care. (3)

9. Identify the physical difficulties service users may experience accessing health or social care services. (4)

10. Describe the precautions designed to minimise lifting injuries in care staff. (5)

References

Department of Health (2000) *Your Guide to the NHS*, NHS London

R. Rogers, J. Salvage (1998) *Nurses at Risk*, Palgrave Macmillan, Basingstoke

The Terrence Higgins Trust for information on HIV and Aids

NUPE, trade union for information on health and safety of health care workers

R. Adams (1994) *Skilled work with people*, Collins Educational, London

B. Hopson, M. Scally (1994) *Communication, Time to Talk*, Mercury, London

A. Pease, B. Pease, (2005) *The Definitive Book of Body Language*, Sheldon Press, London

P. Burnard (1992) *Communicate!* Hodder Arnold, London

A. Jaskolka (2004) *How to Read and Use Body Language*, Foulsham, London

N. Moonie (2000), *AVCE Health and Social Care*, Heinemann, Oxford

Y. Nolan (2001), *S/NVQ Care Level 3*, Heinemann, Oxford

Useful websites

Please see www.heinemann.co.uk/hotlinks (express code 1554P) for links to the following websites which may provide a source of information:

* Health Development Agency

* NHS Direct Wales

* NHS Direct

* NHS 24

UNIT
2

Effective communication

You will learn about:

2.1	Types of communication
2.2	Communication difficulties and strategies to overcome these
2.3	Barriers to communication and factors affecting the effectiveness of communication skills
2.4	Communication when working in teams
2.5	Clients and care settings
2.6	Giving a talk
2.7	Feedback research
2.8	Evaluating communication skills

Introduction

This unit focuses on communication skills. It explores different types of communication, together with some of the factors that affect the effectiveness of communication skills. Communication skills relevant to specific service user groups and care settings are discussed in depth. For this unit you are required to produce a report based on a short talk that you will prepare and give to a small audience. This talk should be about good practice in communication skills for one type of service user in one care setting.

How you will be assessed

This unit is internally assessed. You will need to produce a report based on a short talk which you will prepare and present to a small audience.

2.1 Types of communication

We use words when we speak – oral communication; and we use words when we write – written communication.

Oral or verbal communication

Thompson (1986) writing about health work, argues that communication is important for two major reasons. Firstly, communication enables people to share information, and secondly, communication enables relationships between people. Teresa Thompson states that 'communication is the relationship' (1986: 8). Speaking or signing is central to establishing relationships between people and care workers need to have highly developed social skills in order to work with the wide range of emotional needs that service users will have. Face-to-face, oral (or mouth) communication involves using words and sentences (verbal communication) together with a range of body language messages (non-verbal communication).

Oral communication may be central to the kind of tasks listed in Figure 2.1.

Oral communication is central to emotional work as well as communicating information

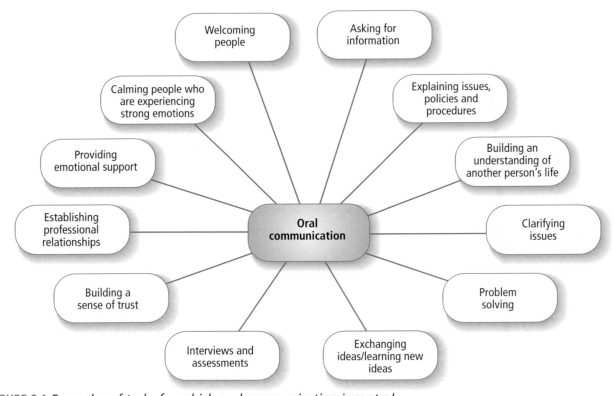

FIGURE 2.1 *Examples of tasks for which oral communication is central*

Written communication

There is an old Chinese saying that the weakest ink is stronger than the strongest memory! Written records are essential for communicating formal information that needs to be reviewed at a future date. When people recall conversations they have had, they will probably miss some details out, and also change some details. Written statements are much more permanent and if they are accurate when they are written they may be useful at a later date.

Some examples of important written documents are listed in Figure 2.2.

When an issue is recorded in writing it becomes formal. It is important that records of personal information are as factual and accurate as possible. You should describe only the facts or the events that happened, without giving your own interpretation or saying how you feel about the person.

Many organisations use printed forms to help staff to ask important questions and check that they have taken accurate information. Service users' personal records are likely to be written on forms that use headings.

Non-verbal communication – Para language

Tone of voice

Tone involves the way our voice resonates as we speak. It is not just what we say, but the way that we say it. If we talk quickly in a loud voice with a fixed voice tone, people may see us as angry. In most UK contexts, a calm, slow voice with varying tone may send a message of being friendly. A sharp tone may be associated with angry or complaining behaviour. A flat tone might be associated with exhaustion or depression. A faint tone might be associated with submissive behaviour.

Pitch

Pitch relates to the sound frequency of the voice. Some people might speak in a monotonous high-frequency voice or a monotonous low-frequency voice. It is important to vary the type of sound

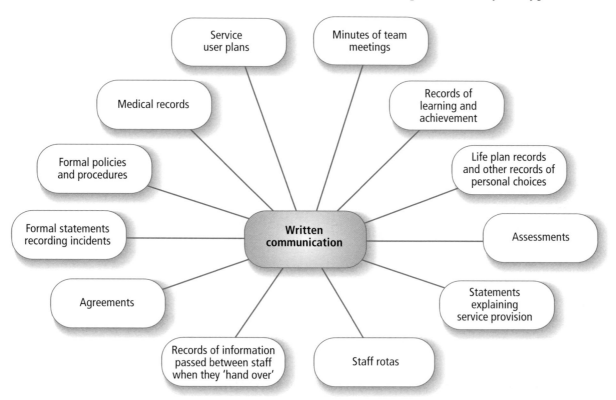

FIGURE 2.2 *Examples of important written documents*

that we make. And culturally there may be expectations as to how high or low our voice should sound.

Speed of speech

Bostrom (1997) states that announcers (such as radio or TV presenters) speak at a rate of between 100 and 125 words per minute. This speed might represent an ideal pace for explaining information. A great deal of speech is used to express emotional reaction rather than simply explaining issues to an audience. A faster speed of speech might indicate that the speaker is excited, anxious, agitated, nervous, angry or seeking to impress or dominate the listener. Alternatively, a fast speed might simply mean that the speaker is in a hurry!

Exactly what a fast rate of speaking means can only be worked out by interpreting other non-verbal body language and the cultural context and situation of the speaker. People who wave their arms, wide eyed and smiling, while talking rapidly about exam results might be interpreted as being excited at the news of having done well.

A slow speed of speech can indicate sadness or depression. Slow speech may sometimes be associated with impairment of thought processes. Slow speech might indicate tiredness or boredom. Slow, loudly spoken speech might be used to convey dominance or hostility. Sometimes slow speech can indicate attraction, love and affection between individuals who know each other. Once again, this aspect of communication can only be interpreted once the non-verbal, social, cultural and practical context of the conversation is understood.

In formal communication work, such as, for example, if you were meeting people at an information desk or hospital reception, it might be important to maintain a normal pace of speech. This is because your work might focus on a formal exchange of information. Informal situations often involve a need to communicate emotions, such as, for example, talking to a service user you know well. In this situation you might want to speak faster or slower in order to communicate your emotions clearly.

Volume – how loud you speak

Talking or shouting loudly often sends a message that you are excited, angry or aggressive, unless you are in a situation where it is obvious that you are trying to overcome background noise or communicate with someone who is a long distance away. Talking quietly sometimes sends a message that you lack confidence, or that you are being submissive in the presence of a more important person. Once again, talking quietly is an obvious strategy if you do not want everybody to hear what you are saying.

Clarity of voice

It is important not to mumble, slur or drawl our words when speaking, and also not to stress words inappropriately, or clip words when speaking if we are to communicate effectively. Clarity of voice can be affected by our emotional state and many people need to imagine themselves speaking clearly in order to achieve a clear voice.

Hesitation

In order to speak clearly we need to think through what we are about to say. A long pause in which nothing is said is often interpreted as an indication that the speaker has finished talking. One way of showing that you intend to continue speaking is to use sounds such as 'uhm' and 'ah' so that it is obvious that you intend to continue speaking, even though you are not actually communicating. In an informal setting, friendly listeners can often cope with this behaviour. When giving a formal speech, too many 'uhms' or other meaningless pause fillers may mean that listeners lose track of the content of your communication.

Non-verbal communication – body language

When meeting and talking with people we usually use two language systems. These are:

* a verbal or spoken language
* a non-verbal or body language.

Effective communication in care work requires that care workers have the ability to analyse their own and other people's non-verbal behaviour. Our body sends messages to other people – often without our deliberately meaning to send these messages. Some of the most important body areas that send messages are outlined below.

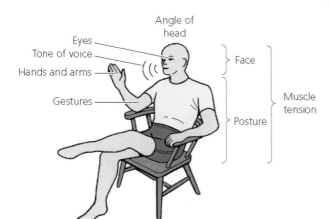

FIGURE 2.3 *The use of body language*

FIGURE 2.4 *Facial expression*

Eye contact

We can guess the feelings and thoughts that another person has by looking at their eyes. One poet called the eyes 'the window of the soul'. We can sometimes understand the thoughts and feelings of another person by eye-to-eye contact. Our eyes get wider when we are excited, attracted to, or interested in someone else. A fixed stare may send the message that someone is angry. Looking away is often interpreted as being bored or not interested, in European culture.

Facial expression

Our face can send very complex messages and we can read them easily – see Figure 2.4.

Our face often indicates our emotional state. When people are sad they may signal this emotion with eyes that look down; there may be

tension in their face, and their mouth will be closed. The muscles in the person's shoulders are likely to be relaxed but the face and neck may show tension. A happy person will have 'wide eyes' that make contact with you and a smiling face. When people are excited they may move their arms and hands to signal this emotion.

Proximity and personal space

The space between people can sometimes show how friendly or 'intimate' the conversation is. Different cultures have different assumptions about how close people should be (proximity) when they are talking.

In Britain there are expectations or 'norms' as to how close you should be when you talk to others. When talking to strangers we may keep an arm's-length apart. The ritual of shaking hands indicates that you have been introduced and you may move closer. When you are friendly with someone you may accept their being closer to you. Relatives and partners may not be restricted in how close they can come.

Personal space is a very important issue in care work. A care worker who assumes it is all right to enter a service user's personal space without asking or explaining, may be seen as being dominating or aggressive.

Face-to-face positions (orientation)

Standing or sitting eye to eye can send a message of being formal or being angry. A slight angle can create a more informal, relaxed and friendly feeling (see Figure 2.5).

If you are facing an audience of people in order to deliver a formal talk you might wish to face your audience 'squarely' or eye to eye in order to look confident, prepared and ready to deliver your talk. The further your audience are away from you, the less they will be able to see your face and eye contact and the less feedback

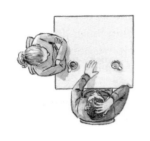

FIGURE 2.5 *Face-to-face interaction*

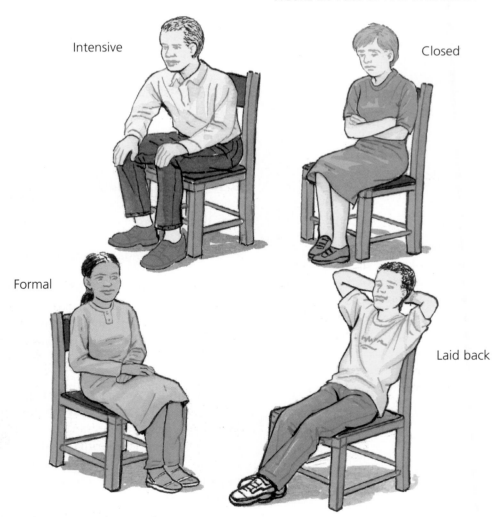

Intensive

Closed

Formal

Laid back

FIGURE 2.6 *Body postures that send messages*

you will get from them. This creates more formality. Again, if you are some distance from your audience you will need to increase the volume of your voice in order to be heard clearly. As a general rule – a rule that is not always right – the larger the group you are talking to, and the further away you are, the more formal your body language will need to become.

Body movement

The way we walk, move our head, sit, cross our legs and so on, sends messages about whether we are feeling tired, happy, sad or bored.

Posture

The way we sit or stand can send messages. Sitting with crossed arms can mean 'I'm not taking any notice'. Leaning back can send the message that you are relaxed or bored. Leaning forward can show interest. The body postures shown in Figure 2.6 send messages.

Muscle tension

The tension in our feet, hands and fingers can tell others how relaxed or how tense we are. When people are very tense their shoulders might stiffen, their face muscles might tighten and they might sit or stand rigidly. A tense face might have a firmly closed mouth with lips and jaws clenched tight. A tense person might breathe quickly and become hot.

Gestures

Gestures are hand and arm movements that can help us to understand what a person is saying. Some gestures carry a meaning of their own. Some common gestures are shown below.

'I don't know'

'stop, don't do that'

'success – everything's going well'

'perfection' or 'perfect'

FIGURE 2.7 *Some gestures common in Britain*

2.2 Communication difficulties and strategies to overcome these

Sensory impairments of vision and hearing

Some service users will have sensory impairments such as impaired vision or hearing. Many people who are 'registered blind' can sense some images and can tell the difference between light and darkness. However, low vision often means that a person cannot see your non-verbal behaviour. Because of this, it is important to remember that a person with low vision may not understand your emotions unless you can communicate using your tone of voice. It will also be important to remember to explain things that sighted people take for granted. For example, an explanation of issues like the weather may benefit people with low vision, though obvious to a sighted person.

Many older service users lose the ability to hear high-pitched sounds, although they can still hear low-frequency sound. This means that many older people have difficulty in understanding some speech. Sometimes a service user may understand their relatives because they are used to their style of speaking and may even be able to read their lips. A service user may have difficulty understanding the speech, or the lip movements of somebody whom they do not know. People who have been Deaf since birth often learn to use British Sign Language and they therefore have a different language to English. Learning to sign is a useful skill for communicating with members of the Deaf community. People who develop a hearing impairment in later life are unlikely to have learned British Sign Language. Many people with a hearing loss may prefer to communicate using speech and reading replies written in English if they cannot interpret non-verbal communication and the sounds that others make.

Aphasia

Aphasia is a disability that can involve an inability to speak and/or an inability to understand spoken language. Certain types of head injury can result in aphasia. A person with expressive aphasia may be able to understand language but unable to respond with speech. A person with receptive aphasia may be unable to understand what you are saying. Sometimes a person who cannot speak can nevertheless answer your questions using signs, pointing to pictures or even writing answers.

Overcoming communication difficulties

British Sign Language

The British Deaf Association states that British Sign Language 'is the first or preferred language of nearly 70,000 Deaf people in the United Kingdom'. The British Deaf Association explains that British Sign Language (BSL) 'belongs to Deaf people. It is not a communication system devised by hearing people. It is a real language which has evolved in the UK's Deaf community over hundreds of years'. The British Deaf Association campaign for the right of Deaf people to be educated in BSL and to access information and services through BSL, arguing that the Deaf community is a 'linguistic and cultural minority and is not measured in medical terms'.

Note: the use of a capital 'D' in Deaf is deliberate. It denotes culturally Deaf. Culturally Deaf means that deafness is about belonging to a different language community – and not about being an impaired-hearing person.

Please see www.heinemann.co.uk/hotlinks (express code 1554P) for further details about BSL, signs and finger spelling alphabet, and the website of the Royal Association for Deaf People.

Makaton

Makaton is a system for developing language that uses speech, signs and symbols to help people with learning difficulties to communicate and to develop their language skills. People who communicate using Makaton may speak a word and perform a sign using hands and body language. There is a large range of symbols that may help people with learning difficulty to recognise an idea or to communicate with others. Further information on Makaton can be found at www.heinemann.co.uk/hotlinks (express code 1554P).

Braille

Braille (a system of raised marks that can be felt with your fingers) provides a system of written communication based on the sense of touch for people who have limited vision. The communication system known as Braille was first published by Louis Braille, a blind 20-year-old, in 1829. The system is now widely adopted as the form of writing and reading used by people who cannot see written script.

Nowadays, computer software can translate written material into Braille, which can be printed out using special printers. Further detail on Braille can be found at www.heinemann.co.uk/hotlinks (express code 1554P).

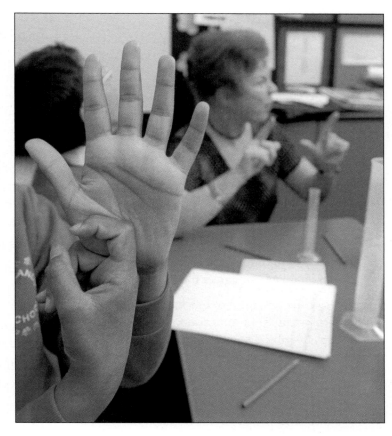

Sign language is used by nearly 70,000 Deaf people in the UK

2.3 Barriers to communication and factors affecting the effectiveness of communication skills

Communication can become blocked if individual differences are not understood. The three main ways that communication becomes blocked are:

1. A person cannot see, hear or receive the message.
2. A person cannot make sense of the message.
3. A person misunderstands the message.

Examples of the first kind of block, where people do not receive the communication, include visual disabilities, hearing disabilities, environmental problems such as poor lighting, noisy environments, and when speaking from too far away.

> ### Key concept
>
> *Barriers:* effective communication depends on identifying barriers that may block understanding. Barriers can exist at a physical and sensory level, at the level of making sense of a message and at a cultural and social context level where the meaning of a message may be misunderstood.

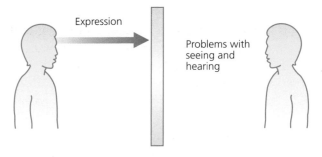

FIGURE 2.8 *Environmental problems like noise and poor light can create communication barriers*

Examples of situations in which people may not be able to make sense of the message include:

* the use of different languages, including signed languages

* the use of different terms in language, such as jargon (technical language), slang (different people using different terms), or dialect (people from different communities use different sounds to say words)

* physical and intellectual disabilities, such as dysphasia (difficulties with language expression or understanding, aphasia (an absence of language ability) being ill, or suffering memory loss, or learning difficulty.

Reasons for misunderstanding a message include:

* cultural influences – different cultures interpret non-verbal and verbal messages, and humour, in different ways

* assumptions about people – about race, gender, disability and other groupings

* labelling or stereotyping of others

* social context – statements and behaviour that are understood by friends and family may not be understood by strangers

* emotional barriers – a worker's own emotional needs may stop them from wanting to know about others

* time pressures can mean that staff withdraw from wanting to know about others

* emotional differences can sometimes be interpreted as personality clashes, or personality differences. Very angry, or very happy, or very shy people may misinterpret communication from others.

In order to minimise communication barriers it will be important to learn as much as possible about others. People may have 'preferred forms of interaction'. This may include a reliance on non-verbal messages, sign language, lip-reading, the use of description, slang phrases, choice of room or location for a conversation and so on. Everyone has communication needs of some kind.

Different language systems

When people use different language systems there may be an obvious barrier to understanding. It may be necessary to use the services of an interpreter or translator in order for people to communicate across a language barrier. Interpreters are people who communicate meaning from one language to another. Translators are people who change recorded material from one language to another.

Translating and interpreting involve the communication of meaning between different languages. Translating and interpreting are not just the technical acts of changing the words from one system to another. Many languages do not have simple equivalence between words or signs. Interpreters and translators have to grasp the meaning of a message and find a way of expressing this meaning in a different language system. This is rarely a simple task even for professional translators.

Interpreters can be professional people but they may also be friends, or family members. For example, a mother might learn sign language in order to communicate information to a Deaf child. It is sometimes possible for family members to interpret for each other.

Terminology

The actual words or terms that you use will influence both what another person understands and the relationship that you have with the person you are communicating with. Words can create a sense of formality or informality. The use of technical terminology also identifies the social groups that you identify with.

The degree of formality or informality is called the language 'register'. For example, suppose you went to a hospital reception. You might expect the person on duty to greet you with a formal response such as, 'Good morning, how can I help you?'. An informal greeting of the kind used by white males in the south-east of England might be, 'Hello, mate, what's up then?' or 'How's it going?'. It is possible that some people might prefer the informal greeting. An informal greeting could put you at ease; you might feel that the receptionist is like you. But in many situations, the informal greeting might make people feel that they are not being respected.

The degree of formality or informality establishes a context. At a hospital reception you are unlikely to want to spend time making friends and chatting things over with the receptionist. You may be seeking urgent help. Your expectations of the situation might be that you want to be taken seriously and put in touch with professional services as soon as possible. You might see the situation as a very formal encounter.

If you are treated informally, you may interpret this as not being treated seriously, or in other words 'not being respected' (see Figure 2.9).

FIGURE 2.9 *Informality and informal humour may be perceived as disrespect*

Speech communities

Another issue is that informal speech is very likely to identify a specific speech community. Different localities, ethnic groups, professions and work cultures all have their own special words, phrases and speech patterns. An elderly, middle-class woman is very unlikely to start a conversation with the words 'Hello, mate'. Some service users may feel threatened or excluded by the kind of language they encounter. However, the use of formal language in itself will not solve this problem. The technical terminology used by social care workers may also create barriers for people who were not part of that 'speech community'.

Service user: I come about getting some help around the house, you know, 'cause it's getting 'ard nowadays, what with me back an everything.

Service worker: Well you need to speak to the Community Domiciliary Support Liaison Officer, who can arrange an assessment in accordance with our statutory obligations.

The two statements above use different levels of formality, but they also represent speech from different speech communities. Can you work out what each person is saying? How do you think the service user will feel given such a response? Will the service user feel respected and valued?

Cultural beliefs and assumptions

Skilled carers have to get to know the people that they work with in order to avoid making false assumptions about them. In getting to know an individual, carers will also need to understand the ways in which class, race, age, gender and other social categories influence the person. A person's culture may include all social groups that they belong to.

There are many different ethnic groups in the world, many different religions, many different cultural values, variations in gender role, and so on. Individuals may belong to the same ethnic group, yet belong to different religions or class groups. Knowing someone's religion will not necessarily tell you all of their beliefs, or about their general culture.

You can acquire background knowledge on different ethnic and religious customs, but it is impossible to study and learn about all the differences that can exist for individual service users. The best way to learn about diversity is to listen and communicate with people who lead very different lives.

It is important to be able to identify the different interpretations that words and body language have in different cultures. This is not a straightforward issue, as words and signs can mean different things depending on their context. For example, the word 'wicked' can have different meanings. If older people use this phrase to describe their experience of World War II, it would mean 'horrific' or 'terrible'. In a TV comedy written and produced 15 years ago the

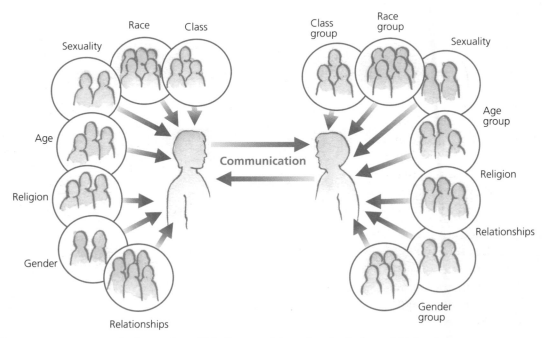

FIGURE 2.10 *The groups a person belongs to will influence his or her beliefs and behaviour*

phrase would mean 'cool' – something very desirable. In a religious context 'wicked' might relate to the concept of sin.

Making sense of spoken language requires knowledge of the context and intentions of the speaker. Understanding non-verbal communication involves exactly the same need to understand 'where the person is coming from' or, to put it more formally, to understand what the circumstances and cultural context of the other person are. For example, in Britain the hand gesture with palm up and facing forward means 'Stop, don't do that'. In Greece it can mean 'You are dirt' and is a very rude gesture.

Why do the same physical movements have different meanings? One explanation for the hand signs is that the British version of the palm-and-fingers gesture means 'I arrest you, you must not do it'; whereas the Greek interpretation goes back to medieval times when criminals had dirt rubbed in their faces to show how much people despised them.

Using care values means that carers must have respect for other people's culture. People learn different ways of communicating, and good carers will try to understand the different ways in which people use non-verbal messages. For instance, past research in the USA suggests that white and black Americans may have used different non-verbal signals when they listened. It suggests that some black Americans may tend not to look much at the speaker. This can be interpreted as a mark of respect – by looking away it demonstrates that you are really thinking hard about the message. Unfortunately, not all white people understood this cultural difference in non-verbal communication. Some individuals misunderstood and assumed that this non-verbal behaviour meant exactly what it would mean if they had done it. That is, it would mean they were not listening.

Key concept

Cultural assumptions: communication is always influenced by cultural systems of meaning. Different cultures interpret body language differently.

There is an almost infinite variety of meanings that can be given to any type of eye contact, facial expression, posture or gesture. Every culture develops its own special system of meanings. Carers have to understand and show respect and value for all these different systems of sending messages. But how can you ever learn them all?

No one can learn every possible system of non-verbal message – but it is possible to learn about those that people you are with are using! It is possible to do this by first noticing and remembering what others do – i.e. what non-verbal messages they are sending. The next step is to make an intelligent guess about what messages the person is trying to give you. Finally, check your understanding (your guesses) with the person.

Skilled interpersonal interaction involves:

* watching other people,

* remembering what they do

* guessing what words and actions mean and then checking your guesses with the person

* never relying on your own guesses, because these might turn into assumptions

* understanding that assumptions can lead to discrimination.

Think it over...

Imagine you are working with an older person. Whenever you start to speak to her she always looks at the floor and never makes eye contact. Why is this?

Your first thought is that she might be depressed. Having made such an assumption, you might not want to talk to this person. But instead you could ask: 'How do you feel today; would you like me to get you anything?' By checking out how she feels you could test your own understanding. She might say she feels well and is quite happy, and then ask you to do something for her. This suggests that she cannot be depressed.

Why else would someone look at the floor rather than at you?

Using care values involves getting to understand people – not acting on unchecked assumptions. Non-verbal messages should never be relied on; they should always be checked.

Prejudice

It is easy for people to begin to believe that their system of speaking and communicating verbally is the right one. People who are different can then become stereotyped or labelled as being stupid, difficult or in some way defective because they are different. Stereotyping and labelling people results from a prejudiced view that our way is the only right way.

Where prejudice exists it will obviously create a major barrier to communication but other words and non-verbal communication are likely to be misunderstood and misinterpreted.

A willingness to value difference and to explore what another person means is vital if we are to overcome prejudice.

Think it over...

Many years ago an adolescent girl was interviewed by a psychiatrist. The psychiatrist asked what the girl hoped for in the future. The girl responded by saying that she hoped to get married and live in a banjo. 'But a banjo is a musical instrument,' replied the psychiatrist. 'Yes, I know that' replied the girl, 'but many of my friends live in banjos and I think that's much better than living in an ordinary street'. The psychiatrist is said to have concluded that the girl had a mental disorder.

The psychiatrist did not know that in the local area the term 'banjo' was used to mean a no-through road with a turning circle at the end.

How can you prevent misunderstandings such as the misunderstanding in the story above by using your communication skills?

Lack of confidence

It is vitally important to have the ability to check assumptions and to be prepared to learn when involved in communication work with other people. Overconfidence can lead to our making inappropriate assumptions about people. The opposite, a lack of confidence, might have a positive outcome if it results in people being prepared to listen, ask questions and learn.

Sometimes a lack of experience can create a sense of threat, however, and a care worker or practitioner may have a strong emotional desire to withdraw and not to ask appropriate questions or build an understanding of other people. Unless you are actively involved in checking your understanding of another person's communication, communication is likely to go wrong. If a lack of confidence results in a lack of interaction then there is a barrier to overcome.

Most people develop their confidence by mixing with people who are not neighbours, friends or family. If you gradually learn the skill of checking what other people mean you can increase your confidence in communication work.

Hostility

Within health and care work, professional workers sometimes have to communicate with people who are hostile towards them. Sometimes people in health settings become anxious or afraid. Fear can create hatred and hostility that can be focused on health care workers. Social workers also encounter people who are afraid that their lifestyle will be criticised or judged. Sometimes bad reports about hospital or care services make people suspicious of care staff.

If you are faced by people who are angry or hostile it will be important to stay calm and to use good listening skills in order to try to build a sense of trust with the angry person. It is quite difficult to follow this advice, because you have to be able to control your own emotions and this is a skill that can take time to learn. See the section on coping with angry behaviour on page 27.

2.4 Communication when working in teams

Communication in teams may be about sharing information and/or it might be about developing the relationships between people.

Bales (1970) put forward a theory of task and maintenance activity within groups, such as teams found within health and social care. Teams may have to transmit the following information:

* details of events that have happened while staff have been on duty need to be 'handed over' to new staff that are just coming on duty. This activity is usually called a 'hand over'

* details of the service user plan. When a service user goes into a care home there will be a care plan based on the initial assessment of the service user's need. Staff usually need to know the details of this assessment. In addition staff need to update their knowledge of individual service user's needs

* staff may need to transmit information about policies and procedures to ensure that everybody is up to date with the organisation's policy.

Transmitting this information would form the task of a staff team group discussion. But working together in a team is a social activity. People cannot just concentrate on their work as if they were machines. People need to feel that they belong and that other people in the group respect them. Relationship work might include:

* using humour to defuse tension and conflict

* discussing individual thoughts and feelings about training needs and the development of caring skills

* providing emotional support and encouragement for members of the team.

Bales argued that there needs to be a balance between the practical work of achieving a task and the social needs of group members. Bales (1970) suggested that observers could understand and analyse what was happening in a group by using an interaction analysis of individual members' behaviour. Such an analysis might enable the observer to understand how a group was moving between the focus on task activity and a focus on social activity. An interaction analysis involves classifying the way people behave using defined categories. Bales's categories are outlined in Table 2.1.

BALES'S CATEGORIES	
Group task (including transmission of information)	* Gives suggestion (including taking the lead) * Gives opinion (including feelings and wishes) * Gives information (including clarifying and confirming) * Asks for information * Asks for opinion * Asks for suggestion
Group maintenance (relationship work) (called 'Social-emotional Area' by Bales)	* Seems friendly * Dramatises * Agrees * Disagrees * Shows tension * Seems unfriendly

TABLE 2.1 *Bales's categories*

Using categories can be a useful way of gaining an insight into how an individual is influencing the work and the emotional maintenance or feeling involved in group communication. It is possible to design a grid that can be used minute by minute to try to categorise the task and maintenance behaviours occurring in groups. An example is shown in Table 2.2.

	1	2	3	4	5	6	7	8	9	10
Group task										
Starting discussion										
Giving information										
Asking for information										
Clarifying discussion										
Summarising discussion										
Group maintenance										
Humour										
Expressing group feelings										
Including others										
Being supportive										

TABLE 2.2 *A grid designed for use in categorising the task and maintenance behaviours of individuals in groups*

Think it over...

In a group of five or six people, take four matchsticks each and agree on a topic for group discussion. Next, agree the following rules for the discussion. Only one person may speak at a time. Whenever that person speaks, he or she must place a matchstick on the floor. When people run out of matchsticks they cannot say anything. No one may say anything unless others have finished. Non-verbal communication is allowed. People should not speak for more than one minute.

This exercise should emphasise the importance of group maintenance activity. The matchstick game can make people very focused on the task to the exclusion of much of the social maintenance activity. So being in the group might make you feel awkward or tense.

Relationship work is very important because teams need to develop a sense of belonging that gives the members a 'group feeling'. This could be described as a group identity. In teams people need to:

* know each other and understand each other's feelings
* have a 'feeling of belonging' shared by people in the group
* share a set of beliefs or norms.

How do people get to know each other and develop a sense of belonging, common purpose and norms? Some researchers claim that there is a pattern to the way the communication develops in individual relationships and in group formation.

Tuckman's theory of group development

Tuckman (1965) analysed around 50 studies on group development and concluded that groups of people generally go through a process of development that can be identified as the four stages of Forming, Storming, Norming and Performing (see Figure 2.11). In 1977 Tuckman and Jensen identified a fifth stage of Adjourning in order to describe the process of ending a group.

Tuckman's four stages of group formation

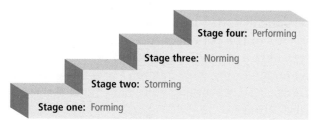

Stage four: Performing
Stage three: Norming
Stage two: Storming
Stage one: Forming

FIGURE 2.11 *Tuckman's four stages*

An explanation of how a group of people comes together to form a team

Forming: when people first get together there is likely to be an introductory stage. People may be unsure about why they are attending a meeting. The purpose of the group may not be clear. People may have little commitment to the group and there may be no clear value system.

Storming: there may be 'power struggles' within the group. Different individuals may contest each other for the leadership of the group. There may be arguments about how the group should work, who should do tasks and so on. Groups can fail at this stage and individuals can decide to drop out because they do not feel comfortable with other people in the group.

Teams might split into sub groups who refuse to communicate with each other, if they become stuck in the storming stage.

Norming: at this stage group members develop a set of common beliefs and values. People are likely to begin to trust each other and develop clear roles. Norms are shared expectations that group members have of each other. Norms enable people to work together as a group.

Performing: because people share the same values and norms the group is able to perform tasks effectively. People may feel that they are comfortable and belong in the group. There may be a sense of high morale.

Adjourning: the group has to conclude their activities and find an acceptable way for group members to part. The group has to complete and end the existence of the group's identity.

> **Key concept**
>
> *Team norms:* for a group to perform effectively, members will need to share a common system of beliefs, values or norms relevant to the purpose of the group. It may be very important to identify the extent to which a team does share a common set of beliefs and norms when observing a team or discussing communication within groups.

2.5 Clients and care settings

Particular communication barriers

Some examples of communication barriers in specific settings are outlined in Table 2.3.

Infants and young children

Infancy is the stage of life before children develop language. Infants communicate with their carers through eye contact and through sounds that later develop into words. Carers usually try to attract the interest of infants through placing their face close to the infant and making eye contact. Most people instinctively talk to infants using a high-pitched voice and it is believed that infants have an in-built tendency to respond to a high-pitched voice with varied voice tone.

When communicating with children it is very important to remember that children do not understand language in the same way that most adults do. Adults and adolescents understand that words are symbols that stand for things. Adults can easily understand that a word like 'wicked' can have many different meanings, but children are likely to have trouble with this idea. If a child has grown up in a family that uses the word 'wicked' to mean 'evil' they may become very upset to be told that they are wearing a wicked T-shirt. When you are only 3–5 years old a word has to have a fixed meaning. If you say something is 'scary' then a young child is likely to understand that you are talking about monsters; children usually do not generalise their understanding of words until they get older.

Children simply do not think the same way as adolescents and adults. If you use leading questions such as 'Do you think it is time to have a drink now?', children will often answer 'Yes', not because they have carefully thought through the issues and come to the considered conclusion that they do want a drink, but because they are used to trusting and wanting to please adults by agreeing with them. It is therefore very easy to 'put words into children's mouths' and get them to say things that they do not really believe in. Care workers may often use leading questions in order to try and guide children into new activities.

Children can be easily frightened by adults who do not appear friendly or supportive, especially if they are tall or 'big' and talking using a loud or fast pattern of speech. It is important to establish a sense of emotional safety before communicating with children – and this principle is also true of working with many other service user groups.

Naturally, children have a much smaller vocabulary than adults and children often do not understand the concepts and words that an adult might use. When communicating with children it is very important to use simple words and phrases that the child may be able to recognise. Some children may not be familiar with very formal communication styles, and it may be important to talk in an informal way that is appropriate to the culture and speech community that the child belongs to.

Some specific skills that you might observe care workers using when they communicate with young children include the following:

* care workers may use a different range of voice tone than they might use with adults

* care workers may come much closer to young children than they would when interacting with adults

* you might see more examples of touch – for instance, holding hands – than you would expect to see in adult interactions. Touch may create a feeling of friendship and safety between a child and familiar carers

* care workers are careful to make eye contact when speaking to children; eye contact is sometimes more fixed during a conversation than it might be with adults

* care workers might use lots of questions – not really as questions but to guide children – for example, 'shall we leave the sand tray now'.

* care workers might be careful to speak softly and constantly change the tone of their voice; this might help to keep children interested in the conversation and help to create a friendly relationship between the worker and the child.

SETTING	BARRIERS
Hospitals	* Staff time may be limited, preventing effective support and understanding * The professional role of medical experts may exclude patients from management of health needs * Technical terminology and formal language may create a barrier to understanding * Staff may make assumptions about lifestyle habits * Emotional distress may create a specific problem for communication
Family home	* Emotional relationships may not be understood by outside people * Individuals may have developed private systems of language and communication * There is the risk of stereotyping or making assumptions about diverse cultures
Day centres	* Staff time and other resource constraints may prevent effective communication and support * Different speech patterns may create a barrier between members * Individuals may make inappropriate assumptions or stereotype people * Emotional distress may create a specific problem for communication
Nursing and residential homes	* Staff time and other resource constraints may prevent effective communication support * Sensory disabilities * Specific disabilities associated with mental health needs * Emotional distress * Person-centred communication approaches for valuing individuals may not be used * Individuals may make inappropriate assumptions or stereotype people
Early years settings	* Staff time and other resource constraints may prevent effective communication support * There is the risk of stereotyping or making assumptions about diverse cultures. * The use of adult speech patterns and non-verbal communication may not be understood by young children * Children will have a limited vocabulary and a different way of understanding concepts compared with adults
Special educational settings	* Staff time and other resource constraints * There is the risk of stereotyping or making assumptions about diverse cultures. * The use of adult speech patterns and non-verbal communication may not be understood * People with a learning difficulty may have a limited vocabulary and different ways of understanding concepts.

TABLE 2.3 *Examples of communication barriers in specific settings*

Talking to children keeps them interested

People with a specific learning difficulty

Specific learning difficulties may include issues such as:

* autism, a disorder involving difficulty in understanding human relationships

* dyslexia (a disturbance in the ability to read and write)

* dysphasia (a disorder of speech).

Autism

People with autism may not produce or understand non-verbal language in the same way that many people are used to. Certain words may have a significance that is hard to understand without getting to know the individual. Care workers who communicate with individuals who have a specific learning difficulty will be very concerned to learn about the individual thought patterns and ways of communicating that the person may be able to develop. Makaton provides a system which is useful for encouraging the development of language and communication skills for people who have a learning difficulty.

Dyslexia

Like many conditions, dyslexia does not result in a simple set of problems. One person's dyslexia may be different from another's. Dyslexia can delay the age at which a child learns to read; it is also associated with a serious difficulty in spelling words and understanding how letters are arranged to make words. Some people with dyslexia can communicate very effectively using spoken language, and modern information technology can sometimes compensate for the difficulties experienced by those suffering from dyslexia with spelling and writing. Voice-recognition software, for instance, can be used to enable a person with dyslexia to convert speech into writing.

Dysphasia

When people have a disturbance with their use of language this disability is called dysphasia. People who have had a stroke often have difficulty in saying certain words. Sometimes people with dysphasia become distressed because they cannot speak clearly. If you are communicating with a dysphasic person it is important to be calm and patient; sometimes you may be able to guess a word the person is struggling with and the individual may nod to indicate that you are correct. People with dysphasia are likely to become tired and stressed if they feel that they are expected to communicate verbally for any length of time.

Learning difficulty

People with learning difficulty may have a limited vocabulary (range of words that they can use) and may sometimes use words or phrases in a way that is difficult to understand without knowing about their lives and preferences. As with many other communication difficulties it is important to understand as much as possible about the person you are working with in order to understand his or her speech, and to make them feel at ease and comfortable.

With respect to general learning difficulty, current practice emphasises the importance of person-centred care. It is vitally important for care workers to learn about the individual needs and preferences of the people that they work with. The skill of active listening and asking skilled questions is therefore a very important skill when working with adult service users.

Speech disability

If you are communicating with someone with a speech disability it is important to be calm and patient and to learn as much as possible about the person's use of sound to help you understand their words.

> **Key concept**
>
> *Person-centred care:* care that places 'the person' at the centre of decision-making and activities. Person-centred care is care that seeks to value the individual 'personhood' of service users.

In services for people with learning difficulty, the government White Paper 'Valuing People' (2001) argues that services should use person-centred approaches when planning care. 'Person-centred' means that care must be focused on the specific needs and wishes of the service user. Service users plan their own life and make their own choices using help from family, friends and professionals. Service users are empowered to control their own life; their life is not controlled by the wishes of other people.

People with sensory, speech or other communication impairments

Visual impairment

People with a visual impairment will not be able to interpret your body language. Because of this, it may be important to use words to describe things that a sighted person may take for granted. You may also be able to explain your feelings through voice tone. This might include how you feel about an issue; for example, it might be obvious to someone who can see your face that you feel sad, but you might need to put your emotions into words so that a person with a visual disability can understand you. Touch may also be important; some registered blind people can work out what you look like if they can touch your face in order to build an understanding of your features. You can often explain how you feel using touch, but it is important to be sure that a service user is comfortable with being touched. You must never take it for granted that a person

with low vision would expect to be touched even on the hands or arms.

Hearing impairment

People with a hearing impairment may be able to use a hearing aid in order to increase the volume of sound that they can sense. One problem with hearing aids is that they often increase the volume of background noise as well as the volume of a person's voice. Some people with a hearing disability use partial lip-reading in order to understand what a person is saying. It does make sense for a person to say, 'I'm sorry I can't hear you, I need to put my glasses on.' It is very important that a person with a hearing disability can see your face, read your body language and watch your lips.

Hayman (1998) notes the following points for communicating with people who have hearing impairments:

* make sure the person can see you clearly
* face both the light and the person at all times
* include the person in your conversation
* do not obscure your mouth
* speak clearly and slowly. Repeat if necessary, but you may need to rephrase your words
* do not shout into a person's ear or hearing aid
* minimise background noise
* use your eyes, facial expressions and hand gestures, where appropriate.

People who are born Deaf often learn to use British Sign Language; this is a different language to English and is not a set of signs for English words. The ability to use some signs in BSL will enable care workers to communicate with members of the 'Deaf community' in the UK.

Some people have difficulty making the sounds that we expect to hear in relation to words. Speech therapists provide a service that may help people to develop their ability to communicate more effectively using speech. As with all disabilities, getting to know the individual person and creating a safe and supportive atmosphere will be central to improving your ability to communicate with a person who has a speech impairment.

People with disabilities – the risk of stereotyping

People with mobility disabilities can usually communicate in exactly the same way as mobile people. However people with disabilities are often stereotyped as being 'defective people'; in other words a person who needs a wheelchair to get around is seen as somebody who is not competent to express their own thoughts and feelings. The classic way of understanding this stereotype is the 'does he take sugar?' situation.

A service user is wheeled into a tea room by a carer, and the person serving the tea communicates only with the carer. Why ask the person in the wheelchair if they take sugar? The person serving the tea has assured that a person who needs a carer is a 'non-person' incapable of communicating choices!

FIGURE 2.12 *A disability does not mean an inability to communicate*

Disabled people are at risk of being patronised and sometimes being talked to as if they were children. It is possible that some people only understand caring as something you do with children. Because of this there is an assumption or stereotype that anybody who needs care must be childlike. There is, therefore, the risk that people will automatically use more fixed eye contact, a higher tone of voice and simple language with anybody who has a carer. Many people with coordination or mobility problems are vulnerable to the assumptions of other people. You may be, for example, an expert on astrophysics but people will attempt to communicate with you as if you were only five years old.

As with all interpersonal communication it is vital to get to know the individual needs, preferences and abilities of the individuals that you work with. Active listening provides a central tool for achieving this goal.

People attending an accident and emergency unit – working with distressed people

People and their relatives in an accident and emergency unit are likely to experience stress and perhaps distress. It will usually be important to use calming skills in order to help communicate effectively with people who are stressed. There is always the possibility that people who are stressed or in a state of distress may become aggressive or hostile. Aggression is an issue that can occur in many health and care settings; it involves some important communication skills, and these skills might be particularly useful in coping with people who experience distress

Preventing aggression

One of the key ways of showing respect for other people is to be assertive. The word 'assertion' is often misunderstood. Many people see assertion as 'sticking up for yourself', but being assertive involves much more than this. Being assertive is about remaining calm, and showing respect and value for other people. Assertion involves being clear about your own needs and intentions and being able to communicate in a clear, controlled and calm manner.

Fear and aggression are two of the basic emotions that we experience. It is easy to give in to our basic emotions and become either submissive or aggressive when we feel stressed. Assertion is an alternative way of coping that involves controlling the basic emotions involved in running away or fighting. Assertion involves a mental attitude of trying to **negotiate**, trying to solve problems rather than giving in to emotional impulses.

Assertion is different from both submission and aggression, Assertion involves being able to negotiate a solution to a problem.

Winning and losing

During an argument aggressive people might demand that they are right and other people are wrong. They will want to win while others lose. The opposite of aggression is to be weak or submissive. Submissive people accept that they

Aggressive response:

'Can't you read the sign – we don't deal with medicine here. In any case, you should know the times, we are not your servants, you know.'

The aggressive response meets the needs of the care worker and not the service user. An 'I win you lose' situation.

Angry service user

'Look, I came in here to get the tablets I need – and the pharmacy is shut. I want my medicine right now or I'm making a complaint.'

Assertive response:

'I'm sorry that the pharmacy is shut. It will be open again this afternoon. I cannot get your tablets, but if you do want to make a complaint then that is your right.'

The assertive response is aimed at meeting the needs of both the worker and the member of the public. 'We both win.'

Submissive response

'I'm terribly sorry. I don't know what to say. I'll try and get somebody who can get your tablets.'

The submissive response meets the needs of the service user and not the worker. The service user may dominate the worker. 'You win I lose.'

FIGURE 2.13 *How assertion enables both people to win*

will lose, get told off, or be put down. Assertive behaviour is different from both of these responses. In an argument an assertive person will try to reach an answer where no one has to lose or be 'put down'. Assertion is a skill where 'win-win' situations can happen – no one has to be the loser. For example, consider the following scenario in which a member of the public is angry because of being unable to get some tablets (see Figure 2.13).

Assertion can help care staff to cope with difficult and challenging situations.

To be assertive a person usually has to:

* understand the situation that they he or she is in – including facts, details and other people's perceptions

* be able to control personal emotions and stay calm

* be able to act assertively using the right body language

* be able to act assertively using the right words and statements.

Table 2.4 compares some of the different characteristics commonly associated with assertion, submission and aggression.

If you behave assertively, your calm, respectful behaviour may help to prevent aggression in other people. This is because you will not 'set yourself up as a target' for other people's emotions. If you lose control of your own emotions and become angry you may increase the threat experienced by another person. They may feel emotionally justified in abusing or even physically attacking you – because 'attack is the best defence'. If you appear weak and afraid you may invite abuse and attack because this may increase the frustration experienced by another person. A person who is weak and afraid my also appear to be an easy target – easy to dominate and control. If you listen and show respect for another person you may create an emotional environment in which that individual feels encouraged to respond with listening and respect.

Coping with aggression

Anger is a powerful emotion and it often looks as though people suddenly lose their temper

SUBMISSIVE BEHAVIOUR INVOLVES:	ASSERTIVE BEHAVIOUR INVOLVES:	AGGRESSIVE BEHAVIOUR INVOLVES:
Main emotion: fear	Main emotion: confidence	Main emotion: anger
Letting other people win	Negotiating so that everyone wins	Wanting to win
Understanding and acceptance only of other people's needs	Understanding and accepting your own and other people's needs	Understanding only your own needs
A mental attitude that other people are more important than you	A mental attitude that it is important to negotiate in order to get the best outcome for yourself and others	A mental attitude that you are more important than other people
Not speaking or only asking questions to find out what is wanted	Listening carefully	Not listening to others – making demands
Lack of respect for self	Respect for self and others	Lack of respect for others
Speaking quietly	Speaking in a clear calm voice	Shouting or talking loudly
Submissive body language including: ✳ looking down ✳ not looking at others ✳ looking frightened ✳ looking tense.	Relaxed body language including: ✳ varied eye contact ✳ looking confident ✳ keeping hands and arms at your side.	Threatening body language including: ✳ fixed eye contact ✳ tense muscles ✳ waving or folding arms ✳ clenching fingers.

TABLE 2.4 *Characteristics commonly associated with assertion, submission and aggression*

without a justified reason. A service user might suddenly start shouting or start making abusive comments. In many situations, this service user might have felt stressed long before the outburst of anger. Frustration and tension can grow as individuals fail to control their own emotions and their circumstances.

Triggers

As tension mounts, it may only take a single remark or some little thing that has gone wrong, to push the person into an angry outburst. People who feel stressed may only need a trigger incident to set off an explosion of anger that has built up inside them.

After an explosion of anger, stressed people can still feel tense. Very often they may feel that is someone else's fault that they have been made to feel so angry. Anger can flare up again if the person is not given respect and encouraged to become calm. As time passes, tension may reduce as stress and levels of high emotional arousal decrease.

Not all angry outbursts follow this pattern. Some people learn to use aggression to get their way and some people can switch aggressive emotions on and off as they wish. Being angry can sometimes be a reaction that a person has chosen. But it is wrong to assume that most outbursts of aggression and anger are deliberate. A great deal of aggression experienced by care

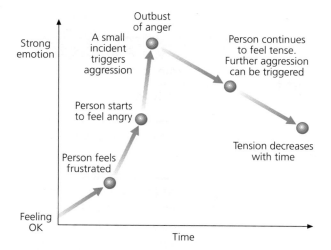

FIGURE 2.14 *Stages in the development of aggression*

workers will be an emotional response to frustration or distress.

The desire to fight or run

When people are aggressive or abusive they may make care workers feel threatened. The simple in-built emotional response to threat is to want to run or fight. An unskilled response to aggression is to be aggressive back. This will almost certainly escalate into a conflict situation, which is unlikely to have a positive outcome.

Even in mildly aggressive encounters one or both people are likely to feel resentment towards each other following the incident. A professional skilled response is to stay calm, be assertive rather than aggressive, calm the other person, and resolve the situation without creating resentment.

Care workers are unlikely to be able to switch off feelings of being threatened simply by wishing them away. Usually, workers will switch off the threat using positive thoughts about their own past experiences, their skills in being able to calm people, or just by using their own professional role to protect themselves from feeling 'got at'. If care workers can think 'this person is distressed because of his or her situation', rather than 'this person is out to get me' they may be able to switch off the emotions that create the feeling of being threatened.

Staying calm

Being calm depends on the thoughts that we

have, but it is also a practical skill which can be acted out and rehearsed. If care workers can appear to be calm their own behaviour may have

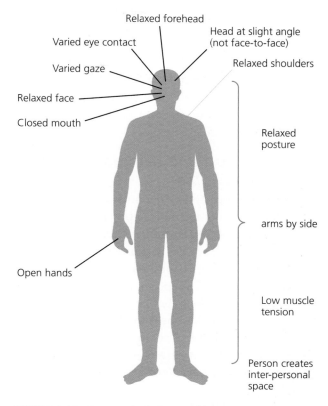

FIGURE 2.15 *Non-verbal signs of being calm*

a calming effect on others. Non-verbal signs of being calm are summarised in Figure 2.15.

It is important to remember to breathe gently and slowly. Slow, careful breathing can help to create relaxation and calmness as well as looking calm to others. Sometimes it is appropriate that body posture should be at a slight angle towards an angry person. A face-to-face posture is sometimes interpreted as an attempt to dominate or be threatening. The volume of speech should not be raised, it is important to talk in a normal tone and volume and to display that you do not feel threatened or angry.

Communicating respect and value

It is important to acknowledge the feelings and complaints that distressed people may be experiencing. If the other person feels that he or she is being taken seriously and is being listened to, this may have a calming effect. Active listening skills and the ability to keep the conversation going will be very important. A professional conversation should be warm and sincere while also seeking to build an understanding of the situation. Thanking a person for clarifying issues may be one way in which a worker can reduce the frustration that another person may feel. If a worker can communicate an understanding of the other person's point of view this may go a long way toward calming a situation and preventing further outbreaks of anger.

Creating trust and negotiating with distressed people

If you can successfully calm an angry or distressed person, the next step will be to try and establish a sense of common ground or liking between each other. It is at this stage that a skilled worker will attempt to build an understanding of the other person's viewpoint. Creating trust involves meeting the other person's self-esteem needs. In some situations it may be necessary to make the other person feel important. Sometimes it may be appropriate to say just a little about your own feelings, background, and so on, if this helps to build bridges and create a sense of safety with the other person. It is usually appropriate to convey that you are open-minded and supportive, but it is important that you do not agree with everything that the other person demands. It will be important to keep the conversation going and to keep the other person talking – perhaps using questioning and active listening skills.

Once you have built a level of understanding with a distressed person, it may then be possible to try and sort things out and to negotiate what kind of help or support you can offer. At this stage in the interaction it may be possible to take a problem-solving approach. Problem solving may start off by clarifying the issues that are involved and exploring alternative solutions.

Sometimes it may be necessary to structure expectations. This means gently introducing ideas of what is and is not possible. It is important not to argue with a distressed person, as arguing may only force him or her back into being aggressive or withdrawn. If you have to say 'no' to a demand, it may often be better to slowly lead up to the expectation that you will say no, rather than directly confronting a person with a 'stone wall' rejection of their views. For instance, 'I understand what you're saying and I'll see what I can do, but it would be wrong to promise anything', or 'We can try, but I am not hopeful'.

Only after you have developed a sense of trust and friendliness with the distressed person should you try to resolve the issues involved in the aggressive incident. During this stage of negotiation it may be important to bring factual information into the conversation. It is important not to appear patronising when offering information. It is also important to clearly explain technical information that the other person may not fully understand.

Sometimes it may not be possible to reach agreement with a distressed person, and in these circumstances it is important to conclude the conversation, leaving a positive emotional outcome, even if agreement has not been reached. It may be possible to agree to resume a conversation tomorrow, or to thank the person for his or her time and offer to talk again. It will always be important to leave the person with an increased sense of self-esteem even if he or she did not agree with your viewpoint.

While you cannot always give other people what they want, you can always give respect and a little time in supportive communication. Listening and respect may go some way to creating a positive emotional environment. Steps to take in order to manage a conversation with an angry person are shown in Figure 2.16.

Real conversations do not always follow simple stages but it is important not to attempt to negotiate and solve problems before listening and building trust.

People resident in a hospital ward – providing emotional support

As with many health care settings, people within a hospital ward may experience distress and it is important to provide emotional support. You can use active listening skills in order to build an understanding of people receiving medical care. Good listening skills and supportive body language can lead to effective emotional support.

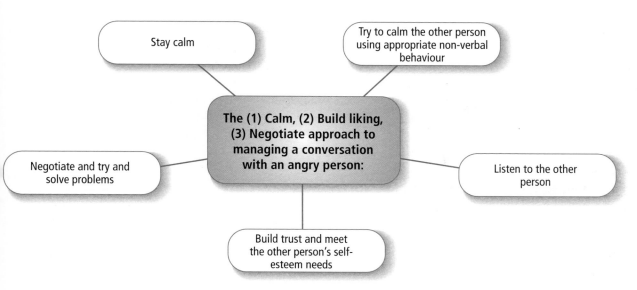

FIGURE 2.16 *Managing a conversation with an angry person*

Emotional support

Supportive body language involves looking friendly. When meeting a person it is usually appropriate to smile, to express interest through eye contact and to maintain a relaxed posture – free of muscle tension – which indicates a readiness to talk and listen. It is difficult to define a simple set of rules for supportive body language because each individual will have their own expectations about what is appropriate and normal. The most important thing about supportive body language is to learn to monitor the effects that our behaviour is having on the other person. Being supportive involves being aware of your own non-verbal behaviour and monitoring how your non-verbal behaviour is affecting others.

It is important for service users to feel emotionally safe and able to share experiences. The skills for creating a sense of emotional safety were first identified by Carl Rogers (1902–1987). Originally, these skills were seen as a basis for counselling relationships, but they have since become adopted as a basis for any befriending or supportive communication. There are three conditions for a supportive conversation and these are that the carer must show (or convey) a sense of warmth, understanding and sincerity to the other person. These conditions sometimes have other names:

* warmth (sometimes called acceptance)
* understanding (originally called empathy)
* sincerity (originally called genuineness).

Warmth

Warmth means being perceived as a friendly, accepting person. In order to influence another person to view you this way you will need to demonstrate that you do not stereotype and label others. You will need to show that you do not judge other people's lifestyles as good or bad, right or wrong. This is sometimes referred to as a non-judgemental attitude.

Conveying warmth means being willing to listen to others. It means having the ability to prove that you are listening to a person because you can remember what they have said to you. Warmth involves using active listening. That is, you give your attention to individuals when they talk, and remember what they say. You can then reflect their words back again.

In the scenario in Figure 2.17, the nurse is able to show the patient that she is listening by repeating some of the things that he has said. The repetition is not 'parrot fashion'; the nurse has used her own way of speaking. The nurse has also avoided being judgemental. When the patient said that no one cared, the nurse did not argue with him. Warmth makes it safe for the

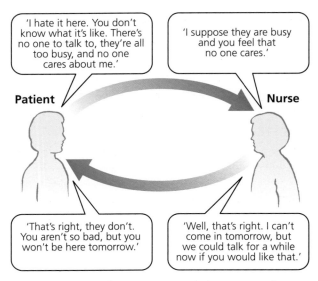

FIGURE 2.17 *developing a supportive sense of warmth involves being non-judgemental*

patient to express his feelings. Warmth means that the nurse could disagree with what a patient has said, but the patient needs to feel safe that he will not be put down.

In developing the skill of showing warmth, it is important not to judge. Carers should accept that people have the right to be the way they are, and to make their own choices. While you may disapprove of someone's behaviour, you must show that you do not dislike them as a person.

Active listening provides a useful tool that enables staff to learn about people. If a person is listened to, he or she may experience a feeling of being understood. If a care worker is warm and non-judgemental, it becomes safe for a service user to talk about his or her life. If the care worker checks that he or she understands the person, this may result in the service user feeling valued. As the person feels that they are valued, so he or she may talk more. The more the person talks, the more the care worker has a chance to learn about that service user.

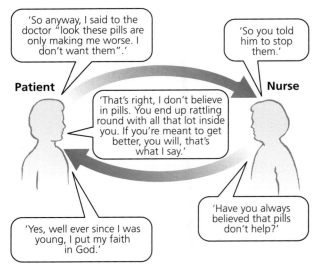

FIGURE 2.18 *developing a supportive sense of understanding involves active listening*

By listening and conveying warmth the health care worker is being given the privilege of learning about the patient's religious views. Understanding can grow from a conversation that conveys value for the other person. A sense of trust may develop out of a sense of understanding. If you feel you are understood then you may feel it is safe to share your thoughts and worries.

Sincerity

Being sincere means being yourself – honest and real. It means not acting, not using set phrases or professional styles, which are not really you. Being real has to involve being non-judgemental though – trying to understand people, rather than trying to give people advice. If being honest means giving other people your advice, don't do it! However, when you listen and learn about other people, do use your own normal language.

| Patient | 'But what's the point in talking to you? I mean, you don't really care, it's just your job.' |
| Nurse | 'It is my job, but I do care about you, and I would be pleased to talk with you. I chose this work because I care and because I can make the time to listen if you want to talk about it.' |

Learning to create a supportive relationship with people involves practice and a great deal of reflection. A care worker may be able to tell if his or her communication is effective because the other person may reflect his or her behaviour. This means, if you are warm and understanding you may find that others are warm and friendly towards you. If you are honest and sincere, people may be honest and sincere with you in return. The quality of a supportive relationship becomes a two-way process.

Think it over – developing supportive skills

You could try the following ideas for developing your supportive communication skills.

1. Work with a friend. Take turns in imagining that you are upset or sad whilst the other person uses reflective listening skills. Tape-record the conversation. Play the tape back and evaluate your performance in terms of warmth, understanding and sincerity.

2. Watch videos of conversational skills or counselling situations where warmth, understanding and sincerity are demonstrated. Discuss how this is effective and how you might develop your own conversational skills.

3. Think about your own conversations with service users – keep a logbook to reflect on your own skills development.

4. Write up examples of being warm, understanding and sincere. Discuss your examples with your tutor and ask for feedback.

Creating a caring presence

Verbal conversational skills are very important in enabling people to feel supported, but part of what is needed may simply be to provide a 'caring presence'. Sometimes just sitting with someone – simply being with a person because you care about that individual – creates a sense of being valued and supported. Engebretson (2004) explains this sense of being valued and supported without words as the creation of a caring presence. She explains the importance of being open to the experience of other people. Health and care work cannot simply be about 'doing things' to people. Creating a caring presence is about sharing an understanding of the feelings that service users have. Engebretson explains how nurses can work on an emotional level in order to make a real difference to what people experience when they receive health care.

People in consultation with a medical practitioner

The term 'patient' has been around for many centuries and the idea is that the people needing help are patient while the expert medical practitioner works on them. Many people who consult medical practitioners expect to be passive and expect simple pharmaceutical (to be given a tablet) solutions to their problem. Half a century ago a visit to the doctor would involve patients explaining their problem and accepting the advice received in return. The term 'doctor's orders' was sometimes used to describe the treatment plan that a patient had to follow. Patients often thought of doctors as being senior people who were entitled to give orders – rather like officers in the army.

Some patients and some medical practitioners may find this idea of giving and receiving orders a satisfying prospect. But there are problems with communications that assume this kind of power relationship.

Many people's health problems are associated with economic and lifestyle issues. For example, some people develop health problems associated with being overweight or with smoking. Just giving people information or orders to eat less and exercise more, or to stop smoking is almost wholly ineffective in helping patients. There is no simple tablet or procedure that enables people to change their lifestyle. In order for 'the patients' to become healthier they must stop being patient, and instead become actively involved in their own health issues.

In order to encourage active involvement, consultations may need to involve a more empowering approach where the patients take responsibility for understanding and managing their needs – in partnership with a health professional – rather than delegating total responsibility for treatment to health staff.

Medical practitioners should communicate their knowledge to service users and enable service users to make their own decisions and choices about care plans or medical treatment. Empowering communication is communication that aims to give service users choice and control of the service that they receive.

> ### Key concept
>
> *Empowerment:* this enables service users to make choices and take control of their own life. Empowerment involves patients taking some responsibility for the management of their health needs.

An example of empowerment

In 2001 the government launched the 'Expert Patient Initiative'. The idea of an 'expert patient' is that a person with a long-term, or chronic, illness such as arthritis can learn to take control of the management of his or her condition. Expert medical staff can provide advice and guidance, but the patient is the expert on his or her own body. Thus patients work in partnership with medical staff in order to build their own treatment plan.

The 'expert patient' is empowered to take control of his or her own medical condition. The expert patient does not simply have to comply with the treatment prescribed.

Getting empowerment to take place

There are pressures that may limit the degree to which service users are empowered.

* some care workers may enjoy a sense of prestige and power that might come from making decisions for other people. In reality, some care staff may be reluctant to share their expert status

* lack of time may represent a problem for some care workers. Working in partnership may require longer conversations than a more directive approach

* some service users may resist 'working in partnership'. Some service users may find it preferable to delegate responsibility for meeting their needs to others. Taking responsibility for your own life may require a well-organised self-concept, a degree of confidence in your own abilities and perhaps some energy and enthusiasm for being in control. Many vulnerable people may initially prefer 'to be looked after' by professionals.

Christine Descombes (2004) provides evidence that within medical practice, 'It is still the doctor who controls the whole patient-practitioner encounter. It is the doctor who decides just what information will be given and how much use can be made of it' (2000: 94). Establishing an empowering approach will require much more than simply giving clear information to service users.

Older people

As with all adult service user groups, it will be vitally important that care workers are skilled in using active listening and supportive skills. The section on supportive skills and caring presence related to residents in hospitals is equally important when working with older people.

There are special problems that may arise when working with people who are disorientated or who have memory problems. A 90-year-old service user might say, for example, 'My mother visited me yesterday.' On the surface, such a statement appears to be irrational. From a care perspective it is very important not to challenge the irrationality of what is being said. The most important thing is to make the older person feel valued and respected. People with memory disorders, often substitute inappropriate words. The person has said that her mother visited and perhaps the care worker knows that the visitor was, in fact, a daughter. The service user has simply used an incorrect word, although she knew what she meant; perhaps, too, the care worker knew what the service user meant. The technical inaccuracy is not important. It is much more important that the service user feels safe and respected.

Sometimes disorientated service users may make statements about needing to go to work or to go home to look after their children. Once again, it is important not to argue, but rather to try and divert the conversation in a way that values the person, as is illustrated in the following scenario.

Active listening skills are important for care workers

Care workers often develop the skills of managing a conversation in a way that demonstrates respect and value and prevents aggression. The conversation below takes place in a care home for older people and illustrates how difficult encounters can sometimes be resolved by taking an assertive approach that also seeks to value others.

Relative: What have you done to my mother? She's so much worse than before. You aren't looking after her properly. She can't eat because of the rubbish food you give out.

Worker: Your mother does look worse today. Perhaps you would like to sit down and we can talk.

Relative: Well, you tell me what is going on, then, and why the food is such rubbish!

Worker: I'll explain what we're doing if you like, and I'm sorry that your mother doesn't like the food. Could you tell me what sort of things she really does like to eat?

Relative: Not the rubbish here.

Worker: Sometimes it's possible to increase someone's appetite by just offering a very small tasty piece of something that person really likes, perhaps fruit or a tiny piece of bread and jam?

SCENARIO

Service user: I must go home and get the tea ready for my children.

Care worker: All right. Shall we walk to your room then – you might want your coat?

Service user: Yes, that's right, you are so kind.

Care worker: [now in service user's room] Is this photograph a photograph of your son and daughter?

Service user: Yes, that's right.

Care worker: They've both got married now. Haven't they both grown up?

Service user: Yes, I'm very proud of them. They're coming to visit me tomorrow.

Care worker: That's wonderful. Why don't we go downstairs and have a cup of tea?

Service user Yes, that would be very nice. You are so kind to me.

In this script, the carer has avoided arguing about logic, and instead the carer has gently helped the service user to remember the age of her children now. Throughout the conversation, the carer has shown respect and value for the service user.

Relative: What, and you are going to sort that out, are you!

Worker: I've found that it works for a lot of people. But can you give me some ideas of what your mother would like?

Relative: Well she likes pears and cherry jam, but good stuff – not like here.

Worker: OK, could you possibly bring some of her favourite things in and we could try and see if that would help.

Relative: Why should I?

Worker: Well, it might help. Everyone is different and you are the person who would really know what your mother is likely to enjoy.

Relative: Can't you do something about the food here?

Worker: I'm afraid that the choice of food is limited, but we might be able to work together to improve your mother's appetite as a first step to making things better.

Relative: I suppose it's not up to you to change the food. I'll bring the jam in, but I still think it's not right.

Worker: I'm sorry that you're not happy about the food, but perhaps we can talk again tomorrow.

Relative: Well, thank you for your time – at least I could talk to you.

Discussion

This conversation starts with the relative in an angry mood. The worker responds by remaining assertive and not arguing, or going straight into discussing the complaints that the relative has raised. Instead, the worker attempts to calm the situation and invites the relative to sit down. By inviting the relative to sit down the worker is taking control of the conversation and creating a situation where he or she can use his or her listening skills.

At several points the angry relative is still challenging the worker with complaints and aggressive statements. The worker is careful not to respond to these challenges and risk triggering more aggression. The worker is able to stay calm and to build a sense of trust by keeping the conversation going. The worker is able to ask the relative questions about his mother's needs. The worker is also able to meet the relative's self-esteem needs by pointing out that he is the person who would really know what his mother likes and dislikes.

In this conversation the worker negotiates that the relative will bring some food in. The worker structures the relative's expectations by mentioning the limited choice of food. Because the relative has been listened to, he is willing to stop complaining. He compliments the worker with the statement that at least she listened.

The conversation ends on a positive emotional note, even though the problems of catering in this care setting have not been resolved. The point of this conversation was to meet the emotional needs of the distressed relative and not to find technical solutions to catering problems!

2.6 Giving a talk

Whilst some people feel quite comfortable with the idea of giving a talk, others are filled with emotions that range from nervousness to fear. If you are one of those for whom giving a talk is a daunting prospect, be reassured that many people feel this way. However, there are a number of things that can be done to make it likely that the talk will be a success, and one of these is to prepare adequately for the event. The planning process described in this section, if followed carefully, will increase your chances of giving an interesting presentation in a confident manner. There are also a few tips for dealing with pre-talk nerves.

Remember, too, that it is quite normal, and indeed desirable, to be nervous before making a presentation. As someone once said, 'It's OK to have butterflies in your stomach – you just have to make sure that they fly in the same direction!' The steps described in this section will help to make sure that your butterflies behave themselves.

Being a little nervous may actually improve your presentation

Identifying a topic

Fairly early on in your studies for this unit, you should identify a type of service user and a care setting as the subject for the presentation. You might, for example, choose to consider an aspect of communication with an older person who lives in a residential setting. Alternatively, you may be interested in communication with younger children, perhaps in an early years centre. People with learning disabilities have specific communication needs, as do people with sensory disabilities. If you are able to visit a centre or unit attended by people with the kinds of need you are interested in, this will help you tremendously in preparing and researching your talk.

Remember that the talk is only to last about 5–10 minutes. It will be important to select a topic that can be dealt with adequately in that relatively short time span. For example, it would be hard to explain to people how to use British Sign Language (BSL) in ten minutes. It would be more realistic to explain to people why it can be useful for a hearing person to know BSL, or to point out the kinds of situation where BSL makes a difference (e.g. in theatres, law courts, etc.).

One way to find a good topic is to focus on a particular event, and the learning points that arise from it. In this section, the progress of a typical A-level student, Natalie, is followed as she works on her presentation for this unit.

Natalie is interested in communication issues for people with learning disabilities, and her tutor has arranged for her to visit a day unit run by the local social services department. At the day unit she meets Ellen, a young woman who is about to take part in a facilitated session led by a staff member. Like many people with a learning disability, Ellen is not used to being asked to say what she wants, and usually gives answers that she thinks the staff wants to hear. She also has a limited knowledge of what kinds of things are available to her.

Learning about what's available

At Ellen's day unit, Person Centred Planning has just been introduced by social services, and staff have come up with a way of finding out what each service user wants. One of the workers had been on a special training course to learn how to lead groups to do this, and there is now a weekly meeting at the unit in which people are helped to discover what they like.

This week, the subject is 'fruit'. Staff have brought in a very wide range of fruits for everyone to try. As each fruit is tasted, service users explain their reaction to it by pointing to a face-symbol: a smiley face for 'love it', a grumpy face for 'don't like it', and so on.

Ellen discovers that she loves fresh pineapple, something she has never tasted before, but she is not very keen on kiwi fruit.

Natalie is fascinated by what has happened, and the way it was done. The meeting was led by a **facilitator**, who had been specially trained to help people with learning disabilities to express themselves, asking the right questions, and adapting her listening style to suit the needs of each person. Sometimes, this can be as simple (and as complex) as learning to observe (and correctly interpret) the non-verbal signals that a person gives.

> **Key concept**
>
> *Facilitator:* a person who helps to make something happen. This is often associated with decision-making or planning.

Natalie has also been introduced to the concept of **Person Centred Planning**. The staff at the unit give her some information about this, but she realises that now she will have to go away and do some more research. How she did this is described in the next section.

Collecting information

Natalie does some Internet research to find out more about Person Centred Planning. She discovers that it was introduced for people with learning disabilities by a government initiative called Valuing People, which was launched in 2001.

> **Key concept**
>
> *Person Centred Planning* 'A process for continual listening and learning, focused on what is important for someone now and in the future, and acting upon this in alliance with family and friends.'
>
> Source: *Planning With People: Guidance for Implementation Groups* (Department of Health, 2002), p. 12.

Natalie's search reveals several websites with further information about how Person Centred Planning may be carried out, including the Valuing People website, People First and the website for In Control. (Further details of these sites, which have a lot of information about communicating with people with learning disabilities, and empowering them to say what they want, may be found at www.heinemann.co.uk/hotlinks (express code 1554P).)

Besides finding out more about facilitation, Natalie also comes across the concepts of **advocacy**, **self-advocacy** and **self-directed support**.

> **Key concepts**
>
> *Advocacy:* the act of speaking on behalf of someone else, to make sure that his or her views and wishes are heard.
>
> *Self-advocacy:* the act of speaking up for yourself.
>
> *Self-directed support:* a process that involves the service user playing a key role in decision-making about the services he or she wants.

Natalie also spends some time at her local library, to find out more about communicating with people with learning disabilities. By combining what she learnt from her visit to the day unit with Internet and printed information, she finally decides on a topic for her talk (in discussion with her tutor). She decides to call the presentation 'Finding out what people with learning disabilities want'.

Planning your talk

There are a number of factors that Natalie will have to consider when preparing a presentation. These are set out in Table 2.5.

Who are my audience?

Doing an analysis of your audience in advance of giving the talk is essential. Who they are, what they will expect and how many of them there will be are all factors that will have an effect on what you say and how you say it. Social workers, for example, may be very interested in a talk that includes lots of theoretical material, whereas parents or carers may want to hear more about practical issues.

Similarly, the size of the group will also have a bearing on the kind of talk you give. Group size has implications both for the venue that you will need (size of the room, need for a microphone, etc.) and also for the possibility of interaction between speaker and audience. The atmosphere is more likely to be relaxed with a small group and, therefore, people may be more willing to ask questions. If audience participation is a key element of your presentation, the size of the group may be critical.

A more detailed checklist of aspects of the venue is given at the end of this section (p. 90). At this stage, you should have the following broad considerations in mind.

Natalie will be giving her talk to a group of fellow students. There will be nine people, plus her tutor. She feels that it would be useful for her talk to include both theoretical and practical aspects of communication. She is the only person studying people with learning disabilities for this unit, so she wants to take the opportunity to share some of the key issues with her colleagues.

When will the presentation take place?

Besides forming a clear picture of who your audience is going to be, it is important to find out what time of day you will be giving your talk, and how it fits in with other activities that may be scheduled to take place.

PLANNING A TALK		
Checklist		**Notes**
Who?	– Who is my target audience? – What are their expectations? – What is the size of the group?	
When?	– When will the talk take place? – What time of day? – What is happening before and after my talk?	
Where?	–– Where will the talk take place? – Will I have support, facilities and equipment? – What else will be going on at the time?	
What?	– What are the aims and objectives of my presentation? – What should the content of the talk be?	
Note. You might like to take a photocopy of Table 2.5 to use when planning your talk. You could also include it in your report.		

TABLE 2.5 *Factors to consider when planning a talk*

If, for example, you are making your presentation to staff in a care setting such as a residential unit, it would be wise to make sure that your event does not clash with something else that is taking place at the time (such as serving tea or other group sessions like dancing). Although your talk will only last 5–10 minutes, you will need to allow extra time for setting up, people arriving and settling down, the general conversation that usually goes on after a presentation (and you may wish to collect feedback from your audience immediately after you have finished), and then clearing away. This means you will need to schedule about an hour for the whole process.

A detailed checklist concerning the setting and timing of the event is given at the end of this section.

Natalie has to schedule her talk for a time when there will be no other lectures or teaching sessions, so that her fellow students are free to attend. She also needs to make sure that her tutor can be present. After checking it out, she decides that a Thursday afternoon would be the best time to make her presentation.

Where will the talk take place?

It is vital to find out where your talk will take place as early as you can. You will need to know whether it will be in a room that is normally used for something else (in which case, you will have to allow plenty of time for setting up, arranging furniture and so on), or whether it is a room dedicated to this kind of activity.

The room must be big enough to accommodate the number of people you are expecting, with adequate heating and ventilation. There must be enough chairs for everyone, and you may choose to include tables if you plan to ask people to write or to do some other kind of activity that requires surfaces to lean on.

It may be important to check out whether or not there will be another activity taking place at the same time that may affect your talk. For example, if you will be presenting in a day unit, and there is a music class taking place at the same time, you need to be sure that the noise from this group will not disturb your talk.

Natalie is lucky. Her college is making

available a seminar room for the event to take place. The seminar room is fully equipped with flipchart, whiteboard and OHP, although Natalie may use Powerpoint for her support materials. The room is soundproof, so there will be no danger of disturbance from outside. Good heating, lighting and ventilation are a feature of this room. The talk is taking place in January, but Natalie doesn't need to worry that her group will be too cold, as the temperature in the seminar room is thermostatically controlled.

What are my aims and objectives?

The setting of clear aims and objectives is critical to the success of a presentation. As the saying has it, if you don't know where you are going, the chances are you will end up somewhere else.

You can think of an aim as the point you want to be at the end of a process, in this case a presentation. Objectives are the small steps you need to take to get there. Some examples of aims and objectives are set out in Table 2.6.

For a short presentation of 5–10 minutes it is likely that there will be only one aim. You will have noticed, by studying Table 2.6, that an aim can be expressed as what you hope to achieve by giving your talk. In the three examples in Table 2.6, the speakers have set out where they want to get to in very broad terms. It will take only ten minutes, after all, so the aims are limited by time. It is important, therefore, that your aims are realistic. The first speaker hopes simply to create an awareness of the kinds of problems faced by Deaf students. The second focuses specifically on one kind of activity with service users – the reminiscence session (in which intellectual activity is stimulated by the use of objects to trigger memory). The third (which is Natalie's presentation) looks at one aspect of working with people with learning disabilities – that of empowering them to make their views known.

Objectives deal with the steps needed to achieve the aim. They can be expressed in terms of what the audience will be able to do as a result of the information contained in your talk. Because the presentation is so short, these will often be limited to cognitive outcomes like 'knowing' or 'recognising' something. However, if you choose

AIM (WHAT YOU PLAN TO ACHIEVE WITH YOUR TALK)	OBJECTIVES (WHAT THE AUDIENCE WILL BE ABLE TO DO AT THE END OF THE TALK)
Create an awareness of the problems encountered by Deaf students.	Recognise specific issues for Deaf students with particular reference to: ＊ missing key points in class ＊ misunderstanding what people are saying (social issue) ＊ being excluded from social and study activities
Explain how reminiscence sessions can be used to build relationships between staff and service users in a day unit for older people.	Know how communication can be stimulated by the use of: ＊ old photographs and objects to trigger memories ＊ active listening by staff ＊ skilled facilitation
Explain some methods that can be used to ensure that people with learning disabilities can express their views and wishes.	Know how facilitation can be used to help people with learning disabilities express their views. Recognise other techniques including: ＊ advocacy ＊ self-advocacy ＊ self-directed support

TABLE 2.6 *Aims and objectives of a presentation*

to talk about something practical like using a couple of BSL signs, the objectives might refer to practical outcomes like 'using the signs for . . .'. Specific objectives will make for a successful presentation.

In Natalie's case, she wants to focus specifically on how facilitated sessions can be used to find out the views and preferences of people with learning disabilities. She really only has time in the ten minutes allowed to explain this technique fully. However, she has researched other techniques such as advocacy and self-directed support, so she wants to explain these briefly, and decides to give her audience some additional material about these in a handout. She also hopes that the group will ask her questions, giving her the chance to give them some further information.

The analysis that Natalie did in answering the questions 'Who?', 'When?' and 'Where?' has

helped her to focus on her aims and objectives. She feels that her fellow students will be interested to hear about the facilitated session she took part in at the day unit, and some more theoretical material about a range of communication techniques. She hopes that the relatively small group size will encourage questions, and she feels that the group will appreciate having a handout to support the presented material.

Natalie still has to arrange the information she has collected into the order in which she will present it. There is more advice on how to do this in the next section.

Delivering the talk

When delivering a presentation a speaker has to manage three things: the material (i.e. the content of the talk), the audience and him or herself.

GIVING A TALK INVOLVES MANAGING

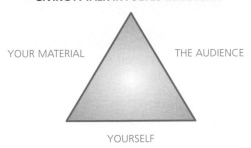

FIGURE 2.19 *Managing Your Material*

There is a saying about giving a good talk. First of all you tell the audience what you are going to tell them (the introduction); then you tell them (the main body of your talk); then you tell them what you've just told them (the summary and conclusion at the end).

The structure of a talk

TELL THEM what you are going to tell them

TELL THEM

TELL THEM what you've just told them

This is a tried-and-tested approach used by public speakers, whether they are politicians, salespeople or entertainers. Good teachers and lecturers also use this structure. The important aspect of this system is that it uses the principle of repetition, which is also a central aspect of teaching and learning.

If you set out what your talk will be about in a clear and memorable introduction, you have created an expectation in your audience about what they will hear. The central body of your talk should then elaborate on these points, using only information or material that is relevant. A summary and conclusion will remind the audience about what they have just heard, and make it more likely that they will remember the key aspects of the talk. People who are taking notes at a talk always appreciate a speaker who keeps to the point, and follows a structure as laid out in the introduction.

The key points of a talk will be designed to achieve the aims and objectives that have already

been decided. This is critical. There is no point is telling your audience to expect a talk on communicating with children, and then digressing to include a mass of anecdotes about working with older people.

The same is true of any supplementary material that you decide to use. Visual material should enhance the points you are making. This might be carefully chosen photographs, or projected images showing the points you are making in bullet-point form. It is a mistake to show too much printed or written material on an overhead – it will be too much for your audience to take in, and can detract from what you are actually saying.

If you are using audio-visual aids such as a video, DVD or CD recording, make sure that you know how to use the equipment that will be available to you on the day. For a short talk, it is advisable to keep the use of such supplementary material to a minimum.

If there is too much material for 10 minutes, but you feel it is really vital to tell the audience about certain things, handouts can be used to give out additional information. Handouts can also be used to reinforce the key points of the talk.

Although you will have to write out the text of your presentation in full to put in the report, you might like to consider using a more abbreviated form for the actual presentation. Some people use prompt cards, on which are written the main points. They then speak naturally when elaborating on these key items. Other people write out the key points onto a sheet of paper.

Whatever method you use on the day, it's a good idea to have a rehearsal beforehand, and to time yourself. You may be surprised at how short 10 minutes is, and find that you have too much material for the time allowed. Record how much time you spend on each topic, and decide whether or not you have the balance right. Make sure you allocate more time to the most important items, but also make sure you don't run out of time completely.

Natalie has decided to introduce her topic with a short account of the facilitated session she attended at the day unit. This will allow her to tell her audience what the talk is to be about. She

MANAGING YOUR MATERIAL	
Structure your talk	Introduction Body of talk Summary/conclusion
Link your talk to your aims and objectives	Choose relevant material that supports your case
Audiovisual material	Keep to a minimum for a short talk Make sure you can use the equipment
Aides memoires	Options include: Reading from full text Prompt cards Notes on sheets of paper
Visual aids	Should be clear and concise Use white space to effect (do not clutter your overheads with too many words) Should enhance (not detract from) your talk
Supplementary material	You can use handouts to give extra material
Rehearse your talk	Always have at least one run-through before the actual event Make sure you keep to time Allocate time to each item

TABLE 2.7 *Tips for managing your material*

then makes several key points about the technique of facilitation. She gives these in bullet-point form on an overhead to complement what she is saying. She then briefly explains that there are a number of other techniques that can be used to help people with learning disabilities to express their views, listing them in the form of bullet-points on an overhead. She tells her audience that she does not have time to describe these fully, but that she is giving them a handout with additional information, including how they can find out more if they are interested.

Managing the audience

Giving a talk is not just a simple matter of standing in front of a group of people and speaking to them. An audience has to be managed in order to create the right environment for listening and learning.

It is important to establish a rapport with a group by exhibiting a friendly and open demeanour. Eye contact can play an important part in this, but it is necessary to maintain a balance between avoiding eye contact completely and making people feel intimidated by staring at them. Remember, too, that some cultural groups may find too much eye contact insulting. Some people (for example, some Muslims) may avoid making eye contact with a speaker.

The physical conditions in the room are also an important consideration. People's concentration will be affected if a room is too hot or cold, too stuffy or too crowded. It is really important for an audience to be comfortable and therefore able to concentrate well if the message is to be delivered effectively.

Creating the right furniture arrangement is also essential in ensuring that your audience is comfortable. Assuming that the chairs are not

A semi-circular arrangement can enhance communication with a small group

fixed, you might want to consider whether the group should sit in a semi-circle or in rows. Larger groups are easier to manage in rows, but the semi-circular arrangement can help to enhance communication between speaker and audience when the group is small.

It is important to make sure that the room is safe. For example, there should be no trailing cables for people to fall over, and the room should not be overcrowded with furniture.

Finally, but no less important, you should take into account the potential needs of people with disabilities, or people for whom English is not a first language. A Deaf person, for example, may need to have a Signer present, and you will certainly need to think about where you position yourself in relation to someone who has a hearing problem. If the audience is to include a Blind person, you should consider having your material prepared in Braille, or make someone available to read the content of the handouts or to take notes. Someone with a physical disability may need more space (for example, if he or she uses a wheelchair). A person with a learning disability may wish to bring along a helper or advocate to make sure that he or she is fully included in the event. Someone for whom English is not a first language may need an interpreter to help explain the key points of the talk.

Natalie's group includes a Deaf student, so she allows space for this person's signer to join. She has opted for a semi-circular chair arrangement, and places a table centre-front on which she can put her laptop, her notes and the handouts. The signer will stand next to Natalie and opposite the Deaf student, who will sit in the centre of the semi-circle. The seminar room has good lighting, heating and ventilation, but she goes along well in advance of the start of the talk to set the thermostat at an appropriate setting for the temperature that day. All cables are properly covered by ducting in this room. However, it is a good idea to take along some masking tape if you are working in a room where equipment is not fitted – any loose cables can then be taped to the floor for the duration of the session.

MANAGING THE AUDIENCE	
Creating a rapport	A friendly attitude is helpful. Eye contact should be appropriate.
Physical comfort	Make sure the room temperature is comfortable. Ventilation should be adequate. Lighting should be adequate.
Furniture	Consider how best to arrange furniture: rows, semi-circle, small groups around tables.
Health & safety	Safety is paramount: ensure no trailing cables, no overcrowding.
Special requirements	Plan for people with sensory, physical or learning disabilities, and people for whom English is not a first language.

TABLE 2.8 *Tips for managing the audience*

Managing yourself

You will be the centre of attention during your talk, so how you manage your voice and body language will be critical.

It is important to speak at a speed that is neither too fast (which will leave people wondering what you have said) nor too slow (which may be boring and result in inattentiveness). Pacing out your talk, not being afraid of making short pauses to allow people to assimilate your words, is also helpful. A silence of about two or three seconds may seem like a long time to you, but in fact it does not seem very long to those who are listening and can be of tremendous help when people are concentrating on what you are saying.

Your voice should be loud enough to be heard by people sitting at the back of the group, although if there is amplification it will be important to speak at a more normal level. Try to vary the pitch of your voice, giving emphasis to the words or phrases that you consider to be more important than others.

Taking a few deep breaths before you start will improve your performance, as will keeping your head up, your spine straight and your shoulders back. Slouching will give a negative impression, and will also prevent you from breathing properly.

Choose your words carefully, and adapt your style of speaking to suit the needs of the audience. A group of non-specialists, for example, may not appreciate being bombarded with a lot of jargon or acronyms that they are unfamiliar with. It is always a good idea to explain any abbreviations or acronyms that you use, just in case there is someone in the audience who is unfamiliar with these terms; specialist terminology (such as Person Centred Planning, or Valuing People) also needs to be explained.

Just as when writing a report or essay, it is a good idea to open each topic or item with a straightforward sentence or statement about what you are going to talk about. For example, 'I am now going to describe three methods that can be used to communicate with people who have a hearing impairment.' It can be a good idea to alternate longer and shorter sentences.

Consider where you will stand in relation to your audience, and whether or not you will need to move about at all. Carefully paced movement (perhaps from one side to the OHP to change an overhead, and than back to your original place) can sometimes enhance a presentation by giving the audience the chance to alter their focus. However, in a very short presentation such as this one, such a tactic would only be of use perhaps once. Too much movement can be distracting.

Similarly, you should avoid unnecessary distracting mannerisms such as head-scratching or hand-waving. These can get in the way of the audience's concentration.

You may choose to sit to give your presentation. This would be appropriate for an intimate group where one of your aims is to engage in a significant amount of interaction. On the other hand, perhaps you have a particular condition which prevents you from standing for any length of time. If sitting down is your choice, for whatever reason, it is important to consider how you can maximise your impact as a speaker – perhaps by ensuring that you are a little higher than the audience, or allowing a little more space between yourself and them so that everyone can see you clearly.

Eye contact should be appropriate (see above), as should your facial expression. You should aim to communicate confidence, interest in the topic and responsiveness to your audience. If you have allowed space for the audience to ask questions, show that you appreciate their response, and treat each questioner with respect, even if you think that the question is irrelevant, or that you have already dealt with that topic.

Sometimes, a speaker will open a talk with a joke or amusing anecdote. This is usually best left to people who are very experienced, as a badly told joke can fall very flat. At worst, it may offend somebody. Only use humour if you are totally sure about your audience's background. You should never tell jokes that stereotype or offend somebody's race, religion or disability.

Finally, using the technique of visualisation in the run-up to the event can help to keep nerves under control. The idea is to imagine yourself in the exact room where you will give your talk, with the audience as far as you know it to be. In your mind's eye, go through the talk, imagining that you are confident and clear, and that your audience is responsive and positive. Sportspeople often use this technique to maximise success in sporting events. It can work just as well for presentations. Creating an expectation of a positive outcome can make the difference between a mediocre performance and an outstanding one.

In the week before she is due to give her talk, Natalie rehearses several times, using the cards she has prepared. She also spends some time each day visualising herself in the seminar room, giving a successful presentation to her fellow-students. On the day, before the event, she has a few quiet minutes during which she does some breathing exercises. She is very excited about the topic, and this enthusiasm helps her to present naturally and clearly. As the group is fairly small, she does not need to raise her voice, and she is helped by the acoustics in the seminar room, which are good. There are some questions, which she is able to deal with very well (she has done her homework).

MANAGING YOURSELF	
Before the event	✳ Visualise yourself giving a superb presentation ✳ See the audience appreciating your talk, asking interesting questions ✳ See yourself after the talk, discussing it with your tutor
Just before you start	✳ A few deep breaths will calm the nerves
Voice	✳ Consider pitch, tone and volume ✳ Speed should be neither too fast nor too slow ✳ Short pauses can assist assimilation of information
Words	✳ Choose words carefully ✳ Make sentences appropriate to needs of your listeners ✳ Explain any acronyms or abbreviations ✳ Explain any specialist terminology ✳ Explain each topic/item clearly
Position	✳ Consider whether you will stand or sit ✳ Choose your position carefully ✳ A little movement can assist concentration ✳ Too much movement can be distracting ✳ Mannerisms may annoy
Eyes and face	✳ Eye contact should be appropriate ✳ Facial expression appropriate ✳ Convey confidence, interest, responsiveness
Humour	✳ Be careful about using humour ✳ Only use if you are totally sure about your audience

TABLE 2.9 *Tips for managing yourself*

2.7 Feedback research

Collecting feedback

It is essential to get feedback on your performance. This can help you to improve your technique for future occasions. It is also a requirement of this unit that properly documented and researched feedback is obtained.

Structured data

Data of this kind can be **structured** or **unstructured**. Structured data is the kind of information which is uniform – that is, it is collected in the same format from everyone who gives information or feedback. A questionnaire requiring the ticking of boxes, or allocation of a rating to specified parameters provides structured data. Some examples of structured data are given in Table 2.10.

Data can also be structured by asking all respondents the same questions in the same way. Closed questions (i.e. those that can be answered 'yes' or 'no') will give responses that can be directly compared with each other.

Examples of closed questions:

* Did you find the presentation helpful?
* Did the speaker use his/her voice well?
* Did the speaker allocate time appropriately?

Closed questions and structured data are useful if you want to make a **quantitative analysis** of the feedback. Quantitative analysis gives results that can be expressed in terms of numbers or percentages. Table 2.11 gives an example of a quantitative analysis of a presentation from a questionnaire.

To make the presentation clearer, you might choose to set out this table with only the 'Yes' column. However, if some people left boxes

EXAMPLES OF STRUCTURED DATA:		
Tick box questionnaire		Agree Disagree
	Visuals were effective	☐ ☐
	Presentation was clear	☐ ☐
Rating scale questionnaire	Give a rating for each of the following parameters by circling the appropriate score (1 = low; 5 = high)	
	Low Score High Score	
	Visual aids 1 2 3 4 5	
	Presentation 1 2 3 4 5	

TABLE 2.10 *Some examples of structured data*

ANALYSIS OF END-OF-SESSION QUESTIONNAIRE 15 PEOPLE ATTENDED THIS TALK; 12 QUESTIONNAIRES WERE COMPLETED.				
	YES		NO	
	Number	Percentage	Number	Percentage
Was the presentation clear?	11	92%	1	8%
Were the visual materials effective?	11	92%	1	8%
Were the handouts helpful?	7	58%	5	42%
Was the venue pleasant?	7	58%	5	42%

TABLE 2.11 *Example of a quantitative analysis of a presentation*

unticked, you might want to make this clear by adding an additional column for a 'no answer'.

Using this method of data collection and analysis, it is possible to conclude that over 90 per cent of those attending the talk felt that the presentation was clear and the visual materials were effective. There was less satisfaction with the quality of the handouts, and also with the venue.

The rating scale method of structured data collection makes possible a more precise analysis of what the audience really thought of a presentation, as Table 2.12 shows.

This analysis of the audience's response to the same talk is more specific. It shows that while 11 people gave the presentation and visuals a very high score (4–5 on the rating scale), the level of dissatisfaction with handouts and venue was considerable. Ten people (83 per cent) rated the handouts at poor to adequate (scores 1–3), while all 12 gave a similar low rating to the venue. The scores can be aggregated for presentation purposes, as Table 2.13 shows.

Collected rating-scale information has given this speaker clear information to take into account when evaluating the talk. There was something about the handouts that the majority of people did not like, and a review of this material is called for. However, the audience was unanimous in having reservations about the venue, and unless there are very good reasons for this (perhaps the room was too hot or too cold) the speaker would be advised to think very carefully before booking this venue again. He or she should certainly investigate this response further.

Presenting quantitative data

As well as presenting quantitative material in the form of tables, bar charts and pie charts may also be used to give a more graphic representation of audience response. An example of both a bar chart and a pie chart are given in Figure 2.20, using data from Table 2.13.

ANALYSIS OF END-OF-SESSION QUESTIONNAIRE 15 PEOPLE ATTENDED THIS TALK: 12 QUESTIONNAIRES WERE COMPLETED 1 = LOW SCORE: 5 = HIGH SCORE					
Parameter	**Rating**				
	1	**2**	**3**	**4**	**5**
Clarity of presentation			1	9	2
Effectiveness of visual aids			1	9	2
Helpfulness of handouts		5	5	2	
Venue		6	6		

TABLE 2.12 *Example of analysis of end-of-session questionnaire using the rating scale method of structured data collection*

ANALYSIS OF END-OF SESSION QUESTIONNAIRES AGGREGATED SCORES		
	Poor–Adequate	**Good–Very good**
Clarity of presentation	1 (8%)	11 (92%)
Effectiveness of visuals	1 (8%)	11 (92%)
Helpfulness of handouts	10 (83%)	2 (17%)
Venue	12 (100%)	

TABLE 2.13 *Analysis of end-of session questionnaires showing aggregated scores*

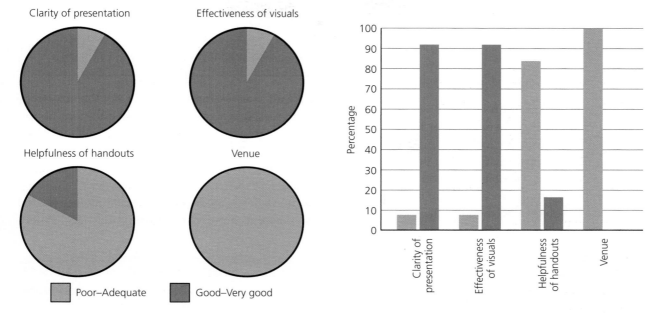

FIGURE 2.20 *Graphic representation of audience response*

Unstructured data

Many questionnaires contain areas for respondents to add their own comments on whatever topics they wish, and in their own words. This kind of information is known as unstructured data. Such information is harder to quantify than structured data, and is sometimes referred to as **qualitative data**. Qualitative data is also often collected by interview. (Quantitative data can also be collected in this way. If so, the researcher ticks the boxes for the respondent.) Open questions are often used to collect this kind of information. Open questions are those that cannot be answered 'Yes' or 'No'. They often begin with the words 'What' and 'Why'.

Examples of open questions are:

* What are your views about the talk you have just heard?

* What did you think about the venue?

* Why did you choose to attend this talk?

Sometimes, this kind of data is referred to as semi-structured, because it invites responses about a specific topic, while leaving respondents free to answer in their own words.

Examples of questions to collect semi-structured data:

* Were there any topics not covered in the talk that you would like to have had included?

* What did you think of the time allocation for each topic?

* How could this talk have been improved?

Totally unstructured data is collected by leaving a space on the questionnaire for audience members to express their own views in their own way on whatever issues they want. This may give some valuable information that was not anticipated. In the case of the hypothetical talk analysed in the tables above, some of the audience may have used free space to explain why they gave the venue such a low score. Perhaps the chairs were uncomfortable in the room, or maybe the facilities in the venue were less than adequate.

A good questionnaire will usually gather a mixture of quantitative and qualitative data. The quantitative data set will allow for some precision in measuring audience satisfaction, while space for the freer qualitative material may raise valuable points that would otherwise not have been mentioned.

2.8 Evaluating communication skills

Evaluating your performance

An essential aspect of professional work is reflection and self-assessment, in order to evaluate what has been achieved.

A good way of evaluating your performance is to check it against the objectives you set at the start of the planning process. If you have achieved the objectives, then the chances are you gave a good talk.

As well as assessing whether or not the objectives were met, it is a good idea to ask questions about the way in which you performed, and about other aspects of the total event. The planning checklists in this unit might be used as the basis for a self-evaluative exercise, as the questionnaire demonstrates. Feedback from the audience is vital if you are to improve your communication skills.

EVALUATING YOUR PERFORMANCE USE THIS QUESTIONNAIRE TO EVALUATE YOUR PERFORMANCE AFTER GIVING YOUR TALK. GIVE YOURSELF A RATING FROM 1–5 FOR EACH OF THE FOLLOWING PARAMETERS (1 = LOW SCORE, 5 = HIGHEST SCORE).	
MANAGING THE MATERIAL	**Score (1–5)**
Introduction to the talk	
Main body of talk	
Summary/conclusion	
Meeting aims/objectives	
Visual aids	
Audiovisual material	
Supplementary material	
Use of notes/written text, etc.	
MANAGING THE AUDIENCE	
Creating a rapport	
Physical comfort of audience	
Furniture arrangement	
Health & safety Issues	
Use of equipment	
Attention to special requirements (e.g. use of signer, etc.)	
MANAGING YOURSELF	
Use of voice (pitch, tone, volume)	
Speed of delivery	
Choice of words	
Use of humour (if applicable)	
Use of body: position, mannerisms, etc.	
Eye contact/facial expression	
On reflection, would you do anything differently next time?	
Use this space to record anything else about your performance that you feel is relevant.	

TABLE 2.14 *Example of a questionnaire*

PLANNING TO GIVE A TALK: SOME PRACTICAL CONSIDERATIONS		NOTES
Is your talk one of a series of presentations planned for the same day?	If 'yes', you will need to be very clear about how your talk fits in, both in terms of timing and content.	
What time of day would be best for the talk?	Is your audience likely to be tired, or to be distracted by something that is happening afterwards?	
What else may be going on at the same time?	If you are giving your talk in a social services unit, for example, make sure that your activity does not clash with other important daily events, or that another activity does not impinge on what you are doing (e.g. a noisy activity in the room next door).	
Is the room the right size for the expected audience?	How big will the audience be?	
What furniture and/or equipment will you need?	Tables? Straight-backed chairs? TV/video/DVD player? etc.	
What facilities will you need?	Powerpoint? Loop system? Strong lighting? etc.	
Is there easy access to the room/building?	Do you need a ramp/lift? Handrails? Wide doors for access by people in wheelchairs? etc.	
What additional help will you need?	Signer/communicator for people who are Deaf/hearing impaired? Personal helper for someone with a mobility problem? Communicator/translator for someone who does not use English as a first language?	
What other aids or equipment will you need?	Braille translation of written materials? etc.	
What health & safety issues do you need to consider?	Condition of all furniture and equipment (including electrical equipment); Safe access and exit (all emergency exits to be easily accessible) Trip hazards to be eliminated Adequate heating and ventilation, etc. Note. There will be guidance on health & safety in the setting where you give your talk. Be sure to check this out with the manager responsible.	

TABLE 2.15 *Planning to give a talk: a checklist*

The questionnaire in Table 2.14 uses a mix of structured, semi-structured and unstructured data collection. You might consider asking your tutor to use the same questionnaire to record his or her views on your performance.

As with collection of audience feedback, quantitative and qualitative information can be combined to give a balanced evaluation of your performance.

Natalie has saved all the checklists she used during the planning process for her talk. She has designed a feedback questionnaire that uses a mix of structured, semi-structured and unstructured data collection, and has used the format suggested in this unit to self-assess (Checklist Table 2.15, page 95). Her final report uses a mix of quantitative and qualitative data to give a balanced analysis of her performance. She is able to identify a number of areas where she could have done better, but on the whole both she and her tutor are pleased with her performance. It has demonstrated her knowledge of relevant communication skills and issues, together with her ability to self-assess and to collect and analyse data from a variety of sources.

UNIT 2 ASSESSMENT

In the report you produce for this unit, you will need to demonstrate a knowledge of communication skills (together with barriers to communication) in two areas. The first relates to the service user and the setting that you have chosen to study. The second relates to the act of giving a talk.

With respect to the former (i.e. work with a service user), you must demonstrate a theoretical knowledge of communication issues, in terms of the content of your talk and the material you use. With respect to the latter (giving a talk), the actual act of presentation itself constitutes a practical demonstration of your communication skills in this domain. The feedback that you collect from your audience and your tutor will contribute to your evidence about your communication skills. Planning documentation, together with research materials, will also enhance your evidence.

AO1 Knowledge of communication skills; knowledge of chosen topic

You will need to show that you have understood the issues explored in this unit, together with issues that are important for the particular service user you have chosen to describe.

Good marks will be obtained by demonstrating knowledge of:

* a range of verbal skills (e.g. using appropriate words and language, etc.)

* non-verbal skills (e.g. adapting the voice, observing body language, using eye contact appropriately, respecting personal space, etc.)

* barriers to communication (e.g. with people who have a sensory impairment or a learning disability, with people who have a different first language to yourself, conditions such as aphasia, etc.)

Higher marks will be obtained by demonstrating the above plus:

* an explanation of techniques and strategies that may be used to overcome barriers to communication (e.g. use of facilitator, use of communicator or signer, etc.)

* a clear explanation of the communication issues that are important to the service user in the chosen setting.

* use of specialist terminology or key concepts (e.g. para-language, speech community, cultural assumptions, prejudice, etc.).

AO2 Application of communication skills

In giving your talk, good marks will be obtained by:

* confident management of the material, the audience, yourself
* using a range of types of question to collect feedback that includes both quantitative and qualitative data.

Higher marks will be obtained by demonstrating the above, plus:

* evidence of thorough planning for the event
* a thorough exploration of the communication issues that are the subject of the talk.

AO3 Research and analysis

Good marks will be obtained for:

* use of relevant material gathered from a range of sources (including the Internet, printed sources and relevant experts)
* a clear analysis of feedback collected from the audience and your tutor
* a thorough written account that sets out all relevant information, using clear headings to guide the reader.

Higher marks will be obtained by the above, plus:

* a confident and appropriate use of both quantitative and qualitative data collection techniques
* use of specialist vocabulary to interpret information
* use of a comprehensive range of source material to research the talk
* use of a range of expressive devices to present your material, such as tables, bar charts, pie diagrams
* an excellent written account that gives a clear, well-reasoned analysis, combining visual presentation of data with the written text in a complementary way.

Evaluation

After the talk, you will need to reflect on the experience, and then collate your personal thoughts and reactions with the feedback collected from the audience and your tutor.

Good marks will be obtained by:

* a balanced and sound judgement of the effectiveness of the talk and of your own communication skills
* an appraisal of the decisions you made concerning the choice of material and the order in which you presented it
* some suggestions for improving the design of the talk and/or its content
* a clear written account of this analysis, that uses headings to guide the reader.

Higher marks will be obtained by the above, plus:

* effective use of audience feedback in making an evaluation of the talk
* achieving a balance between accepting criticism that is justified, and an assertion of what you did well
* explaining which of your planning decisions you consider (on reflection) to be sound, whilst identifying things that you would do differently
* an excellent written account in which written text and visual presentation of material are complementary.

References

Bales, R. (1970) *Personality and Interpersonal Behaviour,* Holt, Rinehart & Winston, New York

Bostrom, R. N. (1997) 'The process of listening' in Hargie, O.D.W. (Ed.) *The Handbook of Communication Skills* 2nd Ed. Routledge, London and New York

Department of Health (2001) *Valuing People: a new strategy for learning disabilitiy for the 21st century. Planning with people: Guidance for Implementation Groups.* Department of Health, London. Can also be accessed via www.valuingpeople.gov.uk

Descombes, C. (2004) *The smoke and mirrors of empowerment: a critique of user-professional partnership* in *Communication, Relationships and Care* Robb, M., Barrett, S., Komaromy, C., and Rogers, A. (Eds) OU & Routledge, London & New York

Engebretson, J. (2004) *Caring Presence: a Case Study* in *Communication, Relationships and Care* Robb, M., Barrett, S., Komaromy, C., and Rogers, A. (Eds) OU & Routledge, London & New York

Hayman, M. (1998) *A Protocol for People with Hearing Impairment* Nursing Times, 28 October, Volume 94, No 43

Rogers, C. R. (1951) *Client Centred Therapy,* Houghton Mifflin, Boston

Tuckman, B. (1965) 'Development Sequence in Small Groups', in *Psychological Bulletin*, Vol 63, No 6

Thompson, T. L. (1986) *Communication for Health Professionals* Harper & Row, New York

Useful websites

Please see www.heinemann.co.uk/hotlinks (express code 1554P) for links to the following websites which may provide a source of information:

* The Valuing People website set up by the government is an excellent source for articles/research about work for and with people with learning disabilities.

* The People First website is a good place to find out about what people with learning disabilities, their advocates and their carers, are saying.

* The In Control organisation promotes communication with people with learning disabilities, especially ways to empower them to express their views and to be involved in Person Centred Planning.

* The British Deaf Association website contains details of BSL.

* The British Sign website includes details of signs and finger spelling alphabet.

* Website of the Royal Association for Deaf People.

* Information on Makaton can be found on their website.

* Further details on Braille are on the Braille Plus website.

Health, illness and disease

You will learn about:

Introduction

This unit begins by exploring the attitudes and understanding of the concepts of both health and ill health and how individuals and groups of people may view 'health' differently. In developing this theme, an investigation is made into the importance of a selection of major factors affecting health and well-being and the interrelationships between them. Finally, an examination is made of major preventative measures currently being taken to promote health and avoid illness.

How you will be assessed

This unit will be internally assessed. You will need to produce a portfolio containing a questionnaire and two reports.

3.1 Concepts of health and ill health

Defining 'health' is a difficult task to do, as it means different things to different people, rather like 'stress' or 'happiness' does. These socially abstract words are almost indefinable except in the utmost general terms. We must, however, have some idea of the meaning of 'health', as we use the word in all sorts of titles such as health visitor, health care worker, healthy living, health foods, health education and health promotion. Where the word health prefixes an occupational title, it is particularly desirable to understand the meaning of the word in order to establish the nature of the job role.

At this stage, you might like to think about how *you* might define health, bearing in mind the difficulties with care terminology already referred to.

Think it over...

How would you explain your health?

The World Health Organisation, part of the United Nations organisation, was set up in 1948 and at that time defined 'health' as being *'a state of complete physical, mental and social well-being and not merely the absence of disease or infirmity'*. Later on, criticisms about the idealistic nature of 'complete state of well-being' and the unreal, implied view that health is static throughout one's lifespan led to an expansion of this definition by several groups and individuals in the mid-eighties. In effect, this means that there is no single definition of health that everyone uses, so in this unit we will consider three of the most common concepts currently in use. These are:

✳ a holistic concept of health

✳ a positive concept of health

✳ a negative concept of health.

Concepts of health

Holistic

A favoured concept of health might produce a more wholesome or 'holistic' view of health as being in the peak of physical, intellectual, social and emotional fitness. Holism means giving attention to the whole, in this case the whole person. The term must also encompass the environment or surroundings of the individual and take on board social and psychological factors.

Health can be affected by all that is around us, and the individuals whom we have contact with. Although our basic health needs do not change as we progress through the life stages, our surroundings and contacts change all the time, suggesting that in holistic terms, our health changes too. Most care professionals will agree that addressing physical health only is not enough and that we must appreciate the emotional, social, spiritual and intellectual health as well – in fact, the whole person. This concept provides some practical difficulties, as it means that there is no limit to the boundaries of responsibility of health professionals, and consequently the focus of care becomes blurred. Once the focus is regained, there is a risk of

FIGURE 3.1 *The concept of holisitic health*

becoming limited to treating a particular condition or part of the body again – this is often called reductionism.

The broader, holistic focus has been absorbed for some professionals into the term well-being.

Positive

There is also a positive concept of health, which can be equated to the achievement of physical fitness and mental stability. When considering the negative concept below, and discussing that the absence of disease and illness represents health, then that in itself assumes a background of 'normal' health represented by efficient, fully operational physiological and mental function.

The positive concept goes a little way to describing what health is, rather than what it is not.

Seedhouse (1986) proposed health 'as a foundation for achieving a person's realistic potential'. The WHO later offered a revised concept of health as 'the extent to which an individual or group is able, on the one hand, to realise aspirations and satisfy needs, and on the other hand, to change or cope with the environment'.

Health is now seen as a positive concept that focuses on personal and physical capacities together with social resources, adaptability and responsibility.

Negative

If you ask friends or members of your family what they understand by 'health' or 'being healthy', you will collect varied responses.

Most people will respond in terms of 'not being ill', indicating a rather negative view that health is something that you do not think about until you have not got it. In other words, health is something that you have until your daily life is disturbed by illness and you are unable to carry out your normal programme. When it is difficult to explain a term using clear and definite attributes, people often resort to describing what it is not – a somewhat negative viewpoint. Some individuals might describe happiness as not being sad or regretful, but many people might describe themselves as neither sad nor happy – so there is

a middle position. Similarly, being poor might be thought of as not being rich, but once again many individuals would say they were neither wealthy nor poor, but possess enough money to supply their basic needs. Clearly then, negative descriptions, while they might be helpful, do not provide a full picture and are simple to use in the absence of positive characteristics.

Terms such as these are also relative to their context; a wealthy businessman who has lost several hundred thousand pounds in a bad business venture, might describe himself as poor, even though he has several functioning businesses and a large bank account. An elderly senior citizen, having just won £20 on a lottery ticket might describe herself as rich. The context of such words can therefore be extremely important in their interpretation. Health and well-being can thus be considered as a negative concept when described as the absence of physical illness, disease and/or mental disorder. This concept has fallen out of favour in current care concepts, but it is a description that the general public still frequently employs.

Other terminology in current use

Well-being

Well-being is just as difficult to explain as health! Even theorists cannot agree on the meaning although many feel that it is partly subjective, what we wish it to be for ourselves, and partly objective because it must have something to do with 'wellness' and some people do not make healthy lifestyle choices. Dictionary definitions do not help either; some equate well-being with welfare, a person's satisfactory condition, and others with flourishing and thriving.

Personal notions of health

Some people might provide you with a very personal notion of health, such as 'when my rheumatism isn't giving me trouble'. Personal views like this might depend on age, social background, culture, circumstances and experience as seen in the mini-case studies below.

SCENARIO

* Simon is 24 years old and has used a wheelchair following a road accident, which left him paralysed four years ago. He has totally recovered from the accident and travels by car to his local leisure centre to play basketball with other wheelchair users. Simon hopes to take part in national events next year and international competitions in a year or two. When asked, Simon replies that he is in excellent health.

* Maria and her four children have lived in bed and breakfast accommodation for three years. Before that, Maria was homeless and the children were in residential care. Last month, Maria and her family moved into a partly furnished council house; she obtained two nursery places for her pre-school children and managed to get a part-time job in the local supermarket. When she met her friend yesterday Maria told her that she felt 'on top of the world'.

* Stan is a 68-year-old ex-miner who is a widower, living alone. He smokes 20 cigarettes a day and enjoys a few pints at the local with his friends when he can manage the walk. Stan has chronic bronchitis and moderately severe arthritis, a legacy from his working days. On the days when he can meet his friends and spend a few hours chatting about old times, Stan says that he 'is in great shape'; on other days he will say that he is 'soldiering on'.

* Simon probably links the perception of his health to his basketball prowess and considers himself 'ill' if he cannot attend to practise due to physical ailments.

* Maria associates health with decent accommodation and being with her family; she is unlikely to worry about minor problems of physical health, like colds.

* Stan is likely to concentrate on meeting his friends; he is likely to dismiss his bronchitis and arthritis as being natural because of his age and previous occupation. When he cannot manage his little outing then life is more of a burden.

Disability does not prevent people from being active

The scenarios show how each person's view of 'health' is different and closely linked to feelings, moods and being able to cope with daily activities, jobs or events.

Other people, especially those with different cultural inheritances, may view health as a spiritual form of well-being; for example, in Islam, consuming alcohol is seen as an unholy thing to do, as it leads to loss of self-control.

Many Christians believe that they can only be truly healthy when they have accepted the teachings of Christ and not whether they feel ill or not. Vegans and vegetarians often believe that eating meat is not healthy. Other religious and non-religious groups have different views of health.

Concept of ill health

Terms signifying ill health are in general parlance interchangeable, but in health terminology, they have more specific meanings. Illness tends to be a word that we use ourselves (i.e. a subjective sensation) to describe a situation that exists if we feel less than well, either physically or mentally.

For example, we may say 'I have to leave because I am feeling ill'. Rarely, do we say, 'I have to go home because I have a disease', probably because we feel unqualified to make that statement. This example illustrates the difference between illness and disease, although we have a tendency to interchange them in prose. Illness, then is something that we feel, a sense of 'unwell-ness' that is personal to us at certain times. Disease is more specific, an 'unwell-ness' that has some pathological basis; it can be diagnosed and named, has certain signs and symptoms, possible treatment and an outcome.

We can feel ill without having a disease and have a disease without feeling ill; we can also feel ill with a disease.

Another term, more easily defined, is disorder that, as the name suggests, is a malfunctioning of part of the body but once again is often used as a replacement for illness and disease.

Summary

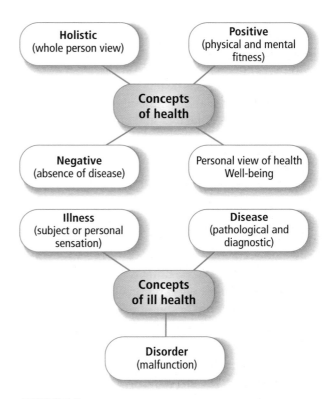

FIGURE 3.2

3.2 Factors affecting health and well-being

Not everyone is fortunate to be healthy and many factors affect an individual's quality of health. Some factors may be outside a person's control, such as poverty and inherited diseases, and thus lead to a low health experience. For a large number of people, however, good health is dependent on lifestyle choices and habits; yet still individuals gamble with their health. Many healthy people are fully aware of the risks they take but feel that poor health is an experience that others suffer from and not themselves.

There are many factors that affect health and well-being and many are inter-related in an important ways. Some factors to be considered are shown in Figure 3.3.

Eating sensibly in order to maintain a balanced diet

A balanced diet is an important part of a healthy lifestyle. Food is a basic human need, as it drives the body processes; we can think of food as fuel rather like the petrol or diesel that drives a motor car. A lack of food fuel, or the wrong type, can result in poor physiological performance and, consequently, less effective work and play and the likelihood of illness and even death.

Food contains nutrients (substances that nourish) that allow the body to grow, develop and function in the correct way. Some components of food, chiefly fats and carbohydrates, provide energy to carry out physiological work, while proteins are necessary to form the structures of the body such as cells, many hormones and vital enzymes. These three named components all contribute to our calorie (or in SI units, joule) intake and should form the bulk of a diet.

Vitamins and minerals, on the other hand, do not contribute to energy requirements, but are, nevertheless, just as essential to the normal functioning of the human body, although they are only required in small quantities. Water constitutes a major part of the human body and is essential to life processes. An individual who is deprived of both water and food would die from lack of water first. Fibre, or roughage, is also an important part of a diet, as it assists in moving food along the digestive tract, prevents many bowel disorders and adds bulk to food without providing calories.

Table 3.1 provides a list of some of the major foods supplying dietary requirements.

A balanced diet is one that provides carbohydrates, fats and proteins in the correct proportions and adequate vitamins, mineral elements, fibre and water for healthy living.

Planning a balanced diet can be a complex process in terms of energy requirements, size of portions and so on; most people, however, manage diets without recourse to lengthy volumes of food energy tables. Approximately 60

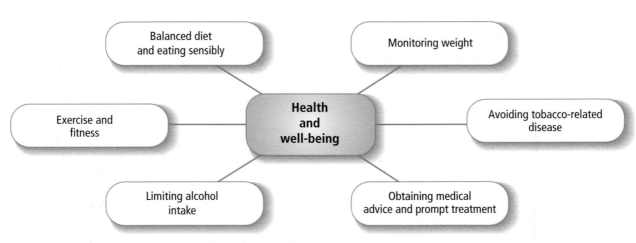

FIGURE 3.3 *Factors that affect health and well-being*

FOOD COMPONENT	COMMON FOODS SUPPLYING BASIC NEEDS FOR THE COMPONENT
Carbohydrate	Bread, pasta, rice, potatoes, cakes, biscuits, cereals
Fats	Butter, lard, suet, oils, margarine
Protein	Meat, milk, fish, eggs, milk, soy beans, legumes
Vitamins	Fresh fruit, fresh vegetables, dairy products
Mineral elements	Fresh fruit and vegetables
Fibre (roughage)	Cereals, fresh fruit and vegetables
Water	Water in drinks, most foods

TABLE 3.1 *Some major foods supplying dietary requirements*

per cent of meals should be in the form of carbohydrates, 20 per cent as fats and 20 per cent as proteins. Meals should also contain substantial proportions of fruit and vegetables to fulfil the vitamin, mineral and fibre requirements in individuals diets.

One of the major problems of nutrition in the twenty-first century is the relatively large quantity of hidden fat, sugar and salt found in convenience foods. The pace of life is so much faster than it used to be; many people live very busy lives, which leave little time for food preparation. There is little wonder that convenience foods have become a way of life.

The UK government is so concerned about the growing epidemic of obesity, particularly among school children that there are now a vast number of organisations and committees trying to resolve the issues. One change in the pipeline is the more accurate labelling of food, so that the hidden components are more obvious. Whether busy parents can afford the time to read labels on groceries and have the inclination to act upon that information, however, remains to be seen.

So-called 'healthy' food alternatives are often more expensive and the term in itself can be misleading.

> ✳ DID YOU KNOW?
>
> Half a can of well-known baked beans contains 10.4 g of sugar (although total carbohydrate content is actually 27.1 g), so a boldly advertised can of low-sugar baked beans may still contain 9.4 g of sugar. Customers who purchase the low-sugar alternative can pay more and feel worthy, although they have in fact only saved 1 g of sugar.

Cans of tuna and sardines in oil or tomato sauce can be bought quite inexpensively, especially in multi-packs, but single tins, in water, are twice as expensive to buy. Manufacturers claim that they have to make them specially and there is not much demand for them. People have been conditioned to taste high salt and sugar levels in prepared food and consequently feel that other preparations do not taste the same.

Another major problem of highly processed foods is the lack of fibre content, most of which has been removed in the processing. An individual who consumes such food rapidly feels hungry again and looks for more food to eat. Wholegrain foods, fruit and vegetables, in addition to containing lower calories, have a 'feel full' factor to them, so dispel hunger for longer periods and provide protection for longer periods. The government-backed 'Five a day' campaign has highlighted a simple message that consuming five pieces/portions of fruit and vegetables each day is an important aid to health for all levels of society.

NACNE and COMA dietary advice

Other recommendations made by NACNE (National Advisory Committee for Nutrition Education) and COMA (Committee on Medical Aspects of Food Policy) include those that are outlined below.

Reduce overall fat intake

Reduce overall fat intake and when fat is part of the diet make sure that as much as possible is polyunsaturated and not saturated (basically, this means minimising animal fats and using plant lipids instead). Lipids or fats and oils contain twice as many calories as carbohydrates and proteins – they are energy-rich. When consumed in a greater quantity than is needed, fat is stored around the body tissues, causing weight gain. As weight increases, the demand for more food to sustain the extra cells also increases and so, too, does the demand for oxygen, pumped blood, hormones like insulin and more substances taking part in metabolism.

Overweight people have a higher risk of developing diabetes, heart disease, strokes, respiratory difficulties and mobility problems, as the excess load on legs, ankles and feet over a period of years takes its toll. Having developed health problems, they are then more likely to suffer accidental injury and problems with surgical care. Organs function less well as arteries become narrowed due to fatty deposits (atheroma) coating the inner walls.

There may be social and emotional problems associated with being overweight to contend with as well as physical problems.

There has been a great deal of recent publicity in the media about the 'epidemic' of eating disorders, both anorexia nervosa and bulimia, and the failure of doctors to recognise these conditions until a late stage has been reached. Indeed, even when such disorders are recognised, there are no specialist services for referral. This is the other side of the coin, and although a distorted perception of body image is considered to be a psychological condition, it has also been appreciated that psychiatric wards are not appropriate care environments for the young people (mostly teenage girls and young women) who have these disorders. Clearly, this too has to be considered as an example of individuals *not* eating sensibly. Individuals who suffer with these complaints have a morbid fear of being fat, and see themselves as fat even when they are several stones underweight. Induced vomiting is common and regular in both disorders, that of bulimia following bouts of binge eating.

Eat less salt

Salt attracts water and when combined they are thought to contribute to raised blood pressure with consequent, heart and circulation problems, kidney disorders, cerebral strokes and haemorrhages. The human body requires some salt, but there is enough in natural plant materials without the need to add more salt in cooking. We have become conditioned to a high salt intake as a result of eating processed foods. People who suffer from hypertension are advised to refrain from adding salt to cooking or plated meals. Herbs and spices can be used to flavour food instead of salt.

Reduce intake of sugar

Sugar provides calories without providing any other benefits; this is often known as 'empty' calories. Excess sugar is converted into fat for storage, so eating too much sugar leads to the same health problems as too much fat. Consider the effect of consuming only 'junk' food containing surplus energy-rich fat *and* surplus sugar; obesity is just around the corner!

Eat more fibre

The benefits of fibre, fruit and vegetables on food and eating are examined on page 105, but rather like a see-saw, feeling satisfied hunger-wise from eating more fibre will also enable us to eat less fat, salt and sugar.

Drink less alcohol

Just like sugar, alcohol provides 'empty' calories resulting in weight gain. (See also limiting alcohol consumption on page 109).

Limit the consumption of certain other foods

There is also good advice on limiting the consumption of red meat and substituting fish or vegetable protein on at least two days of the week.

Think it over...

You need to be aware of different food patterns within different cultures and that by choice or religion many people are vegan, vegetarian or a variation of these.

Taking regular exercise to maintain physical and mental fitness

The Chief Medical Officer in his report 'Call for Action' (April 2004) quotes:

'The message in this report is clear. The scientific evidence is compelling. Physical activity not only contributes to well-being, but is also essential for good health. People who are physically active reduce their risk of developing major chronic diseases – such as coronary heart disease, stroke and type2 diabetes – by up to 50 per cent, and the risk of premature death by about 20–30 per cent. The annual costs of physical inactivity in England are estimated at £8.2 billion – including the rising costs of treating chronic diseases such as coronary heart disease and diabetes. This does not include the contribution of inactivity to obesity – an estimated further £2.5 billion cost to the economy each year.

This report must be the wake-up call that changes attitudes to active lifestyles in every household. Being active is no longer simply an option – it is essential if we are to live healthy and fulfilling lives into old age.'

The report suggests that a total of 30 minutes of moderately intense physical activity each day for five or more days per week will improve the general health of adults. Furthermore, this can be made up of shorter bouts of activity, such as walking briskly rather than taking motorised transport or using stairs rather than lifts. For many people, 45 minutes to 1 hour of activity may be necessary to prevent obesity. More intensive exercise will bring even greater benefits

For children and young people, a total of at least 60 minutes per day is necessary with intense activity at least twice a week (such as jumping, skipping, running, gymnastics) to improve bone health, muscle strength and flexibility.

The adult recommendations are also appropriate for older people to enable them to keep moving and retain mobility. More specific activities to improve strength, coordination and balance are particularly beneficial. Independence is further promoted by avoidance of diseases prevalent in older people such as osteoporosis, circulatory disease and depression.

The Chief Medical Officer further states that 'physical activity needs to be seen as an opportunity – for enjoyment, for improved vitality, for a sense of achievement, for fitness, for optimal weight, and – not least – for health. It needs to be seen as enjoyable, and as fun – not as unnecessary effort. Perceptions need to be changed – too many people think they are already active enough.'

This report identifies physical inactivity as ranking alongside cigarette smoking and unhealthy diets as agents for chronic disease.

Games help develop balance and coordination

Maintaining an active lifestyle is important in order to avoid weight gain, but the most potent combination is physical activity and a healthy diet. This maximises fat loss, keeps lean tissue and promotes both fitness and health benefits.

Exercise improves health and strength in children

Research has also shown that moderately intense exercise is beneficial for depression, anxiety, sleep disorders, the effects of stress and cognitive function in older people. Group recreational sports/activities have social and emotional benefits but activities, best described as rhythmic, such as dancing, jogging, cycling, swimming and brisk walking, are most effective.

Children are in danger of becoming 'couch potatoes'

Protection against some cancers is also enhanced with an active lifestyle; the incidence of colon cancer is 50 per cent less likely in those who are intensely active than in inactive people. There may also be reductions in breast cancer in post-menopausal women and lung cancer amongst those who are physically active.

Physical inactivity is not an option; the encouragement of an active lifestyle is essential in order to reduce the number of chronic conditions and to promote better health.

Many girls and women, particularly from Asian cultures, do not undertake much sport or exercise because of strict dress codes; and other groups, like older people, consider exercise is only necessary for young people.

This section has shown how regular exercise and eating sensibly are interrelated in the way that health is maintained.

Monitoring weight in order to avoid weight-related illness or even premature death

Weight or mass in relation to height and frame size is a routine measurement of physical health. It is also used as an indicator of growth in children. Healthy adults can maintain a fairly stable weight, as input of energy in the form of food and drink should balance the amount of energy loss from physical activity and metabolic activity. When there is an imbalance, there are implications, certainly in the long-term for health and well-being. Here, we can see the interrelationships between eating sensibly, exercising regularly and monitoring weight.

Most people monitor their weight informally on bathroom scales, noticing whether they have gained or lost weight since the last time they weighed themselves. Few people actually act on this knowledge by redressing the balance – either cutting down on food intake, or selected parts of it, or increasing physical activities. People are even less likely to refer to charts or graphs for monitoring purpose (see Figure 3.4). Some might attempt a slimming diet for a few weeks or join a gymnasium, but this is usually short-term.

Commercial interests make huge sums of money from both gymnasium members who never actually use the gym and slimming foods and meals that work in the short-term. Even the

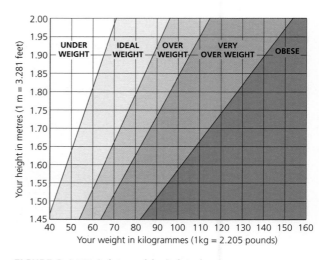

FIGURE 3.4 *Weight and height charts*

media have joined the bandwagon! In January of every year, practically every tabloid newspaper and magazine publishes a 'guaranteed' slimming diet and reality TV features celebrities and non-celebrities trying to lose weight.

The sad fact is that it takes a long time to regain a normal weight for height, often years, because individuals watch their weight increasing by a few pounds each year before they act. Apart from using weighing scales, there are other signs that people ignore such as:

* normal clothing is too loose or too tight
* requiring larger or smaller sizes in clothing
* being uncomfortable in hot or cold weather
* friends remarking on changed appearance
* being disinclined to undertake physical activity.

An individual is considered to be obese if his or her body weight is 20 per cent or more than that given in a standard height/weight chart. Obesity results in significantly increased incidence of:

* high blood pressure
* stroke
* coronary artery disease
* type 2 diabetes (mature onset)
* cancers of the colon, rectum and prostate
* cancers of the breast, cervix and uterus
* aggravation of osteo-arthritis, hip, knee, and back pain
* decreased mobility causing a vicious circle of more weight gain.

Only a very few people are overweight because of gland disorders but many have a genetic predisposition to obesity. Fat people are often part of fat families.

Weight loss may occur as part of a deliberate weight reduction plan, or because food intake has been reduced or activity increased. More serious implications for loss of weight are:

* depression lowers motivation to eat
* ulcer pain may cause food avoidance

* eating disorders such as anorexia nervosa or bulimia
* illness causing severe vomiting
* untreated type 1 diabetes (juvenile onset)
* nearly all cancers
* chronic infection such as tuberculosis
* hormonal problems such as hyperthyroidism.

It is clear from these two lists that it is important to monitor weight to avoid chronic illness and premature death.

People from ethnic groups who wear loose clothes may not be aware of weight changes quite as easily as those who wear Western styles; they are also less likely to use scales regularly, as weight is not important to them. Older people, too, are not so concerned about monitoring weight.

Limiting alcohol consumption to avoid alcohol-related deaths

This is another health issue that seems to be regularly newsworthy and topical. Currently, it has been re-fuelled by the extension of licensing hours for bars and public houses and by the media highlighting alcohol-related social issues, particularly 'binge drinking' among young women, many sports fans and tourists abroad. Many social commentators have compared Britain to the European continent and theorised that the UK seems to have an alcohol-culture problem that does not exist elsewhere. It is certainly of great concern to the government, health authorities and local councils. The individuals concerned appear to have no anxiety about alcohol-related illnesses and premature deaths. The same people have total disregard for safe recommended drinking levels; their only goal is to have a 'good time' and this apparently cannot happen unless they have consumed excess alcohol.

Recognising that alcohol drinking has become part of society and that group and peer pressures are difficult to resist, it is still incomprehensible that some people persist in drinking to the extent that they feel very unwell, risk chronic illness,

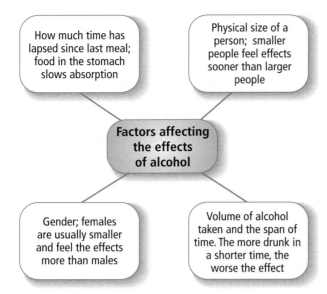

FIGURE 3.5 *The factors affecting the effects of alcohol drinking*

lose their sensibilities and even die.

The effects of alcohol drinking can be different for individuals, depending on a number of factors, as shown in Figure 3.5.

Over-consumption of alcohol produces both short-term and long-term effects; the long-term effects clearly take place over a period of several years. Table 3.2 identifies some of these effects.

People who are dependent on alcohol (alcoholics) are also likely to smoke and this increases their risks to health and well-being far more than the effects of each added together. They are also likely to suffer from malnutrition even though they appear to be of normal weight or, more likely, overweight. Like sugar, alcohol provides calories without nutrients – so-called 'empty calories'. The affection for or addiction to alcohol usually means that these individuals spend a lot of their time drinking and thus, do not take, or are incapable of, regular exercise.

Some religious groups forbid the consumption of alcohol and will be offended by questions investigating alcohol consumption.

Not smoking in order to avoid tobacco-related diseases

Like alcohol, smoking has also been very much part of society but is declining rapidly and is

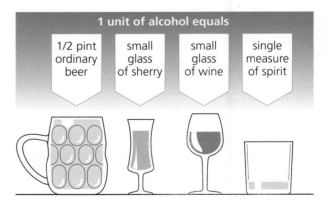

FIGURE 3.6 *Alcohol units*

considered by many to be unacceptable. One of the factors contributing to this decline is the degree of publicity that both active and passive smoking has received in relation to health risks. There has also been a number of, again, well-publicised cases of employees who have developed cancer as a result of working in smoky areas. Employers now have to provide a smoke-free healthy environment for workers. Bars, pubs and restaurants that serve food will also be required to be smoke-free in the near future by law, and many food establishments already

THE EFFECTS OF EXCESS ALCOHOL CONSUMPTION	
SHORT-TERM	**LONG-TERM**
Brain functioning is affected and errors of judgements are made, e.g. estimating distances	Very heavy drinking causes dehydration, the brain becomes inflamed and shrinks; this may lead to loss of intelligence
Although alcohol initially stimulates the mind, it is actually a depressant	Increases risks of cancer of mouth, throat, oesophagus, larynx and liver
More risks of accidents and at risk of crime attacks such as robbery, rape	Chronic liver diseases such as fatty liver and cirrhosis over several years
Loss of inhibition and more talkative; more likely to get into trouble	Nervous system disorders of walking gait, pain, cramps, tingling, etc.
Social effects, arguments, domestic violence, child abuse	Social effects, arguments, domestic violence, child abuse
Facial flushing and general dilatation of skin arteries; this can lead to exposure on very cold nights	Gastritis, pancreatitis, stomach ulcers more common
Large amounts of alcohol in a short time can lead to alcohol poisoning, a serious life-threatening condition	Anxiety, depression, dementia and suicide are more common
More urine produced (diuresis)	Increased urine produced, if prolonged can cause renal failure
Disorientation, incoherence, unconsciousness, coma, death	Increased risks of hypertension, coronary heart disease and stroke
Alcohol increases the desire for sexual intercourse but decreases the performance of it	Impotence
Slurring of speech	Foetal alcohol syndrome in pregnant women. Serious abnormalities of development can occur and low birth weight. More risk of miscarriage
Unsteady gait, risk of falls	Associated with malnutrition, particularly vitamin deficiencies. Obesity

TABLE 3.2 *Short- and long-term effects of excess alcohol consumption*

comply with this due to public demand.

The risk of lung cancer has long been known, but, until relatively recently, the risks of heart disease and other cancers were less public.

Effects of smoking on health

Some of the effects of smoking on health are shown in Figure 3.7.

Risks to health are increased in people who started smoking at a young age and in proportion to the number of cigarettes smoked.

Exercise makes people feel healthy

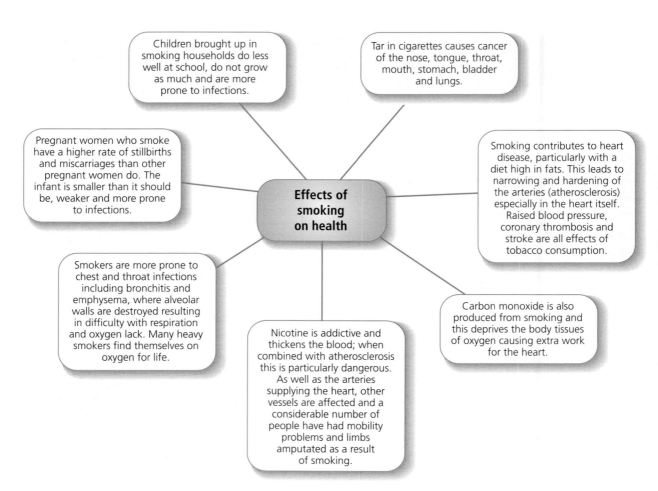

FIGURE 3.7 *Effects of smoking on health*

Smoking taints the taste of food so salt and other additive uses are common. Many smokers also consume alcohol as public houses and bars have been favourite meeting places. Smokers are disinclined to carry out regular exercise as they have less dissolved oxygen circulating in their blood.

Many smokers are reluctant visitors to their GP, as they know that they will be encouraged to give up and that their illness might be smoking-related.

Visiting the general practitioner to obtain medical advice and appropriately prompt treatment

At first, this might seem an obvious thing to do if you are ill – you go to the doctor!

However, many people do not visit their GP until they have had the symptoms or signs of illness for too long. Very often it is regrettably too late; the individual is seriously ill; recovery takes a long time and may not be complete. At times, there will be no recovery and death follows in due course. This is extremely sad when treatment could have been offered earlier.

Fear of being told that they have cancer or other serious illness stops many people from consulting a doctor promptly. Other people might feel that fate has intervened and that the illness is pre-destined. Many individuals consult physicians extremely rarely and are very reluctant to visit them. Smokers,

alcoholics and drug abusers tend to shy away from medical personnel. Cultures that are different from our own have varying attitudes to doctors; people may have come to live in the UK because they were oppressed and are now frightened of anyone they see 'in authority'. Women from some ethnic minorities are not allowed to speak to men that they do not know and most doctors are still male. Some religions and groups of people do not hold with blood transfusions and injections.

There is also a type of 'bureaucracy' involved in making medical appointments such as the use of the telephone early in the morning, getting past a receptionist who asks the purpose of the visit,

fitting in with work or getting time off work. These factors tend to cause people to put off making appointments, particularly timid and hesitant people or those with poor communication skills.

Summary

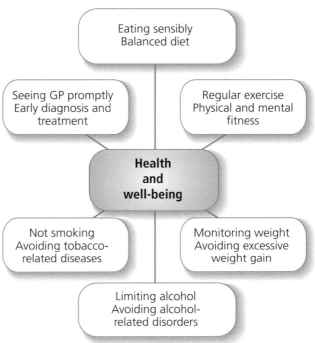

FIGURE 3.8 *Health and well-being*

3.3 Immunisation against disease

Immunity is the ability to resist infectious disease arising from microorganisms such as viruses, bacteria and fungi. The body can produce special proteins known as antibodies that neutralise the invading pathogens or disease-causing organisms. Immunisation – a term often used interchangeably with vaccination – is the process of artificially producing immunity by the use of a vaccine.

White blood cells are concerned with the defence of the body; lymphocytes produce antibodies and phagocytes eliminate foreign substances and antigen/antibody complexes to prevent further damage to the body.

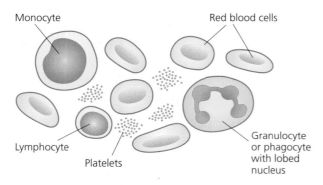

FIGURE 3.9 *Blood cells*

Pathogens have certain proteins embedded into their surfaces that are known as antigens. Antigens are generally specific to the microorganisms and have characteristic features such as shape. Antibodies have complementary shapes that attach themselves to the antigens rendering the microorganisms ineffective. The phagocytes eliminate the antigen/antibody complex. Antibodies must also be specific as they must 'fit' the antigen. In other words, the antibody for a disease like pertussis (whooping cough) is of no use in a service user with measles. Some bacteria produce poisonous proteins called toxins; these may be exotoxins that are secreted outwards or endotoxins only released when the organisms die. Clearly exotoxins produce effects quickly while endotoxins are much slower. Toxoids are inactivated

toxins used to stimulate antibody formation and are often used in vaccinations; for example, diphtheria and tetanus toxoids are constituents of DPT vaccine (see under Diphtheria).

No vaccine is known to give 100 per cent lifelong immunity to a disease.

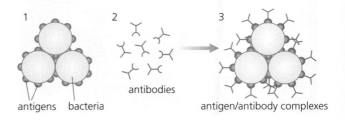

FIGURE 3.10 *Antibodies and antigens*

Innate (inborn) immunity

Each individual has a level of immunity with which they are born, known as *innate immunity.* This type of immunity consists of natural barriers to infection such as the dead, cornified layers on the outer surface of the skin, the hydrochloric acid secreted by the stomach lining, the phagocytes in blood and the lysozyme (an anti-bacterial substance) in tear fluid.

Acquired immunity

Immunity that is developed after birth is called *acquired immunity.*

Acquired immunity can be further divided into *active* and *passive types.*

Active immunity is so called because individuals produce the antibodies in the blood from their own lymphocytes. There are two ways of doing this, by *natural* means and by *artificial* methods. The immunity produced by active means is usually for a very long time, even for life; however, it takes time to develop so is of no use in giving immediate protection in an epidemic situation.

Acquired, natural active immunity

When an individual contracts a disease in the usual way from another infected person or contaminated food or water, the microorganisms multiply rapidly producing the signs and symptoms of the disease. Over a period of time the blood lymphocytes respond and begin to produce antibodies to control the infection and the individual recovers. When the person is exposed to further episodes of infection by the same microorganisms, the lymphocytes pour millions of the relevant antibodies into the blood and the progress of the disease is halted very quickly. The individual might never know that they have been in further contact with the infecting organisms or might feel a little unwell for a short period of time.

Some of these antibodies are always circulating in the blood of an individual who has recovered from a disease and there are laboratory techniques to measure the immune status of a person in this way. There has to be a certain level of specific antibodies circulating in the blood for a person to be designated 'immune'. Sometimes an individual might have a second illness of the same type, although usually milder, because their level of circulating antibodies has not been high enough to make them immune.

Acquired active artificial immunity

This is by immunisation with a vaccine. Killing the microorganisms will still leave the antigenic nature of most pathogens intact and if a sterile solution containing killed organisms is injected into an individual, it will still evoke the antibody production but without producing the effects of the disease. Two or three injections (shots or jabs) may be necessary to produce a high level of antibodies to confer immune status. In some cases, the killed vaccine is deemed to be inferior to a live, but very much weakened, dose of microorganisms. The individual may feel a little unwell with this type of vaccine but nothing as severe as the actual disease or its side effects.

Acquired passive immunity

Passive immunity occurs when the individuals have not produced the antibodies from their blood lymphocytes, and they have been introduced from elsewhere – another person or animal's blood. This means that passive immunity will confer almost immediate protection, but will not last, as the antibodies will eventually be destroyed as foreign material. Passive immunity then is useful in an epidemic or treatment situation but not as a way of providing long-term protection. There are two types of this immunity, called again *natural* and *artificial,* as shown in Table 3.3.

TYPES OF ACQUIRED PASSIVE IMMUNITY	
Acquired, natural passive immunity	The foetus in the womb will acquire maternal antibodies from the exchange across the placenta and after birth, through the mother's colostrum and breast milk. This is the main reason why mothers are urged to breastfeed a newborn infant for at least a few weeks, even if they intend to use formula milk food at a later stage. The very young infant will thus be protected against those conditions that have produced immune status in the mother. The valuable immunity received lasts only for approximately four months; thereafter, the infant is once again susceptible to diseases, so vaccination begins a little earlier to confer some degree of overlap.
	Note. Infants cannot receive antibodies that are not present in the mother.
Acquired, artificial passive immunity	Sometimes in epidemic situations, the authorities need to prevent further spread of a disease and can do so by providing injections of the relevant antibodies, often produced in animal bodies who themselves do not contract the disease because they are from a different species. This will provide temporary protection and hopefully stop further spread.
	Occasionally, antibodies are also used in treatment, particularly of an uncommon serious disease. Stocks of antiserum (serum containing antibodies) are kept in reserve for such conditions. These may have come from donated blood of individuals who have had the disease and recovered from it or from animals as described above.

TABLE 3.3 *Types of immunity*

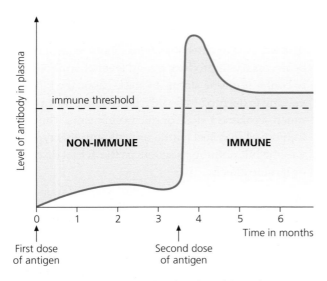

FIGURE 3.11 *How immunisation is achieved*

Some common illnesses and vaccination programmes

Diphtheria

Diphtheria is an acute bacterial illness caused by *Corynebacterium diphtheriae*; although now uncommon in developed parts of the world, it was a major cause of death in children until the 1930s.

> ✳ **DID YOU KNOW?**
>
> Children still die from diphtheria in countries that have yet to develop good health care systems. The bacteria, carried largely in the throat or on the skin of immune people, can cause disease in non-immune persons; this is why it is of paramount importance that a high percentage of the population is immune; currently in the UK 94 per cent of the population is immune to diptheria. Some cases still occur in the UK and these are mainly among immigrants who have become carriers after a minor diphtheria infection. It is possible for immunised people to contract diphtheria but deaths are rare and the disease is mild. The disease is characterised by sore throat, lymph node enlargement of the neck and fever.

Rapid multiplication of the bacteria can lead to the formation of a membrane across the interior of the throat, often causing difficulties with air intake and a hoarse voice. The bacteria secrete a powerful exotoxin into the bloodstream and this can cause heart failure and collapse or paralysis of limb and throat muscles, so threatening life.

It is particularly important for those travelling to developing countries to have their immune status for diphtheria checked to avoid infection and to be re-immunised if warranted. One rare death in the UK occurred in a 14-year-old boy who had visited Pakistan and there appeared to be no known immunisation record. The risk is deemed by the authorities to be greater in Southeast Asia, South America, the Indian sub-continent and the former USSR.

DTP vaccination

Immunisation in infants is by three spaced injections of DPT (Diphtheria, Pertussis and Tetanus) in their first year of life. The ages at which these doses are given varies, although most commonly they are given at ages nine months, three years and five years. Approximately half a million school-leavers have also been vaccinated with DTP.

Treatment of diphtheria consists of both antibiotics (like penicillin) and antitoxin to counteract the effects of the exotoxin. Surgical opening of the airway might be necessary to overcome breathing difficulties and isolation to prevent further infection.

The installation of immunisation programmes in all countries should lead to virtual eradication of the disease.

Pertussis or whooping cough

Pertussis exists worldwide and, although it can affect adults, half the cases are in children under two years of age and those newly born are most susceptible. Infection is by airborne droplets containing the bacteria *Bordetella pertussis* being breathed in, usually from coughing. The infection results in severe inflammation of the whole respiratory tract, resulting in bouts of coughing that end in a characteristic 'whoop' or gasp. Vaccination takes place in the first year of life by DTP.

The infection can last up to three months and as it is worse at night the whole family suffers. Complications such as vomiting, dehydration, pneumonia and collapsed lung can occur.

> **✶ DID YOU KNOW?**
>
> A press campaign alerting the public to the dangers of pertussis vaccine in the 1970s caused the immune population of children to fall below 50 per cent and there were serious outbreaks of pertussis every four years. When this was later found to be a mistake, immunisation figures rose again and the incidence of the disease fell once more.

The risks of vaccination are far less than the dangers of the disease itself; the infant may develop mild fever and irritability for a day or so. Some infants, who have a fever, a history of fits or a more severe reaction to a previous dose of the vaccine, may not be given the injection. This is because about 1 per 300,000 babies may develop permanent brain damage, but the risk is very small.

Tetanus or lockjaw

The causative bacteria of this serious condition are *Clostridium tetani*, which thrive in soil, manure and intestines. They are anaerobic bacteria; this means that they thrive in poor oxygen environments. The bacteria enter the body through contaminated deep wounds such as dog bites involving the long canine teeth, pitchfork or garden fork accidents, penetrating shards of glass and even occasionally thorn pricks. In such incidents, the skin moves back over the wound leaving the bacteria deep inside in a poorly oxygenated space where they begin to multiply, producing a deadly toxin.

This toxin affects motor nerves that supply muscles, causing paralysis.

In developing countries, some infants have contracted tetanus through the umbilical cord after birth in dirty conditions.

> **✶ DID YOU KNOW?**
>
> In the UK approximately 20 cases of tetanus or lockjaw occur each year mainly in older, non-immune people. Most people recover after prompt treatment with antitoxin. People who have suffered accidents like those named above are usually given a 'booster' dose to enhance immunity if it is some years since vaccination. Ideally, people should have booster doses every ten years.

Infection results in stiffness of the jaw (hence the more common name), the facial muscles (producing a grimace), the neck, abdominal and back muscles. Asphyxia may result necessitating assisted breathing. Children are given DTP vaccination in the first year of life.

MMR (Triple) vaccine

This is a live-attenuated vaccine for measles, mumps and rubella that is given in the second year of life and again before starting school. Two doses are given at 12 and 15 months of age and at three to five years. It was developed in the early 1970s and is part of the immunisation programme in over 90 countries. In the UK there has been, and still is, a raging controversy over the safety of the vaccine to the extent that there is a government/NHS website available to the public, which gives the facts about the MMR vaccine.

Journalists regularly ask high-ranking politicians whether their own children have received the vaccine. Most decline to reply and claim privacy, but this issue does not seem to go away. The General Medical Council has issued statements, which categorically state that there is no proven link between MMR vaccination and autism or bowel disease.

Many members of the public have asked for three separate vaccinations, believing that this is a safer option. The World Health Organisation claims that the triple vaccine has an outstanding safety record and that no recommendation for separate injections is given in any country using this immunisation programme. Consequently, the government, through the NHS, declines use of separate doses of the vaccine under normal circumstances. Caution should be exercised in infants who are known to have an egg allergy, a history of fits or a positive HIV result.

One or two side effects may occur in some individuals:

* swelling of the parotid glands (salivary glands in the cheeks, mumps-like swelling)
* jerky movements particularly with walking
* pain in muscles and joints
* redness, pain and hardness at the injection site
* headache, general malaise, fever and irritability
* fits
* diarrhoea
* rash and signs of allergy.

The vaccine should not be given during pregnancy or breast-feeding.

Measles (a viral disease)

This is one of the most contagious and dangerous childhood diseases that produces a rash because of its complications. It is spread through airborne droplets, contaminated clothes, toys, etc. After an incubation period of one to two weeks, the victim complains of sore throat, cold symptoms, red eyes and coughing with a high temperature. The red rash starts near the ears and spreads to the trunk and parts of the limbs in a day or two. The individual is infectious for about four days before the rash appears, but Kopliks spots, fancifully likened to 'grains of salt on a bed of red velvet', can be seen around the molars a day or two before the rash comes.

The affected individual can be quite ill with fever, lymph gland enlargement in the neck and photophobia (dislike of light). Complications such as pneumonia, middle ear infection (otitis media) and inflammation of the nervous system can be very dangerous. Pregnant women can also be in danger. There is lifelong immunity after infection.

Mumps (a viral disease)

Mumps has a long incubation period of up to three weeks and, once again, the individual is infectious to others one week before any signs or symptoms develop, although this is the least contagious of the childhood diseases. Children between the age of one and five years are the most vulnerable, but older children and adults can contract the disease, which is spread through airborne droplets. The sufferer experiences swelling of the parotid glands on the cheeks in front of the ears, fever and difficulty opening the mouth. Some 20–30 per cent of men develop orchitis (inflammation of testes) in one or both testes and in 10 per cent of cases may become sterile in the affected organ/s. Other complications are pancreatitis (inflammation of the pancreas) and meningitis.

Rubella (a viral disease)

This mild disease, also known as German measles, is only of concern to pregnant women when it might cross the placenta in the early months and cause Rubella syndrome in the foetus.

> **✳ DID YOU KNOW?**
>
> A syndrome is a collection of signs and symptoms characteristically grouped with a distinct disease.

Spread by airborne droplets, Rubella was most common in primary school children, but through the immunisation programme, it is now less prevalent. At first, rubella vaccination was offered only to teenage girls and women planning babies and the number of cases of rubella syndrome in babies continued. Now, through the MMR vaccine, all infants are vaccinated and the number of cases has reduced.

Vaccination for travellers

Although few immunisations are compulsory for travel to countries abroad, many are advised for travellers outside Europe, North America, Australia and New Zealand.

Most UK citizens have been immunised in childhood but booster doses may be required on medical advice. Regular travellers will need to keep their immunisations up to date.

Common examples of diseases that travellers may need to be protected against are shown in Table 3.4.

EXAMPLES OF COMMON TRAVEL IMMUNISATIONS		
NATURE OF DISEASE	**WHERE?**	**EFFECTIVENESS**
Cholera (bacterial disease) from contaminated food or water, often by sewage. Produces severe, watery diarrhoea that can rapidly cause dehydration and death if untreated	Most Asian and African countries (may be compulsory immunisation in some of these countries)	Moderate protection for about six months. Bottled drinks from reliable sources should only be consumed as well
Hepatitis A (viral disease) from sewage-contaminated food and water produces a 'flu-like' illness with jaundice or may be symptomless	In countries where hygiene standards are low, particularly with respect to food hygiene	Passive immunisation is short-lived (approximately 3 months) and offers some protection. Food and personal hygiene is important
Typhoid fever (bacterial disease) major life-threatening disease causing fever, rash, diarrhoea and serious gastro-intestinal complications. Spread by contaminated food and water, flies or typhoid carriers	Most countries outside Europe, North America, Australia and New Zealand	Moderate protection for about three years (two doses recommended)
Rabies (viral disease) transmitted by a bite or lick on an open wound from a rabies-infected animal, e.g. foxes wolves, jackals, skunks and dogs. Causes a fatal inflammation of the nervous system	Very few countries are rabies-free – the UK, Scandinavia, Australia and New Zealand	Highly effective vaccine. When a bite has been given, passive immunisation is given with the least delay for treatment (limited duration)

TABLE 3.4 *Examples of common diseases that travellers may need to protect against*

Malaria

This is a disease of tropical climates, prevalent in over one hundred countries; it affects between two and three hundred million people globally each year. Malaria is spread by bites of female mosquitoes of a particular type (*Anopheles*) that carry a parasite called *Plasmodium*. The parasite spends part of its complicated life cycle in humans and part in mosquitoes, forming the most important disease hazard to people who travel to warm countries.

The disease causes severe fever and complications involving kidneys, liver, blood and brain, which can often be fatal.

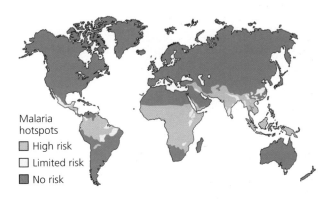

FIGURE 3.12 *Areas of the world where malaria occurs*

Research and development for an effective long-lasting vaccine is taking place in many clinical research facilities with varied results. However, it is not yet available for ordinary travellers who have to prepare themselves before their journey with courses of anti-malarial drugs.

Some individuals do not believe in processes like vaccination, believing that it can be more harmful than having the disease or that it is interfering with nature. Religious groups such as Jehovah's Witnesses and Christian Scientists also have different beliefs, particularly where blood transfusions and receiving blood products are concerned, although the former in recent years, have permitted vaccinations and left the matter to individual conscience. The latter believe that healing can only be spiritual by reading the words of the founder and the Bible.

Summary

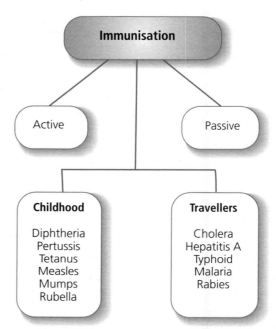

Consider this

Tania is very worried about immunisation schedules for her infant, as she has read some very scary stories in the tabloid press about immunisations causing side effects and more permanent damage such as autism. Her partner says that it is all exaggerated and to forget it. Tania cannot just dismiss these stories and it is making her very anxious. They are also planning a wonderful holiday in Kenya the following spring to show the baby to her mother-in-law who lives there.

Using concepts, can you?
1 Explain the immunisations that Tania's baby should have over the next two years.

2 Justify the vaccinations that Tania and her partner should have prior to their holiday.

Going further – can you analyse the issues?
3 Explain how immunisation works.

4 Clarify the difference between active and passive immunisation and provide examples

Going further – can you evaluate?
5 Evaluate the process of immunisation and clarify the benefits obtained.

3.4 The value of screening

Screening takes place when people are routinely tested in certain ways to aid the detection of disease at an early stage to make treatment more effective. There is no point in testing for conditions that do not respond differently when detected early. Tests for large sections of the population must be inexpensive, simple and not unpleasant for the individual. People will not attend for routine tests if put to inconvenience and discomfort. Such tests should also be reliable and accurate, not giving high figures of false positives and false negatives. These occur when the test result is judged to be different to the actual result; this has happened in the past with tests like cervical smear results, and the media are quick to highlight such errors.

Nevertheless, screening provides valuable information that protects the health of different client groups and saves many lives. The first screening tests occur even before birth, as a part of antenatal care of pregnant women.

Antenatal screening tests

Two membranes surround the developing embryo, the amnion and the chorion; the amnion also known as the amniotic sac is a bag-like structure containing the embryo and amniotic fluid. As development proceeds, foetal skin cells are shed into the fluid and certain chemicals accumulate there. The chorion further develops into the placenta, which consists of microscopical projections of tissue containing loops of foetal blood capillaries (chorionic villi) lying in small 'lakes' of maternal blood. Small molecular materials can pass to and fro between these two blood streams across the intervening delicate membranes, although the actual blood does not mix. Amniocentesis and chorionic villus sampling are usually undertaken when special blood tests have revealed 'markers' or pointers for genetic disorders and when there is evidence of advancing maternal age. These blood serum markers are alphafetoprotein, human chorionic gonadotrophin, oestriol and inhibinA; a pointer from ultrasound scanning of nuchal translucency can be used as well. A foetus with Down's syndrome has a thicker layer of amniotic fluid at the base of the neck resulting in different translucency (the amount of light permitted to pass through).

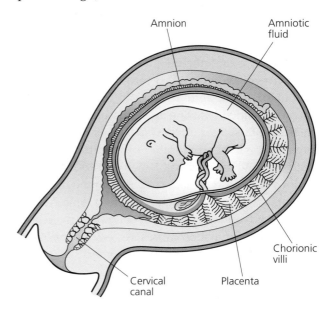

FIGURE 3.13 *A foetus*

Chorionic villus sampling (CVS)

This can be performed earlier than amniocentesis, within the first 12 weeks or later. The test is used where there is a family history of a genetic abnormality or the individual is deemed to be of special risk of inheriting such an abnormality. The cells of the chorionic villi have the same genetic make-up as the foetus and, after removal, are grown in a culture medium so that the chromosomes can be analysed.

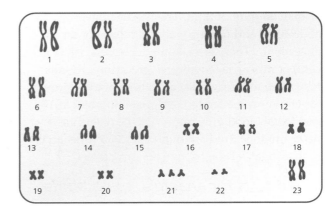

FIGURE 3.14 *Karyogram showing 3 chromosomes at position 21 – Down's syndrome*

Typical genetic abnormalities investigated using CVS are Down's syndrome, haemophilia, thalassaemia, muscular dystrophy and sickle cell disorders.

The test is usually carried out as an outpatient and takes about 30 minutes. The sample can be obtained from the foetal side of the edge of the placenta by a cannula (thin, hollow tube) attached to a syringe. Access is either through the vagina and uterus or the abdominal wall. The former method is aided by using an endoscope (an instrument used for direct visual access of a hollow organ or cavity) and the latter by an ultrasound scan to locate the placenta. When evidence of a serious chromosome abnormality is found, the parents can be given the choice of termination or not. The advantages of CVS over amniocentesis are that earlier termination carries less emotional stress and less risk to the health of the mother.

Risks of CVS are:

* puncturing the amniotic sac

* bleeding

* infection.

There is also a 1–2 per cent increased risk of miscarriage.

Amniocentesis

Small amounts of amniotic fluid are withdrawn from the amniotic sac for skin cell culture and chemical analysis. The technique is performed during the sixteenth and eighteenth week of the pregnancy, and the positions of the foetus and placenta are located by ultrasound scanning to allow the free passage of a hollow needle to remove a small amount of fluid. The needle penetrates the abdominal and uterine walls with local or no anaesthetic. There is a slightly increased risk (1 per cent) of miscarriage with this procedure. Results take three to four weeks, as cells have to be grown for chromosome analysis. Alphafetoprotein levels and foetal blood groups can also be determined from amniotic fluid although the main function is to investigate chromosomal abnormalities.

Blood tests for anaemia, spina bifida and blood groupings

The mother's blood provides vital dissolved oxygen for the growing foetus and this exchange takes place across the placenta (see Antenatal screening on page 121). When the mother is anaemic, that is her blood has a lack of oxygen-carrying capacity, most probably due to iron deficiency, then her foetus will not receive the desired supply of oxygen for its needs. The baby will be small for date and function might be impaired. A sample of blood taken from a vein in the forearm will enable laboratory determination of the level of iron-containing haemoglobin in the red blood cells.

When this is deemed to be inadequate, the pregnant mother can be provided with relevant medication. At the same time, testing against specific antisera assesses the mother's blood group; the blood group may be important if, as happens rarely, complications develop necessitating blood transfusion. In a small number of cases, the mother and foetus may have incompatible blood groups and, although the two bloods do not actually mix, some special precautions may have to be taken, especially at birth.

When a mother has Rhesus negative (D -ve) blood and the foetus Rhesus positive (D +ve) blood, the first foetus may sensitise the mother by causing Rhesus antibodies to develop. This usually happens during the birth as the placenta is breaking away from the uterine wall. An injection of anti-D serum will 'mop up' the antibodies, and prevent sensitisation. This is necessary because in a second or subsequent pregnancy with a Rhesus positive baby, the mother's antibodies will start to destroy the blood of the foetus, causing severe jaundice and even death.

Blood levels of certain chemicals will also provide pointers to other risks such as spina bifida, which causes high levels of alphafetoprotein.

Infant and child screening tests

Blood tests for CH, PKU and thalassaemia

After the infant is born, certain screening tests are carried out to ensure that the child is not affected by detectable conditions that were not apparent during antenatal care.

Congenital hypothyroidism (used to be called cretinism, now more commonly referred to as CH) and phenylketonuria (called PKU) are conditions that should never be missed, as both seriously affect growth and development – particularly mental development – and both are treatable conditions.

PKU is tested by a small prick on the heel of an infant and the drop of blood produced is mopped up on to a specially treated card. This is known as the Guthrie test and looks for high levels of phenylalanine that the infant is unable to metabolise due to a genetic inborn error of metabolism. The infants are usually blue-eyed and have blonde hair, as melanin is unable to be produced from the phenylalanine, although this is often difficult to tell in the newly born.

Thalassaemia is an inherited blood disorder and is most common in families originally from the Mediterranean area, South East Asia and the Middle East. Red blood cells are easily broken and are pale, due to a fault in haemoglobin manufacture. The infant and child will thus suffer from anaemia and insufficient oxygen carriage. A microscopic analysis of blood and haemoglobin estimation will diagnose this condition.

> ✳ DID YOU KNOW?
>
> As the UK becomes increasingly multicultural and mixed race unions are common, an increasing number of cases of thalassaemia, sickle cell anaemia and other blood disorders now occur. There are moves to make these blood tests part of routine infant care throughout the whole of the UK. This already occurs in some geographical areas of Britain, where there are large numbers of people from the countries mentioned.

Dental examination for dental caries

Children should have regular examinations of their milk or deciduous teeth from an early age so that monitoring for dental caries (decay) and the formation of the permanent teeth can be carried out. At the same time, advice regarding good personal mouth hygiene can be given. The dentist will examine and record the status of each tooth using a mirror and probe.

Currently, depending on the individual and the health status of the teeth, the dentist will determine the interval between examinations;

although this used to be half-yearly, the shortage of dentists working for the NHS has determined re-planning. In some areas, there are no NHS dentists and the community is experiencing much longer delays.

Eye tests for visual defects

A health professional will observe whether the baby looks at the mother when feeding and in many areas a pupillary red reflex test is carried out using an ophthalmoscope (a special instrument for looking into the eye. Most people will have seen flash photographs where the flash has illuminated the back of the eye, causing the person to have red eyes. This is essentially the same principle as using the ophthalmoscope. When an infant or child has congenital cataracts the red-eye reflex is absent.

The pupil reaction to light test is also carried out. When a bright light is shone on to the pupil of the eye, the pupil becomes smaller and vice versa in dim light conditions. When the infant is six to eight weeks old, the mother is asked for her opinion regarding the infant's eyesight, the red reflex test is again carried out and the observer notes the fixation of the eyes on the mother's face.

FIGURE 3.15 *The Sheridan-Gardner test being carried out*

At the eight-month check, the infant should follow moving objects and be able to focus on and reach out for a small object.

The child is assessed for squint at each eye test from this stage. At three years of age, visual acuity is measured using a letter-matching chart with the observer showing single letters and asking the child to point out a matching letter (Sheridan-Gardner test, see Figure 3.15).

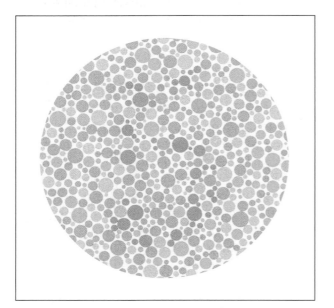

FIGURE 3.16 *An Ishihara chart*

At school, the familiar Snellen chart with letters of different sizes is used to test visual acuity. Near vision, colour vision (Ishihara charts (see Figure 3.16) or wool) and myopia (short-sightedness) are also tested for.

✳ DID YOU KNOW?

In the UK at the present time, there is controversy surrounding pre-school and schoolchildren's visual testing, Many visual impairments are not picked up until later in life. Many children are taken to the general practitioner following parental or teacher concern. It is likely that revised testing will take place in the coming years. It is particularly important for visual impairment to be diagnosed early for schoolwork, reading and play to be optimal. Infants who fail to see properly from an early age will not develop full vision.

Hearing tests for deafness

In the UK about 700 children are discovered to have severely impaired hearing each year. Early treatment leads to improved language skills and fewer emotional problems. However, like visual tests, there is much controversy over current hearing tests and these may be replaced in time with some form of electronic tests that may be more reliable and quantitative. Infants are observed for their reactions to noise, particularly voices. Babies will usually quieten in these conditions. From eight months onwards, infants will first move their heads sideways to locate noise and a little later up and down movements are added, giving full rotating head movement towards sound. This is used in distraction testing – various noises, like a shaken rattle, siren or whistle, are made in different locations to watch if the infant turns the head to the sound. After a child's second birthday, word-object testing is used; the care professional whispers the name of an object and asks the child to point to it.

Word-object testing is used to check hearing

A further test requests the child to carry out a particular task when certain sounds are made. It is also important to listen to the mother's views on the ability of the child to hear well, such as reaction to television sound, a doorbell ringing, or a dog barking and so on. If there is any doubt about the child's hearing, specialist advice is sought.

Physical examination for hip dislocation

The femur is the longest and strongest bone in the body; the head is a round ball that fits snugly in a cup-shaped depression in the pelvis. Sometimes the cup is not deep enough to hold the femoral head and it moves outwards, so-called dislocation. Some infants are born with permanent dislocated hips (one or both). This condition has been re-named developmental dysplasia of the hip, or DDH for short. When the condition is not discovered for some time, the child may walk with a painless limp, but osteo-arthritis of the joint occurs much earlier in life than normal and the hip joint becomes very painful. With early diagnosis and treatment, there is no limp and no early onset of osteo-arthritis.

The physical examination should take place at birth, at six to eight weeks old, and six to eight months. With the infant lying on its back, the doctor flexes the hip and knee to 90° vertically, with the thumb on the inner side of the knee and the forefinger on the outer bump of the head of the femur, the hip is turned smoothly and gently outwards (see Figure 3.17). When the hip joint is unstable there is a 'clunk' that can be both felt and heard as the head of the femur slips out of the socket (acetabulum) on the pelvis. Each hip is examined separately. The absence of the 'clunk' indicates that the hip joints are stable.

Recent research studies have demonstrated that two out of three of cases of children requiring surgery at a later date for this condition were not 'picked up' by this test. This has caused great concern and moves are being made to add to or replace this test by ultrasound scanning.

> **✳ DID YOU KNOW?**
>
> One of the main problems of DDH examination is that newly born infants are frequently affected by a hormone circulating in pregnant mothers and this makes their ligaments slack. Infant musculature is also weak and these two factors can cause unstable hips that clear up without any treatment. More than one in 100 infants born have unstable hip joints. Interestingly, DDH is six times more common in girls, and the left hip is affected four times more than the right hip. In one to three of the cases in which both hips are affected, there is a family history of the condition.

Treatment is by splints, plaster casts or surgery if this fails.

Adult screening tests

Screening tests may be suitable for the whole population, such as those for infants and children; however, others may be applicable to groups of people at special risk such as a particular age group or gender, certain hazardous occupations or those with family histories of disease.

Blood pressure tests for hypertension

Increasingly, more young adults are affected by a higher resting blood pressure than normal (hypertension) whereas the condition used to be thought of as relevant only to middle-aged and older people. GPs are urged to routinely measure blood pressures of service users on visits to the surgery. Other clients are urged to visit the practice at least once a year to have their blood pressure checked. Clients with hypertension, or raised blood pressure not yet deemed to be clinical hypertension, are advised to attend regular clinics for monitoring purposes. Hypertension increases the chances of life-threatening conditions such as strokes and heart disease, particularly coronary thrombosis.

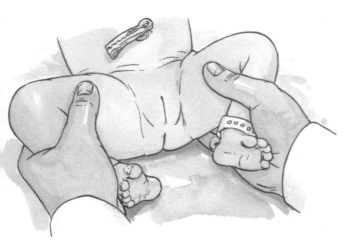

FIGURE 3.17 *Testing a baby for hip displacement*

It is normal to experience raised blood pressure during periods of stress or physical exertion. Hypertension is raised blood pressure at rest. Blood pressure rises naturally with age because of hardening and narrowing of the elastic arteries. It also rises with kidney disease, narrowing of the aorta (the main artery serving the body), alcohol consumption, smoking tobacco products and hormonal disorders. Pregnant women may experience raised blood pressure in a serious condition known as pre-eclampsia.

Nowadays, blood pressure is usually measured electronically as the old mercury devices are banned. A device for measuring blood pressure is called a sphygmomanometer or 'sphygmo' for short and is usually used on the upper arm over the position of an artery. An inflatable cuff is blown up to stop the blood flowing through the artery and slowly deflated until the point is reached when blood is just able to push through. This is the systolic pressure and represents the force, which the blood is pressing on the artery walls, when the heart ventricles are contracting (systole).

The cuff is further deflated until blood is first flowing naturally and the heartbeat disappears; this is the diastolic pressure measuring the resistance of the arteries against which the heart has to pump blood. This is seen as the most important reading, as the systolic pressure is frequently raised due to excitement, anxiety or physical exertion. Individuals should sit quietly for about ten minutes before having their blood pressure recorded. The two, recorded pressures are usually given as a fraction with the larger systolic as the numerator and the diastolic as the denominator. The first instruments measured in millimetres of mercury (mm.Hg) and this is still the most frequently used unit, although units are frequently omitted; thus BP 120/80.

Most normal healthy young people have blood pressures around 110/75 or even less, although the average normal BP is quoted at 120/80.

Hypertension is quoted to be BP consistently over 160/95 mm.Hg, but there is no absolute line and many individuals with borderline hypertension are carefully monitored by their GP and advised accordingly. Males are more frequently affected with hypertension than females and for many individuals there appears to be no underlying cause. Clinical investigation for any underlying cause is carried out and anti-hypertensive drugs are effective in lowering blood pressure.

Smear test for cervical cancer

This is a test recommended that women take six months after first sexual intercourse, then after one year and every three years, ideally until the end of their lives. In the UK at present, cervical smear tests cease at the age of sixty-five years unless there is a particular reason for continuing monitoring. The test detects abnormal cells in the cervix or neck of the womb. Abnormal cells usually indicate a pre-cancerous condition and the smear test has a 95 per cent chance of detecting these. Cancer of the cervix is one of the most common cancers in the world and the chances of a cure are very much improved with early detection. Herpes simplex (a troublesome virus infection) and genital warts can also be detected.

A woman lies on her back, with knees raised and pressed open, and an instrument (speculum) opens the vagina so that a specially shaped spatula can be inserted to scrape off some cells to be smeared on to a microscope slide. The quick test is carried out in family planning and well woman clinics, or by a GP, but the results are not routinely ready for several weeks. When abnormal cells are found, the test is usually repeated and the abnormality graded by experts. Sometimes a biopsy (removal of a small piece of tissue) is carried out to determine the extent and full nature of the abnormality. When the area of abnormality is well defined this can be eradicated and destroyed by extreme heat or cold. The cervical smear test is free under the NHS.

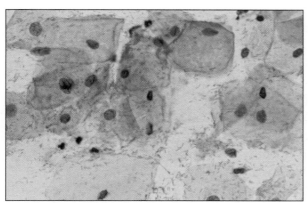

Light micrograph of a cervical smear containing normal squamous cells (pink and blue) and numerous rod-shaped bacteria

Eye tests for glaucoma and other visual defects

Some of the titles used by eye professionals are confusing and it is important to understand the different terms.

Ophthalmologists are doctors who specialise in eye disorders and treatment; ophthalmic opticians are trained to perform eye examinations and prescribe glasses to correct visual defects.

Ophthalmic opticians are not doctors who treat eye disorders and will refer any concerns in this regard to ophthalmologists. Opticians fit and sell glasses. It follows then, that the professional (other than a doctor) who might carry out a routine eye examination should be an ophthalmic optician and not an optician,

The eyeball is fluid-filled to enable the shape of the eye to be maintained. The volume of fluid entering the eye must balance with the volume leaving the eye; in glaucoma, the exit of fluid is narrowed so more fluid enters than leaves, causing the pressure inside the eyeball to rise.

A raised intra-ocular pressure damages the optic nerve at the back of the eye, causing patchy loss of vision. The extent of visual loss depends on the type of glaucoma and how long the raised pressure has been undiagnosed. When intra-ocular pressure is monitored regularly, damage will be minimised. This is important because any long-standing damage will cause the visual loss to be permanent. The individual will not necessarily be aware of the patchy vision because most tasks are carried out by central vision, such as reading and watching television, for example, and central vision only becomes affected at a later stage in glaucoma.

Glaucoma usually affects both eyes. Individuals over the age of 40 years are generally tested regularly; those with a family history of the condition from thirty-five years of age, but Afro-Caribbean people, diabetics, people with myopia and heavy smokers should be tested earlier, as glaucoma is significantly more common in these groups.

An applanation tonometer is used to measure the intra-ocular pressure, a specialist piece of equipment. The ophthalmoscope is also used to examine the back of the eye where the optic nerve disc can be viewed.

Measurement of visual fields can also be important for checking on peripheral vision and clearly the accuracy of vision using Snellen charts is vital (see eye tests in children on page 124).

> ✳ **DID YOU KNOW?**
>
> Glaucoma is responsible for 15 per cent of blindness in adults in the UK and is the most common major eye disorder in people over 60 years of age.

Astigmatism is a 'bumpy' cornea that causes some parts of vision to be clearer than others are;

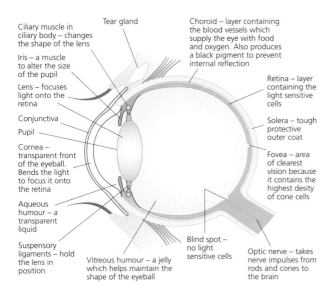

Ciliary muscle in ciliary body – changes the shape of the lens

Iris – a muscle to alter the size of the pupil

Lens – focuses light onto the retina

Conjunctiva

Pupil

Cornea – transparent front of the eyeball. Bends the light to focus it onto the retina

Aqueous humour – a transparent liquid

Suspensory ligaments – hold the lens in position

Tear gland

Vitreous humour – a jelly which helps maintain the shape of the eyeball

Blind spot – no light sensitive cells

Optic nerve – takes nerve impulses from rods and cones to the brain

Choroid – layer containing the blood vessels which supply the eye with food and oxygen. Also produces a black pigment to prevent internal reflection

Retina – layer containing the light sensitive cells

Solera – tough protective outer coat

Fovea – area of clearest vision because it contains the highest desity of cone cells

FIGURE 3.18 *A section through the eyeball*

it is often tested for using a series of black lines arranged as spokes of a wheel on green and red backgrounds. Some spokes appear blacker than others do. Corrective lenses in glasses are able to cancel the effect out.

Myopia (short-sight), hypermetropia (long-sight) and presbyopia (long-sight of old age) are investigated using trial spectacles into which loose lenses can be placed until vision is near perfect.

Mammography for breast cancer

This is an X-ray procedure for screening for breast cancer and lumps. Like the cervical smear test, mammography can reveal small lumps that are not apparent to touch even if the women practices breast self-examination; and early diagnosis is an important factor in the reduction of fatalities from this disease. Each breast in turn is gently compressed between a plastic plate and the X-ray plate to spread the tissue over a wide area. Views are taken in more than one plane. Specialists inspect the X-ray photographs looking for dense masses of tissue. When a lump is found, a biopsy is arranged to determine further treatment. Currently, most small tumours are surgically removed and combined with radiotherapy and/or anti-cancer drugs.

Mammography is available as routine screening for anyone aged 40 with a family history of the disease and, for other women, from 50 until 65 years. It is simple, safe (uses only a low dose of radiation) and effective. Screening

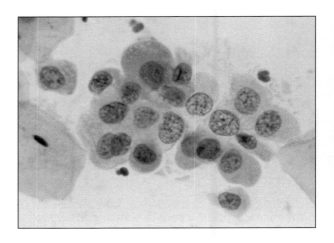

should be repeated every three or four years, as this is the most common cancer in women. Mammography is free under the NHS.

Physical examination for testicular cancer

Testicular cancer is rare in puberty and old age; conversely it is most common in young adults and middle-aged men. Both testes should be regularly felt over the whole surface, moving the loose skin of the scrotum from side to side. It is easy and simple to do and should not cause discomfort. Any firm lumps, not usually painful or tender, should be followed up promptly by the GP, who will treat any lump as malignant (invasive) until proven otherwise. Testicular cancer has an extremely good cure rate when caught in the early stages.

Summary

Screening tests

Antenatal screening
Amniocentesis
CVS
Blood tests

Infant and child screening
Blood tests (PKU, thalassaemia)
Dental examination (caries)
Eye tests (visual defects)
Hearing tests (deafness)
Hip dislocation examination

Adult screening
BP monitoring
Cervical smears
Eye tests (defects)
Mammography
Testicular examination

Tania has just learned that she is pregnant with her first child; both she and her partner are very happy, as they have been wanting to start a family for a year. Tania is 39 years old, and five years ago had a small lump removed from her left breast. The lump was discovered after a routine mammography. She also has had cervical smears every three years, all of which have been negative. Her blood group is Rhesus negative and her partner is Rhesus positive, and she has had mild iron-deficiency anaemia for most of her adult life due to heavy menstrual periods.

Tania has had annual eye tests because she is short-sighted and astigmatic. Her older sister has four children and began her family when she was 23 years old. She has three girls and one boy, the youngest, has Down's syndrome.

Using concepts, can you identify?

1 The antenatal screening tests that Tania would be advised to have by her health care advisors.

2 The screening tests her newly born infant will have.

3 The adult screening tests that Tania has experienced.

Go further – can you analyse issues using theory?

4 The scientific basis for each of the antenatal, infant and adult tests you have named.

5 How positive and negative results would be obtained for each screening test.

Go further – can you evaluate using a range of theory?

6 Explain the values of the screening tests to the health of Tania and her baby.

UNIT 3 ASSESSMENT

You will need to produce a portfolio of evidence containing a questionnaire and two reports. The work should be wholly your own work and not shared with other candidates or part of a group exercise.

A: The Questionnaire

You will need to construct a sound questionnaire to demonstrate the differing attitudes to the concept of health and ill health and to determine how the understanding of people is different. Further questions should then examine all the factors affecting health and well-being, focusing on their relative importance, the reasons for them and how they link into one another.

You will need to decide on the number of people to be surveyed by the questionnaire and include as many different individuals and groups of people of different culture, beliefs and settings as you can. Your questionnaire should be designed so that when you collate the responses you can analyse the results and provide evidence showing how you assessed the validity and accuracy of the data that you have collected. You will need to draw conclusions from your survey and justify how you reached those conclusions.

✳ DID YOU KNOW?

Questionnaires are an effective way to gather information on people's thoughts, views or activities; however, they need to be carefully designed and planned.

First of all, make sure that you are fully briefed on the topic and while you are doing your research, jot down any ideas on possible questions to ask. At this stage, do not try to write the question because you may decide on a special format later, just a note will do. When your research is concluded, check whether you have covered all the aspects required.

Decide on the breadth of your survey, by considering the number of people you will question, who these will be and where you can find different people from different groups of society. You will also need to consider how many questionnaires will be returned and increase your number to offset the shortfall. For example, if after careful consideration, you think that you will survey 50 people in total and there will be 1 in 5 who will not complete the questionnaire, then you will need to increase the number of people surveyed to 60.

The style of the questionnaire is important, as it can make the difference between getting it completed or not, so you should bear in mind the people who will be answering it. The questionnaire should not be too long and make people give up, or so short that you have too little material to analyse. Design your questions so that there is a mix of different formats with not too much writing; short answer questions and boxes for completion are good. A brief introduction giving the purpose of the request is useful, particularly if you plan not to give out each questionnaire yourself.

It is useful to give the questionnaire to an individual and provide a short time interval for completion. If you hover over someone while they are completing the questionnaire, you are less likely to get honest and detailed responses. You will also need to consider how the completed questionnaires will be returned to you.

✳ DID YOU KNOW?

Questions can be in different formats. When seeking an opinion or view, you can ask an open question (often beginning with what, how, why, where or when) such as:

What does being healthy mean to you?
Responders would need a few lines for their answer. Open questions are more difficult to answer because, hopefully, the answer is more detailed and considered.

When you are seeking facts, you are more likely to ask closed questions; these require yes or no answers or just a simple fact such as:

Have you seen a doctor for advice or treatment in the last six months?   Yes/No
In this case you can provide options for the responder to use by circling, ticking or underlining the correct answer. You will need to provide the instruction for completion, such as 'please circle your answer'.

You can also provide a small number of choices to limit the response types. This makes analysis easier for you, but also can be frustrating for the individual if the response they wish to give is not available.

How many times have you seen a doctor for advice and/or treatment in the past twelve months?
Please tick one box only

None ☐   Once ☐   2–3 times ☐   4–8 times ☐   more than 8 times ☐

You can also use restricted options to simplify responses for analysis by making a statement and asking for agreement or disagreement. This is a verbal rating scale.

All tobacco products should be banned from public places immediately.

Please tick one box only

Strongly agree   ☐
Agree   ☐
Neither agree nor disagree   ☐
Disagree   ☐
Strongly disagree   ☐

You can also use ranking questions, asking the responder to rank a list in order of importance, such as:

Please rank the following in order of importance to your health.

(1 = most important, 6 = least important.)

Eating sensibly ☐

Regular exercise or physical activity ☐

Monitoring your weight ☐

Limiting alcohol consumption ☐

Avoiding smoking ☐

Visiting the GP promptly for medical advice and appropriate treatment ☐

Another way of gauging opinion is to use a graded scale on which the responder makes a judgement, such as:

Estimate your health status by placing a mark in the appropriate place on the line below:

|_____|

Not healthy   Full health

You will need to consider your notes and decide which format is most suitable to investigate the questions you wish to ask. When you have written your questions in your desired format, it is worth carrying out a small trial to test whether the questionnaire 'works' and whether adjustments need to be made. At this stage, it will be useful to consider how you will collate and analyse your results in order to achieve high marks. Careful planning now will save hours of work later on.

You are recommended to make regular perusals of the assessment objectives and marking grids to maximise your achievement. For example, when using a graded question like the one above, you may wish to have a copy with divisions marked on so that you can place it over the response and transfer to a percentage or number for collation purposes.

B: Report 1

This report assesses your understanding of the Immunisation against Disease part of the specification. You will need to carry out original research to accurately explain the rationale behind both active and passive immunity. Each listed disease should be covered by a brief description of aetiology (study of the causes), signs and symptoms and the importance of immunisation to prevent specific long-term damage. You will also need to evaluate immunisation against non-immunisation and include a consideration of the side effects of immunisation. To gain high marks, you will need to provide depth and breadth of understanding in your report, use a variety of research sources and different contexts.

You are recommended to make regular perusals of the assessment objectives and marking grids to maximise your achievement.

C: Report 2

The second report assesses the Value of Screening section of the specifications. The report should explain the value of screening for different client groups. Each screening test should be briefly described, including the way in which it is performed and how results are interpreted. Clearly referenced research resources from a variety of sources should explain the scientific basis of the test and the results obtained from it. To gain high marks, you must show depth and breadth of understanding of the importance of screening tests for different client groups and stress the scientific principles underlying each test.

You are recommended to make regular perusals of the assessment objectives and marking grids to maximise your achievement.

References

Any good health or medical encyclopaedia will have details of screening tests.

Aggleton, P., (1990) *Health (Society Now),* Routledge, London

British Medical Association, (2000) *Complete Family Health Encyclopedia,* Dorling Kindersley, London

Ewles, L., Simnett, I., (2003) *Promoting Health – a Practical Guide,* Bailliere Tindall, London.

Kassianos, G. C., (2001) *Immunization: Childhood and Traveller's Health,* Blackwell Science, Oxford

Naidoo, J., (1997) *Health Studies: An Introduction,* Palgrave Macmillan, Basingstoke

Neustaedter, R., (2002) *The Vaccine Guide: Risks and Benefits for Children and Benefits,* North Atlantic Books, Berkley, California

Neustaedter, R., (1990) *The Immunization Decision: A Guide for Parents,* North Atlantic Books, Berkley, California

Romm, A. J., (2001) *Vaccinations: A Thoughtful Parent's Guide,* Healing Arts Press, Rochester, New York

Seedhouse, D., (1986) *Health: The Foundations for Achievement,* John Wiley, Chichester

Senior, M., Viveash, B., (1997) *Skills-based Sociology,* Macmillan, London

Taylor, S., Field, D., (1998) *Sociological Perspectives on Health, Illness and Healthcare,* Blackwell Science, Oxford

Useful websites

Please see www.heinemann.co.uk/hotlinks (express code 1554P) for links to the following websites which may provide a source of information:

* The Department of Health and Human Services has a website of Centres for Disease Control and Prevention.

* The NHS Immunisation information site provides information on MMR.

* Trekmate is an outdoor and store which carries trekking and extreme weather equipment for sale or rent.

* The Association for Clinical Biochemistry and the American Association of Clinical Chemistry has a non-commercial lab tests online site.

* The website of the UK government has information on disabilities and many other topics.

* Surgery Door provides an online health service.

UNIT 4

Child development

In this unit you will learn about:

4.1   Growth and development

4.2   Factors affecting development

4.3   The importance of play

4.4   Health and safety

Working with children can be interesting and rewarding but also challenging. To work well with children, practitioners need to have a good understanding of how children grow and develop. It is important to understand the factors that can affect children's development as well as those ways in which practitioners can actively promote development through play. Safety is also a major consideration when working with children. This means that practitioners need to know how to keep children safe and be able to recognise dangers in different environments.

Ages of children

It is common when talking about children to categorise them according to age. Exact ages and even terms can vary in child development, but in this qualification the following are used.

AGE RANGE	TERM
Less than 2 years	Infant
2 to 3 years	Toddler
3 to 5 years	Pre-school child
5 to 8 years	School aged child

4.1 Growth and development

The physical growth and development of children underpins other aspects of their development.

The difference between growth and development

The term 'growth' refers to the way in which cells subdivide to, for example, allow bones to lengthen. Development refers to the skills that the child masters. Many aspects of children's development are firmly intertwined with growth; for example, babies cannot walk until their bones are long and strong enough to take their weight.

Why physical growth is important

Growth provides the background for development

Physical growth is essential in helping children's development as it makes certain movements possible; for example, children's hand movements are linked to the growth of the bones in their wrists. This in turn means that new opportunities for stimulation are available for the individual child. Once children can walk, for example, they can see their environment from a new height.

Growth affects adults' responses

The size and shape of a child affects the way adults respond. A tall child may be given more responsibility. Development as a result of growth also affects adults' responses. Adults may, for example, start to expect more of children once they are able to dress themselves.

Growth can affect self-esteem

As children begin to grow, so they often start to feel more capable. Taller children, for example, usually have higher self-esteem. The shape of a child's body can also affect how that child feels about him or herself. A child who is obese may have lower self-esteem.

Physical growth is not smooth and continuous

The rate at which children grow is not smooth and continuous. The first two years are marked by significant growth, after which children grow more steadily until the onset of adolescence.

> **✳ DID YOU KNOW?**
>
> Infants gain in height and weight very rapidly. They gain around 30 cm in height in the first year and by the age of 2 years children have reached half their adult height and weigh three times more than they did at birth (see Figure 4.1).

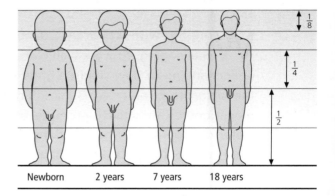

FIGURE 4.1 *Growth charts*

Allometric growth

The rate at which a child's body parts grow is not even. This means that a child's body shape changes throughout childhood. A good example of this is head size. For example, the head of a two-year-old will be roughly one quarter of his or her total height, whilst an adult's head makes up between one eighth or one tenth of total height. During adolescence, allometric growth can be seen again as hands and feet grow more quickly and reach their full size earlier than other parts of the body.

Measuring growth

During children's early years, and especially the first year, health professionals measure children's growth. Height, weight and head circumference are all noted. Measurements are plotted onto a growth chart which some professionals refer to as a centile chart (see Figure 4.2). There are separate charts for boys and girls, which reflect that boys are usually heavier and taller than girls. Health professionals also have to take into account a child's ethnic background, as some races are lighter or shorter than others.

How the growth chart works

Each area has nine bands, known as centiles. A height measurement on the seventy-eighth centile means that for every hundred children, only 12 will be this height and taller. Where, for example, a child's height falls above or below the centile bands, the child will be unusually tall or short.

The chart shows the growth rate curve that children's measurements should follow for normal development. Whilst many children will vary slightly, their measurement curve should look similar. Reasons why there might be short-term changes in the rate of curve might include difficulties in feeding because of a cold. Significant variations from the norm growth rate curve are always investigated, as there might be an underlying medical reason such as a heart condition or diabetes.

What the growth charts show

Key factors identified in the growth chart are shown in Figure 4.3.

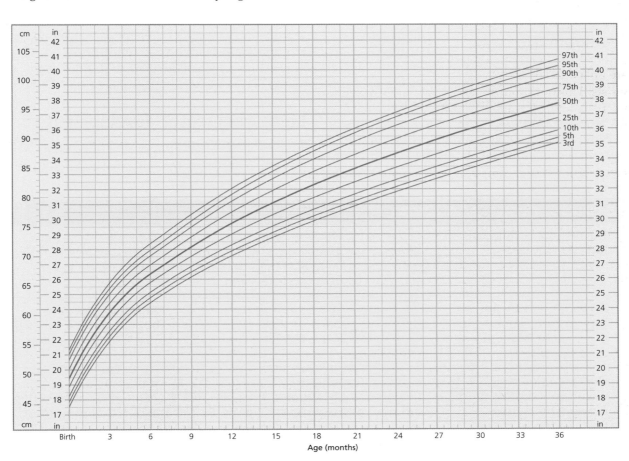

FIGURE 4.2 *Length-for-age percentiles for boys, birth to 36 months*

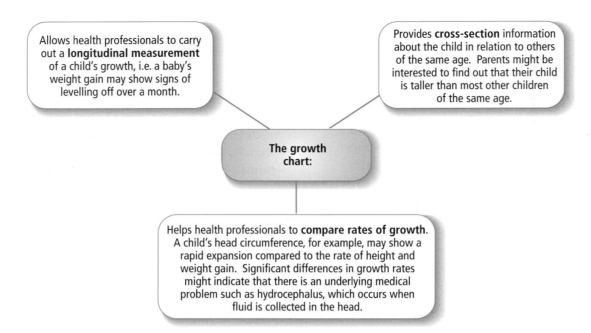

Allows health professionals to carry out a **longitudinal measurement** of a child's growth, i.e. a baby's weight gain may show signs of levelling off over a month.

Provides **cross-section** information about the child in relation to others of the same age. Parents might be interested to find out that their child is taller than most other children of the same age.

The growth chart:

Helps health professionals to **compare rates of growth**. A child's head circumference, for example, may show a rapid expansion compared to the rate of height and weight gain. Significant differences in growth rates might indicate that there is an underlying medical problem such as hydrocephalus, which occurs when fluid is collected in the head.

FIGURE 4.3 *Information obtained from the growth chart*

Key principles of physical development

There are three principles of physical development, which were first suggested by Arnold Gessell, an American paediatrician. These are shown in Table 4.1.

As an adult you may have had a learning experience similar to that of a young baby if you have learnt to use a computer with a mouse. Most people find that at first they can only just manage to keep the mouse visible on the screen before they gradually learn how to refine their movements which allow them to position the mouse accurately where they choose.

Measuring motor development

To measure children's physical development, professionals look at the skills that children have

PRINCIPLES OF PHYSICAL DEVELOPMENT	
1. Development follows a definite sequence	As we watch children grow and develop, we see that a pattern emerges and that certain movements have to be in place before others can follow; e.g. children have to be able to walk before they can skip (see also page 150)
2. Development begins with the control of head movements and proceeds downwards	Babies at first gain control of their head and top of the spine before other parts of their bodies. This is thought to be a survival mechanism, as it is important for babies to be able to turn their heads to feed.
3. Development begins with uncontrolled gross motor movements before becoming precise and refined.	At first the young baby's arm and leg movements are uncontrolled, but some control is quickly gained, first of the arms and then of the wrist and hands. By the age of six months, most babies are usually able to take an offered toy reasonably easily.

TABLE 4.1 *Principles of physical development as suggested by Arnold Gessell*

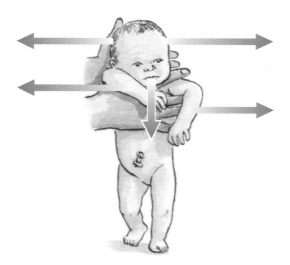

FIGURE 4.4 *Principles of physical development as suggested by Arnold Gessell*

acquired. These skills are sometimes referred to as *milestones* and are linked to children's ages. The milestones have been determined by looking at large groups of children's development and considering what the 'norm' for each age is. This means that there will always be some variation, with some children showing development that is in advance of the milestones. Significant delays in reaching milestones are likely to monitored and investigated.

Gross and fine motor movements

Gaining physical control of the body is an extremely important process for children. It allows them to gain mobility and independence. Movements can be divided into two broad categories. Children need to be able to combine both types of movements in order to gain physical independence. By the age of six or seven years, most children have mastered both types of movements at a basic level. After this age, children perform better at using these movements and are able to refine and make them more complex, i.e. an eight-year-old will be able to draw a more detailed and intricate picture than a six-year-old.

Fine motor movements

These are small movements involving the hands. Fine motor movements use smaller muscles. They often include skills that require the coordination between the hands and the eye, such as, for example, threading beads and putting a lid onto a bottle.

Gross motor movements

These are the large movements that involve the whole limb or whole body. Gross motor movements use large muscles. They include movements such as walking and crawling as well as throwing or lifting up an arm. Gross motor movements develop before fine motor movements. Development of fine and gross motors skills are shown in Table 4.2.

Consider this

Figure 4.5 shows Ali's growth chart. Ali's mother has taken her son to the clinic to be measured. He is now 17 months old. His father's ethnic background is Chinese. Ali has been well, although he has had one bout of diarrhoea since he last came to the clinic.

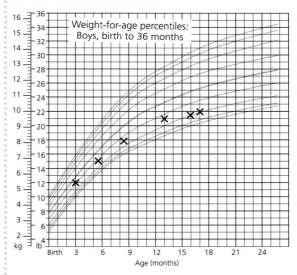

FIGURE 4.5 *Centile chart for Ali*

1. How old was Ali when the last measurements were recorded?

2. Explain what the chart shows in terms of Ali's growth rate so far.

3. Explain what the chart shows in terms of Ali's weight compared to other children.

4. Give one reason for Ali's size.

	AGE	FINE MOTOR SKILLS	GROSS MOTOR SKILLS
Infant	3 months	* Watch their hands and play with fingers * Clasp and unclasp their hands * Can hold a rattle for a moment	* Lifts head and chest up * Waves arms and brings their hands together over their body
	6 months	* Reach for a toy * Can move a toy from one hand to another * Puts objects into mouth	* Move their arms to indicate that they want to be lifted * Can roll over from back to front
	9 months	* Can grasp object with index finger and thumb * Can deliberately release objects by dropping them	* Can sit unsupported * Is likely to be mobile, i.e. crawling or rolling
	12 months	* Uses index finger and thumb (pincer grasp) to pick up small objects * Can point to with the index finger	* May stand alone briefly * May walk holding onto furniture (although some children may be walking unaided)
	18 months	* Can use a spoon to feed with * Can scribble * Can build a tower of three bricks	* Can walk unaided * Can climb up onto a toy * Can squat to pick up a toy
Toddler	2 years	* Can draw circles and dots * Can use spoon effectively to feed with	* Can run * Climbs onto furniture * Use sit and ride toys
	2 years six months	* May have established hand preference * Can do simple jigsaw puzzles	* Can kick a large ball * May begin to use tricycles
Pre-school age	3 years	* Turns pages in a book one by one * Washes and dries hands with help * Holds a crayon and can draw a face	* Can steer and pedal tricycle * Can run forwards and backwards * Throws large ball
	4 years	* Buttons and unbuttons own clothing * Cuts out simple shapes * Draws a person with head, trunk and legs	* Walks on a line * Aims and throws ball * Hops on one foot
School age	5 years	* Forms letters, write own name * Colours pictures in * Completes 20 piece jigsaw	* Skips with a rope * Runs quickly and is able to avoid obstacles * Throws large ball to a partner and catches it
	6-8 years	* Is able to join handwriting * Cuts out shapes accurately * Produces detailed drawings * Ties and unties shoe laces	* Hops, skips jumps confidently * Can balance on a beam * Chases and dodges others * Can use bicycle and other wheeled toys such as roller skates

TABLE 4.2 *Development of fine and gross motors skills*

Cognitive development including language

Cognitive development is about the way in which children develop thinking skills such as the ability to reason, match and use information to solve problems. One of the key features in children's cognitive development is the way in which most children learn to start to think in the abstract. Four-year-olds, for example, might need to see counters in order to add them together, but seven-year-olds will be able to do a simple sum in their head.

Nature versus nurture

How much of a child's cognitive ability is down to their genetic inheritance and how much is due to the amount of stimulation and experiences they have received? This nature versus nurture question is interesting and is still unresolved. The key difference between people of different cognitive abilities appears to be the speed at which connections in the brain can be made and the quantity of information that they can process at once. This revolves around the structures in the brain known as neural pathways.

In terms of nature, it would seem that some basic structures are already in place when we are born, but stimulation or damage to the brain will affect how the pathways will develop and be used. Savants, for example, who may have a particular and extreme ability in one area, such as the ability to remember phone books or multiply thousands of digits, are thought to have damaged or unusual structures in their brains. This means that information in the brain is handled differently.

In terms of nurture, a key difference to cognitive development is the amount of stimulation, language and support that children are offered in their earliest years. Brain scans of children in Romanian orphanages in the early 1990s suggested that the lack of stimulation had affected their brain development.

Stages and sequences of cognitive development

It is very difficult to give milestones for cognitive development, as children's acquisition of concepts will depend on their play experiences, individual pattern of development and the quality of the stimulation they have received. Figure 4.6 outlines some of the cognitive skills that children often show at different ages.

> ## ✱ DID YOU KNOW?
>
> Intelligence tests were designed to help educators decide the potential academic ability of children. Intelligence or cognitive ability tests are still used in schools today. Whilst the general public often believes that they show a child's potential, this is not quite so. It is thought to be impossible to design a test which really looks at underlying potential, as this would mean that no knowledge or experience would be needed in order to complete them. Interestingly, as we learn more about the brain, we know that the brain continues to grow and develop if stimulated. This means that intelligence test scores can actually change during a person's life.

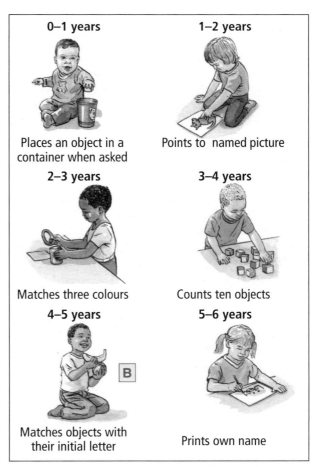

0–1 years
Places an object in a container when asked

1–2 years
Points to named picture

2–3 years
Matches three colours

3–4 years
Counts ten objects

4–5 years
Matches objects with their initial letter

5–6 years
Prints own name

FIGURE 4.6 *Cognitive skills that children often show at different ages*

Piaget's tests of cognitive functioning

One of the most influential theories of how children's thinking develops was put forward by Jean Piaget (1896–1980). Piaget began his interest into children's thinking and logic whilst working on intelligence tests. He was fascinated by the way in which children regularly gave similar, but wrong, answers to some of the questions. From this he came to the conclusion that children's logic was different to adults and began to explore why this was. He designed several tests to look at children's logic at different stages.

Piaget outlined stages in children's cognitive development: these are shown in Table 4.3.

Piaget's tests

Object permanence

From around the age of eight months onwards, babies begin to realise that objects do not disappear, even when they are out of sight. Piaget's test of object permanence was to show a baby a toy and then to hide it in front of the baby, i.e. a rattle would be shown and then hidden under a cushion near the baby. He then observed whether the baby tried to look and find it. Interestingly, if the game is played a few times and the object is put in a new place, the baby at the age of eight or nine months will keep looking in the place where it was previously hidden, not the new place. At twelve months of age, the baby will look in the last hiding place.

Conservation

One of Piaget's tests to see which stage children might be at is related to children's ability to 'conserve'. Conservation means understanding that certain things do not change even if their appearance is different. Piaget suggested that young children found it difficult to conserve and that they were easily taken in by appearances. This explained why they come to different conclusions to adults. A three-year-old may for example think that a man wearing a women's dress has become a woman.

STAGE	AGE	FEATURES
Sensori-motor	0–2 years	The child develops physical schemas as he gains control of his movements. At around 8–9 months, the baby begins to understand that objects continue to exist even if he cannot see them. This is known as object permanence and may explain why most babies begin to protest when their carer leaves the room.
Pre-operational	2–7 years	Children begin to use symbols to stand for things; for example, a piece of dough represents a cake. Language is also a way of using symbols (see page 156). Children also show **egocentrism**, i.e. a belief that everyone will see the same things as they do or have the same thoughts. Piaget felt that children in this stage were easily tricked by appearances as was evidenced in his experiments involving **conservation** (see below)
Concrete operations	7–11 years	Piaget felt that this stage marked a significant change in children's logic. They were less easily deceived by appearances and could apply rules and strategies to their thinking. The term 'concrete' is used because Piaget felt that children were helped in their thinking when they could do and see things in practical ways, e.g. physically counting out items

TABLE 4.3 *Stages in children's cognitive development (outlined by Piaget)*

Put out six buttons in a line. Ask a child to count how many buttons there are.

In the presence of the child, spread the buttons out. Ask the child how many buttons are there. Children who can conserve will not need to count the buttons again, as they will understand that unless some have been taken away or added, the same amount will remain regardless of their position. Repeat this observation with different ages of children.

1. From your observation, can you identify the age at which children understand this type of conservation?

Decentration

As part of Piaget's pre-operational stage, Piaget felt that children's thinking was based only on their own experiences and a belief that everyone would have the same experiences as themselves. He felt that this would mean that young children would have difficulty in 'decentring'. Decentration was the ability to imagine someone else's perspective. To test children's ability to decentre, Piaget constructed a model of three mountains. Each mountain was a different colour and had a different feature on it. Children could walk around the model and then were asked to sit down on one side of the model. A doll was put on the other side. Children were then shown pictures of different views and were asked to choose the

Consider this

Anthony is watching a puppet show. Both puppets – a mouse and fox – are on the stage,. The mouse hides a ring in a box and then goes off to play. The fox takes the ring and hides it under a hat. The mouse comes back and starts looking for the ring in the box it had been left. Anthony cannot understand why the mouse does not go straight to the hat.

1. Why does Anthony think that the mouse should look under the hat?

2. What does this tell you about Anthony's ability to decentre?

view that the doll would have. Whilst four-year-olds chose the picture that represented the view that they could see, seven and eight-year-olds consistently selected the view that the doll would see.

Animism

Many children in the pre-operational stage draw pictures with human faces or believe that inanimate objects such as puppets and teddy bears, for example, have real feelings. This is thought to be linked to egocentrism, as children believe that if they have thoughts and feelings, so must everything else.

FIGURE 4.7 *Children may see animals as having human characteristics*

Language is fundamental to cognitive development

Learning how to communicate and use language is hugely important for children. It helps children to socialise with other children and also express their needs. It can help them to understand what is happening and ask questions.

Language also allows for much more complicated thoughts. We use it to store and categorise information, i.e. a simple word can trigger a host of images and memories, to organise ourselves and to help us reason and speculate. It also allows us to control our behaviour and this is one reason why children's behaviour often radically changes once they have begun to master language at around three years of age.

Think it over...

What have you used language for today?

What things might you not have achieved without language?

The development of language

Whilst babies arrive in the world without being able to speak or even to understand what is being said, the development of language has already begun. Research now shows that babies can recognise their mothers' voice at birth as well as music that she has been listening to! The process of how children learn language follows a definite pattern and whilst there are differences between children, the sequence remains broadly similar. The stages in language development are shown in Table 4.4.

Pre-linguistic phase

The first stage in the process of language development is known as the pre-linguistic phase. This phase usually lasts 12 months, or so, and ends once babies' first words begin to emerge. In this phase, babies learn to tune into the language that they are exposed to and also learn the skills of communication including eye contact, smiling and turn taking. Babies also learn about the meanings of words as well as practising or vocalising the sounds that they will need. This often takes the form of babbling, which becomes increasingly tuneful and reflects the sounds of the language babies are exposed to. By the end of the pre-linguistic phase, most babies will have also understood the meanings of some words that are used. Words that we understand but may or may not use form what is known as our receptive vocabulary. By the age of 9 months, it is thought that most babies will have 15 words in their receptive vocabulary.

Key concepts

The *pre-linguistic phase* is the first stage in the process of language development.

Receptive vocabulary consists of words that are understood but may not be used.

Linguistic phase

First words often are used at around 13-months-of-age although, as with other areas of child development, there is some variation. Common first words include dada, mama, bye, together with words that have significant importance for the child. Words may not be recognisable to others, but parents and carers realise that these words have meaning for the child and they are used with consistency. From using their first words, toddlers quickly learn to use one word to stand for several things. In describing this usage, linguists use the term 'holophrase'. A good example of this is the toddler who uses the word 'dink' to stand for 'drink'. Very quickly he is likely also to use the word 'dink' to ask for food or to point out to his parents that his beaker has fallen down! To differentiate between the meanings of the word, he may simply alter the tone of his voice.

Key concept

A *holophrase* is a word used to stand for several things.

Alongside the use of holophrases, toddlers' vocabularies begin to increase. They build up a stock of words, most of which are linked to objects and people in their environment with a few useful additions such as 'more' 'no' and 'come'. Whilst at first this is a gradual process, once children have fifty words or so in their expressive vocabulary, they enter a new phase during which it becomes increasingly hard to keep track of their store of words. This phase has been dubbed as the 'language explosion'.

Key concept

Expressive vocabulary is the stock of words which builds up rapidly after a child has learnt about fifty words.

At the same time as children's store of words rapidly expands, they also begin to put two words together into a simple sequence. These are

STAGE	AGE	FEATURES	COMMENTS
Pre-linguistic	Six weeks	Cooing	Babies making cooing sounds. Cooing sounds are made to show pleasure. These early sounds are different to those made later on mainly because the mouth is still developing.
Babbling (Phonemic expansion)	6–9 months	Babies blend vowels and consonants together to make tuneful sounds, e.g. ba, ma, da	Babbling has been described as learning the tune before the words. The baby seems to be practising its sounds. Babies increase the number of sounds or phonemes. This is sometimes called phonemic expansion. All babies, even deaf babies, produce a wide range of sounds during this period.
Babbling (phonemic contraction)	9–10 months		Babies seem to repeat the same sounds in long strings e.g. bababababa. Babies are also learning that they can use communication skills to direct adults. They begin to point to objects that they want to show the adult
Echolalia	11-12 months	Babies babble but the range of sounds is limited	The range of sounds or phonemes that babies produce becomes more limited and reflects the phonemes used in the language that they are hearing. At this stage, it would in theory be possible to distinguish between babies who are in different language environments. At 10 months babies also understand 17 or more words.
Linguistic stage			
First words	Around 12 months	Babies repeatedly use one or more sounds which has meaning for them	The first words are often unclear and so gradually emerge. They are often one sound, but are used regularly in similar situations – for example 'ba' to mean drink and cuddle. Babbling still continues.
Holophrases	12–18 months	Toddlers start to use one word in a variety of ways	Toddlers use holophrases to make their limited vocabulary more useful for them. One word is used in several situations, but the tone of voice and the context helps the adult to understand what the toddler means. Most toddlers have a vocabulary of between 10–15 words by 18 months.
Two word utterances – telegraphic speech	18–24 months	Two words are put together to make a mini sentence	Toddlers begin to combine words to make sentences. They seem to have grasped which are the key words in a sentence – 'dada gone' or 'dada come'.
Language explosion	24–36 months	A large increase in children's vocabulary combined with increasing use of sentences	This is a period in which children's language seems to evolve rapidly. Children learn words so rapidly that it becomes hard for parents to count them! At the same time the child uses more complicated structures in their speech. Plurals and negatives begin to be used, e.g. no dogs here!

TABLE 4.4 *Stages in language development*

continued overleaf

STAGE	AGE	FEATURES	COMMENTS
	3–4 years	Sentences become longer and vocabulary continues to increase	Children are using language in a more complete way. Mistakes in grammar show that they are still absorbing the rules and sometimes misapplying them! Mistakes such as 'I wented' show that they have learnt that 'ed' makes a past tense. These type of mistakes are known 'virtuous errors'.
Fluency Fully developed speech	4-5 years	Mastered the basic skills of the language	Children have mastered the basic rules of English grammar and are fluent, although will still be making some 'virtuous' errors.

TABLE 4.4 *Stages in language development*

often two word utterances such as 'dink gone', which are in effect sentences stripped back to the essentials. This feature in toddlers' language is known as 'telegraphic', referring to the style of communication that used to be sent by telegrams. Years ago, when not everyone had a telephone, urgent communications would be sent by telegram. An operator would take down the message and it would be sent onto to its destination and then delivered. It was expensive, so people kept the length of their messages to an absolute minimum.

Key concept

Telegraphic language is the short communication style used by toddlers.

Moving towards fully developed speech

From telegraphic speech, children begin to use longer and more complex speech. The length of children's sentences increases and they begin to use questions and plurals in addition to negatives. From around three-years-of-age, most children's speech becomes intelligible to people who are not familiar with the child, although all children will have some sounds that they find hard to pronounce. This is a good reminder that

language development is linked partly to maturation. Children's tongues, jaws and teeth need to develop in order to allow them to clearly make all the sound that they will need. The use of 'w' instead of 'r' in the word rabbit is a good example of this, as some children do not master this sound until they are seven years old.

The correct use of grammar takes a while for children to learn. This is learnt naturally and in context. Roger Brown, the famous linguist, suggests that one of the reasons why children make interesting mistakes such as 'tooked' or 'swimmed' when they will not have heard this from adults is that they are in the process of experimenting with grammar. He dubbed these types of mistakes as 'virtuous errors', as children are simply trying to apply rules that they have instinctively learnt to all verbs. Virtuous errors continue to appear in children's speech even after the age of six or seven years, by which time mostly their speech will be fluent. This does not mean to say that their language will not develop further. Children will continue to learn new vocabulary and will hopefully also become increasingly aware of how their speech and language affects others.

Key concept

Virtuous errors are the result of children experimenting with grammar.

The social dimension of language

Research looking at the way that parents and carers talk to babies is very interesting. It would seem that whilst babies are primed to learn language, parents may also instinctively know how to help them. The way in which adults communicate with babies and toddlers has been called 'motherese' or 'parentese'. Parentese helps babies to learn about communication but also gives them clues about the specific meanings of words. For example, a parent may point to a cat and then say to the baby 'look at the cat. There's a cat. Look at the cat'.

Below is a list of some of the ways in which you might see adults communicate with babies:

* high levels of facial expression e.g. exaggerated smiles, eye contact

* close physical contact – cuddles, bouncing

* drawing a baby's attention to objects e.g. pointing out of the window

* higher pitched voice

* emphasis on key words in sentences

* simplified sentences

* repetition of key words.

Most parents and adults tend to be good at responding to children and pitching their language at a level that a child can understand. Conversations between adults and young children often concentrate on events and objects that are in the here and now and some adults are good at helping children to make connections through speech; for example, 'that cat is like the one Auntie Margaret has. Auntie Margaret's cat has stripes. This cat has stripes too'. This is important in helping children to learn to use language to remember and to also to draw children's attention to particular features such as in the example above 'stripes'.

Social factors

The social dimension that is needed to promote language also means that some children for whom language use is restricted will be disadvantaged. Children who spend time with responsive adults, who spend time interacting with them, generally score higher in simple cognitive tests.

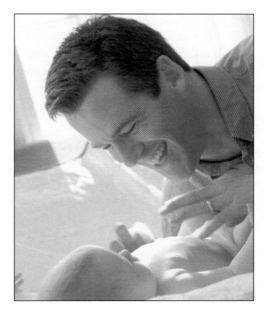

How adults communicate with babies

> **Consider this**
>
> Aysel is three-years-old. She talks using telegraphic speech. Her mother can understand her, but other people find it difficult. Aysel also has twin sisters who are one-year-old. Aysel's mother finds it difficult to spend time with her as her other daughters are very demanding and she gets very tired.
>
> 1. Discuss the level of Aysel's language development.
>
> 2. Give two reasons why Aysel's language may be delayed.
>
> 3. Explain ways in which adults normally help children to develop language.
>
> 4. What effect might Aysel's language have on her overall development?

Social and emotional development

For many years, the focus for caring for young children was on meeting their physical needs including nappy changing, bathing and feeding. Caring for young children literally meant attending to their physical needs. Now we know that babies and young children also need to build relationships in their earliest years and that there are serious consequences when children's emotional needs have not been met in this respect or where the relationship for some reason has come to an end. Attachment theories look at the way in which children need to develop a special bond or attachment with their parents and also the people who care for them.

Attachment as a process

Psychologists have studied the ways in which babies form early attachments. It is generally accepted that unlike geese that immediately start to follow the first creature they see after hatching, babies gradually form attachments. There seems to be a general pattern to the way in which children develop attachments and Table 4.5 summarises the stages.

Is attachment instinctive?

There is some support which suggests that the need for babies to form attachments is instinctive. Most newborn babies are quick to recognise the smell and voice of their mothers and even fathers. Babies are also quick to work out familiar faces.

It is interesting to see that around the time that babies begin to become mobile they also develop a fear of strangers. There is some speculation as to whether this is a device to prevent babies from straying too far from their parents.

Attachment behaviour

There are four broad indicators that babies and children might show which indicate that a child has made an attachment to a parent or carer.

* actively seeking to be near the other person
* crying or showing visible distress when that person leaves, or for babies is no longer visible
* showing joy or relief when that person appears

AGE	STAGE	FEATURES
6 weeks – 3 months		Babies begin to be attracted to human faces and voices. First smiles begin at around the age of six weeks.
3 months – 7/8 months	Indiscriminate attachments	Babies learn to distinguish between faces showing obvious pleasure when they recognise familiar faces. They are happy to be handled by strangers, preferring to be in human company rather than left alone – hence the term indiscriminate attachments.
7/8 months	Specific attachments	At around 7 or 8 months of age, babies begin to miss key people in their lives and show signs of distress – for example crying when they leave the room. Most babies also seem to have developed one particularly strong attachment – often to the mother. Babies also show a wariness of strangers even when in the presence of their 'key people'. This wariness may quickly develop into fear, if the stranger makes some form of direct contact with the baby – for example by touching them.
From 8 months	Multiple attachments	After making specific attachments, babies then go on to form multiple attachments. This is an important part of their socialisation process.

TABLE 4.5 *Stages in attachment*

＊ acute awareness of that person's presence – for example, looking up at them from time to time, responding to their voices, following their movements.

What happens when children are separated from their main attachments

The term separation anxiety is used to describe the behaviours that babies and children show when they are separated from their main attachments even for short periods of time; for example, a parent might leave the room or a child might start in nursery. Separation anxiety can be seen in most babies from around the age of seven months. Up until this point, most babies are quite content to be left with someone that they do not know. After the age of seven or eight months, the majority of babies begin to show clearly that they want to stay near or with their main attachment by crying or only settling when they are with that person. Separation anxiety reaches a peak at around 12–15 months of age but does not fade away until children reach the age of three years or so. For some children with poor experiences of leaving their main carer, separation anxiety may last for longer and they may for example cry when they start school.

Key concept

Separation anxiety Separation anxiety describes the behaviours babies and children show when apart from their main attachment, even for a short term.

John Bowlby outlined three distinct stages in separation anxiety and noted that as the length of separation grew, it affected the way in which children reacted (see Table 4.6). Where children reached the final stage of separation anxiety, they had literally broken off the relationship as a way of coping. He called this final phase 'detachment'.

Consequences of short separation

Most babies and young children will experience being left in the care of someone other than their

STAGE	FEATURES
Protest	Children may cry, struggle to escape, kick and show anger.
Despair	Children show calmer behaviour almost as though they have accepted the separation. They may be withdrawn and sad. Comfort behaviour such as thumb sucking or rocking may be shown.
Detach-ment	Children may appear to be 'over' the separation and start to join in activities. The child is actually coping by trying to 'forget' the relationship – hence the title detachment. The effects of detachment may be longer lasting as the child may have learnt not to trust people they care for.

TABLE 4.6 *Three stages in separation anxiety (outlined by John Bowlby)*

parents or main carers, especially as increasing numbers of women return to work following the birth of their children. Leaving their babies and toddlers can be hard for mothers, as they too have an attachment with their children. Happily, it is now known that babies and toddlers can form surrogate attachments who will give them temporary security whilst their parents or main carers are not with them. Most nurseries and pre-schools therefore operate a system using keyworkers. Where babies and young children are put into situations where they can make an alternative attachment, it is thought that this can mitigate the effects of separation anxiety.

Key concept

Keyworkers are designated people within a nursery or pre-school who spend time getting to know the child and developing a close relationship with them.

Consequences of long-term separation

The effects on children who have been separated or 'deprived' of their main attachment can be quite significant. The death of a parent, a parent leaving the family home or a child being taken into foster care are examples of ways in which children might experience long-term separation. It was through researching the case histories of juvenile delinquents that Bowlby was first alerted to the link between maternal deprivation and later anti-social behaviour. One of the long lasting consequences for children who have been separated from a significant person in their lives at an early age appears to be their lack of trust and inability to 'give' themselves completely to new relationships.

This can mean that in adult life, they find it difficult to commit to relationships. Long-term separation can also affect the way in which children go on to learn the skills of empathy and develop a 'conscience'. It is important here to recognise that not all children who have experienced a long-term separation and who have detached from a main carer will be affected in the same way. Other supportive family members who act as a long-term surrogate can make significant differences; for example, a grandparent may bring up a child who has been left. It is also known that children who have experienced traumatic separations need to be given opportunities to talk about their feelings in order that they can be helped.

Self-concept and self-esteem

The way we think about ourselves can influence our feelings, behaviour and also relationships with others. The development of self-concept in children is now given more attention for these reasons.

The development of self-concept

Who are we? What are we like? These are fundamental questions for children, almost like being able to place oneself on a map. In some ways, the development of self-concept is the process by which we gather information about ourselves. The development of self-concept is important because it is closely linked with self-esteem. It is useful to understand the difference between the terms used when talking about self-concept.

> ### Key concepts
>
> *Self-concept* is our vision of our whole selves, which includes our self-esteem, our self-image and our ideal self.
>
> *Self-image* or self-identity is the way in which we define ourselves – who we are, where we live, our gender, and so on.
>
> *Ideal self* is our view of what we would like to be.
>
> *Self-esteem* is also referred to as self-confidence. Once we have developed a self-image and an ideal self, we then judge ourselves – how close are we to being the person we want to be? This judgment either gives us a high self-esteem or a low self-esteem.

Developing self-image

Children gradually develop self-image. The first step for children is to be able to recognise themselves. A well-known test to see if children can recognise themselves is to put a touch of red lipstick on a baby's nose and then put the baby in front of the mirror. A child who is beginning to recognise themselves will touch their nose, rather than the nose in the reflection. Most babies do this by the time they are 21 months old.

Looking glass effect

One of the ways in which we might develop a self-image is by considering the reactions of others to us. This established theory was put forward by Charles Cooley who suggested that in order to for us to know what we are like we need to see how others react to us. This theory is particularly important for adults to consider, as it means that we must be positive towards children so they are able to see themselves positively.

Symbolic interactionalism

A slightly different approach was taken by Herbert Mead (1934) who suggested that we developed self-image as a result of interacting with others and that role play was an important part of this process for children. Mead suggested that children's role play allowed them to understand different points of view. This would suggest that the home corner play is particularly valuable for young children.

How self-esteem and self-image are linked

Once we have established what we think we are like – our perceptions of ourselves – we then consider whether we are happy with the result! Those people with a high self-esteem will be reasonably happy about their self-image, whereas those with a low self-esteem feel that they are not 'measuring up'. This means that self-esteem and self-image are linked together.

It is always fascinating to discover that people who we might feel have everything may actually have quite low self-esteem. How can this happen?

The process of how we come to make our judgments has been researched. There seems to be three main factors that affect this process which carries on through our lives. These are:

* reaction of others to us
* comparison to others
* ideal self-image.

Reaction of others

This is a combination of the looking glass effect. Children may listen to what their parents say about them or notice how carers talk and treat them. If children perceive that they are wanted, liked and loved they will have positive self-regard. If they are constantly criticised they will come to the conclusion that they are not good enough or naughty. Children may also link performance to praise in believing that they must always achieve if they are going to be liked or loved by their parents and carers.

We also notice the reaction of others to our achievements. If we are good at a skill that is valued, we are likely to feel positive; but if we are good at a skill that others do not value, it does not become a positive part of our self-image. This becomes an issue particularly when children reach school age; for example, a boy who is an excellent dancer will not necessarily have a high self-esteem if dancing is not valued by his friends and peers.

Comparison to others

As children become older, they begin to compare themselves to others. They may notice that they are not running as fast as others in their class or that they cannot read as fluently. The process of comparison helps children to work out 'their place' but it can also lead children to feel that they are not as good as others. As adults we continue to compare ourselves to others.

Students may consider their essay marks, home owners may look at their neighbour's new kitchen, and so on. It is interesting to note that sometimes children who are doing well at school may still have low self-esteem, simply because they are comparing themselves to their friends who they may perceive to be doing better. On the other hand, children who receive praise and feel that they are achieving well in school, may have a higher self-esteem.

Ideal self

As part of the process in developing our self-esteem, we seem to judge ourselves according to our own ideal-self. This means that although someone may be attractive and intelligent, that individual may not necessarily have high self-esteem. They may still not match their ideal. Research by Susan Harter (1987) seemed to indicate that a child's level of self-esteem is a product of two judgments – what they think they are like and what they would like to be (their ideal self). Where there is a great difference between the self-image and ideal self, children have low self-esteem.

Effects of low self-esteem and poor self-image

How confident children feel can affect their achievement. Children who do not believe that they are 'good' readers or are good at maths may quickly learn to avoid situations in which they believe that they might fail. This can lead to situations whereby they do not put in the necessary practice or effort. This in turn affects their results. Sadly, this can become a vicious circle, as their poor performance serves to confirm and consolidate their self-image. Children's self-image can also be a root cause of some unwanted behaviours. Children, for example, who are constantly told that they are 'naughty' can begin to believe that their behaviour is a part of them. This means that they may not feel that they can control their behaviour and may actually learn to gain attention from acts of unwanted behaviour.

Pro-social behaviour

Pro-social behaviour is the type of behaviour that we tend to encourage in young children, such as, for example, comforting another child or sharing equipment. As with other areas of child development, there is some discussion as to whether nature or nurture is responsible for pro-social behaviours.

Is pro-social behaviour instinctive?

It is a commonly held belief amongst some psychologists and social scientists that pure altruistic behaviour (e.g. helping others for no obvious gain) does not exist. They believe that all acts of pro-social behaviour are linked to a greater human instinct to preserve our species. Thus a person who jumps into the sea to save a child, is reacting to an instinct which is to save the young. Pro-social behaviours do after all help us to survive as humans who live together and need each other in order to survive.

Pro-social behaviours are learnt – social learning theory

Alongside theories that pro-social behaviours are instinctive, there is also some belief that they can be learnt. The social learning theory suggests that children who observe significant adults and other children showing pro-social behaviours are more likely to copy and learn them. This theory is based on the idea that children observe and model themselves on others. As well as the social learning theory, pro-social behaviours might also be learnt in situations in which children have been rewarded in some way. A group of children might be praised because they have helped another child who has fallen in the playground. The praise acts as a reward or positive reinforcement and so encourages children to repeat the same types of behaviour. This theory is known as 'operant conditioning'.

Anti-social behaviour

All children at times show behaviours that are unwanted. Sometimes these behaviours are linked to children's stage of development; for example, many two-year-olds bite others and many children under three years-of-age find it hard to play cooperatively and share.

Reasons for children who show anti-social behaviour that is not connected to their stage of development can be complex. In some cases, they can be linked to the child's self-image. Other times, anti-social behaviour is linked to a child's inability to empathise with others. This can be a result of feeling insecure and in some cases is linked to early difficulties in making attachments.

There is also some research that some types of anti-social behaviour such as swearing and aggression can be learnt. Children may copy behaviours that they have seen; for example, a child who has an older sibling who hits him or her may begin to hit other children. This is the social learning theory at work, which we looked at earlier in the context of pro-social behaviour (see above).

Children can also learn to show anti-social behaviours in order to gain attention or, in the case of older children, status amongst peers. The theory of operant conditioning comes into play here. By hitting another child or shouting, a child may get immediate adult attention or sometimes admiration from peers. For children who are desperate to gain attention, this acts as a reward or positive reinforcement, thereby encouraging them to repeat the anti-social behaviours. Many approaches to guiding children's behaviour now caution against giving children attention when they show anti-social behaviour for this reason.

Developing relationships

Whilst babies and toddlers are extremely reliant on their parents and main carers, children gradually become aware of other children. This is a process

DEVELOPMENT OF RELATIONSHIPS	
0-2 years	Children are attached to the parents and main care givers, but in their second year begin to notice other children although are not interested in making contact or playing.
2–3 years	This age group begins to be increasingly interested in other children and will play alongside each other. They will for example notice another child and want to join them, even though they will not interact or actively play with them.
3-5 years	From three years onwards, children begin to have favourite playmates, which tend to be linked to play activities that are enjoyed by the child.
5-8 years	Children actively look to be with other children and have stable friendships. These are often same-sex friendships. Shared play interests are often the reason behind friendships.
8-11 years	Friendships are based on compatibility. Same-sex friendships are stronger and there are gender differences in the group size. Girls tend to meet in stable pairs or small groups, whilst boys' friendships are more fluid and they gather in larger groups.

TABLE 4.7 *Development of relationships*

that is linked to language, cognitive skills and also experience. From around the age of three years, children begin to be more interested in other children and by five or six-years-of-age, friendships are very important to children. Not having friends becomes a problem and can affect children's self-esteem. Children who show pro-social behaviour such as thoughtfulness and are gentle are more likely to find making friends easier. Children also seem attracted to others who smile and are confident. Table 4.7 shows the ways in which relationships are developed throughout infancy and childhood.

Consider this

Beth is finding it hard to learn to read. She has an older sister who is good at reading and who constantly tells Beth that she is on baby books. Beth's mum is keen for Beth to read and keeps correcting her when she makes a mistake. She sometimes gets cross with Beth, especially if Beth is not concentrating. Beth is now beginning to refuse to look at books at home.

1. How might this situation affect Beth's self-image and self-esteem?

2. Explain why Beth is refusing to read at home.

3. How might this situation affect Beth's reading in the longer term?

Summary

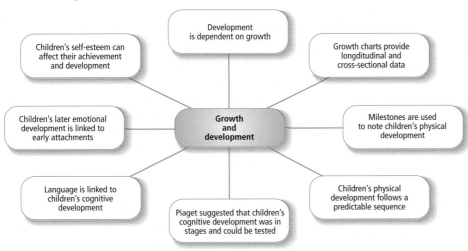

Growth and development

- Development is dependent on growth
- Growth charts provide longditudinal and cross-sectional data
- Children's self-esteem can affect their achievement and development
- Milestones are used to note children's physical development
- Children's later emotional development is linked to early attachments
- Language is linked to children's cognitive development
- Piaget suggested that children's cognitive development was in stages and could be tested
- Children's physical development follows a predictable sequence

FIGURE 4.8 *Section 4.1 summary*

4.2 Factors affecting development

For years, educators and psychologists have been interested in why children can be so different even at the same age. It is now recognised that there are many important factors that can affect children's development. Some are linked to the environment and experiences that a child has, whilst others are biological such as the colour of eyes or growth. The extent to which children are influenced by either their environment or instinctive and biological factors is sometimes called the *nature v nurture* debate. Today it is recognised that both are important and are interrelated i.e. a child might be born with a pre-disposition to asthma, but the asthma is triggered by living in damp housing.

Social factors influencing development (nurture)

Social class

There are many interesting statistics that look at the social class of parents in relation to their children's academic performance. Generally, children from middle and upper class backgrounds are more likely to achieve at school and go onto take degrees. It is important that whilst understanding that social and economic backgrounds can be significant, there are plenty of examples of children from working class families who perform extremely well academically. The statistics which show that children from middle and upper class backgrounds are favoured by the education system has meant that the government is currently looking at ways to help children from low-income families.

Some of the benefits for children from higher socio-economic groups are outlined in Table 4.8.

Parenting

Whilst social class is an important factor, parenting appears to be equally or even more important in children's early years.

Attachment

The way parents feel about their children and form a relationship with them in the first years is important. Babies need to have developed strong attachments in order to promote healthy social and emotional development. Where strong attachments are made, babies and toddlers are less likely to show demanding behaviour such as clinginess, as

BENEFITS	REASONS
Higher standard of education and care	✳ Parents may understand the education system and know how to help their children ✳ Parents may be able to afford housing in areas where schools are performing well ✳ Parents may choose to send their children to private schools where teacher–child ratios are more favourable or use tutors to coach them in particular areas ✳ Parents may choose childcare where staff have higher levels of
High parental expectations	✳ Parents who have been well educated are more likely to have high expectations for their children
Better access to provision and stimulation	✳ Parents are able to provide better housing and diet for their children. This can reduce the risk of infections and time off from schools. ✳ Parents are able to provide toys and equipment for their children to stimulate play and to build their all-round development ✳ Parents may have access to transport to take their children to enriching activities such as sport, music and dance

TABLE 4.8 *Some of the benefits for children who are from high socio-economic groups*

they are likely to feel more confident. In the longer term children who have strong attachments are likely to have high self-esteem and be more confident. Whilst early attachments are important, children need the attachment to continue.

Factors affecting attachment

There are many reasons why the attachment process might not go smoothly. Figure 4.9 outlines some common reasons, although those working with children and their families are careful not to stereotype and to see each child and family as individual cases.

Parental approval and interaction

Throughout childhood, relationships with parents are important. Parents who are able to provide unconditional love give children a secure base, which helps them to feel confident. Children with confidence and high self-esteem are more likely to try out new skills and be ready to persevere rather than believe that they are simply 'not good' at a skill.

As well as the emotional security that a warm relationship with a parent brings, children also benefit in other ways. Good interaction between parent and child can help young children's language development. Parents who are able to expand children's statements and also encourage their children to think and problem solve as they play will contribute to their children's cognitive development. Parents can also help their children by showing them how to interact with others. Children observe the way that adults behave towards others and can learn pro-social behaviour.

Parental expectations and interests

Parental expectations can make a difference to children's development. Parents who enjoy music

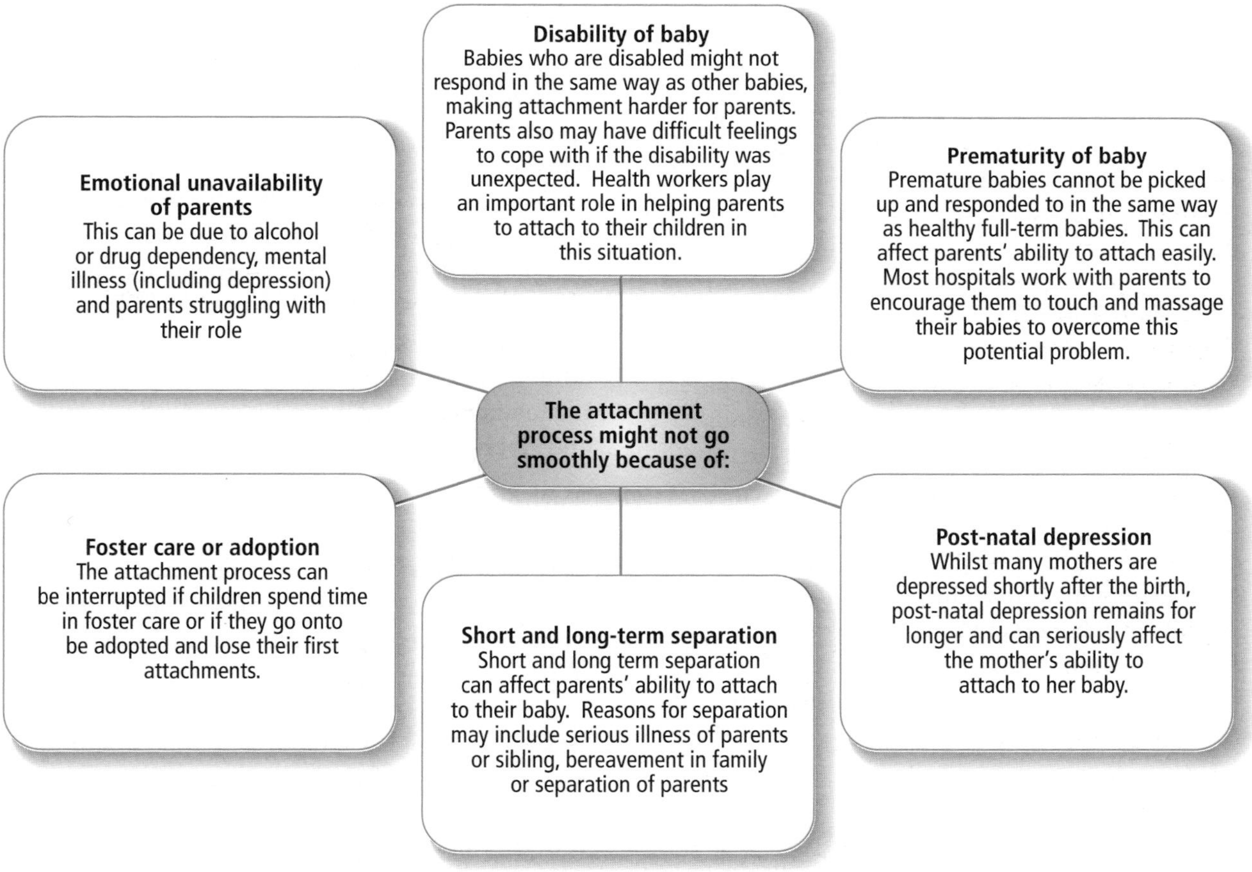

Disability of baby
Babies who are disabled might not respond in the same way as other babies, making attachment harder for parents. Parents also may have difficult feelings to cope with if the disability was unexpected. Health workers play an important role in helping parents to attach to their children in this situation.

Emotional unavailability of parents
This can be due to alcohol or drug dependency, mental illness (including depression) and parents struggling with their role

Prematurity of baby
Premature babies cannot be picked up and responded to in the same way as healthy full-term babies. This can affect parents' ability to attach easily. Most hospitals work with parents to encourage them to touch and massage their babies to overcome this potential problem.

The attachment process might not go smoothly because of:

Foster care or adoption
The attachment process can be interrupted if children spend time in foster care or if they go onto be adopted and lose their first attachments.

Short and long-term separation
Short and long term separation can affect parents' ability to attach to their baby. Reasons for separation may include serious illness of parents or sibling, bereavement in family or separation of parents

Post-natal depression
Whilst many mothers are depressed shortly after the birth, post-natal depression remains for longer and can seriously affect the mother's ability to attach to her baby.

FIGURE 4.9 *Some of the factors affecting attachment*

may foster their children's creativity by encouraging them to play instruments, whilst parents who take part in sport may provide more physical games and play. Parental expectations also make a difference in education. Parents who read are likely to encourage their children to look at books and will be keen for them to learn to read. Difficulties can arise where parental expectations are unrealistic and children feel that parental approval is based on meeting these expectations. This can lead to children having low self-esteem, as they may feel that they are not measuring up to their parents' wishes.

Parental involvement in education

The Effective Provision of Pre-school Education is a project that looks at the effect of early education on children. Whilst the project shows that attending a nursery from the age of three years, part or full time, is important to achievement, it also shows that parental involvement in children's early years is also crucial. The project also cites that parental involvement is more important even than the parents' backgrounds. Parental involvement is likely to help children feel that education is valued and also helps parents to understand the needs and strengths of their children.

Parenting styles

Three types of parenting styles have been noted. Most parents do not decide what type of a parent they wish to be unless they make a conscious decision to raise their children very differently to their own parents, i.e. a parent whose own parents were extremely authoritarian may use a permissive style. Difficulties arise where children have extremely authoritarian or permissive parents or where parenting styles keep changing. It is worth noting that whilst parents do have different parenting styles, the majority of parents care about their children and only want the best for them.

Authoritarian style

Authoritarian parents are likely to have high demands and expectations of their children's behaviour and achievement. They are likely to be dictatorial in their style and see things in black and white. Children may be expected to conform to given rules and be punished when they have broken them. Parents find it hard to explore their children's preferences, strengths and needs. They may, for example, not give children choices in whether or not they participate in an activity. Highly authoritarian parents tend to restrict the way in which their children play or only provide structured activities.

Children of highly authoritarian parents might lack confidence and be overly concerned about doing things well or getting positive feedback.

Permissive style

Permissive parents are at the other extreme. They may not set guidelines and rules for their children; for example, children may go to bed when they choose or eat only when they like. Parents may focus on the needs and particularly the happiness of the child. They may blur the distinction between parent and friend. Permissive parents are likely to be positive with their children, which results in the children having high self-esteem. The lack of boundaries, however, may mean that children when in school or other group situations can find it hard to share, cooperate with others or conform. For some children the lack of boundaries can mean that they find it difficult to learn how to manage their behaviour. This in turn can affect their ability to settle to activities or take instruction from adults. Some children take on the role of parent in the relationship and begin to organise the parents and siblings.

Authoritative parents

Authoritative parents are middle-of-the-road parents. They are keen for their children to do well, but are ready to listen and respond to their children's needs. Authoritative parents are confident enough to establish and maintain boundaries on behaviour, but are also likely to explain and negotiate them with their children. Authoritative parents are positive with their children and support them. Children of authoritative parents are more likely to be popular with other children and also cope well with the demands of nursery and school. They are also likely to have high self-esteem.

Housing

Where children live and the condition of the housing can be an important factor in children's development. Figure 4.10 shows how poor housing can affect children's overall development

Housing and education are linked. Schools in areas of poor housing are not always as valued and may not achieve the same level of results as in areas of affluent housing.

Education

Education can make a significant difference to children's development. Children are able to develop skills, use a range of equipment, play alongside other children and also become independent from their parents. The extent to which children will benefit from education can vary. It is dependent on several factors such as how well the education provision meets their learning and social needs as well as parental expectations. Other factors also include whether children develop a sense of belonging and whether they are able to attend consistently.

Children who change schools frequently, or who have significant periods of absence, can find it hard to settle in which can affect the benefits of education.

Physical development

Children benefit from larger spaces e.g. playgrounds, halls as well as equipment and varying activities. This can develop their co-ordination and gross motor skills. Children's fine motor development can be enhanced through activities such as playing with dough, paint as well as writing activities.

Intellectual development

Teaching and non-teaching staff who have been trained in child development are able to promote children's intellectual development. They may help children by providing stimulating activities such as jigsaws, junk modelling but also as they get older by introducing them to concepts such as number and shape as well as the books and skills involved in literacy.

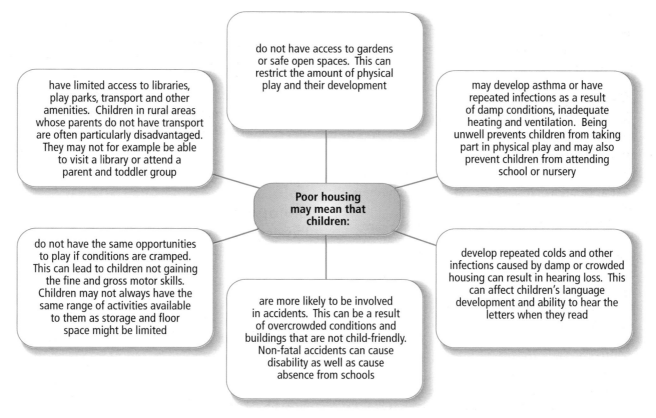

FIGURE 4.10 *How poor housing can affect children's overall development*

Children's language development can also benefit through the skilled interactions such as questions and giving children new materials and activities to talk about.

Social and emotional development

In educational settings, children learn to separate from their parents and in doing so learn to take responsibility and gain in confidence. Children also learn to mix and socialise with other children, which can promote their self-confidence and esteem. Their confidence and self-esteem can also be raised as they learn new skills such as reading, counting and writing.

Note that high self-esteem is linked to children having a positive experience in education. In situations where children are unhappy because they have not made friends, are bullied or realise that they are not achieving as well as their peers, self-esteem can be low.

Culture

The culture in which children are raised can make a difference to children's development. Culture is partly about expectations and social codes.

Physical development

In some cultures, girls may not be encouraged to take part in physical play and activities. Boys may be seen as needing more time outdoors and requiring more boisterous activities. This can mean that boys develop high levels of gross motor skills whilst girls might have fine motor skills from 'quieter' activities such as drawing, threading or playing in the home corner.

Expectations about how much time children should play can also affect physical and intellectual development. Cultures that regard play as unimportant may place more emphasis on children sitting and being taught.

Intellectual development

Expectations of the importance of learning and education can vary. Some families place great emphasis on education and will encourage their children to do homework and will take an interest in children's education. Other families might rate practical skills more highly and encourage children to gain these skills.

Some cultures place a higher value on boys gaining education whilst other cultures may consider that education and learning is 'girlish'. This can affect attitudes to learning, concentration and the type of activities children engage in; for example, whether a boy decides to read quietly in the book corner.

Children may also be learning more than one language. This can have significant benefits provided that fluency is gained in each language. Some children who begin school with an additional language may need extra support in order to build on the level of their English or their home language.

Social and emotional development

Children may be in a culture where family is important. They may spend time with family members and friends, which can help children's social and emotional development. Children who have a wider supportive network can feel secure.

Children whose home culture is a minority one can face discrimination. This can result in lower self-esteem, as they may find it harder to make friends or may be bullied.

Biological factors influencing development (nature)

Children come into the world already primed to a certain extent because of their genetic makeup or genotype. In addition, other factors such as disease, circumstances during pregnancy and birth and maturation of the body will influence children's development.

Genotype and maturation

Physical development

Children's physical development is influenced by both their genotype and also maturation processes and often accounts for the variation in which children are able to master certain skills. A good example of this is toilet training. The central nervous system has to be sufficiently developed in order for messages to be sent from the brain to the nerves. Some children are ready for toilet training at the age of 18 months whilst others will be ready at three-years-of-age. The average age for most children is around two to two-and-a-half years of age.

Intellectual/cognitive development

It is still unclear how much of children's cognitive abilities are inherited as research studies are conflicting. It is, however, known that the brain develops in response to stimulation and that it builds up pathways as a result. This accounts for the tripling in weight of a child's brain in the first year of life. As the brain grows, we can see that the way children store and interpret information also changes. This is one reason given for the common errors that young children make as they are interpreting information differently.

Social/emotional development

How much of our personalities result from the interaction of our genetic inheritance and our life experience, both of which influence our development? Brain research does show us that there are parts of the brain associated with detecting others' feelings. Scientists are also aware of chemicals in the brain which are associated with feeling happy, depressed and angry.

Disease and illness

Disease and illness can affect children's development in numerous ways depending on the severity and the duration. Whilst the odd cold will not adversely affect a child, long term absence from school or frequent bouts of hearing loss from ear infections can make a lasting difference.

Physical development

Some medical conditions, such as asthma and sickle cell disease, for example, can restrict children's physical activity. This in turn can affect children's gross motor development as they may not be able to run around and take part in vigorous physical activity. Children who are not feeling well because of a disease or treatment that they are undergoing may lack the energy to take part in physical activity.

Cognitive/intellectual development

Children who are unwell may not have the energy to concentrate on activities. Drugs for conditions such as epilepsy can make children

drowsy. Repeated absences from schools can also affect children's achievement as they miss out on vital stages. When children stay in hospital or need to stay at home, teachers are usually provided for them so that children can catch up. Children with a hearing impairment or who have a learning difficulty because of a birth injury may be slower to learn language.

Social and emotional development

Children who are often ill may miss out on friendships. They may not be able to mix with other children because of the risk of infection. They may also find it can be hard to form relationships if they are infrequently there.

Where children have a chronic medical condition or have been extremely poorly, parents and other adults might have the tendency to be overprotective. This can mean that children miss out on becoming independent which in turn can affect their self-esteem. Children's self-esteem can also be low if they feel that they are 'different' to other children and often find themselves in situations when they cannot do the same as other children, for example, sitting out during swimming lessons.

Disability

Some children may have a disability as a result of an accident, birth trauma or chromosomal difficulty. The extent to which a disability handicaps children will depend on the situation in which they find themselves and the support that they gain from parents, teachers and early years staff. Below is a list of common ways in which disability may affect a child's development.

Physical development

Children may be overprotected and not have opportunities for self-help skills.

Some disabilities can make physical movements difficult for children although sometime these difficulties can be overcome through the use of specialist equipment, for example, a standing frame to support a child who requires more strength in their legs.

Intellectual/cognitive development

Some disabilities affect children's ability to learn, concentrate and use language, for example,

Down's syndrome and autism. Other children may find that low expectations and stereotyping mean that they are not given sufficient opportunities and challenges; although parents, teachers and early years staff are more aware of this now.

Social and emotional development

Discrimination is a major factor facing children with disabilities. Access to the same level of education is sometimes difficult, although there is now legislation in place to combat this. Discrimination also means that some children might find it harder to make friends and be accepted by other children. Bullying and teasing can influence a child's self-esteem and is one reason why there are preventative bullying strategies in place in educational settings.

Children's self-esteem might also be low if children begin to feel that they are 'different' from others. Some types of disability affect children's ability to make friendships e.g. children on the autistic spectrum disorder find it hard to imagine other children's needs and feelings.

Summary

Consider this

Leman is five-years-old. Her parents are both professionals who have a high income and they live in a large house in a pleasant area. Leman is a healthy girl who has a good balanced diet and gets enough sleep each night.

Leman's parents spend plenty of time playing and talking with her and her younger brother. Leman enjoys playing in the garden and loves the climbing frame, tree house and bicycles. She loves looking at books at home and continually asks questions and is very imaginative. Leman goes to a local school which has excellent resources and teachers. She is very happy there and has made several friends. Leman's parents are confident parents who try to make sure that whilst there are boundaries, they also listen and think about their children's needs.

1. Predict how well Leman is doing at school.

2. Explain the reasons for your prediction.

3. Discuss the factors in Leman's life that are likely to contribute towards her development.

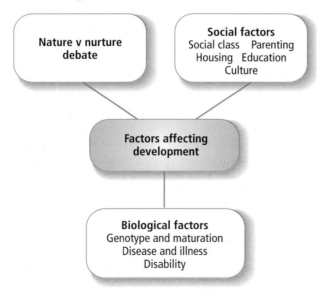

FIGURE 4.11 *Section 4.2 summary*

4.3 The importance of play

Play is considered to be an essential ingredient in children's development. It is also argued that play meets an instinctive need in children. Today, in the United Kingdom play is used as a key way in which to help children, particularly those under the age of five years, to develop skills and concepts. Play is essentially a pleasurable activity for children, so they are happy to play for hours at a time. Whilst they are playing, they are, without realising it, practising movements, social skills, and problem solving as well as learning new skills. This is why play is an effective way of helping children to learn. Structuring children's play by, for example, introducing new materials or showing them how to play a game can mean that children learn a new concept or skill without feeling under pressure. As most play activities involve several skills, children make progress in more than one area of development at a time as they play. The ways in which play contributes to individual areas of development are discussed below.

Play contributes to development

Physical development

Repeated movements and practice are needed in order for muscle strength and coordination to develop. Play motivates children to make these movements. A baby sees a rattle and is stimulated to reach out for it. A toddler wants to put teddy to bed, so works hard at wrapping him up in a blanket. A pre-school child wants to make a pretend necklace and threads beads onto a lace.

Play also builds children's physical stamina, as they are motivated to run, crawl, throw or kick balls around or use wheeled equipment such as tricycles and bicycles.

Intellectual (cognitive) development

Play has an important role in stimulating the brain as children use their senses to explore materials, toys and equipment. It also helps children to concentrate and focus their attention; for example, a baby might spend a few minutes looking at a mobile and a toddler might concentrate on building a tower with bricks. Play helps children to build ideas about what they are seeing and doing (see schemas p.152). It can help their imagination and problem solving skills. Some play activities can encourage children to use language; for example, a toddler playing with a toy telephone, older children using language to negotiate rules of a game.

Social development

Playing with others help children to learn some social skills. Early play begins with parents and carers making eye contact and holding toys; and later on, playing simple games such as peek-a-boo. Later children begin the process of learning to play with each other. This helps the development of learning to negotiate, listen and to take account of other's feelings and needs; for example, two seven-year-olds agree which game to play on the computer.

Emotional development

Children learn to express their feelings through play and also work out the meanings of what they have experienced; for example, a pre-school child might scold a doll in the home corner, imitating what she has heard adults do.

Play also helps children gain in confidence if they are organising their own activities and trying to do things for themselves. A toddler may try to snip dough using scissors and then feel pleased that he has done it by himself. A school-aged child might build a den out of fabric in the garden and show it to her friend.

Stages in social play

As children's social and language skills develop, we can see that they learn to play more cooperatively. This is a process, but it can be grouped into stages. Learning how to play with other children helps children's social and emotional development. They learn to make relationships with others, take turns and learn

AGES	STAGE	FEATURE
0–2	Solitary	Up until the age of two years, children usually play alone and explore material and toys by themselves. They may look at adults for reassurance and enjoy directed games such as peek-a-boo. They are not likely to pay much attention to other children.
2–3	Onlooker/ parallel	From about two-years-of-age, toddlers begin to notice other toddlers and they may happily play alongside each other. They do not try to play and their games and ideas are very separate. Toddlers may sometimes stand and watch others play without joining in, hence the name 'onlooker'.
3–4	Associative	From around three years of age, the pre-school child will start to play alongside other children and copy what they are doing. For example, children may both be in the role play area. One might start to cook and the other might join in.
4+	Cooperative	As children reach the age of four years, they begin to cooperate as they play. They talk more about what they are going to do and often spend time planning and agreeing with each other. A child might suggest to another that they go together and play with the train set and then talk about how they ought to set it up.

TABLE 4.9 *The social stages of play*

that others have needs too. Table 4.9 outlines the social stages of play, but it is important to recognise that the ages given are only guides as children's development can vary. Table 4.10 shows the potential benefits of different types of play.

Play types

Play can be grouped into different types, as shown in Table 4.11.

Play in different environments

The way in which children play may vary according to the environment in which they are playing. This is because some learning environments have more space than others, but also because the aims of each environment can be different. One of the differences that we might see between environments is the way in which play is organised. A distinction may be made between structured and free play, as shown in Figure 4.13.

FIGURE 4.12 *Development of children's drawings as they get older*

AGE	FEATURES OF PLAY	EXAMPLES OF TOYS AND EQUIPMENT	ROLE OF THE ADULT
0–1 years	Learning by trial and error Repeated movements at first uncontrolled and then more controlled	Rattles Baby gym Pop up toys	Interaction with baby Awareness of safety
1–2 years	Learning by trial and error Repetitive play Developing coordination and mobility reflected in play – e.g. pushing a brick trolley Talk as they are playing	Posting toys, e.g. shape sorters Push and pull toys Baby swing Brick trolleys Toy telephones	Awareness of safety Interaction with child
2–3 years	More interest in other children Learning by trial and error Pretend play starts to appear Repetitive play Children become restless and need frequent changes of toys and equipment	Mark making and paint Cuddly toys Tea sets, prams Simple jigsaw puzzles Tricycles Dough Small world play, e.g. play people	Awareness of safety Regular changes of activity Support during play, e.g. adding a new toy or playing alongside
3–5 years	Children are starting to cooperate with each other. Play becomes more complex and children begin to use symbols, i.e. drawings have meaning. Children begin to plan and negotiate their play from around 4 years Gross and fine motor skills are more coordinated	Small world play e.g. farm animals Tricycles Dressing up clothes Paint, dough, sand and water Building bricks Jigsaw puzzles Slides, swings and see-saws	Awareness of safety Supervise Show children how to use large equipment safely Encourage children to resolve their own difficulties
5–8 years	Children's play becomes more complex. Rules appear in games Children plan for play and negotiate with each other Children are more independent of adults Children show problem solving during play	Den building Painting, drawing Musical instruments Large equipment e.g. climbing frame, slides Wheeled toys including bicycles, skate boards Junior sports e.g. football, tennis	Unobtrusive supervision Provide new opportunities for children Give children independence and responsibility

TABLE 4.10 *Development of play from 0-8 years*

TYPE OF PLAY	EXAMPLES	POTENTIAL BENEFITS	0-2 YEARS	2-3 YEARS	3-5 YEARS	5-8 YEARS
Creative play	Sand Water Dough Painting Drawing/ mark making Junk modelling Collage Musical instruments	Fine motor skills Self-expression Confidence Independence Concentration Relaxation Opportunities to learn about properties of different materials Language* Cooperation* Negotiation Painting and drawing also helps children to learn about symbolic representation, e.g. that marks can have meaning.	Children of this age enjoy bath time and playing with water. Mark making begins from 18 months. Rotational patterns are common. Note: Sand, dough and paint are not usually provided for children until they are around 18 months of age and then only with supervision.	Creative play is popular and children usually have opportunities to play with all types. Repetitive play is seen, e.g. pouring, scooping. As children approach three-years-of-age, they begin to ascribe meaning to marks as they make them. Collage and junk modelling allow children to experiment with different materials.	Creative play remains popular. Children may try and combine it with pretend play e.g. dinosaurs in the sand tray or pouring 'tea' from the teapot in the water tray. Children may also play cooperatively and share materials. From four years of age, children draw recognisable pictures. Junk modelling and collage also shows representations.	Children continue to enjoy creative play, but play becomes more complex, e.g. a whole fortress is made in the sand and boats are designed for the water tray. Drawing and paintings are more skilled and representational. Towards the end of this age range, some children become conscious of their ability to draw or paint.
Pretend play	Cuddly toys Dressing up clothes Home corner Superhero play, e.g. running around the playground pretending to be superman. Small world play, e.g. farm animals, dolls houses.	Fine motor skills Self expression Independence Exploration of roles Learning about relationships Language* Cooperation*	Early pretend play often involves transporting dolls, teddies and is seen from 18 months of age onwards.	Children begin to use objects to represent items. Children may involve adults in their play e.g. give a piece of dough as a pretend cake.	Pretend play become more complex. Children are more cooperative and agree roles. Toys for small world play become more detailed and smaller. Play is more complex.	Superhero play is seen and can be influenced by television and media. Pretend play becomes more gender orientated. Boys may play more 'action games'. Some children begin to drop pretend play as they become more self-aware.

TABLE 4.11 Types of play and potential benefits

TYPE OF PLAY	EXAMPLES	POTENTIAL BENEFITS	0-2 YEARS	2-3 YEARS	3-5 YEARS	5-8 YEARS
Manipu-lative play	Building bricks Duplo Lego Jigsaw puzzles Interlinking train tracks	Fine motor skills Problem solving Language* Cooperation* Gross motor skills if equipment is on a large scale	Early manipulative play includes knocking towers of bricks down as well as trying to build them. Shape sorters and pop up toys often help to develop children's fine motor skills and problem solving.	From around two-years-of-age, children begin to build towers using bricks. They also begin to try out simple jigsaw puzzles. This type of play is usually supported by adults.	From three-years-of-age onwards, children's hand-eye coordination and confidence means that they enjoy manipulative play. They may also combine this type of play with small world play. A duplo house might have a farm animal in it.	Manipulative play becomes more complex. Toys become more detailed and often smaller e.g. technical lego. Gender differences in the choice of equipment may also be seen.
Physical play	Wheeled toys including sit and rides, tricycles, bicycles Throwing and catching Climbing frames Slides Sport	Gross motor skills Hand/foot eye coordination Balance Spatial awareness Learning concepts such as speed, distance, time, gravity Independence Confidence Cooperation*	From 18 months of age, children enjoy using simple sit and ride toys that are pushed along with their feet. They also enjoy sensations such as being helped down slides and on swings.	At around two years of age, children begin to try out simple tricycles but will not begin to pedal and still until they are around three years. They enjoy small slides and swings.	From age three years onwards children become confident at using tricycles and other wheeled toys. Play is often cooperative and might include pretend play.	Children begin to use equipment that requires more skill such as bicycles and rackets. In this age range, children may begin to show skills and preferences for certain types of play. They may also begin to take up a sport such as football or swimming.

*If children are playing together and co-operatively

TABLE 4.11 Types of play and potential benefits

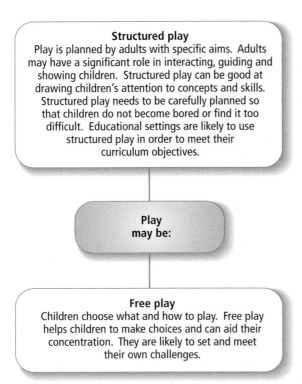

Structured play
Play is planned by adults with specific aims. Adults may have a significant role in interacting, guiding and showing children. Structured play can be good at drawing children's attention to concepts and skills. Structured play needs to be carefully planned so that children do not become bored or find it too difficult. Educational settings are likely to use structured play in order to meet their curriculum objectives.

Play may be:

Free play
Children choose what and how to play. Free play helps children to make choices and can aid their concentration. They are likely to set and meet their own challenges.

FIGURE 4.13 *How play may be organised*

Home environment

Children at home tend to be more responsible for their own play and mostly it is free play. They may have favourite toys and choose how and even when to play with them. Pretend and manipulative play are popular play types in homes. Children may also combine toys and equipment in order to make their play more fulfilling; for example, farm animals will appear in the garden tent or in the bath. Children at home also have opportunities to play by themselves unless they have a sibling that is close in age or friends visiting. This gives children opportunities to explore for themselves without the need to share or consider others. Play can sometimes be very repetitive, although this can be relaxing for children. Where children have a slightly older sibling, they may show play that is in advance for their age as they might try to copy their sibling's activities.

Physical resources

The quantity and variety of toys can vary enormously between individual children's homes.

Most homes do not have space for large-scale equipment, so physical play may be limited especially if there is no access to a garden.

Human resources

The amount of time that parents have available to supervise and interact with their children may be limited especially if parents work full time. This time can, however, be very enriching as the parent is only focusing on one or two children at a time.

Limited time also means that creative play, where paint or materials are 'messy' or very noisy, are less likely to be provided on a regular basis.

Some parents are more skilled than others at recognising the play needs of their children and so will provide toys in a more strategic way.

The type of play that children show may also reflect parents' interests especially when children become older, for example, families that enjoy sport may have children who are interested in sport.

Educational settings

When children spend time in educational settings such as schools and nurseries, play is likely to be more structured. This is because it is used to promote particular areas of development, learn skills or understand a concept. Specific activities, toys and equipment may be put out with key learning intentions in mind; for example, in a nursery the water tray may contain objects that will encourage pouring skills, whilst in a school a board game might be used to help children's maths. From around seven- years-of-age though, the amount of time 'playing' is often reduced inside classrooms, although children may enjoy less structured play at playtimes.

Physical resources

Most educational settings can provide for physical play. They may have an outdoor area such as a playground and may also have an indoor hall. This means that large apparatus such as climbing frames can be used as well as hoops, balls and skipping ropes. In nurseries, tricycles and wheeled toys are often provided, but most of these items are not generally provided in primary schools.

Educational settings are also likely to have a good range of resources and will usually aim to provide for each area of play.

One restriction on children's play will be time. Most educational settings will need to structure sessions and make sure that all children are given similar opportunities. This means that children might not be able to play at their own pace or follow their own ideas.

Human resources

Staff working in educational settings are likely to have a good knowledge of child development and the way in which it can be promoted. This means that they are able to plan for children's development and choose appropriate materials and activities. They may also be aware of children who need particular support.

Staff will also have to follow the early years or national curriculum that is appropriate for the country in which they work. The adult-child ratio in primary schools is often 1:30; this means that children may not receive individual attention and time for interaction. In nurseries, the adult–child ratios are more favourable.

Children at play

Public environments

Parks, fields and sports centres are often areas where children can play. These environments are particularly good at providing for physical play. Wide open spaces also allow children to experience a sense of freedom and to gain spatial awareness. They also help children to feel independent and devise their own challenges. Play areas are particularly popular with children as they can use a variety of large equipment that may not be available at home or in other settings. Children gain from play parks as they can socialise with other children, but also gain in confidence as they develop and are able to do things for themselves.

Physical resources

Most play parks offer a range of physical activities that will promote children's balance and spatial awareness whilst also encouraging gross motor movements such as climbing. Most play parks are designed to help children develop skills in safety, whilst presenting children with some challenges. Parks often have paths which children can use with wheeled toys such as tricycles, bicycles and skate boards.

The quality of public environments can vary enormously. In some areas, equipment is new, paths are maintained and areas are fenced in to keep children safe.

Human resources

Most public environments do not have dedicated staff who supervise and work with children unless children are taking part in some kind of organised activity. Parents often have to take responsibility for children's welfare and safety. This means that the amount of time that children spend in these areas can be very variable. Ease of access, time and parking can be factors that determine whether or not parents take their children into these environments.

Care settings

Care settings that look after children often provide a range of toys and equipment for them. Care settings include childminders, parent-and-toddler groups, crêches as well as hospitals. Many care settings will provide for each type of play, although some care settings will not have outdoor areas and will find it hard to provide for physical play. The type of play that takes place in many care settings is a balance between structured play and free play. Some activities may be planned to help children to develop certain skills, whilst children may also be free to play in ways of their own choosing.

Physical resources

The quantity and quality of toys and equipment in care settings can be variable. Where care settings share their facilities e.g. a church hall might be used to for a parent and toddler group, storage can be a problem.

Human resources

Adult-child ratios can be very good in care settings. Staff are likely to have a knowledge of child development and will plan for areas of child development. In hospitals some staff may work on particular aspects of a child's development such as physical movement.

Consider this

Some parents have asked you to choose some new toys and equipment for their child who is two years old. Their budget is £150. They have some storage indoors and they also have a small fenced garden.

1. Choose a range of toys that will meet this child's developmental needs.

2. Produce a list complete with prices.

3. Discuss the reasons for your choice of toys and equipment including the developmental benefits to the child.

Summary

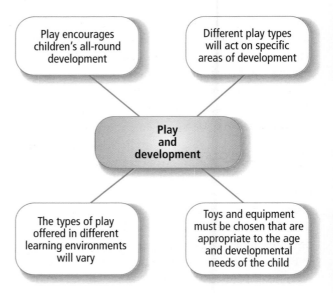

FIGURE 4.14 *Section 4.3 summary*

4.4 Health and safety

Keeping children safe is a major role for adults who work with children. Young children, particularly toddlers and babies, are vulnerable. This is because developmentally they are impulsive and will not have the ability to think through the consequences of their actions. It is therefore the role of the adult to provide complete protection and to be aware of the risks involved in different situations so that they can manage the children.

Statistics relating to accidents

> ### ✳ DID YOU KNOW?
>
> ✳ Accidental injury is the commonest cause of death in children over one-year-old.
>
> ✳ Children aged 0–4 years are the most at risk of an accident in the home.
>
> ✳ Older children are likely to have accidents outside of the home, reflecting where they spend more of their time.
>
> ✳ 2 million children under the age of 15 years are involved in reported accidents each year. Half of these accidents will happen at home.
>
> ✳ Boys are twice as likely to have accidents as girls.
>
> ✳ In 2002 320 children died in the UK as a result of accidents.
>
> ✳ More accidents occur late afternoon, early evening, weekends, summer and school holidays.
>
> ✳ Many accidents go unreported as they may not require medical attention.
>
> ✳ Children from lower income families are more at risk of accidents. Poor standards of housing, cramped living conditions and difficulties in affording safety equipment are thought to be contributing factors.

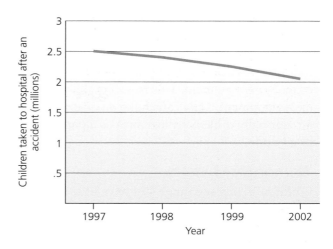

FIGURE 4.15 *Number of children taken to hospital after an accident each year*

Types of accidents

Some common types of accidents are shown in Figure 4.16.

FIGURE 4.16 *Common types of accidents*

0–18 months

Accidents are the commonest cause of death in children over one year of age. Adults who work with children in this age range have to constantly supervise and be aware of objects in the environment that may present hazards as well as the child's developmental stage.

Babies and toddlers can be determined to reach, walk or even climb objects that they have noticed and have no sense of danger. Babies and toddlers will also put things in their mouths in order to explore them. This is part of their stage of development. They can choke on objects that are normally quite harmless such as a paper clip or a button.

18 months–3 years

Children in this age range still have little sense of danger and need careful supervision. Their physical and thinking skills have developed so they are able to remain focused and think about how to get what they want. They also copy and notice what adults do. A two-year-old might climb onto a chair to reach a cupboard where he has seen biscuits put away by adults.

3 years–5 years

Children are beginning to play in a more physical way and are also keen to explore. Falls are common in this age range as children may fall off tricycles or off play equipment. Boys are twice as likely to have accidents as girls, partly because they are more likely to engage in more physical activities. Adults must provide good supervision even when children appear to be playing cooperatively.

5 years +

Older children begin to be more aware of safety, but still need supervision and adults to look out for hazards. They are likely to try things out to impress other children or simply be impulsive. Boys particularly have more accidents because they take more risks. Older children are also likely to want to try out activities that they have seen adults do, such as use matches, or try out stunts that they have seen on television.

Safety equipment

A range of safety equipment is available to help prevent accidents both indoors and outdoors. Using safety equipment can help to prevent accidents, but it is important to stress that safety equipment alone is not a substitute for careful adult supervision.

Table 4.12 outlines some key pieces of equipment commonly used in a variety of settings to protect children under the age of five years.

It is important to remember that:

* safety equipment must be used according to manufacturer's instructions

* the age, weight and height of a child have to be taken into consideration for many types of safety equipment such as car seats, highchairs and harnesses

* safety equipment must be regularly checked to ensure that it is still effective, e.g. reins are not frayed

* safety equipment is not a substitute for adult supervision.

FIGURE 4.17 *Where's Harry?*

Promoting safety in different contexts

The environment in which children has a significant effect on the type of accidents that children have.

The home

Most accidents involving children under seven years of age occur in the home. Supervision and

TYPE OF EQUIPMENT	REASON	HOW TO USE
Harnesses and reins	To prevent children from falling out of pushchairs, highchairs To prevent children from running into the road or straying	* Should be a snug fit * Make sure that you can release babies and toddlers easily when they are being fed in case they choke
Play pens	To keep mobile babies in a safe environment for a short period	* Do not use for long periods * Are not a substitute for adult supervision * Must be suitable for the age and stage of baby
Socket covers	To prevent children from poking electric sockets	* Must be consistently used
Corner covers	To prevent toddlers from catching their heads or eyes on furniture	* It is always better to remove unsuitable furniture
Drawer and cupboard catches Window catches	These prevent children from opening drawers, cupboards and windows	* It is always better to make sure that children are not allowed in areas where there are dangerous items such as chemicals * Some catches can weaken over time and so are not completely childproof
Safety gates	To prevent toddlers and young children from falling down stairs or having access to certain areas, e.g. kitchen	* Adults must use them consistently * Check that they are securely in position
Cycle helmets Protective clothing	To prevent serious head injuries and cuts if children fall off bikes and other wheeled toys	* Must be consistently used

TABLE 4.12 *Key equipment commonly used to protect children under the age of 5 years*

the constant use of safety equipment is often a problem for parents. Children of different ages also pose challenges. Toys and equipment that are suitable for an older child might be hazardous for a baby or toddler. Parents may also find it hard to supervise several children at once.

Transporting children

Many accidents occur when children are moving from one place to another. Road accidents account for the largest numbers of fatalities and serious injuries. In 2002 33,000 children were involved in road accidents.

Pushchairs

Pushchairs should be maintained and the brakes checked. They need to be correct for the height and weight of the child. Children should be strapped in securely at all times. Older children should not be encouraged to stand on the back of the pushchair or pram unless this is part of the design, as there is a danger that the pushchair might topple over or parts might collapse from metal fatigue.

Walking with children

Toddlers and young children who can walk should be put on reins or harnesses. They should

AREAS OF THE HOME	HAZARDS	PREVENTATIVE STRATEGIES
Kitchen/ dining room	Cleaning products Hot liquids and food Cooker, kettle Knives Tumble dryer Freezer Highchair Gas and open fires	Keep young children out of the kitchen, e.g. safety gate Use play pen with babies Keep cleaning products out of reach or in a locked cupboard Use a pan guard on a cooker Use safety catches on drawers containing knives Keep floor areas clear of toys Supervise older children as they cook Use catches on freezers Do not leave babies and toddlers unattended in high chair Be wary of toddlers who might try and climb into a highchair and topple it over Strap babies and toddlers in highchairs securely Do not leave babies, toddlers and young children alone with food or drink in case they choke or have an allergic reaction Make sure that gas and open fires have fireguards to prevent burns
Bedroom	Sudden Infant Death Syndrome (cot death) Suffocation Falls	Make sure latest guidelines to prevent Sudden Infant Death Syndrome are followed. These currently include placing babies down to sleep with their feet touching the foot of the cot and not using pillows or duvets Make sure that toys in the room are suitable for the age range Check that clothing does not have ribbons or ties or anything that is loose which could cause strangulation or suffocation Make sure that windows are locked
Bathroom	Medicines Cleaning products Water	Do not leave children unattended in the bath or shower Use a bath mat to avoid falls in shower and bath Check temperature of water to avoid scalds. Run cold water into a bath before hot water Keep medicines out of reach and in a locked cupboard Keep cleaning products out of reach and in a locked cupboard Do not allow children to play in bathroom
Stairs	Toys and objects	Use a stair gate at the top and bottom to prevent babies and toddlers from falling Keep stairs clear of objects Do not allow children to play on stairs
Garden	Garden ponds Paddling pool Garden tools Dog mess Poisonous plants Steps Canes or sticks	Supervise children as they play Give clear guidelines for older children as to what they can do Keep garden tools locked away Fence off garden pond Constant supervision if paddling pool is out Dig out poisonous plants or fence around them Put safety rail around steps or help children Put away canes or sticks or give strict guidelines for the way in which older children can play with them

TABLE 4.13 *Hazards in the home and strategies to prevent accidents* continued

AREAS OF THE HOME	HAZARDS	PREVENTATIVE STRATEGIES
General	Electrical appliances Electric sockets Lighters, matches Glass doors Furniture Iron Toys Windows and balconies Plastic bags	Use plug covers to prevent young children from poking their fingers in sockets Do not use iron when young children are around or leave it out Keep lighters and matches out of reach. Avoid using when children can watch Use covers on corners of furniture to prevent toddlers from hitting their heads Keep floor areas tidy and clean. Teach children to tidy away Replace glass with safety glass. Use plastic covering if this is not possible. Use wedges to avoid door being slammed Make sure that toys are clean and age appropriate. Check that they conform to European standards of manufacture Use window locks or block the window to restrict opening. Lock balcony and keep key out of reach Make sure that carrier bags or plastic bags are kept out of reach of young children. Teach older children about why they are dangerous.

TABLE 4.13 *Hazards in the home and strategies to prevent accidents*

be given clear instructions as they walk and be kept in away from the kerb.

Car journeys

Young children must be put in a car seat that is correct for their age/weight. Front seats should only be used with young babies and the air bags in the car must be turned off. Car booster seats should be used until the age of 11, when children can sit comfortably with the seat belt across their chest. Food and drinks should not be given to a child during the journey unless there is a free adult in the car because of the risk of choking.

Cycling

Children on cycles need to wear cycle helmets wherever they are. Young children should not cycle on the roads. It is advisable for young people who want to cycle on the roads to be trained in road safety. Cycles must be properly maintained and young people must wear reflective clothing and use lights on the cycles.

Play areas

Most play areas have been designed with children's safety in mind. This does not make them a risk-free zone. Adult supervision is still necessary. Older children and young people can also be involved in sports injuries.

It is important to:

* check that play areas are free of dog's mess, as this can contain the toxacara worm which if ingested can cause blindness
* wash children's hands after playing outdoors and before eating or drinking
* check that there are no obvious hazards such as broken glass, syringes or overflowing bins that might attract wasps in the summer
* make sure that children use the equipment in the way it has been designed
* make sure that children are using equipment that is correct for their age/height
* Teach children to be aware of other children and to wait their turn
* do not leave young children unattended and teach older children not to leave with strangers
* make sure that children wear cycle helmets when using bicycles, tricycles, skateboards and roller blades
* teach children rules of games and intervene if games are becoming heated or aggressive
* show children how to use sports equipment safely.

Care settings

Care settings such as nurseries, pre-schools, crêches and hospitals cater for many children at a time. Working with groups of children requires good organisation, supervision and strong awareness of health and safety. Some of the health and safety prevention strategies are the same as in children's homes, but certain activities and areas of care settings need specific attention.

AREA	HAZARD	GOOD PRACTICE
Feeding	Choking Allergic reaction Falls from highchairs Infection Burning and scalds	Adult-child ratio should be high to ensure that children are supervised and can react if children choke Staff have to be aware which children have food allergies Harnesses should be used with highchairs. Children should not be left unattended Good hand washing and food hygiene procedures required Food and drink to be checked for temperature before being served to children
Nappy changing	Falls Infection	Nappy changing should take place where the danger of babies or toddlers rolling is minimised Hand washing and correct disposal of human waste is essential to avoid infections
Nap time	Sudden Infant Death Syndrome (cot death) Falls Suffocation	Sleeping babies and toddlers should be monitored Latest advice to prevent Sudden Infant Death Syndrome should be followed Sides of cots should be securely fastened Age-appropriate beds Avoid over heating rooms Pillows and soft toys should not be given to babies and toddlers
Outdoor play	Falls Collisions	Good adult supervision Tricycles, bicycles should be age and stage appropriate Cycle helmets should be provided Children should be taught to wait their turn Sufficient space should be provided for children to use wheeled toys Toddlers may need separate times from three and four-year-olds to play
Doors and fencing	Children may escape	Good supervision and also systems such as electric doors Fencing to be checked outdoors
Kitchen	Cuts from knives Poisoning Scalds and burning	Safety gates to prevent children from gaining access Cleaning products to be locked away
Toilets	Drowning	Good supervision when children are using toilets Systems in place to know which children are using the toilets

TABLE 4.14 *Potential hazards and strategies to promote health and safety in care settings*

Providing and using toys and equipment

When providing toys and equipment for children, it is important to take into account the age and stage of development the child has reached. It is also essential to consider how the toys and equipment are to be used. A tricycle that is being bought for a nursery needs to be of a stronger construction, as it is likely to be used for more hours than if in a private home.

Where children of different age ranges are together, care must be taken that toys and equipment that could be dangerous for babies and toddlers are put out when they are not around.

Some accidents are caused by adults and children falling over toys and equipment. Children should be encouraged to tidy up when they finish playing. Thought also has to be given to layout so that there is enough space for children to play safely.

It is important to:

* keep and follow manufacturer's instructions and warnings

* make sure that toys and equipment are clean and regularly checked, especially moving parts

* remove broken or faulty toys and equipment immediately. If not safe to repair, throw away

* provide cycle helmets and protective clothing for tricycles, cycles, roller blades and skateboards

* toys and equipment should conform to safety regulations and be bought from reputable sources.

Potential hazards near water

Water has a fascination for children. They enjoy playing in it and if it is properly supervised water can provide many benefits for children.

Swimming pools

Children must be supervised at all times in and around swimming pools. Adults should be in the water with children even when lifeguards are available. It is recommended that there should be

POTENTIAL HAZARD	NATURE OF ACCIDENT	GOOD PRACTICE
Sand	Falls from slipping on sand on floor Sand in eyes can be serious Hygiene hazard	* Clear up spilt sand promptly * Stop children from throwing sand * Take children to hospital if sand gets in eyes * Sieve and change sand regularly
Water (trays and buckets)	Falls from spilt water Drowning Hygiene risk	* Mop water up * Supervise children as they play * Do not leave buckets and water unattended * Make sure that water is changed daily
Tricycles, bikes	Falls Collisions	* Make sure that surface is smooth * Check that children's feet can touch the ground * Provide cycle helmets * Give children particular areas in which to ride * Maintain equipment and check moving parts
Climbing frames, slides	Falls	* Make sure that children take their turn * Check that the equipment is appropriate for children's height and weight * Make sure that equipment is secure and is placed on appropriate surface, e.g. special tarmac, grass

TABLE 4.15 *Potential hazards and practices to promote health and safety*

one adult for each non-swimmer in general sessions. When children can swim, strict monitoring is still necessary as many children overestimate their abilities.

Private pools that have covers have also been known to be a source of fatal accidents. Children have attempted to walk on the covers and slipped in unnoticed or have tried to swim underneath the cover.

Rivers, streams, canals and beaches

These are places where older children may enjoy playing. Children who can swim can often overestimate their abilities and find themselves in trouble. Dangers such as rocks, metal structures and strong currents can lurk beneath the surface. Children should only swim in places that are designated as safe and where there is adult supervision and preferably lifeguards on patrol. Warning signs and flags must be heeded. Icy rivers, streams and ponds can tempt children who want to skate. The danger is that the ice may not hold their weight and they may slip underneath. This can result in a child drowning.

Paddling pools

Paddling pools can provide opportunities for sensory play and learning, but can also be hazardous. Children need to be constantly supervised. Bath mats can be put in the bottom of paddling pools to prevent toddlers from slipping. Water should be changed frequently to avoid the risk of contamination. Paddling pools should be emptied when they are not in use.

It is important to remember that:

* inflatable rings, dinghies, arm bands or buoyancy aids can lull adults and children into a false sense of security. They are not designed as life savers and must be seen in terms of aids to swimming

* garden ponds, paddling pools or private swimming pools are serious hazards; children should be supervised and measures should be taken to fence them off

* children must always be constantly supervised near water

* adults need to know what to do in an emergency and should also be able to provide resuscitation.

Labelling of toys and equipment

There is a range of labels that appear on toys and equipment. These labels provide information for the public. Most labels are declarations that products have met European directives for safety, but do not mean that they have been independently tested to check that they do.

Regulations covering the safety of toys and equipment

Choosing safe toys and equipment for children is important. Fortunately, there is legislation in place to prevent toys, equipment and materials being sold that could be dangerous for children. From the Consumer Protection Act 1987, there are the Toys (Safety) Regulations 1995. The Regulations define a toy as: 'any product or material designed or clearly intended for use in play by children of less than 14 years of age'. Under the regulations third parties, as well as the actual users of toys, must be protected against health hazards and physical injury when the toy is used.

Understanding the symbols

Contrary to popular belief, you should be aware that the CE mark is not a guarantee of a safe toy or piece of equipment. This is a symbol that shows that the toy or piece of equipment has been manufactured for sale in the European Union. The mark acts as a declaration that the toy should comply with the essential safety requirements that are applicable to it. The mark, however, is not a seal of approval or quality and this means that toys with this mark can still be unsafe.

FIGURE 4.18 *The CE mark*

The lion mark symbol was created in 1988 by the British Toy and Hobby Association (BTHA). They were concerned

FIGURE 4.19 *The lion mark*

that the CE mark was misleading consumers into believing that the mark guaranteed safety. The lion mark can only be used by manufacturers that are licensed and it is designed to show consumers that the toy is safe and conforms with all relevant safety information.

The age warning symbol began to appear on toys in 1995 and is designed to warn consumers if a toy is unsuitable for young children. The reason for the warning is also included on the pack, e.g. contains small parts. This warning should not be ignored.

FIGURE 4.20 *The age warning symbol*

Consider this

Mandy lives on a low income in a flat with her baby of 8 months and five-year-old son, who likes playing outdoors. The flat is not very well maintained, but Mandy does not like to complain in case her landlord does not renew the tenancy agreement.

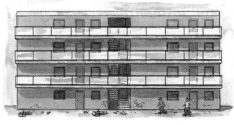

FIGURE 4.21 *The area Mandy lives in is not very safe*

1. For the flat and outside area make a list of at least twenty dangers.

2. For each danger, explain how to minimise the risk.

3. Where safety equipment is required, research the cost of it.

4. Explain the difficulties that Mandy faces in keeping her children safe

5. Is the five-year-old son more likely to have an accident indoors or outdoors? Give reasons for your answer.

Summary

Safety equipment has to be used according to the manufacturer's instructions

Most accidents to children under the age of seven years occur in the home

Children from low income families are more likely to be involved in accidents

Health and safety

Children under 18 months of age have no sense of danger and need complete protection

Toys and equipment have to be appropriate to the age of children

Adults need to be aware of the risks in different environments

FIGURE 4.22 *Section 4.4 summary*

UNIT ASSESSMENT

The assessment for this unit takes the form of a short exam. To prepare for this exam, make sure that you:

* can plot measurements onto a growth chart

* can read a growth chart

* learn gross and fine motor milestones for different ages

* learn the cognitive functioning tests of Piaget

* know the stages of language development

* know factors that can affect children's progress in each of the areas of development

* learn how play contributes to children's development

* learn the stages of social play

* know what activities and equipment are used for different play type

* identify safety risks in different settings

* consider factors that affect children's health and safety.

1 Explain the importance of physical growth to children's overall development. (2 marks)

2 What is meant by the term allometric growth? (1 mark)

3 Mark is three-years-old. Give one fine and one gross motor movement that he is likely to show. (2 marks)

4 Identify two factors that might affect children's physical development. (2 marks)

5 Explain the test used to see if children have acquired object permanence. At what age is it usually seen? (2 marks)

6 Identify two factors that might affect a child's language development and outline how each may have an effect. (4 marks)

7 Discuss how play may contribute to children's physical development. (4 marks)

8 Give two reasons why more accidents occur in the home for children under five-years-of-age. (2 marks)

9 Suggest three ways in which the risk of falls can be lowered in the home. (3 marks)

10 Explain why more accidents occur outside of the home in children aged 6 years and over. (2 marks)

References

Meggit, C., Sunderland, G. (1999) *Child Development: an illustrated guide*, Heinemann, Oxford

Useful websites

Please see www.heinemann.co.uk/hotlinks (express code 1554P) for links to the following website which may provide a source of information:

* Child Accident Prevention Trust

UNIT
5
Nutrition and dietetics

This unit covers the following sections:

This unit looks at nutrition and dietetics. It aims to develop your understanding of food components and their nutritional content. It also covers the importance of eating a balanced diet and how the nutritional needs of different client groups can be met.

There are five main nutrient groups in food. They are divided into macro and micronutrients. Macro nutrients are large nutrients and include protein, fat and carbohydrate. They are needed in larger quantities in the body. The micronutrients are needed in smaller quantities in the body and these include vitamins and minerals. The other two essential constituents which the body needs to function effectively are water and fibre or non-starch polysaccharide – but these are not strictly nutrients.

Protein

Protein is made up of carbon, hydrogen, oxygen, nitrogen and small amounts of sulphur and phosphorus. Protein is an essential constituent of all cells. It is an essential component of the human diet as it is the only source of nitrogen, which is vital for cell formation and therefore growth. It is a large and complicated structure called a polymer. Proteins are water-soluble and can diffuse through the cell walls.

Each protein is built up from units known as amino acids. Amino acids link together to make peptide chains and the number of constructions possible is almost limitless.

There are 22 amino acids known; 8 of these are essential to adults for repair and maintenance of the body cells and 10 are essential to children for growth and repair. They are essential because they must be obtained from the diet. Some amino acids can be synthesised in the body from other amino acids, but the essential ones cannot and, therefore, must be in the diet.

Key concepts

High biological value (HBV) foods are those which contain all the essential amino acids known.

Low biological value (LBV) foods are sources of protein but do not contain all the essential amino acids.

✳ DID YOU KNOW?

The essential amino acids for adults and children are: valine; leucine; isoleucine; phenylahanine; theonine; methionine; tryptophan and lysine. In addition, children also need arginine and histidine.

High biological value (HBV) foods come from animal sources of protein including meat, fish, eggs, milk and cheese. Soya is also classed as an HBV food as, although it does not contain all the essential amino acids in the correct quantities, it is fortified during the manufacturing process.

Foods containing protein

Low biological value (LBV) foods include peas, beans and lentils. If two LBV foods are eaten together, one may compensate for the deficiencies in the other; for example, beans on toast. This is known as the complementary action of proteins.

Vegetarians and vegans can be at risk of consuming too little protein in their diet. However, if they combine a range of vegetable protein in their diet, they should have as good an intake of protein as an omnivore.

Think it over...

Think about other examples of where two LBV protein foods might be combined to complement each other.

Function of protein in the body

Protein has the following functions in the body:

* essential for body cell growth – this is particularly important for babies and children and for a woman during pregnancy

* required for repair and maintenance of body cells, i.e. general wear and tear and after injury

* a secondary source of energy for the body. This means that the body's first source of energy is fat and carbohydrate, but if energy is not available from these sources, it will use protein

* it is used to form enzymes, hormones and antibodies.

Adults require 1 gram of protein per kilogram of body weight per day. Children require more protein in proportion to their size as they are growing intensely.

✻ DID YOU KNOW?

After an injury or operation, the protein in the body is broken down. This results in weight loss and nitrogen loss which is detected through the urine. It also occurs if lying in bed for a long time such as, for example, after an operation or if immobile in the way that elderly people sometimes are. Therefore, protein needs increase at this time.

Protein deficiency

A lack of protein might result in: retarded growth; degeneration of the body cells as worn out cells are not replaced; organ malfunction due to hormone and enzyme deficiency; and the body may be more susceptible to disease due to the lack of antibodies. Protein deficiency is not common in this country.

✻ DID YOU KNOW?

Protein Energy Malnutrition (PEM) is the name used to describe a range of disorders which occur mainly in underdeveloped countries. It affects children under five-years-of-age and is the result of too little energy and protein in the diet. Marasmus and Kwashiorkor are the most common.

Think it over...

Find out how marasmus and kwashiorkor occur and the effect they have on the child.

Fats

Fats are made up of carbon, hydrogen and oxygen. They contain the highest amount of energy at 9 kilocalories per gram. Therefore, too much fat in the diet can contribute to obesity. Sources of fat in the diet can be divided into four groups:

* animal, e.g. fat on meat, lard, dripping

* vegetable, e.g. olive oil, nut oils

* marine, e.g. fish oils such as cod liver oil or oily fish such as herrings or mackerel

* dairy, e.g. cream, milk, yoghurt.

The building blocks of fat are fatty acids and glycerol. A fatty acid is made up of a chain of carbon atoms with a methyl group at one end and an acid group at the other. Each carbon atom has one or two carbon atoms attached and this determines if it is a saturated or unsaturated fat.

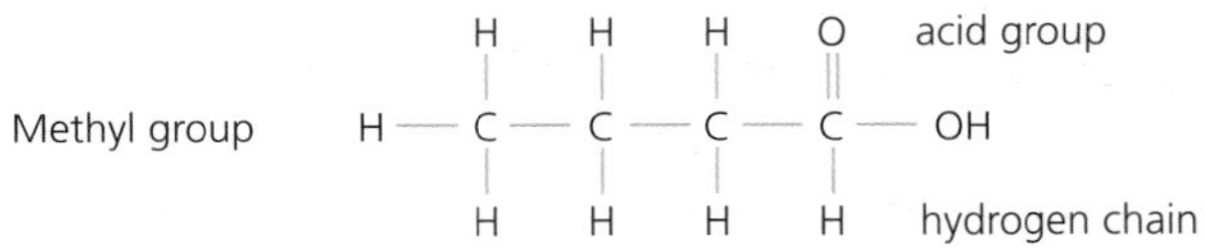

FIGURE 5.1 *Composition of a fatty acid*

If the fatty acid has all the carbon atoms it can hold then it is 'saturated'. If some of the hydrogen atoms are missing, it is 'unsaturated'. If this happens once, it is 'monounsaturated', if more than once it is 'polyunsaturated'.

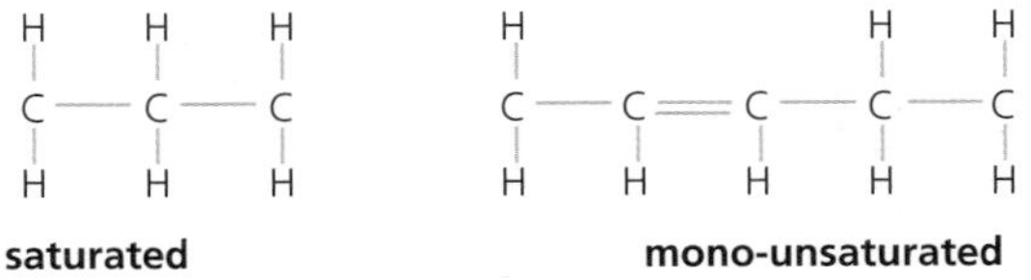

saturated   **mono-unsaturated**

FIGURE 5.2 *Types of fatty acids*

Saturated fats are usually of animal origin and are solid at room temperature; butter and lard are examples of saturated fats. Unsaturated fats tend to be liquid at room temperature and of vegetable origin such as corn oil, olive oil or sunflower oil.

Saturated fats, cholesterol and coronary heart disease

The Western diet is often very high in fat, particularly saturated fat. A high saturated fat intake has been associated with a raised cholesterol level, which is one of the risk factors in coronary heart disease. Cholesterol is used in the body to make bile, which is used in the digestive process. The body therefore uses some of the cholesterol that is eaten; however, excess cholesterol is carried in the blood stream by low density lipoproteins (LDLs) and can be laid down in the arteries, causing the walls of the arteries to narrow.

In some cases, the build-up can be such that the artery blocks and prevents the blood flow. It is also possible for blood clots to get stuck in places where the arteries have narrowed, causing the same effect. Both can lead to thrombosis, a stroke or, if in the arteries around the heart, a heart attack.

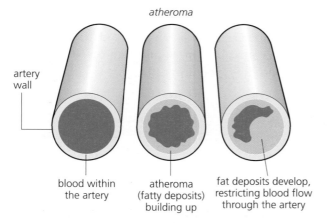

atheroma

artery wall

blood within the artery

atheroma (fatty deposits) building up

fat deposits develop, restricting blood flow through the artery

FIGURE 5.3 *Arteries showing atheroma*

Saturated fat is believed to increase the amount of low density lipoproteins in the blood and a raised level of LDLs is associated with an increased risk of heart disease. However, it is believed that polyunsaturated fats actually lower the amount of cholesterol in the blood, as they lower the amount of LDLs in the bloodstream but also increase the amount of high density lipoproteins (HDLs), which in turn counter the action of LDLs by carrying cholesterol away from sites it has accumulated in. Monounsaturated fats reduce LDLs but do not increase HDLs. Therefore, besides reducing the overall amount of fat in the diet, it is suggested that the ratio of saturated fat to polyunsaturated fats or mono unsaturated fat in the diet is reduced.

Manufacturers have tried to respond to this by producing a wide range of low fat products. It is also possible to reduce the amount of fat in the diet by taking simple actions such as choosing lean cuts of meat and grilling instead of frying where possible.

Think it over...

Make a list of the different ways in which you could reduce the amount of saturated fat in the diet.

Functions of fat in the body

Fat has the following functions in the body:

✳ it is the main source of energy for the body

✳ it provides the body with warmth, as it provides a layer of insulation just under the skin known as the adipose layer which helps to reduce heat loss

✳ fat lubricates food and makes it more palatable (think about eating a dry piece of bread against a piece of bread and butter)

✳ fat protects the vital organs such as the heart, kidneys and lungs from damage as it acts as a shock absorber

✳ fat carries the fat soluble vitamins A, D, E and K in the bloodstream – without fat, these vitamins cannot be carried in the body

✳ fat provides essential fatty acids which have a vital role in the formation of cell membranes and nerve tissues.

Fat has some essential functions in the body and, therefore, we cannot survive with a completely fat-free diet; however, the type of fat chosen can affect health.

Carbohydrates

Carbohydrate is a macronutrient. Some 50–60 per cent of the energy in our diet should come from carbohydrates. Carbohydrates are composed of carbon, hydrogen and oxygen. They have an energy value of 3.75 kilocalories per gram. Structurally, they are divided into three main groups.

Carbohydrates in food are usually classified into

Sources of carbohydrate

Disaccharides or sugars
These are formed when two monosaccharide molecules are joined together. Examples of disaccharides are sucrose (found in cane sugar) and lactose (found in milk).

Polysaccharides or complex carbohydrates
These are made up of many monosaccharide molecules joined together and include starch, glycogen, cellulose and pectin.

Carbohydrates are divided into three main groups

Monosaccharides or simple sugars
These are the simplest carbohydrate molecule. The most commonly occurring monosaccharides in food are glucose, fructose and galactose. These are the simple building blocks that all carbohydrates are broken down into for digestion.

Sugars (simple or double sugars)	These are found in sugar itself and therefore in sweet foods. Sugar is easily digested and therefore can provide the body with an instant source of energy.
Starch (polysaccharide)	Starch is found in cereals, potatoes and flour. As they are complex carbohydrates, they take longer to break down in the body and therefore provide a slow release of energy.
Cellulose (polysaccharide)	It is one of a mixture of substances which are also called dietary fibre or non-starch polysaccharide. These cannot be digested by the human digestive system but pass into the large intestine where they are fermented by bacteria. They provide bulk to the diet and aid the digestive process. Dietary fibre helps the stools to remain soft as it helps to increase the water content and, therefore, move through the digestive system with ease. This bulk helps to encourages peristalsis (the name for the contraction and relaxation of the muscles of the digestive system). Therefore, fibre helps prevent constipation and diverticular disease.

TABLE 5.1 *Carbohydrates in food*

sugars, starch and cellulose, as shown in Table 5.1.

Dietary fibre also contributes to general health in the following ways:

* it helps to reduce the risk of colon cancer as faeces move through the digestive system quicker and carcinogens or cancer-producing substances have less time to develop

* it is believed to help to reduce the risk of cardiovascular disease as the increased transit time for waste products means that bile is excreted rather than being reabsorbed and reused. Therefore, the body then uses new cholesterol from the bloodstream to make new bile for digestion, leaving less to be laid down in the arteries

* a high fibre diet can contribute to weight control as it provides bulk and gives a full feeling. The slow release of glucose makes individuals feel full up for longer and therefore they are less likely to over-eat.

Function of carbohydrate

The main function of carbohydrate in the body is to provide energy. The body needs a constant supply of glucose and this is supplied by carbohydrates. If this is not available then the body will use protein to provide glucose and therefore protein will not be available for growth, maintenance and repair of tissues. Therefore, carbohydrate is also known as a 'protein sparer'. It also has a key role in the effective functioning of the digestive system.

Vitamins

Vitamins are organic compounds. They are essential to life even though they are only needed in small quantities. They are fairly complex chemically and are different from each other in both structure and function. But for a few exceptions, the body cannot synthesise vitamins and therefore they must be in the diet. However, many vitamins can be synthesised in the laboratory and can be manufactured in bulk. The body cannot tell if a vitamin is synthetic or natural.

Vitamins are divided into two groups according to how they are dissolved and carried in the body:

* fat soluble – A, D, E and K

* water soluble – C and B complex.

Characteristics of water soluble and fat soluble vitamins are shown in Table 5.2.

WATER SOLUBLE VITAMINS	FAT SOLUBLE VITAMINS
Soluble in water – have a hydrophilic group which sticks out in water and allows vitamins to dissolve	Insoluble in water – have a hydrophobic group which repels water and dissolution
Found in aqueous foods	Found in fatty foods
Leaching may occur in cooking, resulting in heavy vitamin loss	No leaching occurs which results in less loss
Absorbed into the blood stream via the capillaries	Transported in fat and absorbed via the lymph
Remains in the blood plasma	Moves from the lymph to the liver where it combines with protein to make the vitamin soluble in water to be transported in the blood
Not stored in the body – excess is excreted by the kidneys	Stored in association with fat, e.g. in the liver
Intake needed often as there is no store in the body to fall back on	Not necessary to eat daily as body has a store to draw on
Unlikely to get symptoms from excess as it is excreted	Excess symptoms may occur as it is stored in the body

TABLE 5.2 *Characteristics of water soluble and fat soluble vitamins*

Fat soluble vitamins

Vitamin A or retinol:

Vitamin A is found in two different forms in food. In animal products it is found in the form of retinol and this is the form the body uses. In vegetables, it is found in the form of beta-carotene. It is found in the form of yellow pigments called carotinoids, some of which are converted to vitamin A during absorption through the small intestine. It is a less efficient source of vitamin A than retinol.

Vitamin D:

This is also known as the 'sunshine vitamin'. It behaves like a hormone in that the body can make vitamin D itself with the action of sunlight on the skin. Also, it can be made in one area of the body and used in another.

Vitamin D is found in two forms: vitamin D3 – cholecalciferol, which is the form found in cod liver oils and other foods. It is the most effective form for children. It is also the form the body produces itself.

Vitamin D2 or ergocalciferol is a form found in

VITAMIN A OR RETINOL

Function	Sources	Requirements
Essential for vision in dim light. Retinol is vital for the formation of the visual purple (rhodopsin) or 'purple pigment' which helps the eye adjust to the dark. Contributes to the maintenance of the skin – epithelial layer Used in the development of the skeleton including the skull and the vertebral column	Sources of vitamin A can be divided into very rich sources, good sources and useful sources: **Very rich** – liver oils such as cod liver oil or halibut liver oil **Good** – Liver, carrots, spinach, butter, margarine **Useful** – cheese, eggs, tomatoes, milk, salmon, herrings	Vitamin A is easily obtained from a mixed diet. It is stored in the liver so a daily intake is not always required. Adults need around 750 micrograms per day; however; a lactating or breast feeding woman needs 1,200 micrograms per day

TABLE 5.3 *Vitamin A*

VITAMIN D

Function	Sources	Requirements
Essential for the formation of bones and teeth Promotes the absorption of calcium and phosphorus by the small intestine Aids the withdrawal of calcium from the bones to try to maintain the correct amount of calcium in the blood Promotes phosphate absorption by the kidneys	The main sources of vitamin D are fatty fish such as herring, salmon and sardines and dairy products such as milk, cheese, butter, eggs and margarine. The action of ultra violet light on the skin causes 7-dehydro-cholesterol found under the skin to convert to choecalciferol or vitamin D3	It is not known if adults need to obtain any vitamin D from their food due to the body's ability to manufacture it itself. However, it is recommended that children have 7.5 mg/day and all other age groups 10 mg/day.

TABLE 5.4 *Vitamin D*

fungi and yeast. When irradiated by ultra violet light, the molecular structure of the ergosterol is modified to produce ergocalciferol which has strong vitamin D activity.

Vitamin E:

Vitamin E or tocopherol was discovered in 1923. Studies have shown that a deficiency in rats leads to sterility in males, death of foetuses in the womb in females and a fat degeneration of the muscles, but this has not yet been proven in human beings.

Vitamin K:

Vitamin K or phylloquinone is needed in small amounts in the body. Many diets are deficient in Vitamin K; however, it is produced by bacteria in the large intestine. Half the daily requirement can be met by this.

> **✳ DID YOU KNOW?**
>
> Margarine is fortified with vitamin A and D during the manufacturing process. This helps to prevent diet-related disorders. Flour is fortified with calcium for the same reason.

> **✳ DID YOU KNOW?**
>
> Newborn babies are born with sterile guts. Therefore, newborn babies are often given a vitamin K injection to ensure their blood clots if they bleed for any reason. A lack of vitamin K leads to excessive bleeding and this can contribute to brain haemorrhage in newborns.

VITAMIN E		
Function	**Sources**	**Requirements**
Essential for normal metabolism Acts as an antioxidant preventing fats from going rancid as a result of reaction with oxygen in the air It may prevent cell damage as it reduces destructive oxidation of polyunsaturated fatty acids in cell membranes	Most foods have a trace of vitamin E in them; however, it is mainly found in seed oil, particularly wheat germ. It is also found in eggs and liver.	A safe intake is considered to be above 4 mg/ day.

TABLE 5.5 *Vitamin E*

VITAMIN K		
Function	**Sources**	**Requirements**
Important component in blood clotting	Vitamin K can be found in liver, green leafy vegetables and milk	A safe intake is considered to be 1 microgram per kilogram of body weight per day.

TABLE 5.6 *Vitamin K*

Water soluble vitamins

Vitamin C or Ascorbic Acid

Vitamin C is a white crystalline substance, which is highly unstable and therefore easily lost in cooking and food preparation through heat and oxidation. Up to 75 per cent of vitamin C can be lost during cooking. Vitamin C can be lost from the cells of fruit and vegetables as they are cut. The vitamin oxidises into the air. Vitamin C is also destroyed by heat and leaches into the cooking liquids. Therefore, it is recommended that in order to maximise vitamin C intake, you should cut fruit and vegetables as close to the cooking time as possible, cook in as small amount of liquid as possible for the least amount of time and use the cooking liquid in gravy and sauces.

Vitamin B complex

There are eight different vitamins in the B group. They are grouped together because they are often found together in food, for example, in yeast extract. Table 5.8 (see page 186) outlines the function, sources and requirements of six of these vitamins.

VITAMIN C OR ASCORBIC ACID		
Function	**Sources**	**Requirements**
To make the connective tissue which binds body cells together Essential in the manufacture of blood and cell walls of blood vessels Aids resistance to infection – it is believed it helps fight the common cold but there is no definite evidence to prove this	Citrus fruits, blackcurrants and vegetables Tinned tomatoes Potatoes are also a good source of vitamin C for the British as, although there is not a high amount in them, it is a staple of the British diet and many are eaten, so they make up a significant source. Potatoes have the greatest amount of vitamin C during active growth in the spring and summer. When stored, the amount of vitamin C diminishes.	As vitamin C is a water-soluble vitamin, it is not stored in the body and therefore, a daily intake is required. Recommendations are: 15mg/day for infants under 1 20mg/day for children 1–8 years 25 mg/day for children 9–14 30 mg/day for 15 years to adults During pregnancy and lactation, the amount needed increases to 60 mg per day

TABLE 5.7 *Vitamin C*

VITAMIN	FUNCTION	SOURCE	REQUIREMENTS
Vitamin B1 – Thiamin	Essential for the release of energy from carbohydrates Needed for growth and normal functioning of the nervous system Maintains muscle tone	Brown rice Offal: liver, kidney Milk, eggs Fruit and vegetables Flour and most breakfast cereals – added by law	Children: 0.3–1.0 mg/day (varies with age) Adult males: 1.2mg/day Adult female: 0.9mg/day
Vitamin B2 – Riboflavin	Involved in the metabolism of proteins, fats and carbohydrates and therefore has an effect on growth	Liver, kidneys, meat Eggs Green vegetables Some manufactured by bacteria in the large intestine	Children: 0.4–1.7 mg/day (varies with age) Adult males: 1.7mg/day Adult female: 1.4 mg/day
Niacin or Nicotinic acid	Involved in the metabolism of proteins, fats and carbohydrates and therefore has an effect on growth Essential for healthy skin and nerves	Meat and poultry especially offal Wholewheat flour and fortified white flour Manufactured in the large intestine (Can be converted in the body from amino acid tryptophan which is found in eggs and milk)	Children: 5–16 mg/day (varies with age) Adult males: 18 mg/day Adult female: 15 mg/day
Vitamin B6 – Pyridoxine	Affects the metabolism of proteins especially the conversion of tryptophan to niacin Acts as a catalyst Essential for the formation of haemoglobin (red blood cells)	Widespread in foods but good sources include: liver and kidney, yeast and yeast products, wholegrain cereals, eggs	Bottle fed babies: 0.4 mg/day Children: 1.5mg/day Adults : 2 mg/day
Folic acid	Essential for the formation of red blood cells Important in foetal development	Liver, kidneys, dark green vegetables, wholegrain cereals and bread, pulses (peas, beans and lentils)	300 micrograms but 400micrograms for pregnant and lactating women
Vitamin B12 – Cobalamin	Essential for the formation of red blood cells Essential for a healthy nervous system	Liver, kidney, eggs, milk, cheese and meat. There is no B12 in vegetables. Added to some breakfast cereals	3.0–4.0 mg/day

TABLE 5.8 *Some vitamins in the B group*

Minerals

Minerals are organic substances which the body requires in minute quantities in order to function effectively.

Iron

There are about 4 grams of iron in the body. Some 60–70 per cent of this is in the form of haemoglobin in the red blood cells. Red blood cells have a lifespan of about four months after which they are withdrawn from circulation. Most of the iron is released and used to form new red blood corpuscles in bone marrow. Ten per cent of the iron is found in the body cells and the remaining 20–30 per cent is stored in the liver, spleen and bone marrow in a complex of iron, phosphate and protein called 'ferritin'.

Animal sources of iron ('haeme' or 'ferrous' iron) are the form of iron that is best absorbed by the body. Vegetable sources of iron such as 'non-haeme' or 'ferric' iron are not easily used by the body. The body has to convert the ferric iron to the ferrous state before it can use it. This occurs in the stomach during digestion. Both protein and vitamin C also have to be present for it to occur.

Protein absorption can be inhibited by phytic acid which is found in wholegrain cereals. This acid binds with the iron and makes absorption difficult.

Elderly people can be at risk from a low intake

Foods containing iron

of iron, as they often exist on a relatively cheap diet, low in vegetable sources of vitamin C.

Calcium

Calcium works hand-in-hand with phosphorus. If there is a lack of calcium in the diet, this can lead to stunted growth and rickets in children. Adults with a poor diet may suffer from osteomalacia (malformation of the bones), badly formed teeth or muscle spasms. Calcium is essential in pregnancy, as it is needed for the development of the foetus. If the mother's diet is lacking, the body will withdraw calcium from the mother's bones to meet the needs of the developing child. This could result in weakened teeth and bone structure for the mother.

IRON		
Function	**Sources**	**Requirements**
Formation of haemoglobin in red blood cells, which enables cells to carry oxygen around the body to the cells and tissues	Iron is found in both plant and animal food sources Animal sources include offal such as liver, black pudding, eggs and fish (known as 'haeme' or 'ferrous' iron) Vegetable sources of iron include green vegetables, cocoa, parsley and flour (known as 'non-haeme' or 'ferric' iron)	Adults need about 10mg/day to remain healthy. Iron is important during growth spurts and therefore is needed during adolescence. An increased intake is also needed to cover the blood lost through menstruation each month. Increased amounts are also needed in pregnancy (13mg/day) and lactation (15mg/day)

TABLE 5.9 *The function, sources and requirements of iron*

CALCIUM

Function	Sources	Requirements
Needed for the formation of the skeleton – strong bones and teeth Needed to help the blood to clot Helps the normal functioning of the muscles including the heart muscles and the nerves Involved in the activation of enzymes An essential component of the blood	Calcium can be obtained form various foods but the best sources are: ✳ milk and milk products e.g. yoghurt ✳ tinned fish particularly where the bones are eaten e.g. salmon ✳ hard water ✳ green vegetables ✳ flour as it is fortified during manufacture	Children require 600mg/day; adults 500mg/day but pregnant and lactating women 1200mg/day

TABLE 5.10 *Calcium*

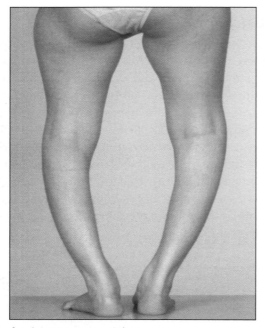

Lack of calcium causes rickets

Think it over...

Pregnant and breast feeding women need a lot more calcium in their diet than others. How could calcium be increased in their diets to meet this need?

Phosphorus

Phosphorus works in conjunction with calcium. An adult body contains about 900 grams of phosphorus, most of which is in the bones as calcium phosphate. It is the second most abundant mineral in the body. Excess phosphorus is removed by the kidneys.

Iodine

There is between 20 and 50 mg of iodine in the body – 8 mg is found in the thyroid gland. A deficiency of iodine can lead to lack of energy and

PHOSPHORUS

Function	Sources	Requirements
Contributes to the formation of bones and teeth – it provides the strength Essential component of the blood Necessary for metabolism of energy from foods – component of certain enzymes and hormones	Phosphorus is present in most animal and vegetable foods and therefore a deficiency is unknown. Phosphates are also added to a number of foods during manufacture.	No specific requirements given

TABLE 5.11 *Phosphorus*

Function	Sources	Requirements
Essential component of hormones manufactured by the thyroid gland in the neck including thyroxine. These control the body's metabolic rate	The most reliable sources of iodine are seafood and seaweed. Iodine can be found in plant foods but the amount depends on the soil in which they are grown and therefore the amount if irregular.	The recommended daily intake is very small – 0.05 – 0.30mg/day.

TABLE 5.12 *The function, sources and requirements of iodine*

obesity. It can also lead to goitre which is a swelling thyroid gland in the neck.

Zinc

Zinc is a trace element which is found in most foods (see Table 5.13), particularly in association with protein.

Less than half the amount of zinc consumed is absorbed and this can be reduced even more if wholegrain cereals, rich in fibre and phytic acid are eaten, as this combines with the zinc and makes it unavailable to the body.

Water

Water is not considered a nutrient but it is essential for life. It makes up two thirds of the body's weight. It forms part of the cell liquid cytoplasm and the surrounding extra-cellular fluid. The blood, bodily secretions such as sweat and tears, digestive juices and lymph are mainly water. Even bone is 25 per cent water. Water has a number of key roles in the body:

* it is a medium of transportation from one part of the body to another, e.g. nutrients

* it enables the distribution of heat generated by the metabolism. Water keeps the body at a temperature required for body functions, i.e. 37°C

* water helps to keep the lining of the membranes moist, e.g. lungs, eyes and joints

* water dissolves food during digestion, forms secretions for enzymes and assists absorption

* its ability to dissolve substances enables chemicals to mix with each other so hydrolysis takes place (hydrolysis is the reaction of a compound with water to break it down)

* water is needed for the removal of bodily waste products

* water, in the form of perspiration, cools the body by taking heat from the skin.

Function	Sources	Requirements
Essential for tissue growth Required for enzyme reactions including carbonic anhydrase which is the quick liberation of CO_2 from red blood cells in the lungs as part of respiration Involved in the development of the foetus during pregnancy	Good sources of zinc include: oysters, kidney, green vegetables and wholegrain cereals.	Adult males require 9.5 mg day whereas adult females require 7.0 mg day.

TABLE 5.13 *The function, sources and requirements of zinc*

Humans cannot last without water and, in fact, can last longer without food than they can without water. Adults should consume between 2–4 litres of water per day in food and liquid.

Summary

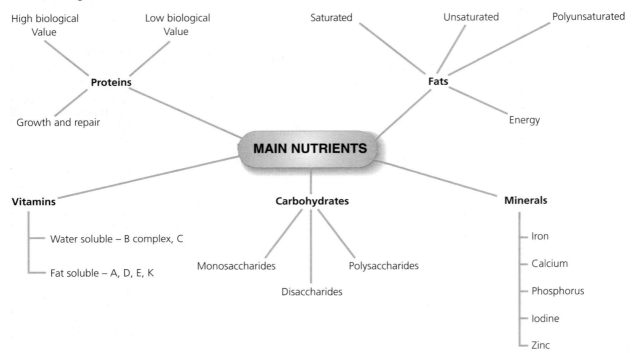

FIGURE 5.5 *Section 5.1 summary*

The Smith family consists of:

> Nicola Smith – mother – aged 47
> Martin Smith – father – aged 48
> Norelle Smith – student – aged 17

Their current diet is not very healthy. The family eat a lot of fried and highly processed foods.

Norelle has recently been feeling more tired than usual. Tests have shown that she is suffering from slight anaemia.

Martin has been diagnosed with high cholesterol levels and needs to address this.

1. Which two nutrients are likely to be lacking from Norelle's diet? Give an example of a food high in each nutrient.

Nutrient 1   Food
Nutrient 2   Food

2. Give reasons why Norelle's diet may be low in the nutrients identified.

3. Explain how the family needs to adjust their fat intake to reduce cholesterol levels.

4. All the family would benefit from a diet which is higher in Non Starch Polysaccharide or fibre.

   What advice would you give the family to help them to increase their intake of fibre-rich foods?

5. Critically evaluate the effects of a high fibre diet on the health on one family member.

5.2 Food additives

Pre-prepared, processed foods

Modern diets often contain a lot of pre-prepared, processed foods. There are many reasons for this:

* many people want to use their leisure time in different ways and look for quick solutions for eating

* shopping habits have changed – we no longer shop on a daily basis and therefore foods need to have keeping qualities

* traditional roles have changed – in the past, women often stayed at home and prepared the meals. Now many women choose to work and do not have time to prepare food from natural ingredients

* supermarkets are based around pre-packed foods which are easy to store

* people demand foods out of season and preservation methods can provide this.

Functions of food additives

Besides the expected ingredients in these foods, food additives (chemicals) may be added in small amounts to perform a special function including those outlined in Figure 5.6.

Regulation of food additives

The use of additives in food is regulated to ensure they are used safely and effectively and in the minimum amounts to achieve their objectives. Additives are listed on the ingredients list and are depicted as E numbers. Table 5.14 outlines some of the common additives and their functions.

Convenience foods contain additives

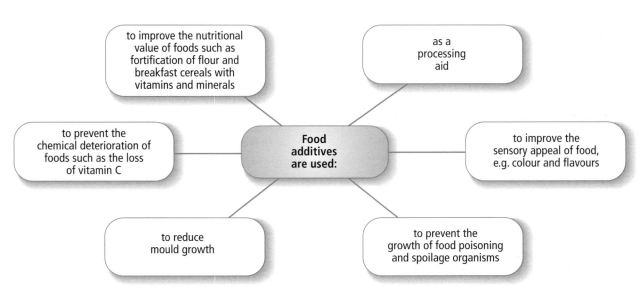

FIGURE 5.6 *Some of the special functions performed by food additives*

ADDITIVE	PRIME FUNCTION	EXAMPLE OF USE
Preservatives	Prevents or limits the growth of micro-organisms. In most cases a particular preservative is used in a particular food	Benzoates – soft drinks Nitrate – preserved meat
Antioxidants	Stop fatty foods going rancid Prevents fruits going brown	Natural antioxidants, e.g. vitamin E in oil and margarine
Stabilisers	Help to blend two substances together which do not normally mix. It prevents them from separating by dispersing tiny droplets of one substance through the other. This gives a smooth texture	Mayonnaise
	Also has a preserving effect where a higher proportion of water to fat than normal is needed	Low fat spreads
Thickeners and gelling agents	A texture modifier, which depending on the amount used can act as a stabiliser, thickener or gelling agent	Pectins Lecithin Guar gum Alginates
Colours	Used to improve or enhance the colour of foods Some have been linked to hyperactivity in children	Sunset yellow-squash, fish fingers Cochineal
Flavourings	Used to give taste to food. Can be completely artificial	
Anti-caking agents	Stops dried products like powder from sticking together. Prevents active ingredients working until needed.	Baking powder
Flour improvers	Used to make dough more elastic so improving the baking quality	Vitamin C in bread making

TABLE 5.14 *Some common additives in food and their functions*

Many people feel food additives should not be used as freely as they are in food manufacture. Some arguments against their use include:

* they are dangerous chemicals and there is evidence that use of some additives is linked to increased cancer risks

* additives can be used to disguise inferior quality food

* some additives can trigger adverse reactions such as hyperactivity in children

* preservatives can be used by manufacturers to compensate for poor hygiene practices

* it is believed that many of the cosmetic additives such as those for colour are unnecessary.

Think it over...

Look at different packet/processed foods. Make a list of the ingredients and identify the role of each of the additives in the product.

Summary

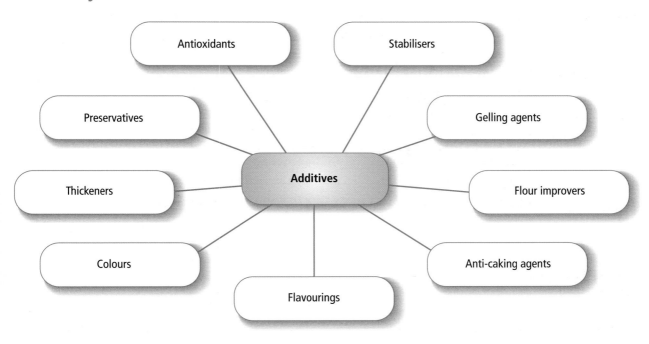

FIGURE 5.7 *Section 5.2 summary*

5.3 The principles of a balanced diet

A balanced diet is one that provides individuals with all the nutrients required in the amount needed for their age and stage of life. A balanced diet contains a mix of the different food groups so that nutrients come from a range of sources. It also follows healthy eating goals to be:

* low in saturated fat
* low in refined sugar
* low in salt
* high in dietary fibre.

Energy intake

A balanced diet is also one in which energy intake does not exceed the energy output. An imbalance can lead to either weight loss or excessive weight gain. The amount of energy needed will vary for each individual depending on their metabolic rate and their levels of activity and exercise.

FIGURE 5.8 *Energy intake and expenditure*

Factors affecting energy intake

Gender

Males need more energy intake than females because they are physically larger and, therefore, their Basal Metabolic Rate is higher.

Activity levels

This includes the levels of activity needed for the job an individual does as well as the energy needed for recreational activities. Certain jobs, such as coal mining or construction, are very demanding and require high levels of energy. Other roles such as administration or working in some health and social care fields would be classed as sedentary and, therefore, do not require as much energy.

Some people take part in recreational activities which use lots of energy, such as football, hockey or swimming, whereas others prefer fishing or reading. All aspects of an individual's lifestyle need to be taken into account when considering energy levels.

FIGURE 5.9 *High and low energy activities*

Age

This is another important factor that influences energy needs. Children need a high amount of energy for their size because they are growing. However, as we get older, the amount of energy needed stabilises and then factors such as activity levels are more important. The body naturally slows down with ageing so it is fair to assume that an elderly person needs less energy intake than a younger adult.

State of health

Healthy individuals should aim to eat a balanced diet, which contains all the nutrients they need in the right quantities. When ill, however, individuals often run high temperatures and have little appetite. Therefore, their diet should contain a lot of liquid to quench thirst and prevent dehydration. Once an individual starts to recover, they can be given small amounts of solid foods. Easily digested protein foods are particularly important as are those supplying calcium, iron and vitamins A, B complex and C. Fat and carbohydrates should be limited at this stage as there is little demand on energy levels. They should be provided with light appetising meals, which are easily digested. Fried food, fatty meat and fish, heavy puddings and strong flavours should be avoided.

Think it over...

Plan a meal suitable for someone who is recovering from an illness.

Dangers of excess or poor intake

An excess intake of energy and nutrients will lead to obesity. Excess calories that are not burned up as energy are converted to fat by the body and laid down in the adipose tissue. Excess weight can put a strain on the body's organs and also can make individuals less mobile. They are more prone to illness and have a higher risk of heart attacks, varicose veins and thrombosis. Statistics show overweight people also have a higher percentage of accidents.

Poor intake may lead to signs of deficiencies. There is likely to be a lack of energy and individuals may find themselves more prone to minor illnesses which take longer to clear up.

Planning a balanced diet

There have been several different systems for helping individuals to choose a balanced diet. One popular method is the food pyramid which places the four main food groups at various positions on the pyramid in relation to the amount that should be consumed in the diet. Therefore, foods at the bottom of the pyramid should be consumed in larger quantities than those that appear at the top. In this case, fats and

sugars, which contain few nutrients but are high in calorie content, are at the top to indicate they should be used sparingly in the diet, whereas starch foods such as bread and pasta are at the base of the pyramid to indicate they should be consumed most frequently as a daily food choice.

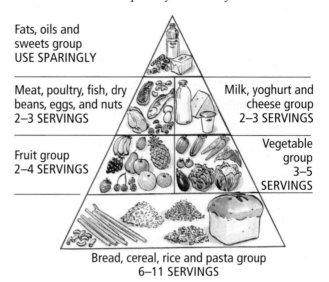

FIGURE 5.10 *The Nutrition Pyramid*

Another popular method of meal planning is the food plate. This aims to indicate the percentage of different food groups on any plate or meal. The recommendations are shown in Figure 5.11.

FIGURE 5.11 *Recommended portions of different foods types*

	DIETARY REFERENCE VALUE (DRV)		4–6 YEARS		7–10 YEARS		11–14 YEARS		15–18 YEARS	
			BOYS	GIRLS	BOYS	GIRLS	BOYS	GIRLS	BOYS	GIRLS
Energy	EAR	kcals	1,715	1,545	1,970	1,740	2,220	1,845	2,755	2,110
Fat	DRV: average 35% of food energy	g	66.7	60.1	76.6	67.7	86.3	71.8	107.1	82.1
Saturated fat	DRV: average 11% of food energy	g	21.0	18.9	24.1	21.3	27.1	22.6	33.7	25.8
Total carbohydrate	DRV: average 50% of food energy	g	228.7	206.0	262.7	232.0	296.0	246.0	367.3	281.3
Non-milk extrinsic sugars (loosely termed as 'added sugars')	DRV: average 11% of food energy*	g	50.3	45.3	57.8	51.0	65.1	54.1	80.8	61.9
Fibre	Proportion of DRV for adults (18g)/CRV**	g	13.7	12.4	15.8	14.0	17.8	14.8	22.1	16.9
Protein	RNI	g	19.7	19.7	28.3	28.3	42.1	41.2	55.2	45.0
Iron	RNI	mg	6.1	6.1	8.7	8.7	11.3	14.8	11.3	14.8
Zinc	RNI	mg	6.5	6.5	7.0	7.0	9.0	9.0	9.5	7.0
Calcium	RNI	mg	450	450	550	550	1,000	800	1,000	800
Vitamin A	RNI	µg	500	500	500	500	600	600	700	600
Vitamin C	RNI	mg	30	30	30	30	35	35	40	40
Folate	RNI	µg	100	100	150	150	200	200	200	200
Sodium	SACN recommendation	mg	1,177	1,177	1,961	1,961	2,353	2,353	2,353	2,353

FIGURE 5.12 *Dietary reference values*

The structures of both of these diets cover similar recommendations. They both avoid giving specific recommendations about portion sizes but give a guide on how a meal might be made up.

Dietary reference values (DRVs)

For many years, dietary standards have been set. These have outlined the nutritional needs of different subgroups of the population according to their age and gender. There are also subgroups for groups with particular nutritional needs such as children, as they are actively growing, and pregnant women. The tables are intended for use with healthy people and take no account of the effects of illness or injury on nutritional needs. They represent another way to work out what can be eaten.

Key concept

Dietary Reference Values are used to cover a range of differently defined values. Rather than making one recommendation, which implies a minimum required intake, three values are offered from protein, vitamins and minerals to show the range which may occur. The highest of these is the Reference Nutrient Intake which is the highest need for that nutrient. The other two figures are the Estimated Average Requirement (EARs), which is the estimated average for most people, and the Lower Reference Nutrient Intake (LRNI), which is the best estimate of the needs of those people with a low need for the nutrient concerned. The assumption is that the requirement of almost everyone should lie within the range of the LRNI and the RNI.

Think it over...

Look at the recommended daily intake table. Analyse the data to answer the following questions.

1. How many kilocalories per day should a moderately active 23-year-old male consume?

2. How many more kilocalories per day should a 28-year-old-pregnant women consume compared to a woman of the same age who is not pregnant?

3. How many grams of protein per day should an 8 year-old-child consume?

4. Using the data provided, how and why does the intake of iron change for females between 9 and 17 years?

Nutrition tables which analyse the nutritional content of different foods can also be used. These allow you to calculate the nutritional and calorific content of foods which have been eaten.

Summary

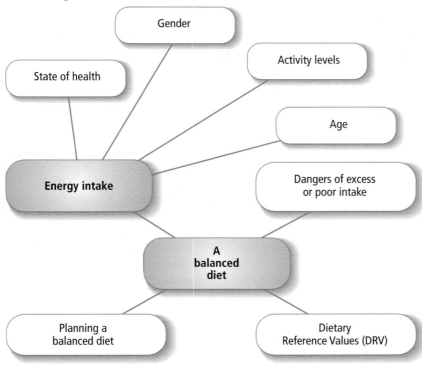

FIGURE 5.13 *Section 5.3 summary*

It is often stated that adolescents have poor diets that include a lot of convenience foods. Katie, a 17- year-old student, asks for some dietary advice. Before the meeting, she completes a food diary and her nutritional intake for one day is analysed as a percentage of the estimated average requirements (EAR).

NUTRIENT	% OF (EAR) ENERGY
Protein	130
Fat	102
Iron	150
Fibre	70
Vitamin D	50
Calcium	40

1. Assume that the data provided is reflective of a typical day's intake for Katie. Which nutrients are (i) in excess and (ii) deficient in Katie's diet?

2. What are the health risks that could result if this diet continued?

3. What does Katie need to do to improve her diet?

4. What might affect Katie's ability to change her diet?

5.4 Nutritional needs in pregnancy

Individuals have different dietary needs but there are certain ages and stages of life that make particular nutritional demands. Some people also have a restricted or special diet due to a particular physical condition or allergy. In addition, the food people eat can be affected by their culture or religion. In this section we will look at a number of different diets that you may come across when working in the health and social care field.

Diet in pregnancy

When analysing food tables, you will notice that the requirement for most nutrients increases during pregnancy. The diet of a pregnant woman needs to provide enough of the right nutrients to cope with the demand of the growing baby as well as the needs of the pregnant woman's own body. Therefore, there needs to be some change in nutritional intake but 'eating for two' is nutritionally unsound and can lead to weight gain. Certain nutrients are needed more than others. These are outlined below.

Energy

During pregnancy and lactation, energy requirements are increased. Growth of both the foetus and the placenta need energy for synthesis. Also, to prevent potential damage to the foetus as it develops, the body lays down extra fatty layers as a defence mechanism. Energy intake should be increased by about 200 kilocalories per day.

Protein

Protein is one of the most essential nutrients for the foetus and the mother. If the diet does not include enough protein, the cells are broken down to provide protein for the baby regardless of the needs of the mother.

Iron

A deficiency in iron can lead to anaemia in the mother and a failure to build up a store in the foetus. It is important that the mother has a good iron intake in the 'haeme' form which is readily used by the body. However, it is recommended that pregnant women should avoid liver, although it is a good source of iron, as it also contains high levels of vitamin A, which is linked to foetal abnormalities.

Folic acid

Folic acid is important during pregnancy, as it is believed to reduce the risk of foetal abnormalities. Pregnant women are advised to take folic acid supplements during the first three months of their pregnancy.

> ✳ DID YOU KNOW?
>
> Milk, both breast and bottle, which is a newborn's only source of nutrients, does not contain iron. Therefore, babies do not take in iron until they are weaned. This means that they must build up a store which is used until weaning occurs. This is between the age of three and four months.

Calcium and phosphorus

Calcium and phosphorus are important for the development of the baby's skeleton. If the mother does not increase her intake of these nutrients, calcium and phosphorus will be taken from the mother's bones and teeth to satisfy the needs of the foetus. This may lead to osteoporosis later in life. In addition, a low calcium intake can lead to pre-eclampsia.

Dietary fibre

Pregnant women need to increase their intake of dietary fibre as they are more prone to constipation. The reason for this is that the digestive system tends to slow down during pregnancy as the body attempts to gain maximum nutrients from the food consumed. Also, as the pregnancy progresses and the woman gets larger, physical exercise is likely to be reduced, which also contributes to constipation.

Fat and carbohydrate

It is important for a pregnant woman not to increase her intake of these foods as they lead to excess weight gain, which is difficult to lose after the birth. However, an intake of fat is important as it provides essential fatty acids for the foetus, which are linked to brain cell division in the third trimester of pregnancy.

Think it over...

What foods would you advise a pregnant women to increase in the diet to meet these needs?

Summary

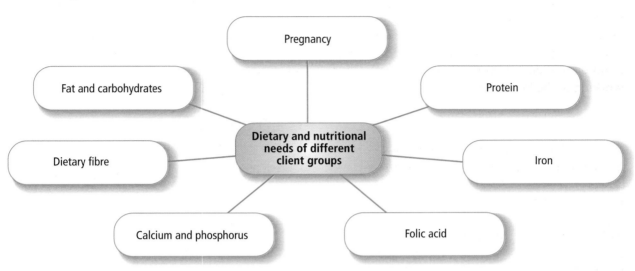

FIGURE 5.14 *Section 5.4 summary*

Consider this

Sharon is pregnant. Table 5.15 sets out the Reference Nutrient Intake (RNI) for females aged 19-50 in general compared to that of a pregnant woman.

1. Explain the reasons for the differences in each of the nutrients stated.

2. How would you recommend Sharon adapts her diet to meet the increasing needs?

3. Give example of foods which will help her to meet those needs.

4. It is easy to put on excess weight during pregnancy. If this happened to Sharon, how might she try to control her weight?

NUTRIENT	FEMALES 19–50	PREGNANT WOMAN
Energy (cal)	1940	2140
Protein (g)	45	51
Vitamin A (microgram)	600	700
Vitamin C (milligram)	40	50
Iron (milligram)	12	15
Calcium (milligram)	500	1200

TABLE 5.15 *The RNI for females aged 19–50 compared with that of a pregnant woman*

5.5 Dietary variations

Why do people choose the food they eat?

There are many reasons why people choose the food they eat.

Think it over...

Make a list of all the food you ate yesterday. Write down why you ate the foods you did. How do they fit with the diagram below?

LIST ALL FOODS EATEN AND AMOUNT				
	BREAKFAST	LUNCH	DINNER	SNACKS
Sunday				
Monday				
Tuesday				
Wednesday				
Thursday				
Friday				

FIGURE 5.15 *List the food you ate today*

For many people their choice of food is limited by external factors. For example, some elderly people may have their choice of food limited by cost because they are on a limited income, and by their own mobility. They may not be able to get to the large supermarkets for a greater choice of food due to lack of transport. Therefore, they may have to use local corner shops where prices are higher and there is less choice. They may also have medical conditions such as arthritis, which make it difficult for them to prepare and cook fresh foods and may have to rely on convenience foods.

Think it over...

Think about another client group, e.g. children, pregnant women or clients with special needs. What factors might affect what they eat?

Figure 5.16 outlines some of the factors which influence food choice and therefore food intake.

Special diets

Some individuals need or choose to have special diets as a result of lifestyle choices, cultural or religious issues, or health issues. This section covers some of these special diets.

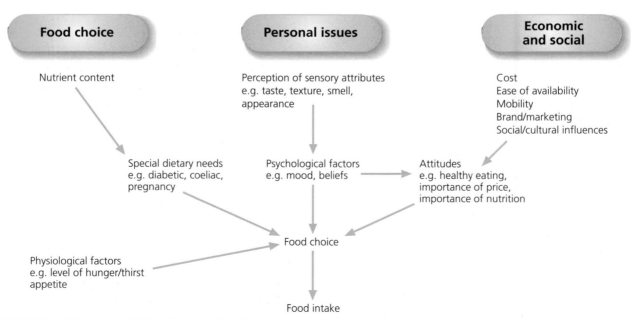

FIGURE 5.16 *Factors which influence food choice*

Culture and religion

All religions of the world have their own beliefs, morals, ceremonies and celebrations. Many of these are linked to food, either in relation to food eaten at particular times, or to restrictions on the diet. These can set one religion apart from others and give a sense of belonging to those who share the religion. A strict follower of the religious laws is considered to be orthodox. However, many are more relaxed about certain practices today. Table 5.16 outlines some dietary practices of certain religions.

Consider this

Mr Mohan Samarakeon is a strict Muslim. He is also a widower and lives alone. He is 78-years-old, slightly overweight and has high blood pressure, which is controlled by tablets. He is not very active but enjoys sweet foods. Identify the type of diet he could eat using the following headings:

* Dietary restrictions

* Dietary requirements

* Foods to avoid due to health problems

* Foods to include in the diet and their nutrient content

Lifestyle choices

Vegetarianism

A vegetarian is someone who chooses not to eat foods from animals and by-products of animals, such as cheese and eggs. Many people choose to be vegetarian and with careful food choices, all nutrients can be obtained from the diet. There are several different types of vegetarian:

* Lacto vegetarian – those who eat milk and cheese but not eggs, meat, poultry or fish

* Lacto-ovo vegetarians – those who will eat eggs, milk and cheese but not meat, poultry or fish

* Vegan – those who are strict vegetarians who will not eat meat, fish, poultry, eggs, milk or

cheese. Vegans do not use any products that may have animal by-products in them such as makeup or soap and they will not wear leather.

Therefore, vegetarians cut out major sources of protein from the diet. Any diet in which one or more of the major food groups is omitted is not ideal; however, the different types of vegetarian diet each present difficulties of their own.

Lacto or lacto-ovo vegetarians

Few problems exist with this type of vegetarian as they consume high biological value proteins and therefore the essential amino acids in the form of milk, cheese and, in the case of lacto-ovos, eggs. They can also obtain protein from peas, beans and lentils.

Soya or textured vegetable protein is a source of protein for this type of vegetarian. They may also eat Quorn, another source of vegetable protein made from soya beans.

However, lacto/lacto-ovo vegetarians need to pay particular attention to the amount of saturated fat they consume, as it is easy to eat large amounts through high consumption of dairy products.

Vegans

Vegans may find it difficult to obtain the correct amount of protein from their diet as they choose to omit all forms of animal protein. They rely on vegetable sources of protein and this can make the diet bulky and monotonous. They may also have low intakes of some of the vital micronutrients that are found in protein foods and dairy products such as vitamins A, B1 and D and calcium, phosphorus and iron.

Think it over...

Look at food tables and identify sources of vitamin A, B1 and D and iron, calcium and phosphorus that a vegan could eat.

In order to ensure they obtain enough protein, vegans should:

* eat a good supply of vegetable proteins that complement each other and therefore provide all the essential amino acids

FOOD RESTRICTION	TIME OF YEAR/DAY	HOW FOOD IS PREPARED	FASTING PRACTICES
Judaism Only eat animals with cloven feet and who chew the cud e.g. beef, sheep, goats, deer, Do not eat pork Will only eat forequarters of the animal Only eat fish with fins and scales Will not eat shellfish Must not eat foods containing meat and milk at the same meal Do not eat blood	Do not prepare food on the Sabbath (Saturday)	Meat and poultry have to be killed in a particular way to drain the maximum amount of blood from the animal. The meat is then soaked in a salt water mixture and finally drained. This is called kosher. Separate utensils and cooking vessels must be used for meat and dairy products and fish	There should be six hours between eating meat and dairy foods. If dairy products are eaten before meat, one hour must pass Fasts occur in the Jewish calendar to represent sad events which have happened. All females over 12 years and 1 day and males over 13 years and one day must take part in fasting Some fasting incorporates eating special foods which symbolise events in Jewish history
Muslim diets (Islam) Do not eat blood Do not eat pork or pork-related products Do not consume alcohol	Ramadam is a period of fasting where Muslims do not eat between sunrise and sunset. Therefore they eat light meals during the hours of darkness. Ramadam lasts for one month and occurs during the 9th lunar month. This varies from year to year. Strict muslims also fast on Mondays and Thursdays and also between the 13th and 15th of each month	Animals must be ritually slaughtered with a blow to the head. Certain words must be spoken whilst this happens. Meat slaughtered in this way is called halal meat	Males are deemed to have reached the age of responsibility at 15, females at 12. All who have reached the age of responsibility must fast except for menstruating, pregnant and lactating women, sick or elderly people, those travelling long distances or those doing hard physical work. Must only eat with the right hand – left is considered unclean
Hinduism Do not kill or eat any animals Usually lacto-vegetarians Strict Hindus are vegan	Varies according to caste, family, age and gender	Ritual bathing and clean clothes are put on before food is prepared. Will not eat Western cheese	Hindu society is based on castes. Hindus from the upper casts cannot eat with the lower castes. Hindus from higher castes are more likely to be vegans

TABLE 5.16 *Dietary practices of some religions*

* avoid too many foods which contain phytic acid, e.g. wholegrain cereals as this will bind with any iron or calcium in the diet and make it unavailable to the body

* avoid too much bulk in the diet – vegetables are naturally more bulky and many absorb more water during cooking so increase their bulk. This can lead to constipation.

* eat a broad range of fruit and vegetables in the diet as this will help cover the nutrient range needed.

> ## * DID YOU KNOW?
>
> Vegans cannot eat Quorn, as egg white is used in its manufacture, which means that it is not totally animal free. They can eat soya protein. This is a good source of high biological value protein for vegans, as it contains all the essential amino acids at the correct levels as they are added during manufacture.

The vegan diet can contain less energy because it is bulky. There is also a risk of anaemia due to lack of iron; and the lack of calcium, phosporus and vitamin D can affect the bone density. It is not advised that children should follow a vegan diet as the bulk of the diet means that they do not consume enough energy to meet their growth needs.

Food intolerance

The term food intolerance can be used in three different groups as outlined in Table 5.17.

> ### Think it over...
>
> Are there any foods which you choose to avoid because you do not like them?

Food intolerance can affect many different parts of the body. Individuals suffering from food intolerance may not suffer all the symptoms and each individual's symptoms will be different. The types of symptoms that food intolerance can cause are outlined in Figure 5.17 (on page 204).

Diabetes Mellitus

Diabetes Mellitus is a disorder caused by insufficient or absent production of the hormone insulin by the pancreas. Insulin is responsible for the absorption of glucose into the cells for their energy needs and into the liver and fat cells for storage. A deficiency of insulin means that the level of glucose in the blood becomes abnormally high, causing excessive urination and excessive thirst. The inability to store glucose results in weight loss, hunger and tiredness. Diabetes tends to run in families. There are two main types of diabetes.

MAIN GROUPS OF FOOD INTOLERANCE	
Food allergy	This is a form of intolerance which causes reproducible symptoms including abnormal immunological reactions to the food eaten. This means that the body produces antibodies when a particular food is eaten, as it believes it is harmful. These antibodies can be detected in a blood test.
Food intolerance	This is a more general term and includes all reproducible adverse reactions to food which are not psychologically based. It includes reactions to additives, e.g. hyperactivity, natural components of food and inborn errors such as Coeliac disease and Diabetes Mellitus. The body does not always produce antibodies in the case of food intolerance but the body reacts in the same way each time the particular food is eaten.
Food aversion	These include foods which individuals choose to avoid for psychological reasons although there is no medical reason why they cannot be eaten. For example, some people cannot eat oysters because they do not like the texture or salty taste. This can make them feel physically sick.

TABLE 5.17 *Main groups of food intolerance*

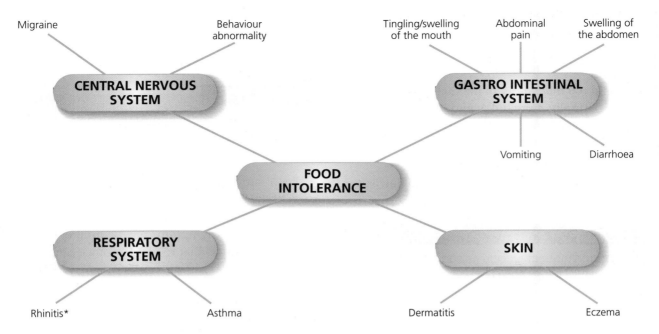

(*inflammation of the mucus lining of the nose)

FIGURE 5.17 *Symptoms caused by food intolerance*

IDDM – Insulin Dependent Diabetes Mellitus (Type I)

This is a more severe type of diabetes which usually appears in the under 35s and is often known as teenage onset, as it most frequently appears in 10–16-year-olds.

It develops rapidly and the pancreatic cells are completely destroyed, probably after a viral infection, and therefore insulin production ceases immediately. The condition has to be controlled by hormone injections without which the sufferer would fall into a coma and die.

NIDDM – Non Insulin Dependent Diabetes Mellitus (type II)

This type of diabetes is characterised by its gradual onset. It usually appears in the over 40s and is often so weak in the early stages that it is not obvious and only detected in medical checkups. With NIDDM, insulin is still produced by the body but not enough to meet needs. It is often linked to obesity. It is the common form that elderly people suffer. This type of diabetes is usually controlled by diet, weight loss and oral medication if needed. Injections are not required.

How to control diabetes

Diabetics should aim to keep the blood glucose levels as near to normal as possible thorough:

* maintenance of normal body weight for height
* regular physical exercise
* careful dietary management
* careful monitoring of blood glucose levels and insulin injections or oral medication if needed.

Dietary management

Doctors, dieticians and the British Diabetic Association all recommend a diet which follows the principles of healthy eating:

* high fibre/unrefined carbohydrates i.e. starchy food such as wholegrain cereals, pulses, potatoes including the skin, brown rice, and most fruit and vegetables. Fifty per cent of energy should come from this. These carbohydrates are broken down and absorbed more slowly than others and therefore help to maintain the stability of the blood sugar
* low sugar intake – refined sugar is released into the blood stream very quickly and can cause a rise in blood sugar levels

* low fat content – to help manage weight

* low salt content.

It is important to ensure food is eaten regularly throughout the day as this helps to maintain the stability of the blood sugar levels.

Key concepts

Hyperglycaemia occurs when too little insulin or too much carbohydrate for insulin levels means that the blood sugar level rises too high.

Hypoglycaemia occurs when too much insulin or too little carbohydrate means blood sugar levels are too low.

Consider this

Your teenage friend, Julie, has just been diagnosed with Insulin Dependent Diabetes Mellitus (IDDM).

1. What is the most likely cause of the diabetes?

2. How might Julie's eating habits need to change as a result of IDDM?

Coeliac disease

Coeliac disease is a condition in which the body reacts to gluten, the protein that is found in wheat and some other cereals such as rye, barley and oats. Coeliac disease affects the small intestine, which is the part of the digestive system where both digestion and absorption of food takes place.

A healthy small intestine is lined with millions of finger-like projections called villi. These are important for the absorption of nutrients (see Figure 5.18).

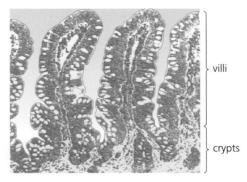

FIGURE 5.18 *A healthy small intestine*

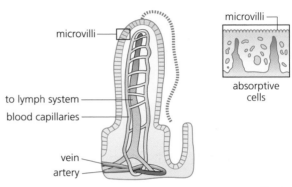

FIGURE 5.19 *The villi of someone who is suffering with Coeliac disease*

In Coeliac disease, the gluten in food damages these villi and they are almost lost. They become very flat and are described as atrophic. Any microvilli that might remain become shortened and irregular. The result is malabsorption of nutrients, weight loss and deficiencies of vitamins and minerals.

Coeliac disease often becomes apparent in babies once they are weaned onto solids. Coeliac disease in babies can be very dangerous, as they

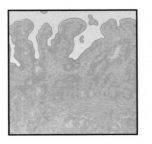 

FIGURE 5.20 *(a) Biopsy of normal intestine (b) Biopsy of Coeliac intestine*

do not have the reserves of energy to survive on. This is one of the reasons why a common first food is rice, as it does not contain gluten.

Babies with Coeliac disease are likely to be irritable, miserable and cry constantly. They will have diahorrea and vomiting. They will not thrive or gain weight.

> ✳ DID YOU KNOW?
>
> Coeliac disease occurs in Europe, North America and Australasia but is rare in India, Africa and China where they have different dietary habits. Rice and maize do not contain gluten and can be eaten by suffers of Coeliac disease.

The most common time for the onset of Coeliac disease is between 20–50 years of age. If a parent has Coeliac disease, there is a 1:10 chance of his or her children developing it.

Dietary control of Coeliac disease

Coeliac disease can be kept under control with the complete elimination of gluten from the diet. This must continue throughout life, as any gluten intake will result in a relapse. Generally, eating a diet of fresh healthy food should be adequate. Those suffering from Coeliac disease will have to avoid any foods that contain flour such as pastries, bread and biscuits. Also, they need to be cautious about manufactured and processed foods, as flour is often used in the manufacturing process.

Some supermarkets now provide gluten-free ranges of food, which are labelled as such. The Coeliac Society regularly tests convenience foods for gluten and provides its members with a list of safe foods. However, manufacturers change their recipes and processes regularly and the Coeliac Society is aware of this and regularly re-checks foods. Therefore, it is important for those who suffer with Coeliac disease to continually receive up-to-date lists. Foods approved by the Coeliac Society usually carry the sign of the 'crossed grain', as shown in Figure 5.21.

Sufferers of Coeliac disease also need to take care when eating out as it is difficult to know exactly what the food ordered contains; they should therefore choose food which is nearest to its natural form.

There are some flours which a coeliac may consume and these can be used to make baked products. However, the results produce different textures, colours and flavours than the same product made with wheat flour. Gluten-free flour produces a product most similar to wheat flour but is very expensive. Other flours include soya flour, rice flour, potato flour and cornflour. With careful meal planning, a coeliac can eat a well-balanced diet.

FIGURE 5.21 *Symbol used on packaging of food approved by the Coeliac Society*

> Think it over...
>
> Visit your local chemist, health food shop and supermarket to carry out a survey of price differences between foods and flour suitable for non-coeliacs compared to similar products for coeliacs.

> Consider this
>
> Many older people suffer from some form of food intolerance. Arden Care Home has a new resident who suffers from Coeliac disease.
>
> 1. What component of food do coeliacs react to?
> 2. Explain the effects of Coeliac disease on the digestive system?
> 3. Discuss how the care home can cater for the needs of this new resident in the food it provides.

Food allergies

Allergies to food seem to be on the increase. This is partly because of better recognition of symptoms and partly because there seems to be an increase in the number of people suffering from food allergies. Some of the most common foodstuffs that give rise to allergies are milk, eggs, shellfish and peanuts.

Allergies are quite difficult for carers to deal with, as they vary so much according to the individual. With acute food allergies, the first sign is usually a tingling in the mouth and a swelling of the lips. This may be followed by vomiting or diarrhoea if the food is swallowed. This is called an anaphylactic reaction.

An anaphylactic reaction is caused by the sudden release of chemical substances in the body, including histamine, from cells in the blood and tissues where they are stored. The release is triggered by the reaction between the allergic antibody with the substance causing the anaphylactic reaction. In the case of food allergy, the allergen could be any ingredient in the food.

Key concepts

IgE is the term for an allergic antibody.

An *allergen* is a substance which causes an anaphylactic reaction.

✳ DID YOU KNOW?

An anaphylactic reaction is so sensitive that minute quantities of the allergen can cause it. Therefore, even having peanut oil on a utensil which is then used to prepare another dish can cause a reaction. This is why you often see a warning on processed foods that the food is made on a production line on which products containing nuts are also made, as the manufacturer cannot guarantee that every trace of nut has been removed before they make the next product batch.

A severe reaction to food allergies is anaphylactic shock and is at the extreme end of the allergic spectrum. The whole body is affected, usually within minutes of exposure to the allergen, but sometimes the reaction is delayed and will occur hours after contact. This makes the cause more difficult to identify. Peanut allergy and nut allergy are frequently severe and for that

reason have received widespread publicity. Other foods can also cause anaphylaxis as can other triggers such as insect stings, latex and drugs. On very rare occasions anaphylaxis may occur with no obvious trigger. The signs and symptoms of anaphylaxis are shown in Figure 5.22.

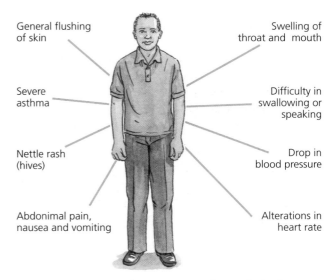

General flushing of skin

Severe asthma

Nettle rash (hives)

Abdonimal pain, nausea and vomiting

Swelling of throat and mouth

Difficulty in swallowing or speaking

Drop in blood pressure

Alterations in heart rate

FIGURE 5.22 *Signs and symptoms of anaphylaxis*

There may also be a sudden feeling of weakness as a result of a drop in blood pressure. The individual often collapses and falls unconscious. An individual would not necessarily experience all of these symptoms.

Treatment

Any individual who suffers from anaphylactic shock will need adrenaline. Adrenaline injection kits are available on prescription for those believed to be at risk and those people generally carry kits with them. The kits are available in two strengths – adult and junior.

The injection must be given as soon as a serious reaction is suspected and an ambulance must be called. If there is no improvement in 5–10 minutes, a second injection must be given.

Think it over...

Plan one meal that is suitable for as many different special diets as possible. Explain why the meal meets the different needs.

Milk intolerance

The most common reaction to milk is due to lactose intolerance, (lactose is the sugar found in milk). The body lacks or is unable to produce sufficient lactase, the enzyme necessary for the digestion of milk. As the milk sugar cannot be digested, it passes into the large intestine where it causes irritation and consequently pain and diarrhoea.

Sufferers from milk intolerance do not necessarily have to avoid all milk and dairy products, as usually small amounts can be tolerated with little ill effect. Cheese has so little lactose that it does not produce the symptoms. Yoghurts also contain very little lactose as most is converted to lactic acid during fermentation, which does not cause the same symptoms.

Sufferers may choose goat or ewe's milk and cheese and these are low in lactose.

Consider this

Matthew's mother thinks he may suffer from hyperactivity. Matthew is six years old. Hyperactivity is a reaction a child may have to a food or food constituent.

1. What signs and symptoms might Matthew display if he was suffering from a food intolerance?

2. Name two foodstuffs that are commonly known to cause to hyperactivity.

3. Explain ways in which Matthew's mother could reduce the risk of hyperactivity through the choice and preparation of food.

Summary

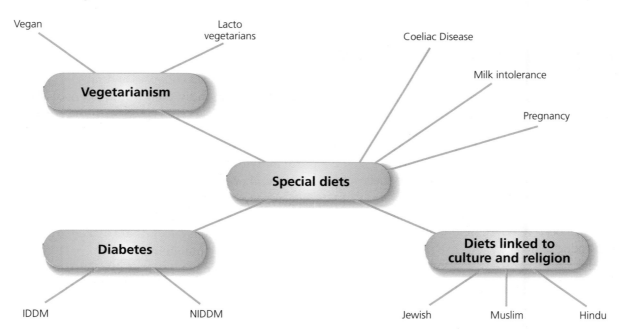

FIGURE 5.23 *Section 5.5 summary*

5.6 Food preparation and food hygiene

Poor food hygiene and poisons in foods

Food poisoning as a result of poor food hygiene is on the increase. Reasons for this include:

* increase in eating out where more food is prepared in a commercial setting in which hygiene faults can occur easily and one fault affects many

* mass catering, e.g. in hospitals, schools, care homes where one fault can affect many

* greater use of convenience foods where temperature control is very important and is commonly misunderstood. This can also affect cook-chill food provided for the elderly

* increased consumption of takeaways where food is kept at room serving temperature for long periods of time

* more cases are being reported as the public are more aware and there are also better laboratory techniques to identify causes.

Food may be poisonous or cause illness for several reasons:

* some foods are naturally poisonous because they contain natural toxins, e.g. some mushrooms, red kidney beans (if not cooked correctly)

* food may be contaminated with toxic chemicals such as lead, copper, agricultural pesticides and herbicides; or chemicals such as disinfectants can contaminate food during growth, storage, preparation and/or cooking

* food may be contaminated with pathogenic micro-organisms or toxic chemicals produced by micro-organisms. This is the most important type of food poisoning and is generally a result of poor food hygiene practices.

The main reasons for food poisoning are poor temperature control and/or incorrect storage. This often occurs because food is prepared too far in advance, cooled too slowly, stored incorrectly (for example, at room temperature), not reheated sufficiently or incorrectly thawed.

Groups particularly at risk from food poisoning include vulnerable groups such as children, pregnant women, the elderly and those suffering from illness or convalescing. They are less able to cope with the symptoms of food poisoning.

Conditions in which bacteria multiply

Growth conditions need to be understood as preventing these conditions will help to prevent the growth of harmful bacteria. Conditions for the

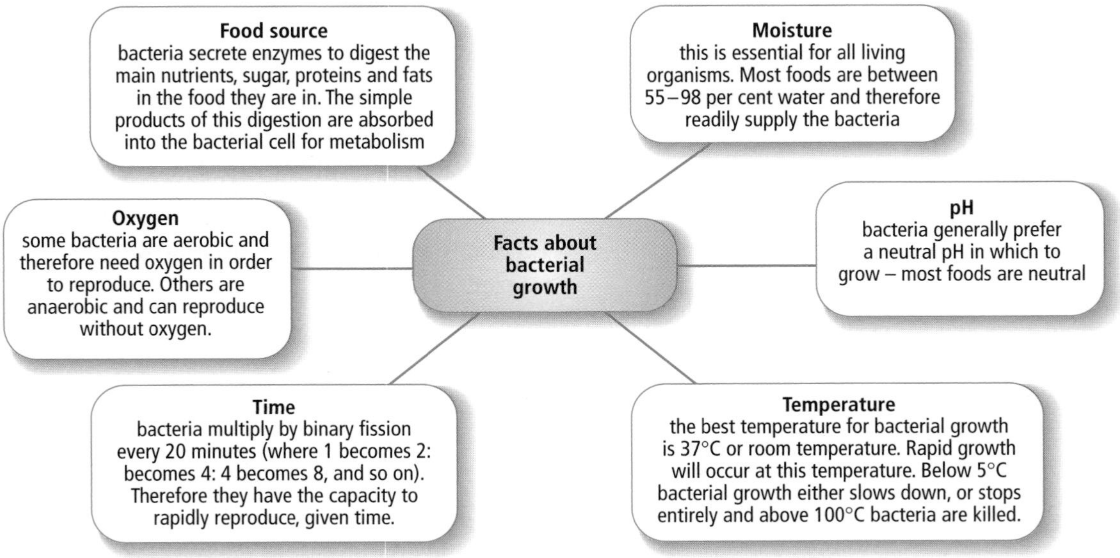

Food source
bacteria secrete enzymes to digest the main nutrients, sugar, proteins and fats in the food they are in. The simple products of this digestion are absorbed into the bacterial cell for metabolism

Moisture
this is essential for all living organisms. Most foods are between 55–98 per cent water and therefore readily supply the bacteria

Oxygen
some bacteria are aerobic and therefore need oxygen in order to reproduce. Others are anaerobic and can reproduce without oxygen.

Facts about bacterial growth

pH
bacteria generally prefer a neutral pH in which to grow – most foods are neutral

Time
bacteria multiply by binary fission every 20 minutes (where 1 becomes 2: becomes 4: 4 becomes 8, and so on). Therefore they have the capacity to rapidly reproduce, given time.

Temperature
the best temperature for bacterial growth is 37°C or room temperature. Rapid growth will occur at this temperature. Below 5°C bacterial growth either slows down, or stops entirely and above 100°C bacteria are killed.

FIGURE 5.24 *Conditions that promote the growth of harmful bacteria*

growth and reproduction of bacteria are shown in Figure 5.24.

Most methods of food presentation aim to remove one of these growth conditions. For example, freezing reduces the temperature to a level at which bacteria cannot multiply; canning heats food to a level at which bacteria are killed; dehydration removes the moisture and pickling renders the pH too acidic for most bacteria to be able to grow.

Common types of bacteria that cause food poisoning

There are many types of food poisoning bacteria. Table 5.18 sets out some of the most important types and how common they are.

Preventing food poisoning

There are a number of simple precautions which can be taken when preparing food that will help to reduce the risk of food poisoning. These can be divided into food choice and storage and preparation and cooking.

Food choice and storage

When choosing and storing food it is important to make sure you:

* always choose fresh foods which look fresh
* choose foods that are within 'sell by' dates
* use a cool bag to transport cold foods from the supermarket to home
* do not allow frozen foods to thaw between cooking and storage
* make sure the fridge is between 0° and 5°C and the freezer below −18°C
* store cooked and raw food separately
* store cooked meat above raw meat to avoid blood dripping onto cooked meat.

Food preparation and cooking

When preparing and cooking food it is important to make sure you:

* use separate utensils to prepare raw and cooked foods
* wash hands before preparing food and between handling different foods
* wash hands after using the lavatory
* ensure that you do not touch face, hair or nose when preparing food
* ensure that you do not cough or sneeze over food – if you are preparing food for others, do not do this if you are ill
* clean work surfaces and utensils as you go
* eat foods by the use by dates
* keep animals away from food preparation areas
* thoroughly defrost food that needs defrosting before cooking
* make sure cooked foods reach a temperature of over 63°C – they should be piping hot
* follow the instructions for pre-prepared foods and make sure that reheated meals are piping hot
* check meat and poultry with a food thermometer to make sure that the right temperature has been reached. Juices should run clear
* keep hot foods hot and cold foods cold
* do not keep food warm for long periods of time and particularly not between 5° and 63°C where bacteria multiply rapidly
* cool foods as quickly as possible and within 1.5 hours cover and store in the fridge or freezer.

NAME	HOW FOOD IS CONTAMINATED	AFFECTED FOODS	SYMPTOMS	ONSET	DURATION	SPECIAL COMMENTS INCLUDING GROUPS MOST AT RISK
Salmonella	Found in the guts of humans, animals and insects; therefore their excreta are both a direct and indirect source of this bacteria. Poor hand washing habits after using the toilet may be a cause of infection. Salmonella can also survive outside the body for long periods and therefore door handles, work surfaces and equipment can be contaminated. Meat and poultry may be infected at the slaughter house	Meat, especially cooked meat, and poultry, eggs, shellfish from polluted water, custards, cream and ice cream	Some fever, vomiting and diarrhoea	12–36 hours as the bacteria produces the poisonous substance in the cells and this is only released into the body when the cell dies	1–7 days	This is the most common type of food poisoning and is responsible for two thirds of cases. Salmonella can survive for up to 3 hours on unwashed hands. It is particularly dangerous for the very young and the elderly and can lead to death. It is easily destroyed by adequate cooking – food must reach a high enough temperature to kill the bacteria
Staphylococcus aureus	Found in the human nose, throat and on the skin. Also found in whitlows, infected burns and wounds and in nasal secretions after a cold. Introduced to food directly from the hands or by droplet infection from coughs and sneezes or indirectly by licking spoons or handkerchiefs	Foods which are handled and then served without cooking, e.g. cream-filled cakes, pre-cooked or processed meats and pies. Also meats that are pre-cooked then reheated to serve as this allows the food handler to contaminate them after cooking	Vomiting, diarrhoea, abdominal cramp (unpleasant but not serious)	1–6 hours (very rapid as the toxin is produced by the bacteria before it is eaten)	6 – 12 hours	Toxin is produced in the food before the food is eaten and therefore onset is quick but so is the course of the illness. Bacteria are easily destroyed by heat but the toxin can survive 20 minutes of boiling
Clostridium perfringens	Found in soil and therefore infects fruit and vegetables. It can form spores and therefore can survive dry atmospheres – it is often found in dust, on floors and on kitchen surfaces	Meat, gravies, stews and large joints which are cooked and allowed to cool slowly	Diarrhoea and severe stomach pain	8–22 hours – because the bacteria produces the toxin when it reaches the intestines	12–24 hours	The spores are heat resistant and are not killed until exposed to a temperature of 100 °C plus. They germinate as meat and meat dishes start to cool

continued overleaf

NAME	HOW FOOD IS CONTAMINATED	AFFECTED FOODS	SYMPTOMS	ONSET	DURATION	SPECIAL COMMENTS INCLUDING GROUPS MOST AT RISK
Clostridium botulinum	Found in soil and decaying matter	Bottled or canned foods particularly those which are not acidic. Vegetables, meat, fish and meat pastes where the processing temperature has not been high enough to kill the spores	Central nervous system is affected leading to paralysis and eventually death	13–36 hours	Prolonged illness which is sometimes fatal	Very rare disease. The bacteria produce a spore, which if it survives processing can reproduce without air and produces a very dangerous toxin
Listeriosis	The bacteria can grow in low temperatures where other bacteria are usually dormant and it produces a toxin as it develops	Found in pre-prepared salads, soft crusted cheeses, processed meats and pates, cook chill foods and shellfish	Moderate flu-like symptoms – can cause miscarriage in pregnant women. Sometimes causes blood poisoning	5 days to 6 weeks	Various	Toxin damages the human cells involved in immunity and therefore abnormally weak people do not stand up well to an attack of this toxin. It is difficult to treat as it gets inside the cell which protects it from antibiotics

TABLE 5.18 *Some of the most common types of food poisoning bacteria*

Summary

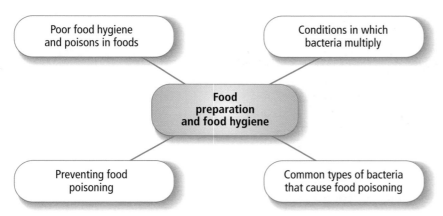

FIGURE 5.25 *Section 5.6 summary*

Consider this

Hamed Ali is an active 78-year-old who is still living in his own home. He has meals on wheels delivered on Mondays and Thursdays.

As the meals provided are cook-chill, it is important that Hamed understands how to store and reheat the cook-chill meals correctly. Hamed's daughter visits on Sunday and finds that he has been keeping his meals in the kitchen cupboard until he eats them. Hamed still prepares some food from fresh produce. He particularly likes chicken and is therefore at risk from cross contamination.

1. Identify four conditions that bacteria need to multiply.

1. What advice could Hamed's daughter give him to help him prevent food poisoning?

3. What advice would you give Hamed about safe food handling?

UNIT ASSESSMENT

This unit is assessed through a written examination which lasts for one-and-a-half hours. The exam will assess your knowledge, understanding and skills in relation to nutrition and dietetics. This will be applied to health and social care situations.

The exam consists of four compulsory structured questions, which will include short answers as well as free response. Some questions will require you to analyse data relating to nutrition and dietetic issues and to evaluate evidence, make judgements and draw conclusions.

The paper will cover all the areas of the unit; therefore, you need to revise all topics thoroughly. To gain high marks, you need to ensure that:

* you provide detailed relevant answers which show a depth of understanding and are accurate

* you relate your answers to the scenario in which they are presented

* you analyse any data thoroughly and present your comments clearly. You should be able to show logical reasoning and judgements

* your conclusions are details, relevant and consistent with the data provided

* you should be able to support suggestions and opinions with information gained through the study of this unit.

Unit test

1   Explain what is meant by DRV. (1 mark)

2   Why is it essential that protein is included in the diet? (1 mark)

3   Explain the difference between saturated and unsaturated fats. (2 marks)

4   Why is it unhealthy for a pregnant woman to 'eat for two'? (2 marks)

5   What is Coeliac disease? (2 marks)

6   Explain the difference between a vegan and a lacto vegetarian. (2 marks)

7   How can you tell if an individual has a food allergy or a food intolerance? (4 marks)

8   Explain the dietary restrictions of one culture. (2 marks)

9   Explain how salmonella bacteria may get into food. (2 marks)

10 Outline the different measures individuals can take in their choice of food to help them reduce the risk of CHD. (4 marks)

References

Barasi, M. (2003) *Human Nutrition: A Health Perspective*, Hodder Arnold, London

Bender, A., Bender D. (1989) *Food tables and labelling*, Oxford University Press, Oxford

Fox, B, Cameron, A. (1995) *Food Science and Nutrition*, Hodder Arnold, London

HMSO (1995) *Manual of Nutrition*, HMSO Books, London

Tull, A. (1997) *Food and Nutrition*, Oxford University Press, Oxford

Useful websites

Please see ww.heinemann.co.uk/hotlinks (express code 1554P) for links to the websites of the following, which may provide a source of information:

* Coeliac Society
* Food Standards Agency
* BBC Food
* Food Commission
* Foodlink
* Vegan Society

UNIT 6

Common diseases and disorders

You will learn about:

Introduction

This unit aims to help you to understand the causes and symptoms of a range of common diseases and disorders. The unit is externally assessed by an examination lasting one-hour-and-a-half.

6.1 Infectious disease

Infection is caused by micro-organisms which include bacteria, fungi, viruses and parasites. They can enter the body through the respiratory system, the digestive system and open wounds, and some can cross through the placenta from a mother to an unborn baby.

Although everyone is potentially vulnerable to infection, there are certain groups of individuals who are more at risk than others, depending on their age, state of health or lifestyle. Those most particularly at risk are the very young, very old and people with underlying conditions, for different reasons:

* the very young have immature immune systems that cannot fight off infection

* the very old have immune systems that are less efficient than when they were younger

* people with underlying conditions may have immune systems that are unable to cope with fighting off infection, which could be a gross assault on the body.

Bacteria

Bacteria are single celled micro-organisms that are invisible to the naked eye and can only be seen under a microscope. They reproduce by binary fission, which means that they divide, in some cases very quickly. Most bacteria in existence are harmless to humans and are known as non-pathogenic micro-organisms. The bacteria that are harmful are considered to be pathogenic or disease causing bacteria. Some bacteria are beneficial as they are used in food production such as bread, cheese and yoghurt making and for use in sewage works to treat waste. Other bacteria live naturally on or in the body, such as *Escherichia coli* (*E. Coli*), which helps to keep the large intestine healthy. It is only when it contaminates food that it can cause food poisoning, which is potentially fatal.

Some bacteria cause disease and are known as pathogenic bacteria. A pathogen is a disease-causing organism. Other bacteria will feed on food, which makes it go bad. Most bacteria release toxins, and these can change the cell chemistry or invade body cells where they can multiply and cause disease.

Bacteria are classified according to their shape. There are four shapes:

* cocci – spherical e.g. *Staphylococcus aureus* – causes food poisoning

* bacilli – rods – e.g. E. coli and *Salmonella* – cause food poisoning

* spirilla – spirals – an example is syphilis

* vibrio – crescents – an example is cholera.

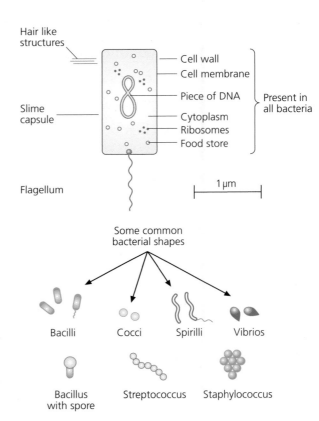

FIGURE 6.1 *Different types of bacteria*

Fungi

Most people are aware of different types of fungi – mushrooms, toadstools, yeasts and moulds. Some are edible, such as mushrooms, and others are used beneficially such as in beer making, bread and for the manufacture of antibiotics.

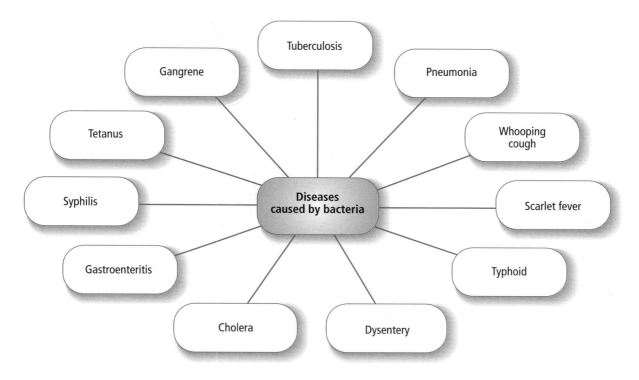

FIGURE 6.2 *Bacteria can cause serious diseases*

Most fungi that cause disease in humans will not cause serious illness, but they can cause irritation and discomfort. Examples of more common fungal infections are:

✳ athlete's foot, a contagious fungus that attacks the feet

✳ thrush, a yeast that can affect the skin, mouth, gut and vagina (candidiasis)

✳ ringworm (tinea), a fungus that can affect all areas of the body.

Fungi can form spores that can be carried on wind and rain and spread disease, or they can spread by growth.

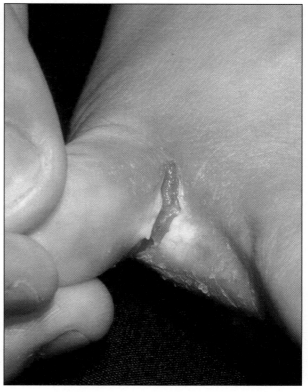

Athlete's foot affecting the skin between a 14-year-old boy's toes

Viruses

Viruses are even smaller than bacteria and can only be seen under an electron microscope. They are made up of DNA or RNA surrounded by a protective protein coat. They cannot multiply so have to invade a cell in order that they can use the cell's structures to make more viruses. Eventually, the cell will burst which releases the viruses. They then are able to invade other cells and the process starts again. Epithelial linings such as in the respiratory system are particularly vulnerable to virus invasion because they are not covered by skin, which provides protection as long as it has not been broken.

Although people can be immunised against many viruses, and some such as smallpox have been eradicated in recent years, colds and influenza are still very common. In recent years new strains of influenza have originated in Hong Kong and China, and have in some cases reached epidemic proportions. Because viruses cannot be treated by antibiotics, this makes them very difficult to treat.

The spread of viruses and bacteria

Viruses and bacteria are spread in similar ways, as shown in Table 6.1.

Some bacteria and viruses can be transmitted through sexual contact or through infection by instruments or blood contaminated with blood or other body fluids. It is for this reason that standard

Droplet infection	Infected droplets of moisture in the air are breathed in by the victim, e.g. colds and flu
Via digestion	Contaminated food or water is ingested, e.g. cholera
Via the placenta	Some viruses can pass through the placenta from the mother to the foetus; an example is rubella or German measles
Via broken skin	A example is hepatitis B through a needlestick injury

TABLE 6.1 *Ways in which viruses and bacteria are spread*

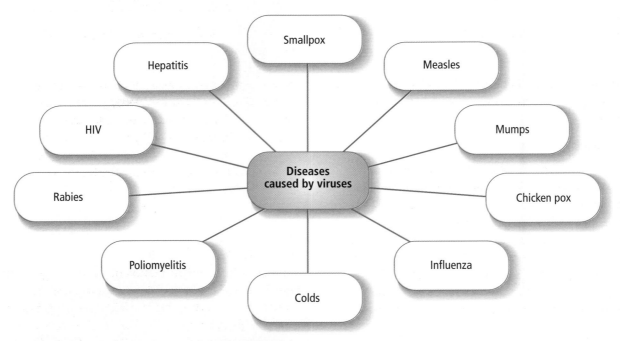

FIGURE 6.3 *Viruses can cause a variety of diseases*

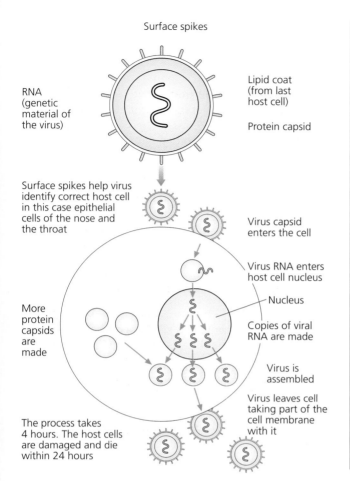

Surface spikes

RNA (genetic material of the virus)

Lipid coat (from last host cell)

Protein capsid

Surface spikes help virus identify correct host cell in this case epithelial cells of the nose and the throat

Virus capsid enters the cell

Virus RNA enters host cell nucleus

Nucleus

More protein capsids are made

Copies of viral RNA are made

Virus is assembled

Virus leaves cell taking part of the cell membrane with it

The process takes 4 hours. The host cells are damaged and die within 24 hours

FIGURE 6.4a *Influenza virus: infection cycle*

Disease		Some symptoms
AIDS		Prolonged tiredness, fever, diarrhoea and excessive weight loss
Common cold		Sneezing bouts, runny nose, shivering, streaming eyes
German measles		Small pink spots covering the skin, swollen glands, mild fever
Hepatitis		Headache, muscle pain, nausea, vomiting, jaundice
Influenza		Same symptoms as the common cold plus aching muscles, fever and a cough
Measles		Runny nose, streaming eyes, followed by spots on the back and arms, white spots in mouth
Mumps		Fever, sore throat, shivering and swollen glands
Polio		Mild fever, stiffness of muscles and eventually paralysis
Rabies		Headaches, muscular spasms and breathing difficulties

FIGURE 6.4b *Some common viral diseases and their symptoms*

precautions should be followed by all personnel who are likely to come into contact with bacteria and viruses.

Spores

Spores are like overcoats that will encase some bacteria and fungi. This acts as a protective mechanism and allows the bacteria and fungi to withstand higher temperatures and other circumstances that would normally kill them. For this reason, foods that might be likely to be infected by these organisms must be heated at higher temperatures and for a longer time than those that do not develop spores in order to destroy them.

Parasites

A parasite is an organism that lives in or on a host, obtaining nourishment without causing benefit or killing the host. They can cause damage within the body. Examples of parasites that are seen in the United Kingdom include head lice, scabies and tapeworms. There are many parasites that cause illness and disease, especially in Third World countries. Many of these are caused by people drinking and washing from contaminated water supplies.

Specific bacterial infections

Meningitis

Meningitis is the inflammation of the meninges – the three layers of the brain. Meningitis can also be caused by a virus but this is a fairly benign infection and there is no specific treatment for it. Bacterial meningitis, however, is generally much more serious.

There are three main types of bacterial infection that cause meningitis. These are:

✱ *Haemophilus Influenzae type b* (Hib)

* *Meningococcus*
* *Pneumococcus.*

> ## ✳ DID YOU KNOW?
>
> Before Hib vaccination was introduced in October 1992 about four in every 100 children aged between 1 and 4 years of age were Hib carriers, with 1 in 600 children going on to develop some form of Hib disease by their fifth birthday. Each year around 30 deaths were caused by Hib infection and it left about 80 children with permanent brain damage (in England and Wales). Following the introduction of Hib vaccine into the immunisation schedule there was a 98 per cent drop in laboratory confirmed cases of Hib disease.
>
> *Source:* Department of Health website

Meningococcus

Groups B and C *Meningococcus* are the most common in the UK. The bacterium cannot survive outside the body. As well as meningitis, people can also suffer from septicaemia (an infection of the blood caused by the bacterium).

Who is at risk? Although it can affect anyone, the most at risk groups are children under five-years-of-age and teenagers aged 15, 16 and 17. About one in four people are carriers of the bacterium which lives in the nose and throat. It is spread by close contact such as kissing, coughing or sneezing.

Symptoms A variety of symptoms may occur, but not necessarily all of them:

* rash – this is red or purple in colour and develops as small spots. They can occur anywhere on the body and can grow to look like small bruises. The tumbler test can be carried out to check whether the rash is meningitis. A clear glass is pressed firmly on the rash, and if the rash does not fade, medical help must be sought immediately
* fever, sometimes with cold hands and feet
* stiff neck with inability to bend forward
* headache which becomes severe

* photophobia – the victim will close their eyes and turn away from bright light
* aches and pains
* confusion or drowsiness
* repeated vomiting.

Babies can display other symptoms including:
* a different cry from usual – may be high pitched or moaning
* high temperature
* will not feed
* irritable if handled
* sleepiness
* the fontanelle or soft spot on the baby's head may bulge
* jerky movements and stiffness of the body or floppiness
* fits (convulsions).

Symptoms can develop over a few hours although in some cases this may take longer and cause doctors to diagnose a different illness, such as a more minor viral infection. However, if the victim's condition starts to deteriorate, then it may be meningitis or septicaemia.

Treatment Urgent antibiotic injections in high doses are given and intensive care may be required. If meningitis is treated early enough then most people will make a good recovery. Most people who do not receive treatment will die.

> ## ✳ DID YOU KNOW?
>
> In the UK about one in ten people who have meningococcal meningitis without septicaemia die. Of those who survive, some are left with some permanent damage such as brain injury or deafness. If septicaemia occurs then up to half of cases may die, depending on how quickly treatment is given.
>
> *Source:* www.patient.co.uk

Prevention In 1999 a vaccine was developed and introduced to prevent Group C *meningococcus*. Babies are now routinely given this as part of their immunisation programme. In addition 15, 16 and 17 year olds were also targeted to receive the vaccine, as they were the second most at risk group. As a result, the incidence of Group C meningitis has been dramatically reduced. Group B *meningococcus* infection is now the most common type in the UK. A vaccine has not yet been developed against this type.

Pneumonia

Pneumonia can be caused by bacteria, a virus or a fungus. It is inflammation of the lung tissue. Pathogens enter the respiratory tract, and the immune system can normally fight off such assaults. However, if someone has an inefficient immune system then the bacteria will multiply and cause infection in the lungs. *Streptococcus pneumoniae* is the main bacterium responsible for pneumonia.

Who is at risk?   People who are chronically ill or have weak immune systems: this can include those suffering from asthma, diabetes, heart conditions, smokers, HIV, people who have had their spleen removed, alcoholics and children and older people.

Symptoms These include the following:

∗ high temperature

∗ cough

∗ sweats and shivers

∗ feeling unwell

∗ aches and pains

∗ sputum (phlegm) – may be yellow/green or bloodstained

∗ tight chest and breathlessness

∗ chest pain if the pleura (the lung membranes) are infected

∗ a crackly chest when listened to with a stethoscope.

Diagnosis will often be confirmed by having a chest x-ray.

About 50 per cent of pneumonia cases are caused by viruses but these tend to be in small children. Adults usually suffer from the bacterium *Streptococcus pneumoniae*.

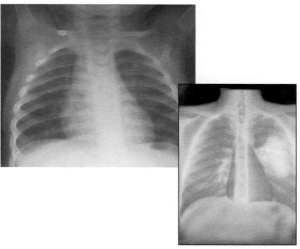

A normal (above) and abnormal (right) chest x-ray

Treatment People suffering from bacterial pneumonia will be treated with antibiotics. It may also be necessary to administer oxygen to help with breathing. In some cases chest physiotherapy will be required to help to clear sputum.

Prevention Vaccination against *pneumococcus* is available and recommended for those who are at risk. Approximately five years after immunisation, a blood test should be taken to ensure continued immunity.

Gonorrhoea

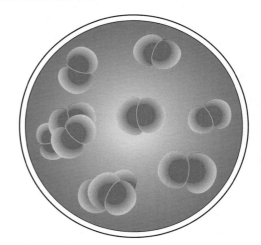

FIGURE 6.5 *The Gonorrhoea bacterium*

Gonorrhoea is a sexually transmitted disease caused by the bacterium *Neisseria gonorrhoeae*. It is the second most common sexually transmitted disease in the United Kingdom and typically affects 15–24 year olds. About one half of the women and one third of the men who suffer from this infection do not experience any symptoms, and this obviously delays treatment. If the infection is left untreated it can cause pelvic inflammatory disease in women and pain and swelling of the testicles and prostate gland in men. Pelvic inflammatory disease can result in fertility problems.

Gonorrhoea can be transmitted from mother to baby during birth. Gonorrhoea cannot be transmitted by lavatory seats or by sharing towels, only by sexual contact.

Who is at risk?   The people who are most at risk are those who have multiple partners and those who do not practise safe sex. The most effective way for people who are sexually active to prevent becoming infected is to practise safe sex and use condoms.

Symptoms In men include the following:

* pain when urinating
* discharge from the urethra – initially slimy but becoming thick and yellow or green
* inflammation of the prostate gland and testes
* irritation or discharge from the anus
* possible sterility

  In women symptoms include the following:
* pain on urination
* vaginal discharge that smells strongly and may be thin and watery or yellowish green in colour
* discharge from the anus
* low abdominal pain.

Infected people who practise oral sex can also develop a throat infection.

Diagnosis This is made by taking swabs from the penis or vagina and urine samples. This can be done by the sufferer's general practitioner or by specialist staff working in a genito-urinary medicine (GUM) clinic.

Treatment Gonorrhoea can be treated very simply with a single dose of antibiotics. One month later a second test is carried out to ensure that the infection has cleared up. Infected people are generally instructed to inform all sexual partners so that they can be tested and treated if necessary.

Specific fungal infections
Athlete's foot

Athlete's foot is also known as *tinea pedis*. It is caused by anthropophile fungi (fungi preferring humans). It is a form of the skin fungal infection known as ringworm. The main fungi that cause such infections are microsporum, epidermophyton and trichophyton. Although athlete's foot generally affects the feet, it can be transferred to the palms of the hands. The fungi can live quite normally on the skin feeding on dead skin cells, but if the conditions are right the fungi will invade the skin. The infection is very contagious and can be passed on by direct contact, the shared use of towels and on floors in communal areas such as swimming pools or shower areas.

Who is at risk?   The conditions for growth of the fungi are warm damp environments so occur in people who wear tight fitting training shoes, do not dry their feet and between their toes properly and wear shoes made from synthetic materials.

Symptoms Development of a small rash between the fourth and fifth toes, which may include scaling and pustules. This may spread all over the foot and to other parts of the body.

Diagnosis This is generally made by a doctor who will recognise the symptoms easily. This may be confirmed by scraping some of the skin cells and checking them under a microscope.

Treatment There are many different brands of anti-fungal treatments, which can be bought without prescription, that come in many forms including prescription powders, creams and sprays. They must be used regularly and treatment must be continued for at least two weeks after the symptoms have disappeared to ensure that treatment has been effective.

Prevention There are measures that can be taken to prevent athlete's foot or to ensure that it does not spread:

* feet should be washed at least once a day and dried very carefully, ensuring that particular attention is paid to the areas between the toes. A separate towel should be used just for the feet and this should not be shared

* socks should be made of natural materials such as wool or cotton and should be changed at least twice a day or if they become damp

* sandals or leather shoes should be worn and shoes made of synthetic materials should be avoided.

Ringworm

Ringworm is caused by the same fungal infection as athlete's foot. When the body is infected this is known as tinea corporis and infections of the scalp are known as tinea capitis. The name is somewhat misleading as the infection has nothing to do with worms. The fungus can be picked up from contact with pets or farm animals and also through person-to-person contact and sharing items such as towels and hairbrushes.

Who is at risk? Anyone can be infected, although people with weakened immune systems may be more at risk.

Symptoms Include the following:

* ring-shaped scaly reddened patches on the skin

* bald patches may appear inside the rings on the head

* itching.

Diagnosis This is made quite easily by medical staff, as this infection is quite easily recognisable. Some fungal infections can be identified under ultraviolet light, but as many do not fluoresce this may not be a conclusive way to make the diagnosis.

Treatment As with athlete's foot, ringworm is treated with anti-fungal creams and lotions. They must be used for some weeks after the symptoms have disappeared to ensure that the fungus is completely cleared from the skin.

Candidiasis

Candidiasis is more commonly known as thrush. It is caused by a yeast called *Candida albicans*, which normally lives quite harmlessly in the skin, mouth, gut and vagina. Sometimes the yeast can multiply very quickly and thrush can break out.

Who is at risk? Thrush cannot be transmitted from lavatory seats, kissing or sharing towels, but it can be transmitted through sexual contact with an infected person. It can affect people who:

* wear tight trousers

* wear nylon underwear

* are taking some antibiotics

* are pregnant

* suffer from diabetes

* have a weakened immune system

* suffer from some diseases such as leukaemia.

  Newborn babies can also suffer from thrush.

Symptoms In women include:

* a thick white vaginal discharge that is cheesy and strong smelling

* soreness, itching and redness in the vulval and vaginal area

* painful sexual intercourse

* painful urination.

  In men symptoms include:
* a similar white discharge from under the foreskin of the penis

* burning, itching and redness under the foreskin or at the tip of the penis

* painful urination

* difficulty retracting the foreskin.

  In babies symptoms include:
* a white cheeselike coating on the mouth and tongue

* red patchy areas under the white coating

* soreness.

Diagnosis Thrush is quite easily identified by the discharge and sufferers' descriptions of the itching and soreness. It can be diagnosed by taking a swab for culture in the laboratory.

Treatment Thrush is easy to treat with antifungal creams, tablets or pessaries (which are inserted into the vagina). Advice to sufferers would include the following:

* avoid using highly scented soaps, deodorants, bubble bath or talcum powders – wash with water only

* wear loose fitting underwear made of natural fibres – not nylon

* use sanitary towels instead of tampons during menstruation.

There have been suggestions that more natural remedies such as using live yoghurt to treat thrush may be useful, but there seems to be little evidence that these are effective.

Some specific viruses

The common cold

About 200 different viruses can be responsible for the common cold. The common cold is not very contagious although adults suffer between two and five colds per year and children seven to ten colds per year. It is thought that the most usual way for the virus to be passed on from person to person is through coughs and sneezes, where droplets are spread through the air, or by hand contact, where the virus is passed by people wiping their hands across their noses and mouths and then passing the virus onto surfaces that other people touch, such as door handles. It is thought that the best way to avoid passing the virus between family members is to wash hands thoroughly. A person is most contagious from the day before the symptoms appear until about three days after they begin to feel better.

> ### ✳ DID YOU KNOW?
>
> On average one person out of sixty will currently be suffering from a cold. This means that in the UK alone, in any one day, 930,000 people will have a cold. As around 30 per cent of the population work, 279,000 people should be away from work on any one day, suffering from cold symptoms. This means that over a full year, one-hundred-and-one-million – 101,000,000 – workings days would be lost to the rhinovirus, costing industry, at a minimum wage of £4 an hour, a staggering £2.8 billion per year; no wonder it is called the **common** cold!
>
> *Source:* www.commoncold.co.uk

Who is at risk? Young children probably carry the virus most commonly and adults with children or who work regularly with children are most at risk of catching a cold.

Symptoms

* sneezing and/or coughing

* runny nose – at first this will be a clear fluid but it becomes thicker and more yellowish in colour

* a feeling of being 'bunged up' and unable to breathe properly

* sore throat or painful swallowing

* the ears might feel blocked

* children might have a high temperature.

Diagnosis Usually people are able to diagnose themselves, or parents will be able to diagnose children quite easily. It is not necessary for a doctor to provide a diagnosis.

Treatment As the common cold is caused by a virus, antibiotics are not given as they will not be effective. Some of the symptoms can be relieved by medicines that can be bought over the counter such as paracetamol, or specifically made cold remedies. A cough mixture can be given to relieve any cough, and there are decongestant inhalers and drops that can be used to relieve the blocked up feeling. In general, people get better within one to two weeks.

In general, people who have colds will not experience a more severe illness, but in some cases, there may be additional problems such as sinusitis (inflammation of the sinuses), tonsillitis, pneumonia or a middle ear infection. These may be caused by the irritated mucous membrane becoming infected by bacteria. In such cases, sufferers may need to see the doctor for treatment, usually antibiotics.

Influenza

The influenza virus was first identified in 1933, although one of the most serious epidemics of influenza occurred in 1918. The virus first affected soldiers in the trenches during the First World War and spread to Britain where 228,000 people died. Worldwide it was estimated that over 70 million people died.

There are two main types of influenza virus that cause infection – influenza A and influenza B. Influenza A usually causes a more severe infection.

Flu is passed on in the same way as the common cold but it is much more contagious. The incubation period – the time between becoming infected and symptoms appearing is about three days. People are infectious from the day before their symptoms appear and remain infectious for about three to five days.

Who is at risk? There are various groups who are more at risk during influenza epidemics. These include:

* young people who have not developed immunity

* people aged 65 or older

* people who have poor immunity

* people with conditions such as diabetes, lung disease, kidney disease, heart disease, or liver disease.

People at higher risk because of underlying illnesses or an underefficient immune system may develop more serious illnesses such as pneumonia. In very severe cases, death may occur.

Symptoms Some of the symptoms are similar to the common cold, but influenza symptoms are usually much more severe. They include:

* headache

* high temperature

* cough

* sore throat

* generalised all-over aching

* shivering.

Many people who are suffering from the common cold believe that they have 'flu', but 'flu' symptoms are much more severe and sufferers are often completely unable to get out of bed for about three days and may need as long as three weeks off work to recover.

Diagnosis This is usually made by a doctor after establishing the symptoms with the sufferer. Laboratory diagnosis is not necessary and is considered to be expensive and time consuming.

Treatment Plenty of rest, fluids and pain relief such as paracetamol or aspirin.

Prevention Immunisation is available against flu and is routinely offered to at-risk groups of people during the autumn of every year when the virus is most likely to cause widespread infection. However, people are advised to be vaccinated every year as the strain of the virus changes frequently and the previous year's vaccine may not protect against a new strain.

Specific parasites

Head lice

Pediculosis capitis, or the head louse, is a small insect that lives on the scalp and feeds on the blood. It has six claws and uses these to cling onto the hair. The female lays eggs or nits in the hair. These are usually pale in colour, which makes them difficult to see, especially in fair hair. The eggs hatch after seven to ten days and it takes about fourteen days to reach maturity. Because of the speed of reproduction, infestation can be very rapid.

Who is at risk? Head lice are very common among school children. Head lice spread by direct contact – that is, they walk from one head to another. There is no evidence to suggest that poor hygiene is a reason for head lice infestation. In fact, there is more evidence to suggest that head lice like clean hair.

Symptoms The main symptom for sufferers is intense itching which leads to scratching and redness of the scalp. The lice may or may not be visible depending on hair colour.

Diagnosis Diagnosis will often be made by a parent or teacher who notices a child scratching his or her head.

Treatment there are various treatments available from pharmacies to treat head lice. They are available as lotions, shampoos and creams. The instructions must be followed carefully as head lice can be very difficult to treat. Treatment may have to be followed according to geographical region, as different chemicals may be more effective in a particular area.

One of the most effective methods of treatment is the 'bug busting' or combing method. This is carried out on wet hair which has had conditioner applied. A fine-toothed comb (nit comb) is then used to comb through the hair in sections. It is a good idea to use plain white kitchen paper or towels round the neck so that the lice can be seen as they are combed out. As long as this treatment is carried out thoroughly, the lice can be removed. It can also be carried out on a regular basis to ensure that the head has not been reinfested.

Other alternative treatments have been used, some with good effect. These include tea tree oil and other herbal remedies.

Scabies

Scabies is caused by a tiny mite called *Sarcoptes scabiei*. It is a highly contagious skin condition caused by the mite burrowing under the skin and laying eggs, after which they die. The eggs hatch after about three weeks and infestation continues.

Who is at risk? Scabies is most common in children and young adults. It can be passed on by close physical contact including sexual contact.

Scabies can affect people of any age but is most common in children and young adults. It is highly contagious and is spread by close physical contact, especially in overcrowded living conditions. There are sometimes outbreaks in schools and residential or nursing homes. It can also be passed on by sexual contact, shared clothing or bed linen. There is some evidence to suggest that a non-infected person can become infected by standing too close to an infected person. Scabies can be common in schools and nursing homes.

Symptoms Itching due to a red, raised rash caused by an allergic reaction to the mite. Some parts of the body are more likely to be affected than others. These include between the fingers and toes, the palms of the hands and soles of the feet, the wrists, the armpits, skin around the navel and the nipples.

Diagnosis Some doctors will have had extensive experience of scabies and will be able to diagnose the resulting rash quite quickly. However it can be quite difficult to diagnose unless a skin scraping can be taken and examined under a microscope and there is a mite present.

Treatment This is simple and efficient and treatment in the form of lotions can be bought from pharmacies without a prescription. The lotions are left on the skin for a prescribed length of time and then washed off. Medical advice should be sought before using these treatments on small children. The whole family should be treated at the same time to ensure that the mites are killed and reinfection does not occur. Once the mites are killed it takes about three weeks for the body to break down the bodies of the mites and itching will continue until they are eliminated. If the itching is very irritating, antihistamines can be taken to help relieve it.

Tapeworms

A tapeworm (*Taenia*) is a ribbon like parasite that can infect the digestive tract. There are two species that are common in humans – *Taenia saginata* (the beef tapeworm) and *Taenia solium* (the pork tapeworm). Although the life cycles of these tapeworms are slightly different, the eggs of both are ingested in infected undercooked meat and develop into adult tapeworms. They are hermaphrodites so can fertilise themselves and produce many eggs. The beef tapeworm can grow to between five and seventeen metres in length; and the pork tapeworm can grow to between three and eight metres long. Tapeworms are transmitted to others by eggs being passed in the faeces, and infecting water or surfaces where they can be picked up and ingested.

Who is at risk? People who eat undercooked infected meat.

Symptoms of beef tapeworm This is variable and infected people may not suffer from any symptoms at all. However, in others there may be obstruction of the intestinal tract. Vitamin deficiency may be evident due to the worm absorbing nutrients from the host's body (although this is more common in people suffering from fish tapeworm). There may be abdominal pain, digestive disturbances, fatigue, anaemia, excessive appetite or loss of appetite, weakness and loss of weight.

Symptoms of pork tapeworm Inflammation of the mucosa of the digestive tract. There may be very few symptoms but infected people may suffer from constipation, pain and diarrhoea. Other parts of the body can be affected because the larvae when hatched can travel into the bloodstream and form cysts in the brain, eyes and under the skin.

Diagnosis The sufferer may report any of the symptoms described above or may notice that they have passed a worm or segment of a worm in their faeces.

Treatment There are two types of oral medication that can be taken to kill the adult worm. These are Miclosamide and Praziquantel. They do not kill the eggs so it is important to keep checking stool samples for some time after the treatment to ensure that the worms have been eliminated.

Prevention In order to prevent tapeworm infestation, steps can be taken to kill the tapeworm larvae in food during storage and cooking. Meat should be cooked at a temperature of at least 65°Celsius or frozen for more than 12 hours. Fish should be frozen for at least 24 hours.

Think it over...

Carry out some research into different types of infectious diseases. You could do this in groups or individually. Find out what type of disease each is, how it is caused, the spread of the disease and symptoms, and how to treat it.

Some examples of infections that you could research are Malaria, Dysentery, HIV, Rubella, Measles, Salmonella, Cholera and Tuberculosis. You could then make a booklet or poster about the diseases you have researched, putting all your findings together.

Summary

This section has covered different forms of infectious diseases, their signs and symptoms, people most at risk and treatment.

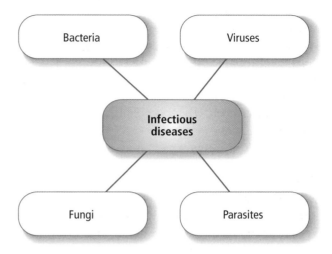

FIGURE 6.6 *Section 6.1 summary*

Consider this

Jackie is 24-years-old and has a six-month-old son, Jacob. Jackie is very worried because when he woke up this morning Jacob seemed to be very hot. He has developed a high-pitched cry and will not settle. He is not keen to take his bottle at breakfast time. A rash is starting to develop on his tummy.

1. Why might Jackie have good cause to worry about Jacob's health?

2. What illness or problem might she suspect?

3. What should she do?

6.2 Allergies

What is an allergy?

An allergy is a reaction by the body's immune system to a substance, which is called an allergen. In many people the particular substance is harmless but about one in four people in the UK develop or have an allergy at some time in their life. Some allergies can be quite minor and slightly irritating, but others can cause severe reaction, resulting in anaphylactic shock, which is potentially fatal.

When someone is exposed to an allergen for the first time, the immune system makes IgE (immunoglobulin E), which is an antibody. The antibodies attach to mast cells in human tissue. On the next occasion that there is exposure to the allergen, the allergen and antibodies attach to the mast cell. The result is that powerful chemicals like histamine are released and cause the symptoms of an allergic reaction. Most of the substances that cause allergies are proteins or contain proteins.

Genetic and environmental influences are factors that can increase the chances of people suffering from an allergy. A person is more likely to suffer from an allergy if there are other members of the family who also suffer from it. However, it is not necessarily the case that a person will suffer from the same allergy. Some people will grow out of the allergy that they suffer from, and others may develop allergies in later life.

Environmental factors may include food (especially nuts, seafood, eggs and dairy products), insect bites and stings, or airborne allergens such as pet dander or feathers, plant pollens, cigarette smoke, chemicals in the atmosphere, and house dust.

Airborne allergies

An airborne allergy is an abnormal reaction to normally occurring substances in the environment. Most substances that are carried in the air are very small and can travel many miles on the wind.

Pollen

Airborne allergies often vary by season, with grasses and trees pollinating in the late spring and early summer and weeds creating problems from late summer to the first hard frost of winter. Depending on which pollen an individual is allergic to, hay fever symptoms may be present at any or all of these times.

Animal dander or feathers

Dog and cat allergies are the most common,

✳ DID YOU KNOW?

The number of people with allergies is increasing. This is probably partly because the condition is recognised by doctors more often than before, but other factors which seem to be important include:

✳ a rise in the number of people, particularly mothers, who smoke

✳ an increase in the number of dust mites in houses as more homes have central heating and carpets, and windows are opened less often because of security fears

✳ a loss of 'normal' immunity in children. This could be the result of better overall hygiene, increased treatment with antibiotics or a reduction in the number of serious childhood illnesses thanks to vaccination programmes. Smaller families also mean a lower risk of infection. Overall, these developments have substantially improved child health and cut death rates

✳ an increase in air pollution

✳ a rise in the number of allergens to which people are exposed. This is due partly to human civilisation over the last 10,000 years and particularly to developments over the last 50 years. New plant species are brought from overseas and people travel abroad much more often, which brings them into contact with new inhaled allergens. The introduction of animals as domestic pets over the last few hundred years may also have had an effect.

However, there is no medical evidence to back up any of these unproven theories.

Source: Institute of Child Health

although many allergy sufferers react to birds, horses, cows and pigs. It is not the cat or dog hair itself that causes the allergy, but the old skin cells (dander) that are constantly being shed.

A person who is allergic to a cat or dog will suffer when animal dander becomes airborne and is inhaled. It is not necessarily the case that a sufferer will be allergic to all cats or all dogs, or that a long-haired animal will produce more dander than a short-haired animal.

Dust mites

House dust allergy is caused by the excreta of house dust mites. These are tiny insects about 0.3 mm in length that are related to ticks and spiders. Every house contains dust mites and a female dust mite lays up to 50 eggs every 3 weeks. They like to live in warm and humid conditions, commonly in beds where humans shed skin, which provides them with food. The excreta contains enzymes which the mites use to digest the dust. It is these that cause asthma and other allergies. Unlike pollen allergy, house dust allergy is perennial – it carries on all through the year.

Mould spores

Moulds are unable to produce their own food so live on other living organisms which they decompose and use for nourishment. Many moulds reproduce by releasing spores into the air which are carried in the atmosphere. It is the spores that cause allergies and they are probably the most common allergy-causing organism. Although they are not generally considered to be seasonal, moulds will be most abundant in warm humid conditions, so will be present in shady damp outside areas and in damp areas in the house such as showers and basements. They can be widely dispersed in the air and can enter a house from outside. They will live on decaying substances where there is enough moisture to support them.

Symptoms of airborne allergies

Sufferers from any of the above sources may experience any or all of the following symptoms:

* runny or blocked nose
* sore, red and itchy eyes
* coughing
* dry, itchy throat and tongue
* itchy skin or a rash
* diarrhoea and/or vomiting
* wheezing and shortness of breath.

Food allergies

Although many people have a reaction to something that they have eaten and believe that they have a food allergy, in reality only about three per cent of children and one per cent of adults suffer from a true food allergy. The difference between food allergy and food intolerance is that an allergy is an abnormal response to a food that is triggered by the immune system. Even though the symptoms of food intolerance can be similar to an allergy, the immune system is not responsible for intolerance.

It is very important that food allergies are identified, because they can cause serious illness and may even be fatal.

Signs and symptoms of food allergy

These include:

* nausea
* vomiting
* flatulence

* abdominal pain

* cramping

* diarrhoea

* rashes

* eczema

* swelling

* nasal allergy

* wheeze

* angioedema (swelling)

* in some cases, life threatening anaphylaxis.

Strawberry allergy

Strawberries are a common cause of hypersensitivity reactions, especially in young children. Skin manifestations are common symptoms in individuals reacting to strawberries. The reaction caused by strawberries may not be due to IgE, but by the aromas and colours found in the fruit.

Egg allergy

This is a reaction to proteins in eggs. IgE is produced in response to the proteins because the immune system thinks that the proteins are harmful. When a person with an egg allergy eats anything that contains egg proteins, histamines and antibodies are produced. Most people who have an egg allergy are allergic to proteins in the white of the egg but some are allergic to the proteins in the yolk. The allergy usually appears in very young children, but most grow out of it by the time they are five years old.

Shellfish allergy

Shellfish allergy is an adverse reaction to the proteins found in shellfish. It is the third leading cause of food allergy (after eggs and milk) and includes both fish and shellfish. People with shrimp or prawn allergy often suffer from skin, stomach or respiratory problems, but people can also suffer from nasal congestion, hives, itching, swelling, wheezing or shortness of breath, nausea, upset stomach, cramps, heart burn, gas, diarrhoea, lightheadedness, or fainting. Reactions can occur as soon as two hours after eating, inhaling cooking vapours or handling seafood. Sufferers must be very cautious about eating in food outlets as often seafood is cooked in the same oil as other foods. Shellfish reactions are not often seen in young children and more usually present in teenage years or adulthood. Fish allergy on the other hand may begin in childhood and is likely to be lifelong.

Nut allergy

There has been a marked increase in recent years in the number of children suffering from nut allergy. Nuts that commonly cause allergies are peanuts and nuts that grow on trees, such as almonds, walnuts, pecans and cashews. Nut allergies cause difficulty in breathing and some people may stop breathing altogether. Nut allergies are known in some cases to be fatal. Many foods contain nuts and even foods that do not contain nuts can be dangerous to those who are allergic because they may have been contaminated with nut products during the manufacturing process. Foods most likely to contain peanuts or tree nuts include:

* cakes, biscuits, pastries, ice cream, desserts

* cereal bars, confectionery

* vegetarian products such as veggie burgers

* salads and salad dressings

* pesto sauce

* satay sauce, curries, Indian, Chinese, Thai or Indonesian dishes

* marzipan and praline (confectionery products made with nuts).

Although it is possible that an individual may only be allergic to one type of nut, it is often more sensible to avoid them altogether so that the possibility of being affected by cross contamination does not arise.

Anaphylaxis

Anaphylaxis or anaphylactic shock is a very serious allergic reaction, which can be fatal if not treated urgently. Although this may not occur until some hours after exposure to the allergen, sometimes anaphylaxis can occur very rapidly. Any or all of the following symptoms can occur:

* generalised flushing of the skin

* nettle rash (hives) anywhere on the body

* sense of impending doom
* swelling of throat and mouth
* difficulty in swallowing or speaking
* alterations in heart rate
* severe asthma
* abdominal pain, nausea and vomiting
* sudden feeling of weakness (drop in blood pressure)
* collapse and unconsciousness.

Diagnosis of allergies

There are different ways to diagnose allergies and the method used will depend on the type of allergy that is being tested for. It is advisable to be diagnosed by a doctor specialising in allergies. Although there are testing kits available for purchase, they may not be reliable, and this is also the case for some other tests such as pulse testing, where the pulse is taken after eating certain types of foods. The belief is that a food that will cause an allergy will raise the pulse. The different ways to diagnose allergies are shown in Table 6.2.

Treatment

The easiest way to avoid developing symptoms for people who have allergies is to avoid the cause.

However, this may not always be easy, especially if the allergen is a food product. People at risk have to become experts in reading food labels and many food manufacturers and providers will indicate if a certain food might contain an allergen, for example nuts.

Anti-histamine drugs are useful in the relief of allergic symptoms. Anti-histamines mimic the allergen enough to fool the body, but they are not enough like histamine to cause the symptoms. As a result they stop histamine working in the body.

In some cases, a desensitising programme may be undertaken, in which very small amounts of the allergen are injected. The body's immune system produces inhibitors that prevent the allergic reaction from occurring. Gradually immunity to the particular allergen increases and symptoms decrease. This form of treatment is not suitable for food allergies, and is most commonly used for insect bites and stings and pollen allergy.

Anaphylactic shock must be treated immediately to prevent serious illness and possible death. The greatest threat to sufferers is that they experience swelling of the face and neck. This is because histamine affects smooth muscle, which causes the airways to swell and difficulty in breathing. People who know that certain substances are likely to trigger such a serious attack will usually carry adrenaline in the form of epinephrine. This is an injection 'pen' which they

TESTS FOR ALLERGIES	
Skin prick test	A needle is used to prick the skin (usually of the forearm) and an allergen is dropped into the broken skin. If the person is allergic to the substance, a raised red itchy patch will appear. The more severe the allergy, the stronger the reaction will be. Often a person will be tested at the same time for several possible causes. This may not be a useful diagnostic tool in someone for whom there is a fear that the allergic reaction might cause anaphylaxis.
Blood test	A sample of blood is taken and levels of IgE antibodies of different substances are measured. The higher the level, the more likely a person is to suffer from an allergy.
Patch test	This can be carried out for people who suffer from eczema or dermatitis conditions. A small amount of different allergens are placed on the skin and covered with a small aluminium patch. They are left for 48 hours and the reaction is then observed and measured.
Challenge test	This can be done by directly introducing suspected allergenic substances into the eyes, nose or lungs to measure the reaction.

TABLE 6.2 *Ways of diagnosing allergies*

Girl at the beach wearing a EpiPen adrenaline syringe round her neck

can self-administer as soon as they know that they are in danger. Most injection kits are easy to use and can even be injected through clothes to ensure the quickest possible treatment. Even people with very little knowledge can use them in emergency situations.

Summary

In this section you have learned about different types of allergies, what causes them, how they are treated and the signs, symptoms and treatment for anaphylactic shock.

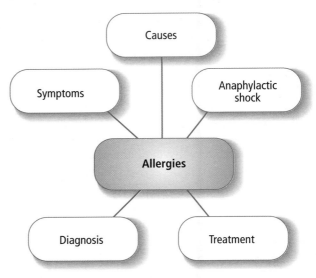

FIGURE 6.7 *Section 6.2 summary*

Consider this

Mr Jones is a very unadventurous eater and has been invited to a business dinner in a very well-known restaurant. When he arrives, his boss tells him that the dinner has been ordered in advance, and not wishing to cause offence, Mr Jones decides that he will have to eat everything put in front of him. The menu consists of mussels, pasta with a pesto sauce and almond and plum tart. About three hours after going to bed, Mr Jones wakes up feeling very ill. He has difficulty breathing and feels nauseated. He rushes to the bathroom where he vomits and has diarrhoea.

1. What might be wrong with Mr Jones?

2. What tests might he undergo to find out what is wrong with him?

3. What advice might he be given after he has been given the results of his tests?

6.3 Disorders of the eye and ear

The eye

There are two eyes situated in the front of the skull in cavities known as orbits. The eyes are organs of sight. Sensory nerve cells in the eye pick up images and transmit them to the brain via the optic nerve where they are translated to form pictures. Having two eyes is a great advantage, as they allow humans to see large areas and to have three-dimensional vision. This means that the depth, height and width of objects can be interpreted, and is known as binocular vision.

The structure of the eye

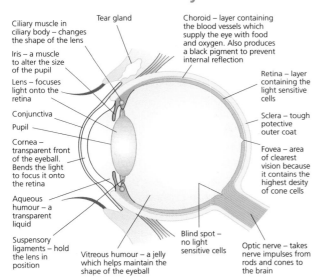

Ciliary muscle in ciliary body – changes the shape of the lens

Tear gland

Choroid – layer containing the blood vessels which supply the eye with food and oxygen. Also produces a black pigment to prevent internal reflection

Iris – a muscle to alter the size of the pupil

Lens – focuses light onto the retina

Retina – layer containing the light sensitive cells

Conjunctiva

Pupil

Sclera – tough potective outer coat

Cornea – transparent front of the eyeball. Bends the light to focus it onto the retina

Fovea – area of clearest vision because it contains the highest desity of cone cells

Aqueous humour – a transparent liquid

Suspensory ligaments – hold the lens in position

Vitreous humour – a jelly which helps maintain the shape of the eyeball

Blind spot – no light sensitive cells

Optic nerve – takes nerve impulses from rods and cones to the brain

FIGURE 6.8 *The structure of the eye*

The eye is a spherical object held in place in the orbit by six muscles, which can move the eye in all directions. It has three layers:

∗ the sclera, which is a tough outer coat to protect the eye

∗ the choroid, which is highly vascular to provide blood supply to the eye

∗ the retina which contains cells that are sensitive to light.

There is a bulge at the anterior (front) of the eye; this is separated from the posterior (back) by the lens, which is held in place by suspensory ligaments. Tear or lachrymal glands produce tears, which are secreted onto the surface of the eye through the tear ducts. They keep the front of the eye lubricated and have antibacterial properties. The eyelashes and eyelids are also protective, preventing debris from entering the eye. Blinking helps to spread tears over the surface of the front of the eye, keeping it moist.

The eye is divided into two chambers, the anterior (front) and posterior (back). Aqueous humour is a thin fluid that fills the anterior chamber between the cornea and iris. The fluid is needed to nourish the cornea and lens and gives the front of the eye its shape. Vitreous humour, much thicker than aqueous fills the posterior chamber. It also gives the eye its shape. If the eye is pressed, the vitreous allows the eye to return to its original shape.

The external surface of the eye ball of the eye and the inner surface of the lids is called the conjunctiva. It covers the thick outer coat of the eye called the sclera, and helps to lubricate the surface of the eye.

The iris is the coloured part of the eye, which controls the light levels in the eye. It is a muscular structure and is able to widen and narrow the pupil (an opening in the middle of the iris). In bright light the pupil contracts to reduce the amount of light entering the eye and in dim light the pupil dilates (gets wider) to let in more light.

The cornea is the clear front of the eyeball, which bends light as it reaches the eye. It provides about two-thirds of the eye's focusing power. It enables light to pass through the lens and reach the retina, the layer of the eye that contains light sensitive cells. These cells are rods and cones. Rods detect all colours except red, but they are only interpreted as black and white. They are able to work in areas where light is low or when it is dark. The cones detect the three primary colours, but they can be mixed to make all the other colours in the spectrum. They only work in bright light, which explains why we are unable to see colours clearly in the dark. The rods are situated evenly in the retina, but the cones are mostly situated in one small area known as the fovea.

The fovea is situated in the centre of the macula, which is in the centre of the retina. The macula is responsible for allowing detailed vision for tasks such as reading and close work.

The optic nerve is situated at the back of the eye and transmits nerve impulses from the retina to the brain for interpretation. The only part of the optic nerve that can be seen when examining the back of the eye is the optic disc. There are no light-detecting cells in this area, and this is known as the blind spot.

The ear

The ears are organs of hearing and are situated either side of the skull on the sides of the head. They are designed to pick up sound waves from the atmosphere and transmit them to the brain where they are interpreted. They also have other important functions – detecting movement and gravity to stabilise balance.

The structure of the ear

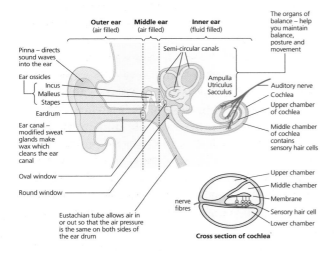

FIGURE 6.9 *The structure of the ear*

The ear can be broadly divided up into three parts – the outer ear, the middle ear and the inner ear.

The outer ear is mainly the visible part of the ear – the pinna and the auditory canal, which ends at the tympanic membrane or eardrum. The pinna is composed of cartilage and picks up sound and vibrations and directs them down the auditory canal towards the eardrum. The auditory canal is lined with skin that secretes wax, which protects

the ear and prevents foreign bodies from entering it.

Sound waves reach the eardrum, which vibrates. These vibrations are transmitted to the ossicles or small bones in the middle ear, an air filled cavity – the malleus (hammer), incus (anvil) and stapes (stirrup), which in turn vibrate and continue to transmit the vibrations to the inner ear. The middle ear is connected to the nasopharynx or throat by the Eustachian tube, whose function is to equalise air pressure on either side of the eardrum. It is normally closed but opens on coughing or swallowing. The base of the stapes sits in the oval window, which leads into the inner ear.

The inner ear is made up of a series of fluid filled bony tubes called the bony labyrinth and inside this is the membranous labyrinth, which is filled with endolymph, another fluid. There are three main sections of the bony labyrinth:

* the cochlea

* the semi-circular canals

* the vestibule

The cochlea is a snail-shaped structure, which contains the organ of Corti. This is spiral shaped and contains hair cells, which convert vibrations into nerve impulses. These impulses are transmitted by the eighth cranial nerve to the brain.

The three semi-circular canals are filled with fluid and lined with hair cells and are arranged in three different planes at right angles to each other. Their function is to detect movement of the head and maintain balance. As the head moves, the fluid moves and impulses are sent to the brain so that imbalance can be adjusted.

The vestibule connects with the cochlea and semicircular canals. It contains the utricle and saccule, which are responsible for balance.

Dysfunctions of the eye

Myopia (short sight)

Myopia or short sightedness is a condition where people are unable to focus on distant objects. It normally occurs when the eyeball is too long from front to back, or the cornea is more steeply curved than normal. This causes light rays to focus in front of the retina. Close-up objects are clear and distant objects are blurred.

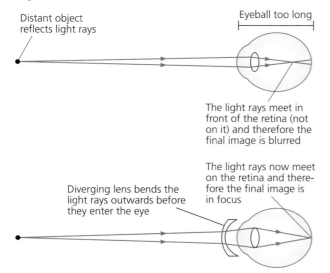

Distant object reflects light rays

Eyeball too long

The light rays meet in front of the retina (not on it) and therefore the final image is blurred

Diverging lens bends the light rays outwards before they enter the eye

The light rays now meet on the retina and therefore the final image is in focus

FIGURE 6.10 *Myopia and how it is corrected*

Myopia can be corrected by the use of glasses or contact lenses, which have concave (diverging) lenses. This then allows the light rays to reach the retina. Laser surgery is available privately to correct myopia, but the long-term effects of such treatment are as yet unknown. Laser surgery is unlikely to be available on the National Health Service until the long term effects are known.

Hypermetropia (long sight)

Hypermetropia or long sightedness is the opposite of myopia. In this disorder, the eye ball is too short so light rays are focused beyond the retina. This has

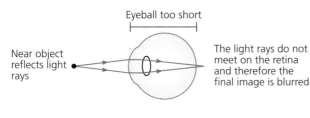

Eyeball too short

Near object reflects light rays

The light rays do not meet on the retina and therefore the final image is blurred

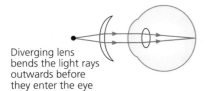

Diverging lens bends the light rays outwards before they enter the eye

The light rays now meet on the retina and therefore the final image is in focus

FIGURE 6.11 *Hypermetropia and how it is corrected*

the effect of making close-up objects blurred and distant objects clear.

Hypermetropia can like myopia be corrected by glasses or contact lenses. Laser surgery can also be used in some cases.

Astigmatism

Astigmatism occurs in people who have an irregularly curved cornea. In a normal eye the light rays hit the cornea and are refracted by it and further by the lens so that the light hits the retina. In astigmatism the cornea is irregular so the light rays cannot hit the same area of the retina, causing blurring of all objects, whether they are close-up or distant.

Astigmatism is corrected by glasses and contact lenses.

Presbyopia

Presbyopia is generally considered to be a condition that is caused by ageing. During middle adulthood, usually in the forties, people begin to experience problems in focusing on close-up work, such as reading, sewing or working on the computer. People generally notice that they have to hold reading material further away from their eyes and are not able to do things like thread needles. Continuous close-up working without correction can lead to eyestrain and headaches. Presbyopia is believed to occur because the lens in the eye becomes less flexible and therefore unable to focus clearly for close work. People who are short sighted or myopic may find that they are able to focus more clearly just by removing their glasses for tasks such as reading.

Again, this is a condition that can be corrected by glasses or contact lenses.

Conjunctivitis

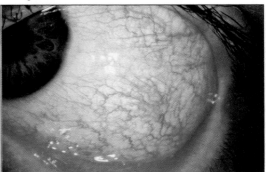

Conjunctivitis is the inflammation of the conjunctiva, which is the mucous membrane that covers the cornea and the inside of the eyelid. It usually affects both eyes at once although it may begin in one eye one or two days before the other. Conjunctivitis is very common and can be very uncomfortable. There are five different types of the condition as shown in Figure 6.12.

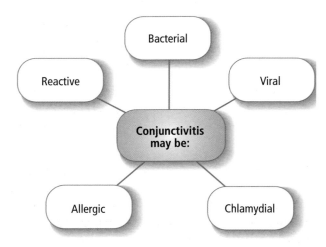

FIGURE 6.12 *Types of conjunctivitis*

Normally, people who suffer from any of the forms of conjunctivitis discussed below will get better within a few weeks, even if they are left untreated. Treatment will usually speed up the healing process, however, and provide relief from the irritating symptoms.

Bacterial conjunctivitis This is caused by bacteria, usually streptococcus, staphylococcus or haemophilus.

The eyes are red and feel gritty. There is a sticky discharge and the eyelids may be stuck together on waking.

Bacterial conjunctivitis is usually treated with antibiotics in the form of drops or ointment. The eyes should be cleaned with cool boiled or sterile water to remove any discharge. The infection will usually clear within a few days.

Viral conjunctivitis This is a viral infection which is very contagious. It often occurs when a person has a cold and is commonly caused by adenovirus.

The symptoms are red and irritated eyes; and the infection may spread to the corneas. It may last for several weeks.

As this is a viral infection there is no antibiotic treatment that can be used effectively. Ointment may be used that will soothe the eyes. It is very important that people suffering from viral conjunctivitis maintain strict standards of hygiene to prevent its spread. This includes not sharing items such as flannels and towels with others.

Chlamydial conjunctivitis This type of conjunctivitis is caused by *Chlamydia trachomatis*, which can affect other parts of the body and can also be a sexually transmitted disease. The eyes are red, sore and produce a sticky discharge.

Treatment is by antibiotics and sufferers who may have the sexually transmitted form of the infection must be treated for this. In addition, partners of the sufferer should be treated.

Allergic conjunctivitis This form of the infection is usually associated with allergies and hay fever. The eyes itch intensely and are often red. Because of its link with hay fever and pollen, it may be more common during spring and summer when the pollen count is high.

The eyes may be treated with anti-histamine drops, and this may be long-term. If the sufferer knows what has triggered the attack, they should avoid this substance if they can.

Reactive conjunctivitis – chemical or irritant conjunctivitis This is the reaction of the eyes to chemicals such as those used in swimming pools or to dust or smoke. The eyes are red, uncomfortable and watery.

Treatment is to avoid the irritant causing the condition as far as possible.

Cataract

A cataract is the gradual clouding of the lens of the eye, which results in deteriorating vision. This is because light rays cannot reach the retina through the cloudiness. It is the most common cause of vision loss for people over 55-years-of-age in Western countries. The clouding causes blurring of vision, but cataracts will not cause permanent blindness. Treatment is a simple operation, normally under local anaesthetic, to remove the cloudy lens and replace it with an intraocular lens implant (a plastic lens), which will restore sight. People who have cataracts in both eyes will not have them operated on at the same time. Diabetics are more susceptible to the development of cataracts.

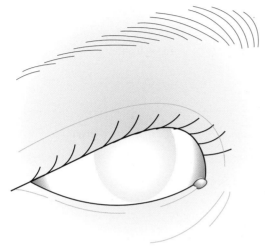

FIGURE 6.13 *A cataract*

Dysfunctions of the ear

Glue ear

Glue ear or secretory otitis media is a common cause of hearing impairment in children. This is not usually a problem if it occurs in only one ear, but if it occurs in both then developmental delay can occur.

Glue ear affects the middle ear, which is normally an air-filled cavity. Fluid builds up behind the eardrum and prevents efficient transmission of sound waves into the ear. It is usually a common problem in young children that gets better without treatment. It is thought that glue ear occurs because the Eustachian tube collapses. This prevents air flow in the middle ear and causes the production of mucous.

Who is at risk?   Those at risk include:

* children under the age of seven (with the highest risk at two years of age)
* children who have a parent who smokes
* children who suffer from frequent coughs and colds

* boys
* children with a brother or sister who has also suffered from glue ear
* children who have been bottle-fed
* children who attend day care and come into contact with other children during winter or spring
* children with certain genetic conditions, such as Down's syndrome
* children with an anatomical abnormality affecting the face, such as a cleft palate.

Diagnosis   This is usually made by inspecting the inside of the ear. The doctor can usually see that there is fluid behind the eardrum. Hearing tests can be carried out to determine the level of hearing loss.

Treatment   There is often no treatment because in about half of cases the glue ear will get better within three months. Antibiotics may be used but there seems to be little evidence that this will prevent further attacks.

Autoinflation is a technique that can be used. A small tube can be placed into the Eustachian tube and inflated to open it up. This allows air to circulate and may dry up the mucous.

In some cases an operation will be required. This is called myringotomy and insertion of grommets. A myringotomy is a small cut into the ear drum. Any mucous is sucked out and a grommet is inserted into the hole that is made. The grommet is a tiny tube shaped like a cotton reel that will help the air to circulate in the middle ear. This may be carried out with the removal of the tonsils and adenoids. The grommets normally fall out spontaneously and the hole in the ear drum closes, but about half the children treated with surgery will need grommets to be reinserted within five years of the original operation.

Tinnitus

Tinnitus is a condition in which people hear sounds that no-one else can hear. The sounds may be ringing, whistling, buzzing or other sounds and can be present constantly or they can come and go. It usually occurs with some level of hearing loss. Tinnitus can be caused by different ear disorders, such as a perforated ear drum, middle ear infection, an obstruction in the ear canal or Ménière's disease, which is a disease of the inner ear caused by a change in the fluid pressure. It is not known what causes this disease but it can appear suddenly and may possibly be linked to stress.

Tinnitus can be treated but there is no cure. Some recommended treatments include:

✳ wearing a hearing aid

✳ using a tinnitus masker – this produces white noise that can help to cut out the tinnitus

✳ tinnitus retraining therapy in which people learn to live with the noise.

Most people who suffer from tinnitus can learn to manage the problem and do not suffer unduly, but about 25 per cent of sufferers do experience more severe problems such as difficulty in concentrating, inability to sleep (insomnia) and depression.

Progressive hearing loss in older people (Presbycusis)

Presbycusis is a normal part of ageing and can worsen as a person gets older. Different parts of the ear are affected. The eardrum becomes less elastic and the ossicles (the small bones in the middle ear) are less able to vibrate. This means that fewer sound vibrations are transmitted to the inner ear. In the cochlea in the inner ear, hair cells become less efficient and although sufferers can hear speech they will probably have difficulty in interpreting it.

There is no treatment for presbycusis, but older people who experience this type of hearing loss should be prescribed hearing aids. This will help to overcome some problems such as isolation and exclusion, which may result from the condition.

Summary

In this section you have learned about the anatomy and physiology of the eye and ear, different disorders that may affect them, diagnosis and treatment.

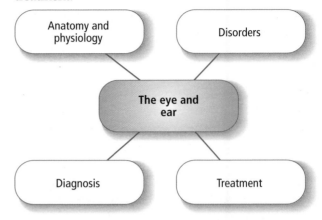

FIGURE 6.14 *Section 6.3 summary*

Consider this

Mrs Jackson is 75-years-old and lives alone. Her family all live close by and her three children take it in turns to visit her every day to check that she is all right. She has diabetes, and recently all of her children have noticed that she is becoming clumsy. She is not able to find things when she puts them down and reads and watches television much less than usual. She loves doing needlework, but she has also stopped doing this recently. When asked, she complains that her vision is blurred. She also says that when she does watch the television she has to turn the sound up very loud in order to hear it.

1. What do you suspect could be wrong with Mrs Jackson?

2. What would you advise her to do?

3. What treatment might she need?

6.4 Dental caries (tooth decay)

Dental caries or tooth decay is the destruction of the hard outer surfaces of the tooth. This is often caused by the consumption of foods that are high in sugar and by lack of fluoride in drinking water.

The structure of teeth

Humans have two sets of teeth – milk or deciduous teeth and adult or permanent teeth. Normally, babies are born with their teeth buried beneath the gums, although there have been some reported cases of babies being born with teeth. Children have twenty deciduous teeth, which loosen and fall out as the adult teeth push up from under the gums. Adults have 32 teeth.

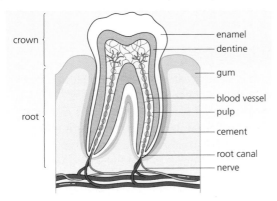

FIGURE 6.15 *An adult tooth*

The crown is the visible part of the tooth which is above the gum line. The outermost layer of the crown is the enamel, which is the hardest tissue in the body. It is mainly made up of calcium. Dentin is the layer situated under the enamel. It is also made up of calcium but is not as hard as enamel. The pulp is the soft central part of the tooth where nerves and blood vessels are situated. The root makes up about two thirds of the tooth and anchors the tooth into the bone of the upper or lower jaw.

The formation of dental caries or tooth decay

The teeth are coated in a substance called plaque, which is made up of bacteria. It occurs naturally in the mouth and helps to protect the mouth from infection. When a meal is consumed, sugar provides nutrition for the bacteria, which then produce acid and will attack the enamel of the teeth. Saliva is produced, which neutralises the pH of the mouth within 20–30 minutes, helping to prevent dental caries. Chewing sugar-free gum after a meal promotes the production of saliva.

If sugary food continues to be eaten, particularly by people who 'graze' all day, the acid is not neutralised and will attack the enamel and form a cavity. If the cavity is not treated, the acid will eat through the enamel and attack the dentin underneath. This can happen quite quickly because of the softer properties of the dentin. As a result, a large cavity could be forming in the dentin that is not visible because the dentin is situated below the enamel. Eventually, the decay will reach the pulp. This produces infection, which in turn causes inflammation and toothache.

Left untreated, dental caries can cause an abscess. This is a collection of pus that builds up as bacteria take hold. It can be very painful and cause the root of the tooth to die. If this happens, the pain may stop, but the bacterial infection will remain without treatment, and spread to other tissues.

The stickiness of the food that is eaten will have an effect on the acidity of the mouth. Food that sticks to the teeth and stays there for a long time will have a greater effect on acid production than those that do not. Dentists are reporting an increase of tooth decay among children who eat large quantities of dried fruit, as these stick to the teeth. So although there are benefits to the body of eating dried fruit, there are also less beneficial effects for dental health.

Gingivitis

Gingivitis is inflammation of the gums, which is

> **Think it over...**
>
> Carry out further research into the causes of tooth decay. Produce a leaflet for parents on how to encourage their children to look after their teeth. The leaflet should include how dental caries are formed and dietary and hygiene advice.

usually caused by poor dental hygiene. Dental plaque builds up in the area of the mouth where the teeth and gums meet. This irritates the gums and makes them sore, swollen and red. The gums bleed easily, especially when brushing the teeth.

Left untreated, this could lead to receding gums, infection and eventually possible loss of teeth. There are other factors that can contribute to gingivitis:

* poor diet

* smoking

* injury to the gums

* pregnancy

* diabetes that is not well controlled

* some drugs

* stress

* anatomical problems with alignment of the teeth.

There are various preventive measures that can be taken to reduce the risk of gingivitis occurring. These include good dental hygiene – regular brushing of teeth with a fluoride toothpaste and flossing between the teeth – visiting the dentist regularly and maintaining a healthy diet that does not contain too many sugary foods.

Good oral hygiene, regular dental checks, not smoking, eating a healthy diet and keeping stress under control help to reduce the risk of gingivitis.

Think it over...

Find out how clean your teeth are. You can obtain dental disclosing tablets at a chemist. These are small tablets that can be chewed for a few minutes and then spat out. The disclosing agent is coloured and stains the plaque on your teeth. You can easily see the amount of plaque on your teeth by looking in a mirror. You can then remove this by thorough brushing and flossing of your teeth.

Summary

In this section you have learned about the structure of teeth, how dental decay occurs and dental disorders.

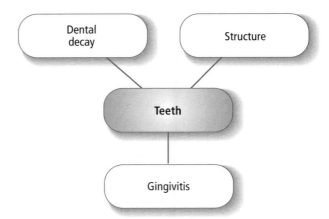

FIGURE 6.16 *Section 6.4 summary*

Consider this

Sarah is seven-years-old and has just had her yearly dental check up. The dentist is concerned that she is showing signs of quite advanced dental decay. He is not sure that Sarah and her mother understand the importance of good dental hygiene and nutrition. He has asked you to find out what Sarah eats and what her dental hygiene routine is. She eats a packet of sweets every day and loves fizzy drinks such as cola. She brushes her teeth when she gets up in the morning.

1. What dietary advice would you give to Sarah's mother to improve her dental health?

2. What advice would you give Sarah about brushing her teeth?

6.5 Skin, spots and rashes

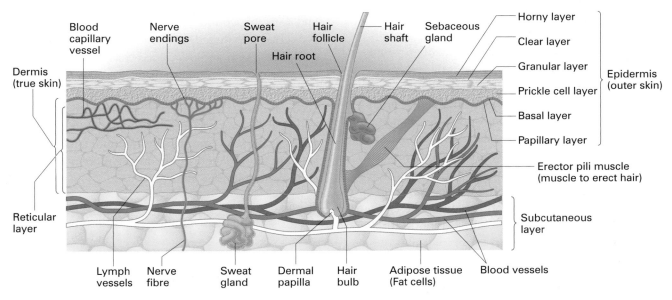

FIGURE 6.17 *The skin*

The skin

The skin is the largest organ of the body. It is made up of three layers, the epidermis, the dermis and the subcutaneous layer.

The epidermis is the outermost layer of the skin. It provides a waterproof protective covering and is made up of five layers. The top three layers – the horny layer, the clear layer and the granular layer – are made up of dead cells which are shed constantly. The two layers beneath them are the prickle cell layer and basal cell layer, which contain living cells. New skin cells are formed in the basal cell layer and are pushed upwards as new cells form beneath. The prickle layer is protective and prevents bacteria entering the body. The granular layer contains keratin, a protein that prevents loss of moisture through the skin. The clear layer is found on the palms of the hands and soles of the feet and provides cushioning and protection. The horny layer is the dead layer of skin from which skin cells are shed.

The dermis contains two layers, the papillary layer and the reticular layer. This is the layer where most of the functioning parts of the skin are situated, such as blood and lymphatic supply, nerve endings, sebaceous glands, hair follicles and sweat glands. These layers provide protection and nourish the skin.

The subcutaneous layer is a fatty layer, which provides insulation and protection for the body.

Blackheads (comedones)

Sebaceous glands are situated in the dermis close to hair follicles. They produce a greasy substance called sebum, which lubricates the hair and skin. A comedone or blackhead is formed when skin cells and sebum form a plug inside the hair follicle. The pore of the follicle is open, and the plug is exposed to the outside air. This gives the comedone a black appearance. This is not dirt but is due to the exposure of the oil to the air. These are also known as closed comedones. Whiteheads are formed in the same way, but the pore of the hair follicle is closed. Because of this, the plug is not exposed to the air so this type of comedone, known as a closed comedone, is a small bump in the skin.

Comedones often appear with acne or spots. They are most common at puberty when the release of testosterone causes the sebaceous glands to produce more sebum. The sebum blocks the pore of the hair follicle and a bacterium, propionobacterium acnes, which lives normally on the skin, multiplies within the blocked pore, causing inflammation. This causes redness and a spot appears, which is filled with pus. Spots can be localised, or as in a case of acne, generalised with spots commonly appearing on the face and neck, chest, shoulders and back.

People who suffer from acne are often young and feel very self-conscious about their skin because it is often red and angry looking with spots in various stages of development. There is often a great temptation to pick at or squeeze spots but this should be avoided as it can lead to scarring. Any affected areas should be washed twice a day with an unperfumed mild cleanser, which may contain an anti-bacterial substance. Sunshine can often aid in improving the skin condition, but sufferers must be aware that it can take weeks or months for the condition of the skin to improve. Over-the-counter remedies and prescription medicines can be used to help treat acne, including antibiotics, which may need to be taken for as long as three months. The antibiotics will help to prevent infection of the pores of the skin but will not make a significant difference to blackheads and whiteheads, so the use of a lotion such as benzoyl peroxide should be used at the same time. It is often the case that the use of lotions initially will cause the skin to look worse for a few days before improvement is noticeable. For some young women, the contraceptive pill can help to alleviate the condition, but in others it can make the problem worse.

Blisters

Blisters are small fluid-filled swellings that appear on the skin. Usually, they are formed by friction as skin is rubbed by something, often in the case of the feet by ill-fitting shoes. Serum, the liquid part of the blood, leaks into the skin as a result of the friction, causing the area to become red and sore. There are other causes of blisters, such as burns, including sunburn, and some medical conditions such as chicken pox or impetigo. Skin continues to grow and the growing skin beneath the blister absorbs the fluid and the outer layer of skin dries and falls off. Although many people are tempted to burst a blister to release the fluid, this should never be done because the breaking of the skin could cause bacteria to enter the blister site and cause infection.

Scabs

Scabs are part of the healing process of injured skin. When a person cuts him or herself, the blood clots and seals the wound. Fibrinogen, a blood protein, is converted into threads of fibrin which form a mesh over the wound and trap blood cells, forming a clot. The clot dries out and forms a seal over the cut, preventing entry of bacteria and infection occurring. New skin cells form underneath the cut and push upwards to form new skin. As this happens the scab comes away. In minor cuts the skin heals completely but in deeper more major cuts, a scar might be left.

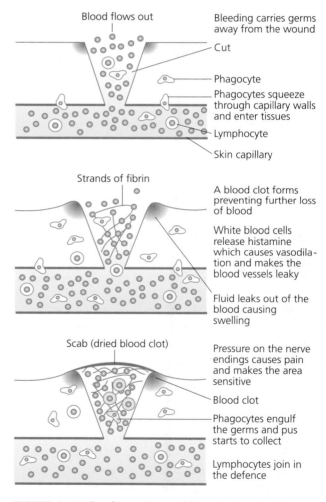

FIGURE 6.18 *The formation of blood clots and scales helps to prevent germs entering broken or cut skin*

Rashes

A rash is a change to the colour or texture of the skin and is usually seen as redness or inflammation. Rashes can be accompanied by itching or fever, and can be very uncomfortable for the sufferer. They can be caused by allergic reaction, infection or occur as a symptom of a medical condition.

There are different types of rashes that will present in different ways as shown in Figure 6.19.

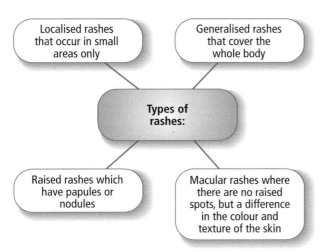

FIGURE 6.19 *Types of rashes*

Localised rashes

Localised rashes are rashes that occur in isolated patches on the skin. In some cases they may appear in one area of the body, but in others there may be patches on the skin in different parts of the body.

Dermatitis means inflammation of the skin and there are different types of dermatitis, which are often referred to as eczema.

Contact dermatitis

There are two types of contact dermatitis that can affect humans.

* Allergic contact dermatitis can be caused by an allergic reaction to contact with a specific material. It is often seen when a person wears jewellery that contains nickel, and only affects the area of skin that has been in contact with the material.

* Irritant contact dermatitis can be caused by prolonged or repeated irritation of the skin, such as exposure to chemicals such as bleach or washing the hands many times a day, which is often known as 'dish-pan hands'.

Although contact dermatitis cannot be cured, it can be treated. Avoidance of the substance that causes the problem and treatment by creams will relieve the rash, but further exposure will cause the rash to return.

Contact dermatitis is not contagious, and spread will depend on the amount of skin that has been exposed to the irritant. The sensitivity of the skin differs in different parts of the body, so some areas may appear unaffected or less affected than others.

Atopic dermatitis Atopic dermatitis often occurs in young children and is thought to be hereditary. It is also known as atopic eczema, and begins with itchy skin progressing to thick discoloured patches of skin on the scalp, torso, arms and legs. It is often associated with allergies. The skin tends to be very dry and can often crack, causing fissures, which can be very sore.

Generally most children will grow out of the condition, but it can return in some people as adults, and sometimes adults will acquire the condition having never had it as a child.

Atopic dermatitis cannot be cured, but it can be treated so that the symptoms disappear. It is not contagious, so you cannot 'catch' it.

Nappy rash

Nappy rash is a rash that will affect babies if a wet or dirty nappy is left for too long in contact with the skin. The skin becomes irritated by contact with ammonia, and becomes very red and sore. In some babies this may occur very infrequently, but a baby with more sensitive skin, may suffer more than others.

Treatment for nappy rash is as follows:

* frequent changing of nappies

* washing the area carefully – rinsing with warm water if the nappy was wet, and using a small amount of soap and rinsing well if the nappy was dirty

* exposure of the skin to air several times a day

* the use of a barrier such as zinc cream to protect the skin

✳ in some cases a change from fabric to disposable nappies may help as disposable nappies are generally more absorbent.

Generalised rashes

Generalised rashes are rashes that can cover the entire body. They can be a symptom of many different types of disease or infection, and may need to be diagnosed formally by a doctor. Two different types of rashes are macular and raised rashes.

Macular rashes Macular rashes are rashes that are not raised from skin level. They are generally of a different texture or colour than normal skin. A macular rash can be a symptom of various diseases and infections, such as rubella (German measles), measles, scarlet fever or an allergy. Before any treatment can be given, accurate diagnosis must be made.

Raised rashes Raised rashes are characterised by papules, blisters or nodules that are raised from the surface of the skin. Again they can be caused by infection or allergy. Common examples of infections causing blistering are chicken pox, herpes zoster (shingles) and meningitis. Allergic reactions can often manifest themselves as hives or urticaria. These are large red itchy wheals on the skin, which can be relieved by preparations such as calamine lotion. It the substance that caused the hives to appear can be identified, it should be avoided as further exposure may cause further reaction.

Summary

In this section you have learned about the anatomy and physiology of the skin, different skin disorders and how to treat or alleviate the symptoms.

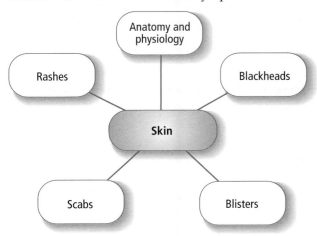

FIGURE 6.20 *Section 6.5 summary*

Consider this

Steve is 17-years-old and is taking a catering course at his local college. He has just started his first work experience placement in a local pub. One of his main duties as a junior kitchen hand is to wash the dishes, which can take three hours each evening. One morning his mother notices that his hands look very dry and red. When questioned, Steve says that his hands are very sore. His mother makes an appointment for him to see his GP.

1. What might the GP diagnose?

2. What advice might he give Steve, when Steve says that he loves his job and is planning that catering will be a long-term career?

3. What arrangements might Steve have to make with his work placement supervisor to ensure that his hands get better?

6.6 Headaches

Headaches are one of the most common forms of pain and are caused by the irritation of different parts of the head and neck. Pain will not be experienced in the skull or brain tissue as they have no pain receptors. Most headaches are caused by tension in the muscles of the head or neck or changes to the blood flow in the vessels of the head. There are four types of headache: vascular, muscle contraction (tension), traction, and inflammatory; and many causes, with some types of headache being more common than others. Headaches are rarely an indication of a serious underlying disease, and can be relieved by over the counter medicines or a change in lifestyle.

Causes of headache

Stress or tension headache

Tension headache accounts for about 70 per cent of all headaches. It is most common in adults and adolescents. There are different causes of tension headache, but in general they are caused by contraction of the muscles in the head and neck. They can be caused by stress, tiredness, poor posture, eye-strain, and tobacco and alcohol use. Women can also suffer from headaches around the time of their menstrual period due to hormonal changes.

Sufferers usually experience general pain and muscle tightness in the head and neck, which does not last very long if treated early with some form of pain relief.

Dehydration and hangover

Water makes up about 70 per cent of the human body and is necessary for many vital functions. A headache is often a symptom of dehydration. There can be many causes of dehydration, such as lack of water intake especially during and after exercise, diarrhoea and vomiting, fever and excessive alcohol consumption. The common term for the after-effects of drinking too much alcohol is a hangover, and a symptom of this is dehydration. Alcohol is a diuretic, which means that it causes water to be lost from the body by urination. In addition, the body is adjusting to a rapidly falling blood alcohol level, and both of these factors contribute to a headache.

Prolonged travel

Long haul travel often involves time changes and a general change in daily routine. Headaches during prolonged travel can be caused by many factors. Aircraft descent for landing can often cause blockage of the sinuses, which can cause a headache, and many people do not drink enough during a long haul flight or are tempted to drink alcohol, especially if they are nervous travellers. People who drink a large quantity of alcohol during flights should be advised to alternate each alcoholic drink with water. Nervous travellers may develop a stress headache, especially if they are afraid of taking off and landing.

Foods

There are certain foods that can trigger a headache, most commonly the four Cs – chocolate, cheese, caffeine and citrus fruits, which are covered further in the following section on migraine.

Stuffy atmosphere

Rooms that are stuffy, over-heated and poorly ventilated can cause headaches and congested sinuses. Central heating can have a very drying effect, and it is advisable to have a window slightly open to provide some fresh air. People who work in offices with central air conditioning sometimes complain of headaches. It is advisable to take breaks for fresh air if at all possible. Some people find that air quality is greatly improved in offices when an ionizer is used to negatively charge the ions in the atmosphere.

Hunger

People can suffer from hunger headaches if they experience a sudden drop in blood sugar levels. It is important to try to keep blood glucose levels steady by regular snacking on slow release complex carbohydrate foods. Although sugary snacks can give an instant 'lift', when the effect wears off the blood glucose level can drop again quite quickly, triggering another headache.

Migraine

Migraine accounts for about 20 per cent of all headaches. It is caused by the constriction of blood vessels on one side of the head, which is accompanied by photophobia (sensitivity to light) and nausea. It occurs in approximately 20 per cent of women and 6 per cent of men. A migraine can last from four to 72 hours.

Who is at risk?   The following factors increase the risk of migraine:

✳ where there is a family history of migraine

✳ smoke or alcohol use

✳ stress or fatigue

✳ menstrual periods and oral contraceptives

✳ certain food – the 4 Cs – chocolate, cheese, citrus fruit and caffeine, food containing sweeteners and additives and those containing tyramine, an amino acid found in red wine, mature cheese and smoked fish.

Symptoms   Include the following:

✳ an aura (often vision disturbance) before the pain begins

✳ pain on one side of the head

✳ sensitivity to light (photophobia) and sound (phonophobia)

✳ nausea and sometimes vomiting.

Diagnosis   There is no specific test that will diagnose migraine, but it is often useful for a sufferer to keep a detailed diary for a few weeks. Incidents of migraine are recorded together with details of food eaten as this may give some indication of a cause.

Treatment   People who suffer from migraine are usually advised to rest in a dark quiet room and to take pain relief as soon as possible after symptoms start to appear. Over the counter analgesia can be sufficient for some people, but others may require a stronger prescription drug to relieve the pain. People who suffer frequent and prolonged migraines may be prescribed preventive drugs, to be taken on a daily basis.

It is important to try to identify any dietary related causes as these can then be avoided.

Summary

In this section you have learned about the signs and symptoms of headaches and migraine, causes and treatment.

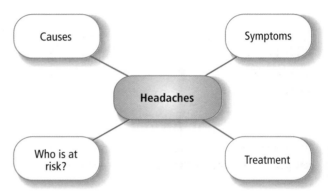

FIGURE 6.21 *Section 6.6 summary*

6.7 Food poisoning

Food poisoning is the term used for any illness which is caused by the consumption of food or drink that is contaminated by bacteria. The bacteria multiply to dangerous levels, are consumed and cause illness. The most common symptoms tend to be nausea, vomiting and diarrhoea although with some bacterial or viral infections, sufferers could also complain of fever or abdominal cramps and may even collapse.

Food-borne diseases

Food-borne disease is caused by bacteria that are passed on to humans by micro-organisms in food or water. Relatively small amounts of these micro-organisms are needed to cause illness.

Causes of food poisoning

There are different causes of food poisoning which can produce symptoms with a range of severity. These are:

* bacteria or viruses that live on food

* moulds on food

* foods that are poisonous to humans

* contamination of food by chemicals or by foreign bodies.

Infective food poisoning

Infective food poisoning is caused mainly by bacteria, viruses and parasites, which can already be present in the food or can come from people, surfaces or equipment. Food usually becomes contaminated from poor personal hygiene or lack of care in preparation. Food handlers who do not wash their hands after using the bathroom or have some kind of infection can cause contamination. Food that is poorly packaged and stored can also cause contamination.

People at risk

Although anyone can become infected and suffer from food poisoning symptoms, those most at risk include young children, because they have immature immune systems, and pregnant women because food poisoning bacteria (especially listeria) can cause stillbirth, premature labour and miscarriage. People who are suffering from other diseases can have reduced immunity due to the illness or the drugs prescribed to treat it, and older people's immune systems tend to be weakened with age.

MICRO-ORGANISM	SOURCE	SYMPTOMS	INCUBATION PERIOD
Salmonella	Raw poultry, eggs, raw meat, milk, animals, insects and sewage	Abdominal pain, vomiting, diarrhoea, fever	12–36 hours
Staphylococcus aureus	Unpasteurised milk, people	Abdominal pain or cramp, vomiting, low temperature	1–6 hours
Clostridium perfringens	Raw meat, animal and human waste, soil, dust, insects	Abdominal pain, diarrhoea	12–18 hours
Clostridium botulinum	Raw fish and meat, vegetables, smoked fish, canned fish and corned beef	Difficulties in breathing and swallowing, paralysis	12–36 hours
Bacillus cereus	Cereals, soil and dust	Abdominal pain, diarrhoea and vomiting	1–5 hours or 8–16 hours depending on the form of the food poisoning

TABLE 6.3 *Types of food poisoning bacteria*

MICRO-ORGANISM	SOURCE	SYMPTOMS	INCUBATION PERIOD
Campylobacter	Raw poultry, raw meat, milk, animals (including pets)	Diarrhoea, often bloody, abdominal pain, nausea, fever	48–60 hours
E. coli	Human and animal gut, sewage, water and raw meat	Abdominal pain, fever, diarrhoea, vomiting, kidney damage or failure	12–24 hours or longer
Listeria	Soft cheeses, cheese made from unpasteurised milk, salad vegetables, patés	Symptoms like flu	1–70 days
Shigella	Water, milk, salad vegetables	Diarrhoea, sometimes bloody, fever, abdominal pain, vomiting	1–7 days

Source: Chartered Institute of Environmental Health

TABLE 6.4 *Food-borne diseases*

Norwalk virus

Norwalk-like viruses are the commonest food borne viral infection and are usually spread from person to person, by environmental contamination and contaminated water. Food-borne infection may be associated with sewage contamination of shellfish or fresh produce, or contamination by an infected food handler. Outbreaks occur most frequently in places like nursing homes and hospitals due to person-to-person spread.

Norwalk-like viruses cause an acute gastro-enteritis and are the commonest cause of viral gastro-enteritis epidemics. Symptoms include vomiting and diarrhoea. The symptoms take 12–48 hours to develop, and last for about 2 days. The virus is destroyed by thorough cooking of food.

Non-infective food poisoning

Non-infective food poisoning is, as its name suggests, not infective. It will usually only make the consumer ill because its cause is not a bacteria, virus or parasite and the contamination is usually physical – that is, something is in the food that will cause illness.

Foods poisonous to humans

There are some foods that are poisonous to humans and can cause illness when eaten. These include toadstools and poisonous fish, such as the Japanese puffer fish. Other foods, such as red kidney beans, are toxic if they are not cooked thoroughly. Canned beans are cooked so do not present a problem but dried beans should be soaked and then boiled in rapidly boiling water for a minimum of 20 minutes before eating.

Contamination of food

Food can be contaminated in a variety of ways – both physical and chemical. Physical contaminants include bones, shells or pips and stalks from food, food packaging, nuts or bolts from equipment, jewellery, hair, fingernails, plasters, dust and dirt and insects and their droppings and eggs.

Chemical contamination can be caused by cleaning chemicals if they are not kept separate from food and food preparation areas, and agricultural chemicals, e.g. on fruit and vegetables if they have been sprayed. They must be cleaned thoroughly or peeled before eating.

Leftover food or drink from metal containers

should always be transferred to a non-metallic container and stored covered in a refrigerator. Acidic and salty food can attack the metal once a can is opened.

Consider this

Carry out research into how to store and prepare different foods safely. Produce a poster that gives information on:

* optimum storage temperatures for freezers and refrigerators

* the temperature danger zone for hot and cold foods

* requirements for bacteria to multiply on foods

* how to store different foods in a refrigerator

* an explanation of 'use by' and 'best before' dates on food packaging.

Summary

In this section you have learned about different types of food poisoning, their symptoms, incubation periods and how to prevent food poisoning and food contamination.

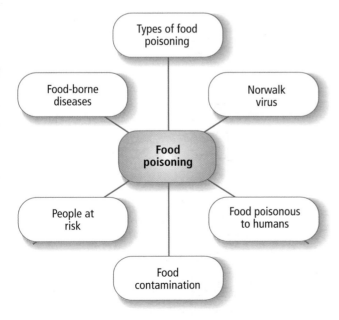

FIGURE 6.22 *Section 6.7 summary*

Consider this

Sunnybank is a residential home for 24 elderly people ranging in age from 78 to 97 years. The cook, Mavis, who has been working there for 16 years has fallen and broken her leg and is unable to work for three to four months. The owner of Sunnybank has contacted an agency to find a replacement for her. They are unable to find a qualified chef, but have just received a call from Andy, a young man who claims to have experience of cooking in residential homes. Because he is desperate, the owner agrees to give Andy a trial before taking up references. Andy produces an excellent lunch for the residents that they all enjoy. Between four and 24 hours later, 18 of the residents start to feel quite ill and start to vomit. Some have a fever and others have a high temperature. The doctor visits and confirms food poisoning. Jane, the senior care assistant, tells him that she observed Andy using the toilet on two occasions during the morning, after which he did not wash his hands. She also said that he licked his fingers to taste the food while cooking it.

1. Why are the residents particularly at risk of food poisoning?

2. What types of food poisoning might they have?

3. What should the owner do?

UNIT ASSESSMENT

How you will be assessed

This unit is externally assessed.

Test questions

1 Which groups are most at risk from infectious diseases and why?

2 Name the four different shapes of bacteria and give an example of each one.

3 How can bacterial and viral infections be spread?

4 What are the signs and symptoms of meningitis?

5 What is tinea pedis and how can it be treated?

6 What is pediculosis capitis and what are possible methods of treatment?

7 Why is the incidence of allergies increasing?

9 Explain the body's response when it is exposed to an allergen.

9 Describe two different ways of testing for allergies.

10 What are the signs and symptoms of anaphylactic shock?

11 Draw a labelled diagram of the eye.

12 Explain how sound waves are transmitted from the outer ear to the brain.

13 Explain astigmatism.

14 What is glue ear and how can it be treated?

15 How does sugar cause tooth decay?

16 Explain how a scab is formed.

17 What is a macular rash?

18 What are the four Cs and what can they trigger?

19 What are the sources, symptoms and incubation periods of salmonella and E. Coli?

20 What is physical and chemical contamination of food?

References

Beckett, B.S. (1981) *Illustrated Human and Social Biology*, Oxford University Press, Oxford

Givens, P., Reiss, M. (1996) *Human Biology and Health Studies*, Nelson Thornes, Walton-on-Thames

Chartered Institute of Environmental Health (1998) *Food Safety First Principles*, Chadwick House Group, London

Hiscock, J. and Lovett F. S., (2002) *Beauty Therapy*, Heinemann, Oxford

Meggit, C. (2003) *Food Hygiene and Safety, A Handbook for Care Practitioners*, Heinemann, Oxford

Wright, D., (2000) *Human Physiology and Health*, Heinemann, Oxford

Useful websites

Please see www.heinemann.co.uk/hotlinks (express code 1554P) for links to the websites of the following, which may provide a source of information:

* Department of Health

* Institute of Child Health

* Chartered Institute of Environmental Health

Needs and provision for elderly clients

You will learn about:

7.1 Health conditions

7.2 Social conditions

7.3 Health care

7.4 Social care

7.5 Interview research with older people

Introduction

This unit explores some of the health and social conditions that influence the quality of life for older people. The nature of – and access to – health and social care services are also explored. The assessment for this unit requires you to undertake an informal interview with one person who is more than 70-years-old. Within this unit, therefore, there is an explanation of how to organise an informal interview and a discussion about the ethical issues involved in interview research. The methodology for writing a structured report is explained and some ideas for covering the report topics, including a comparison of experience, are provided.

7.1 Health conditions

The 2001 National Census asked people about their experience of long-term illness and disability. The percentages given in Table 7.1 show the proportion of people who rated their general health as being good, fairly good or not good.

	GOOD HEALTH	FAIRLY GOOD HEALTH	NOT GOOD
Males			
65 to 74 years	42%	39%	19%
75 years and over	31%	43%	26%
Females			
65 to 74 years	39%	42%	19%
75 years and over	28%	44%	29%

Source: Table 7.3 Social Trends 2004

TABLE 7.1 *How people rated their health in the 2001 National Census*

As you can see from the table, the majority of older people experience good or fairly good health. However, one in four men over the age of 75 and almost one in three women reported that their health is not good.

As people age there are a number of changes to the body. Some of these changes may be due to the cumulative effects of damage during a lifetime. For example, if a person has been exposed to loud music throughout their life there may be accumulated damage to the systems in the inner ear, resulting in a hearing loss. Injuries to the eye may prompt the development of cataracts. Some of the changes to the body involve an ability of body tissues to renew themselves effectively. It is likely that the wasting and thinning of bone, the weakening of muscles and perhaps some impairment within the nervous system are due to a genetic limit on the ability of cells to renew and repair themselves. It is important to understand that people do not wear out – if anything, regular activity and exercise are likely to prolong a healthy life. It is simply that our genetic design does not allow us to go on forever. Some problems associated with ageing are described below.

Heart disease

The heart is a pump, which pushes blood to all the living cells within our body. Heart muscle needs to be fed with blood and the oxygen that it carries in order to stay alive. As people age, fatty deposits can build up in the arteries and this build-up may restrict the flow of blood. When the flow of blood in the coronary arteries to the heart becomes restricted, a person may experience angina; this may be experienced as a feeling of pressure in the chest and it can also feel like indigestion or be experienced as a tightening sensation. Other symptoms of angina involve breathlessness or trapped air. A major blockage to an artery can prevent the flow of blood to the heart and this causes a heart attack known in medical terminology as myocardial infarction. A heart attack can cause permanent damage to the heart and can be fatal.

> **Key concepts**
>
> *Angina* a feeling of pressure in the chest when arterial blood flow is restricted.
>
> *Myocardial infarction* a major arterial blockage which prevents blood flow to the heart, causing a heart attack.

In later life, heart muscles can deteriorate and heart valves can become less elastic. If the heart becomes too weak to pump blood effectively heart failure can occur. Heart failure is often associated with a fluid build-up in the lungs.

Older people can lower their risk of heart disease by eating a healthy diet – avoiding saturated fats and by taking exercise. As with most health problems, smoking dramatically increases the risk of heart disease.

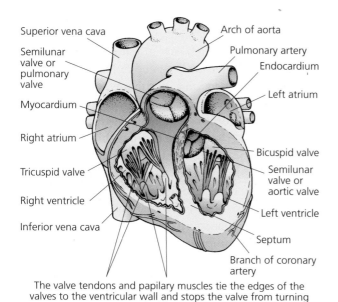

Superior vena cava
Semilunar valve or pulmonary valve
Myocardium
Right atrium
Tricuspid valve
Right ventricle
Inferior vena cava

Arch of aorta
Pulmonary artery
Endocardium
Left atrium
Bicuspid valve
Semilunar valve or aortic valve
Left ventricle
Septum
Branch of coronary artery

The valve tendons and papilary muscles tie the edges of the valves to the ventricular wall and stops the valve from turning inside out.

FIGURE 7.1 *Diagram of the human heart*

Cerebrovascular accidents

A cerebrovascular accident occurs when a blood vessel within the brain is blocked or bursts. Following a burst or blockage, an area of brain tissue does not receive the blood supply it needs, so some brain cells will die. Cerebrovascular disease involves damage to the arteries that supply blood to the brain. Some older people will have a narrowing of the arteries due to fatty deposits. It is sometimes described as the arteries furring up. A blockage can occur if a blood clot forms (this is called a thrombosis) or if some other substance, such as cholesterol, travels in the blood until it causes a blockage (this is called an embolism). When a blockage completely blocks the blood supply to a part of the brain, or when a burst causes bleeding within the brain, this is called a stroke.

Key concept

A *stroke* occurs when blood supply to part of the brain is blocked or bleeding in the brain occurs.

High blood pressure is associated with the narrowing of the arteries and it is important that older people have their blood pressure checked because of the risk of stroke. A stroke can result in brain damage that causes problems with speech, vision, movement of arms and legs and sensation (the ability to feel things like touch).

Older people can lower the risk of cerebrovascular disease by following the health advice to take regular exercise, enjoy a good diet and avoid becoming overweight. Smoking is particularly dangerous and can cause the narrowing of arteries, thereby increasing the risk of cerebrovascular accidents or stroke.

Sensory impairments

Vision

As people grow older they often have difficulty in focusing their eyesight to read small print. A large number of older people therefore need reading glasses to be able to read or use computers. Some people develop long-sightedness as they age: this involves difficulty in seeing close objects, and a person without appropriate glasses may need to hold a book at a distance in order to read it.

More serious problems include cataracts, which may start to develop between the ages of 50 and 60 years and often take time to develop. As people grow older the lens can become hard and cloudy. This process stops the lens of the eye from being able to change shape or transmit light appropriately, resulting in symptoms such as blurred vision. Diabetes can also lead to the development of cataracts. Another serious problem is glaucoma. Glaucoma involves damage to the optic nerve and nerve fibres to the retina. Diabetes can increase the risk of glaucoma. If glaucoma is not detected and treated it can result in blindness.

Key concepts

Cataracts result from changes in the lens of the eye, which can become hard and cloudy as people age.

Glaucoma is caused by a build-up of pressure within the eye, or poor blood supply to the optic nerve.

Older people may be able to reduce their risk of visual impairment by having regular eye tests, in order to check their visual needs and to detect the risk of eye disease. Much visual impairment associated with ageing can be corrected with appropriately prescribed lenses or glasses. Glaucoma can often be treated if detected early. It is thought that protecting eyes from harmful ultraviolet sun rays may also help to reduce the risk of cataract.

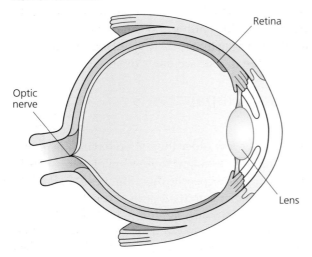

FIGURE 7.2 *The parts of the eye*

Hearing

The ability to hear high-frequency sound is often affected by ageing, as the sensitivity of nerve cells within the inner ear may decrease. This means that some older people find it increasingly difficult to understand certain words or voices. It is not simply that there is insufficient volume – talking more loudly may not help – it is that certain sounds become harder to hear. Hearing loss is often gradual and is sometimes associated with increasing frustration as older people find increasing difficulty in understanding speech. The RNID estimate that there are between eight and nine million people suffering with hearing impairment within the United Kingdom.

Some older people develop tinnitus; this is a problem whereby the person hears sounds within their ear such as ringing, hissing, whistling, roaring or buzzing noises. These sounds are somehow generated within the ear or head and do not come from outside. Tinnitus can create a great deal of stress for some people, as it can disturb sleep and concentration.

There is a saying that hearing impairments cut you off from the world of people. This saying may not be true for everyone, but many people find hearing disorders particularly difficult to live with. Many older people experience a degree of isolation because a deterioration in hearing ability disrupts their ability to communicate and enjoy social activity.

Older people who experience difficulty with hearing may be able to reduce disability following medical assessment, which may present the possibility of managing hearing loss with the assistance of equipment such as hearing aids.

Skeletal mobility problems

Problems with the cardiovascular system are responsible for many mobility problems such as the ability to climb stairs and so on. Many older people also have problems with painful joints that can limit their ability to travel or even to move about the house. Two medical conditions that older people may be at particular risk of are osteoarthritis and osteoporosis.

Osteoarthritis

Osteoarthritis is a type of arthritis in which the cartilage between the bones within a joint gradually disappears. This loss of cartilage can lead to the bones rubbing together, creating pain when limbs are moved. In some cases, pieces of bone or cartilage can break off and float within the joint; as the disease progresses the joint lining can become inflamed. Osteoarthritis most frequently affects the hands, spine, knees and hips, although it can also affect the neck, finger joints and toes. The risk of osteoarthritis increases with age and NHS Direct estimates that around 12 per cent of people over 65 have osteoarthritis. Another type of arthritis – rheumatoid arthritis – can occur at any age, although it is more common after 40-years-of-age. Rheumatoid arthritis is probably caused by a problem with the immune system.

Older people may be able to reduce the symptoms of arthritis by avoiding weight gain, as increased weight will place extra stress on joints. Exercise may also help because exercise helps to strengthen muscles that support the joints.

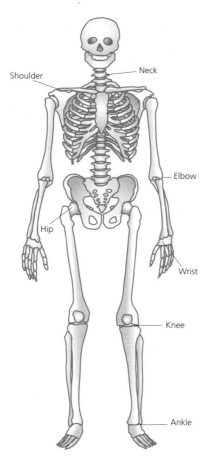

FIGURE 7.3 *The joints of the body*

Labels on figure:
- Shoulder
- Neck
- Elbow
- Hip
- Wrist
- Knee
- Ankle

Osteoporosis

NHS Direct state that approximately three million people in the United Kingdom have osteoporosis and that there are over 200,000 fractured bones every year as a result of osteoporosis. Bone is part of our body and, like other body tissue, it needs to regenerate and rebuild itself. As people become older this ability to regenerate bone becomes less effective. The bones of older people often become thinner and more likely to break than when they were young. Women are more at risk of osteoporosis than men because bone strength is affected by sex hormones. Men continue to produce the male sex hormone testosterone, but women often experience a major decrease in the hormone oestrogen after the menopause. Some people are more at risk of developing osteoporosis because of genetics, i.e. it 'runs in their family'. People who live a lifestyle that involves little exercise may also be more at risk because exercise helps to strengthen bones.

Older people may be able to reduce their risk of osteoporosis by taking regular exercise in order to strengthen bones. A calcium-rich diet may also help. As with so many diseases, smoking will increase the risk of the disease. Excessive drinking of alcohol may also contribute to problems associated with osteoporosis.

If you trip over or fall, brittle bones can result in fractures so much more easily than in a younger person who has strong bones. Because of this, it will be important for older people to avoid hazards, especially within their own homes, that might result in their falling over or knocking themselves against hard surfaces.

Diabetes

Diabetes is known to affect 1.3 million people in the United Kingdom. Diabetes is caused by too much glucose or sugar in the blood; this happens because sugar is not being processed properly because of a lack of the hormone insulin. Type 1 diabetes (sometimes called insulin-dependent diabetes), often starts in adolescence or early adulthood. Type 2 diabetes (sometimes called non-insulin dependent diabetes) mostly occurs in people over the age of 40. Nine out of 10 people with diabetes in the UK have Type 2 diabetes. According to NHS Direct, 80 per cent of these people are overweight and Type 2 diabetes is therefore closely associated with obesity. In Type 2 diabetes the body does not produce enough insulin or cells do not react appropriately to the insulin produced.

High glucose levels in the blood can damage blood vessels and is important that people with diabetes receive appropriate treatment.

Older people can lower their risk of diabetes by taking regular exercise, maintaining a healthy diet that is low in fat, salt and sugar and avoiding smoking or excessive alcohol intake.

Respiratory disorders

Some older people develop problems with breathlessness that is associated with heart problems. If the heart is not effective in pumping blood around the body, fluid can build up in the lungs. Older people may have to take diuretics; these are tablets that help to get rid of excess fluid from the body. Some breathing problems are therefore associated with heart disease.

If chest muscles become weaker and breathing becomes shallower an older person may be more exposed to the risk of an infection such as bronchitis. Bronchitis involves a swelling and inflammation of the airways that connect the windpipe to the lungs. Persistent or chronic bronchitis can result in conditions such as emphysema. People with emphysema may require oxygen to be given by mask. Ultimately, emphysema can result in respiratory failure or effects on the heart that result in death.

Key concept

Emphysema a condition in which less oxygen gets into the blood and the waste gas, carbon dioxide, is not expelled from the lungs efficiently because the lungs do not work so well.

Chronic bronchitis, emphysema and chronic obstructive airways disease sometimes occur together and chronic obstructive pulmonary disease (COPD) is the name given to a general problem involving these illnesses. According to NHS Direct COPD is one of the most common respiratory diseases in the UK, resulting in 300,000 deaths each year. A diagnosis of COPD means that a person's lungs are damaged and that breathing problems are likely to continue to worsen with time.

Incontinence

Incontinence means not controlling the disposal of urinary or faecal waste from the body. Urinary incontinence involves a partial or total loss of control of the bladder. In a healthy person the brain is aware when the bladder is full. The person then chooses a convenient time to empty the bladder in a toilet. Incontinence occurs because nerves do not work appropriately or because the muscles involved in retaining urine do not work properly. The muscles controlling the bladder can become weaker as a result of ageing.

Stress incontinence occurs when a small amount of urine leaks out when a person coughs, sneezes or performs some other physical activity. Stress incontinence, which is most common in women, occurs because muscles in the pelvic floor are weak.

Urge incontinence occurs when the bladder contracts and empties without being controlled by the central nervous system or brain. This happens because of a problem with the nerves that send messages between the bladder and brain. Regular voluntary emptying of the bladder may help to prevent urge incontinence in some people.

The problem of overflow incontinence results from an enlarged prostate gland in men. The enlarged prostate makes it difficult for the bladder to empty completely and the bladder may release a small dribble of urine without conscious control.

Incontinence can also occur because an older person has mobility difficulties that prevent them from accessing toilet facilities in time. The side-effects of drugs can result in incontinence and constipation can cause pressure on the bladder which results in incontinence.

Faecal incontinence involves the inability to control the loss of solid or liquid faeces from the anus. Faecal incontinence may be caused by diarrhoea – liquid matter can be harder to retain – or by constipation. When a person becomes constipated liquid waste may gather behind the solid blockage and leak around it.

Constipation is a common problem that can result from insufficient exercise, lack of dietary fibre or insufficient liquid intake. Chronic or long-term constipation may be associated with more serious problems, such as those involving the nerves or muscles in the digestive tract, for example. Some older people become immobile because of heart or skeletal problems and may also be used to a low-fibre diet. These factors may contribute to the development of constipation, which in turn can result in the leakage of faecal waste.

People with dementia may also develop urinary and faecal incontinence due to a loss of ability to control the nerves and muscles associated with continence.

Without assessment and treatment, incontinence can create a highly embarrassing problem which might greatly restrict the quality of life of an older person. However, there is often a great deal that can be done to manage or treat a problem with urinary or facial incontinence and incontinence should not be regarded as an expected outcome of ageing.

Obesity

The risk of developing diabetes, heart disease, cancer and arthritis is higher in obese adults. People put on weight and become obese when they take in more energy (calories) than they used up in bodily activities. The spare energy (calories) is then stored as fat. Many older people are less active than they were when they were young. If people continue to take in or eat the same amount of food as they did when they were young there is an obvious risk of weight gain. There are several reasons why older people are likely to have difficulty maintaining a healthy weight.

Some of these difficulties are shown in Figure 7.4.

SCENARIO

Imagine you had overheard the conversation below.

Care worker: 'Hello Bill I've got the home's menu here, perhaps you'd like to choose something – the cook has produced a lovely vegetarian salad.'

Resident: 'I'm not eating all that muck – all that sweetcorn rubbish – we used to feed that to the chickens when I was young. I want proper food – food that fills you up!'

Care worker: 'But you are putting on weight Bill, you ought to try to cut down.'

Resident: 'So what – if nice food kills me then you'll know what I died of won't you!'

What possible explanations can you think of for Bill's attitude towards eating?

Reasons why older people find it difficult to maintain healthy weight include:

Eating Habits
some people may have learned to eat regular portions of high energy giving foods; regular eating is fixed by habit. When activity levels change, the person carries on eating as normal. Individuals do not respond to a lower need for energy by reducing food intake or eating a healthier diet.

'Cheering oneself up'
tasty, interesting food and drink is one of life's pleasures. When people feel low or depressed, eating is one way of making yourself feel better

Cultural assumptions about food
historically, high energy foods (foods high in fat or sugar) were seen as desirable. Sixty years ago food was rationed in the United Kingdom and some people had difficulty getting enough food to maintain an appropriate energy balance – in other words they went hungry! Some older people may have come to regard salad and other low-energy foods as low-status food. Some care services may tend to provide high-energy meals such as meat pie, fish and chips, jam sponge, and so on because service users expect and feel valued by, the presentation of such food.

The impact of health problems
restricted mobility may mean that individuals lose the ability to increase their energy needs. Restricted mobility because of arthritis, for example, may in itself create a feeling of depression in the individual. Paradoxically, a person may begin to eat more because they have a problem that stops them from exercising, thus creating a 'double whammy' of increased eating and lowered energy needs.

FIGURE 7.4 *Some of the reasons for weight gain amongst older people*

Physical ageing – at a glance

* Skin becomes thinner, less elastic, and wrinkled

* Bones can become more brittle and more likely to fracture

* Joints can become stiffer and may become painful as the cartilage on the bone ends reduces

* The ligaments which reinforce joints can become looser

* Height can be reduced because the cartilage separating the vertebrae becomes compressed. The spine may also become more rounded

* Muscles become weaker

* Sense of balance can become impaired

* Taste and smell receptors deteriorate

* Vision can deteriorate because the lens of the eye starts to block light; cataracts can develop

* Hearing can deteriorate with a failure to hear high-pitched sounds

* Lack of skin sensitivity can lead to increased risk of hypothermia

* Muscles in the digestive tract become weaker – creating a risk of constipation.

* The heart is less efficient at pumping blood

* Blood pressure becomes higher

* Nutrients from food are not absorbed as well as in earlier life

* Breathing is less efficient because respiratory muscles are weaker

* Gas exchange in the lungs becomes impaired as the elastic walls of the alveoli become damaged

* Body metabolism is reduced due to lowered performance of the endocrine glands.

Confusion and dementia

Describing and categorising mental health issues is not easy. Historically, the term neurosis was used to classify disorders involving distorted thinking. Neurosis included disorders such as

depression and anxiety and irrational fear, called phobia. More serious disorders involving a loss of rationality and seriously disordered thinking were classified as psychotic illness. Dementia was understood as a disorder with a physical cause and was understood as being different from neurosis or psychosis.

Nowadays, mental health problems are classified as 'disorders'. Many psychologists and psychiatrists use the classification system developed by the American Psychiatric Association, called the Diagnostic and Statistical Manual of mental disorders or DSM for short. The DSM is a complex system for interpreting disorders but the fourth version of the DSM includes the categories listed in Table 7.2, within its interpretation of clinical disorders.

Mental health and income

Social Trends 2004 reports that among people aged 60–74 the likelihood of having a neurotic mental illness such as depression, anxiety, obsessive compulsive disorder, panic or phobia increases with low income. Older women who had a weekly household income of £500 or more in the year 2000 were three times less likely to experience a 'neurotic' mental illness than women living on a household income of under £200. It is very likely that the stress of living on a low income increases the risk of anxiety and depression.

DISORDER	BRIEF EXPLANATION
Delirium	Thinking and behaviour are disordered perhaps due to a physical illness, or perhaps due to the effects of drugs. Delirium results in 'confusion'. Many older people who are labelled confused are likely to be experiencing the effects of physical illness or drug effects or drug 'side-effects'
Dementia	A disorder resulting from a physical condition in the brain. There are different types of dementia
Schizophrenia	A serious disorder of thinking and emotion that can result in irrational beliefs about persecution and power, withdrawal from other people, disorganised thinking or even rigid, withdrawn body postures
Mood disorders: depression	A loss of ability to function effectively and to cope with practical and emotional issues in life
Anxiety disorders: panic disorder	An overwhelming emotional reaction that disables a person. May be associated with issues such as agoraphobia – a fear of open and usually public spaces, e.g. a fear of going out from home
Anxiety disorders: specific phobia	A specific fear which interferes with daily living, such as a fear of dogs, spiders, or of looking down from tall buildings. A phobia may prevent an individual from leading a satisfactory life

TABLE 7.2 *Some of the disorders listed in the fourth version of the DSM*

Dementia

The Alzheimer's Society estimates that over one-quarter-of-a-million people in the United Kingdom are affected by dementia and that approximately 5 per cent of people over the age of 65 have dementia. The risk of developing dementia increases with age. The Alzheimer's Society estimates that as many as 20 per cent of people over the age of 80 are affected by dementia. This still means that dementia is not a normal part of ageing. Four out of five people who live to extreme old age will never experience dementia.

Dementia involves damage to the structure and chemistry of the brain. Because a person's brain becomes damaged, he or she is likely to experience problems with understanding, communicating, reasoning, becoming lost, and remembering important recent events. It is wrong to assume that older people who cannot find their glasses are exhibiting the first symptoms of dementia. Dementia always involves a range of problems with mental functioning. Forgetfulness can be caused by a wide range of issues,

including physical illness and stress. Many older people report that they find it difficult to remember items of shopping and so on, but this type of forgetfulness is different from the problems associated with dementia.

There are many different kinds of dementia and research is constantly improving our understanding of the nature and potential causes of these illnesses. With respect to Alzheimer's disease, there is no straightforward explanation of what causes this disorder even though there are many theories. There is no cure for Alzheimer's disease although there is a range of drug treatments that may help to improve the mental abilities of people with Alzheimer's disease. Some of the main types of dementia as identified by the Alzheimer's Society are described in Table 7.3.

Carers should never attempt to diagnose psychiatric disorders. Even highly experienced professionals with extensive training will find difficulty in interpreting and understanding individual need. On the other hand, it is important that carers do not make assumptions

TYPE OF DEMENTIA	EXPLANATION
Alzheimer's disease	The Alzheimer's Society state that Alzheimer's disease is the most common form of dementia, making up to 55 per cent of all cases of dementia. Alzheimer's disease will involve problems with understanding, remembering and making sense of things. As the illness progresses people may lose the ability to make sense of their surroundings and recognise close friends and relatives. People with Alzheimer's may eventually become extremely dependent and may eventually lose the ability to speak clearly, to swallow and retain continence
Vascular disease	The blood supply to the cells of the brain becomes disrupted, so parts of the brain die. This type of dementia is also called multi-infarct dementia. An infarct is a dead area of tissue. Some people with this problem may experience mental decline as a series of steps, as if they were having multiple strokes. The disabilities experienced, and the pattern of this illness, may be different from Alzheimer's disease
Dementia, with Lewy bodies	Lewy bodies are microscopic deposits within the brain, which are associated with the death of nerve cells. The Alzheimer's Society states that more than half of people who have this type of dementia show symptoms of Parkinson's disease. The Alzheimer's Society state that this type of dementia is associated with visual hallucinations and difficulty in judging distances. Abilities can often fluctuate from day to day
Fronto-temporal dementia and Pick's disease	This type of dementia is associated with damage to the front and side sections of the brain. The front of the brain (frontal lobes) is associated with the ability to control behaviour. People with this kind of dementia may show a loss of inhibition and may appear to have changed their personality. Some people who are affected by this disorder may be labelled as being rude or aggressive by other people. Memory abilities may be relatively unaffected during the early stages of this kind of dementia
Rarer causes of dementia	There are many other kinds of dementia, including sub-cortical dementia, where the inner part of the brain appears to be more damaged than the outer part of the brain. A person with these problems may experience a wide range of physiological problems including difficulty staying awake

TABLE 7.3 *Types of dementia*

about ageing and start to see all older people as suffering from dementia.

Unusual or challenging behaviour may result from a whole range of issues, and it is dangerous to assume that an unusual behaviour is a symptom of a mental disorder.

Some examples of issues that may cause unusual behaviour are listed in Figure 7.5.

FIGURE 7.5 *Some reasons why people may display unusual or challenging behaviour*

Summary

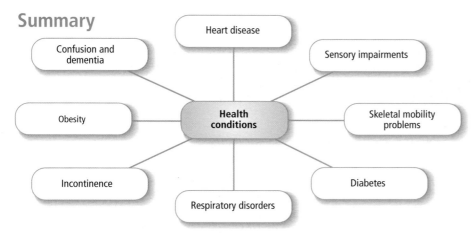

Health conditions
- Heart disease
- Sensory impairments
- Skeletal mobility problems
- Diabetes
- Respiratory disorders
- Incontinence
- Obesity
- Confusion and dementia

FIGURE 7.6 *Section 7.1 summary*

Consider this

Consider the five short descriptions of people below. There is nowhere near enough information for you to be able to be sure about the needs of any of these people. But what would your best guess be about the reasons for these people's problems?

Person A: this person spends a lot of time wandering outside his house or just standing indoors looking blankly into space. He rarely speaks; he has a poor appetite and is unable to explain why he wanders. He sometimes calls the name of his wife, who died six months ago, and he seems unable to accept that she is dead.

Person B: this person rarely gives a sensible answer when she is asked questions. She avoids talking to other people at the day centre she goes to and sometimes becomes agitated when other people try to communicate with her. She has moments of sitting and crying.

Person C: this person accuses care workers of spying on him and stealing his property. He says that his next door neighbour is trying to kill him by feeding poison gas under the door at night. This person has a problem with breathing and is at risk of developing pneumonia.

Person D: this person used to be quite sociable, but for the past week she has spent most of the day in total inactivity within the lounge of a care home. When this person is not actually asleep she will still have a vacant and detached expression. She is not responsive to care staff who try to talk to her. This person is incontinent of urine, and this problem has become worse in the last week.

Person E: this person lives in a sheltered housing complex, but has great difficulty in orientating herself and often becomes lost within the complex. She often forgets whether her son has visited her and other details such as what she may have eaten for lunch. This person enjoys company and enjoys talking, but often repeats herself and sometimes seems insensitive to what other people are saying.

PERSON	BEST GUESS?
Person A	Bereavement, grief – appropriate social support may help
Person B	Hearing impairment – check communication aids
Person C	Fear or Schizophrenia or both. The person has an unreasonable belief that he is being attacked (paranoia). The person may be seriously stressed by his breathing problem. Clinical support may help and carers may be able to reduce stress by using effective communication
Person D	Delirium, perhaps due to urinary infection, or possibly the effects of medication. Urgent medical attention is needed. The disorder could also be due to some other physical illness
Person E	Dementia – although there is not enough information to be sure.

7.2 Social conditions

Life expectancy

In 1901 the average life expectancy for a newborn baby was only 49 years for a girl and 45 years for a boy. Many children died in the early years of their life and this resulted in a low figure for life expectancy. The Office for National Statistics (2004) reported that by 2002 female life expectancy at birth was 81 years and male life expectancy at birth was 76 years.

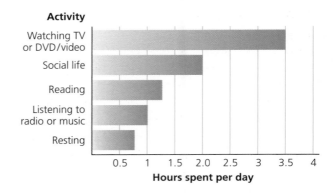

FIGURE 7.7 *Time over-65s spend on activities*

Work patterns and lack of occupation

According to the Office for National Statistics (2004) the great majority of older people who are beyond the state pension age do not work; 91 per cent of men and 90 per cent of women are classed as 'economically inactive'. Some people do continue to work; one per cent of men over the age of 65 and two per cent of women over the age of 60 remain in full-time employment. Some three per cent of men aged over 65 and 6 per cent of women aged over 60 work part-time. Four per cent of men over retirement age were self-employed, but only one per cent of women over 60 were self-employed. It may be that, in the future, an increasing number of older people will remain in employment, but at present it seems reasonable to describe the majority of women over 60 and men over 65 as being 'retired'. For many people, retirement represents a time of opportunity for relaxing and enjoying leisure pursuits. For some people, retirement may involve a loss of earnings, contact with work colleagues, and possibly a loss of status and identity associated with work. For many people, retirement will be seen as a positive change, but for a few retirement may result in significant stress.

Older people often have more free time for leisure than younger people. Health and mobility problems can sometimes limit the activities older people can choose. The Office for National Statistics (2004) reports an average time spent on the activities set out in Figure 7.7 by the over 65 year-old age group.

Risk of isolation

Many older people live alone. The 2001 census reported that 21.8 per cent of men and 43.5 per cent of women over 65 live alone. Among the 85-year-old and older age group 36.9 per cent of men and 54.5 per cent of women live alone.

The Office for National Statistics (ONS) (2004) reported that 79 per cent of people aged 65 and over saw a relative or friend at least once a week. Only a small minority (two per cent) of over 65-year-old people had no contact with friends or relatives. A further 19 per cent saw friends or relatives less than once a week.

Once again, as with the majority picture on health, the majority of older people appear to enjoy effective social networks; only about one person in five may experience a degree of isolation, and only about two per cent of people are isolated from friends and relatives.

> ✳ DID YOU KNOW?
>
> Sixty years ago, many people lived in extended families, where grandparents, parents and children all lived together in the same building. Older people would not be isolated, because they lived with their adult children. Coleman and Salt (1992) report that in 1951 15 per cent of households contained adult relatives. By 1990 only 4 per cent of households included adult relatives; and today the figure is smaller still. Parents are increasingly less likely to live with their children when they become old.

Another factor is that people are geographically mobile; this means that people move away from the area where they were born a lot more than they may have done in the past. Older people often move home when they retire. Sometimes people move in order to 'downsize' and live in a smaller cheaper property in order to save money. Sometimes, people move in order to live in what they consider to be a more desirable area. For example, over 30 per cent of the population of East Devon are over state retirement age. This geographical mobility may result in some older people losing touch with networks of family and friends. As well as older people choosing to move, many older people find that their children have to relocate in order to take advantage of cheaper housing or better job opportunities. A lack of contact may result from people living long distances apart. It might be wrong to assume that isolation is caused by attitudes, i.e. because children no longer care about their parents.

Having access to a car may be an important factor in maintaining social contact

Difficulties with travel

Older people may find it difficult to travel and to keep in contact with friends and family, who do not live nearby. One factor that may increase isolation is lack of car ownership. The 2001 census reports that nearly 90 per cent of 50–54-year-olds have access to a car within their household. However, only 45 per cent of men and 25 per cent of women aged 85 and over have access to a car according to Arber and Ginn (2004). Some older people may not be able to afford to run a car; other people may give up driving for health reasons. Part of the reason that only a quarter of women over the age of 85 have access to a car is that historically women did not learn to drive, and instead relied on their husbands to own and drive a car. The loss or illness of a husband may

therefore result in a loss of ability to travel for many women in this age group. If you do not drive or cannot afford a car, you can, of course, use public transport. Arber and Ginn (2004) explain that many older people may be prevented from using public transport, because of frailty, disability or fear of crime. Public transport may be difficult to reach in many rural areas.

Mobility problems

There is an increased risk of developing physical problems with movement as people grow older. Serious physical disability may include difficulties with walking and difficulties in transferring from a bed to a chair, and so on. The 2001 health survey for England interviewed a sample of people about disabilities that they experienced. Table 7.4 reports the percentages of people in the survey who reported a serious disability with respect to body movement.

Table 7.4 suggests that mobility problems increase dramatically with age. The survey

AGE GROUP	16–24	25–34	35–44	45–54	55–64	65–74	75–84	85+
Men	0 %	1 %	1 %	2 %	4 %	6 %	10 %	22 %
Women	0 %	1 %	1 %	2 %	5 %	6 %	16 %	32 %

TABLE 7.4 *The percentage of adults in England with serious 'movement' or locomotor disability*

Source: Table 3 Health Survey for England 2001

detected very few people under the age of 24 with serious mobility problems. Yet nearly one in three women over the age of 85 reported a serious disability in relation to body movement. Physical disability will limit the amount of travel that people can engage in. Some people may experience a sense of isolation because their physical health limits the amount of travelling they can do to meet with friends and family.

Risk of poverty

The over 65-year-old age group includes many people who are extremely well off and who enjoy high levels of saving and property ownership. For example, the Office for National Statistics (2004) reports that in 2000, 61 per cent of people aged 65 and over owned their homes outright (they had paid off any mortgage). Social Trends (2004) reports that 16 per cent of one-person households and 30 per cent of two-person, pensioner households have over £20,000 in savings. This compares with only 15 per cent of households across the age range.

On the other hand, the ONS report that some 40 per cent of people aged 85 and over live in rented accommodation. Social Trends (2004) reports that 28 per cent of one-person pensioner households and 17 per cent of two-person pensioner households have no savings of any kind. Arber and Ginn (2004) report that some 21 per cent of people aged 65 and over may be considered to live in poverty within the United Kingdom. This figure compares with 17 per cent of the population in general.

For some people, old age can be a time of wealth and affluence but for others it can be a time of poverty. Writing about differences in income, Arber and Ginn (2004:10) state: 'These differences in older people's incomes reflect mainly inequalities in their ability to build private (occupational or personal) pension entitlements during the working life' Arber and Ginn (2004) point out that 'since 1980, the value of the basic state pension has declined relative to national earnings while those retiring with private occupational pensions received increasingly large amounts'. Although there is a range of benefits available to pensioners who would only

otherwise receive the state pension, the possession of a large private pension may make a huge difference to quality of life.

SCENARIO

Martin is 65-years-of-age and enjoys a company pension that pays him over £20,000 a year. He has received this pension since he retired at the age of 60. Martin received a substantial inheritance from the sale of his parents' house when they died. Martin travels abroad with his wife on activity holidays for about eight weeks each year. At home, he spends much of his time playing golf or socialising with old friends or other retired work colleagues. Martin buys a new prestige car every three years and jointly owns his home outright. Martin's only concern is that his health might limit his ability to drive and to mix with friends as he grows older.

Marc is 65-years-of-age and receives the state pension together with income support, housing benefit and council tax benefit. Marc's parents lived in rented accommodation, as Marc does. He did not inherit any money when they died. Marc worked in a range of semi-skilled jobs when he was younger, none of which involved a company pension. He never had enough money to invest in a private pension. Marc has enough money to get by on but he cannot afford to run a car and finds it difficult to get to the supermarkets. Marc talks to his neighbours but he has lost touch with some of his relatives and old friends because they do not live nearby. He does much of his shopping at a local shop that actually charges higher prices than most supermarkets. Marc constantly worries about having enough money to make ends meet and pay the bills.

How far do you believe that income might influence issues such as health and the quality of social life?

Inadequate housing

A majority of older people over the age of 65 – six out of 10 according to National Statistics – own their own home outright (without a mortgage). National Statistics explain, however, that a large proportion of people over the age of 85 – some 40 per cent – live in rented accommodation. Renting is less common in people aged 65–84 (just 28 per cent). Only one per cent of people over the age of 50 live in overcrowded conditions, but National Statistics report that just over half of all people aged 50 or over live in a property which is under-occupied. So in general the majority of older people may enjoy living in the house that they have chosen, and they may have an excess of space and facilities.

National Statistics reports that about 12 per cent of older people said their house was too cold in winter whilst one in ten older people complained of issues such as rising damp or problems with insects or mice, or a house being too dark. Some 93 per cent of people aged 50 to 64 have central heating, whereas only 86 per cent of people aged over 85 have central heating.

In general it would appear that the majority of older people in the United Kingdom enjoy good or adequate housing but a small minority of older people may be living in poorly heated cold, damp, dark or infested properties.

Reduced independence

A significant number of older people experience long-term illnesses such as heart problems, arthritis and rheumatism. These illnesses may restrict daily living activities such as shopping, cooking and travel. National Statistics (2004)

suggest that approximately 70 per cent of people over the age of 85 experience a level of disability that restricts daily living activities. Interestingly, some people who experience disability may still report their health as being good.

Many people who have long-term illnesses are assessed for support, such as home care. Social Trends (2002) reported that nearly half of personal social services expenditure was spent on older people.

Many older people with disabilities become dependent on relatives. Data from the 2001 census suggests that 21 per cent of people in their 50s claimed to be providing some level of care for a relative. Much of the support provided by relatives involved 'keeping an eye on a person' or 'keeping them company', or 'taking them out' or other practical help such as shopping. But a smaller number of relatives provided physical help or personal care.

For some older people the thought of being dependent on others creates a threat to self-esteem. A mother, who has always guided and advised her daughter, may be unhappy about being dependent on or, indeed, a burden for that daughter. A father might worry about imposing on his children, who are still in full-time work. As well as threatening self-esteem, dependency might lower a person's satisfaction with life. If you can no longer cook for yourself you may not find 'meals on wheels' to be an adequate substitute. If you have to rely on someone else to do the shopping for you, you may become frustrated when they do not return with exactly what you would have chosen. Dependency can cause some people to give up trying to cope with their life. This can result in a process called 'learned helplessness' (Seligman, 1975). According to Seligman, who developed the theory of learned helplessness, giving up and withdrawing from daily living activities can result in the onset of clinical depression.

Illness or disability can therefore start a process of feeling frustrated, followed by becoming withdrawn and losing confidence and motivation to cope with daily living activities. A further issue is that many older people do not feel that they are useful or valued by others.

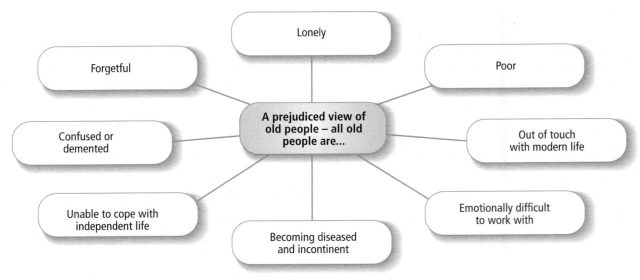

FIGURE 7.8 *Some perceptions of old people*

Many people are aware of a prejudiced attitude towards older people. Ageism, as this prejudice is sometimes called, is often based on assumptions (or stereotypes) such as those listed in Figure 7.8.

Perhaps the most extreme danger of this kind of prejudice is that some older people may come to believe in this view themselves; they may say things such as 'you can't expect much at my time of life'. When people have very limited expectations this may add to the risk of withdrawal and isolation that some elderly people experience.

Increased likelihood of potential danger

Poor physical health or poor mental health might result in an increased likelihood of danger to self or others. Some potential dangers are listed in Table 7.5 opposite.

What does it take to be happy?

Seligman (2002) published a textbook exploring what it takes to be happy. Although his research was not focused on older adults, as such, his conclusions may still be worth noting. His research suggests that happiness mainly results from the way people apply their abilities in life, rather than on external circumstances. However,

his research did suggest that being married, having a rich social network of friends and family, being religious and being good at avoiding negative experiences and emotions are associated with happiness for many people. Seligman did not find a meaningful link between wealth and happiness – although poverty may be associated with unhappiness. When it comes to health the key issue seems to be whether you believe that you are healthy or not; he did not find a strong association between genuine health and happiness. So happiness does not depend on what you've got, instead happiness depends on how you think.

What is old age like?

From the brief evidence presented so far it is fair to say that the majority of people over state retirement age experience reasonable health, a satisfactory social life and, in some cases, a high standard of material well-being. There is evidence that a minority of older people experience poor health, poverty and isolation. A small section of the older population may experience high levels of stress due to social and economic factors. Social care workers are more likely to be in touch with people who have health, social or economic problems. But it is important to guard against the assumption (or stereotype) that later life is a story of decline and misery for everyone.

	RISK	WAYS IN WHICH INFORMAL CARERS CAN HELP
Risks from poor physical health	Hypothermia – risk from under-heated housing.	Provide thermometers to help monitor temperature in the home – make regular visits
	Falls	Provide home alarm system
	Not taking medication as scheduled	Monitor medication – provide tablet boxes to help organise medication
	Self-neglect	Provide company/provide assistance
Risks from poor mental health	Security in the home	Make regular visits – try to organise a routine to check safety and security issues
	Memory problems	Provide orientation sheets – written details to remind a person what to do each day/what to do if there is a problem
	Withdrawal/depression	Provide company, try to interest the person in talking perhaps by discussing the past (reminiscence)
	Frustration and aggression	Try to stay calm and use conversational skills to calm the person
	Wandering and/or dangerous behaviour, such as turning gas taps on	Consult medical and social services for additional support

TABLE 7.5 *Potential dangers faced by older people*

In many ways old-age will be like any other life stage. Whether or not an older person is leading a happy and fulfilled life will have a lot to do with his or her approach to life. Life satisfaction may not always be predictable from measurements of health, time spent with relatives, or money in the bank!

Services for older people

Where services come from

Services to older people are provided from a number of sources, set out in Figure 7.9.

Each of these providers and the type of service they provide will be discussed in much more detail below. In reality, a service user is likely to receive support from a number of different providers. Consider the scenario on page 268,

which gives an idea of how one person might receive services from a number of providers.

FIGURE 7.9 *Providers of services for older people*

Staying at home

Betty is 84-years-old and has problems in walking due to arthritis. She can get around indoors, but has trouble using the stairs.

She has paid to have a stair-lift installed (by a private company), but social services have provided her with a commode to use downstairs. She has a Home Help to do the cleaning and laundry once a week. The Home Help is employed by a private company, but the service is paid for by social services. An NHS chiropodist (from the local health centre) visits Betty at home to treat her feet every six weeks. Betty is well-known at the health centre, and can ring up to be issued with repeat prescriptions from her GP, which a neighbour takes to the chemist for her. She uses a personal alarm service run by the charity Age Concern.

The neighbour does Betty's shopping every week.

Betty's support network is thus made up of a combination of provision from the health service, social services, private and voluntary sectors and informal support.

Key concept

Statutory sector refers to organisations set up to provide services that are required by law. It includes the NHS and local authorities.

Private sector refers to businesses that offer services on a profit-making basis.

Voluntary sector is those organisations that provide services to bridge gaps in statutory provision. Sometimes voluntary organisations provide services without charge. They are non-profit-making organisations.

A charity is an organisation that is officially registered as having charitable status.

Background to current service provision

It is important to be aware that the political and social background to service provision changes over time. The information given in this section is based on the situation that is current at the time of writing (2005), and as part of your studies you should always check out details of current law, policy and guidelines for providing services.

At present, services are provided according to the Fair Access to Care Services Guidance. This guidance says that people are entitled to services according to the level of risk to independence that a person will suffer if his or her needs are not met. There are bands of need/risk, ranging from low to critical. Local councils have to work out their own eligibility criteria in order to determine how complex an assessment needs to be. Four types of assessment can be offered:

* initial assessments

* assessments to take stock of wider needs

* specialist assessments

* comprehensive assessments.

Source: Fair Access to Care Services: Guidance on Eligibility Criteria for Adult Social Care (Department of Health 2002)

These Guidelines apply to all people in need of assessment. However, there are further guidelines on planning care for older people. The National Service Framework (NSF) sets out standards for the management of care for older people, together with the principles that should underpin the provision of care.

The NSF covers intermediate care, hospital care, stroke, falls and mental health issues. It also has sections on age discrimination, and the promotion of health and an active life. Most importantly, it promotes the concept of person centred care. This is summarised below. Putting the person at the centre of care is one of the main ways to ensure that care values respect service users diversity, rights and beliefs.

Person centred care Standard Two of the National Service Framework for Older People says that: 'Older people should be treated as individuals and receive appropriate and timely packages of care which meet their needs as individuals, regardless of health and social services boundaries.'

Source: National Service Framework for Older People, Standard Two (Department of Health, 2001)

Another key concept in the implementation of services for older people is that of the single assessment process.

Key concept

Single assessment process: a process by which everyone concerned (including the service user, his or her carer, health services, social services and any other providers) works together to make sure an individual gets exactly what is needed. This working together begins at the assessment stage.

SCENARIO

Compare two care settings

What evidence can you find of a person centred approach in either of the two care settings below?

'The Meadows' is a modern purpose-built care home that accepts service users with dementia. The home is often short staffed but residents are always well fed, and the home is clean and well equipped. Residents always have a choice of food, although communication difficulties often result in service users not understanding what they are being offered. A 'service user plan' is kept in the office for each service user, but some care workers say they do not have time to use these plans.

At 12 Springfield Road there is a specialist unit caring for people with dementia. There is a good ratio of care workers to service users and staff try to build a supportive relationship. All care workers understand the personal history and interests of the service users. Carers spend time listening to and reminiscing with service users, despite the fact that service users often repeat statements, and say things that are not easy to follow. Care staff understand that people with dementia often have important

emotional needs that may not be clearly expressed in verbal communication. Carers explain that 'you need to listen for the message behind the words – and not just for the words themselves'. Some care workers have learned basic aromatherapy and foot massage techniques, which are offered to service users. Carers explain that these approaches can help anxious people to relax and feel safe.

Discussion: although The Meadows offers choice, and a clean well equipped setting there is little evidence of a person centred approach here. Springfield Road offers:

Comfort	Foot massage and aromatherapy
Attachment	Staff try to build supportive relationships
Inclusion	Staff listen – despite the difficulties
Occupation	Some reminiscence activity and foot massage and aromatherapy
Identity	Concern for service users' identity (staff learn their history)

Summary

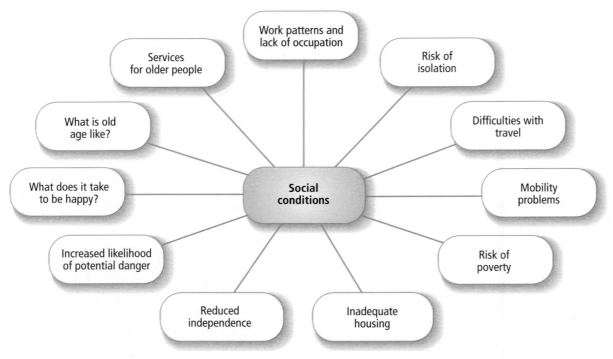

FIGURE 7.10 *Section 7.2 summary*

Consider this: coming out of hospital

Mrs Green has spent several weeks in hospital after breaking her hip in a fall. She is now ready to go home.

The hospital discharge team have been responsible for preparing a care plan to meet Mrs Green's needs. The care manager from the discharge team has coordinated information from a number of people. These have included the hospital consultant, the physiotherapist and the occupational therapist (who has done an assessment of Mrs Green's ability to perform a number of basic personal and domestic tasks for herself). Mrs Green lives alone as she is a widow, but she has a son and a daughter who live nearby.

The care manager has had to take all these facts into consideration when drawing up a plan for Mrs Green. Not least, she has to take into account Mrs Green's wishes for the kind of support she would like.

The resulting care plan includes support from a number of sources, including Home Care, and physical support from the district nursing team (to help Mrs Green get up and dressed in the morning, and to get to bed at night). Mrs Green lives in a flat, so she does not have the problem of getting up and down stairs. Her son and daughter will shop for her, and will call in every day to make sure she has had something to eat. Mrs Green has decided that she would also like Meals on Wheels.

The care manager has arranged for the situation to be re-assessed in a few weeks, as Mrs Green may not require intensive nursing support for longer than that.

7.3 Health care

Health care services

The National Health Service (NHS) is responsible for a range of health-care services. The NHS is itself divided up into a number of smaller organisations, some of which have a strategic or planning role, and others that deliver services. For example, in England there are 28 Strategic Health Authorities (SHAs) which are responsible for the quality of the services provided. Each SHA contains a number of Primary Care Trusts (PCTs), and NHS Trusts.

PCTs are responsible for commissioning and funding local health-care services. NHS Trusts provide some services commissioned by the PCTs. The range of health-care services is listed below.

HEALTH CARE SERVICES
Commissioned by PCTs

Community Based Services eg.

GP	NHS walk-in centre
Dentist	NHS Direct (telephone service)
Optician	Chiropodist
District Nursing Service	Mental Health Services

Hospital Based Services eg.

Consultant	Nursing Care
Physiotherapist	

Continuing NHS Health Care Services
Nursing care in a care home or other setting
Rehabilitation and recovery services
Palliative care
Intermediate Care
Respite health care
Specialist health care support
Specialist health care equipment
Specialist transport

If the person's main need is for health care (i.e. related to his or her medical condition) then the responsibility for providing care rests with the local PCT. This means that if because of an existing medical condition or problem someone needs continuing specialist nursing care, this must be arranged by the PCT, even if this is in a care home provided the client meets local eligibility criteria.

Rehabilitation services are those that help a person to regain a normal life. Such support may include physiotherapy (to help regain mobility or the ability to use the hands), speech therapy (to help with swallowing problems or speech difficulties) and occupational therapy to assist a person to do basic tasks and assess the need for aids and/or adaptations in the home.

> **Key concept**
>
> *Rehabilitation:* the process of helping a person to resume his or her normal life (after an illness or accident) by regaining physical skills and emotional confidence.

Palliative care is that provided to someone who has a life-threatening condition or disease that is not responding to treatment. Palliative care focuses on the care and comfort of the person, including pain-management, and the provision of emotional support both to the person with the condition and his or her family and carers.

> **Key concept**
>
> *Palliative care:* nursing, practical and/or emotional support to people with life-threatening conditions or illnesses that are not responding to treatment. Such care often includes pain-management and help to improve quality of life.

If the carer of a person with a medical condition or disability needs a break, then a short period of respite care can be arranged. This means that the person with the illness or medical condition can be given care elsewhere, perhaps for a week or two, to allow the regular carer to take a rest.

> **Key concepts**
>
> *Respite care:* a short period of residential and/or nursing care given to someone to enable his or her usual carer to take a break.
>
> *Intermediate care:* health care that can include social care services and is intended to promote recovery after a stay in hospital, or to prevent admission to hospital.

Health care workers

Older people may be supported by a very wide range of health-care workers, some of whom will work within the NHS, and others who will work for private organisations. Some of these workers (like ward nursing staff) may be generic, that is to say, they do not necessarily specialise in the care of one particular patient group. Others (such as a Consultant Geriatrician) are specialists who work only with older people. Table 7.6 lists some of the professionals you might expect to work with older people.

Key concept

Generic: the opposite of specific or specialist. A generic social worker will serve a range of service users with many different needs.

TITLE	ROLE	LOCATION
GP	Assessment, advice on and treatment of illness and medical conditions	Community
Consultant Geriatrician	Assessment, advice on and treatment of illness and medical conditions	Hospital
Psychogeriatrician	Assessment and treatment of psychiatric conditions in older people	Hospital
Community Psychiatric Nurse	Assessment and planning for people with mental health problems	Community
Nursing staff	General nursing care	Hospital
Nursing staff: District Nurse, Health Visitor	General nursing care	Community (often in patient's own home)
Occupational Therapist	Assessment/treatment of physical, psychological or social problems using specific, purposeful activity to prevent disability and/or promote independent function in daily life	Hospital, Community
Speech Therapist	Assessment/treatment for people with speech, language and communication problems (e.g. with patients who have suffered a stroke, or have Parkinson's disease)	Hospital, Community, Patient's own home
Continence Adviser	Information and practical help for people with incontinence problems	Hospital, Community
Optician	Advice and assessment on visual problems	Hospital, Community
Dentist	Assessment and treatment of dental problems	Hospital, Community
Chiropodist	Advice, treatment of problems relating to the feet	Hospital, Community, Home
Complementary Therapists	Examples include art and drama therapy, acupuncture, homeopathy, osteopathy	Hospital, Community

TABLE 7.6 *Health-care professionals (older people)*

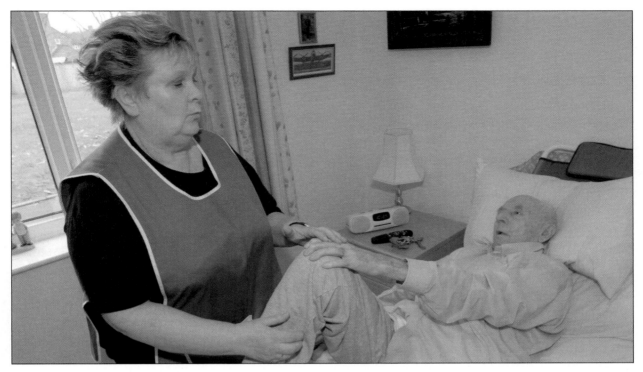

A wide range of care workers support elderly service users

As the current situation is that of a mixed economy of care, health-care professionals may be employed by a number of different organisations. Some are NHS-funded and managed; others may be in multi-disciplinary teams and be funded by the local authority. Some professionals, e.g. nursing staff, now work privately and are employed by nursing agencies. The situation is very complex and varies locally.

Summary

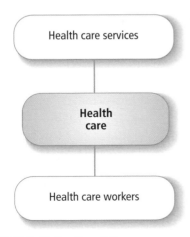

FIGURE 7.11 *Section 7.3 summary*

Consider this: recovering from a stroke

Arthur has had a stroke, and now has trouble both in speaking and in swallowing.

A Speech and Language Therapist, Liz, has been assigned to him as part of a rehabilitation package put together by the care manager and the hospital discharge team. Liz is based in an NHS community health centre, but she also visits people at home.

Liz visits Arthur regularly in his home to give him specialised sessions that will enable him to swallow properly, and also to begin to regain his speech.

7.4 Social care

Services provided by local authorities

Local authorities are responsible for providing a range of services to older people, including social care and housing. Figure 7.12 shows some of the services that local authorities may provide.

You can see from Figure 7.12 that the role of the local authority (in particular social services) has been changing. Most of the services shown used to be delivered directly by social services (or the housing service). However, the role of social services has become more of assessing need and purchasing the services required. Sometimes these services are bought from private businesses (e.g. companies that provide home care or frozen meal delivery) or from voluntary sector organisations (e.g. the provision of day care by Age Concern, or mental health care from MIND). Local arrangements vary, and you should check out those for older people in your area.

Social care staff

As with health-care professionals, the picture is now quite complex. Some staff are employed directly by local authorities, others may be privately funded or work for voluntary agencies and/or charities. Table 7.7 gives information about the roles of some of these professionals, and where they might work. As with health-care workers, some of these people will have a generic role, others will be more specialist in their remit.

Social workers may be employed directly by a local authority, but they may also work privately for social work agencies. Care workers, too, may work directly in a local authority facility, but this is becoming increasingly rare, because many residential homes are now run as private businesses. Day centre workers may work for local authorities, but are also just as likely to be employed by voluntary organisations such as MIND, or to be volunteers.

The scenario opposite describes the role of a care worker in a private residential home for older people.

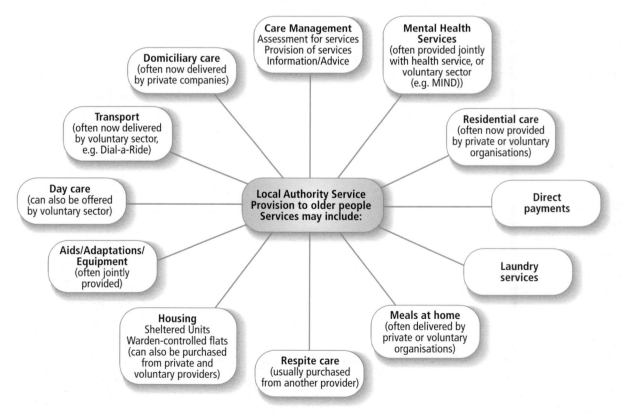

FIGURE 7.12 *Main kinds of services provided by local authorities*

TITLE	ROLE	LOCATION
Care manager	A social worker who has the designated role of assessing need and producing a care plan. The care manager will also ensure that services are provided according to the care plan, and will monitor and evaluate service provision and the effectiveness of the plan	Hospital, Community
Social worker	Assessment of and planning to meet need	Hospital, Community
Specialist social worker	As for social worker, but with a specialist responsibility (e.g. for older people)	Hospital, Community
Care worker	Provides daily physical care, often in a residential or day care setting. Also gives support for intellectual, emotional and/or social needs	Residential or day care settings
Home Help (Domiciliary care worker)	Practical support to someone in his or her own home. May include help with personal tasks such as washing, shaving, bathing etc.	Client's own home
Day centre worker/support worker	Support to users of day facilities. Such staff may have a range of job titles. Support can be practical; can also include support with intellectual, emotional and social needs	Community

TABLE 7.7 *Social-care professionals and workers (older people)*

SCENARIO

Home from home

Vikram works in a private residential care home for older people. He works shifts, and this week he is on earlies, starting his duties at 7.00 am. His first task is to help people to get up, washed and dressed. Some of the residents also need help in going to the toilet.

After this, the residents have breakfast in the communal dining room. Vikram helps to serve. Some people also need assistance with eating. After breakfast, residents like to listen to the radio or to watch TV. However, today a specialist reminiscence therapist is coming in to run a memory session with anyone who cares to join in. Vikram makes sure that all the residents know about the session, and helps people in settling down comfortably before the session begins. The session is all about what the town centre looked like in the 1940s. The therapist has some photographs to start off the discussion, which becomes very lively.

Vikram sits in on the session and enjoys listening to the stories that people have to tell. He will use some of these at another time to encourage people to talk.

Later, he helps with lunch. He then gets the medicines trolley ready for the afternoon round.

His shift ends just after the residents have had afternoon tea.

Social care services provided by voluntary and charitable organisations

There are many voluntary organisations that provide a valuable service to people in need of care or support. Not all of these have charitable status (see above, page 268). Some organisations (e.g. Age Concern) are very large and cover the whole country, with local branches in each area. (NB Scotland, Wales and Northern Ireland often have their own nationally based organisations.) Others are local and specific to particular groups and their needs. The kinds of service offered by such organisations are discussed below.

Services for older people offered by voluntary and charitable organisations

Such services might include:

* Day care (e.g. social centres, lunch clubs)

* Specialist support (e.g. for people with mental health problems)

* Transport

* Information/Advice

* Personal alarm service

* Special deals on insurance products

* Special deals on power supplies

* Training for professionals working with older people.

Like private sector companies, the voluntary sector is now an important provider of services within the mixed economy of care.

Consider this

Find out what local voluntary and charitable organisations provide services for older people in your area.

You might start with the local telephone book, and also contact your local council. There may be a Volunteer Bureau, or a branch of the Council for Voluntary Services in your area that has a list of such organisations.

Voluntary workers

Many people like to offer their services as voluntary workers. Their contribution to health and social care service provision is considerable. According to a report by the National Association of Hospital and Community Friends (NAHCF, 2005), 16 million people did some kind of voluntary work in 2003, and 39 per cent of adults give time to volunteering activity at least once a year (citing figures provided by the National Council for Volunteering Organisations). This report also finds that the contribution of volunteers in health settings not only enhances quality of life for patients, but also gives much-needed support to health-care staff.

Voluntary workers are found in many settings. They provide support in facilities run directly by voluntary organisations such as day or social centres run by MIND or Age Concern, in charity shops or by staffing telephone advice lines. As the NAHCF Report shows, they also make a contribution in statutory settings such as hospitals. A recent Internet advertisement for a London hospital asked for volunteers to fulfil a number of roles including staffing advice and information desks, taking the tea or library trolleys around the wards, staffing the hospital shop, and simply befriending and talking to individual patients. However, volunteers can be involved in other, less traditional tasks. Other activities noted in the NAHCF Report (not specifically in the health-care sector) include such activities as website building, boat-building and restoration work.

The NAHCF Report stresses the benefits of voluntary arrangements. These include that of having diversity amongst volunteers, which ensures that support is available to meet the particular requirements of people from different religious and ethnic groups. Where joint training is given (to include both paid staff and volunteers), volunteer retention is improved, and some of these people go on to become professional health or social-care workers. The NAHCF Report also finds that many hospital patients will talk more freely to volunteers than to professionals (who are often very busy). Patients value having attention from someone who sees them as individuals, rather than as people with particular symptoms or medical problems.

Volunteering can also offer older people the opportunity to have meaningful employment. Kitwood (1997: 82) has stressed the importance of meaningful employment to the well-being of older people. Occupation, he says, contributes to the maintenance of personal abilities and skills, and also to a feeling of self-esteem. This does not have to be paid employment, and services given in a voluntary capacity will provide as much social, intellectual and emotional satisfaction as many well-paid and significant jobs. The following scenario demonstrates how regular volunteering enhanced Bob's retirement.

SCENARIO

Life begins at 65

Bob retired five years ago, but he is very fit and does not like to stay indoors. He had a responsible job as fleet manager for a road haulage company, and when he first retired he badly missed the stimulation of the job, and the friendship of his colleagues.

After a few months, Bob saw an advertisement in his local paper. A local charity (with a focus on people with disabilities) wanted people to help in their shop. They also wanted drivers to help in taking people to hospital, to day centres and to the shops. Bob volunteered for everything, and now works for three days a week, either in the shop or on driving duties.

He loves his new role, as it gives him plenty of time to talk to people (shop customers and the people he drives about). He has learned a lot about disability issues, benefits and other matters that concern people with disabilities. He is now on the committee of the organisation (which has charitable status).

Bob now wonders how he ever found the time to go to work.

If you are considering a career in either health or social care, it would be a good idea to gain some initial experience as a volunteer. The range of opportunities is immense, and there may also be some training and development opportunities, depending on where you gain your experience. The resources section of this unit lists some of the major national organisations that give information and help to people wishing to work as volunteers.

Informal social care

A very significant amount of care to older people (as with other groups) is provided informally by family, friends or neighbours. Anyone who plays a significant role in the care of an individual is known as a carer.

Key concept

Carer: anyone who looks after someone who is ill, disabled or otherwise unable to look after him or herself. This term usually refers to someone who provides informal (unpaid) care, rather than to a paid worker.

The carer could be a husband or wife, an adult son or daughter looking after a parent, any other relation, or even a friend or neighbour. The kinds of (unpaid) service that such carers provide are set out below.

Services to older people

Informal carers Support might include almost anything, but common tasks include:

* help in getting up in the morning and going to bed at night
* help with washing and dressing
* help with bathing or showering
* preparing snacks and meals
* cleaning and shopping
* helping with the taking of medicines
* providing transport/escort support
* giving social and emotional support
* advocacy
* help with filling in forms.

Sometimes, an older person may place a great deal of reliance on the support given by an informal carer. Even when carers are very close to their relative or friend, they may experience stress because of the work they have to do. Looking after someone who is incontinent, for example, can be very physically and emotionally demanding.

✳ DID YOU KNOW?

There is now a National Strategy for Carers (1999), published by the Government and acknowledging their value, and also the fact that they have needs themselves.

The *Carers (Recognition and Services) Act* 1995 says that carers who provide, or intend to provide 'substantial and regular' care can also have their own needs assessed when a care assessment (or reassessment) takes place (see below).

There are also several organisations that offer advice and support to carers (e.g. Carers UK and Crossroads – Caring for Carers; see resources section for website details).

Many care packages for older people are likely to involve the services of an informal carer.

Integrated service provision

Another important change to the way in which services are delivered is the provision of joint services, often in teams that contain staff from both health and social services, or from social services and the voluntary sector.

One example of this might be the hospital discharge team (see above, page 270). The care manager in this team may be provided by social services. His or her function will be to make assessments and to draw up care plans. However, within the team there may also be health service staff such as a nurse and an occupational therapist. The fact that these staff are part of the same team makes it easier for a care plan to be made, and makes service delivery more efficient.

Another example of joint working might include a day facility run by a voluntary or charitable organisation, but funded by social services with the addition of sessional support by, for example, Benefits Advisers or Housing Officers. There might also be sessions provided by an NHS chiropodist.

Consider this

Contact your local authority to find out what services are available for older people in your area.

Find out who pays for and who provides each of these services.

Are there any jointly provided services (i.e. teams containing a mix of staff from health and social services, or from social services and the voluntary sector)?

Many of the services formerly provided by social services are now often delivered by private companies, run on a profit-making basis:

Services to older people provided by private companies

✳ Hospital treatment

✳ Dental treatment

✳ Residential care

✳ Nursing home care

✳ Home care

✳ Home meals delivery.

An older person can, of course, opt to have private medical care, just like anyone else who has the funds to do so. The provision of private hospital treatment has grown in recent years, with companies offering insurance schemes linked to treatment. Since the 1990 *NHS and Community Care Act* created the distinct concepts of care purchasers and care providers, the notion of a mixed economy of care has developed. It is now seen as quite normal for a care plan to be made up of services delivered by a combination of statutory, voluntary and private care suppliers.

Key concepts

Purchasers and providers: the care purchaser is the organisation that controls the funding to buy care – usually the local authority or the PCT.

The *care provider* is any organisation that delivers a service, e.g. a home meals delivery company, an NHS Trust etc.

Key concept

Mixed economy of care: the notion that care can be provided by a range of different service providers, e.g. statutory agencies, private and voluntary organisations and informal carers.

Summary

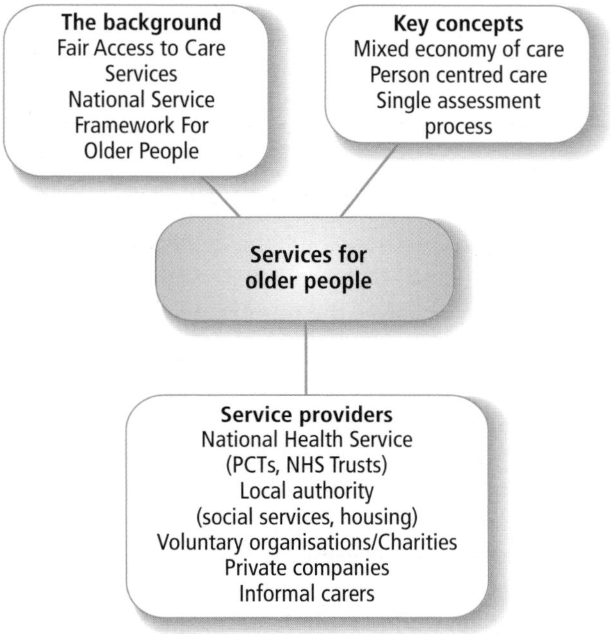

The background
Fair Access to Care Services
National Service Framework For Older People

Key concepts
Mixed economy of care
Person centred care
Single assessment process

Services for older people

Service providers
National Health Service (PCTs, NHS Trusts)
Local authority (social services, housing)
Voluntary organisations/Charities
Private companies
Informal carers

FIGURE 7.13 *Section 7.4 summary*

Consider this: A vision for the future

Mr Goldstein is 80 years old and a widower. He lives alone in a warden-controlled flat. For many years, he has had a lively social life. He attends a social centre run by a local voluntary organisation, taking lunch there once a week and spending time socialising with his friends. He is also a steam train enthusiast, and likes to attend the meetings of the local Steam Society, going on outings with them at weekends to visit local steam railways and old stations.

Unfortunately, Mr Goldstein has been having trouble with his sight. Because he dislikes what he calls 'making a fuss', he hasn't told anyone about this. However, it has now reached the point where he is reluctant to go out on his own. He is having trouble with distinguishing signs and numbers (e.g. on the front of the bus), and also cannot tell when it is time to get off the bus. He missed the last meeting of the Steam Society, and is quite upset about this.

Finally, he confides in the social centre manager. With Mr Goldstein's permission, this manager contacts the care manager in the social services team for older people.

1. Who will be responsible for assessing Mr Goldstein's needs?
2. Who else might be involved in this process?
3. What kind of support and/or medical treatment might Mr Goldstein require?
4. How will the care manager ensure that Mr Goldstein receives person centred care?

7.5 Interview research with older people

When carrying out interview research, you must consider the following points:

* structuring your report
* ethical considerations
* the life stories of older people – interpreting findings

Recognising personhood

The assessment for this unit is based on the observation of and an informal interview with one older person. The interview will be a key event both for yourself, and for the person you interview. It is essential that you go about it in the right way so that it is a positive experience for both of you.

Before considering practical issues such as how you conduct the interview itself, how you collect and structure information, and how you go about interpreting it, it is vital that you reflect upon how you will approach this task. The older person you are going to interview is not simply a source of data for your project, he or she is a unique individual with a complex identity. You will need to have the right attitude if the interview is to be a success.

A good place to start is with the concept of personhood. Tom Kitwood (1997) has written extensively about personhood with particular reference to people with dementia. People with this disease were often understood in terms of 'no cure, no help, no hope', or 'the death that leaves the body behind' (Kitwood, 1997:67). However, Kitwood emphasises the importance of recognising the principle of personhood when working with people with dementia, and those working with or caring for them need to establish a relationship involving recognition, respect and trust. The first task of care is thus to maintain a service user's sense of being a person.

Kitwood summarised the needs that must be met if a sense of personhood is to be nurtured. These are set out in Table 7.8. Although Kitwood relates these needs directly to people with dementia, in fact all of us have these needs as human beings.

NEED	EXPLANATION
Comfort	'the soothing of pain and sorrow, the calming of anxiety, the feeling of security which comes from being close to another. To comfort another person is to provide a kind of warmth and strength which might enable them to remain in one piece'.
Attachment	'without the assurance that attachments provide it is difficult for any person, of whatever age, to function well'.
Inclusion	Kitwood argues that all people need a distinct place in the 'shared life of a group'.
Occupation	People need a sense of purpose and to be involved in personally significant activities that draw on their abilities.
Identity	'To have an identity is to know who one is.' This includes 'having a sense of continuity with the past, and hence a 'narrative', a story to present to others.

TABLE 7.8 *Needs and Personhood*

Source: Based on Kitwood (1997)

When conducting your interview with an older person, you must make sure that you approach the task with the right attitude – that of respect for that individual's personhood. If you do this, there is a strong possibility that taking part in the interview will actually meet some or all of these needs for the person concerned. If you have a warm and friendly approach, the person may derive some *comfort* from talking to you. Focusing on the task in hand (by answering your questions) provides meaningful *occupation*, especially if the person is fully aware that taking part will help you in gaining your qualification.

Telling and retelling personal stories reinforces a sense of *identity*. This is something that everyone does, and some writers on narrative psychology (the study of such storytelling) have gone so far as to see the creation of spoken narratives as an 'organising principle' in human life, and that 'human psychology has an essentially narrative structure' (Michelle Crossley, 2000, p. 46). The importance of helping someone to tell his or her own stories will be discussed in further detail below. Before that, however, it is important to be aware of some ethical considerations.

Ethical considerations

You will be asking an older person to help you to develop your understanding of their past life. You will be asking them to tell you their life story. This story will enable you to compare your life conditions with the conditions that your informant lived in over 50 years ago. The person is helping you – you are not providing a service to them. Because you are asking for their help it is vital that you get their permission to write about them. You must therefore explain the nature of your research, and explain how you will use any information they give you. You must guarantee that you will not use the person's real name or any details (such as addresses, details of their relatives or photos) that could identify who they are. This is called providing a guarantee of anonymity. You must ask for permission to write about their perception of their needs and their perception of service provision.

In order to be sure that your informant is comfortable with your research you might offer to feedback the outline notes you have taken so that they can check that you have understood. It will be important to stress that the person can ask you not to repeat any information that they may decide should not be mentioned. It is important that your informant should be in control of how the interview material is used.

The British Psychological Society has produced a code of ethical principles for conducting research with people in order to guide psychologists. Although you are not a psychologist the BPS code does provide a point of reference for the ethics of interview research. The British Psychological Society emphasises the key principles as follows:

Key principles for conducting research

* obtaining consent
* avoidance of deception
* provide debriefing – talk about your research at the end
* enable withdrawal from the investigation – a person can withdraw their consent at any time
* maintain confidentiality and the anonymity of participants
* protect participants from harm.

Protecting individuals from harm is a particularly important issue. The Code of Ethics states: 'The essential principle is that the investigation should be considered from the standpoint of all participants; foreseeable threats to their psychological well-being, health, values or dignity should be eliminated'.

'It should be borne in mind that the best judge of whether an investigation will cause offence may be members of the population from which the participants in the research are to be drawn'. (*Source*: The British Psychological Society Ethical Principles for Conducting Research with Human Participants (2000)).

Part of your preparation for the research should involve preparing your questions and any checklists you intend to use in advance. You must check out how you intend to conduct the interview with a tutor, in order to be sure that your approach and the kind of questions you ask will not cause offence, or in any way threaten the person you are working with. The single most important thing about interviewing an older person is that you must not fail to show respect or threaten, or fail to value the person you are talking to.

Conducting an interview

Practical considerations

Thorough planning is essential to conducting a successful interview. There are several practical considerations that you will have to bear in mind, and these are set out in the following checklist.

Time

Choose a time that is convenient for both the interviewee and yourself. Make sure that the interview does not clash with something that the older person would normally be doing (e.g. appointment with the chiropodist, taking part in a group session etc.)

Venue

Choose a venue that is convenient for both of you, and also suitable for holding a private and quiet conversation.

The room needs to be comfortable, neither too hot nor too cold, and well-ventilated

Furniture

Furniture should be comfortable, but not so as to cause drowsiness. Consider whether you will need a table to lean on (to take notes) or whether you will have your papers on a clip-board

Accessibility

Another factor to consider with respect to the venue. If the older person has a mobility problem, make sure that he or she can have easy access to the building/room you have chosen.

Conversely, if you yourself have mobility problems, make sure that the venue is accessible to you.

Additional help

Consider whether the older person will need a

signer, or an interpreter if English is not his or her first language.

If you have your own sensory or language needs, then check out whether the venue is adequate to accommodate both yourself, your helper and the older person.

The same applies to the presence of a helper for physical needs.

Recording the conversation

Consider how you will record what you are told:

* tape recorder
* questionnaire with tick boxes (for service data)
* taking notes
* second person to take notes

NB The interviewee must be quite comfortable with whatever recording methods you choose to use.

You might wish to make your own checklist using the categories above. Thorough planning makes for success, whatever the task in hand.

Aims and objectives

It is important to go into an interview knowing exactly what you want from it. Of course, you may get more than you bargained for, and the person may give you lots of material that you had not anticipated. This can be an enriching experience, both for the interviewer, and also for the interviewee (who has the pleasure of telling stories that are of personal meaning and value). However, there will be some core data that you must collect in order to do this task successfully, and it will be essential to plan how you will make sure that you get this information.

The needs description

You must describe the person's health and social needs in your report, and it may be useful to have some sort of checklist to work from in the first instance. If you choose to interview someone who is already a service user (perhaps in a health or social care setting), then there may be some kind of needs checklist already in existence that you may use to base your enquiries on.

The following checklist serves as a reminder of the broad areas of need.

Assessing need

Health needs:
* existing medical conditions
* developing health needs

Needs arising from a disability:
* physical needs
* emotional needs
* social needs

Circumstances:
Needs associated with:
* financial circumstances
* living conditions

Emotional needs:
* comfort
* attachment
* inclusion

Needs arising from:
* personal circumstances

Social needs:
* attachment
* inclusion
* identity

Needs arising from:
* isolation
* lack of inclusion

Intellectual needs:
* occupation
* continued stimulation
* continued interest

If the older person has a disability, or a medical problem, then you might need to go into more detail about the nature of the physical need that results. It will be significant, for example, to note whether a person has mobility problems (gross motor ability), or is not able to open small containers like bottles and jars (fine motor ability). Any sensory difficulties (such as visual or hearing impairment) should be noted. The older person may also have a learning disability, and you may wish to note how this affects his or her daily life.

Description of service provision

It may be useful to use a checklist of possible services to make sure that nothing is missed. You can then ask the older person whether he or she receives any of the services listed, and you can read these out, ticking those currently received. You might also consider having a second column to indicate those services not received, but which the person might need or want in the next five years. Using a checklist or questionnaire in this way is also known as structured data collection.

You will find a list of Health Care Services on page 271. Social care services are set out in Figure 7.12 (local authority service provision to older people). Be sure to add services provided by the voluntary and charitable sector to your checklist, together with informal care (provided by family, friends or neighbours).

> ### Key concept
>
> *Structured data collection:* getting information from someone in a tightly controlled way, often by using a checklist or a questionnaire.

Option: comparisons or consequences

For the optional topic, you will choose between making a comparison between the older person's experience of growing up with your own experience, or doing an analysis of the person's perspective on growing old.

Older people sometimes enjoy the opportunity to recall the events of their life. You may be able to work with an older person who will enjoy explaining their experiences of education, work and mixing with other people when they were young. You must work with a person who is over 70-years-old so it is likely that you will be able to compare the living conditions of more than 50 years ago with the conditions in which you live. You will find that 50 years ago technical developments were dramatically different from those of today. Almost any older person you speak to will have grown up in a world of mechanical rather than electrical technology. In the 1940s and '50s many homes did not have a telephone. It was not until the 1960s that the majority of homes had TV. The majority of homes in the 1940s and '50s would not have owned a car. The way people communicated, socialised and shopped would have been very different from today. Part of your comparison will, no doubt, note the huge changes that have happened over the last 50 years – but this might be the least interesting part of your research. Although you can gather lots of historical information about activities, employment and customs of the past you should also be interested in the unique human experience of the person you are listening to.

To gather this information, using checklists might be a useful starting point to make sure that nothing relevant is omitted from your discussion. You might include items such as education (schools attended, subjects studied, what the teachers were like etc.), cultural background (e.g. religion, where the person was born and grew up, the language or languages used, beliefs and values etc.), social background (the community where the person grew up, what their house was like, brothers and sisters etc.), occupation (where the person worked, what this was like etc.) and leisure (what did the person do for fun, whether he or she had a favourite sport etc).

Using a semi-structured approach

However, in this situation (i.e. the optional topic) using **a semi-structured** approach to information gathering may be more fruitful than simply checking items off on a list. You can still use the checklist as a starting point, but then allow the person to tell you about personal experiences in his or her own words. Open questions or prompts (see below) are very useful for collecting this kind of data.

Key concept
Semi-structured data collection: a method of collecting information that starts from a number of open questions, and then allows interviewees to talk about a topic in their own way.

Topic	Open questions/Prompts
Social circumstances	What was it like when you were growing up?
	Tell me about your home life at that time.
Education	Tell me about your experiences of going to school.
	What were you teachers like?
Work	What kind of work did you do when you first left school?
	What were conditions like at work?

Unstructured data collection occurs when interviewees are allowed to talk about anything they want to, without any further prompting on the part of the interviewer.
Although the interviewer will probably initiate the topic, after that there will be little attempt to control what the interviewee wants to disclose. This method is also sometimes known as in-depth interviewing, as they often allow interviewees to say what they really think about something.

Key concept
Unstructured data collection (in-depth interviewing): a method of collecting information using a very loose structure. This method allows interviewees to express themselves in their own way, often on topics they choose themselves.

Topic	Opening prompt
Personal perspective on growing older	Give me your views on what's good and not so good about growing older.

In this case, the interviewer wants the older person to talk about the consequences of growing older. Using a totally unstructured approach, the conversation may go anywhere that the older person wishes. The interviewer may choose to clarify certain points.

The semi-structured approach will probably be the best one to choose for the optional topic, as there may be a number of areas that you would like the older person to talk about.

It is likely that in this part of the interview, the older person may begin to tell you some personal stories, and you will need to develop listening and questioning skills in order to encourage the storytelling. The telling of personal stories is actually a collaborative affair, as the following sections will show. The way in which you ask questions and listen to the response will affect the way the story is told to you.

Skilful questioning

The semi-structured method of data collection starts from the asking of **open questions**. These are questions that cannot be answered 'yes' or 'no', and they often begin with 'how', 'what' or 'why'. In contrast, closed questions may be answered with a 'yes' or 'no'. Examples of open and closed questions are set out below.

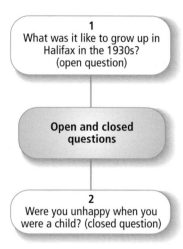

FIGURE 7.14 *Examples of open and closed questions*

Of course, someone who does not feel like answering may refuse to give a detailed response to a question like number 1 in Figure 7.14. He or she might avoid answering by replying 'I can't remember', or 'It's a long time ago, now', but it is not possible just to say 'yes' – another strategy has to be found if the person does not want to open up. Conversely, a very talkative person is not likely to stop at a simple 'yes' or 'no' in reply to question 2. He or she may go on to elaborate on his or her response without any further prompting, particularly if the person has agreed to the interview, which should be the case here.

However, the open question is more likely to encourage a person to talk freely, and can prove a very fruitful starting point, as the interviewee is free to select a topic or an angle, and to go on to develop a narrative around it if he or she wishes. Another good way of starting off a topic in this way is to say 'Can you tell me about when you were growing up in Halifax?' The open question is thus rephrased as a request for information.

Closed questions can, of course, be useful when you want to check out a point of detail in a narrative or a particular response, and can be specific questions. If your interviewee starts to tell you about the family, you might want to ask 'How many brothers and sisters did you have? '(a specific question), or 'Were you at work when that happened? '(a closed question). In practice, the distinction between closed and specific questions is not important; it is important to grasp that some kinds of question are designed to elicit specific responses, whilst others serve the purpose of encouraging people to open up and talk freely. Too many specific and closed questions may stop the flow of a story.

Leading questions can also affect the flow of a narrative, especially if the storyteller has to spend too much time dealing with such an interruption. Leading questions indicate that the questioner is expecting a particular answer. If that answer is not what the storyteller wants to give, more time will need to be spent in dealing with the question before he or she can return to the main storyline.

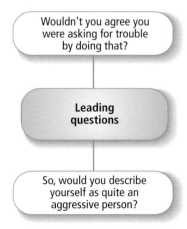

FIGURE 7.15 *Leading questions*

Figure 7.15 gives two examples of such questions.

When you are listening to someone telling a story, reflective questions and reflective statements can be very useful to encourage the speaker to carry on talking. These are simply devices to reflect back to the speaker something he or she has just said. They show the speaker that you are following and understanding the emerging story, and that you are sympathetic to the angle that the teller is seeking to present.

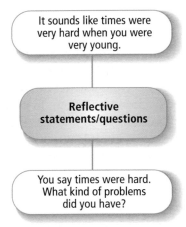

It sounds like times were very hard when you were very young.

Reflective statements/questions

You say times were hard. What kind of problems did you have?

FIGURE 7.16 *Examples of reflective statements/ questions*

Reflective questions differ from leading questions in that the questioner will often re-use or paraphrase the storyteller's own words, rather than try to impose a new concept into the story.

Questions are on one side of the interviewing coin. On the other is skilful listening, and aspects of being a good listener are considered in the following section.

Being a good listener: active listening

Being a good listener is a very skilful business. There is an activity that is sometimes used in training courses where participants work in pairs to experiment with different ways of listening. One member of each pair has to speak for two minutes about something that is of interest or importance to him or her. The others, who are the listeners, are asked either to keep absolutely silent, or to keep interrupting the speaker. Both these tactics drive the speakers to distraction (as

well as causing some distress to the people who are supposed to be listening) and there is a great feeling of relief all round when the two minutes are up.

Listening in complete silence is something that many people in Western culture find very unnatural. Although this kind of listening is appropriate at times (perhaps during a lecture or when watching a play or film), it is perceived as unfriendly by the person who is speaking. To avoid making your interviewee feel uncomfortable, you can give small acknowledgement responses every few seconds. Nodding your head and keeping an interested expression will also help to make the speaker feel that what he or she is saying is interesting to you.

Using acknowledgement responses and appropriate facial expressions help to encourage a speaker to carry on talking

Conversely, too much interruption can stop the flow of a story. An interviewee can tolerate a certain limited amount of interruption (such as asking for a point of detail on a particular point), but too much is inhibiting. You will need to take care that you support the older person by not interrupting. However, some reflective statements (such as 'That must have been very hard for you', see above, p. 285), if used carefully, will also encourage the older person to carry on talking to you about their experiences.

Hearing the story

The information that you collect, by observation and interview, will result from a combination of structured and unstructured data collection methods. Structured methods (such as using checklists or a questionnaire) can be used to collect basic factual information, for example about services used, medical conditions and/or the degree of disability experienced by the person being interviewed.

However, a more unstructured approach will probably work better for collecting information about the older person's early life or perception of growing older. Unstructured (or qualitative) data is more descriptive, and often concerned with attitudes, opinions and values. Although (as has been suggested) you can start from a partly structured approach (perhaps with a list of open questions), with careful active listening and skilled questioning an older person can be encouraged to talk about his or her personal views and experiences.

The telling of a personal story is a collaborative affair. It depends as much on the listener as on the storyteller. The older person you interview will be looking for an interested and positive response from you; otherwise he or she may decide not to continue. If the older person is from a different cultural group from yourself, you may encounter some differences in the way that he or she discloses information, or tells stories. If he or she has a disability of some kind (particularly a sensory disability) this may also affect the way the interview proceeds. You will need to keep these factors in mind when listening.

Make sure that you hear what the person wants to tell you, and not just want you want to hear. If someone is telling you a personal story, there will be clues built in which tell you why the story is being told, and why it is important to the teller. For example, you might be asking the older person to talk to you about the advantages and disadvantages of growing older. However, the person suddenly starts to tell you a personal story about something that happened many years ago, perhaps from a time when he or she had very young children. The story might be about having sleepless nights when one of the children was a baby. Your first reaction might be 'So what? Why am I being told about this? 'However, if you are patient and listen for the clues, it should become apparent why this story is relevant. Clues can be given by tone of voice, by repetition of important elements, or even by a pause in the telling where the person addresses you directly to make the purpose of the story clear.

In the middle of a description of a sequence of sleepless nights, the person might then say: 'Children are lovely, but I don't miss being exhausted every morning, I can tell you! I let my son do that now, with his children! ' This might tell you something about what the older person values about growing older, including not having parental responsibilities.

Use the checklist on the next page to check out your interviewing skills. You might want to practise interviewing a friend as preparation for conducting the interview with the older person.

Reporting your findings: re-storying the narrative

It is important to observe the key aspects of reporting when a real person is the subject of the enquiry you are making.

You should observe confidentiality at all times, and not discuss the older person's details with anyone except your tutor and, possibly, a care worker or key worker if there is one. You should make it clear to the older person that you wish to discuss the information given to you, in order to learn how best to make a report; and you should only proceed with his or her permission. Ideally,

Give yourself a score out of five for each of the following aspects of interviewing.

Alternatively, interview a friend, then ask him or her to give you a rating on your performance.

	Score
Using prepared questions	
Using open questions to encourage the person to talk	
Using acknowledgement responses to show that I am listening	
Using reflective statements to show that I am listening	
Using appropriate questions for clarification	
Being aware of body language (my own and the other person's)	
Being aware of tone of voice and facial expression (my own and the other person's)	
Recognising the possible significance of cultural differences	
Recognising the possible impact of physical, sensory or learning disabilities	
Staying positive if I encounter a conversational style I am not used to	

you should show the report to him or her once it has been finished.

Keep your notes (and the tape recording, if you have made one) in a safe place, and make sure that all written notes are kept anonymous. Destroy all your notes once the project is finished.

When you write up your report, be sure to give details as accurately as possible, and not to misrepresent what the person has told you. To some extent, you will be creating a new version of the person's life, by editing and selecting from the mass of information that you collect. This representation of someone's details is also referred to as re-storying. This is something that professionals, such as doctors or social workers, do all the time. A doctor's account of a patient, for example, will just concentrate on their medical condition, any disabling factors and what the person has difficulty with, together with a prognosis for his or her further development (or deterioration). A social worker's case study will

focus on the person's needs, and the services that he or she is likely to need. Both of these are, to some extent, 're-storyings' of the person's own narrative, as they focus on particular aspects of that person's situation. This is not to suggest that you are doing something wrong by writing an account of the person that focuses on services and needs. It is inevitable that the provision of a specific service will need its own recording formats in order to make the delivery of those services more efficient and effective. However, it is important for you to recognise that in writing an account of an older person that is heavily focused on services and need you are, in reality, re-storying a personal narrative. It is essential that you do this responsibly and with respect for that person's individuality.

This brings us back to the concept of personhood, which is where this section of this unit began. Never lose sight of the personhood of the individual you work with for this unit, and you will produce a sensitive and insightful report.

Summary

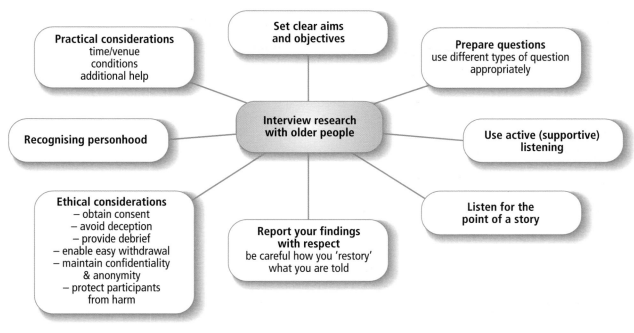

FIGURE 7.17 *Section 7.5 summary*

Your report

In the report you produce for this unit you will set out what you have found out about an older person aged 70 years or over.

The report must include three topics:

1   Needs description

   * health
   * social circumstances

2   Service provision

   * current
   * future need

3   Either (a) comparisons, or (b) consequences:

   (a) Comparisons
      *   the older person's experience of growing up compared to your own experience
   (b) Consequences
      *   the older person's perspective on the advantages and drawbacks of growing old

The report will contain information from a number of sources, including an interview with the older person concerned. Other sources of information might include informal carers and key or care workers, if this is appropriate. If you do wish to consult other people, you should make this clear to the older person, and seek permission to do this.

You may also wish to supplement your understanding with research from printed or Internet sources, and there may be existing documentation that can help (for example, existing assessment forms). If you are given access to such personal information, you should treat it with the utmost confidentiality.

AO1: Knowledge of conditions affecting the participant. Knowledge of relevant services

You will need to describe any medical conditions affecting the health of the older person, together with any disabilities they may be experiencing. You might want to supplement this with extra research from Internet or printed sources.

You will also need to describe the older person's social circumstances, and any services currently received.

Good marks will be obtained by:
*   a detailed description of the older person's health and social conditions
*   a detailed description of the services received together with supporting evidence

Higher marks will be obtained by including all of the above, plus:
*   provision of a comprehensive account of the person's health and social conditions, and current service provision
*   accurate use of medical terminology as appropriate, e.g. cerebrovascular accident, glaucoma, tinnitus etc.
*   accurate use of key social concepts, e.g. social isolation, level of independence etc.
*   appropriate and accurate use of the terminology of service use, e.g. informal care, statutory sector, private sector, voluntary sector, person centred care, single assessment process etc.

AO2 Report structure, application of ethical precautions

The report should be in four sections as follows:

A: Introduction
*   scope of the report
*   brief description of the older person

B: Method
*   description of how the information was collected
*   dates, times of interview(s) etc.

C: Findings
*   health and social circumstances of the older person
*   current service provision
*   suggestions for additional future services
*   advantages and disadvantages of the services described
*   comparisons or consequences

D: Appendix
*   documents to support your findings, such as questionnaires you have designed or used, existing assessment schedules, letters seeking consent and copies of responses
*   a list of all informants (anonymised, giving only their relationship to the person studied)
*   references to printed and electronic sources

Good marks will be given to:
*   a well-structured report, clearly laid out and observing the designated headings
*   good use of paragraphing, and clear sentence structure
*   a clear explanation of the ethical issues as they relate to the person studied.

Higher marks will be given for achieving all of the above, plus:
* * logical arrangement of material within each section
* * concise, coherent and well-organised work
* * confident use of Key Concepts and specialist terminology.

AO3 Preparation of interview materials. Effectiveness of recording methods

You will need to demonstrate evidence of more than one recording method. It will be advisable to collect both structured and unstructured data.

Good marks will be obtained by producing:
* * well-designed interview schedules (e.g. checklists, questionnaires) that aim to elicit a range of information
* * evidence that questioning/listening techniques were adapted to suit the needs of the interviewee (e.g. use of signer, other helper etc. as appropriate)
* * use of suitable specialist vocabulary to organise and interpret the information collected.

Higher marks will be obtained by producing all of the above plus:
* * comprehensive and thoughtfully designed interviewing schedules that aim to ensure that all potentially relevant items of information are included in the interview
* * evidence that both structured and unstructured techniques were used to obtain information from the older person
* * evidence of positive use of questioning and active listening during the interview(s)
* * analysis of unstructured data that shows clearly that you have identified what the older person wanted you to understand (the point of telling the story, or giving you the information)
* * evidence of respect for the older person in the way that you have re-storied their narrative.

AO4 Evaluation of appropriateness of current service provision and of suggested provision

In discussing this issue, you will need to be aware that there may be a difference between what the older person would like and what is available to him or her, particularly with respect to social care services. There may also be differences of opinion between the older person and other people, such as an informal carer, or a medical professional.

Good marks will result from:
* * sound analysis of the advantages and disadvantages of all suggested provision
* * clear acknowledgement of the older person's perspective on what is proposed.

Higher marks will result from all of the above plus:
* * evidence of an awareness of current regulations on service provision (e.g. the Fair Access to Care Services guidelines)
* * evidence of an awareness of local eligibility criteria and how these may impact upon any future service provision
* * a written analysis that conveys something of the complexity of an individual's situation
* * an in-depth analysis of the person's needs that takes into account both structured and unstructured data in such as way as to give an insight into the realities of the older person's requirements.

References

Age Concern (2004) *Finding Help at Home*, Factsheet 6, Age Concern, London

Age Concern (2004) *Continuing NHS Healthcare, NHS funded registered nursing care and intermediate care*, Factsheet 20, Age Concern, London

Arber, S. and Ginn, J. (2004) 'Ageing and Gender: Diversity and Change' in *Social Trends*, Vol. 34, HMSO, London

Coleman and Salt, (2000) *The British Population*, Oxford University Press, Oxford

Crossley, Michelle L. (2000) *Introducing Narrative Psychology: Self, trauma and the construction of meaning*, The Open University Press, Buckingham, Philadelphia

Department of Health (2001) *National Service Framework for Older People*, HMSO, London

Department of Health (2002), *Fair Access to Care Services: Guidance on Eligibility Criteria for Adult Social Care*, HMSO, London

Kitwood, T. (1997) *Dementia Reconsidered*, Open University Press, Buckingham UK and Bristol USA

Seligman, M. (1975) *Helplessness*, W. H. Freeman and Co., San Francisco

Seligman, M. (2002) *Authentic Happiness*, Nicholas Brealey Publishing, London

Social Trends, Vol. 32 (2002), HMSO, London

Social Trends, Vol. 34 (2004), HMSO, London

Useful websites

Please see www.heinemann.co.uk/hotlinks (express code 1554P) for links to the websites of the following which may provide a source of information:

* Age concern
  Information, advice and a range of other services for older people in England. Scotland, Wales and northern Ireland have their own Age Concern organisations.

* Alzheimers Society

* Website of the Better Government for Older People network. Encourages Older People to 'achieve participation and citizenship', and to bridge the gap between what policies say, and what actually happens in practice.

* British Psychological Society: Ethical Principles for conducting Research with Human Participants

* Community Care
  News on latest developments in social care, including policy and law, jobs, agencies, projects, funds and new initiatives.

* Community Service Volunteers Website
  Information about volunteering and training opportunities.

* General Social Care Council

* Joseph Rowntree Foundation. Research on social issues.

* Health Survey for England 2001 – University College London: published by HMSO.

* National Audit Office. Access to reports on current developments in services.

* National Council for Voluntary Organisations. Umbrella body for the Voluntary Sector in England. (Scotland, Northern Ireland and Wales have their own VCO organisations.) Represents the views of the voluntary sector to policy makers and government. Consultation and research; telephone helpdesk, information, publications.

* National Electronic Library for Health

* The Office for National Statistics

* NHS careers
  NHS website giving full details of all jobs/ professions within National Health Service.

* Nursing older people:
  online journal from RCN publishing.

* Social work careers:
  a Department of Health website. Gives information on professions/jobs within social work. Relates to social work in England only. There are links to sites for Northern Ireland, Scotland and Wales. Also links to Jobcentre Plus.

* Website of the Women's Royal Voluntary Service.
  Help and information about volunteering, especially to support older people and to keep them in their own homes. Useful case studies about volunteering.

UNIT
8

Needs and provision for early years clients

You will learn about:

8.1 The needs of early years clients

8.2 The formal services which are available to meet the needs of early years client

8.3 The informal services which can meet the needs of early years client

8.4 The origins and development of services

8.5 Access to services

Introduction

This unit looks at the different needs of early years service users and the variety of provision available to meet those needs.

8.1 The needs of early years clients

Children have a range of needs which can broadly be divided into health, social care and educational needs. These needs have to be met in order to allow the children to develop to their full potential.

It has generally been accepted for a long time that children need both care and education in order to develop successfully. 'Care' means to provide for physical needs or comfort and 'education' is defined as the process of imparting knowledge by formal instruction. Modern approaches to early years care and education are based on integrating these two areas – learning cannot take place if a child's physical needs are not met.

Maslow's hierarchy of human need can help us to understand why care and education have to be integrated in order to provide the most effective support for children. Maslow identified physical, intellectual, social and emotional needs when he developed his hierarchy. He suggested that each 'layer of need' has to be met before the next can be achieved. Therefore, physical needs such as feeling warm and well-fed must be met before a child's emotional needs can be satisfied. A child who feels hungry will find it difficult to concentrate. The higher up the pyramid you go, the more satisfaction is aligned to social and intellectual rather than physical needs. The pyramid puts education or intellectual needs near the top.

Think it over...

Think about the common needs in each classification for children. Why do you think children learn best when their physical or care needs are met?

Foundations of early years care and education

Some of the first nursery schools that were founded at the beginning of the twentieth century by early childcare theorists, such as Maria Montessori (1869–1952), Rudolf Steiner (1861–1925) and particularly Margaret McMillan (1860–1931), developed their theories on both care and education. These early theorists have had a great influence on the ethos of early years provision today.

Maria Montessori (1869-1952)

Maria Montessori was born in Italy in 1869. She trained as a doctor and worked as an assistant doctor in a psychiatric clinic for 'mentally deficient' children. From this and her experience as the head of a state institute for the education of such children, Montessori formed her own ideas about early childhood education. Her methods are based on the fact that Montessori felt that children under the age of six have the most powerful and receptive minds. This gives them a once in a lifetime opportunity to learn. The Montessori method gives children the opportunity to learn about the world around them through exploration. They are given the freedom to move within it, manipulate and touch it. She developed a number of 'educational toys' to support this process. There is a lot of repetition in the activities, such as card stitching. These toys were designed to help a child acquire skills, competence and confidence.

There was also a lot of emphasis on the development of social skills and these took

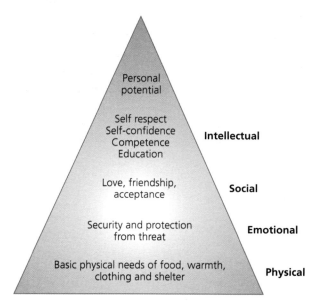

FIGURE 8.1 *Some human needs*

preference over early reading and writing.

The role of the teacher is important. The teacher will never interfere or correct a child. A Montessori teacher assesses a child and presents him or her with one of the toys. If a child is able to use it correctly, then it has been presented at the right time. If the child is not yet ready to use it, then the teacher will put the material away for another day. The child is never made to feel inferior. This method has been used in thousands of schools around the world.

Rudolf Steiner (1861–1925)

Steiner was born in Austria in 1861. His ideas about teaching young children are known as the Waldorf education system. For Steiner, childhood was a separate period of life and his methods aimed to develop all aspects of the child. The curriculum he designed aimed to provide children with equal experience of the arts and the sciences. Play is often with natural materials and there are no manufactured toys. Imaginative play is therefore central to the Waldorf scheme. Children are free to choose whether to play together or alone.

Steiner also felt it was important to develop other aspects of the child as well as the intellectual. He placed a lot of emphasis on relationships and the community. Children in Steiner schools often stay with the same teacher for the whole of their primary education. The teacher also gets to know the family well through home visits. The type of link is seen as central to the child learning effectively.

The teacher has an important task as a role model for the children. They have to encourage a child to think imaginatively through songs, games or activities such as cooking or painting. The teacher also makes up or retells stories as a way to encourage a child to think. These stories are not read from a book. Through close observation of the child, a teacher can decide what material a child may need next in order to develop.

Steiner also felt children should be educated in a happy and joyful atmosphere. Children are often not taught about or told of some of the dangers or less pleasant aspects of society.

Margaret McMillan (1860–1931)

McMillan was born in Britain in 1860. Initially she designed her approach to the curriculum around toys which developed a child's fine and gross motor skills and manual dexterity. However, as her ideas developed, she saw the children being able to experience things themselves or 'first hand' as increasingly important. Relationships and emotions were given as high an importance as physical play and movement. Play became the way in which children applied what they knew and understood. Free play was seen as important.

McMillan introduced the Nursery School. She saw this very much as the extension to the home and put great importance on working closely with parents. The outdoor environment was as important as the indoor and McMillan recognised that children could learn a lot from the natural environment. She opened the first open-air nursery school in 1911.

McMillan saw care and education going hand in hand. One of her biggest messages was that children cannot learn effectively if they are hungry, cold or ill. These needs have to be satisfied if learning is going to take place. Therefore, she promoted the importance of school meals and medical services to help to ensure that all children could benefit from their education.

Many services now aim to integrate these two important aspects of a child's' development.

Summary

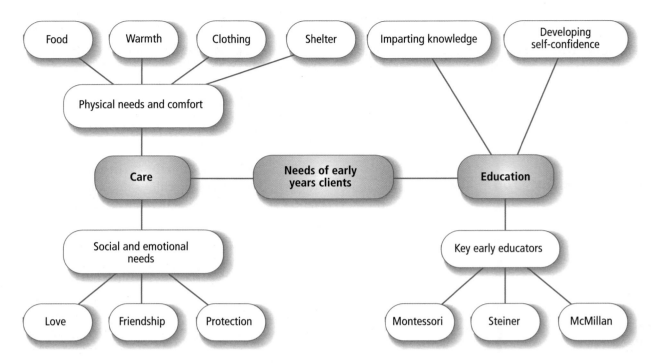

FIGURE 8.2 *Section 8.1 summary*

Consider this

Think about an early years setting you are familiar with.

1. Identify how the setting provides both care and education for its children.

2. Are the two aspects delivered independently or is it an integrated approach?

3. Give an example of an activity in which care and education are integrated.

4. Explain how you think an integrated approach might benefit the children.

8.2 Formal services

There are many different types of formal care and education services in Britain today. These have increased significantly in the last 30 years as the number of women working outside the home has increased. This is partly due to the reduction in the size of the workforce, accompanied by changes in the age structure of the population, and partly due to a much greater acceptance that mothers may choose to continue working once they have children.

There has been a range of legislation passed by Parliament to encourage and support working mothers. The National Childcare Strategy aimed to ensure the provision of high quality early years provision and after-school facilities. The government has also provided free pre-school places for all children from the term following their third birthday through the 'voucher scheme' for a limited number of sessions per week and offers tax incentives for working mothers.

✳ DID YOU KNOW?

The early years voucher scheme does not always cover the full cost of a session at an early years facility. Parents are offered 15 hours per week for 33 weeks of the year and often have to pay a 'top up' fee to cover the care required. It certainly does not cover full-time care for a working parent but does provide some help to parents for the cost of childcare.

How national policies influence the provision of care and education

National policies are produced by central government. Central government sets taxes and determines what is spent on areas such as education and health. The government is divided into different departments. The Department for Education and Skills (DfES) is responsible for all aspects of education.

Many laws and Acts of Parliament have influenced the provision of early years care and education. One of the most important ones was the Children Act 1989.

The Children Act 1989

This Act of Parliament resulted in a number of changes in the way young children were cared for and protected. It covered care in the home including issues around parenthood and arrangements that took place if parents separated. It also covered services provided outside the home such as, for example, child protection care (See also pages 313–314)

The Children Act 2004

The Children Act 2004 established a new Children's Commissioner for England, who will raise awareness of issues relating to children and young people and report annually to Parliament, through the Secretary of State. The role is to look at how both public and private bodies listen to children and report on improvements. It also calls for cooperation between key agencies to improve children's well-being. It places a duty on people working with children and young people to have systems in place which ensure they safeguard and promote the well-being of children through their work. It also calls for a basic database to hold information on children to help joined up work between agencies.

Local authorities are required to have a Director of Children's Services, who brings together education and social services.

Every Child Matters – what's next?

Every Child Matters: Change for Children outlines how the Children Act 2004 will be implemented. It applies to all children, from birth to the age of 19. Through the *National Service Framework for Children, Young People and Maternity Services* (NSF), an integral part of the programme, the government aims to support parents from pregnancy onwards. The vision is to create a joined-up system of health, family support, childcare and education services so that all children get the best start possible in the vital early years. It is a shared programme of change to improve outcomes for all children and young people. It takes forward the government's vision of radical reform for children, young people and families.

Children and young people identified five outcomes that are central to well-being in childhood and later life: being healthy, staying safe, enjoying and achieving, making a positive contribution and achieving economic well-being. This programme aims to improve those outcomes for all children and to close the gap in outcomes between the disadvantaged and their peers.

In the next 10 years (2004–2014) the government's aim is to offer parents greater help with childcare, often located conveniently in schools and/or provided in partnership with the voluntary and private sector. The DfES *Five-year Strategy for Children and Learners* set an expectation that primary schools should, over time, offer childcare between 8.00 am and 6.00 pm, 48 weeks per year. This builds on the extended school programme and could form the basis of arrangements made by groups or clusters of schools.

National Childcare Strategy

Another key government strategy that has influenced the provision of early years services is the National Childcare Strategy. The government has put major resources into this strategy, which aims to ensure provision of good quality early years services. It also aims to increase the availability of before- and after-school clubs, including homework clubs for 5–15 year olds. The strategy planned to make childcare more affordable. In addition, it had a direct influence on increasing the demand for early years provision and, in doing so, the number of childcare facilities available.

Early years curriculum

The curriculum covered in many pre-school groups and reception classes reflects the National Curriculum. This is outlined by the DfES and sets out the curriculum areas and the knowledge and skills which must be covered. It also outlines what level children are expected to achieve by specific ages. The way the material is delivered is left to the individual provider. Ofsted (Office for Standards in Education) will monitor if providers have an appropriate curriculum when carrying out inspections.

Any pre-school provider that accepts nursery vouchers has to deliver the Foundation Stage Curriculum. This is the first stage of the National Curriculum and it focuses on the distinct needs of children aged three until the end of the reception year of primary school. It is a broad, balanced and purposeful curriculum, delivered through planned play activities to ensure that all children have the opportunity to reach their full potential and experience the best possible start to their education. This has greatly influenced the work which is carried out in all education settings.

Think it over...

Many early years setting use circle time as an opportunity for children to talk about something they have done. Imagine a nursery in which a group of children are asked to talk about what they did at the weekend. Which early learning goals would be covered by this activity?

Early learning goals: these identify six areas of learning which must be included in the curriculum designed by a provider. These are: language and literacy; mathematics; knowledge and understanding of the world; physical development; creative development and personal, social and emotional development. Personal, social and emotional development is a topic covered through the other five areas and is almost a core theme running through every activity. Many activities will cover more than one area.

Educare

It has been accepted for a long time that children need both care and education. The concept is known as 'Educare' – a combination of care and education. 'Care' means to provide for physical needs or comfort and 'education' is defined as the process of imparting knowledge by formal instruction. Modern approaches to early years care and education are based on integrating these two areas – learning cannot take place if a child's physical needs are not met.

Formal services are those which provide care and education in a structured way. Provision, whether formal or informal, can also be classified as statutory, private or voluntary as outlined below.

Statutory services These are services which are required by law and organised and run by local authorities. State-run nurseries are examples of statutory provision. These are usually attached to primary schools and provide term-time nursery classes for the year before the child reaches the age for entry to reception. Another example of a statutory service for children is the family centre. These centres are often run under social services and provide support for children and their families.

Private services These are childcare services which are run for profit. The owner of the provision will see the childcare business as a business opportunity and its main aim will be to make money from the service provided. Many nurseries are privately owned. This category also includes independent schools, many of which will have a pre-school section. Childminders also provide a private service. They are self-employed and work from home.

Voluntary groups These services are run by non-profit-making organisations and often provide services when the organisation feels that statutory and private provision are inadequate in an area. Voluntary services are usually funded by grants, fundraising from the public and contributions from individuals. Voluntary services can be staffed by volunteers or employ paid staff. An example of a voluntary service would be a church-run parent and toddler group.

Provision of formal care

Many providers of formal care have to meet legislation such as that already discussed in this unit. Many are regulated by local authorities or other government departments. They may receive funding from central government and therefore have to be accountable for the provision they offer. They are often monitored by those who fund them. Different types of formal provision are outlined below.

Playgroups

Playgroups provide care in sessions for two to five-year-olds. They tend to provide for certain localities in a town and are often run in local church halls and community centres. Provision can be either private or voluntary. Playgroups are often run by a committee of volunteers who oversee the running of the group. They do not have large budgets and often rely on fund raising. Their fees are generally lower than those charged by private nurseries. Playgroups are valuable in helping children to develop social skills. They effectively develop links within a neighbourhood between the parents and carers of young children.

The playgroup leader is qualified; however, playgroups may rely on untrained staff and parent helpers to meet ratio requirements. Playgroups are often held in premises that were not built to meet the needs of children.

As this type of service is provided in sessions, it does not meet the needs of working parents.

Nursery education

Nurseries provide both full day care provision and morining or afternoon sessions. They can provide care for children between the ages of six months and four years depending on their registration. Many nurseries are open all year round and therefore cater well for working parents. Other nurseries operate during term- time only. Nurseries tend to be more expensive than some other forms of child care.

They aim to develop independence and social skills and also to prepare the child for the routine of school through specialist rising fives groups. These are special groups for children about to start school. They work in a more structured manner to help the children become familiar with the expectations in a classroom setting.

Children generally have a 'key worker' who is their main carer and with whom they form a strong relationship. Staff are generally well qualified and experienced in early years care and education. The manager is trained to at least level 3 and 50 per cent of the staff must also be qualified. Nurseries have high adult to child ratios; however, higher staff ratios can result in children finding it difficult to adapt to the lower ratios in schools.

Family centres

Family centres are usually run by local authority social services departments or by voluntary organisations such as NCH Action for Children. Their aim is to teach parenting and relationship skills to families that are experiencing difficulties. Family background and parenting practices are extremely important in influencing how a young child develops. A poor start often means children will be behind intellectually and lack the social skills to mix with other children. Family centres help to support families to improve these skills so that their children have a better start in life. They aim to keep families together. Unfortunately, some parents feel there is a stigma attached to such support and do not take full advantage of what is offered.

Family centres are staffed by social workers and early years workers who are well qualified. They work with families who have children of all ages. They generally provide sessions rather than full day care.

Crèches

A crèche can be run privately or voluntarily. Crèches provide short-term care in sessions, which frees the parent to carry out certain tasks such as shopping. Crèches have become increasingly popular in recent years in shopping centres and other places in which care is needed for short periods of time. The advantage of a crèche is its convenience for parents if they need to be free to focus on a particular task for a short period of time. The main disadvantage is that the child does not know the carer and relationships can therefore be difficult to build. Even the most confident children are generally reluctant to stay with strangers and therefore may be distressed by the experience.

One point to note is that if the crèche limits the length of time that a child can be left to less than two hours, the childcare provision is not covered by the regulations of the Children Act.

Childminding

Childminding is the provision of day care in the carer's own home. It is one of the most widespread forms of full-time childcare for working parents because the care is provided at times to suit individual parents. Childminders usually live near the child's home and therefore long journeys are avoided. Childminders often start this type of work because they are a parent with young children who wants to work but does not want to work outside the home. Many continue with the service after their children have grown, as they are dedicated to looking after young children.

Childminders offer a flexible service which can fit around the hours that working parents want. Some offer part-time care to more than one set of children to fit around part-time working. Many also offer an after-school collection service as well, so there can be continuity once a child starts school. This means they can build a relationship with both the child and the parents, which will continue through the early years.

A childminder usually cares for no more than three children under the age of five and therefore there is a lot of individual attention. As childminders work from their own homes, the atmosphere is usually more relaxed and less structured than that found in formal childcare, such as a nursery. The home setting is valued by many working parents who choose to use childminders specifically for this reason. Often the childminder will also do daily household tasks such as washing or shopping as part of the normal day.

Many childminders will encourage their children to mix with others by attending parent and toddler groups or playgroups with them. They will also offer activities to engage the children; however, this will not always match the play opportunities and stimulation that a nursery may provide.

Anyone who is paid to look after children for more than two hours per day is classed as a childminder and must conform to regulations. The childminder has to go through a registration process which includes their home being visited. Often adaptations to the home are necessary to make it safe for children. Childminders also have to take out insurance to cover their business and are required to keep records and registers. Parents usually visit a prospective childminder several times before choosing one, as they need to ensure they have childrearing practices and a lifestyle which will reflect their own.

After-school and before-school care

After-school provision is generally a service offered by a private provider. After-school care is provided regularly for school-age children at the beginning and end of the day to enable parents to work. Sessions are often held between 8.00–9.00am and 3.00–6.00pm. Fees are charged, although parents may receive a subsidy through the National Childcare Strategy, and generally after-school care is reasonably priced. Many after-school clubs provide a collection service from local schools in the area. The provision can include a homework club. Staff are generally qualified as play workers, who are specifically trained for working with 5–15 year-olds.

Toy libraries

There are over 1,000 toy libraries in the UK. Toy libraries are a community-based resource for play, which may include equipment, toys for loan, dedicated play space and skilled staff who offer advice and support for parents and carers.

Their main aim is to create and support quality play opportunities by offering a rich variety of high quality toys for loan. Staff appraise the toys, and provide parents and carers with information and ideas about the toys and play activities in general. The libraries provide a wide range of carefully selected toys to borrow that have a high play and education value. The service means that parents can borrow toys that meet the needs and abilities of children of all ages as well as those with special needs. The service helps children to develop vital skills which can be learnt through play.

Toys are loaned to families for a nominal fee (and sometimes for free). They may also offer play sessions, as well as a friendly, informative meeting place for parents and carers. Toy libraries support parents, as they provide a way in which parents can discover the appropriate toys and play activities for their children. This helps them to develop an understanding of the role of play in child development and simultaneously helps them to develop their parenting skills.

The first toy library was started in 1967 by Jill Norris, a Froebel-trained teacher who was a mother of two children with disabilities. The concept developed as families with children who had special needs began to exchange toys at home and raise funds to provide specialist toys and equipment. Toy libraries soon became recognised as a valuable resource for the community. By the early 1970s they had widened their remit to offer the opportunity for all children to borrow toys through local toy libraries.

Each toy library is run independently and is responsible for securing its own funding. Some toy libraries are run by paid workers and others are part of a community-based service, where a range of professionals such as social workers, health workers and pre-school education staff work together to provide a service for the community. Toy libraries may also be a voluntary service and are often run by volunteers, many of whom are parents themselves.

Toy libraries may belong to the National Association of Toy and Leisure Libraries (NATLL) which offers advice and support to members.

Child guidance

The Child Guidance Service works with children from birth to 19 years of age and their families to help with learning, emotional, social and behavioural difficulties. A Child Guidance Service is usually offered by local authorities and includes the services of educational psychologists and social workers. They work together in small locally based teams to offer support to children in school and at home.

Educational psychologists use tests and other assessment methods to help to identify children's strengths and weaknesses and they offer advice to teachers and parents on how to support children who are experiencing difficulties in the classroom or at home.

Child guidance social workers will give support to children and families through counselling and family case work. This may include bereavement counselling, group work with adolescents, play therapy and family therapy depending on the individual circumstances of the child and family.

Both the social workers and the educational psychologists work closely with teachers in schools, other support workers in education, such as the education welfare officer, and with doctors and health visitors, speech and language therapists, social workers and care workers with the aim to provide holistic support for the child and their family.

Parent and toddler groups

Parent and toddler groups provide care in sessions for parents with young children. They are generally run by voluntary groups in local communities and may take place in church halls, for example. They are often run by a committee who oversees the running of the group. The committee is made up of volunteers, who are often parents of children who attend the group. Once their child no longer attends, the committee member ceases to be involved which means that the committee changes on a regular basis. Such groups do not have large budgets and often rely on fund raising.

At a parent and toddler group, parents remain for the session so it is an opportunity for parents to socialise with other parents. They provide a good opportunity for young children to socialise with others before they move onto playgroup or nursery where they may attend alone. One disadvantage is that the children can get used to parents being present so find separation harder once they start pre-school.

Gingerbread

Gingerbread is an organisation, founded in 1970, which supports
lone parent families. Tessa Fothergill, a young parent who struggled for survival in London following the break up of her marriage, decided to set up a self-help organisation. The *Sunday Times* published an article about her and this attracted a response from hundreds of parents in similar situations and Gingerbread was formed. Since then the divorce rate in Britain has trebled, with one in three marriages ending in divorce. In addition, more women are choosing to have children outside a relationship. Therefore, far more children are living in lone or single parent families as a result. It is believed that one in four children are raised in a single parent family in Britain today.

This self-help organisation offers members practical and emotional support. It is also a lobby group, which speaks out for the interests of single parent families in the media and the political arena. Gingerbread offers support in a number of ways, as shown in Figure 8.3.

Gingerbread can provide vital support for children who often lose confidence and self-esteem when they lose a parent either through a relationship breaking down, or the death of a parent. This self-help group recognises that children in single parent families are twice as likely to be poor compared to those in two parent families and therefore unable to afford many things that other children and families can. The organisation aims to ensure that children are not excluded from activities and experiences as a result of their disadvantaged status.

Save the Children

Save the Children is a charity that works for children in the UK and around the world who suffer from poverty, disease, injustice and violence. Save the Children was founded in 1919 in response to conditions in Europe immediately following the First World War. During the war the Allied forces had enforced a blockade that weakened Germany and its supporting countries. An armistice was signed but the allied forces kept the blockage to ensure the Germans accepted the terms for peace.

The continuing blockade meant that many German people, especially in the cities such as Berlin and Vienna, were severely affected. There were food shortages, which meant that many families had nothing to eat but cabbage and turnips. This particularly affected the children

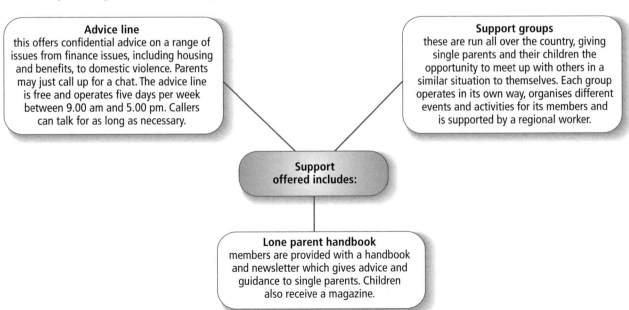

Advice line
this offers confidential advice on a range of issues from finance issues, including housing and benefits, to domestic violence. Parents may just call up for a chat. The advice line is free and operates five days per week between 9.00 am and 5.00 pm. Callers can talk for as long as necessary.

Support groups
these are run all over the country, giving single parents and their children the opportunity to meet up with others in a similar situation to themselves. Each group operates in its own way, organises different events and activities for its members and is supported by a regional worker.

Support offered includes:

Lone parent handbook
members are provided with a handbook and newsletter which gives advice and guidance to single parents. Children also receive a magazine.

FIGURE 8.3 *Some of the support offered to lone parent families*

who became malnourished and showed signs of starvation. They became susceptible to disease like tuberculosis and rickets.

> "Conditions were indeed terrible. Children were actually dying in the street. I saw in the Allgemeine Krankenhaus 38 women who were suffering spontaneous fracture of the hips, their bones having lost all solidity. The children's bones were like rubber. Tuberculosis was terribly rife. Clothing was utterly lacking. Children were wrapped in paper, and in the hospitals there was nothing but paper bandages."
>
> Dr Hector Munro (Save the Children) 1919

Despite the devastation, many British were anti-German. There was an election shortly after the signing of the armistice which was won by the Conservative coalition, whose campaign was based around popular sentiment that wanted to 'hang the Kaiser' and 'squeeze Germany until the pips squeak'.

However, not all people in the UK sought revenge from their former enemies. Throughout the war a group led by Dorothy Buxton had read and translated the European press for the Cambridge Magazine. These 'Notes from the Foreign Press' attempted to provide balance to the propaganda-driven reports in the UK newspapers.

Dorothy and her associates set up the Fight the Famine Council at the beginning of 1919 to campaign for justice and compassion for the defeated nations. The organisation published leaflets promoting its cause and raising awareness of the effect of the blockade on children. The government took a dim view on this, as it was considered to be against the Defence of the Realm Act. One member was fined £5 for handing out such leaflets – a significant amount of money in those days.

Besides campaigning to raise awareness, the Fight the Famine Council realised that practical measures were needed if the suffering caused by the blockade was going to be addressed. Therefore, the Save the Children Fund was launched in May 1919 with the aim of fundraising to raise money to send to children in Europe in the areas so badly affected by the war.

The charity became very successful at fund raising. It received individual donations ranging from two shillings and sixpence from a small boy's money box to a cheque for £10 000 pinned to a Save the Children Fund leaflet.

In the first instance, money was used to support organisations working with children in Germany, Austria, France, Belgium, the Balkans, Hungary and for Armenian Refugees in Turkey. Workers were taken on six-week contracts as it was not anticipated that the organisation would become permanent. However, in the immediate post-war period, Save the Children had to deal with one emergency followed by another.

The following quote is from a child on the Save the Children website:

> "...Thousands of people...tired, sick and hungry. I had to carry my youngest brother. One day I saw that he was not moving nor crying for bread any more. I showed him to my mother and she saw that he was dead. We were glad that he was dead because we had nothing to feed him on."
>
> Armenian refugee child 1921

Save the Children continues to work for children all over the world. It carries out extensive work which aims to improve the life experience of children. The charity:

* provides support in emergencies by helping to prevent food shortages

* responds to emergencies by providing support as part of a longer term plan to help recovery

* provides support for children in emergencies by trying to meet their particular needs, which may include material needs such as shelter and food, developmental needs such as access to education and play opportunities and emotional needs including protection and psychological support. Health care is also provided. The charity also tries to protect children from harm by preventing them from being separated from their families. They will also trace and reunite lost children and families, or find substitute carers if need be. Children are particularly vulnerable in crises, and can be subject to violence, trafficking, and recruitment into fighting forces

* protects refugees and internally displaced

people (IDPs) by providing basics such as shelter, food and clothing

* supports children who are suffering from HIV and AIDS and also works to prevent the spread of the disease through education

Mr. President and Members of Congress

* provides access to health care services for some of the poorest countries. It aims to improve worldwide health by tackling poverty through campaigning for fairer international policies and resources

* provides access to good quality education by tackling poverty, helping communities run schools, training teachers, developing education policies and curricula, supporting flexible learning schemes, developing educational opportunities for very young children, and providing education for children caught up in emergencies

* lobbies to prevent the exploitation of children through crime, trafficking, acting as child soldiers and exploiting child labour.

Think it over...

Look at the Save the Children website and investigate one aspect of its work in more detail. Evaluate:

1. What is the organisation trying to achieve?

2. How might it help the community it is working in?

3. How could this work impact on the future life chances of the children involved?

Foster care

In certain circumstances, social services may have to take responsibility for a child. This may be because the parents are no longer able to look after the child; there may be evidence of abuse or neglect. Removing children from their parents is not carried out lightly. The Children Act 1989 classified such children as 'looked after' children.

In the past, children would have been placed in children's homes and remained there until old enough to leave and live independently. This type of care often institutionalised the child and did not always allow relationships to develop, as the shift-work patterns that employees in residential care followed acted as a barrier.

The preference now is for children to be fostered with foster carers who look after them in their own home as part of their own family. It is felt that this form of care is more like a normal family situation and allows personal relationships to develop. This gives 'looked after' children both stability and affection.

Foster carers are paid an allowance from social services which covers expenses and a small allowance for their caring activities. In certain, more difficult situations, specialist foster carers are recruited and paid more for supporting challenging and difficult children.

Fostering can either be on a long-term or short-term basis. Children who live with a family as if they were part of that family are considered to be in long-term care. However, the children remain under the authority of social services and the foster parents have no legal rights unless they choose to formally adopt the child.

Short-term fostering is used when social services decide to remove a child from its parents and need care at short notice and on a temporary basis. This may be whilst social services work with the family to address the family's problems. Short-term fostering also includes 'relief fostering' which is used to give parents a respite from caring for their children; for example, where the behaviour or health of the child puts a great strain on the family relationship and they need a break.

Fostering can also be temporary because the child is about to move to a permanent home. This is known as a 'bridging arrangement'. Preparation for the move will be made during this time.

The Children Act 1989 requires that fostered children should still retain contact with their natural parents if it is in the best interest of the child. Therefore, foster carers need to be prepared to meet and work with the child's natural parents.

Child protection

Children and young people have a fundamental right to be protected from harm. The law and child protection procedures state that the protection and welfare of the child must always be the first priority. The protection of children and young people is a shared community responsibility. Failure to provide an effective response to any form of child abuse can have serious consequences for the child.

The Children Act 1989 is the legislative authority for child welfare and protecting children from abuse. The Act makes it the duty of a number of agencies to assist social services departments acting on behalf of children and young people in need or enquiring into allegations of child abuse.

In order to understand complex issues relating to child protection, some understanding of children's rights is needed. The UK has supported The United Nations Convention on the Rights of the Child, which states many rights that children should have in modern society, including:

* children have a right to be listened to and their views taken into account, particularly when adults are making decisions that affect them

* governments should ensure that children are properly cared for and not subject to abuse, neglect or violence from parents or anyone else who cares for them

* children should be protected form sexual abuse

* if children have been neglected or abused they should receive special help to ensure they regain their self respect.

More information on the Rights of the Child can be found on their website.

> **Think it over...**
>
> Look at the Rights Site and evaluate the rights of the child. How much do you think children know about these rights?

Despite laws and conventions being in place, a minority of children are either neglected or abused each year, which means their rights and needs are being violated. The aim of legislation and international work on the rights of the child and child protection is to provide broad standards and values around the way children are treated. It will not mean that all children are brought up in the same way, as different cultures and families within cultures will have their own way of doing things. It does mean, however, that children should grow up in a safe environment.

Child protection means protecting children from abuse. Child abuse is a major social problem. Child abuse is complex and has many causes. All sections of society produce adults who abuse or neglect children so it is impossible to describe a stereotype.

There are various types of abuse and neglect. This could include:

* physical abuse or neglect

* emotional abuse or neglect

* sexual abuse

* intellectual abuse or neglect.

Abuse happens to children of all ages, from any social background or ethnic group. The abuse usually involves a parent, another family member, or someone else caring for the child, but it could be anyone.

Indicators of child abuse

Common indicators of child abuse are non-accidental injuries (NAI). These are injuries that

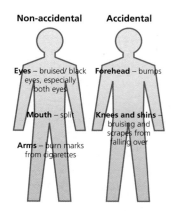

FIGURE 8.4 *Accidental and non-accidental injuries*

NON-ACCIDENTAL	ACCIDENTAL
Eyes – bruised/black eyes, especially both eyes	Forehead – bumps
Cheeks – bruised	Crown of head – bumps
Mouth – split	Spine – bony part from falls
Shoulders – bruising, finger marks from grabbing	Hips – from falls and knocks
Genitals – bruising	Elbows – knocks/bangs
Feet – scalding	Knees and shins – bruising and scrapes from falling over
Skull – fracture	
Ears – bruising, pinch marks	
Neck bruising from being grabbed	
Chest – bruising from being hit	
Arms – burn marks from cigarettes	
Back, buttocks, thighs – bruising in shapes of objects from being hit, burn marks	

TABLE 8.1 *Indicators of accidental and non-accidental injuries*

have been deliberately inflicted upon a child. Table 8.1 identifies the form NAI may take.

Physical neglect may show with a child failing to thrive because of lack of food or sleep. Children may also appear dirty as their clothes are not clean and they do not wash themselves adequately.

Emotional neglect or abuse is harder to identify. This occurs if a child is threatened by an adult, perhaps being constantly shouted at, insulted, ridiculed and undermined. Children may not receive love or attention from the adults who care for them and may become withdrawn or, perhaps, show signs of anger, frustration or sadness. They will appear withdrawn and lack 'fun' in themselves.

Intellectual abuse may occur when adults try to drive their children so hard to succeed that they make them study excessively. Intellectual neglect, on the other hand, occurs when children are given little or no intellectual stimulation and do not develop their own thoughts.

Sexual abuse occurs when adults involve children in sexual acts before the age of consent.

This may involve watching pornographic material, taking part in sexual intercourse or anal intercourse. Children may be encouraged to display sexually explicit behaviour. Indicators might be itching or pain in the genital area, which may make urinating or walking uncomfortable. Undergarments may be bloody or torn and there may be discharge.

Children that are sexually abused often become withdrawn and lack confidence. They may not eat or sleep well. They may also show an unusual amount of sexual knowledge for their age. It is important that this type of abuse is picked up quickly to prevent the abuser from moving onto greater sexual abuse acts with time.

There are many agencies involved in protecting children from abuse. The most well known voluntary agency is the National Society for the Prevention of Cruelty to Children or the NSPCC.

National Society for the Prevention of Cruelty to Children

The NSPCC is the UK's leading charity specialising in child protection and the
prevention of cruelty to children. The charity has been directly involved in protecting children and campaigning on their behalf since 1884.

Residential care

Until the 1970s it was common for children who were unable to live with their parents to be looked after by social workers in residential homes and children would remain there for the whole of their childhood. Today, children who are in residential care are generally those with significant behavioural problems, who find it difficult to accept being in foster care, or they may be difficult to place. They may also have had considerable contact with the police.

Residential social workers work with children in residential settings to help them address their difficulties. The aim will be for children to remain in residential care for as short a time as possible and to be fostered with a family or, if older, be able to live independently.

Long periods in residential care can lead to institutionalisation. This is where everyday decisions such as what to wear and what to eat are made by someone else. Often everyday activities such as going to work or shopping do not take place. The individual in the institution becomes accustomed to this and then finds it difficult to function in normal society. They are said to be 'institutionalised'. Some individuals are unable to live a normal life, as they never develop the confidence and life skills to be independent after living in an institution.

Primary health care services

Primary health care services are those which deal directly with people in the community and include the general practitioner (GP), district nurse, health visitor, practice nurse, community midwife, community physiotherapist, occupational and speech therapists and chiropodists. Dentists and opticians are also classified as primary health care, as they are the first people you would see when you have a health problem.

Think it over...

Find out how dentists are funded. Some operate under the NHS but many are now private or run under an insurance scheme.

The GP provides health care services for a wide range of problems. GPs will also give health education advice with the support of their team on areas such as diet and smoking. They provide a vaccination service and many surgeries will carry out simple, minor operations on site. They work in a team which includes midwives, health visitors and district nurses. Although the GP is generally seen as the central player in the primary health care team, the provision of care in the community is the responsibility of the whole team. They are based in local health centres and responsible for care across a particular patch. If a GP cannot treat a patient, they will refer them to the hospital for specialist care.

✳ DID YOU KNOW?

Primary care trusts (PCTs) are local health organisations responsible for managing health services in local areas. PCTs have the responsibility of making sure that the community's needs are being met and therefore work with local authorities and other agencies to ensure that appropriate health and social care services are provided.

They are at the centre of the NHS and receive about 75 per cent of the overall budget for services. It is believed that as they are based in the community, they are in the best position to know what is required and provide the necessary services. They can also ensure there are enough services to meet the needs of the population and that these are working effectively and efficiently.

Figure 8.5 shows how the different sections of the health service are linked together. More information about the NHS and how it works can be found on its website.

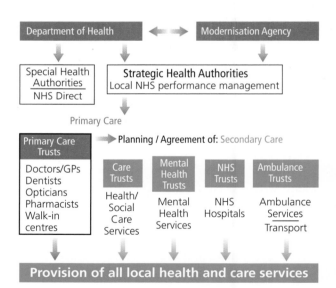

FIGURE 8.5 *How the health service is linked*

Secondary health care services

Secondary health care services are those provided by your local hospital and include out-patient consultancy and in-patient care. If a health problem cannot be sorted out through primary care, or there is an emergency, patients are referred to hospital. If hospital treatment is required, the GP will usually arrange this. National Health Service hospitals provide acute and specialist services, treating conditions that normally cannot be dealt with by primary care specialists.

Primary care trusts are responsible for planning secondary care. They will assess the health needs of the local community and develop plans to improve health and set priorities locally. The trust will then decide which secondary care services need to be commissioned to meet people's needs. Therefore, they work closely with the providers of the secondary care services to ensure those services are delivered.

Secondary health care services therefore include all of the following:

✳ in-patient and out-patient care – of patients who access services during the day as well as those who are admitted for a stay in hospital

✳ surgery – operations, both major and minor

✳ orthopaedics – a branch of surgery concerned with disorders of the spine and joints and addressing deformities in the skeletal system

✳ general medicine – the branch of medicine that deals with general treatment, prevention or alleviation of a broad range of diseases not covered by specialist areas

✳ obstetrics – the branch of medicine concerned with childbirth and the care and treatment of women before and after childbirth

✳ gynaecology – a branch of medicine concerned with women's health, particularly diseases of the genito-urinary tract

✳ paediatrics – the branch of medicine concerned with children's health.

Hospitals are run through NHS trusts and they are charged with making sure that services are provided efficiently and effectively and that the service is of a high quality. They have a strategy for the development and improvement of the service. They have targets to reach and are measured on how effectively they do this. Treatment at NHS hospitals is free.

Some hospitals are now Foundation Trusts, the first of which were established in 2004. Whilst these new trusts are still part of the NHS, they are managed locally and have more freedom over how they spend their budget and how they choose to operate. This is part of the government's drive to decentralise services to a local level.

Think it over...

Many people choose private health care. Why do you think this is? Find out how much private health care costs and consider the advantages and disadvantages.

Speech therapy

The ability to communicate is central to being able to function in modern society. It is necessary for almost everything we do, whether it is at work, in education, at home or in a social setting. Thousands of people have difficulty communicating and this can affect the quality of their life experience.

Communication is very complex and the model below, developed by Nottingham Community Health Speech and Language Service, highlights the complexities. It shows that

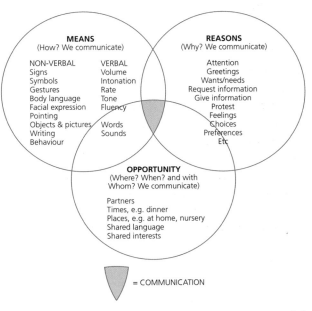

FIGURE 8.6 *Means, reason and opportunity model of communication*

communication is a mix of means, reasons and opportunities. Without the means, individuals cannot express themselves; without reason, there is no point in communicating; and without opportunity, there is no communication.

Speech and language therapists are specialists in communication disorders and work to assess, diagnose and develop the communication skills of the people who are referred to them. They may also support individuals who have difficulty eating and swallowing. The speech and language therapist works to help individuals break down the communication barriers that might exist. They also work with other professionals, such as teachers and social workers, who may support the individual concerned. They will also work with the families. Speech and language therapists are often supported by a speech and language assistant.

Speech and language therapists work in a wide range of settings including schools, nurseries, hospitals, training centres and people's homes. The types of difficulties they might cover include those outlined in Table 8.2.

Speech therapy may be provided through the statutory services (education or health) and access through this route would be via referral from a GP or other professional. This service would be free. Speech therapists may also work as independent practitioners and individuals can pay for their services. Speech therapists' services are not cheap, however, and average costs currently (2005) are in the region of £85 for an assessment and £50 per hour for treatment.

8.3 Informal services

Before the introduction of the Welfare State, the extended family and the community played an important role in providing care. The extent of this decreased with the introduction of centralised services provided by the NHS and social services. In addition, there was a change in work patterns, as the workforce needed to be more mobile in an industrialised society. This meant that families often lived significant distances from each other and could not provide care on the doorstep. Also, communities did not develop in the same way as people moved into and away from the area more often than in the past.

Unregulated care

Nevertheless, there are still a lot of informal arrangements made for childcare, which are not

BABIES	CHILDREN	ADULTS
✳ problems with swallowing and eating	✳ physical disabilities ✳ language delay for any reason including deprivation ✳ specific language impairment ✳ cleft palate ✳ specific difficulties in producing sounds ✳ stammering/dysfluency ✳ autism/social interaction difficulties ✳ Dyslexia ✳ hearing impairment	✳ swallowing and/or communication problems as a result of a stroke ✳ conditions affecting speech including neurological impairments and degenerative such as head injury, Parkinson's, MS, motor-neurone disease, dementia, speech difficulties as a result of cancer of the head, neck and throat ✳ voice and speech problems including stammering ✳ language difficulties associated with physical disabilities, learning difficulties or mental health problems stammering ✳ speech difficulties as a result of hearing impairment

TABLE 8.2 *Types of difficulties covered by speech and language therapists*

covered by any statutory legislation. Many working parents cannot afford organised childcare and look for other solutions, such as using friends or relatives to care for their children. This is often the case with after-school care when organised groups are not available in the area. This type of care also includes babysitting.

Family support

Many families call upon members of their family to help with childcare. This may include grandparents who look after the children whilst the parents are at work. The advantage of such an arrangement is that the children are being cared for by someone who knows them and they are in a family setting. It is a relatively inexpensive form of care. It will also be very flexible as family are more likely to fit around the needs of the parent, whereas formal settings generally work to strict times and are therefore less flexible.

One disadvantage of family support may be that the child does not benefit from the stimulation found in a formal setting and the expertise that trained early years practitioners can bring to support their development.

Support from friends

Again, this is a common form of support for many families with young children. The regulation, however, is that anyone looking after other people's children for more than two hours per day should be registered as a childminder; in practice, this will not happen. This informal support may include children going to their friends before and after school for short periods of care whilst a parent has to do a task which they would prefer to do without a child present. It includes babysitting, which has been a common form of informal childcare for many years.

Babysitters

Babysitters provide an informal type of childcare. Traditionally, babysitters have been used by parents looking for short childcare cover, often for an evening out. They are often teenagers who carry out the role as a means of earning some pocket money.

Babysitters are usually left in sole charge of the children in their care. The role will vary according to the age of the children being cared for and can therefore include all aspects of care, including feeding the children, personal care, entertaining them with activities such as playing games or reading to them and putting them to bed.

Parents usually leave a contact number so they can be reached if the babysitter is concerned about anything.

Some parents operate a babysitting circle whereby a group of parents get together and baby-sit for each other. Each time they baby-sit they are entitled to a baby-sitting session back. No money changes hands in this arrangement.

Baby-sitters do not need to have any formal qualifications, but they must be at least 13-years-of-age to be left in charge of young children. Parents look for mature, sensible young people to carry out this role. They need to be able to form relationships with young children and be confident in looking after them on their own. They are often young people they know or have been recommended to them – perhaps older sons or daughters of friends.

Local support groups

Local support groups may be set up by parents or local voluntary groups that may be attached to churches to give parents an avenue for discussion and support. Looking after children can be a lonely task and, unless parents or carers go out, they may not have access to any other adult interaction during the day. Entertaining children through formal groups and activities has a cost attached and parents will look for other ways to do this without constantly having to pay.

Informal groups may be arranged in which parents and carers meet at each others' houses to give the children opportunity to play together and the parents and carers the opportunity to chat. Nannies often operate informal support groups in this way, as they enjoy the opportunity to discuss issues with other nannies whilst the children play.

Think it over...

Are there any local informal support groups which you are aware of in your area?

TYPE OF CARE	ADVANTAGES	DISADVANTAGES
Formal	✳ Regulated care ✳ Staffed by professionals ✳ Guaranteed provision	✳ Can be expensive ✳ Times may not always suit ✳ May not be locally provided ✳ May be a waiting list
Informal	✳ Generally cheap or free ✳ Can be organised to meet specific needs ✳ Provided by people known to the family ✳ Probably provided in an environment that is familiar to the child	✳ Not regulated ✳ Care may be provided but not necessarily education ✳ Not guaranteed – care may easily collapse

TABLE 8.3 *Advantages and disadvantages of formal and informal care*

Summary

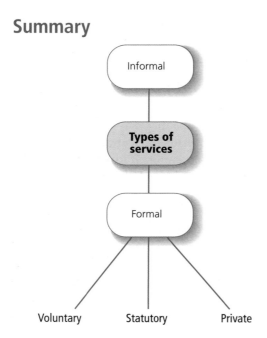

FIGURE 8.7 *Section 8.3 summary*

Consider this

Caroline is a young mother who is considering going back to work. She has one son, James, who is three-years-old. Although he is an only child, he has spent a lot of time with his young cousins who live close by. James has a slight speech impediment and is therefore quite shy. He has not really mixed in at parent and toddler groups.

1. List the different types of care that are available to James – both formal and informal.

2. Discuss the advantages and disadvantages of each.

3. James also needs support from other services. What other services, including primary and secondary health care services might he access?

4. How might these services support James and his family?

8.4 Origins and development of services

To fully appreciate how the services provided for children today have developed, it is helpful to understand the historical development of health and social care services. Many of these services have developed as a result of a number of different government acts and reforms since the conception of the Welfare State in the 1940s.

Historical perspective

The beginning of the concept of a Welfare State began with the Poor Law system, introduced in 1572. The idea was to have a basic safety net that would prevent people from becoming so poor that they had to live on the streets. The belief at that time was that people were responsible for their own misfortune so any help provided had to be worked for. Workhouses were established in towns across Britain, and families who found themselves in desperate circumstances would enter the workhouse. These were unpopular institutions in which people were often poorly treated. Many died in the workhouses.

The 'Welfare State' of modern Britain really grew out of the Beveridge Report of 1942. After World War II, the government wanted to rebuild Britain and William Beveridge was asked to outline how this could be done. The war had raised expectations of a better future. Thousands had died and those returning form the war expected employment and a better standard of living. People did not like the 350-year-old Poor Law and considered that the provision of workhouses as the only State relief from poverty was unacceptable and out of date. The Beveridge Report identified the need to fight the 'Five Evils' of Want, Disease, Ignorance, Idleness and Squalor. It also advocated full employment and the creation of a State system of health care and welfare services. The report led to the establishment of the Welfare State in 1945, which included the statutory provision of education, health and social care services.

The National Health Service was established in 1948 and this included free access to medical care.

A national system of benefits was also developed, providing 'social security' with the aim that the population would be protected from 'cradle to grave'. This system was partly built on the National Insurance Scheme, whereby people in work and their employers had to pay in a certain amount each week as a contribution to these central services. These services became a right of every individual.

There were inadequacies in the system, including the fact that it did not really offer support to those who were unable to contribute, such as disabled, long-term unemployed or divorced individuals. The benefits provided were also set at a level which allowed the people to exist rather than at a level that would allow a basic standard of living.

Think it over...

What do you consider to be necessary for a basic standard of living? Think about food, for example, two hot meals per day, perhaps – holidays, money to spend on alcohol or cigarettes, housing, hot and cold running water?

1. Compare your list with others. Remember that everyone has a different idea about what is essential.

2. Do you think that people should be provided with the basics needed to live on, or should welfare provision take into account the norms of the society in which they live?

Seebohm Rountree did some interesting work into wants and needs.

Since then there have been a number of Acts of Parliament which have established the services provided for children we have today. Some important Acts are described in Table 8.4.

The Children Act 1989

This is a major Act in relation to the care and support of children. It gave local authorities wide-ranging responsibilities in relation to children and particularly children in need. It placed the child's needs at the centre of all service provision and called for the child's welfare to be 'paramount'.

Section 17 of the Children Act gave local

ACT OF PARLIAMENT	EFFECT ON PROVISION
National Health Service Act 1946	Provided a universal health service which was available to everyone. It had three strands – hospitals, local medical centres and welfare services. For children, services included maternity and childcare services, immunisations and vaccinations, health visiting and home nursing. It also established an ambulance service.
Local Authority Social Services Act 1970	Established social services departments which reflect how they operate today. It set out the framework for the services to be provided but not how it should be organised. This was left to each local authority and so there are different patterns of provision across the country.

TABLE 8.4 *Major Acts of Parliament impacting on the provision of services to children*

authorities the general duty of safeguarding and promoting the welfare of children in need. They were charged to promote the upbringing and provide appropriate services to support and meet the needs of children and their families. This included:

* a duty to provide and publicise services including day care for under-fives and family centres

* a duty to take reasonable steps to prevent ill-treatment or neglect of children

* an aim to prevent the need for children to be taken into care or secure accommodation and to encourage them not to commit crime

* the provision of accommodation for children in need where those with parental responsibility are unable to care for the child

* the safeguarding of 'looked after' children and promoting their well-being

* the provision of aftercare service for young people leaving the care of the local authority

* the provision of secure accommodation for children who may run away or have a history of self harm

* the investigation of reports of children who may be suffering and acting to safeguard the children's best interests and safety.

This Act has heavily influenced the provision of services for children today.

Demographic characteristics and the effect on the provision of services for children

Demography is the study of the size, structure, dispersal, and development of human populations to establish reliable statistics including birth and death rates, marriages and divorces, life expectancy, and migration. This information is used to calculate life tables, which give the life expectancy of members of the population by sex and age.

Demography is important for planning services such as education, housing, health and welfare. An example of where this has been used is where the fall in the number of people aged 10–20 in the first half of the 1990s has led to many school closures, a shrinkage in the potential market for teenage clothes, and a fall in the number of young people available for recruitment into jobs by employers. Simultaneously, the forecast rise in the number of people aged 75 plus over the next 20 years will lead to an expansion in the demand for accommodation for the elderly.

> **✳ DID YOU KNOW?**
>
> The UK has an ageing population. Even though the population of the UK has increased in the past 30 years by 6.5 per cent, growth has not been even across all age groups. The proportion of the population over 65 has increased whereas the number of children under the age of 16 is less than that of 30 years ago (see Figure 8.8).

The latest population figures suggests that there were 11, 759,000 children under the age of 16 in the UK in 2005. The number of children under the age of 16 has fallen by over two million

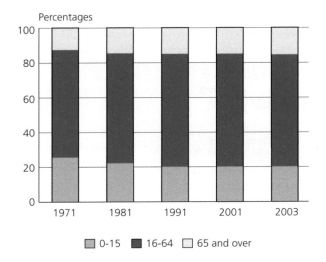

FIGURE 8.8 *Age composition of the population in the UK from 1971–2003*

in the last 30 years. The birth rate has dropped below the replacement level of 2.1 per female to around an average of 1.71 in 2003. This was a slight increase from the lowest recorded fertility rate in 2001 of 1.63. In addition to the low fertility rate, statistics show that the average age for a woman to have her first child is increasing (26.9 in 2003 compared to 23.7 in 1971) and there are higher levels of childlessness. This type of information will influence the planning of health care and education services.

Therefore, over the past 30 years the average age in Britain has risen from 34.1 years to 38.4 years – reflecting the pattern of an ageing population. This ageing is mainly due to the reduction in fertility but increased mortality rates also make a contribution.

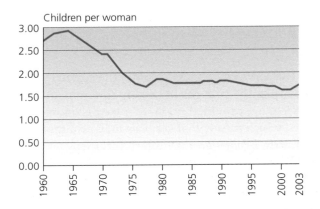

FIGURE 8.10 *The number of children born to women between 1960–2003 (Source: National Statistics)*

Think it over...

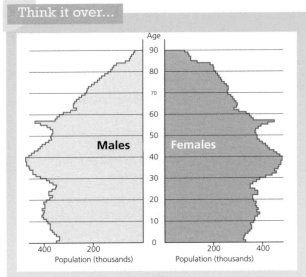

FIGURE 8.9 *Age profile of the population in 2003* *Source:* National Statistics

Look at Figure 8.9 showing the age profile of the population in 2003. Imagine how this will project forward over 10, 20 and 30 years. How might the ageing population affect the provision of services for children? Will there be any other impact on society?

Further details about national and local statistics can be found on the National Statistics website under the neighbourhood link at the top of the home page.

Regional variations

Within the UK there are regional variations in health and this is reflected in the demographic statistics for the country. For example, infant mortality is lower in England than the rest of the UK. Statistics also show that people's health seems to be poorer in the north of the country compared with the south – this is known as the 'north-south' divide. However, there are pockets of significant poverty in both.

The Black Report (1980) highlighted that social and economic circumstances affected health. The report identified that factors that contributed to this included:

* income and wealth including levels of employment

* individual lifestyle choices and the barriers they put up against adopting a healthier lifestyle

* the environment in which individuals live and work including housing, working conditions and air pollution

* access to effective and appropriate health and social care services.

Think it over...

Find out about the incidence of children's diseases in your region of the country. Do the services in the area reflect the patterns shown in the statistics?

The services provided around the country aim to address the patterns of need in different areas. Services are provided under a 'mixed economy of care', which means that services may be a mix of statutory, private and voluntary services. Together, they aim to meet the needs of the community. It is often felt that voluntary services are more adaptable to demographic changes, as they have the flexibility to respond quickly to changing needs. As these services are community based, they understand the changes in the community and have the capacity to innovate and change rapidly.

Private organisations can also respond in this way. An example is the increased number of private nurseries and before and after-school provision that have developed as a result of increased demand for childcare places, brought about by government initiatives such as the childcare 'voucher' scheme for three-year-olds and the tax incentives for working parents.

Summary

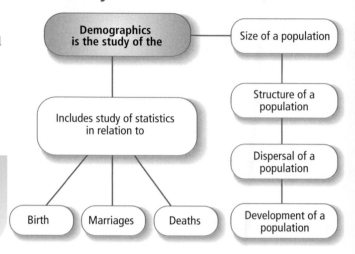

Consider this

Look at Figure 8.9 which shows the age pattern of the population.

1. Describe what the diagram shows.

2. Project what will happen to the age profile of the population in 30 years time.

3. The fertility rate is slowing down. How might this affect the number of young children in the UK?

4. Using the diagram, can you explain why the government is keen to encourage as many of the working population to work as possible?

5. Outline the incentives you feel would encourage more women to work rather than stay at home to look after children.

8.5 Access to services

In general, individuals have certain rights of access to health care services but need to apply for social care services. Once individuals are 'in the system', they will find that they may be referred to different services as necessary. For example, a parent may self-refer a child to the doctor because of a health problem. The doctor may then refer them to a paediatrician at the hospital, who may in turn refer them to another health professional for further treatment.

Main ways to access services

Services provided for children can be accessed in four ways as described below.

Self-referral

Parents may refer themselves to a service. However, to do this, they need to be aware of the service and what it provides. This information may come from word of mouth, as a result of the service advertising thorough the media or posters and leaflets in public places, or as a result of other publicity such as reports in the newspapers. Parents may, for example, self-refer for nursery provision, after first identifying a number of nurseries in their area as a result of studying different information sources and visiting each one before deciding which nursery to send their child to.

Parents will also self-refer to primary health care services such as doctors, dentists or opticians or for other services where they may be happy to pay as a private patient, such as speech therapy.

Referral by a third party

This means referral to a service by another person; this person may be the childs GP, a teacher or other professional. Access to specialist services for children is generally by referral. For example, a teacher may identify that a child has a speech problem and refer the individual child for speech therapy thorough the educational psychologist; or a doctor may notice a developmental problem and refer the child to the hospital for specialist help.

Recall

Once a child has been registered for a service, there may be a recall system in operation so follow up appointments are made automatically. This would be the case with dentists and opticians where regular check-ups are required. It may also occur after certain treatment in a hospital setting, either as an in or out- patient.

Application

Some services need to be applied for and this is particularly the case for social care services. If, for example, parents need respite care for a child because he or she has a disability or behavioural problems, they would need to apply for this support through the local authority.

Services that do not need a referral

Some services are open to anybody and can be accessed without any form of referral. There is no appointment system in place. These services include crêches, libraries and toy libraries and access to voluntary organisations that give advice, such as the NSPCC or Gingerbread. Individuals can also access accident and emergency services without a referral.

Interrelation of services

Many services work together to provide support for children and their families. An appointment with one professional may result in referral to another. For example, a doctor might refer a client for other services such as a specialist at the hospital, out-patient appointments or appointments with another member of the primary health care team. They may also refer to children to speech therapists.

Education services also work closely with other services. They will work with social services and health services if they feel this would support a child or if they have a concern.

The new Children Act 2004 is increasing the importance of all services working together and many local authorities now appoint Directors of Children's Services rather than separate directors of Social Services and Education in an attempt to ensure this happens.

Barriers to accessing services

Some children do not access the services they need. This may be because of:

* cost/economic factors – families are unable to pay for private services

* transportation – some services are not located in the community and transportation links may be poor

* lack of awareness – families may not be aware of the services available to them or the incentives that exist to help them to access these services

* language barriers – children may be part of families for whom English is a second language and therefore parents and carers are not comfortable accessing services

* attitude – some people do not like accessing services, as they feel it suggests that they are unable to cope. Others may choose not to use a service as a result of specific attitudes or belief – for example, some parents choose not to have their child vaccinated against measles, mumps and rubella because of press reports about the vaccination being linked to autism

* previous experience – a poor experience may put an individual off using a service

* child's reaction – a parent may decide not to use a service because the child reacts badly to it. For example, if a child gets very upset in a nursery setting when left by a parent, the parent may decide not to make the child attend again

* environmental factors –there may be a lack of provision in the area in which a family lives.

Think it over...

Can you think of any other reasons why people may not access the services available to them? What could be done to reduce these barriers?

Summary

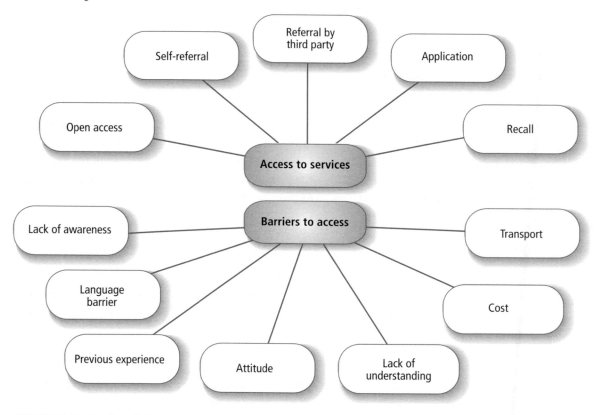

FIGURE 8.12 *Section 8.5 summary*

Ashan has recently arrived in England from India to join her husband, who is already working here. She is five months pregnant and also has an 11-month-old child. Ashan speaks very little English. She needs to access health care for herself and her child.

1. What barriers might exist for Ashan when trying to access services?

2. What support might help Ashan to access the services she needs?

3. List the services that she would need to access and the type of referral required.

4. Which other services might help Ashan and her child to settle into their new environment?

UNIT ASSESSMENT

This unit is assessed through a portfolio. For this unit you need to produce a report on local provision of formal services which meet the needs of children at one main stage of development. The report must include:

* A   Knowledge and understanding of the relevant needs (of the chosen age group)

* B   Application of how those needs are met locally

* C   Research and analysis of the different forms of local provision

* D   Evaluation of the range of local provision

The report must be produced independently and cannot be a shared exercise. It must be wholly your own work. To access the higher mark bands you must complete the work independently.

Structure of your report

The report must contain the following sections.

Section A

You must demonstrate that you have a knowledge and understanding of the needs of children in your chosen age range.

To access the higher mark bands, information about the needs of children must be detailed and specific. It should demonstrate that you have a full and detailed knowledge and understanding of the stage you have chosen. You should cover health, social care and educational needs in depth.

Section B

You must identify the formal provision available in your local area and explain the services each form of provision offers for children in the age range you have chosen.

To access the higher mark bands you need to provide a very detailed and accurate picture of the provision available in your locality. You should also explain, in detail, the services provided by each provider you have identified.

Section C

Having researched the provision, you need to identify how the needs of the children in your chosen age range are being met by the services provided. This will require detailed analysis.

To access the higher mark bands the information must be in depth and show details. There should be no inaccurate information given. You will use specialist vocabulary to describe how the services meet the needs of the age range. The information will explain the complex links between the different services effectively.

Section D

You need to evaluate how well you feel the range of provision in your local area meets the needs of children in your chosen age range. You also need to comment on how the formal services compare with the relative merits of informal care. Comments need to be supported by sound evidence and you should be able to provide a reasoned, detailed evaluation.

To access the higher mark bands all your comments must be relevant. You need to evaluate thoroughly across all the provision identified and you must be able to critically comment on the merit of the services against an informal provision arrangement.

References

Bruce T., Meggitt C. (2002) *Childcare and Education*, Hodder Arnold, London

Moore S. (2002) *Social Welfare Alive*, Nelson Thornes, Walton-on-Thames

O'Hagan M., Smith M. (1999) *Early Years Childcare and Education: Key Issues*, Bailliere Tindall, London

Tassoni P., Hucker K. (2002) *Planning Play and the Early Years*, Heinemann, Oxford

Young P. (2002) *Mastering Social Welfare*, Palgrave Macmillan, Basingstoke

Useful websites

Please see www.heinemann.co.uk/hotlinks (express code 1554P) for links to the websites of the following which may be a source of information:

* Department for Education and Skills
* Gingerbread
* NHS
* Save the Children
* Sure Start
* Government Statistics
* Under-fives

Complementary therapies

You will learn about:

9.1   Definitions relating to complementary therapies
9.2   Criteria for assessing therapies
9.3   Reasons for using alternative and complementary therapies

Introduction

This unit provides you with an introduction to the study of complementary therapies. It gives you the necessary background knowledge to enable you to distinguish between conventional medicine and complementary and/or alternative therapeutic techniques and to assess the value of complementary therapies using a range of criteria.

This unit also contains information about a number of resources that will help you when carrying out your research in preparation for writing your report.

9.1 Definitions relating to complementary therapies

There is no single agreed definition of the term 'complementary therapies'. The British Medical Association used the term 'non-conventional therapies' (House of Lords, 2000) in its description and this tends to be used to cover treatments and therapies that are not encompassed by conventional (or allopathic) medicine.

Allopathic medicine is the mainstream practice within the National Health Service. It treats medical conditions mainly by attacking their symptoms, usually with pharmaceutical products or with surgical interventions. Allopathic medicine makes great use of technology, and relies on scientific research to establish the safety and efficacy of the methods and products used in its practice.

The practice of conventional medicine is also sometimes referred to as the *medical model* of treating illness. This model ultimately makes people into passive recipients of healthcare, as it also maintains that in the final analysis the doctor knows what is best for the patient and whatever the doctor recommends is deemed to be the best treatment.

In contrast, complementary therapies take a *holistic approach* to the treatment of illness. The holistic approach will be described in more detail below (page 327), but first it is necessary to establish how the term 'complementary' will be used in this unit.

> **Key concept**
>
> *Allopathic medicine:* conventional medicine.
>
> *Medical model* of treatment refers to the practice of conventional medicine.

Complementary and alternative therapies

A distinction has been made between those therapies that usually complement conventional medicine (hence the term 'complementary') and those that are seen to provide 'alternative' solutions, both in terms of diagnosis and the nature of the interventions offered. The House of Lords Select Committee on Science and Technology made this distinction in its report on complementary therapies in 2000, and this distinction is shown in Figure 9.1.

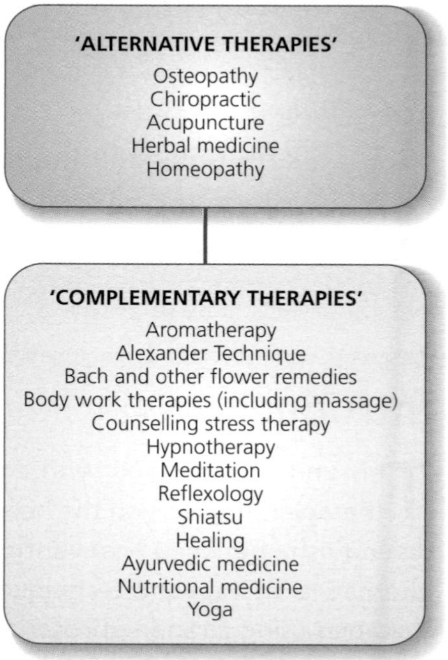

'ALTERNATIVE THERAPIES'
Osteopathy
Chiropractic
Acupuncture
Herbal medicine
Homeopathy

'COMPLEMENTARY THERAPIES'
Aromatherapy
Alexander Technique
Bach and other flower remedies
Body work therapies (including massage)
Counselling stress therapy
Hypnotherapy
Meditation
Reflexology
Shiatsu
Healing
Ayurvedic medicine
Nutritional medicine
Yoga

FIGURE 9.1 *Distinction between 'complementary' and 'alternative' therapies made in the House of Lords Science and Technology Committee, 6th Report, November 2000*

In practice, the two terms 'complementary' and 'alternative' tend to be used interchangeably, and the abbreviation CAM or CAMs is now found extensively in books and articles on the subject. In any case, it can be hard to make a strict distinction between complementary and alternative uses of CAMs. For example, osteopathy (one of those therapies listed as 'alternative' in the House of Lords Report) is sometimes offered as part of an integrated musculo-skeletal service within the NHS, together with physiotherapy and chiropractic. In this case, a so-called 'alternative' therapy is offered very much as a complement to treatment and services provided by conventional medicine.

For this reason, the term CAM will be used throughout this unit to refer to those therapies and approaches that generally fall outside the allopathic tradition, both in terms of treatment types and methods, and with respect to the approach to the patient. The term 'complementary therapy' will also be used to mean the same as 'CAM', and will not distinguish between these and 'alternative' therapies.

Novey (2000) has summarised six key aspects of CAMs that distinguish them from allopathic medicine or conventional medicine (drawing on the work of Dr Catherine Downey):

Six principles of CAMs

* Use the healing power of nature
* Treat the whole person
* 'First Do No Harm'
* Identify and treat the cause of the illness
* Prevention is the best 'cure'
* The physician is primarily a teacher

Source: Donald Novey (2000, pp. 5–6)

These naturopathic principles work on the premise that the body has its own in-built mechanisms for maintaining health. Therefore, CAMs seek to work with these mechanisms as far as possible, removing blocks to health and promoting a healthy human organism. Treating the whole person acknowledges the complex nature of individual human beings. Many factors combine to create health (or illness) including physical, emotional and social aspects (to name but three).

A complementary practitioner is careful to take all aspects of a person's life into consideration. 'First Do No Harm' means that the CAMs therapist should not attack symptoms without first attempting to remove underlying causes. This is because suppressing symptoms without addressing the reasons for them can actually cause more harm in the long run. The main aim of the practitioner should therefore be to identify and treat the actual cause of the problem, and he or she will always be more interested in the root cause than in the symptoms themselves. Indeed, the aim of Naturopathic medicine is ultimately to prevent disease by

giving people information and encouraging healthy ways of living. Ultimately, the healer is a teacher, who is also committed to his or her own personal development (Novey, 2000).

Most CAMs take this approach, as the following scenario demonstrates.

SCENARIO

A pain in the neck

Gemma works in an office, using a computer for several hours a day.

She has recently developed RSI (Repetitive Strain Injury) which affects both her hands. She also has neck pain.

The doctor has given her some painkillers and a neck brace. At work, her manager has advised her to follow health and safety rules, taking regular breaks away from the computer screen. He has also given Gemma a new, fully adjustable chair.

However, she still has pain, and decides to visit an osteopath. She treats Gemma's problems by manipulation, suggests some exercises that may help and also advises her on posture. During the diagnosis, however, Gemma discloses that she is having some relationship problems. The osteopath suggests this may be causing her additional stress, which in turn may be making her musculo-skeletal problems worse. Until Gemma tackles her personal issues, she may not be able to overcome her physical difficulties. Gemma decides to discuss her relationship problems with a counsellor.

In making this diagnosis, the osteopath is taking a holistic approach to Gemma's problems. She looks for the root cause of her physical symptoms, and finds that these may not result totally from the ergonomic factors in her workplace (although these undoubtedly play a part). Instead, she finds that emotional difficulties may not simply be making physical problems worse, but may actually be a main cause of Gemma's injuries.

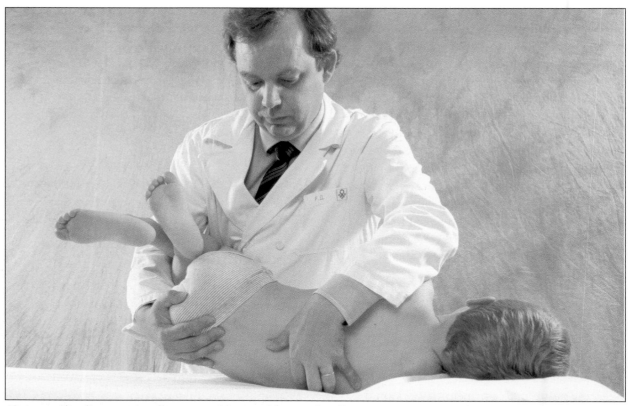

'Osteopaths diagnose and treat problems with muscles, ligaments, nerves and joints to help the body's natural healing ability'

Source: General Osteopathic Council leaflet, *Work Strain*

As public interest in CAMs has grown, especially during the last 30 years of the twentieth century, a number of conventionally trained doctors have also become interested in the use of complementary therapies. This has led to a phenomenon known as *integrated medicine*. Practitioners of this approach are medically qualified, but also recognise the value of some CAMs. They may sometimes practise particular therapies (in addition to using conventional approaches); in other cases, they may be proactive in referring patients on to CAMs therapists where they judge it to be appropriate. The following scenario shows how this might work.

Key concept

Integrated medicine: the use of complementary therapies in conjunction with conventional medicine.

SCENARIO

More than a prescription

Dr Woods has a patient who is complaining of severe fatigue. Blood tests show that he is anaemic (low in iron), and Dr Woods prescribes iron tablets.

However, she also recommends that her patient should visit a nutritional therapist, in order to find out whether changes need to be made to his diet.

She asks the patient to come back in three months, so that they can monitor his progress.

It is important to note that doctors who practise *Ayurvedic Medicine* are very likely to be conventionally medically qualified as well. Ayurveda (pronounced *I-yur-vay-dah*) is an ancient medical system that originated in India. It uses a combination of different treatment techniques including meditation, diet, massage and aromatherapy and herbal remedies. A scenario describing the Ayurvedic practice of a western-trained doctor can be found on page 360.

However, many conventionally trained doctors remain sceptical about the use of CAMs, seeing them at best as therapies that work psychologically to make a patient feel better, and at worst as techniques that do nothing to heal and which can even be dangerous (for example, in cases where patients reject conventional treatments such as chemotherapy in favour of non-invasive healing methods such as meditation). In recent years, the concept of *evidence-based medicine* has been increasingly promoted within the medical profession. This is an approach that emphasises the need to use current best evidence when making decisions about the treatment and care of individual patients.

Key concept

Evidence-based medicine: 'Evidence-based medicine is the conscientious, explicit and judicious use of current best evidence in making decisions about the care of individual patients' (Sackett et al., 1997).

For conventionally trained doctors, sound and reliable evidence comes from properly structured and conducted research, which might include: detailed surveys of large samples of people, cohort studies, clinical trials and systematic reviews of the research literature. (An excellent description of these rigorous research methods is described in a paper by the Research Council for Complementary Medicine (1999), and research methodologies are discussed in greater detail

below, 'Effectiveness of Therapies', pp. 343–344). However, even those who promote the concept of evidence-based medicine note that it has its weaknesses. Evidence-based medicine seeks to combine clinical expertise with external scientifically based evidence to decide what is best for an individual patient. It is recognised that even the findings of scientific trials are limited, as strictly speaking they refer only to those people who were the subject of the study. Furthermore, clinical trials do not take into account people who may have several medical conditions. The website Gpnotebook cautions that 'one must recognise the limitations of adopting a puritan scientific approach'. In some cases, therefore, those who promote the evidence-based approach believe that it may be appropriate to use different kinds of evidence when deciding on the best treatment for a particular person. The following example suggests how this might work in practice.

Consider this: It works for me!

Junaid has a chronic condition for which he is being treated by his GP. He has found that by changing his diet he can modify some of his symptoms. He asks his GP if he can reduce some of his medication.

The GP carries out an Internet search and finds that there are currently no clinical trials into the effectiveness of diet on Junaid's condition, but there are a few anecdotal reports about it (i.e. personal case studies). Having listened carefully he decides to reduce some of Junaid's medication, and to monitor his progress carefully. He asks Junaid to start keeping a food diary, and also to record his symptoms.

How is this GP practising evidence-based medicine?

Summary

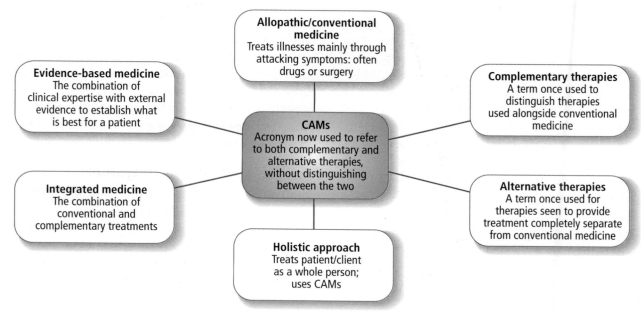

FIGURE 9.2 *Section 6.1 summary*

9.2 Criteria for assessing therapies

This section does not aim to provide a comprehensive A-Z directory of complementary therapies, their uses and associated procedures. Once you have chosen three therapies to study, you will need to do some further research into aspects of their use, and a number of excellent books, guides and websites are listed in the resources section at the end of this unit.

Therapeutic aims and procedures

However, it is useful to begin with a classification of complementary therapies to enable you to think about them in a structured way. Some people make a distinction between therapies primarily designed to maintain or improve health, or to prevent illness, and those aimed mainly at curing or reducing illness (remedial therapies). Under this system, the first category might include health-promoting therapies such as Yoga or Tai Chi, or even music therapy. The second category might encompass treatments such as acupuncture, which is used to treat a wide range of conditions including back, neck or shoulder pain, dental or leg pain, headaches and migraines, rheumatic or arthritic pain, sports injuries, sciatica or trapped nerves, chronic muscle sprain, shingles and pain following surgery (Pinder et al., 2005, p. 25).

However, on further investigation the distinction between preventative and remedial therapies is not so clear cut. Research indicates that yoga, for example, besides promoting general well-being, can sometimes also help with specific conditions such as hypertension, asthma, joint stiffness (in osteoarthritis), epilepsy (Sahaja Yoga), irritable bowel syndrome and mild depression (Pinder et al., p. 49). Music therapy, also considered as something that promotes a positive and healthy state of mind (and thus bringing general health benefits), has been shown to alleviate pain in post-operative patients (in combination with learned relaxation techniques) (Good, 1995); it can be used with people who have mental health problems such as older people who have depression (Hanser et al., 1994); and also to enhance the cognitive development of children (Aldridge et al, 1995).

Furthermore, although there is research to show that many CAMs can alleviate certain conditions, reputable and properly trained CAMs therapists should never claim to be able to cure a specific condition, so it is misleading to suggest that there should be a category of CAMs that can cure conditions (as opposed to CAMs that simply promote wellbeing).

CAMs: a classification system

The observations above warn us to be cautious about attempting a rigid classification of CAMs. Because they act holistically, it is hard to allocate complementary therapies to rigid categories. Music therapy, discussed above, provides a good example of a CAM that works on a number of levels simultaneously. In one sense, it is an expressive therapy, in that it encourages people to experience and express emotions. It acts on the senses (the sense of hearing), and also on the subtle relationship between the mind and the body. However, the physiological benefits of music therapy are apparent in its use to control pain in people who have experienced surgical operations.

This difficulty in allocating CAMs to specific categories is in sharp contrast to the medical model of treatment, where interventions are often categorised according to the kinds of conditions they are used to treat. Thus, in hospitals there are departments such as Neurology (which deals with disorders of the nervous system), Cardiology (which specialises in heart conditions) or Oncology (which provides treatment to people with cancer). Of course, there will be similarities between procedures used across these different disciplines, but conventional medicine remains strictly divided up into specialisms.

Despite these difficulties, however, it is possible to attempt a very broad classification of CAMs, and one such system is presented here. However, you will need to remain aware that some of the therapies listed here fall into more than one of the categories.

The classification used in this unit allocates CAMs to five categories:

* **sensory** – focuses on one or more of the five senses

* **cognitive** – works on the mind-body relationship

* **expressive** – uses expression of thoughts and feelings

* **physical** – works on physiological systems; also uses energy flows

* **medical systems** – complete systems with unique diagnostic techniques, rationale and treatment.

Sensory CAMs work primarily with the five senses of touch, taste, smell, hearing and sight. An example of this would be aromatherapy, which uses primarily both smell and touch.

Cognitive CAMs work on the relationship between the mind and the body to promote healing. Hypnotherapy would fall into this category.

Expressive CAMs use the expression of individual thoughts, feelings and ideas to enable people to identify and work out their problems. Art, drama or music therapies would be classified in this way.

Physical CAMs work on the body's physiological systems to bring about the release of beneficial chemicals such as endorphins, or to promote circulatory systems. Massage would fall into this category. CAMs that use physical manipulation techniques to promote musculo-skeletal health, such as osteopathy or chiropractic, would also be classified in this way. Also in this group would be CAMs which promote the flow of energy that is considered by some complementary medical systems to be essential to good health. Traditional Chinese Medicine calls this energy flow *Chi*, whilst Ayurvedic Medicine refers to it as *Prana*. Reiki and acupuncture would come into this category, as they aim to maximise such energy flows within the human body.

Finally, there are some CAMs that comprise complete *medical systems* in themselves. They have their own rationale and philosophies, and use distinctive diagnostic techniques. Traditional Chinese Medicine (TCM), Ayurvedic Medicine

and homeopathy belong to this category. Such systems use a range of healing techniques that might also be said to fall into several of the preceding four groups. Ayurveda, for example, a system that developed on the Indian subcontinent between 3,000 and 5,000 years ago, has both a spiritual and a healing dimension. It uses meditation (a cognitive technique), diet, massage and herbal remedies (all primarily physical therapies), and aromatherapy (which combines both physical and sensory approaches).

Ayurveda is an ancient healing system closely linked to philosophical and spiritual teachings

Traditional Chinese Medicine is another ancient and complex system of healing. As with Ayurveda, it sees both body and mind as integral components of a healthy bodily system, combining this with the concept of balance. The human body, according to TCM, has vital energy called *Qi* (pronounced '*chee*'), which if blocked can lead to illness. It is vital for the yin and yang energy forces within the body to be in harmony, and also for each person to be in harmony with the external environment. Diagnosis in TCM is very different from that of allopathic practitioners, and includes close examination of the state of the tongue and also of the nature of the pulse. Treatment includes a combination of therapies including acupuncture, herbal medicine, nutrition and Qi Gong (movement used to stimulate the Qi energy through the meridians of the body).

Traditional Chinese Medicine includes the practice of Qi Gong to stimulate Qi energy

Another significant medical system is that of homeopathy, which was developed in the late eighteenth century by Samuel Hahnemann, a German doctor. Homeopathy is based on the principle that 'like cures like', otherwise known as the 'simile principle'. This principle says that an illness is best cured by giving a remedy that would produce symptoms very similar to those already experienced by the patient.

Insomnia, for example, would be treated by an allopathic practitioner by using sleeping tablets. In contrast, a homeopath might prescribe a very

Homeopathy has been available in the UK on the NHS since 1948

small dose of coffee, a substance that would normally induce sleeplessness if given in large doses. Homeopathic remedies are diluted and shaken, then re-diluted, to the point where conventional medical science no longer recognises them as having any active ingredient at all. However, homeopaths believe that the more dilute the substance, the more powerful is the active ingredient. Homeopathy is now regulated in the UK by the Society of Homeopaths. It has been available on the NHS since 1948, and is practised in five homeopathic hospitals.

In Table 9.1 (on page 330), some of the most commonly used CAMs are allocated to one or more of these five categories. Those that may be said to fall into more than one category are marked with an asterisk.

This is by no means a fully comprehensive list of complementary therapies, but it does include sixteen CAMs that are well-regulated, either by law or by self-regulation. These are designated by +. In addition, a number of other CAMs are included in Table 9.1.

The Complementary Healthcare Information Service lists 70 CAMs, and this list is also not exhaustive. There are other organisations and websites that give basic information about a number of CAMs, and some that are devoted exclusively to particular systems or therapies. There are also a number of basic textbooks that describe how CAMs work (see the Resources section). The following exercise will give you the opportunity to research a number of CAMs, and also some practise at categorising them.

Consider this

Investigate three CAMs from Table 9.2, using Internet or written resources for your research. If not already shown in Table 9.1, decide which category or categories you might allocate each therapy to, using the classification in Table 9.1 (ie. Sensory, Cognitive, Expressive, Physical and Medical System). If your three CAMs are shown in Table 9.1, then study each one to decide whether or not you agree with the categories they have been allocated to in that figure.

SENSORY	COGNITIVE
Aromatherapy*+ Bach Flowers Colour Therapy Music Therapy*	Hypnotherapy+ Cognitive and Behavioural Therapies* Meditation
EXPRESSIVE	**PHYSICAL**
Art Therapy Drama Therapy Music Therapy* Cognitive and Behavioural Therapies*	***Manual Therapy:*** Chiropractic+ Osteopathy+ Massage+ (e.g. Swedish, Reflexology+) Acupuncture+ Bodywork (eg. Feldenkrais, Alexander Technique, Rolfing) Aromatherapy*+ Shiatsu+ Craniosacral Therapy+ ***Energy Healing:*** Reiki+ Therapeutic Touch (Spiritual Healing)+ ***Nutritional Therapy+*** ***Herbal medicine+*** ***Exercise Systems*** Qi Gong Yoga+
MEDICAL SYSTEMS	
Anthroposophical Medicine Ayurveda Homeopathy+ Traditional Chinese Medicine Naturopathy+	

* indicates a CAM that falls into more than one category

+ indicates a CAM that is either regulated by law, is self-regulated or is moving towards greater regulation

TABLE 9.1 *Some commonly used CAMs therapies*

As a result of doing this exercise, you may even have found some therapies that are not listed here. Whichever three CAMs you chose, it is likely that you may have experienced some difficulty in allocating each of them to one category alone. As mentioned above, the holistic nature of complementary therapies means that they seldom work purely on one aspect of a person's situation or condition.

Anthroposophical Medicine	Kahuna Bodywork
Aromatherapy	Kanpo
Art Therapy	Kinesiology
Aura Soma	Life-coaching
Autogenic Training	Manual Lymph Drainage
Ayurveda	Massage
Bach Flowers	McTimoney Chiropractic
Bates Method	Medau Movement
Biochemic Tissue Salts	Meditation
Biofeedback	Metabolic Typing
Bodywork	Metamorphic Technique
Bowen Technique	Music Therapy
Buteyko	Naturopathy
Chiropractic	NLP
Cognitive and Behavioural Therapies	Nutritional Therapy
Colonic Irrigation	Osteopathy
Colour Therapy	Pilates
Cranial Osteopathy	Polarity Therapy
Craniosacral Therapy	Psychotherapy
Do In	Qi Gong
Drama Therapy	Radionics
Ear Acupuncture	Reiki
Emotional Freedom Technique	Seichem
Herbal Medicine	Shiatsu
Holographic Repatterning	Thai Yoga Massage
Homeopathy	Therapeutic Touch (Spiritual Healing)
Hypnotherapy	The Journey
Hopi Ear Candles	Thought Field Therapy
Indian Head Massage	Toyohari
Iridology	Traditional Chinese Medicine
Johrei	Yoga
	Zero Balancing

Source: Complementary Healthcare information Service-UK

TABLE 9.2 *Complementary therapies*

The following scenario describes how the use of a CAM treatment for a physical injury led to other benefits.

SCENARIO

Extra benefits

Rick is having a bad time at work. His tasks are piling up, and he is afraid to tell his manager in case she thinks he is incompetent. Not only this, one of his colleagues has stopped speaking to him, and there is a terrible atmosphere in the office.

A friend suggests they have a game of squash to help take Rick's mind off things and to get rid of some of his negative energy. However, Rick sprains his elbow during the game, and has to have a couple of days off work.

Another friend, Sue, is a Reiki healer, and she offers to give him a Reiki session to help speed up the healing process. Although Rick is sceptical, he agrees.

To his surprise, not only does the pain begin to ease but he starts to feel more relaxed, less stressed and more positive. He takes some time to think about the situation at work, and when he goes back he has a meeting with his manager to explain his difficulties. She agrees to take some of the pressure off him.

He still hasn't sorted out the problem with his colleague, but he feels confident that by being assertive and open, he can find a way to discuss things and move towards a solution.

He also decides to carry on with the Reiki sessions.

Think it over...

With respect to the three therapies you have chosen:

1. Identify the medical conditions for which each one is considered to be effective.

2. Identify some conditions that your chosen therapies would not be appropriate for.

3. Identify the diagnostic procedures used in your chosen therapies. (NB Some therapies do not involve diagnosis. It is important to know whether or not a specific therapy encompasses diagnostic techniques.)

4. Identify the treatment techniques used for each of your chosen therapies.

Reiki is a relatively new Japanese therapy developed by Dr Mikao Usui (1865–1926), although its origins lie in Buddhist philosophy and Shintoism, which Usui studied for many years. The Japanese word *Ki* (*Chi* in Chinese) means 'energy', and *Rei* means 'life'. The Reiki practitioner thus aims to stimulate a person's own life energy by connecting it with his or her own *Ki*. This in turn enhances the body's ability to heal itself. This enhanced energy flow can have beneficial effects on the mind as well as the body, as Rick's story illustrates. However, it is arguably not a cognitive therapy as such, because psychological benefits might be said to be a by-product of the enhanced physical energy flows. On the other hand, you might want to argue that Reiki should be classified as a medical 'system', in that it has a complex underpinning philosophy that embraces ethics, behaviour towards others, and taking personal responsibility not only for health (including that of others), but also for living harmoniously and acting positively. However, it is not as comprehensive as TCM or Ayurvedic Medicine, which are clearly sophisticated systems that include not only an underpinning philosophy, but also a wide range of treatment types, together with specific diagnostic techniques. We have already seen how the Ayurvedic system comprises elements of healing that can be categorised as cognitive, physical and sensory (see page 328).

Traditional Chinese Medicine (another medical 'system') uses a variety of methods that may all be classified as 'physical'. Within TCM, acupuncture is used to restore energy flows (*Chi*) by stimulating nerves through the insertion of needles at key points on a number of bodily meridians. Acupuncture would be classed as a physical therapy using the system of classification in this unit. Similarly, herbal medicine, nutrition and Qi Gong, the other key components of TCM, can all be classed as physical CAMs. They are also all practised as separate disciplines outside the TCM tradition.

Another medical system that encompasses a range of types of CAM is *Naturopathy*. This approach was developed in the late nineteenth century, and was declared to be a separate system in 1900. Naturopaths believe that the body wants to heal itself but that disease is caused by imbalance as a result of poor environment, bad nutrition and/or harmful ways of living. Naturopaths will offer one or more of several well-respected CAMs, including acupuncture, chiropractic, Biofeedback or Autogenic Training, meditation, herbal medicine and nutritional therapy, homeopathy, reflexology and physiotherapy. Naturopathy thus encompasses both physical and cognitive types of CAM.

The point of examining these examples in depth is to emphasise that allocating CAMs to specific categories is to some extent artificial. By their very nature, complementary therapies are holistic and therefore act upon several aspects of the human body and mind at the same time. Nevertheless, there are currently a vast number of different therapies in existence, and some kind of simple classification can help to make sense of the range and type of treatments that are available.

New approaches

Some of the CAMs that form part of wider medical systems (both ancient and modern) are now sometimes practised as disciplines in their own right. Chinese Herbal Medicine and acupuncture, for example, are sometimes offered as individual therapies. Some practitioners may combine CAMs that have their origins in different medical systems, as the following scenario shows.

SCENARIO

Building on experience

Sheila studied Swedish Massage at her local adult college and gained her ITEC certificate. This allowed her to set up as a massage practitioner.

She then became interested in reflexology, and studied at a private college, gaining her Practitioner Certificate in Reflexology. This meant that she could then offer reflexology to her clients as well as massage.

After a couple of years, she went to a CAMs conference where she heard about the Bowen Technique. She was impressed by this, and went on to do a short course to allow her to practise this therapy as well.

In following her interests, Sheila has acquired a range of CAMs skills, together with knowledge of several underpinning philosophies and systems. She first studied Swedish Massage, which was developed in the nineteenth century, but then began to learn more about older traditions when she went on to study reflexology. Finally, in studying the Bowen Technique, she added an additional perspective to her work. Thomas Bowen was an Australian who devised his sports-related therapy in 1916. Sheila now offers a range of treatments that reflects her own personal interests and development as a CAM therapist.

Matching CAMS to need

When assessing the value of a particular CAM, it will be important to evaluate this in terms of the kinds of need it can be used to meet. Needs may be physical, emotional and/or social. However, it must be remembered that human beings are very complex and their needs are interrelated. Emotional, social and physical problems can be closely linked, as the following example demonstrates.

Consider this

Jan has just come out of hospital after suffering severe facial disfigurement in a car accident. She is still taking daily medication to control the pain. She also feels ugly and unloved, and has totally lost confidence socially.

Before the accident, she used to be an active member of a local drama group. Now she cannot face seeing anyone, and is becoming quite depressed.

1. What kinds of need does Jan have?

2. What kind of CAMs might be suggested to her to meet each kind of need?

Clearly, whilst Jan still has pain she may not be able to move forward with her emotional recovery, neither will she be strong enough to start work on her social needs. It may be that a course of *Craniosacral Therapy* might help to control the pain, and help her begin to deal with the emotional problems resulting from the accident. Jan's self-image and sense of identity have been damaged as a result of the accident, and some kind of counselling may help her to start to come to terms with her disfigurement. Finally, her interest in drama may help her to regain her social self. With support from friends and family, Jan may gradually regain the confidence to rejoin the drama group, and start to enjoy the intellectual stimulation and social therapy that this membership brings with it. Of course, CAMs can never be imposed on a person, and unless Jan is ready and willing to begin the process of reconstructing her life, any intervention is unlikely to be successful.

In the previous exercise, you were asked to identify the kinds of condition that certain CAMs can be used to treat. It is important to remember that the final choice of any complementary therapy will be determined by a complex range of factors, including personal preference, beliefs and circumstances. Choosing the right therapy (or therapies) for an individual can be complex, and is not a matter of simply selecting from a checklist of possible interventions. Although some CAMs have indeed been demonstrated to be effective for some kinds of problem (e.g. chiropractic for musculo-skeletal problems), in practice individual need can be more complicated

Furthermore, satisfaction of a specific health or emotional need may require a strategy involving a number of CAMs. Many CAMs practitioners will suggest that a client should use other complementary or alternative therapies if need be, even if it means referral on to another person. Integrated Medicine practitioners are very likely to suggest a range of therapies to a patient. The way this might work has been described very thoroughly by Altshuler (2004). For example, for the treatment of chronic pain Altshuler suggests a range of options including dietary changes, exercise, meditation, acupuncture, counselling, bodywork such as the Feldenkrais method, Alexander Technique or Rolfing, Hypnosis, Yoga and Chinese Herbal Medicine. If these methods fail to work, Altshuler will firstly suggest the patient should purchase an over-the-counter pharmaceutical painkiller. If this should be ineffective, he will then prescribe painkillers of increasing strength (Altshuler, 2004 pp. 328-333).

In using therapeutic applications or outcomes as a measure of validity, a holistic view of a person's needs should always be taken.

Professional training, registration and quality control

When selecting an appropriate therapy, the issue of standards is critical. You will need to consider how a particular therapy is regulated (by standards), how practitioners are trained and how the relevant qualifications are regulated.

It may be dangerous to consult a practitioner who is not properly qualified or licensed. In fact, it is still (2005) not a legal requirement for many CAMs practitioners to have completed a specified course of training, or to belong to a professional association. Some CAMs are less well-regulated than others, and many have no single national body to which users may address any complaints or seek redress from as a consequence of receiving poor or harmful treatment.

For these reasons, it is absolutely essential to make a thorough check of both the therapy and the practitioner before embarking on a course of CAMs therapy, or recommending such a course to someone else. The following aspects should always be checked out.

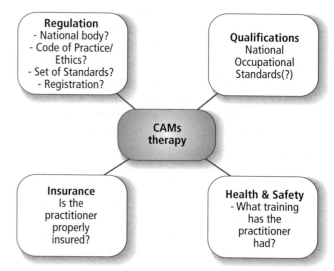

FIGURE 9.3 *Factors to consider when choosing or recommending CAMs therapies*

All of those aspects of CAMs practice shown in Figure 9.3 will be considered in this section.

Consider this: A disappointing experience

Someone has given Claire a gift voucher for a massage at a local beauty salon. She is very excited, as she has read a lot about the beneficial effects of massage. She has not been sleeping well lately, so is hoping the massage will help, and also that the practitioner can give her further advice on health and staying well.

When she arrives at the salon Claire is shocked to find that the treatment room has not been cleaned after the previous session. The floor is dirty (talcum powder and cotton buds are lying around), and there are soiled towels on the massage couch.

The masseuse seems indifferent to Claire, and there is no in-depth questionnaire to be filled in about her current state of health, tablets she is taking, and so on. The treatment is quite rough, and Claire decides that massage is not for her.

1. What are your comments on Claire's experience?

2. Do you think that Claire should report this salon for poor standards? If so, who should she report it to?

3. How would you convince Claire that, when done properly, massage can be very beneficial?

Regulation

In the last ten years, there has been a move towards greater regulation of CAMs, prompted in large part by the great public demand for such therapies. This increasing popular interest led to the commissioning of a House of Lords Select Committee Report (by the Science and Technology Committee) that was published in November 2000. This Report states that CAMs deserve investigation, as it is important for any government to know how they should be regulated by public health policy.

Legislation in 2001 set up the new Health Professions Council (HPC), whose job is to regulate the standards and qualifications of a number of complementary professions. Thirteen groups of practitioners are currently subject to this new regulation, and are shown in Figure 9.4. (NB Not all of these professions are considered to be CAMs.)

Arts Therapists (Art, Drama, Music)*
Biomedical Scientists
Chiropodists/Podiatrists
Clinical Scientists
Dieticians
Occupational Therapists
Operating Department Practitioners
Orthoptists
Prosthetists and Orthotists
Paramedics
Physiotherapists
Radiographers
Speech and Language Therapists

* CAMs practitioners

FIGURE 9.4 *Professions subject to regulation by the Health Professions Council (2005)*

The HPC determines which courses are appropriate to each discipline, and also which colleges are accredited to offer these courses. It keeps a list of properly qualified practitioners in the professions listed above.

It is possible that the HPC may regulate other professions in the future. The establishment of this organisation is recognition by government of the growing importance and use of many CAMs, not only by NHS practitioners, but also by members of the public who are turning increasingly to such practitioners for help.

Alongside this growing public interest and government recognition is a developing tendency towards the self-regulation of CAMs, together with the development of agreed standards for practice in the disciplines.

Centralisation and standardisation

In the last ten years there has been a move towards greater regulation by practitioners of some CAMs. This process has involved initiatives to standardise training courses and qualifications, as well as to establish codes of practice for the

ways in which CAMs are delivered. *Standardisation* has been achieved, in several cases, by the establishment of new national bodies to supervise the new regulations, often by the merging of older organisations. However, not all CAMs are regulated in this way, and it is important for anyone considering any complementary treatment to check out what training and qualifications a good practitioner should hold.

Key concept

Standardisation: A process whereby everything is made to conform to an agreed, common way of doing things: in this case training and qualifications.

Table 9.3 (page 336) gives details of some of the more highly regulated CAMs in the UK, as at December 2004. It should be noted that the situation is changing constantly and new organisations, qualifications and regulations will emerge in the next ten years.

Key concept

Regulation: The control of something by establishing a set of rules that everything must conform to.

Osteopathy and Chiropractic are currently regulated by Acts of Parliament, and this has been the situation since before the House of Lords Select Committee Report into the use of CAMs in the UK was published in 2000 (House of Lords, 2000). Statutory regulation means that practitioners of these CAMs will be required by law to achieve approved qualifications and to adhere to certain standards and codes of practice. This is a safeguard both for clients using these practitioners (who are protected from unqualified therapists, and who can also seek redress if they feel that a registered practitioner has been negligent) and also for properly qualified CAMs practitioners, who benefit from membership of a national organisation. The training of osteopaths is regulated by the General Osteopathic Council

(GOC), and that of chiropractors by the General Chiropractic Council (GCC). (NB Chiropractors do not, in fact, regard themselves as complementary therapists, but rather as primary health care practitioners.)

There is currently (January, 2005) a timetable for passing an Act to regulate Medical Herbalism. The European Herbal Practitioners Association (EHPA), which represents therapists from Ayurveda, Tibetan Herbal Medicine, Traditional Herbal Medicine and Western Herbal Medicine, is an umbrella organisation that sets standards for each of these areas of practice. The EHPA has also agreed a common core curriculum for the training of medical herbalists, with specialist curriculum areas for each of the different traditions noted above. Like osteopathy and chiropractic, the profession has a set of standards to which practitioners must adhere.

The information given in Table 9.3 is by no means comprehensive, but it gives an indication of the ways in which some CAMs practitioners are

CAM/NATIONAL REGULATING BODY/IES	STATUTORY REGULATION	ACCREDITATION	CODES OF PRACTICE/ ETHICS ETC	NATIONAL OCCUPATIONAL STANDARDS	MINIMUM LENGTH OF TRAINING
Osteopathy General Osteopathy Council (GOC)	●	●	●		4/5 years
Chiropractic General Chiropractic Council (GCC)	●	●	●		4/5 years
Medical Herbalism European Herbal Practitioners Association (EHPA)	In progress	●	●	●	Standardis- ation in progress
Acupuncture British Acupuncture Council		●	●	In progress	3yrs F/T & P/T equivalent
Aromatherapy Aromatherapy Consortium/Council		In progress	In progress	●	Standardis- ation in progress
Homeopathy The Society of Homeopaths		●	●	●	3 yrs F/T 4 yrs P/T
Nutritional Therapy Nutrition Therapy Council (NTC) British Association of Nutritional Therapists				●	3 to 4 years
Reflexology Association of Reflexologists		●	●	●	100 hours

NB This table does not always distinguish between full and part-time courses. You will need to investigate qualifications for your chosen therapies in greater depth.

TABLE 9.3 *CAMs: training and regulation, December 2004*

seeking to standardise qualifications and regulate practice. Although only a few CAMs are regulated by law (Statutory Regulation in the Table), nevertheless there have been moves by a number of practitioners to achieve greater standardisation for their own therapies, and the situation at the time of writing (January 2005) is complex. The regulation of aromatherapy, for example, is currently undergoing radical changes. The old Aromatherapy Organisations Council (AOC) has voluntarily dissolved in order to make way for a new group called the Aromatherapy Consortium. In time, this will become the Aromatherapy Council. The register of qualified aromatherapists that was maintained by the old AOC will now be kept by the new Consortium. Aromatherapy already has a set of National Occupational Standards (see below), and the new Aromatherapy Consortium is making these the benchmark for all new qualifications in aromatherapy. A new core curriculum will be produced based on these Standards, and there will be a single National Voluntary Register for aromatherapists.

Aromatherapy is not the only CAM for which there is a set of National Occupational Standards (NOS), setting out how practitioners should deliver their services. Skills for Health, as the Sector Skills Council for the health sector licensed by the DfES, develops NOS in many areas including CAM.

As at August 2005, eight CAMs had National Occupational Standards, four are waiting for approval, and a further three are in development. As these Standards are developed, they will give further impetus to the standardisation of CAMs practice in the UK. CAMs that have agreed NOS, and those that are still open to consultation are listed below.

National occupational standards for CAMs

(January 2005) Existing Standards:

* Aromatherapy
* Herbal Medicine
* Hypnotherapy
* Kinesiology
* Nutritional Therapy
* Remedial and Therapeutic Massage
* Homeopathy
* Reflexology

Standards Awaiting Approval:

* Acupuncture
* Alexander Technique
* Reiki
* Spiritual Healing

Standards in Development:

* Craniosacral Therapy
* Bowen Technique
* Yoga Therapy

Source: Skills for Health website

Courses and colleges

Training courses for CAMs practitioners are offered in a range of educational settings. There are degree courses in some CAMs (for example Homeopathy, Osteopathy, Chiropractic and Nutritional Therapy). For others there are a variety of diplomas and certificates that have different status. The process of regulation described above will eventually result in greater clarity with respect to who is deemed to be qualified to practise.

Courses may be offered at universities, colleges, evening classes and in private training centres. The International Therapy Examination Council (ITEC) offers 17 qualifications that are accredited by the Qualifications and Curriculum Authority (QCA) on behalf of the Department for Education and Skills. Eight of these relate to CAMs professions:

CAMs qualifications (January 2005) International Therapy Examinations Council (ITEC)
Level 3 Diplomas are offered in:

* Anatomy and Physiology
* Holistic Massage
* Aromatherapy
* Reflexology
* On-site Massage
* Lymphatic Drainage Massage
* Diet and Nutrition for Complementary Therapists
* Sports Massage

ITEC also maintains a register of professionals, which was merged with that of the Guild of Complementary Practitioners in April 2003 to form the International Guild of Professional Practitioners (IGPP).

Despite the trend towards standardisation, there is still a great deal of variation in the numbers of courses offered and the bodies that award and accredit them. The discussion in this unit has not included the multitude of short training courses and modules offered by private practitioners in some of the less well-regulated CAMs (e.g. Bowen Technique or Crystal Therapy). Many such trainers may indeed be very well-qualified in some other discipline and be quite competent to deliver training (e.g. someone with a background as an NHS nurse who has branched out into a particular area of Complementary Therapy). However, others will not be so well-qualified. Anyone choosing or recommending a particular CAM is well-advised to do some research into the therapy itself, and the qualifications of the practitioner. Careful research is needed into each of the CAMs chosen for study for this unit, to check on the latest status of qualifications and awarding bodies.

Health and safety

Law and Regulations: In the UK, the practice of complementary therapies is regulated by legislation relating to health and safety at work. Good training courses for CAMs practitioners will cover all aspects of this vital element of the work.

The Health & Safety at Work Act 1974 (HASAWA) provides the foundation for the way in which health and safety issues are managed. Since 1974, there have been numerous Acts of Parliament and guidance documents dealing with all aspects of safety, including manual handling (which includes the moving and lifting of people), managing hazardous substances, provision in case of fire and the use of equipment, to name but a few. These laws and guidelines cover all the things that might go wrong in the workplace including accidents, injuries caused by lifting someone in the wrong way, exposure to dangerous substances, and so on.

Under the HASAW Act, both employer and employee have a 'duty of care' towards everyone on the premises, and both have clear responsibilities. Thus, in the case of a private sports centre the management must make sure that the environment is safe; that any substances (especially potentially dangerous ones) are stored, moved and handled safely; that systems of work, equipment, access to and exit from the premises are safe, and that personal protective equipment is provided to employees. Management must also provide information, training and supervision on safety issues for staff, and have a written safety policy. The protection of members of the public whilst on the premises is also the responsibility of management. Therapists working on the premises on a sessional basis are also covered by HASAWA, and are entitled to the same protection as those who are fully employed.

However, employees (including sessional therapists) also have a personal responsibility for health and safety issues.

Health & Safety at Work Act 1974: Staff responsibilities Section 7 of this Act says that employees must:

* take reasonable care for their own health and safety and that of others affected by their acts or omissions at work

* cooperate with the employer

* report any situation thought to be unsafe or unhealthy.

Practical considerations are also covered by the regulations. Dangers from electricity, gas and fire must be minimised by the proper maintenance of installations and equipment, and by staff training in fire and evacuation procedures. There should also be the correct number of trained First Aiders on the premises (as set out in the Health and Safety (First Aid) Regulations 1981).

Some of the regulations that are relevant to salons and CAMs practitioners are:

* Health & Safety (First Aid) Regulations 1981

* Management of Health & Safety at Work Regulations 1992

* Workplace (Health, Safety and Welfare) Regulations 1992

* Manual Handling Operations Regulations 1992

* Personal Protective Equipment at Work Regulations 1992

NB This list is not exhaustive.

Insurance

Both therapists and the owners of premises where therapies are delivered should be adequately insured. Some professional organisations (e.g. ITEC, the Federation of Holistic Therapists, and so on) arrange access to insurance for practitioners who hold their recognised qualifications. Types of insurance include:

* public liability insurance: to provide protection against bodily injury, and loss or damage to property

* third party insurance: to cover the therapist against claims of negligence.

Other types of insurance, relevant to owners of larger concerns are premises and contents insurance, shopkeepers' liability insurance, and insurance against loss of takings or profit resulting from fire.

Membership of professional bodies

The function of professional bodies in regulating qualifications was discussed above (page 335). Many CAMs practitioners do belong to such bodies. This brings a number of benefits both to practitioners themselves, and also to members of the public. Benefits to therapists may include:

* professional status

* access to insurance

* credibility with customers/clients (especially with respect to safety issues)

* access to information and new techniques

* the possibility of a reasonable relationship with the medical profession

* public listing.

It is in the interests of both CAMs practitioners and their clients that therapists are seen to be well-qualified, properly insured and safe to practise. Membership of professional bodies provides safeguards for both the practitioner and the client.

Codes of Practice and Standards

Many professional bodies and national CAMs organisations have codes of practice. From April 2005, thirteen professions allied to health care will be regulated by the Health Professions Council (HPC) (see pp. 334-336). The HPC sets standards for training, professional skills, behaviour and health, with the aim of securing the safety and well-being of anyone using an HPC registered professional.

The Vocational Training Charitable Trust (VTCT) also has codes of practice governing standards of hygiene and behaviour in the salon or clinic. These guidelines cover the cleanliness of the therapist and equipment, ventilation and heating, and checking for contra-indications before the start of treatment. Practitioners also need to know what to do should contra-actions result from treatment.

Key concepts

Contra-indications: these are reasons why a treatment should not be given. For example, massage is not recommended for people who have some kinds of cancer.

Contra-actions: possible negative side-effects of treatment, e.g. bruising (after massage), mood swings etc.

Quality control: herbs and supplements

Whereas the pharmaceutical products used by conventional medical practitioners are produced to defined, quality-controlled standards and are tested for safety, the production of some herbal products may vary with respect to the standards to which they are produced.

In the UK, such products are currently subject to three different kinds of regulation (Barnett, 2002 pp. 48–49). There are licensed products, which are assessed for quality and safety in the same way as licensed medicine (Medicines Act 1968). Such substances have a product licence (PL) on their packaging. There are also unlicensed medicines, which do not have to satisfy any specific safety standards. However, it is illegal to make written claims about their use on the label.

The third kind of product is the food supplement. These also do not have to satisfy any specific safety or quality standards, but associated claims about health benefits can be made.

The Medicines and Healthcare Products Regulatory Agency (MHRA) gives advice on the safety of both pharmaceutical and other products, and enforces the law when breaches of existing regulations take place. A Registration Scheme for Traditional Herbal Medicines is being implemented (as at March, 2005).

The European Directive on traditional herbal medicines (2002) provides for tighter regulation of such products. Evidence that a product has been in use for at least 30 years will now be required (including 15 years' use in Europe). Another EU Directive, this time on Food Supplements, passed into English law in 2003. This limits the permissible spectrum of nutrients, and also their potential potency by reducing the maximum permitted levels.

The regulation of herbal products and food supplements is likely to change over time, particularly since organisations such as the Alliance for Natural Health and other groups are seeking to challenge the details of regulations such as those imposed by the European Directives. If you choose to study a CAM that uses herbal or similar substances, you should be sure to check on the current status of regulation of such products.

The MHRA has a website containing regularly updated information on the regulation and safety of herbal and other products.

Effectiveness of therapies

It is helpful to assess the effectiveness of therapies with reference to current research. In order to do this, it is important to understand something about research methodologies and their relative value in relation to complementary therapies.

Key concept

Research methodology: the different ways in which scientists and scholars conduct their research.

Different kinds of research methodology are described in this section. However, you should remember that medical opinion varies as to the value of the research that has been done into complementary therapies. Whilst some doctors are proactive in their use of CAMs (e.g. Integrated Medicine Practitioners), others are vitriolic in their opposition to CAMs, seeing them as 'pseudoscientific health cures' that lack 'a coherent, clearly defined explanatory theory that is internally consistent' (Kurtz 2000, pp. 13, 17).

Disagreements about research methodologies lie behind these differences in opinion.

Scientific research methodology

The Research Council for Complementary Medicine (RCCM) has published a very useful account of the nature of research and how it can be done (Research Council for Complementary Medicine 1999). This paper can be accessed quite easily on the RCCM website. It lists a number of types of study, summarised in Table 9.4.

PURPOSE	METHOD
To describe something	Case reports Surveys
To explain something	Qualititative research (e.g. interviews, surveys)
To test a hypothesis	Quantitative research (e.g. clinical trials)
To make generalisations	Multi-centre trials, Systematic reviews of trials

Source: An Introduction to Research, Research Council for Complementary Medicine, 1999

TABLE 9.4 *Types of research study*

It is important to note that different research methods are used to achieve different outcomes. A case report, for example, simply describes something that has happened. An example might be an account of the treatment that a homeopath gave to a specific patient, and the effect that this had. Some surveys, too, simply seek to describe something that has happened – but in this case a greater number of examples will be given.

Researchers also make a key distinction between *quantitative* and *qualitative* studies. Quantitative data is information that can be expressed in numerical form. For example, Table 9.5 gives data about CAMs offered by Primary Care Trusts in UK between 1999 and 2002. This information is derived from actual numbers, and is expressed in this table in terms of percentages. This is quantitative data.

CAMS	
THERAPY	**PERCENTAGE OF TOTAL**
Acupuncture	32%
Osteopathy/Chiropractic	24%
Homeopathy	14%
Hypnotherapy	4%
Aromatherapy/Massage	4%
Reflexology	3%
Herbal/Chinese Herbal Medicine	*
Yoga	*
Other	17%

* = less than 1%

225 references to CAMs in 135 local NHS PCT plans.

TABLE 9.5 *CAMs offered by NHS Primary Care Trusts 1992–2001*

Source: Halpern 2001

> ### Key concept
>
> *Quantitative data:* Data which is expressed in numerical form. Quantitative research methods seek to collect this type of data.

In contrast, qualitative data is that which cannot be expressed in numerical form. This kind of data is descriptive, and is often about attitudes, opinions and values.

> ### Key concept
>
> *Qualitative data:* Data which cannot be expressed in numerical form. It is descriptive information, and is often about attitudes, opinions and values. Qualitative research seeks to collect this type of data.

All scientific research uses a range of methods, depending on the desired outcome of the study. Social scientists, medical researchers and those seeking to determine the effectiveness of CAMs all use techniques drawn from the methods described above. However, medical scientists tend to value quantitative methods over and above qualitative studies. Biomedical researchers and others interested in medical outcomes like to see results from large studies, and most particularly from studies known as *randomised controlled trials*.

The randomised controlled trial (RCT) has become something of a benchmark for medical research. A well-conducted RCT will be fairly extensive, have a carefully selected group of people as the focus of its study, and have clearly defined outcomes. An example might be a trial to investigate the effect of a new drug on a particular medical condition.

In an RCT, the people who are to be studied are selected randomly, that is, they are chosen in order to avoid bias. For example, having a far greater number of females than males in a sample might give different results than if the gender spread of the sample were more equal. Of course, it depends upon the subject being studied, but in general the principle of randomness is held to give a study greater validity.

A trial is said to be controlled when there is a second (or even third) group of people who will provide information about what is likely to happen if no intervention is made. The control group is also selected randomly. So, in a trial to study the impact of a new drug, one group of people is given the drug whilst another (the control group) is either given no drug, or is given a *placebo* (i.e. something that looks exactly the same, but actually has no pharmaceutical properties). Ideally, the people taking part will not know whether or not they have been given the real drug or the placebo. This is known as a *single-blind trial*. Even better, the people administering both drugs and placebos should not know which is which. This avoids any kind of subjective influence onto the people being studied, and is known as a *double-blind trial*. The impact of the new drug (or treatment) on people in both groups is then compared.

Randomised controlled trials are highly valued by doctors who practise conventional medicine. *Systematic reviews* of RCTs also have a high status amongst doctors. Such a review collects together data from a number of RCTs, and presents this data analytically. The methods used in each RCT will be assessed and the results evaluated. Such reviews enable doctors to make an assessment of the validity of research into new treatments and drugs, without having to spend a great deal of time seeking out the data for themselves. These reviews also reveal trends in research; if a number of RCTs produce similar results, then this becomes very compelling evidence.

Conducting such a review is a very skilled task in itself. A very sophisticated form of systematic review is the *meta-analysis*. This uses specific statistical techniques to compare the data from different RCTs, resulting in a single analysis of the effectiveness of whatever is being studied.

In conclusion, then, it should be noted that doctors who practise conventional medicine are more likely to be influenced by research data that is produced from RCTs, particularly when these are validated by comparisons with other studies.

Unfortunately, for people who are interested in CAMs, the RCT has some shortcomings with respect to the investigation of complementary therapies, which are set out below.

Randomised controlled trials and complementary medicine

The problems associated with RCTs in investigating CAMs have been described very clearly by Toby Murcott (2005).

Length of research: RCTs usually have a relatively short time-span (perhaps up to two or three years) which may not be long enough to measure the impact of a complementary treatment on a chronic condition (such as multiple sclerosis).

Multi-factor interventions: RCTs are also not very good at investigating what Murcott terms 'multi-factor-interventions' (2005 p. 81). This problem has been recognised by the Medical Research Council. If a physiotherapist is treating someone for a knee injury, for example, it may be hard to determine precisely whether the treatment itself is responsible for a patient's recovery, or whether other factors such as increased confidence, greater help from a partner or spouse and the long-term application of advice (such as doing exercises or losing weight) have played a part in the process. RCTs tend to focus on specifics (e.g. taking a drug, having a specific surgical procedure), whereas in practice there may be many factors involved in a patient's recovery. This is often true for people who use CAMs, as many of these people have chronic conditions (i.e. conditions that last over a prolonged period of time).

Specifically tailored treatments: Furthermore, the administration of a CAM is sometimes in itself multi-faceted. A homeopath, for example, may see two clients with the same condition. However, she may give each person a different remedy (or combination of remedies) specially tailored to meet that person's individual circumstances. This is also the case with acupuncture and shiatsu, where treatment is varied to suit the client's needs (Murcott, 2005 p. 84). This is because CAMs are designed to treat the patient, rather than the condition as such. Given that CAMs tend to be used in this way, it would be very hard to use the RCT technique in such circumstances, as no two interventions would be exactly the same. This is in contrast to the testing of a drug, where exactly the same substance would be given in order to make the research valid.

The practitioner-client relationship: The relationship between the CAMs practitioner and the client is central to the way in which complementary therapies are delivered. Research into why people opt to use CAMs highlights the value that people place on having a good relationship with the practitioner, in contrast to the negative experience that many people have with their doctor (see Table 9.7). Murcott notes that many CAMs practitioners speak about having a 'depth of interaction' with the people they are working to help (Murcott, 2005 p. 48).

RCTs, however, are not good at measuring this kind of factor. It is not possible to reproduce exactly the interaction between client and therapist, particularly for psychotherapeutic interventions. This would be impossible to reproduce once, let alone on the scale that is normally considered significant for clinical trials.

Problems with placebos: There are also problems with placebos. These can be both ethical and practical. In cases of serious illness such as cancer, for example, it would be unethical to withhold conventional treatment from a group of patients in order to test out the effectiveness of an alternative therapy, e.g. meditation. In practical terms, it can be difficult to administer a placebo. It would be very hard to give a person a 'dummy' massage, for example, although there have been studies in which 'dummy' acupuncture has been given, with needles inserted into the body at places other than would normally be used.

The context effect: Placebos sometimes work simply because a patient has been told that they will. For this reason, the double-blind trial is held to be more effective than the single-blind, because whoever is administering the treatment cannot know if it is a true drug or a placebo. You can see from this that it would be hard to do a double-blind trial with many CAMs, as most involve the therapist engaging quite deeply in conversation with the client.

Murcott describes a study by Di Blasi, which reviewed 25 clinical trials in order to try to distinguish treatment effect from context effect (2005, p. 114–115). Although this study was inconclusive, it did distinguish between cognitive and emotional care in the administration of treatments. Cognitive care involves giving the patient plenty of information about his or treatment; emotional care includes giving

treatment and/or consultation in a relaxed environment. The study suggests that 'physicians who adopt a warm, friendly and reassuring manner are more effective than those who keep consultations formal and do not offer reassurance' (2005, p. 115).

This suggests that the context in which a treatment is given may have some effect on the outcome of that treatment. RCTs are usually conducted in a clinical environment, which may not be conducive to achieving a positive outcome from treatment. This is a factor that may have impacted on some of the clinical studies of CAMs that have been undertaken. It is also something that RCTs do not always take into account.

The foregoing comments should not be taken to imply that there can never be useful RCTs conducted on CAMs and their impact. However, there are sufficient reservations about their use in assessing the effectiveness of some complementary therapies to warrant suggesting that other research methods might be used, either in combination or as an alternative.

Before looking at some alternatives to the RCT, it is necessary to consider another significant factor that may contribute to the success of CAMs, and to assess how far this factor should be taken into account when assessing the effectiveness of complementary therapies. This factor is the power of the mind in relation to the success (or otherwise) of both conventional and complementary therapies.

The power of the mind and the effectiveness of CAMs

Some critics of CAMs like to dismiss their effect as being 'all in the mind'. CAMs will only work, they say, if users believe they will be effective. This argument is strengthened by the relatively low number of good quality RCTs that appear to confirm the effectiveness of complementary therapies. However, since many people claim to have been helped by the use of CAMs (despite the lack of clinical evidence of the kind that meets with broad approval) the 'all in the mind' explanation is a tempting one.

The placebo effect itself is an indicator of the power of the mind in influencing treatment outcomes. Just as the mind can tell a person that he or she is ill (in the case of a 'psychosomatic illness'), the mind can also tell a person that a particular treatment can make them better, particularly if this has been reinforced by a doctor or a CAMs practitioner. Research into placebos, for example, has shown that they will work better when injected, and that pink tablets work better than white tablets in bringing about a 'cure' (Martin 1997, p. 250). Whilst it is undoubtedly true that sometimes a person can convince him or herself of many things, research into the relationship of the brain and the body's physiological systems is now showing that the mind-body association is extremely complex.

For many years, science has separated the study of the mind from that of the body. Thus, medicine has been practised as a totally separate discipline from psychology and psychiatry. Conventional medicine has been concerned with the physical causes of disease (with a treatment focus on physical factors).

On the other hand, psychiatrists and psychologists have tended to see matters of the mind, emotions and behaviours as quite distinct from physiological matters (Martin, 1997).

Psychoneuroimmunology

This rigid divide between the study of mind and body has been breached with the advent of a scientific discipline called *psychoneuroimmunology* (PNI). People who study PNI recognise that the mind-body relationship is very complex, and is a two-way process. On the one hand a person's state of mind can affect the body, and therefore physical health. On the other, physical health can affect the mind, emotions and behaviours. As Martin puts it, PNI 'is concerned with the complex inter-relationships between psychological and emotional factors, the brain, hormones, immunity and disease' (Martin 1997, p. 76).

Two examples demonstrate how these processes can work. The first concerns a study of how stress can have an effect on the immune system.

Cohen's research (amongst other similar studies) shows that if someone is feeling low or

> ## SCENARIO
>
> ### Stress and the common cold
>
> Cohen and colleagues studied 420 volunteers (men and women) who agreed to be given the common cold virus (via nasal drops).
>
> Before doing this, the stress levels of each person were measured. Cohen found that the people with the highest stress measures were more likely to (a) become infected by the virus and (b) develop colds.
>
> *Sources*: Cohen 1991; Cohen 1993; quoted in Martin 1997, pp. 42–43.

experiencing negative emotions, then his or her resistance to infection can be lowered. This is particularly the case if that person has previously suffered a number of stressful life experiences (e.g. bereavement).

On the other hand, the presence of a disease or a medical condition (or even the treatment process itself) can cause stress, as the following example illustrates.

> ## SCENARIO
>
> ### Chronic blues
>
> Tim has Multiple Sclerosis, a chronic condition which in his case has lasted for over 20 years. He is normally cheerful, and has always concentrated hard on taking a positive approach to his condition – using different CAMs and doing all the things that he knows are good for him.
>
> For the last few months, however, his fatigue levels have been very high, which has limited both his ability to work and to go out with his friends.
>
> In turn, this is making him depressed and fearful for the future.
>
> In Tim's case, the continued hard work of living with a medical condition has finally triggered negative emotions and resulted in depression. In this example, the state of Tim's body has had an effect on his mind and emotional state.

The study of PNI is beginning to throw light on this two-way process. Whereas critics of CAMs like to dismiss their effectiveness as 'all in the mind', perhaps it is time to suggest another way of looking at the relationship between any form of treatment (whether allopathic or complementary) and the role of the mind. Perhaps it is time to accept that part of any healing process will be in the mind of the receiver – and quite rightly so. Jenny Cole has described how whilst awaiting the final confirmation of a diagnosis of breast cancer, her enlightened NHS consultant said that he did not want to force her to undergo any treatment she did not believe in, including chemotherapy. If she did not believe in it, he said, she would be fighting it all the time. Jenny was also advised to learn the technique of visualisation, to help her mind to fight the disease (Cole, 1995). Clearly, in this NHS Unit, practitioners acknowledge and use the power of the mind to enhance the effectiveness of conventional treatments.

Thus, research methodologies used to investigate the effectiveness of specific CAMs may need to be designed to take into account the power of the mind together with contextual factors that may influence a person's attitude.

Other research methodologies

RCTs have limitations with respect to the investigation of the effectiveness of certain CAMs. However, other research methods can be used to supplement or replace RCT-based investigations.

Qualitative techniques: These are being increasingly used in the investigation of CAMs.

Observational studies and *interviews* with CAMs users are becoming increasingly popular.

The technique of *conversation analysis* is also being used by linguists and medical anthropologists to investigate what happens during a CAMs consultation. For example, a detailed study of conversations between eight homeopaths and 20 patients has shown how the homeopath works in a subtle, patient-orientated way (Murcott, pp. 108–109).

Combining techniques: Some researchers have combined qualitative with quantitative techniques in their studies.

One example of this is to do some qualitative research in combination with a quantitative study. Murcott describes an example of an investigation into the results of physiotherapy treatment which used both clinical (quantitative) measures, and qualitative data collected from patients by interview after treatment was completed (Murcott 2005 p. 97). Interestingly, there was less than 50 per cent agreement between the results gathered from the two parts of the study, which is significant with respect to the ways in which information is collected, and the questions that are asked. According to Mason, Tovey and Long 'from the user's perspective, it is the beneficial effect itself that matters not how it was brought about' (Murcott 2005, p. 98).

Avoiding placebos: Some of the ethical problems inherent in using a placebo can be avoided by doing *retrospective studies* of clinical data. In such studies, the medical records of patients who had received certain treatments could be examined after the outcome of treatment was known. Using this method, a researcher could look at groups of patients who had received different treatments, and analyse outcomes in a quantitative way.

Another way to avoid the use of a placebo control group is to use RCTs to study groups of patients receiving different kinds of treatment. Thus, researchers could compare outcomes for patients who had opted to use conventional medicine to alleviate symptoms of arthritis, as against a group of patients who had chosen to use acupuncture. *Pragmatic RTCs* often involve such comparisons (Barnett 2002, p. 58).

In using research to assess the effectiveness of a specific therapy, therefore, you should always try to determine what research methodology has been used, the questions that were asked and the specific outcomes the researchers had in mind.

The Resources section of this unit lists a number of websites and publications, and you will find additional guidance on the task of researching CAMs in the Assessment Evidence section of the unit assessment.

Availability and cost

Ease of access to CAMs and the cost are two further criteria that may influence the choice of a particular therapy.

In the UK, CAMs are currently accessed via a number of routes. Figure 9.5 sets out the main ways that people gain access to CAMs.

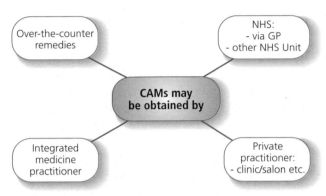

FIGURE 9.5 *Use of CAMs in UK: some access routes*

Over-the-counter purchases and private practitioners

The Royal Pharmaceutical Society (RPS) has estimated that in 1998, people in the UK spent about £93 million on herbal remedies, homeopathic preparations and aromatherapy oils (House of Lords Select Committee Report, 2000, para. 1.20). The RPS also predicted that such sales would rise to £126 million by 2002. Many people are happy to take preparations that they have chosen and bought for themselves, based on information they obtain from magazines, books or the Internet.

Similarly, individuals often take the initiative in consulting CAMs practitioners privately. The reasons for this are complex and are discussed in Section 9.3.

CAMs and the NHS

Research commissioned by the Prince of Wales's Foundation for Integrated Healthcare found that 97 per cent of NHS local plans (Primary Care Investment Plans) for 1999–2000 contained references to CAM services (Halpern, 2001). In other words, of 135 local health plans for England and Scotland, 131 authorities were offering some kind of CAM therapies to patients. Table 9.5 (page 341) sets out the therapies mentioned in these plans.

Some of these local health authorities (Primary Care Trusts or PCTs) were offering integrated services, such as a musculo-skeletal service combining physiotherapy and osteopathy. One GP practice was offering acupuncture to its patients. In some cases, CAMs were on offer to supplement *palliative care* where appropriate. The scenario opposite demonstrates how this might work in practice.

> **Key concept**
>
> *Palliative care:* Long-term health care, often for people with chronic conditions, or people who are unlikely to recover from an illness. Such care aims to give relief from symptoms such as pain, and to enhance quality of life and well-being.

Comfort and pain relief

Gwen is 84 years old and has cancer. Doctors are reluctant to expose her to the risk of surgery, as she is very frail. However, she is in considerable pain from her tumour.

Her consultant discusses Gwen's situation with the hospital Palliative Care Team, Gwen's family and, of course, Gwen herself. It is agreed that aromatherapy may help with pain relief. With Gwen's agreement, treatment goes ahead using a private practitioner who is paid on a sessional basis to treat her in hospital.

Sometimes, the initiative for working in partnership with CAMs practitioners comes from outside the NHS. One such project is described in the next scenario.

Working in partnership

A group of CAMs practitioners has approached the local health primary care trust to see if there is any possibility of providing therapies to NHS patients. The NHS health promotion manager is very interested, and he gives his support to the project.

After careful planning, and making a bid for PCT funding, Reiki is now being made available to people who use mental health services, substance misuse services, and also to people who are carers. Each person has to pay just £5 per Reiki session.

GPs and CAMs

Some GPs are very sympathetic to the use of CAMs by their patients. Indeed, some doctors are now positively seeking to integrate complementary techniques into their own practice. However, other GPs remain unsupportive, and even suspicious of any therapy that is not wholly endorsed by NHS guidelines or recommendations. The situation varies locally.

A survey by the University of Exeter shows that of 461 GPs who took part, 16 per cent actually practised a CAM, 25 per cent had referred patients to a CAM practitioner and 55 per cent had recommended the use of a CAM to patients (White, Resch and Ernst, 1997). The CAMs practised by GPs included acupuncture, manipulation (including massage and osteopathy), homeopathy, hypnotherapy, medical herbalism, reflexology and aromatherapy.

A national survey of access to CAMs via GPs in England was conducted in 1995 and repeated in 2001, based on a target population of one in eight GP practices (Thomas, Coleman and Nicholl, 2003). The findings suggest that in 1995, about 39 per cent of GP practices provided access to CAMs; by 2001, this had risen to about 50 per cent. The researchers note that this rise was mainly due to GPs offering CAMs on-site (rather than to an increase in referrals to NHS-provided CAMs). Over the same period, the financial contribution by patients towards CAMs services rose from 26 per cent to 42 per cent. In both 1995 and 2001, acupuncture and homeopathy were the CAMs most frequently provided via GPs.

Acupuncture at the local surgery

One GP surgery has adopted the use of acupuncture for carefully selected patients. As a result, the practice has noted an 80 per cent success rate, with a reduction in referrals to the physiotherapy department, and in the cost of prescribing drugs.

The project has been so successful that the PCT plans to develop acupuncture services within the whole of its area.

(Adapted from Halpern 2001, p.11.)

This scenario describes a successful initiative by a GP surgery to make use of a complementary therapy (in this case acupuncture). However, in other areas, as a result of changes to the way in which GP practices are funded (changes that took place in 2000), some GPs are no longer able to afford to offer CAM therapies on site, even if they wanted to.

Integrated medicine

Some GPs are now beginning to adopt CAMs into their own practice, and to work more closely with CAMs practitioners in referring patients on when they feel it is appropriate. This combining of the scientific method with the holistic approach of complementary systems and therapies is now being referred to as Integrated Medicine by doctors who adopt this way of working. This is sometimes referred to as a biographical approach to illness, as the focus is always on the whole person, not just the symptoms (Galland, 1998).

Key concept

Biographical approach: a term sometimes used by integrated medicine practitioners to describe how they go about diagnosing and treating an illness.

It takes into account everything about a person (history, lifestyle etc.) and not just the presenting symptoms.

It was previously stated that Ayurvedic practitioners are often also conventionally trained. The work of Deepak Chopra (Chopra, 1990)

SCENARIO

Chemotherapy and meditation

Dr Suman Kohli practises in Nottingham. She has medical degrees from University College London, and has also studied the Ayurvedic system of medicine.

She is consulted by a patient who has cancer, and who is troubled about embarking upon a course of chemotherapy. Dr Kohli advises her to accept the treatment, but also suggests some dietary changes that will help. She then recommends that the patient should spend time each day meditating, and visualising her tumour decreasing in size.

(Adapted from information in Chopra, 1990.)

---

provides a very clear explanation of how Ayurvedic practice may be combined with conventional medical techniques. The following scenario demonstrates how such a practitioner might work with an individual patient.

Outside the Ayurvedic tradition, Western-trained doctors are also seeing the advantages of combining the best of both conventional and complementary treatments. In the UK, the British Association for Allergy, Environmental and Nutritional Medicine works to promote the study and practice of an integrated approach that looks particularly at the contribution of allergies, nutrition and environmental factors to poor health. The Association runs courses, has a register of practitioners and also publishes a quarterly journal on relevant issues. The Prince of Wales's Foundation for Integrated Health promotes research into integrated healthcare, and plays a key part in national developments such as the move towards the statutory regulation of CAMs. A web search based on the term Integrated Medicine will result in a host of hits on UK and other organisations that exist to promote this practice.

Settings for complementary therapies

CAMs are practised in a wide range of settings, from the user's own home through to out-patients departments in NHS hospitals. Table 9.6 sets out a small sample of settings (together with the cost of treatment sessions), showing places in which CAMs could be accessed (as at January 2005).

Table 9.6 shows a variety of settings for the practice of CAMs. Some therapists will visit users in their own homes, taking along all the necessary equipment such as a massage couch and aromatherapy oils. Other practitioners will set up a treatment or consultation room, sometimes in their own homes, sometimes in rented premises such as shop units. Nutritional Therapists in example F in Table 9.6 use subsidised premises made available by an organisation that is a registered charity. The organisation supports research into nutritional therapies, and also the training of new therapies.

Leisure centres and health spas often offer CAMs as an additional service to customers, and

	SETTING	THERAPY	STATUS/SOURCE OF FUNDING	COST TO USER (SESSION)
A	Hospital outpatient department	Reiki	NHS/Private	£5
B	Own home	Massage	Private	£35
C	Leisure centre	Massage Aromatherapy Reflexology	Private	£40-£50
D	Exhibition	On-site Massage	Private	£10
E	CAMs clinic	Osteopathy Chiropractic	Private	£35-40
F	CAMs clinic	Nutrition Therapy	Charity/Private	£35-70
G	Therapist's home	Massage Aromatherapy Reflexology	Private	£35-40
H	Community health centre	Homeopathy Osteopathy	Lottery funding/ NHS	Free
I	Health spa	Range of treatments	Private	From £229 for 1 night stay
J	Private clinic	Integrated Medicine Practitioner	Private	£150

TABLE 9.6 *Sample of CAMs: settings and costs (January 2005)*

many local private gyms and health clubs now have CAM treatment rooms on the premises. CAMs are also sometimes provided on NHS premises. Table 9.6 lists two such examples (in a hospital out-patient department and in a community health centre), and there are also instances of CAMs clinics being established alongside GP surgeries.

Occasionally, short taster-sessions of various complementary therapies are on offer at exhibitions. The fully-clothed, brief massage treatment known as On-site massage is a popular attraction of this kind. Reflexology, too, can be given fairly easily in this kind of environment.

The cost of complementary therapies

Research by White, Resch and Ernst (1997) found that at the time of their study average fees for treatment ranged from £20 to £39 per hour. Table

9.6 suggests that this is still broadly the case, although some practitioners are charging much higher fees than this.

The fee to the user very much depends on the status of the practitioner (i.e. whether he or she is working as a sole trader, in a partnership or for another business), and also whether or not the practice itself has external funding, or must be self-supporting. Some practitioners are actually employed directly by the establishment that offers the therapies.

Example A in Table 9.6 is an instance of collaboration between an NHS Department and a group of Reiki practitioners. Special funding arrangements made it possible to lower the cost to users to £5 per person. Similarly, Example H was initially supported by Lottery funding. By creative management of resources, this health centre could offer free treatment sessions to users.

At the other end of the scale, private practitioners can command fees similar to those charged in private medical practice (Example J in Table 9.6). In-between are a range of practitioners who charge whatever is financially viable in relation to their circumstances. A massage therapist who provides treatment at a local gym, for example, will have to pay rent for the use of the treatment room. A practitioner who rents shop premises will have to take into account the cost of the lease or rent, business rates and cost of utilities (e.g. gas and electricity when calculating the charge to the user. All therapists will need to have indemnity insurance (see page 339), and the cost of this must also be built into the final charge per session. Prestigious establishments such as some health spas can charge higher fees, both to therapists renting their rooms, and directly to therapy users.

Summary

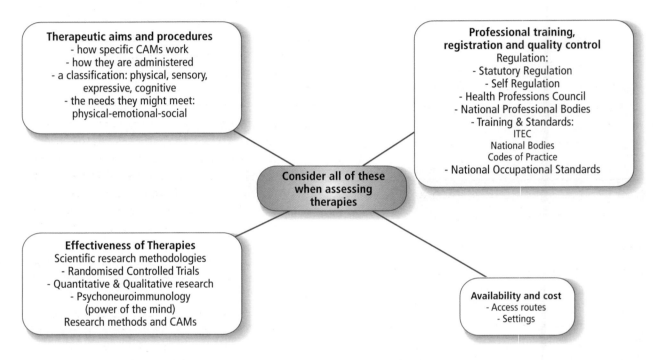

FIGURE 9.2 *Section 9.2 summary*

Consider this: Researching CAMs

Bob has recurrent chest infections, and is taking medication prescribed by his doctor. He has heard that homeopathy might help.

1. Where would you look to find information about research into the effectiveness of homeopathy?

2. From the information you discover, is there enough evidence to make a recommendation to Bob about whether he should try homeopathy?

9.3 Reasons for using CAMs

Why people choose CAMs

Research sponsored by the Prince of Wales's Foundation for Integrated Health (FIH) has highlighted several key reasons why people in Britain today are turning to CAMs (Ong and Banks 2003).

According to this study, patients expect:

* a comprehensive examination
* a satisfactory diagnosis
* effective treatment interventions
* freedom from unwanted side-effects.

The study also sets out both negative and positive reasons for the choice of CAM as a preferred treatment option. These are set out in Table 9.7.

NEGATIVE REASONS	POSITIVE REASONS
Poor outcome from conventional treatment	Good outcome from CAM treatment
Adverse effects from pharmaceutical drugs	Wanting to be an active participant in healthcare
Negative experience of doctor/patient relationship	Positive experience of CAM practitioner/ client relationship
Health views not in line with conventional model	Health views in line with CAM model

TABLE 9.7 *Reasons for Choosing CAMs*

Source: Ong and Banks, 2003, p.14

This research indicates that people who are likely to use CAMs are those who want to have a choice, and who want to take an active role in their own treatment. Such people reject the medical model of illness, which makes them into passive recipients of healthcare. They are more likely to take a holistic view of illness, in which a connection is made between illness, wellness, and all other aspects of a person's life (e.g. diet, lifestyle, beliefs etc.). People who use CAMs are likely to expect a positive working relationship with the practitioner, and to make the final decisions regarding the treatment given to them.

There are a number of other reasons why people may choose CAMs as an alternative to conventional medicine. Some people may object to conventional treatments on an ethical basis. They may strongly oppose the testing of drugs on animals, for example. Others may have religious reasons for objecting to conventional medical interventions such as blood transfusions. However, it should also be noted that some religious groups, such as Evangelical Christians, are deeply suspicious of the use of CAMs. The decision to use complementary therapies (or otherwise) will always be a very personal one.

Murcott (2005) identifies the rise in the number of untreatable chronic conditions as a significant factor contributing to patient dissatisfaction with conventional medicine. Paradoxically, increasing expectations of what medical science can do, and has done in the last century or so (as a result of the development of emergency medicine, transplantation techniques, immunisation and so on), has resulted in disappointment at medicine's failure to address problems such as cancers or diseases of the immune system. As Murcott puts it, 'we have been spoiled by a century of medical success' (2005, p. 30). Although biomedical science offers the possibility of tremendous breakthroughs (e.g. the Human Genome Project), nevertheless these are still in the future.

In the final analysis, people who choose CAMs want to feel empowered and in control of the treatment they receive. They value the special and close relationship that is integral to the therapeutic intervention, and they want to be listened to and treated as a whole person, not just a collection of symptoms.

This may account for the continuing popularity of CAMs, and popularity may be independent of the outcome of research studies.

Neeta is receiving conventional treatment for a chronic condition (arthritis), but she also visits a homeopath every month.

Her doctor tells her that she is wasting her money in visiting the homeopath, as in his opinion there is no medical evidence to support the effectiveness of this therapy.

However, Neeta says she derives great benefit from the treatment, and from the consultation sessions.

1. Why do you think that Neeta refuses to give up her consultations with the homeopath?

UNIT ASSESSMENT

Assessment evidence

To satisfy the requirements of this unit you will need to collect evidence from a range of sources. This will probably include printed reference books and websites.

Several books are listed in the resources section at the end of this Unit. However, you might find the following publications extremely helpful:

Barnett, Helen. (2002) *The Which? Guide to Complementary Therapies* London: Penguin

Pinder, Margot. (ed) (2005) *Complementary Healthcare: a guide for patients.* London: The Prince of Wales's Foundation for Integrated Health

Zollman, Catherine and Vickers, Andrew (2000) *ABC of Complementary Medicine.* London: BMJ Books

There are also some websites that are particularly useful. One is Bandolier which is run by scientists at Oxford University. This site includes data from systematic reviews, meta-analyses, randomised trials and observational studies. Another is that of the Cochrane Collection, which makes available information from systematic reviews of research.

In addition to these sources, interesting material can be collected from newspapers. *The Times*, for example, has a *Body and Soul* supplement on Saturdays. The *Daily Mail* often has articles about health, including features on aspects of complementary therapies.

You may also wish to interview someone who is a CAM-user or a CAMs practitioner. This could be someone you already know (e.g. a family member or a friend). Alternatively, your tutor may be able to arrange for you to meet a suitable person, perhaps at a social services unit, a health care centre or a voluntary sector day centre. You should approach the meeting courteously, and make sure that the person is happy to help you with this project. You will need to explain the project clearly before you start. It may also help to prepare some questions in advance. Your meeting should take place in a venue that is acceptable to the interviewee, and you should make sure that your conversation is private (especially if the person is sharing personal information with you).

Personal information should be kept confidential, and for presentation it will be essential to anonymise the data (i.e. to make it impossible for the person to be recognised). All this information should be stored securely.

As you collect data, it will be important to maintain a good filing system, so that you can find material easily when you come to present your evidence.

Assessment guidance

To satisfy the requirements of this Unit you must produce a report which includes a guide to three different therapies.

Your report must demonstrate competence in each of the following areas.

AO1 Knowledge and understanding

You will need to demonstrate how your three chosen therapies are used to promote health and/or to alleviate the symptoms of illness.

Higher marks will result if you demonstrate an understanding of the following key concepts:

* allopathic medicine
* medical model
* holistic approach
* the six principles of CAMs
* integrated medicine
* evidence-based medicine.

In describing your chosen therapies, good marks will be obtained by a clear description of the procedures used in each case. Higher marks will result if you explain how your chosen CAMs work with respect to cognitive, expressive and/or physical factors.

AO2 Application

You will need to show how a number of criteria have been used in order to assess the benefits of your three chosen therapies, including:

* the therapeutic aims and procedures used
* the training and qualifications of practitioners
* quality control systems for each therapy (e.g. regulatory bodies etc.)
* the potential effectiveness of the therapies
* potential cost to the user
* settings in which each CAM might be accessed.

It is important to remember the six principles of holistic therapies (see above, page 323). CAMs are person-centred, and therefore a key aspect of selecting a CAM for a person is that it should be acceptable to that person in every respect. CAMs are not 'prescribed' in the sense that allopathic medicines are.

AO3 Research and analysis

Marks will be allocated for the way in which you have gathered and presented your evidence.

Good research websites are listed in the Resources section of this unit, together with printed sources of information.

The Research Council for Complementary Medicine publishes a paper on the nature of research (RCCM 1999) which is available on the RCCM website. The information in this report may help you to evaluate some of the research items you identify when investigating your chosen therapies. The Prince of Wales's Foundation for Integrated Healthcare (FIH) has some excellent research papers and booklets which are downloadable.

Good marks will be obtained by:

* demonstrating that you have used a wide range of sources and resources in collecting your evidence

* providing a clear and accurate account of the interview with either a CAMs user or a practitioner.

Higher marks will be obtained by:

* accurate recording of data you collect

* thorough analysis of the information

* a clear statement of what you have found

* accurate referencing of sources.

AO4 Evaluation

To evaluate something is to assess it, in particular its worth, value or importance. When evaluating something, it is important to give a balanced view.

You will need to show knowledge of the potential advantages and disadvantages of the three chosen therapies.

Higher marks will be obtained by a balanced evaluation of each of the three therapies, which will include:

* an objective description of each one

* clear reference to existing research in evaluating each therapy

* an assessment of potential benefits

* guidance about potential disadvantages

* clear and helpful advice to anyone who is considering using each of these therapies.

References

Aldridge, D., Gustoff, G. and Neugebauer, L. (1995) A pilot study of music therapy in the treatment of children with developmental delay, *Complementary Therapies in Medicine*, **3** (4), 197-205

Altshuler, L. (2004) *Balanced Healing*, Harbor Press, Washington

Barnason, S., Zimmerman, L. and Nieveen, J. (1995) The effects of music interventions on anxiety in the patient after coronary artery bypass grafting, Bryan Memorial Hospital, Lincoln, USA. *Heart Lung* (United States), **24**(2), 124-132

Barnett, Helen (2002) *The Which? Guide to Complementary Therapies*, Penguin, London

Chopra, Deepak (1990) *Quantum Healing: Exploring the Frontiers of Mind-Body Medicine*, Bantam Books, New York

Chopra, Deepak (1993) *Ageless Body, Timeless Mind*, Random House, London

Cohen, S. et al (1991) Psychological stress and susceptibility to the common cold, *New England Journal of Medicine*, **325**, 606

Cohen, S., Tyrrell, D. A. and Smith, A. P. (1993) Negative life events, perceived stress, negative affect and susceptibility to the common cold, *Journal of Personality and Social Psychology*, **64** (1), 131-140

Cole, Jenny (1995) *Journeys (with a cancer)*, Pawprints, London

Donnellan, Craig (ed) (2004) Alternative Therapies, *Issues*, **81**. Independence, Cambridge

Ernst, E. and White, A. (2002) The BBC survey of complementary medicine use in the UK, *Complementary Therapies in Medicine*, **8**, 32-36.

Galland, Leo (1998) *Power Healing*, Random House, New York

Gerson, Scott (1993) *Ayurveda: The Ancient Indian Healing Art*, Element Books Ltd, Shaftesbury

Goldstein, Michael S. (1999) *Alternative Health Care: Medicine, Miracle or Mirage?*, Temple University Press, Philadelphia

Good. M. (1995) A comparison of the effects of jaw relaxation and music on postoperative pain, School of Nursing, Case Western Reserve University, *Nursing Research* (United States) **44** (1), 52-57, Cleveland

Halpern, Stephen (2001) *Points of Engagement: the integration of complementary and alternative medicine into NHS primary care*, The Foundation for Integrated Medicine, Occasional Paper 1, London

Hanser, S. B. and Thompson, L. W. (1994) Effects of music therapy strategy on depressed older adults, Stanford University School of Medicine, *Journal of Gerontology*, **49** (6), 265-269, United States

House of Lords Select Committee on Science and Technology, 6th Report, (2000) *Complementary and Alternative Medicine*, The Stationery Office, HL Paper 123, London

Kemp, C.A. (2004) Qigong as a therapeutic intervention with older adults, *Journal of Holistic Nursing*, **22** (4), 351-373

Kurtz, Paul (2000) In Defense of Scientific Medicine, in Wallace Sampson and Lewis Vaughn (eds) *Science Meets Alternative Medicine: What the evidence says about unconventional treatments*, pp.13-19, Prometheus Books, New York

Lantin, Barbara (2004) Draw out fear and stress, accessed at 7th October 2004

Martin, Paul (1997) *The Sickening Mind: Brain, Behaviour, Immunity and Disease*, Flamingo, London

Murcott, Toby (2005) *The Whole Story: Alternative Medicine on Trial?*, Macmillan, New York

National Institute for Clinical Excellence (NICE) (2003) *Multiple Sclerosis: Management of multiple sclerosis in primary and secondary care*, Clinical Guideline 8, National Institute for Clinical Excellence, London

Novey, Donald W. (2000) Basic Principles of Complementary/Alternative Therapies, in Donald W. Novey (ed) *Clincian's Complete Reference Guide to Complementary and Alternative Healthcare*, pp.5-7, Mosby, London

O'Mathuna, Donal P. (2000) Therapeutic Touch: What Could Be the Harm?, in Wallace Sampson and Lewis Vaughn (eds), *Science Meets Alternative Medicine: What the Evidence Says About Unconventional Treatments*, pp.227-243, Prometheus Books, New York

Ong, Chi-Keong and Banks, Bridget (2003) *Complementary and Alternative medicine: the consumer perspective*, The Prince of Wales' Foundation for Integrated Health, Occasional Paper 2, London

Pinder, Margot (ed) (2005) *Complementary Healthcare: a guide for patients*, The Prince of Wales' Foundation for Integrated Health, London

Research Council for Complementary Medicine (1999) *An Introduction to Research*

Sackett, D. L., Rosenberg, W. M. C., Muir Gray, J. A., Haynes, R. B. and Richardson, W. S. (1996) *Evidence-based Medicine: What it is and what it isn't*. Centre for Evidence-Based medicine

Sampson, Wallace and Vaughn, Lewis (eds) (2000) *Science Meets Alternative Medicine: What the Evidence Says About Unconventional Treatments*, Prometheus Books, New York

Thomas, K. J., Coleman, P., Nicholl, J. P. (2003) 'Trends in access to complementary or alternative medicines via primary care in England: 1995–2001. Results from a follow-up national study. *Family Practice* 205, 575–74

Tresidder, Andrew (2000) *Lazy Person's Guide to Emotional Healing*, Newleaf, Dublin

White, A., Resch, K.L. and Ernst, E., (1997) A survey of complementary practitioners' fees, practice and attitudes to working within the National Health Service, *Complementary Therapies in Medicine*, **5** (4), 210-214

Winter, M.J., Paskin, S., Baker, T. (1994) Music reduces stress and anxiety of patients in the surgical holding area, *Journal of Post-Anesthetic Nursing* (United States), **9** (6), 340-343

Zollman, Catherine and Vickers, Andrew (2000) *ABC of Complementary Medicine*, BMJ Books, London

Useful websites

Please see www.heinemann.co.uk/hotlinks (express code 1554P) for links to the websites of the following which may provide a source of information:

* British Acupuncture Council. Information about acupuncture, including research articles.

* Website of the Aromatherapy Organisations Council (AOC).

* Association of Reflexologists website. This organisation absorbed the Reflexologists Society from January 2005. Journal and website containing evidence-based healthcare information.

* British Association for Nutritional Therapy.

* Articles from the British Medical Journal published since 1998.

* Complementary Healthcare Information Service. Basic information about 70 complementary therapies, their history and practice.

* Website of the Cochrane Collaboration, which contains regularly updated healthcare databases. Systematic reviews of research are the main product. Information about careers and professions, including health and social care.

* European Herbal Practitioners Association.

* Website of the Prince of Wales's Foundation for Integrated Health. Many interesting papers and research information.

* General Chiropractic Council.

* The Society of Homeopaths' Website.

* Health Professions Council. The new (2005) regulatory body responsible for standards of professional training, performance and conduct of a number of healthcare professions. Articles about current research projects.

* International Therapy Examination Council (ITEC). Latest information about qualifications regulated by ITEC.

* National Institute for Clinical Excellence. Information about the latest guidelines for the clinical management of a number of conditions.

* Medicines and Healthcare Products Regulatory Agency.

* National Federation of Spiritual Healers website. Information about spiritual healing, access to registered practitioners and research into healing.

* Register of Nutritional Therapists.

* HMSO site. Many key government papers can be downloaded from here.

* Website of the journal *Positive Health*.

* Research Council for Complementary Medicine. An excellent source of information on research into CAMs.

* Sector Skills Council for health. Information on the development of Standards for health professions.

* Hypnotherapy Association website.

* UK Medicines Information website; contains safety information.

Psychological perspectives

You will learn about:

10.1 Different perspectives

10.2 Application and evaluation of perspectives

Introduction

The science of psychology is relatively new to health and social care, but is no less important than the treatment of the physical human body.

This unit challenges the idea that understanding behaviour is 'common sense', and shows how psychologists throughout history have tried to describe the reasons behind human actions. It is through scientific, evidence-based psychology, that a better understanding of human behaviour can be gained, ensuring that care givers have a greater depth of understanding of the human condition.

10.1 Different perspectives

This unit focuses on four main perspectives of psychology: behaviourism, cognitive, social and biological. Behaviourism gives us the technology needed for training and communicating but interprets people as mechanisms, whereas the cognitive perspective encourages individuals to take responsibility for their own health and with professional support to change or modify abnormal thoughts and feelings. Social psychologists place us within a complex society that offers a set of 'norms' within which behaviour is judged, measured and ultimately accepted or changed to fit. Finally, the biological perspective believes that every human is made up of genes, chemicals and electrical impulses. Through the use of drugs and technological intervention, modern medicine has learnt how to control, change and manipulate biologically initiated behaviour. All of these perspectives have an important role to play in maintaining good health and supporting patient-centred care.

The behaviourist perspective

Ivan Pavlov and Burrhus Skinner were two famous behaviourist psychologists. They believed that learning is the main force that controls our behaviour. By performing laboratory experiments they were able to show that the environment has an important part to play in how we act and interpret our surroundings.

It is important to remember that life experiences cause conditioning.

Behaviourists such as Skinner and Pavlov believed that we alter our behaviour due to external factors such as rewards and punishments or flashing lights. This is not the whole story. If I paid you £1 every time you told me that the world was flat, you could become quite rich. However, it is very unlikely that by you repeating the phrase 'the world is flat' that your knowledge or learning has really changed. Learning is many more things than just a collection of learnt responses or changing behaviour due to rewards or punishments. Learning must take into consideration every individual personal

development, life experiences, genetics and much more. In short, the ability to learn is highly individual and totally unique.

> ### Key concept
>
> *Operant conditioning:* learning to repeat an action that produces a favourable outcome.

Operant conditioning

Burrhus F. Skinner (1904–1990) wanted to show that learning is a consequence of our actions and we associate our actions with the pleasure (reward) or discomfort (punishment) that follows them. To demonstrate the belief that we learn from the consequence of our actions Skinner experimented on rats. He placed a hungry rat in a box (known as Skinner's Box), which contained a lever. When the rat pressed the lever a food pellet appeared. The rat learnt that he got food by pressing a lever, so he pressed it more and more often. This is known as the *law of reinforcement*. Reinforcement means to make stronger. The rat was rewarded immediately after it had pressed the lever. If there had been a delay in rewarding the rat then it would not have been so eager to act. Skinner found that the rat soon stopped pressing the lever if it was not rewarded with

> ### Key concept
>
> *Law of Reinforcement:* the probability of a response increases if that response is followed by a reward.

> ### Think it over...
>
> If every time you put your hand up in class to answer a question, the lecturer smiles and praises you, even if your answer is wrong, are you more or less likely to keep trying to answer questions? Why?

food. This is known as *experimental extinction*.

So far we have only considered positive reinforcement in the form of rewards. However operant conditioning is also involved in looking at punishment. Humans learn just as quickly to change a behaviour if it is followed by a punishment. Would you not put your hand up just as often to answer that question if you knew that not doing so meant a detention?

It is important to realise that Skinner's main emphasis should be strongly placed on positive reinforcement. It is possible to change behaviour through punishment, such as taking away playtime for badly behaved children, but punishment loses its effect after prolonged use. It is far better to praise and reward good behaviour than to punish bad behaviour.

Think it over...

Do you respond better to rewards or punishment?

Classical conditioning

If we are driving along a road and the traffic

Consider this

Fatima is two-years-old, she loves going to the supermarket with her mother. Fatima prefers to walk beside the shopping trolley and helping to take the food from the shelves. Like most two-year-olds she sometimes throws a tantrum if she cannot get her own way. Mum always ignores her behaviour and does not talk to her until she has calmed down. Once Fatima starts to behave properly again her mum gives her lots of attention and praise.

Where has the mother used punishment and where has she rewarded Fatima?

Think it over...

Imagine that you have to go to the dentist. As you lie in the reclining chair and gaze into the overhead mirror, you see an arrangement of instruments around you and you begin to feel frightened. Why are you frightened when the dentist has not caused you any pain? The sights and sounds around you have led you to predict that you are shortly to experience pain. This is called forming an association.

lights turns to red, we stop. The smell of baking bread may make our mouths water in anticipation of food. These simple associations help us to make sense of the world around us, by linking actions together. Forming associations between the stimulus of the dentist's surgery and the possibility of pain (as above) is known as *conditioning*.

Key concept

Classical conditioning: a form of learning, which involves the pairing of a stimulus with a response.

Considering how these associations are formed has been the work of many well-known psychologists. The Russian psychologist, Ivan Pavlov (1849–1936), performed laboratory experiments on animals to study the role of stimuli in forming associations and shaping behaviour. During experiments on dogs, Pavlov noted that their mouths watered, known as salivating (*unconditioned response*) before they were given food (*unconditioned stimulus*); in fact, the dogs salivated just at the sight of the person responsible for feeding them. The dogs had learned to anticipate food. Pavlov began to perform further experiments to test this process of association.

Key concept

Unconditioned response: a response in anticipation of an event.

Unconditioned stimulus: a reaction as a result of an event.

Think it over...

Do you think we can understand human behaviour by experimenting on animals?

Pavlov wanted to see if he could get a dog to make an association between the sound of a bell and food. He began by ringing a bell (new stimulus) immediately after food was given to the dog. He then went on to ring the bell but not feed the dog, to see what would happen. Eventually, the sound of the bell on its own (conditioned stimulus) could cause the dog to salivate (conditioned response).

Classical conditioning

What has all this bell ringing and dogs got to do with learning? Well, before the experiment the dog did not salivate at the sound of a bell, but after associating the bell with food the dog soon learnt to expect food when bells ring. The dog had learnt to change its behaviour as a result of an experience. It seems a big jump to relate the experiences of Pavlov's dog to human behaviour, but it's not as far as you think. Lipsitt (1990) was

Stage 1
Unconditioned stimulus

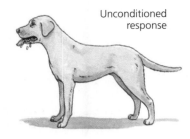

Unconditioned response

Stage 2
New Stimulus + unconditioned stimulus

Unconditioned response

Stage 3
Conditioned stimulus

Conditioned response

FIGURE 10.1 *Conditioning responses*

able to demonstrate that newborn babies were able to form a conditioned response (shutting eyes), to an unpleasant stimulus (puff of air). He began by blowing air into the babies' eyes accompanied by a sound (new stimulus). He was soon able to show that the babies would close their eyes when they heard the sound, 1.5 seconds before the puff of air (conditioned response).

FIGURE 10.2 *Pavlov's dog*

Shakara is in her third year of her nurse training. She has been asked to give a pain relief injection to a patient who is in a lot of pain and is crying out for some pain relief. Rushing to open the glass ampoule containing the drug, she accidentally cuts her finger. It hurts. The staff nurse on duty shows her that there is a piece of special equipment designed to help open glass ampoules, and she did not need to use her bare hands. Next time Shakara is preparing to give an injection the sight of the ampoule reminds her of the pain she suffered, so she quickly learns to use the proper ampoule opening equipment provided.

1. What did Shakara associate with opening glass ampoules using her bare hands?

2. How did she change her behaviour?

Jimmy aged 70, is a new resident at Beeches Nursing home. His favourite pastime is doing crossword puzzles in the daily paper. From time to time he knocks his glasses off the arm of his chair. Staff are quick to notice and pick them up for him. On these occasions staff usually smile or stop for a quick chat before returning to their work. Later, during staff handover, it has been noted that Jimmy has 'become particularly clumsy over the last few weeks, tending to drop his things more often than usual'. Staff show concern that Jimmy may have some coordination problems that cause him to drop things, and are considering informing his doctor.

How would behaviourists explain why Jimmy has become clumsier?

Conditioning behaviour is widely used in many different care settings. In schools children are given stickers or extra playing time for good behaviour. For disruptive behaviour the use of rewards or punishments is known as behaviour modification. One of the most common methods of modifying or changing behaviour is through a token economy.

Ayllon and Azrin (1968) set up a token economy with women patients who had been hospitalised for many years. The women could earn tokens (poker chips) by completing chores such as making their beds and getting dressed. Tokens could be swapped for pleasant activities such as watching a film or extra visits to the café. This token economy was very successful, greatly increasing the amount of chores the women did. A token economy is very effective in a controlled environment such as long-term hospitals or schools. Unfortunately, its effects stop when people return to normal life. In a world outside of care people are not constantly rewarded for good behaviour. Society expects people to behave without continual praise and stickers.

The case study above shows that Jimmy gets positive reinforcement for knocking his reading glasses off the arm of his chair. When the staff return his glasses to him they may smile or stop and chat, reinforcing his behaviour with a pleasurable outcome for Jimmy. The first few times Jimmy lost his glasses and received a smile, he would have formed an association between losing his glasses, and the staff smiling, as predicted by Pavlov. Jimmy soon learnt to act on this association and knock his glasses off on purpose to get attention. Skinner's theory would suggest that Jimmy learnt to perform an action, or change his behaviour, to receive a reward in the form of a smile or company. Care staff need to change their behaviour to modify Jimmy's behaviour. Instead of smiling when returning the glasses to Jimmy, the staff should ignore him and just return the glasses, and Jimmy would not repeatedly drop them. Skinner places emphasis on rewarding good behaviour. In the case of Jimmy, the staff need to spend more time with him when he shows behaviour that is appropriate, such as, for example, helping him with his crosswords.

BEHAVIOUR	OUTCOME	CONSEQUENCE
Drop reading glasses	A smile or chat from staff	Behaviour reinforced
	Glasses returned to Jimmy	Glasses dropped again

TABLE 10.1 *Reinforcing behaviours*

Cognitive perspective

Behaviourism ignores a key aspect of human behaviour: the ability to think things through and make rational decisions. People's thoughts, their beliefs, opinions, motivations and so on, clearly have an impact on their behaviour. The cognitive perspective is an area of psychology that deals with the invisible area of thought. Try, for example, to answer the question, ' What is thought? '. You can see this is a difficult question to answer and it is just as difficult to describe cognitive psychology. One of the most important aspects of cognitive psychology is to look at how information is processed by the brain. This section will look at how humans make sense of the world in which they live by making schema. Sometimes these schema are inaccurate or false and can lead to abnormal behaviour, such as Anorexia Nervosa and Depression, two areas that can be helped by cognitive therapies.

Schema

We have many expectations in our daily lives. For example, we expect a bus to arrive if we stand at a bus stop for long enough. We expect to be served in the supermarket if we wait in the queue at the till.

The list you have written is your schema about eating in a restaurant. Bower et al. (1979) also asked people (participants) to list the things they would expect to happen in a restaurant. He then read them a story about going to a restaurant and asked them to repeat back the story from memory. The people tended to add sections to the story that were not included originally. They told Bower what they expected to happen, i.e. pay the bill and order from a menu. The participants had formed their own schema about restaurants. This schema was so strong that it interfered with their memory of the story. We all use schema to make sense of the world. Schemas are very important when it comes to filling in the gaps in our understanding.

Read the following sentences:

* Mary is in pain.

* She is nine months' pregnant.

* Her husband is getting her overnight bag out of the car.

By now you have probably made several assumptions about Mary. Mary has arrived at hospital with her husband; she is in labour and is about to have her baby. Note none of these points were made in the above sentences, you filled in the gaps from your own schema about what you think is happening. Mary, nine months pregnant, could have just as easily stubbed her toe as she got out of the car, at the hotel where she and her husband are staying for the night.

It is natural that we fill in the gaps to help us understand what is happening. The information we fill in comes from our schema; we draw from our schema to make sense of the information present. Schema change and grow by assimilation and accommodation. Our schema about what to expect in a restaurant does not fit if you try to apply it to going to eat at McDonald's.

FIGURE 10.3 *Assimilating and accommodating*

The first time you ate in a restaurant you will have added to your McDonald's schema to adapt it to the new experience. Your schema will include items such as menus, knives and forks and asking for a bill. This is called assimilation. When we cannot assimilate new information into an existing schema we need to change our schema; this is known as accommodating. Think back to our example of Mary. If you were present when Mary was in pain, you may have noticed that she was in pain at regular five minute intervals (contracting), indicating that she was in the advanced stages of labour. Now you know this new fact, you can accommodate or change your schema about 'labour'.

Stereotyping

The schema we form influences our perceptions of other people. When we consider a particular group of people we think about a set of superficial characteristics, such as skin colour or nationality. The schema we have constructed is best known as a stereotype.

Stereotype: categorisation of people on the basis of superficial features.

Where do stereotypes come from? They are formed from many different influences such as parents, life experiences and the media.

Think about the stereotypes you associate with being old. List them as positive and negative.

1. Which list is the longer?

2. Why is one list longer than the other?

3. How did you form your stereotypes?

4. Does your list have similarities with anyone else's list?

The negative stereotypes that many people have about the elderly may be due to the fact that the elderly are almost invisible in the media. Only 2.3 per cent of fictional characters on the television are over the age of 65 (Gerbner et al.). Negative images of the elderly are very rarely contradicted with positive ones. Have you ever seen pictures of old people taking part in a sporting activity or at a party? If you had no experience of being around the elderly, the schema you form about them will probably be based upon stereotypes.

Self-fulfilling prophecy

When we meet people we often have expectations about the way in which they are likely to behave; these expectations are often based on stereotypes that influence how we interpret behaviour. How we behave towards others often leads to their behaving in such a way that confirms expectations we have about them. This is known as the self-fulfilling prophecy.

> **Key concept**
>
> *Self-fulfilling prophecy:* a prediction that comes true simply because people believe in it.

Suppose you were told that Sarah was a friendly and loving child. When you meet her, this expectation about her behaviour may lead you to be friendly and kind towards her. This may then cause her to act in a friendly way towards you. Therefore, you have confirmed your original expectations of what kind of child Sarah is.

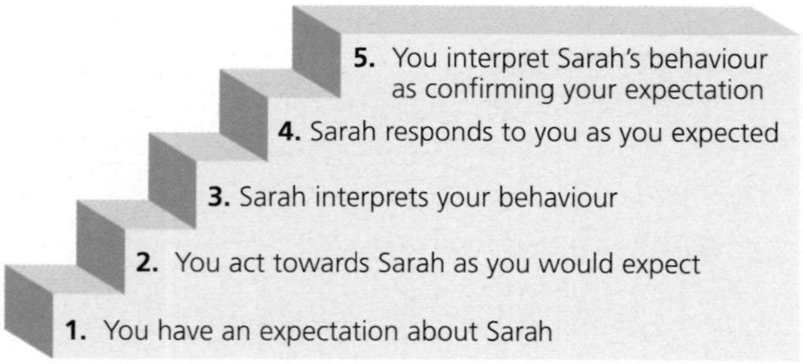

5. You interpret Sarah's behaviour as confirming your expectation

4. Sarah responds to you as you expected

3. Sarah interprets your behaviour

2. You act towards Sarah as you would expect

1. You have an expectation about Sarah

FIGURE 10.4 *Steps involved in self-fulfilling prophecy*

False cognitions

A good example of how our cognitions can be false, or even inaccurate, was highlighted by Rosenhan (1973). Rosenhan asked eight of his friends to pretend they had symptoms associated with schizophrenia, in order to be admitted into psychiatric hospitals. The participants in the experiment were to deceive the staff of several hospitals into thinking that they were real patients; this would be seen as unethical today. But, the trick worked, and they managed to get admitted for treatment. Once inside the hospital they were to stop pretending to be ill, and to try and get discharged without telling the staff that they were part of an experiment. Amazingly, the staff treated Rosenhan's friends as mentally ill patients, often ignoring their requests for information. The staff had formed an inaccurate set of cognitions about the pretend patients, based upon a schema formed about 'mentally ill people'. On average it took the pretend patients three weeks to get out of the psychiatric hospitals, even though there was nothing wrong with them. This example shows us how we rely on schema to help us to decide how to act, and even if those schema are wrong we find it difficult to change them and behave differently.

Changing behaviour from unhealthy to healthy is often the job of health promotion information. Health promotion is designed to makes us think about our behaviour and change it to some thing more appropriate. By understanding how decisions about health are made, and which beliefs are important in making decisions, we may be able to get people to change their behaviour.

Hochbaum (1958) looked at the reasons why people respond to health promotion. Following his research a health belief model was devised. This showed that people firstly consider if they feel that they are personally at risk. They then consider if the benefits of changing their behaviour are greater than the benefits of continuing behaviour. Consider a person who smokes. Before he is prepared to change his behaviour he must decide in what way he will benefit from stopping smoking. He will consider whether the possibility of preventing diseases such as lung cancer and heart disease is of greater benefit than smoking with his friends. The health belief model purports that people must perceive a threat in order to decide to modify their behaviour and then believe that the change has more benefits than costs.

FIGURE 10.5 *Weighing up benefits and costs*

The goal of cognitive therapy is to change abnormal behaviour by changing the way people think. The cognitive perspective sees mental disorders as resulting from distortions of people's cognitions. The aim of cognitive-based therapies is to demonstrate to people that their irrational or inaccurate thoughts are the main reasons behind their difficulties. An example of this would be a woman who shows signs of depression who may say 'I can never do anything right ' or 'Nobody will ever love me '.

If false ways of thinking can be modified or changed, then disorders can be alleviated.

Albert Bandura (1925) suggested that 'people control their behaviour by internal thought processes', i.e. we talk to ourselves. That is, we learn by internal reinforcement. People convince themselves to do something or believe something; they then act on this belief. People with depression tend to favour memory for negative information, which when continually internalised reinforces a state of depression. This is a cycle that is hard to break out of.

Attribution theory looks at how we as individuals attribute cause to events that may happen around us or with in us.

> **Key concept**
>
> *Attribution theory:* the process of assigning causes to things that happen.

For example, a 16-year-old girl with Anorexia Nervosa may attribute the causes of her disease to the pictures of skinny models in the magazines she reads, or to the belief that she deserves the disease for not being pretty enough. However inaccurate attributions may be, they become important parts of our view of the world and may affect our emotional well-being and self-esteem. One of the most influential psychologists who was concerned with looking at disorders from a cognitive perspective was Aaron Beck. Beck based his theories on the negative beliefs that people hold about themselves, especially those suffering from conditions such as depression. He suggested that depression results from three types of negative thinking:

✳ the self: 'I am a real failure'

✳ the world: 'Awful things happen around me'

✳ the future: 'I'm always going to be like this'.

> ## SCENARIO
>
> ### Carol
>
> Hayleigh is a District Nurse. She is 38-years-old, her husband died recently of a heart attack. She has two children aged 7 and 11. Her family live a three-hour drive away and she feels totally alone. At work she lacks interest or motivation. At home she would sit and look at photos of her husband. She stopped taking the children to after-school activities. Carol was convinced that she deserved to lose her husband and that she was a bad mother. She felt that she was no good at her job and that her friends did not like her. When she began to have panic attacks about leaving the house, she sought help from her GP, who diagnosed depression.

Beck believed that people form negative schema about themselves, which cause them to get depressed. Cognitive therapy involves 'standing back' from events and looking at them from an outsider's point of view, then trying to decide what the facts really are; not what Carol, for example, thinks are the facts. Finally, try to look at a more positive alternative view to the world. Through this in-depth process of looking at her own beliefs, and the thoughts that make her depressed, Carol can begin to help herself out of her depression.

Patients with depression are often helped by receiving counselling. Counsellors must have an in-depth understanding of at least one or more of the psychological perspectives. Cognitive therapy takes the view that human unhappiness and problems are often caused by the way we think about and understand our lives. Cognitive therapy aims to help people to re-examine and change the way they think. Cognitive behavioural approaches combine an emphasis on thinking processes with a focus on creating changes in behaviour. Cognitive counsellors do not try to interpret what the client says and do not aim to change the client's behaviour. The job of the counsellor is to help clients to understand how their thinking has 'gone off the rails'. A person might come to counselling saying things like: 'I can't go on, I failed my last test, I've got no future'. A cognitive behaviour counsellor would attempt to challenge these statements and bring out the irrational thinking into the open. The therapist tries to separate the emotion of distress from the thought processes which help to maintain the distress.

Another method of clinical therapy that is used to change thought processes is based on a theory developed by George Kelly (1955). Kelly argued that people have a great need to predict the behaviour of others. In doing so we feel safe and assured about the world we live in. To predict other people's behaviour we each form a set of personal constructs that we use to make sense of the world around us and help us to form impressions about other people.

Each construct has two opposite ends, for example:

* kind – cruel

* frightening – gentle

* confident – anxious.

We form our constructs from our parents' beliefs or environmental factors that have influenced our lives. If your parents attached importance to politeness you might have a polite – rude personal construct. As a result you may pay much more attention to how polite or rude other people are.

Think it over...

List some personal constructs that you consider important. How do these constructs influence your attitudes and behaviour towards other people?

Kelly was interested in helping people with conditions such as schizophrenia to change their personal constructs. People with schizophrenia have a loss of contact with reality and distorted thoughts and emotions. Through therapy exercises such as role-play, Kelly believed that people can practise changing personal constructs in a safe environment to see if it helps them to cope with reality. Advantages to Kelly's theory are that it takes into account individual cognitive processes which if necessary can be changed with clinical treatment. Unfortunately Kelly's theory only considers constructs that the individual is consciously aware of and does not consider that factors such as emotion or social expectations are as important.

Social influence

No man is an island. It is almost impossible for individuals to exist without the society they live in influencing their behaviour. Humans are social animals; they seek the attention and approval of others, but at what cost? We may all consider ourselves as individuals, but once we seek the company of others we become a member of a group. Groups do not allow their members to act in any way that may risk their existence. So as a member of a group you are forced to conform, change or leave, such is the strength of the social influences placed upon you.

Conformity

The social comparison theory suggests that we need our own views, beliefs and opinions to be accepted and recognised by others, so we seek out groups of people whose opinions we value. We have more confidence in our opinions and ourselves if other people share them.

Somebody who smokes is more likely to continue smoking if all their friends smoke as well. Their behaviour is being reinforced and accepted by the group members. Would they feel the same if they were the only one in the group who smoked?

The other people who we compare ourselves with must be similar to us in ways that we feel are relevant to our lives, i.e. smoking, fashion and career aims. By looking for people similar to ourselves we are able to make comparisons between their opinions and ours. But, what happens if the people we find that are similar to us disagree with our opinions? In this situation we must adapt or change our own beliefs to become more similar and therefore conform, or leave the group.

SCENARIO

Shena is 11-years-old. She has just started secondary school and has made a good group of friends that she feels she has a lot in common with. Jasmine, a friend of Shena's from her old school, is also in the class. Shena's group of new friends choose to ignore Jasmine at break times and do not invite her to go with them after school. Shena is very uncomfortable with the situation. To stay in the group she must conform and ignore Jasmine or leave the group.

Does she have any other options?

People fear rejection from a group and often pay a high price of conforming to remain a member of a group and therefore receive its support and sometimes even its protection. In order to remain a member of the group, Shena must shun her friend Jasmine. This would be the price she must pay to keep the respect and support of her new friends. Is the price too high?

Asch (1955) clearly demonstrated the tendency of individuals to conform to the views of other members of the group. Asch devised an experiment where one subject was seated in a room with six other people who were part of the experiment. The seven people sat in a line with the subject in position five. Remember the subject does not know that the others are in on the experiment. They were then shown a card with three lines drawn on it and labelled A, B and C. They were also shown a card with one line drawn on it and asked to say if the line was the same length as A, B or C.

A   B   C

Asch noticed that if four or more people who were in on the experiment all said the wrong answer (on purpose), the subject usually also said the wrong answer. He would lie about the correct answer to conform with the group. If the group were shown a line that was the same length as line C and everyone said A, the subject would also say A, even though he knew the answer was C. It is interesting to think about how much a group member is prepared to change to ensure he or she fits into the group.

SCENARIO

Doris is 80-years-old and a resident of Silver Birch Residential House. When the care assistant asks the residents what they would like for lunch, they each in turn say fish. Doris hates fish. Doris is the last to be asked what she would like to eat and says fish instead of ham, which she would really have preferred.

Individuals take on roles to fit in. Once a person has taken on a role that is expected of them, it can become so much a part of them that efforts are made to act appropriately in that role at all costs. The person must not appear to 'lose face', as that would mean losing their identity within the group.

The expected roles of the group are called the norms of the group. If members do not conform to the group norms they risk being expelled from the group. Being a member of a group can affect individual behaviour in many ways. Individuals may be expected to challenge their personal moral beliefs, as in Joanne's case, or even take part in acts of violence. The power of group roles and rules determine much of a group's behaviour. Campbell (1981) observed aggression in groups of teenage girls and boys. Each gang had its own norms regarding how they expected their members to behave. Within a female gang there are rules. Girls are expected not to take on more than one opponent at a time, not to use bottles or knives and not to report a fight to the authorities. For a member to remain in a gang she is expected to follow the norms of the gang.

Social identity

Henri Tajfel (1978), believed that everyone has a number of social identities, based upon the different groups they belong to such as race, gender, social group, fan club, sports team.

Another aspect of social identity is that of increasing our self-esteem by regarding the groups we belong to as superior to all other groups. Tajfel was able to demonstrate the importance of in-groups (the group you belong to) and out-groups (the other groups) rivalry. He put boys aged 14–15 years old into random groups and asked them to allocate points to the members of their group and the other group. These points were then to be exchanged for money. The members could choose to distribute the points fairly or to favour their group or the other group. Most boys chose to distribute the points unfairly, giving fewer points to the members of the other group, even if it meant that they received fewer points themselves. The

boys discriminated against the other group. By discriminating against groups in society we increase the importance of our own group, therefore increasing the self-esteem of its members. It is easy to see why prejudice is formed. By categorising outer-groups it gives inner groups something to discriminate against, i.e. townies, Goths, punks.

Peer pressure

The actual influence that peer pressure has on adolescents was argued against by Lightfoot in 1992. He found that adolescents were aware of an interest in their peers' way of doing things but did not feel pressurised to copy them and conform. One of the main reasons why adolescents wish to conform may not be due to peer pressure but to a wish for identification with a group. Members of a group wish to dress similarly, listen to the same music, have the same ideals, not because they are under pressure to do so, but because they identify with each other, they feel they belong.

How can studies such as Tajfel, Campbell and Lightfoot be applied to everyday situations? Understanding why groups are formed and the pressure imposed on its members to conform helps us to understand why groups are important within society. Groups have many functions. They maintain and question the morals of a society, for example, Christianity, Fathers for Justice, peace marches and pro-hunting groups. Groups can even support acts of violence or risk taking.

> **Think it over...**
>
> Can you list any groups that allow its members to commit acts of aggression or violence?

Your list may have included our previously mentioned teenage gangs, but what about football hooligans and some animal rights' or peace protesters?

Biological perspective

The biological perspective has dominated the study of behaviour for hundreds of years. Its roots are in the belief that behaviour is due to the physical structure and function of the brain. The relevance of biology to psychology can be illustrated through behaviour such as eating, drug taking and the use of stimulants such as caffeine and nicotine. To understand the application of the biological perspective to psychology, we must first understand the normal structure and function of the brain and nervous system. It is only then that we can study abnormal behaviour as a result of change or damage to these organs. This section will look at two areas of the biological perspective that may explain human behaviour. Firstly, it considers the influence that genes and heredity, play in making us who we are. Secondly it looks closely at how environmental factors can affect neurotransmitters and hormones in the nervous system.

The brain is one of the most complicated organs in the body. It is responsible for regulating the body. The brain controls temperature, blood flow, digestion, and monitors our sensations, breathing and heart rate. It directs our behaviour, tells us to jump, dance, cry or laugh. Every movement and behaviour we show is firstly initiated by the brain.

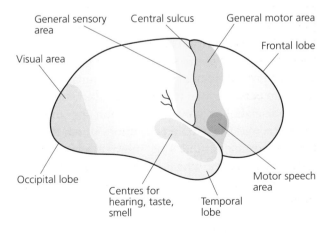

FIGURE 10.6 *The function of the brain*

The brain has only one method of communication, whether an activity is voluntary or involuntary. The brain works by sending and receiving information in electrical and chemical impulses. The brain initiates simple signals, sent at different rates along neurones. Nerve cells, or neurones, collected together make up the nervous system. Neurones carry information to and fro between the central nervous system (brain and spinal cord) and various areas of the body.

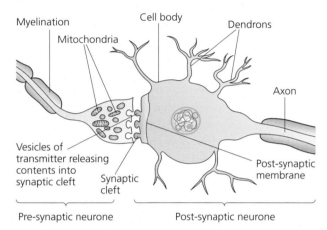

Neurones come in various shapes and sizes, from very small to over a metre long. Each individual neurone carries a small electrical impulse, very much like a battery. When the electrical charge is constant within the neurone then this is known as 'resting'. When the voltage increases or decreases the cell is said to be 'active'. The wave of electrical charge, or wave of excitation, travels down the neurone until it reaches the branching end or the synaptic knob. The gap between two neurones is called the synaptic cleft. The wave of excitation appears to 'jump' across the gap and continues down the post-synaptic neurone. This 'jump' is a result of neurotransmitters, which flood the gap between the two neurones and trigger of receptors on the post-synaptic cell. After the pre-synaptic neurone has fired there is a rest period before it fires again. During this rest period neurotransmitters return to the pre-synaptic neurone. This is called re-uptake. Once the receptors on the post-synaptic neurone have been triggered the wave of excitation becomes transformed into a chemical signal at the synaptic cleft in order that it can

continue its journey. Neurotransmitters are very important in ensuring that the wave of excitation can be transmitted effectively. The brain has hundreds of different neurotransmitters. For example:

* Dopamine – responsible for 'pleasure seeking' and rewarding behaviour. Drug taking increases dopamine production therefore increasing the desire to seek pleasurable activities.

* Serotonin – controls sleep, loss of serotonin causes insomnia. The drug LSD stops serotonin acting effectively, resulting in hallucinations and distorted perception.

Another important way that the brain controls the body is through the neuroendocrine system. The pituitary gland is the control centre for the endocrine system. It is buried deep within the brain and is responsible for coordinating hormone production in glands such as the adrenal and thyroid glands. A hormone is a chemical messenger molecule, larger than a neurotransmitter. Hormones are secreted by glands into the bloodstream, where they travel to locations in order to stimulate the secretion of other hormones. A drop in blood glucose (sugar) levels causes the pituitary gland in the brain to send a signal to the adrenal glands to produce the hormone adrenaline. Adrenaline then causes the liver to secrete glycogen and increase the blood sugar level. The increase in blood sugar increases our energy levels, which will alter our behaviour from tired and lethargic to energetic and responsive. Some stimulants, such as caffeine, cause this adrenaline–glucose cycle to start without a drop in blood glucose levels, therefore changing behaviour.

The brain and nervous system work together to maintain *homeostasis*. By constantly sending electrical and chemical impulses throughout the body the brain ensures that we know: when we are hungry; to put on more clothes when we are cold and take them off again if we get hot. The brain works hard all the time to keep the body in balance and does the same with our feelings and emotions. When feelings of boredom set in, the brain triggers off behaviour to increase levels of arousal. If we get too stressed, excited, or agitated we adopt behaviour to calm down. Many of the behaviours we show are motivated by the need to achieve an optimum level of arousal at which we function best. Everyone's optimum level is different and changes throughout the day. Exercise, music, coffee, studying and rest all change the level of arousal in the body. Consequently, the brain sends chemical and electrical impulses to change behaviour and bring our level of arousal back to its optimum level.

Think it over...

You are working in a nursing home when you notice that Doris has been sitting in her chair for several hours and appears lethargic and withdrawn.

How could you help her to increase her arousal to its optimum level?

Sometimes, as in the case of Doris, we are unable to increase our own arousal levels due to lack of mobility, or physical and mental disabilities. To help Doris increase her levels you may have thought of: playing her music, talking to her, doing an activity with her or just offering her a cup of tea which would, of course, contain caffeine which is a stimulant.

Genes

The nucleus of every cell in the human body (except sperm and egg cells) contains forty-six chromosomes. These chromosomes are composed of twisted strands of deoxyribonucleic acid, DNA. The DNA on each thread carries units of information called genes. From the moment of conception, genes act with environmental factors to influence every aspect of our body's structure and function, from skin colour, height and eye colour to intelligence and personality. Every human being results from the fusion of two cells into a single cell. An egg from the mother joins with a sperm cell from the father. The gene carrying chromosomes from the mother's egg is paired with the gene carrying chromosome from the sperm. The newly formed cell has its own unique set of chromosomes. This new cell multiplies many millions of times to produce,

well, you. Unfortunately, this cell multiplication is subjected to environmental factors that can influence the whole process.

Think it over...

Where did the first two genes that made you come from? Was it your parents or many thousands of generations before them?

Genes and personality

The biological perspective assumes that individual differences in personality may occur because of heredity, that is the genes we inherit from our natural parents. Many personality theorists have argued that personality consists of a number of traits, and it is these traits that are important in determining our personality, not the situation we find ourselves in.

Key concept

Traits: a broad characteristic used to describe and explain behaviour, i.e. talkative, outgoing and shy.

Trait theorists, such as Eysenck, feel that personality can be studied scientifically, relying on analysing results of questionnaires to identify types of personality. They emphasised the importance of biology and genes in determining personality. They did not believe that individual thought had anything to do with personality. They also argued that personality does not change as people grow older but remains the same. Eysenck's theory is based around the belief that people are extraverts or introverts or somewhere in between. Introverts are shy and tend to study a situation carefully before acting, whereas extraverts are more sociable, impulsive and risk takers. He explained his theory by arguing that introversion and extraversion is due to the amount of activity in the brain (arousal). Extraverts have very little arousal so seek out situations that provide them with more arousal. Introverts have too much arousal and look for situations that are quieter to dampen down their level of arousal. This makes sense if you look carefully at the behaviour of extraverts and introverts.

If introversion and extraversion has a biological basis as Eysenck suggests, it therefore follows that personality can be inherited. It is clear that genes are very important in determining physical characteristics, but can they also be responsible for our personalities? One way of studying the importance of genes in forming personality is to look at studies performed on identical twins (monozygotic twins) that were separated at birth. Identical twins have the same genes as they were both formed from the same egg and sperm after fertilisation. Non-identical twins (fraternal twins) share no more similar genes than any other brother and sister would, as they come from different eggs and sperm.

Occasionally, identical twins are separated at birth and brought up by a different set of parents. Therefore, any similarities in the twins could be due to genetics not their environment. Bouchard (1981) studied two brothers who had not met or known each other since being separated at birth. These brothers showed remarkable similarities in their lives since birth. They were both named Jim by their adoptive families and both were security officers; they both enjoyed carpentry and had both built a white bench around a tree in the garden. They dressed the same; they both married twice and their wives had the same names.

Further studies on twins (Shields, 1979), show that the introvert and extravert scores of identical twins bought up separately were found to be very similar. Their scores were closer than the scores of fraternal twins separated at birth. Studies such as those of Shields and Bouchard would indicate that personality may be influenced by genetics, as identical twins separated at birth have similar personality traits.

It would be wrong say that because identical twins have similar personalities, personality must be genetic based. This statement excludes environmental factors and studies that did not find similarities. Loehlin and Nichols (1976) found that parents of identical twins are more likely than parents of fraternal twins to treat them exactly the same. They also found that twins that are treated the same are more likely to have a similar level of intelligence.

It is difficult to say that personality is purely genetic based. The evidence of Loehlin and Nichols suggests that the way in which we are treated by others, and our personal life experiences, may have a strong influence on shaping who we are.

Stimulants

Stimulants and drugs intensify mood, increase alertness, and make you less tired. Drugs and stimulants, such as caffeine and nicotine, stimulate neurotransmitters at the synapses. Drugs interfere with the re-uptake of neurotransmitters, which results in erratic and uncontrolled nerve impulses and this can disrupt levels of consciousness. Dopamine is a neurotransmitter responsible for 'pleasure seeking' behaviour, which causes the person to actively seek rewards, such as food. Drugs, caffeine and nicotine all increase the production of dopamine, which causes us to seek more pleasure and therefore helps to maintain the dependency on the drug.

Alcohol produces particular effects on the body. Alcohol affects the central nervous system; depending on the amount consumed, these effects will range from relaxation and a reduction in levels of anxiety, to serious coordination difficulties. Alcohol passes straight from the digestive system into the bloodstream and is then transported around the body to areas such as the brain. Alcohol first acts on the brain stem; this can result in behaviour such as losing inhibitions, risk taking, exhibitionism and rowdiness. Continual use then affects the brain's cortex area, resulting in lack of muscle control and

can cause depressing thoughts. Alcohol also acts directly on nerves, making them less able to detect signals such as pain, which explains the anaesthetic abilities of alcohol.

Caffeine causes the pituitary gland to produce hormones that affect the adrenal glands, causing an increase in the amount of adrenaline that is released into the bloodstream. Adrenaline is the 'fight or flight' hormone. The 'fight or flight' mechanism is designed to enable us to make quick decisions and responses to sudden or threatening situations. Caffeine causes the body to produce hormones that allow us to tap into this protective mechanism whenever we want, resulting in an increase in attention and an extra boost of energy. Caffeine acts biologically on our body to change our behaviour by giving us a short acting energy burst.

Nicotine acts in a very similar way to drugs and caffeine. There are cholinergic receptors in the brain that are sensitive to nicotine; the continual presence of nicotine causes these receptors to become tolerant of the presence of nicotine. Once these receptors become desensitised a higher level of nicotine is needed to maintain normal brain function.

Summary

This section has described some of the major psychological perspectives and theories that are used to explain human behaviour.

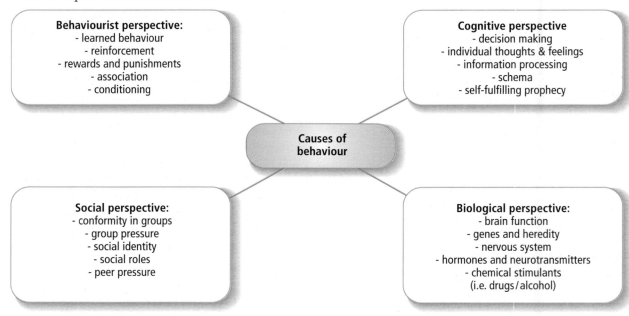

Behaviourist perspective:
- learned behaviour
- reinforcement
- rewards and punishments
- association
- conditioning

Cognitive perspective
- decision making
- individual thoughts & feelings
- information processing
- schema
- self-fulfilling prophecy

Causes of behaviour

Social perspective:
- conformity in groups
- group pressure
- social identity
- social roles
- peer pressure

Biological perspective:
- brain function
- genes and heredity
- nervous system
- hormones and neurotransmitters
- chemical stimulants (i.e. drugs/alcohol)

FIGURE 10.7 *Section 10.1 summary*

Consider this

Stephen is 17 years old. One night Stephen decides to take his girlfriend, Jenny, out on his new motor bike, against his parent's wishes. Unfortunately, they have an accident and Stephen is admitted to hospital with many severe bone fractures. Jenny was not hurt.

Whilst he is in hospital he is visited frequently by many of his friends who enjoy hearing him retell the story of his accident. After the first few weeks the ward staff become concerned about his poor recovery. Stephen is requiring increasing amounts of pain-killing drugs, more than would be expected at this stage of his recovery. He is also showing signs of anxiety when his parents visit and makes excuses not to see them.

1. How is the behaviourist's perspective affecting Stephen's recovery?

2. As the nurse in charge how would you change Stephen's care?

3. How is the fact that Stephen is a boy influencing his recovery?

4. Why should Stephen be referred to a counsellor?

5. Are there any other factors that could be influencing Stephen's recovery?

10.2 Application and evaluation of perspectives

Control and autonomy

Having outlined four of the major psychological perspectives it is important to consider how this knowledge can be applied to health and care. A better understanding of the amount of control and the level of autonomy individuals can exert over their own behaviour may help us to predict abnormal reactions and therefore anticipate any difficulties that may arise.

Predicting behaviour

Many psychologists treat the study of people and their behaviour as a science like any other. The basic idea is that the behaviour of humans can be manipulated and predicted in the same way that chemicals would be in a chemistry experiment; and given enough time and resources it is possible to discover all the causes of behaviour. When carrying out experiments psychologists decide what they are going to manipulate and predict the results that that manipulation would have. The following section considers how the baby forms an attachment with its mother, a predictable behaviour that ensures survival.

Think it over...

What predictable behaviour does a newborn baby show to ensure that its mother cares for it?

John Bowlby (1969) believed that a human baby's behaviour is predictable, as it is purely designed to ensure that it survives. He was very interested in studying the relationship between babies and their mothers, and how they bonded with each other after birth. At birth, babies are physically helpless, needing food, care, love and warmth to survive. The baby must modify its behaviour and form attachments with its carers to ensure that it thrives. It is likely that babies are born with a built-in (innate) ability to form attachments, as this would ensure that they are

fed and looked after. Adults must also have the innate ability to bond so that they become attached to and care for their young. Bowlby was very interested in researching the purpose of attachment, and believed that attachment or 'bonding' is an inherited behaviour and therefore predictable in all humans and animal infants.

If we think of attachment as predictable behaviour, behaviourists would describe bonding in the following ways:

Classical conditioning The newborn baby is born with reflexes. Food from its mother (unconditional stimuli) produces pleasure (unconditional response). The person providing the food is associated with pleasure and becomes the conditioned stimuli. The person who feeds the baby becomes associated with pleasure and the predicted behaviour of attachment is shown.

Operant conditioning Moves this theory forward by suggesting the baby starts the food/pleasure cycle by crying. The mother feeds the baby when it cries; the baby enjoys the experience and has consequently formed an association between crying and its reward of being fed.

Further studies tested the hypothesis that attachment could be due to conditioning, and have shown that this is not a detailed enough explanation to fully understand such a complex behaviour. Scientific studies on young Rhesus monkeys (Harlow and Harlow 1962) have shown that when baby monkeys were presented with two cylinders that gave out milk, one bare and one covered in towelling material, the monkeys bonded with the towelling-covered cylinder. They also used the towelling-covered cylinder as a comforter when they were scared or frightened. This experiment shows that attachment is more than just a need for food as both cylinders gave out food. The young monkeys, like human beings, also needed comfort, care and love to form an attachment. Attachment to the towelling-covered 'mother' was not enough, as the monkeys grew up

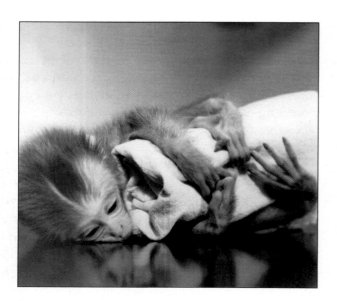

Harlow and Harlow's experiment

violent and abusive and unable to interact with other monkeys. This shows that contact is preferable to food but not enough on its own to ensure normal development.

Studies such as those of Harlow and Harlow convinced Bowlby that a baby needed to form an attachment with a carer, preferably its mother, to ensure that it grew up healthy and well adjusted. In further studies Bowlby attempted to show that teenagers that had not bonded with their mothers at birth were violent and disruptive. Following Bowlby's research, midwives stopped taking babies from their mothers immediately after birth. The practice of putting newborn babies all together in nurseries to allow the mothers to rest was stopped in favour of keeping the mother and baby together to help with bonding.

The biological perspective also tries to predict behaviour, implying that behaviour is due to our genes and the way our bodies work. A good example of how behaviour can be predicted by genes is when considering people with Down's syndrome. Genes are carried on chromosomes; usually people have 23 chromosomes in each cell nucleus. Sometimes people are born with 3 of the number '21' chromosome instead of two. This condition is known as Down's syndrome. The extra

chromosome is responsible for predicting how the individual will behave. People with Down's syndrome will have learning difficulties and some physical abnormalities, ranging from heart defects to reduction in hearing and sight.

It is only in the last few decades that having a child with Down's syndrome has come to be viewed as a positive experience and may not result in the child's premature death or severe abnormalities. Advancement in medical treatment, drugs and technology and the control of environmental factors, now means that a child with Down's syndrome can have a better quality of life than previous generations did.

Albert Bandura (born 1925) wanted to see if it is possible to predict how the environment can affect human behaviour. He predicted that if children watch violence on television they would act violently. To prove this he set up an experiment in which children watched videos of adults hitting a 'Bobo doll' (an inflatable human sized toy that rebounds when hit). He then left the children in a room alone with a 'Bobo doll'. The children who had watched the video began to hit the toy as they had seen the adults do, possibly proving Bandura's prediction that watching violence encourages violence. However, other factors may have explained why the children hit the toy. They could have thought that they were expected to hit the toy. In addition, the toy was designed to be hit.

SCENARIO

Jack attends a college programme for people with learning disabilities. He is 19 years old. Nearly every day he will sit or lie down in the main entrance to the college. He cannot explain why he does this, but his behaviour creates a lot of difficulty for other people using the college.

Controlling behaviour

The behaviourist perspective offers an approach to managing and controlling challenging behaviour. Firstly, it is necessary to define exactly what the challenging behaviour involves. Terms such as 'badly behaved', 'awkward' or 'difficult' are not helpful in understanding or managing behaviour. It is important to record in detail Jack's behaviour, noting how often he sits in the doorway, at what time of day and for how long. Once challenging behaviour is defined it is then possible to monitor what happens before the behaviour occurs and what the consequences might be. Through this careful monitoring it will be possible to identify any reinforcement for Jack's behaviour. For example, Jack may sit in the doorway when he is bored. The consequence of this behaviour is that Jack gets attention, reinforcing his behaviour. Managing behaviour involves reinforcing alternative behaviour. This management may involve encouraging Jack to ask questions when he is bored instead of sitting in the doorway. Positively reinforcing 'question asking' behaviour by responding with praise and support will give Jack the opportunity to learn that the consequences of 'asking questions' are more pleasurable than the consequence of lying in the door.

An example of how behaviour management can control feelings as well as behaviour would be the management of chronic pain. People who are in chronic pain may have learnt how to avoid action that they have previously associated with pain. Operant conditioning attempts to identify and reward well behaviour. Operant conditioning programmes are often organised in the patient's home or care facilities. Care staff and families are shown how to change the patient's environment that may cause pain, and how to reinforce well behaviour with praise.

This method of treatment can be used in all age groups, but it needs supportive families to ensure it works. One of the problems with this method of behavioural management is that sometimes people do not want to get better, as they gain benefit in the form of sympathy and attention through being ill.

Influencing behaviour and feelings

The social perspective has an important part to play in influencing behaviour and feelings.

Think it over...

Does your gender have any effect on the state of your health and how often you access services?

There are many ways in which women's roles affect their health; women are often stereotyped as 'carers'. Consequently, women take on the roles of caring for the young, sick and elderly. Women are more often victims of domestic violence than men are. Women are also more often lone parents, which may lead to poverty, self-neglect and a lack of self-esteem. The behaviour of men is equally influenced by the social perspective. Men are more likely to be involved in accidents and acts of violence. They are also more likely to commit suicide, as well as having higher levels of drug and alcohol use. Men are less likely to seek medical attention when ill and may also die earlier than women.

The roles that men and women take on are not fixed but change constantly. In recent years the use of alcohol has increased in teenage girls and

SCENARIO

Greg suffers from chronic knee pain following a sports injury. He usually hobbles around in pain, relying on pain-controlling drugs. His physiotherapist suggests that he uses crutches, which will take the weight of the knee and allow it to heal. Greg is reluctant to use the crutches. His friends and family have noticed that if they encourage him and praise him when he uses the crutches, he tends to use them more often. Consequently, he is in less pain and needs fewer pain killing drugs.

young women, whereas previously it was associated with working men's clubs and 'lad's nights out'. Social influences affect behavioural 'norms', encouraging roles to be re-defined and behaviour changed to reflect new ideals.

Gender roles are not purely constructed by our society. Martin and Halverson (1987) put forward support for the cognitive perspective, showing that people develop a gender schema. They showed that children as young as two and three-years-old had developed an understanding of their gender. One of the first gender schema to be formed is one of in-group and out-group, where children can identify which toys and games are suitable for boys and which are for girls. This schema then develops on to how to behave in a sex-typed way, for example, a girl's dress and care for dolls.

Gender schemata are used to organise and make sense of experiences. This theory is supported with experimental evidence. Children were shown pictures, such as boys playing with dolls and girls playing with guns. The children were asked one week later to recall the pictures from memory. They replied that the girls had been playing with the dolls and the boys with the guns. The children had changed their recollection to fit their gender schema.

Forming appropriate gender schema is often regarded as desirable and healthy, as it ensures children develop the roles expected of them by society. However, in order that children adopt the roles of their gender they must suppress the 'masculine' and 'feminine' side of their personality. Boys must become assertive, confident and competitive, whereas girls should become sensitive to the needs of others and openly express their feelings.

Think it over...

What could be the advantages and disadvantages of suppressing gender characteristics?

Gaining control of own behaviour

What are the factors that influence individuals to gain control over their own behaviour? In most situations we are aware of having some power of choice over our actions; this is known as having autonomy. You probably feel now that you could, if you wished, choose whether to put down this unit or to continue reading. How can the four perspectives considered in this chapter help you to gain control over this choice?

The behaviourist's perspective would argue that through studying you may receive praise from others, resulting in you feeling good about yourself. The association between studying and praise will encourage you to continue. When this behaviour is reinforced, by achieving a good grade in your studies, you will be encouraged to read more, so you do not put the book down.

The biological perspective could suggest that perhaps the content of this chapter has decreased your arousal levels so that you are under-stimulated, bored and beginning to be distracted. To increase your level of arousal, you need to put down the book and do something else. But wait. What about your parents? The fact that you are intelligent enough to read and understand this unit may be due to the genes your parents passed on to you. Are you going to ignore your genes and put the book down?

Now that you are beginning to think about your actions you are engaging the cognitive perspective. You may have formed a study schema, which involves you setting time aside to study, read this chapter, revise your findings and pass your course work. If you stop reading you will not be fulfilling this schema, but beginning a different schema about, for example, making yourself a cup of tea.

Finally, how could the social perspective help you to gain control of what is rapidly becoming a difficult decision? Perhaps you are reading this to fulfil a social stereotype. If you are female, is it not true that girls do better than boys at their studies? If you do not want to fulfil this stereotype put the book down, but in doing so would you just fulfil another stereotype that young people do not like work? You may be studying with a friend who is encouraging you to continue, in which case are you not reading due to peer pressure?

It is very difficult to truly act autonomously, making a decision without any psychological perspective influencing you somehow. These perspectives exert their own influences on behaviour and can very rarely be separated from each other. The behaviour of people needs to be treated as a whole and not as separate entities. This is known as the holistic approach, whereby every aspect of a person's behaviour is considered in relationship to each other. The person is looked at as a whole.

Evaluation of perspectives

Behaviourist perspective: strengths

Early behaviourists, such as Skinner, devised simple animal experiments to demonstrate how easily behaviour can be changed and modified. By using animals scientists can repeat experiments many times and relatively inexpensively. Their experiments were scientifically performed in laboratories, resulting in data that is clear and concise and experiments that are easily repeated to test their reliability.

As a result of these experiments behaviourists were able to show that with positive reinforcement an individual's behaviour can be changed relatively quickly. In the scenario about Jack, for example, he would quickly learn not to lie in doorways, when positive 'question asking' behaviour was reinforced. Behaviourism has been applied to several areas of care. It can be used to moderate and control unwanted behaviour in care environments, through systems such as token economies. It can also be used to treat phobias by trying to break the abnormal stimulus/response relationship.

Behaviourism controls individual behaviour overriding personal autonomy and choice. This

can be useful when someone is unable to change their own behaviour due to illness, being frail, immature or having learning disabilities. The behaviourist perspective is able to show individuals methods to achieve normal and acceptable behaviour relatively quickly and easily.

Behaviourist perspective: weaknesses

Behaviourists believe that behaviour can be observed only in laboratories where it can be manipulated and explained. Individual thought and consciousness has no place in behaviourism. People cannot show any autonomy or personal choice over their actions. Behaviour is only explainable by responses to stimuli and does not take into account any life experiences, previous learning or social influences.

In the scenario about Jack on page 376, it is important to keep reinforcing his acceptable behaviour on a frequent basis, as without continual reinforcement he may go back to lying in the doorway. As well as keeping up the reinforcement, which can be difficult and impractical, it is also important to ensure that the reinforcement happens quickly after the behaviour. This may be hard to achieve when someone is caring for several people with behavioural problems, who are all demanding attention.

The ethical application of behaviourism has changed over the years, as it is now not so desirable to perform experiments on animals. Also it must be questioned to what extent looking at the behaviour of dogs, rats and pigeons can really be applied to humans. Consent is also an important issue in applying the behaviourist perspective, because it can often be used without consent being obtained. For example, Jack did not give consent for his behaviour to be changed.

Cognitive perspective: strengths

The cognitive perspective takes into consideration the individual's thoughts and beliefs, offering a 'model' of living by. It promotes well being and can be used to correct abnormal thoughts and behaviours. Cognitive therapy requires the full cooperation of individuals and requires them to address their own problems and to seek out their own unique solutions. The cognitive perspective encourages people to take control of their health with the aid of professional guidance. Beck (1967) looked at how cognitive therapy could be used to help people with depression. The treatment teaches people to modify their own behaviour by restructuring the negative beliefs that cause depression. Beck believed that depressed people have characteristics that encourage them to be depressed, such as being gloomy and pessimistic; these characteristics are triggered by life events. Cognitive therapy teaches people to develop coping strategies to overcome abnormal thoughts and behaviours. The cognitive approach to treating abnormal behaviour in care settings is becoming very popular, as it encourages individuals to help themselves by thinking about the reasons why they have abnormal thoughts in the first place.

The cognitive perspective has a high level of *ecological validity*, as it is used with individuals in their own environment. The experiment by Rosenhan took part within real hospitals and looked at the reactions of real staff and patients within those hospitals.

Cognitive perspective: weaknesses

The cognitive perspective emphasises that everyone should be self-sufficient and solve their own problems. This is not always possible. It does not look at the reasons why people have abnormal behaviour in the first place. It ignores social circumstances such as poverty, over-crowding and relationship problems that caused the person to exhibit abnormal thoughts. Beck saw conditions such as depression as indulging in self-defeating thoughts and considered it irrelevant to consider the real causes behind behaviour. Consequently, when abnormal behaviour is treated there is a high chance that it may recur, as the cause has been ignored.

Cognitive therapy involves in-depth discussions with individuals, one to one, which can be time-consuming and needs to be performed by trained professionals. Although it teaches the individual to alter negative disruptive thoughts it does not teach how to alter the situations that cause these thoughts to form. Experiments that look at the cognitive perspective produce results that are hard to measure, as they examine thoughts and perception. Therefore, it is difficult to repeat these experiments as they look at the thought processes of individuals.

In the study by Rosenhan there was a high level of deception used in order to trick the staff of the hospital and to ensure that they did not change their behaviour to suit the experiment. By deceiving people to participate in an experiment the psychologist is unable to get their consent to study them and take notes on any behaviour observed. Therefore, studies such as these may be viewed as unethical.

Social perspective: strengths

The social perspective is mainly interested in observing how people behave in their own environment. Consequently, social studies quite often have a high level of ecological validity. The social perspective covers a very wide area of study and can involve the use of hundreds or thousands of participants. Studies vary greatly; looking at how society can influence a range of behaviours. Behaviours studied include violence, prejudice, obedience, motivation and conformity. A detailed understanding of these subjects can be very useful in care settings.

SCENARIO

Mrs Brown needs to see her GP. The day she visits him there is a locum GP in his place. The locum GP is wearing a smart shirt but no stethoscope or white coat. Mrs Brown is overheard telling her friend that 'the new GP is not a real GP, as he does not dress like one, so I won't be taking the new pills he gave me'. Mrs Brown conforms to the image she expects a GP to portray. She obeys the authority that she believes a GP in a white coat commands. When the GP does not fulfil this image she does not believe that he can be a real GP.

By understanding the influences that can be exerted on an individual, it is possible to develop a greater understanding of normal and abnormal behaviour. The social perspective puts people in their natural context and considers that many other factors affect behaviour than just internal and biological influences.

The social perspective is usually studied through observing behaviour, either in laboratories or in the field (natural environment). By studying people in a natural setting it is possible to observe behaviour without influencing it in any way.

Social perspective: weaknesses

By looking at human behaviour in the wider context of society, autonomy is taken away from the individual. The individual is not responsible for his or her own actions. Consequently, when problems arise such as anti-social behaviour, anorexia nervosa and depression, it is sometimes tempting to blame society rather than allow individuals to take responsibility for their behaviour. Self-fulfilling prophecy may result from the labels that society puts on its individuals, therefore encouraging people to act in a way that is expected of them.

When carrying out social studies it is often necessary to deceive the participants. Deception allows the experimenter to gather data from social situations without effecting natural behaviour. As social studies often look at large groups of people they are unable to obtain full consent from participants, so people can often be involved in studies without their knowledge. For example, if you were studying the behaviour of football crowds, it would be impossible to ask every supporter for their full consent. Sometimes social studies can cause mental harm to the participants, through deception and manipulating behaviour, or possibly failing to stop an experiment from continuing. Zimbardo et al. (1973) set up a study that asked male university students to act as either guards or prisoners in a mock prison. He became so engrossed in the students' behaviour he failed to notice that some of the boys were suffering mental cruelty and humiliating each other. Zimbardo finally stopped the experiment eight days earlier than planned, when another psychologist pointed out to him the suffering the participants were being exposed to.

Biological perspective: strengths

The biological perspective relies on scientific experiments to make new discoveries. Consequently, it is a highly researched field of psychology that is constantly changing as new technology, treatments, therapies and prescriptive drugs are developed. Due to these continual developments there is a large amount of research and study undertaken in this field, producing detailed knowledge of the human body and abnormal conditions.

By studying the human body as a collection of cells, any responsibility for normal or abnormal behaviour is beyond the control of individuals, as they have no control or autonomy over their behaviour. Explanations for behaviour can be seen as a result of chemical and nervous impulses in the body and controlled or eradicated with drugs, surgery or evasive therapies. For example ECT (electro-convulsive therapy) is designed to pass electric currents through the brains of chronically depressed patients. This electric current alters brain activity, hopefully changing the signals responsible for depressive thoughts.

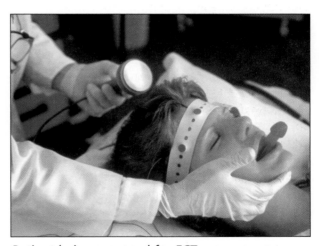

Patient being prepared for ECT

As biological experiments are carried out in laboratories, by professional scientists, they are usually very ethical. Any new proposals for psychological research have to be examined by an ethics committee to ensure that no harm is done to the people who participate.

Biological perspective: weaknesses

The biological perspective believes that behaviour is due to genes, nerve cells and chemicals. This reductionism does not allow for any other explanation as to why behaviour occurs. By looking at genes as the cause of behaviour, the biological perspective fails to address environmental factors. Life experiences, social influences or personal autonomy have no place in the biological perspective.

Biological experiments are very complex and difficult to understand. They need to be interpreted by highly trained and experienced professionals. Therefore, even though experiments are easily repeatable, they can only be performed by experts. Drug treatments may prevent the development of a condition but often do not look at the causes. Once the drugs are stopped, the problem then returns. The biological perspective has problems in establishing cause and effect; for example, an increase in dopamine levels may cause schizophrenia and not be caused by schizophrenia.

The biological perspective encourages people to volunteer to become patients, relying on them to try new drugs and treatments, regardless of the side effects. Patients usually willingly take part in new studies, as they believe that their problems may be cured or relieved. Studies are passed by ethics committees but they often rely on participants' willingness to hand over their 'wellness' to professionals, even though they may not understand the total complexities

Research methods, techniques and ethics

Before psychologists can design a study they must first decide what it is they are testing for and predict what the study will show. This prediction is known as the hypothesis. For example, someone could put forward the theory that noisier children get more attention from their teachers than quiet children do. This theory could be used to put forward several hypotheses or predictions such as: noisy children get attention quicker than quiet children; teachers talk to noisy children more often than other children.

Psychologists can gather a large amount of information from their investigations. This information or data can be collected as quantitative or qualitative data.

Quantitative data are about the 'quantities' of things. They are numbers, percentages, and averages and tell us how much of something

there is. When Tajfel (1970) studied the behaviour of teenage boys he asked them to allocate points to members of another group. Tajfel gathered a lot of quantitative data in the form of numbers, i.e. the amount of points and to whom the boys allocated them.

Qualitative data are about the 'qualities' of things. They are descriptions, pictures, words and meanings and give detail about experiences. Qualitative data is gathered through interviewing people, surveys and questionnaires that ask about opinions and feelings.

Once psychologists have decided what they want to study, they need to decide whose behaviour they are going to study in their investigations, and what method they are going to use.

Selecting participants

The participants are the name of the group of people used in a study. These people are chosen from a larger group or 'target population' i.e. 20 teenage boys (sample) chosen from 100 in a school (target population). Deciding on the size of the sample group is very difficult. If the group is too small it would be difficult to generalise from the findings and apply them to other target groups. If the group is too big it becomes impractical, costly and time-consuming to investigate in any great detail. Sampling can be done randomly or self-selecting.

In a random sample everyone in the target population stands an equal chance of being chosen to participate. A random selection can only guarantee that the participants have been chosen in an unbiased manner.

In a self-selecting sample the participants volunteer to take part in a study; this is usually achieved by placing an advert in a newspaper asking for volunteers. The disadvantages in using a self-selecting sample are that the majority of the target population will probably not apply and that those that do apply may not be a true representation of the population as a whole. For example, Stanley Milgram wanted to test the power of obedience to authority. He placed an advert in the *New York Times* for men aged 20–50 years old to take part in an experiment. The people who applied were a self-selecting sample of men who read the *Times* newspaper. It becomes very difficult to apply the findings of self-selecting studies to the population as a whole.

Experimental method

Experiments are probably the most widely used method of conducting research used in psychology. An experiment is controlled and organised by a psychologist, who aims to prevent any outside influences affecting his findings. By controlling the environment the psychologist can manipulate and alter the variables.

> ### Key concept
>
> *Variable:* anything that can change or vary, e.g. weight, temperature, reaction speeds.

Through controlling the variables, experiments allow psychologists to find out the cause of things and what effect they have. In Pavlov's experiment he controlled the variables of food and bell ringing. Through the control of these variables he could find out the causes of the dog's salivation; this is known as cause and effect.

Advantages of experimental method

An experiment can easily be repeated by other researchers wishing to try and obtain the same results. If the experiment can easily be repeated and the results are similar, then confidence can be increased in the results. The experimental method is the easiest way to control variables and truly measure what it is you set out to test. If all variables are controlled then cause and effect can be measured.

> ### Key concept
>
> *Ecological Validity:* a way of assessing how closely an investigation can be applied to every day, real life situations.

Disadvantages of the experimental method

The experimental method was first designed to be used in scientific subjects such as chemistry and physics, where it is important to have control. It is very difficult to apply the findings of a controlled experiment to human behaviour. Humans have feelings, emotions, opinions and beliefs that cannot be measured during an experiment. Experiments also have a low ecological validity.

Experiments lack ecological validity, as it is difficult to compare experimental findings with normal life situations. Experimenting on people is difficult, as they think about what it is they are being tested for. Sometimes they alter their behaviour in a way they believe will be helpful to the experimenter. They may be feeling embarrassed, awkward or irritated by the experiment and set about deliberately to change the experiment. These unaccountable effects are known as *confound variables.*

Observations

The best way to ensure that an investigation has a high ecological validity is to watch people in their own surroundings, in a natural setting where the experimenter has not manipulated anything. In the study by Rosenhan (1973) he made notes on the behaviour of staff and mentally ill patients in the psychiatric hospitals, when unknowingly faced with pretend patients.

Observations can take place anywhere that human behaviour can be studied; for example, funerals, weddings, and football matches and out-patient departments. Observations do not always take place in a natural environment. Sometimes it is appropriate to set up a fake environment such as a prison or playground to watch behaviour in more detail. The most important aspect of an observation is that the investigators do not interfere with the research and purely observe the behaviour in front of them. It can be necessary for participants to become involved in an observation, as in Rosenhan's study; this is known as a participant observation. A non-participant observation would involve no participants, such as watching children in a classroom or the behaviour of doctors on a ward round.

Advantages of observations

Observations very often have a high ecological validity because they occur in natural environments. The findings of an observation are likely to apply to everyday life and realistic situations. It is possible to use an observation to study large amounts of people. Piliavin et al. (1969) observed 4,450 people over a period of two months in their study, which wanted to find out if train passengers would help a blind or drunk person when they fell. Observations allow the investigators to observe people's behaviour without their knowledge, which means that people are more likely to act normally and reduce the risk of confound variables.

Disadvantages of observations

People have a tendency to 'act' when being observed. Think about the popular TV show 'Big Brother'. Some would argue that it gives us an opportunity to observe people's behaviour, but do the participants of the show ever really forget that they are being watched and act as they usually would? Data gathering can also be difficult during observations, as the investigators may interpret the same situation differently; they may have different ideas about the meaning of actions. For example, one observer may see a gentle tap as an aggressive act whereas another observer may not. Because of the uniqueness of each observation it is not possible to repeat an observation and get the same results. Therefore, it is difficult to generalise from findings and apply the results to other situations.

Questionnaire survey

Have you ever been stopped in the street and asked your views on something? More than likely, you were asked to fill in a questionnaire. Questionnaires can gather a large amount of data very quickly and may be used to find a wide range of information about many social and economic trends. Researchers use questionnaires to target a particular sample of the population, based on certain characteristics, such as age, gender, race, class. Questionnaires can be used in many research situations, asking participants about their feelings, attitudes and intentions.

They can be completed face to face or via the post, telephone, Internet or even text.

Collecting both qualitative and quantitative data

Questions are either open-ended or closed. Open-ended questions allow the person being asked the opportunity to answer how they wish too. For example 'What are your views on smacking children in public?'. Questions such as this allow for a wide range of qualitative responses and do not restrict the choice of answers. The answers to open-ended questions are therefore much more difficult to analyse than the answers to closed questions. Closed questions are questions that have a limited range of possible answers. Participants are usually asked to give their answers by ticking boxes or ringing various choices. They produce quantitative data that is easy to analyse and process.

Advantages of questionnaire surveys

Questionnaires are easy to use and can be used by a lot of people all at the same time, therefore, gathering large amounts of data quickly, effectively and cheaply. Answers from closed questions are easy to analyse and can be used as comparisons in other similar studies. Open-ended questions give participants the opportunity to describe their behaviour in detail.

Disadvantages of questionnaire surveys

It can be very difficult to write questions clearly enough that the participant understands what is being asked of them. People have different interpretations of the same word.

Even when a respondent fully understands the question they may give the answer they want you to hear. In a survey on contraception uses in 16–18 years old girls, would you answer truthfully if asked 'Have you ever had unprotected sex?'. Sometimes even the researchers themselves can influence the answers given. The respondent may be influenced by factors such as age, gender or ethnic group. How would you have answered the question on contraception as a 16-year-old girl if the researcher was an 18-year-old boy? Would your answer have been the same?

Structured interview

Interviews are one of the best ways of getting a large amount of detailed quantitative and qualitative data from one person. They are useful in case studies to gain a deeper understanding of the participant's behaviour. The structured interview is designed carefully before meeting the participant. The researcher would have developed the questions within a framework, ensuring deviation from the set topic is unlikely.

Advantages of the structured interview

Interviews allow for researchers to explore subjects in great detail, gaining a personal perspective on an area of behaviour; for example, interviewing women about the reasons they chose to give birth in a hospital and not at home. Questions can be tailored to carefully fit the subject matter. Interviews can be conducted in a private and confidential manner, which may allow the respondent to talk in detail about more personal issues than those that can be addressed in questionnaires.

Disadvantages of the structured interview

The structured interview will produce a lot of detailed quantitative data, which is hard to analyse and compare to other situations. It takes a great deal of time and skill to interview people effectively. Face-to-face situations, such as interviews, may cause bias with either the researcher or participant manipulating their body language and responses to fit the situation. For example, if you are getting on very well with the interviewer you may expand your answers and give more detailed answers than if you found the interviewer unfriendly and unapproachable.

Ethics

Ethics are the principles that are used in everyday situations to make decisions based on personal and cultural values. Values are the beliefs, customs and characteristics that the individual and society consider important in making choices and appropriate decisions. Psychology is the study of human behaviour and involves performing experiments and studies on humans. Ethical issues are very important within psychology and are primarily concerned with protecting the rights and dignity of the participants. The need for a clear set of guidelines for psychological research led to the development of ethical principles that are used to underlie all psychology research.

Informed consent

All participants in investigations should have access to information that will allow them to make an informed consent as to whether or not they participate in the study. Information should be provided in a format that the participant may fully understand i.e. Braille or provision of an interpreter where necessary. Children under 16-years-old need the consent of an appropriate adult as well as giving their own consent, if at all possible. Participants have the right to withdraw their consent following an investigation. In this case the investigator must destroy any data or measurements that were made on the participant. There are alternatives to informed consent when obtaining consent would be difficult and revealing the purpose of the study would affect the findings. Presumptive consent can be used to study large groups of people such as populations. This involves asking a small percentage of the group to be studied for their informed consent. If they agree it can be presumed that the whole group would have consented.

Deception

Deception involves the withholding of information from the participants. Deception is sometimes necessary when investigating human behaviour. Total honesty in a study may result in the participants modifying their behaviour in some way to fit in with the study. In the experiment by Rosenhan (as discussed in cognitive perspective), where normal people were admitted to psychiatric hospitals because they pretended to have schizophrenia, if the staff of the hospitals were aware of the study, then they would have been on the look-out for fake patients and the study would not have worked. It was

only through deceiving the staff that Rosenhan was able perform his study.

Debriefing

Debriefing is very important, especially where deception has occurred. It is necessary to ensure that all participants are aware that they have taken part in an experiment. Debriefing involves providing the participants and discussing their experiences following the investigation. Debriefing gives the participant the chance to ask questions and to fully understand the true nature of the investigation. The staff of Rosenhan's experiment were debriefed and told that they had been treating 'normal' people as psychiatric patients. The result of this was anger that they had been tricked, but it also encouraged them to re-think how they talk to and treat patients in their care.

A summary of the ethical guidelines for research with human participants. British Psychological Society (2000)

Consent Gaining a participant's informed consent is a very important part of psychology research. Wherever possible, investigators should give all participants sufficient information about the research to allow them to make an informed choice. Wherever possible, the real consent of children and vulnerable groups should be obtained. Also when the participant is under the age of 16 years then consent should be obtained from parents or guardians. The payment of participants must not be used to encourage them to risk harm to their normal lifestyle.

Deception The investigator must never withhold information or mislead the participants. Deception must be avoided wherever possible, although it may be impossible to study some areas of psychology without withholding information about the true purpose of the study.

Debriefing Following any studies in which participants are aware that they have been taking part in a study, the investigator must provide the participants with any necessary information to complete their understanding of the study. The investigators should discuss with the participant their experience of the study in order to monitor any effects that taking part may have had on them.

Right to withdraw from the investigation

From the beginning of the study the investigators should make participants aware of their right to withdraw from the research at any time. Following the investigation, the participant has the right to withdraw retrospectively any consent given, and to require that their own data and recordings should be destroyed.

Confidentiality

Confidentiality Any information gathered about the participant is confidential unless otherwise agreed in advance. The participant has the right to expect that any information that they provide will be treated confidentially and, if published, will not be identifiable as theirs. If confidentiality cannot be ensured the participant must be made aware of this in advance.

Protection of participants The investigator must protect the participant from any physical or mental harm during the investigation. The risk of harm must be no greater than in normal life. Where research may involve the use of personal or private information, the participants must be protected from stress at all times, including the assurance that answers to personal questions need not be given.

Evaluating studies

When you are looking at a psychological study there are many factors to consider over and above the results. Results from experiments can only be of use if they show reliability and validity. The term *reliability* means consistent; if an experiment can be repeated again and the same results found then the experiment can be said to be reliable, Skinner's rat experiment was reliable, as the rats always pressed the lever. *Validity* on the other hand considers if the results measured what they claimed to measure. For example, a rubber ruler would not accurately measure centimetres; therefore, the results it gives would be invalid.

SCENARIO

Mr Brown is in hospital. The staff have decided that it is important that they know how much he is drinking each day. To do this they decide to measure the amount of water they put into his drinking jug each day. This is a *reliable* measure of the amount of water he has available to him, but is not a valid measure of how much he drinks. By only measuring the amount of water in his jug the staff have not really measured his fluid intake. What about the amount he spills, dribbles or even the extra cups of tea? For the results to be reliable and valid the staff need to measure exactly how much fluid Mr Brown is ingesting by also measuring his other drinks and possible spillages as well.

The method used to perform an investigation must be evaluated before its results can be used. Some of the main factors to consider are cause–effect, ecological validity, representative population and ethics.

It is important to consider if the study really does look at cause and effect. For example can a psychologist really say that smoking causes cancer? It is possible to perform experiments that show smoking (cause), may influence the development of cancer (effect), but it would be impossible to say that smoking is a true cause of cancer because it would be impossible to test all the variables that cause cancer.

Think it over...

What are the other variables that may cause cancer?

To really ensure that cause and effect are measured it would be necessary to totally control all the variables in an experiment, but this would reduce the ecological validity. When evaluating studies, it is necessary to look at how ecologically valid an experiment is. An experiment performed in a laboratory with animals will have no ecological validity, as it would be difficult to apply findings to human behaviour in real-life settings. Yet it would be unfair to say that it is not important to look at laboratory experiments when considering human behaviour. Also studies that are performed totally in real life situations, such as Rosenhan (1973), may be high in ecological validity but have low reliability and validity.

Further considerations should be given to the chosen representative sample, that is the chosen people to participate in the study. For example, Milgram in his study on obedience only performed his experiment on American men aged 25–40 years. It would be very difficult to apply Milgram's findings to the general population that includes people such as women, children and old people. Studies must carefully match the participants to the hypothesis. It is no use studying teenage anti-social behaviour and only using teenage boys as participants.

Finally, when all these factors have been considered it is also necessary to consider the ethics of an experiment. Ethical guidelines are necessary to clarify the conditions under which research is performed. Without ethical guidelines, psychological research may be subject to criticism that it does not protect the rights of the participants it is studying. Guidelines are not set in stone, and need to be updated regularly to ensure that they correspond to the morals and values of the society they represent.

Summary

When considering the importance of psychological studies there are many factors to take into account.

FIGURE 10.8 *Section 10.2 summary*

UNIT ASSESSMENT

How you will be assessed

In order to achieve this unit you must produce a report on a chosen topic that gives you the opportunity to describe and apply some psychological perspectives. Your topic should relate to one or more of the following: health, medical treatment, social well-being, social care practice and human development.

Your work should be wholly your own work and not based on a shared exercise. To achieve a higher grade you need to be concise and show a thorough understanding of the topic and relevant perspectives.

Your report may contribute to your Key Skills Communication evidence.

Numerical data gathering through your own research may contribute to your Application of Number evidence.

When writing your report you should include sections under each of the following headings:

A: Introduction Your introduction should state the topic you have chosen.

B: Perspectives You need to refer to several psychological perspectives relating them to your topic.

C: Evidence The evidence section should include relevant evidence supporting or conflicting with the perspectives you have chosen to look at in your report. Evidence should take the form of describing published empirical studies and/or evidence collected by you through your own research.

D: Discussion This section should have relevant criticisms of your chosen evidence, concluding with an evaluation of the perspectives you have described.

E: Appendix The appendix should include references to sources and studies included in your report.

Assessment Preparation – Area A: Introduction

You need to introduce your chosen topic or topic areas. The following list may help you to come up with some ideas regarding appropriate topics to use in your report.

Health: smoking, alcohol, drug taking, obesity, eating disorders, nutrition, diabetes, autism, depression, dementia, stress.

Medical treatment: counselling, genetic screening, immunisation, drug therapy, surgery, diet.

Social well-being: risk taking, modelling, gender differences, attachment, deviance.

Social care practice: care in the home, health promotion, young carers, psychiatric care, patient centred care.

Human development: learning, language, socialisation, senile dementia, adolescence.

Assessment Preparation – Area B: Perspectives

Look carefully at behavioural, cognitive, biological and social psychological perspectives. Choose perspectives that will most accurately relate to your chosen topic. In separate subsections explain each of the relevant perspectives. Do not cover irrelevant perspective whilst not leaving out any relevant perspectives. You should try to explain the perspectives by using everyday examples as well as applying them to your chosen topic.

Evidence

You need to support your choice of perspectives with evidence. This evidence can be taken from published studies and/or through your own research. Your chosen method of research method should be experimental, observational, questionnaire or structured interview.

Undertaking your own research

Planning

1. Identify a research area and narrow it down to the research question to be studied. Produce a description of your study.
2. Identify the population the research concerns; consider the type of data you want to gather. Discuss why you are carrying out the study and how it relates to the perspectives.
3. Decide on the method of research you are going to use to gather data.
4. Plan how to implement your research.
5. Select the participants to take part in your experiment.

Collecting data

1. Contact your participants and collect data.
2. Summarise and organise your data.

Interpreting data

1. Relate the data you have collected to your research question.
2. Draw conclusions from your data. Discuss the extent to which your findings support or conflict with the perspectives.

Assessment Preparation – Area D: Discussion

This is the most skilled part of your report and will help tutors to confirm decisions regarding the award of higher grades. The discussion section should include criticisms, where appropriate, of the all the evidence you have described.

When critiquing research you should carefully consider any ethical objections that have resulted from the research. Also look at strengths and weaknesses of the choice of the chosen method.

Some questions to consider that may help when discussing your chosen research.

1. Was a representative sample used? Y/N
2. Did it have low ecological validity? Y/N
3. Were there any design flaws? Y/N
4. Did it study what it set out to study? Y/N
5. Did it prove the hypothesis? Y/N
6. Could it have been done better? Y/N

This section should conclude with a detailed evaluation of the perspectives you have described, consider carefully how useful they were in explaining your topic.

Assessment Preparation – Area E: Appendix

To achieve a good grade you must add an Appendix to your report includes references to the sources you have studied. You must ensure that you write your references in a conventional form, which can be seen in the 'References' section of any textbook.

References

Asch, (1955) Studies of independence and conformity, a minority of one against a unanimous majority, *Psychological Monographs,* 70, (9, Whole No. 416)

Ayllon and Azrin, (1968) *The token economy: a motivational system for therapy and rehabilitation* Appleton-Century-Crofts, New York

Bandura, A. (1973) *Aggression: a social learning analysis*, Prentice Hall, London

Beck, A. (1967) *Cognitive therapy and the emotional disorders*, International Universities Press, New York

Bouchard, T. et. al, (1981) The Minnesota Study of twins reared apart, in Gellda, L. et al (eds) *Intelligence, Personality and Development*, Liss, New York

Bower, G. H., and Gilligan, S. G. (1979) Remembering information related to one's self, *Journal of Research in Personality 13,* 420–432

Bowlby, J. (1969) *Attachment and Loss Vol 1, Attachment*, Hogarth Press, London

Campbell, (1981) *Girl Delinquents*, Basil Blackwell, Oxford

Eynsenck, H. J. (1967) *The biological basis of personality*, C.C. Thomas, Springfield, ILL

Gerbner et al (1980) Sex roles: A journal of Research, Cited in M. Larson Jan 2003

Harlow and Harlow, (1962) Social Deprivation in Monkeys, *Scientific American*, 207(5), pp 136–146

Hochbaurm, (1958) *Public participation in medical screening programmes; a sociopsychological study*, Public Health Service Publication 572, US Government Washington DC, Printing Office.

Kelly, G. (1955) *The psychology of personal constructs*, Norton, New York

Milgram, S. (1963) Behaviour study of obedience, *Journal of Abnormal and Social Psychology 67*, pp 371–8

Rosenhan, D. L. (1973) On being sane in insane places, *Science*, 179, 250–8

Seligman, M. (1974) *Helplessness; On depression, development and death*, W H Freeman, San Francisco

Shields, J. (1962) Monozygotic Twins, Oxford University Press, London

Tajfel, H. (1970) Experiments in intergroup discrimination, *Scientific American*, 223, 96–102.

Toates, (1986) *Motivational Systems*, Cambridge University Press, Cambridge

Zimbardo P., Banks P., Haney C. (1973) Pirandellian prison; the mind is a formidable jailor, *New York Times Magazine*, 8 April, pps 38–60

Answers to assessment questions

Unit 4

1. Children's physical growth allows them to develop skills. Children's self-esteem is linked to their growth and adults' responses towards children are affected by their size.

2. The term is used describe the uneven growth of children's different body parts.

3. Fine motor movements may include doing a simple jigsaw, building a tower of bricks, threading beads, using a spoon and fork. Gross motor movements may include running, climbing, kicking a large ball, throwing a ball, pedalling a tricycle.

4. Factors that might affect physical development include medical condition, disability, genotype, maturation and environment.

5. An object is usually hidden in front of a baby. The observer looks at whether the child tries to find it. It is usually seen by 9 months.

6. Hearing impairment or learning difficulty. May affect children's ability to reproduce speech or comprehend it.

   Education. Children may have more opportunities to learn vocabulary through interactions with skilled staff.

7. Play encourages children to make repeated movements that are needed for control of movements and muscle strength. Play builds children's physical stamina i.e. running, pedalling or crawling.

8. Supervision of children can be difficult for parents. Homes are not designed with safety of young children in mind. Young children do not have a sense of danger.

9. Safety gates to prevent falls in stairways. Safety locks on windows to prevent children falling out. Bath mats to prevent falls in the bath. Tidying away objects

10. Older children often play outdoors and unsupervised e.g. near canals or rivers. They may try to impress each other. They may imitate things that adults do.

Unit 5

1. Dietary reference values outline the nutritional needs for population groups according to their age and gender.

2. Protein provides the only source of nitrogen to the body and is essential for growth and repair or maintenance and repair of body cells.

3. Saturated fat has all the carbon atoms fully hydrogenated, tends to be of animal origin and is a source of cholesterol. It contributes to heart disease.

   Unsaturated fats are of vegetable origin and their chemical composition means that they can have beneficial effects on the amount of cholesterol in the blood.

4. Eating for two in pregnancy would result in excess weight gain which would be difficult to lose after pregnancy. It would also increase the strain on a woman's heart and contribute to other diet-related disorders such as CHD. A pregnant woman should eat only approximately 200 additional calories per day during pregnancy.

5. Coeliac disease occurs when the body reacts to gluten which is found in starchy foods. Gluten damages the villi in the small intestine affecting the absorption of nutrients and leading to weight loss and other symptoms related to malnutrition.

6. A vegan will not eat any meat, fish or foods derived from animals, for example milk, yoghurt or cheese. A lacto-vegetarian will eat dairy products.

7. An allergy will produce antibodies in the blood as the body attempts to fight the allergen. These antibodies can be detected through a blood test. A food intolerance will produce repeatable symptoms when a particular food is eaten, but the reason for the reaction is not always identified and no antibodies are produced by the body.

8. Any outline of a religious diet is acceptable.

9. One way in which salmonella can be passed to food is through poor personal hygiene. Salmonella can be carried in the human gut and poor hand washing after using the toilet can cause the bacteria to spread.

10. Any acceptable ways of reducing fat intake such as:

    * eating low fat foods
    * choosing a low fat alternative to, e.g. cream, cheese, full-fat milk
    * eating a high-fibre diet which will fill you up and help remove excess cholesterol from the blood
    * grilling or steaming rather than frying food
    * cutting the fat off meat.

Unit 6

1. The very young, the very old and people with underlying conditions that have immune systems unable to cope with fighting off infection.

2. Bacillus – E Coli
   Coccus – Staphylococcus aureus
   Spirilla – Syphilis
   Vibrio – Cholera

3. Droplet, digestion, placenta and broken skin.

4. Fever, stiff neck, headache, photophobia, aches and pains, confusion or drowsiness, repeated vomiting. In babies: a different cry from usual, high temperature, will not feed, irritable, sleepiness, bulging fontanelle, jerky movements and stiffness or floppiness, fits.

5. Athlete's foot. It can be treated by anti-fungal powders, creams and sprays.

6. Head lice which can be treated by lotions, shampoos and creams or by bug busting or combing the hair using conditioner and a nit comb.

7. Allergies are better recognised, a rise in the number of smokers, increase in dust mites, loss of normal immunity in children, increase in pollution, a rise in the number of allergens to which people are exposed.

8. First exposure to an allergen,
   The immune system makes an antibody, IgE (immunoglobulin E)
   The antibodies attach to mast cells in human tissue.
   On the next occasion that there is exposure to the allergen, the allergen and antibodies attach to the mast cell.
   Powerful chemicals like histamine are released and cause the symptoms of an allergic reaction.

9. Blood test – Levels of IgE antibodies of different substances are measured.
   Skin prick test – The skin is broken and different allergens are dropped into the area. A raised itchy red patch will occur if a person is allergic to the substance.

10. Flushing of the skin, nettle rash, sense of impending doom, swelling of throat and mouth, difficulty in swallowing or speaking, alterations in heart rate, severe asthma, abdominal pain, nausea, vomiting, weakness, collapse and unconsciousness.

11. Diagram of the eye.

12. Soundwaves reach the eardrum which vibrates
    The vibrations are transmitted to the ossicles in the middle ear
    They vibrate and transmit vibrations to the inner ear
    The organ of Corti converts vibrations in to nerve impulses which are transmitted to the brain via the eighth cranial nerve.

13. An abnormality of sight where the cornea is irregularly shaped, causing blurring of vision.

14. A build-up of fluid in the middle ear behind the eardrum. Treatment can be by antibiotics,

autoinflation and myringotomy and grommets.

15. Sugar provides nutrition for the bacteria which makes up plaque. The bacteria produce acid which attacks the enamel of the teeth and causes a cavity.

16. Blood clots and seals the wound. Fibrinogen, a blood protein is converted into threads of fibrin which form a mesh over the wound and trap blood cells, forming a clot. The clot dries out and forms a seal over the cut, preventing entry of bacteria and infection occurring.

17. A rash that is not raised from skin level and is generally of a different texture or colour than normal skin.

18. Cheese, chocolate, caffeine and citrus fruit. They can trigger a migraine.

19. See table below.

20. Physical contamination – Items in food that should not be there such as bones, hair, jewellery, plasters, insects.
Chemical contamination – Can be caused by cleaning or agricultural chemicals getting onto the food.

Answer to question 19

MICRO-ORGANISM	SOURCE	SYMPTOMS	INCUBATION PERIOD
Salmonella	Raw poultry, eggs, raw meat, milk, animals, insects and sewage	Abdominal pain, vomiting, diarrhoea, fever	12–36 hours
E. Coli	Human and animal gut, sewage, water and raw meat	Abdominal pain, fever, diarrhoea, vomiting, kidney damage or failure	12–24 hours or longer

Glossary

A

Acquired immunity: Immunity that results from vaccination or being given antisera (medical intervention).

Active immunity: Immunity that results from the manufacture of antibodies from blood lymphocytes.

Active listening: Using the communication cycle, which involves listening with all your senses to what is said and being portrayed and being able to demonstrate what you have understood when you listen to another person. It requires the careful use of a number of devices, including acknowledgement responses, reflective statements and questions, and also questions that ask for clarification.

Acupuncture: A therapy involving the insertion of needles at key points in the body to stimulate *Qi* (energy). Two kinds of acupuncture are currently practised in UK: Traditional Chinese Acupuncture and Western Medical Acupuncture.

Advocacy: Arguing a case for another. In law an advocate argues a legal case. In care work an advocate tries to understand and argue from a service user's perspective.

After school provision: Organised provision for children before or after school.

Allometric growth: Parts of the body grow at different rates.

Allopathic Medicine: This kind of medicine treats medical conditions principally by attacking their symptoms, usually with pharmaceutical products or surgical interventions. It is also referred to as conventional medicine.

Alzheimer's disease: The most common form of dementia, involving problems with the way the nerve cells in the brain work.

Amino acid: The building blocks of protein.

Amniocentesis: A procedure for removing small quantities of amniotic fluid for genetic analysis.

Amnion: A covering membrane surrounding the foetus.

Amniotic fluid: Fluid produced by the amnion that surrounds the foetus in the uterus.

Anaphylactic reaction: A severe reaction that is caused by the sudden release of chemical substances in the body, including histamine, from cells in the blood and tissues where they are stored

Anthroposophical Medicine (AM): A holistic healing system designed to complement conventional medicine.

Antibody: Complementary protein produced by lymphocytes to neutralise antibodies.

Anti-histamine: Drugs taken to counteract the effects of histamine, a chemical released during an allergic reaction.

Antigen: Identification proteins located on the outside surface of disease-causing pathogens.

Application: Some services need to be applied for and this is particularly the case for social care services.

Approval: Being shown positive regard such as affection or praise.

Art therapy: The use of art as a form of psychotherapy, or as a form of personal expression and development.

Arthritis: A condition that can result in pain and restriction of movement within the joints of the body.

Ascorbic Acid: Chemical name for Vitamin C.

Assertion: This is different from both submission and aggression; assertion involves being able to negotiate a solution to a problem.

Attachment: A special bond or relationship between child and parent or care giver.

Autoclaving: Sterilising in a device rather like a professional pressure cooker.

Autonomy: Having the ability and opportunity to influence your own situation and actions. A sense of personal freedom and free will.

Ayurveda: A system of medicine that has both a spiritual and a healing dimension. This system originated in India.

B

Babysitters: Informal care of children, often for short periods of time.

Bach Flower Remedies: Remedies made by boiling or infusing plants in spring water. These work mainly on emotional problems.

Balanced diet: A diet that provides the right amount of energy and nutrients for an individual, according to their age and stage of life.

Barriers to communication: These can exist at a physical and sensory level, at the level of making sense of a message and at a cultural and social context level where the meaning of a message may be misunderstood.

Basal Metabolic Rate: The amount of energy needed just to keep the body functioning when lying down, warm, doing nothing

Behavioural therapy: A psychological system that aims to correct damaging behaviour patterns and attitudes.

Bereavement: The loss of a loved person, such as a partner or other close relative who dies.

Beveridge Report: A report produced by William Beveridge after the World War II, which formed the basis of the Welfare Stare.

Binary fission: A method by which bacteria can multiply. One becomes two, two become four and four become eight and so on.

Biographical Approach: An approach taken by integrated medical practitioners towards making a diagnosis. The focus is on the whole person, his or her lifestyle and life history.

Blood-borne viruses: Harmful viruses transmitted through contact with infected blood and blood-products.

Braille: A system of raised marks that can be felt by people with their fingers. It provides a system of written communication based on the sense of touch for people who have limited vision.

British Sign Language: This is a real language in the same way that English or French is a language. BSL is not a signed version of the English language. BSL has evolved in the UK's Deaf community over hundreds of years.

C

Calcium: A mineral needed in small amounts for strong bones and teeth; works hand in hand with phosphorus.

CAM/CAMs. An acronym that refers to all complementary and alternative systems of medicine and therapy, without distinguishing between the two categories.

Carbohydrate: A macronutrient composed of carbon, hydrogen and oxygen. It should provide 50–60 percent of the energy in the diet.

Care: To provide for physical needs or comfort.

Care provider: Any organisation that delivers a service, e.g. a home meals delivery company, an NHS Trust etc.

Care Purchaser: The organisation that controls the funding to buy care – usually the Local Authority or the PCT.

Carer: Anyone who looks after someone who is ill, disabled or otherwise unable to look after him or herself. This term usually refers to someone who provides informal (unpaid) care, rather than to a paid worker.

Charity: Any organisation that is officially registered as having charitable status.

Child Guidance Service: This works with children, aged 0–19, and their families to help with learning, emotional, social and behavioural difficulties.

Childminders: People who provide day care in own home.

Child Protection: Procedures that protection the child.

Children Act 1989: Act of Parliament that resulted in a number of changes in the way young children were cared for.

Children Act 2004: Update on the 1989 Act of Parliament which established a new Children's

Commissioner for England, who will raise awareness of issues relating to children and young people and report annually to Parliament.

Chiropractic: A system that uses manipulation of the spinal column to ease musculo-skeletal problems. Chiropractors regard themselves as healthcare practitioners, rather than CAMs therapists.

Choice: Being given or having the power to make decisions about one's life or situation.

Cholesterol: A type of fat which is found in foods.

Chorion: One of the membranes surrounding the foetus.

Chorionic villi: Finger-like projections formed from the chorion, which form part of the placenta.

Chronic: A term used to describe a condition that persists over a long period of time.

Clostridium botulinum: Food poisoning bacteria found in soil and decaying matter.

Clostridium perfringens: Food poisoning bacteria found in soil and therefore fruit and vegetables.

Cirrhosis: A degenerative disease of the liver that may occur from prolonged alcohol consumption.

Closed question: The kind of question that has a fixed set of answers. These questions are often used to arrive at quantitative data. Closed questions can also be answered 'yes' or 'no' if the respondent so chooses.

Communication Cycle: The process of building an understanding of what another person is communicating.

Compliance: Agreeing with a recommended course of action

Confidentiality: An important moral and legal right of service users to have their private information restricted to those who have a need to know as part of care practice, thereby promoting safety and security of service users and their property. The maintenance of confidentiality is vital in order to maintain a sense of trust.

Cultural variation: Communication is always influenced by cultural systems of meaning. Different cultures interpret systems of communication such as body language differently.

Coeliac disease: A condition where the body reacts to gluten, the protein that is found in wheat and some other cereals such as rye, barley and oats.

Cognitive therapies: A term used to refer to a number of psycho-analytical approaches.

Confound variables: Something that causes a change in a study that cannot be controlled within the boundaries of the experiment.

Constructive/manipulative play: Play that involves putting things together. It can involve commercial products such as lego, duplo or jigsaw puzzles or natural materials such as dough, sand, and clay.

Contra-actions Possible negative side-effects of treatment eg. bruising (after a massage, mood swings etc.

Contra-indications: Medical reasons why a treatment should not be given.

Craniosacral therapy: A physical treatment involving the application of a very light touch to the head and back.

Creative play: An expression used to describe a wide range of activities including art and craft activities such as drawing and painting through to self-expression through music and dance.

Crèches: Short care which frees the parent to carry out certain tasks such as shopping.

Cross-sectional: Information about a child's rate of growth at a given moment.

D

Dementia: A term used to identify a range of disorders, all of which involve a degeneration of the central nervous system.

Demography: The study of the size, structure, dispersal, and development of human populations

Deoxyribonucleic Acid (DNA): Genetic material contained in each cell in the human body.

DfES: Department for Education and Skills.

Diabetes mellitus: A disorder caused by insufficient or absent production of the hormone insulin by the pancreas.

Diagnostic and Statistical Manual of Mental Disorders or DSM: A complex system for identifying and categorising mental disorders originally developed in the USA.

Dietary fibre: A non-starch polysaccharide, which provides bulk to the diet and aids digestion.

Dietary Reference Value: A term used to cover a range of differently defined values.

Dignity: Being shown respect, the absence of demeaning treatment.

Discrimination: To treat some types of people less well than others. People are often discriminated against because of their race, beliefs, gender, religion, sexuality or age.

Disease: Illness resulting from infection with specific signs and symptoms.

Disengagement: Breaking off an exchange for a short period to achieve an objective such as more appropriate behaviour.

Disorder: A malfunction of an organ or system.

Distraction: Using a diversionary tactic to remove the focus from another feeling such as pain.

E

Early Learning Goals: Six areas of learning which must be included in the curriculum designed by a provider. These are language and literacy; mathematics; knowledge and understanding of the world; physical development; creative development and personal, social and emotional development. Personal, Social and Emotional Development is covered through the other five areas

Early Years Curriculum: The curriculum covered in many pre-school groups and reception classes.

Ecological Validity: The extent to which the findings of a study can be compared to reality.

Economic factors: Income and costs and how money/fees can affect the opportunities a child may have.

Educare: A combination of care and education.

Education: The process of imparting knowledge by formal instruction.

Education Action Zones: Designated areas identified by the Government as areas of significant deprivation, with the aim of putting additional support into both children in schools and in the family setting to raise aspirations and educational success.

Effective communication: This enables a person to access information they need by asking questions, being listened to and being given coherent explanations. **Emphysema**: A disease in which the air sacs within the lungs (alveoli) are damaged. This can cause shortness of breath and result in respiratory or heart failure.

Empowerment: Being given power. Not being dependent on others – taking control of own life decisions.

Endoscopy: A procedure for placing a thin, lighted tube down an orifice to visually examine a tube or cavity.

Endotoxin: A poison produced within pathogens.

Energy intake: The amount of energy taken in by an individual.

Environmental factors: The surroundings in which a child lives which can affect their behaviour and the opportunities available to them.

Epidemic: A disease that can spread rapidly through a community or country.

Equitable treatment: Receiving treatment which might not be the same as the treatment of others but is likely to be seen as fair and not significantly better or worse.

Evaluation: To assess something, in particular its worth, value or importance.

Every Child Matters: The White Paper which outlines how the Children Act 2004 will be implemented.

Evidence-based medicine: The combination of clinical expertise with external evidence in order to establish what is best for a particular patient.

Excellence clusters: New name for Education Action Zones.

Exotoxin: A poison produced externally by pathogens.

Expressive vocabulary: Words that are spoken by young children.

F

Facilitator: A person who helps to make something happen. This is often associated with decision-making or planning.

G

Generic: The opposite of specific or specialist. A generic social worker will serve a range of service users with many different needs.

Group maintenance: The social needs of group members when they are working together as a group. Maintenance activities create an appropriate social atmosphere to enable members to work effectively.

Group task: The work or activities that a group of people have come together to do.

F

Family centres: Designated areas in which professionals work with parents and families who are experiencing difficulties with the aim of teaching parenting and relationship skills.

Fats: A macro-nutrient which is the main provider of energy in the diet; made up of carbon, hydrogen and oxygen.

Ferric iron: Iron which is in a form that is not easily absorbed by the body; generally from vegetable sources.

Ferrous iron: Iron which is in a form that is easily absorbed by the body; generally from animal sources.

Food allergy: a form of intolerance which causes reproducible symptoms including abnormal immunological reactions to the food eaten.

Food aversion: An adverse reaction to certain foods by individuals that is psychological and not medically based.

Food intolerance: A general term which includes all reproducible adverse reactions to food that are not psychologically based.

Food plate: A model that can be used to plan a healthy diet.

Formal services: Services that provide care and education in a structured way.

Foster Carers: People who look after children, who cannot be cared for by their own parents in their own home, as part of their own family.

Foundation Stage: First stage of the National Curriculum.

G

Gingerbread: An organisation that supports lone parent families.

H

Halal: A term used to describe the way meat has been prepared to make it acceptable to Muslims.

Herbal Medicine: The use of herbal preparations to treat disease.

Holiday playschemes: Organised provision for children during their holidays.

Holism: Affecting the whole person, not a part.

Holistic approach: A view of illness that sees the individual as a whole person, who is ultimately in control of any treatment of therapy that may be suggested. This approach sees the causes of disease as complex and often encompasses physical, emotional and spiritual ways of healing.

Holophrase: A single word that has several uses.

High biological value (HBV): Foods that contain all the essential amino acids.

Homeopathy: A system of healing based on the principle that 'like cures like'.

Homeostasis: A state of physiological balance or equilibrium in the body.

Hyperglycaemia: Too little insulin or too much carbohydrate for insulin levels means the blood sugar level rises too high

Hypoglycaemia: Too much insulin or too little carbohydrate means blood sugar levels are too low

Hypertension: Raised resting blood pressure, usually above 160/95 mmHg.

Hypothesis: A prediction of what will happen in an experiment.

I

Illness: A subjective sensation of being unwell.

Imaginative or pretend play: This develops self-expression as well as giving a child the opportunity to explore experiences that have happened to them. Examples include playing 'mums and dads' or 'schools'.

Immunity: Defence against disease.

Informal groups: Arrangements for childcare that are not covered by any statutory legislation.

Innate immunity: Natural defences from birth.

Insulin dependant diabetes mellitus (IDDM): Type 1 diabetes where pancreatic cells are completely destroyed and therefore insulin is not produced.

Integrated Medicine: An approach taken by conventionally trained doctors who want to use both conventional and complementary healing methods with their patients.

Integrated service provision: The provision of services to an individual by different providers, but in a coordinated and carefully planned way. This can sometimes be by multi-disciplinary teams.

Intermediate care: Health care that is intended to promote recovery after a stay in hospital, or to prevent admission to hospital.

Iodine: A mineral that controls the body's metabolic rate.

Iron: Used in the formation of haemoglobin in red blood cells, which enables cells to carry oxygen around the body to the cells and tissues.

K

Key worker: A practitioner who has a special responsibility and relationship with an individual child.

Kosher: A term used to describe the way meat has been prepared to make it acceptable to Jewish people.

L

Lactose intolerance: A reaction to lactose which is the sugar found in milk.

Lacto vegetarian: Vegetarians who choose to eat milk and cheese but not eggs, meat, poultry or fish

Leading questions: Questions that indicate that the questioner expects a particular response.

Lifestyle: The way in which a person spends time and money to create a style of living.

Lipoproteins: A combination of a fat and a protein; there are high density lipoproteins and low density lipoproteins.

Listeriosis: Food poisoning bacteria found in pre-prepared salads, soft crusted cheeses, processed meats and pates, cooked chilled foods and shellfish.

Low biological value (LBV): Foods which do not contain all the essential amino acids.

Lymphocytes: White blood cells that produce antibodies.

M

Maladaptive behaviour: Behaviour that is not appropriate to the needs of local or general society.

Makaton: A system for developing language that uses speech, signs and symbols to help people with learning difficulties to communicate and to develop their language skills.

Maslow's Hierarchy of Human Need: A model which aims to layer different human needs according to the order in which they need to be met. It can be used to explain why care and education have to be integrated to provide the most effective support for children

Massage: A bodywork therapy which uses stroking and kneading movements on the body's soft tissues.

Maturation: Development or growth to eventual adulthood.

McMillan: An early years' practitioner who designed her approach to the curriculum around toys, which developed a child's fine and gross motor skills and manual dexterity.

Medical Model: A view of illness that sees the patient as a passive recipient of treatment. It also often focuses on dealing with the symptoms, rather than seeking the root cause of the problem.

Meninges: The three membranes that cover the brain.

Meta-analysis: The use of statistical techniques to analyse data from a number of trials or research studies.

Minerals: Organic substances which the body needs in minute quantities in order to function effectively.

Mixed economy of care: The notion that care can be provided by a range of different service providers, e.g. statutory agencies, private and voluntary organisations and informal carers.

Modelling: Using socially acceptable behaviour as a role model for others in the hope that an individual will start to copy that behaviour

Montessori: A method of education developed by Maria Montessori, which gives children the opportunity to learn about the world around them through exploration.

MRSA: Methicillin–resistant Staphylococcus Aureus – a bacterial infection that develops in hospital environments, causing death or complications in vulnerable people.

Music therapy: The use of music to allow emotional expression, to promote relaxation and to ease pain. Music can also be used to assist cognitive and personal development.

N

Nannies: Care for children in the child own home.

National Childcare Strategy: Key Government strategy that has influenced the provision of early years' services.

National Health Service: Established in 1948 and gave free access to medical care.

National Policies: Policies that are produced by central Government and apply to the whole of the country.

Natural immunity: Immunity that occurs through natural causes such as recovering from infection or passing from mother to foetus through the placenta.

Needlestick injury: The accidental insertion of a syringe needle into the skin of a person not designated to receive it, usually a carer.

Neglect: A lack of attention and due care which might result in physical or psychological harm to a service user.

Non insulin dependant diabetes mellitus (NIDDM): Type II diabetes where the rate of insulin production by the pancreas slows and therefore does not always meet the demand of the body.

Norms: The expectations that people have of other people within a particular group or culture – i.e. what people regard as normal.

Nuchal translucency: Examining the degree of light shining through the amniotic fluid at the base of the neck (used in investigations related to Down's syndrome).

Nursery care: Fee paying full day care provision or sessional provision.

Nursery nurse: Early years' workers who work in a wide range of early years settings including local authority and private nurseries, crèches, hospital wards and with individual families.

Nutrition pyramid: A model that can be used to plan a balanced diet.

Nutritional therapy: The treatment of disease by eliminating foods to which a person is allergic (or has an intolerance to), and by supplementing the diet with key nutrients.

O

Occupation: Having something interesting or worthwhile to do, either a job or hobby.

Open question: A question to which the respondent replies in his or her own words. Such questions cannot usually be answered by a simple 'yes' or 'no'.

Ophthalmoscope: An instrument with lenses and a

strong light for examining the back of the eyeball.

Osteoporosis: A medical condition involving excessive loss of bone and weakness of the bones and joints.

P

Palliative care: Nursing, practical and/or emotional support to people with life-threatening conditions or illnesses that are not responding to treatment. Such care often includes pain-management, and help to improve quality of life.

Paraphrase: To put what you think a person has said into your own words.

Parent and toddler groups: Sessional childcare provision where parents stay in attendance; provides opportunities for young children to socialise.

Parenting styles: the way in which parents interact with and discipline their children.

Parkinson's disease: A disorder caused by problems with the production of a chemical neurotransmitter that is essential for muscular movement. Parkinson's, disease, can result in serious problems with body movement and mobility.

Passive immunity: Immunity that results from antibodies being introduced into the body.

Pathogens: Disease-causing micro-organisms.

Percentile or centile chart: Chart that is used to measure children's growth.

Peristalsis: The name for the contraction and relaxation of the muscles of the digestive system.

Person centred care: An approach to care set out in Standard 2 of the National Service Framework for Older people: this says that older people should be treated as individuals and receive appropriate packages of care. It is care that places 'the person' at the centre of decision-making and activities; care that seeks to value the individual 'personhood' of service users.

Person centred planning: A way of working with people with learning disabilities. This was promoted by a government initiative called *Valuing People*. It includes the service user, his or her family, carer(s) and friends in the care planning and management process, together with professionals from the relevant services.

Personhood: Recognition and respect for the self-concept and self-esteem needs of a person, which is given to a human being by others.

Pessary: A drug or medicine that is inserted into the vagina.

Phosphorus: A mineral which works with calcium to ensure strong skeleton.

Phylloquinone: The chemical name for vitamin K.

Physical play: Indoor or outdoor play that develops both fine and gross motor skills as well as muscle control. Examples include climbing frames, bicycles, and running.

Phytotherapy: The practice of medical herbalism.

Placebo: A substance or 'treatment' that has no pharmaceutical properties or medical efficacy. Usually given to a control group in a clinical trial.

Play: A learning experience; a child's work.

Playgroups: Local childcare provision in local neighbourhoods.

Poor Law: Beginning of the concept of the Welfare State.

Poverty: Where a person has a low income i.e. worth 40 per cent less than the level of income enjoyed by the average person in the UK (60 per cent of median income) they may be understood as experiencing poverty.

Pre-linguistic phase: The period before an infant begins to use recognisable words.

Primary Health Care Services: Services that deal directly with people in the community such as the General Practitioner (GP), District Nurse, Health Visitor, Practice Nurse, Community Midwife, Community Physiotherapist, Occupational and Speech Therapists and Chiropodists.

Privacy: Opportunities to be undisturbed or unobserved by others in situations likely to cause embarrassment.

Private sector: This term refers to businesses that offer services, but operate on a profit-making basis.

Private services: Childcare services that are run for profit.

Probes and prompts: A probe is a very short question that is used to 'dig deeper' or probe into a person's answer. Prompts are short questions or words, which you offer to the other person in order to prompt them to answer.

Pro-social behaviour: Behaviours that are socially accepted.

Protein: A macro-nutrient and an essential constituent of all cells: made up of carbon, hydrogen, oxygen, nitrogen and small amounts of sulphur and phosphorus.

Protein energy malnutrition (PEM): The name used to describe a range of disorders which occur mainly in underdeveloped countries.

Psychological security: The absence of fear or distressing anxiety.

Psychoneuroimmunology (PNI): A scientific discipline that studies the relationship between the brain and the body.

Q

Qualitative data: Data that cannot be expressed in numerical form. This is often concerned with attitudes, opinions and values.

Quantitative data: Data which is expressed in numerical form.

Qigong A system of movements designed to stimulate the flow of *chi* (energy) within the body.

R

Randomised controlled trials: Research studies that involve the random selection of a study group with an associated control group.

Recall: Once registered for a service, follow-up appointments are made automatically.

Reception classes: First stage of formal schooling.

Receptive vocabulary: Words that are understood by children.

Reductionism: Examining only the part of the body that is not functioning correctly.

Referral by a third party: Referral to a service by another person.

Reflection: Thinking back over your actions.

Reflective questions: Questions that reflect back to the speaker something he or she has just said. Such questions often paraphrase the speaker's own words.

Reflective statements: Statements that reflect back to the speaker something he or she has just said. Such statements often paraphrase the speaker's own words.

Reflexology: The practice of stimulating reflex points on the hands and feet.

Regulation: The control of something by establishing a set of rules that everything (and everybody) must conform to.

Rehabilitation: The process of helping a person to resume his or her normal life (after an illness or accident) by regaining skills and emotional confidence.

Research methodology: The techniques used by scientists and scholars to conduct their research.

Residential care: Homes where children who are unable to live with their parents are looked after by social workers in groups.

Respite care: A short period of residential and/or nursing care given to someone to enable his or her usual carer to take a break.

Retinol: The chemical name for vitamin A.

Ribonucleic acid: Material that transports genetic material from DNA to the cytoplasm in the cells.

Role model: A person who is observed by children and can influence their behaviour and learning.

S

Salmonella: Food poisoning bacteria found in the guts of humans and animals.

Saturated Fat: Fats in which the fatty acid has all the carbon atoms it can hold.

Save the Children: A charity that fights for children in the UK and around the world who suffer from poverty, disease, injustice and violence.

Secondary health care services: Services provided by your local hospital and include out-patient consultancy and in-patient care.

Self-advocacy: Speaking up for yourself to make sure that your views and wishes are heard.

Self-concept: Our vision of our whole selves, which includes our self-esteem, our self-image and our ideal self.

Self-directed support: A process that involves the service user in playing a key role in decision-making about the services that he or she wants.

Self-esteem: How well or how badly a person feels about himself or herself. High self-esteem may help a person to feel happy and confident. Low self-esteem may lead to depression and unhappiness.

Self-image or self-identity: The way in which a person defines him or herself.

Self-referral: Clients refer themselves to a service.

Semi-structured data: Information collected about specified topics, but expressed in the respondents' own words.

Semi-structured data collection: A method of collecting information that starts from a number of open questions, and then allows interviewees to talk about a topic in their own way.

Separation anxiety: Distress caused by the separation of the child from a person to whom they have an attachment.

Septicaemia: Invasion of the bloodstream by virulent micro-organisms from a focus of infection.

Single assessment process: A process by which everyone concerned (including the service user, his or her carer, health services, social services and any other providers) work together to make sure that an individual gets the services he or she needs.

Social contact: Opportunities to be with other people.

Social factors: The norms and values of the society in which a child lives.

Social perception: Recognition of a service user's feelings, needs and intentions.

Social support: Opportunities to be with familiar and trusted people who act in a service user's best interests.

Specific questions: Questions that ask for particular points of information.

Speech communities: A speech community might be based on people who live in a geographical area, a specific ethnic group, or different professions and work cultures. Speech communities are evidenced by their own special words, phrases and speech patterns.

Speech therapy: Help for people who have difficulty communicating.

Spores: Protective coating made by bacteria to prevent damage from adverse conditions such as heat and drying.

Standardisation: A process whereby everything is made to conform to an agreed, common way of doing things (e.g. the practice of a particular CAM).

Staphylococcus aureus: Food poisoning bacteria found in the human nose, throat and on the skin.

Statutory sector: This term refers to organisations set up to provide services that are required by law. It includes the NHS and Local Authorities.

Statutory services: Childcare services which are required by law and organised and run by local authorities.

Steiner: An early educationalist who designed a curriculum that aimed to provide children with equal experience of the arts and the sciences.

Stereotyping: A fixed way of thinking that involves generalisations and expectations about an issue or a group of people.

Stimulation: The presence of factors that increase a person's interest and make life interesting and challenging.

Stimulus: An external or environmental event to which an organism responds.

Structured data: Data that is collected in a uniform way.

Structured data collection: A method of collecting information that follows a well-defined plan or schedule.

Supportive relationship: An encounter between people that conveys warmth, understanding and sincerity.

Sure Start: A Government programme which aims to achieve better outcomes for parents, children and communities by increasing the availability of childcare for all children; improving health and emotional development for young children and supporting parents to achieve their aims for employment. They focus specifically on disadvantaged areas and provide financial support to help parents afford childcare.

Systematic reviews: In research, this is the term used to refer to comparative studies of several clinical trials or other research projects.

T

Telegraphic speech: Abbreviated, but meaningful sentences of two or three words

Tocopherol: The chemical name for vitamin E.

Toxin: A poison that is secreted by a micro-organism.

Toy libraries: A community based resource for play which may include equipment, toys for loan, dedicated play space and a skilled staff who offer advice and support for parents and carers.

Traditional Chinese Medicine (TCM): A traditional and complex system of medicine originating in China. It sees body and mind as integral components of a healthy body system.

Traits: Long-lasting characteristics of a person which influence their behaviour.

Tumbler test: A test used to diagnose meningitis. If a glass tumbler is pressed against a rash and the rash does not fade, this is an indicator of meningitis.

Tyramine: An amino acid found in red wine, mature cheese and smoked fish which can trigger a migraine

U

Unconditioned response: A response that occurs automatically and does not have to be learned.

Unconditioned stimulus: A stimulus which automatically produces a response.

Unsaturated fat: Fats in which the fatty acid has one or more of the carbon atoms without a hydrogen atom attached.

Unstructured data: Data that is not tightly controlled by the interviewer, or by the questionnaire being completed. Such data is expressed in the respondents' own words.

Unstructured data collection: A method of collecting information that allows interviewees to talk about a topic in their own way.

V

Vegan: Strict vegetarians who will not eat meat, fish, poultry, eggs, milk or cheese.

Vegetarian: someone who chooses not to eat foods from animals and bi-products of animals such as cheese and eggs.

Virtuous errors: Mistakes made as a result of a child applying grammatical rules to irregular verbs.

Vitamins: Micro-nutrients needed in small amounts in the body; divided into fat-soluble vitamins (A,D,E and K) and water-soluble vitamins (C and B complex).

Voluntary groups: Those seen as non-profit-making organisations.

Voluntary sector: This refers to those organisations that provide services to bridge gaps in statutory provision. These organisations sometimes provide services without charge. They are non-profit-making organisations.

Vulnerability: Being at risk of some kind of harm – not being protected from risk and harm.

W

Water: Essential for life; makes up two thirds of the body's weight.

Z

Zinc: A trace element that is essential for tissue growth.

Index